MODERN LIFE INSURANCE

THE MACMILLAN COMPANY
NEW YORK · CHICAGO
DALLAS · ATLANTA · SAN FRANCISCO
LONDON · MANILA

THE MACMILLAN COMPANY
OF CANADA, LIMITED
TORONTO

MODERN

LIFE

INSURANCE

A Textbook of Income Insurance

Revised Edition

ROBERT I. MEHR
Professor of Economics, University of Illinois

ROBERT W. OSLER
Vice President and Editor of Life Publications
The Rough Notes Company, Inc.

The Macmillan Company

NEW YORK

To the students of life insurance,
who will, it is fervently hoped, like
this book so well they will make it
a part of their permanent library.

PREFACE

THIS EDITION of *Modern Life Insurance* is actually a new book. It contains perhaps less than 5% of copy lifted verbatim from the last edition and the book has been redesigned in a larger format and completely reset.

There are two reasons for the revision of this book: (1) during the seven years that have elapsed since the first edition was published in 1949, numerous changes have taken place in the life insurance business and in the economic factors influencing it, and (2) as a result of additional experience and study, the authors felt that certain changes in organization and content were desirable to improve its teaching effectiveness.

Perhaps the most unique addition to the text is the subject of Accident and Sickness insurance, making this the first text to combine the discussion of life insurance and Accident and Sickness insurance—not by merely adding a chapter on A & S (and such a chapter will be found), but by discussing Accident and Sickness insurance right along with life insurance, treating the two fields as twins. The modern trend is, and will increasingly be, to look upon life and disability insurance, not as two separate fields of insurance, but as complementary elements of the same field: Income insurance.

Even though this version of *Modern Life Insurance* is a completely new book, it has retained the style used in the first edition and which obtained for it gratifying acceptance both as a college text and as a book for men and women already in the life insurance business. The book is written primarily for the college student, and the language in it is essentially his language. No effort has been made to achieve the complexity of sentence structure and vocabulary so commonly mistaken for erudition. The goal of the book is to make both teaching and learning easier.

Several charges have been made in the organization of this edition. A preliminary chapter on life insurance in the American economy has been added in order to develop the proper setting. The chapters on types of policies have been expanded from three to five, including a summary chapter on the subject of the "best" policy. The material on policy provisions has been enlarged and expanded into two chapters, with one chapter being devoted exclusively to policy options. The chapters on rate making and financial management have been expanded to four and moved to the end of the book. An effort has been made to simplify the discussion of the actuarial principles contained in these chapters. The text actually contains nine parts, as indicated in the table of contents, each of which is self-contained. Since specimen policy forms and applications are readily available from the companies, they have been eliminated from the appendix.

Some classes will find the 27 chapters of this text more than can be taught in the typical one-semester course. If a course in the principles of insurance has preceded it, Chapters 2, 7, 8, 11, 24, 25, 26, and 27 may be omitted. If a non-technical course is desired, Chapters 14, 15, 16, 17, 18, 21, 22, 23, 24, and 25 may be eliminated without sacrificing any of the theory of life insurance.

Throughout the book, the authors have tried to be impartial. They have sought to analyze the life and Accident and Sickness insurance business in the terms of the structure of every business and industry. They have treated it as neither saint nor pariah, recognizing both its faults and its virtues. To those within the business who insist that it should be referred to as an "institution" and explained as something apart from other American business, we say that much of the demagogic misunderstanding to which the "business" is subject stems from past attempts to set it apart from American business as a whole. That which is different is mysterious to the public, and that which is mysterious is ever distrusted.

No book is ever written without the help of others—direct and indirect—of many more "others" than ever receive name acknowledgment.

As authors, we have been preceded by other texts and by trade training courses. To deny we have drawn on them would be to admit to a mental vacuum. We are both widely acquainted in the business, and we have not hesitated to bring into this discussion sound ideas originally imparted to us by acquaintances.

For all *these* helps, we can make no direct acknowledgments. There is a limit to human memory. To anyone who feels he originated any idea contained herein, we concede the credit without argument and with sincere thanks. But for some of the more outstanding aid, memory *does* serve, and we make these name acknowledgments—

Robert W. Mayer, Essel R. Dillavou, Robert W. Harbeson, George A. Steiner, Alden C. Olson, and *Richards C. Osborn* of the College of Commerce and Business Administration of the University of Illinois, for review and technical suggestions in their specialized disciplines: finance, marketing, economics, and law.

Charles Ray, vice president, Associates Insurance Cos., Indianapolis, for his detailed annotations on the chapter on Accident and Sickness insurance which were invaluable.

Bense Leavitt, Life Insurance Agency Management Association, who read several chapters and offered suggestions for improvement.

A. J. Wohlgemuth, president of the Rough Notes Co., Indianapolis, for suggestions resulting in what we have termed the psychological arrangement of the material.

John A. Churchman, of the Great-West Life Assurance Co., who read the chapters on Group insurance and Pensions, and who made helpful suggestions.

William Tozer, a student at the University of Illinois, for assistance in material used in Chapters 1, 20, 21, 22, and 23.

Emerson Cammack and *Robert Hedges,* of the insurance faculty of the University of Illinois, who accepted "invitations" to read certain sections of the manuscript, and who responded with "invitations" to the authors to make several changes, most of which were for the good.

Mrs. Barbara Shoho, Champaign, Illinois, the typist who transcribed those 1,000 manuscript pages with virtually no typographical errors.

To each other, Robert Mehr to Robert Osler and Robert Osler to Robert Mehr, acknowledgment for any errors appearing in the text, each having agreed that such shall be deemed the fault of the other.

And, most of all—

William Beadles, Dean of the University, Illinois Wesleyan University, Bloomington, Illinois, for line-by-line, comma-and-dot reading of the entire manuscript, and catching errors and omissions that otherwise would have lived to haunt the authors.

In closing, the authors wish to say that with all the labor behind, they can declare that writing this text has been fun—fun because both of them are fascinated by the insurance business. The book goes forth with our earnest hope that to the college student it will prove an interesting clarification of one of America's greatest industries, that to instructors it will make the task of teaching somewhat easier, that it will add something to the cause of nonacademic understanding of life insurance, that it will prove of value to the life insurance man who aspires to professionalism and to the layman who seeks clarification of an important phase of American business, and that here and there it will help someone who seeks to know the business only in order to do a sounder job of planning that which is to him the most important thing of all: his family's financial future.

ROBERT I. MEHR
ROBERT W. OSLER

Urbana, Illinois
Indianapolis, Indiana

CONTENTS

PART V. THE USES OF INCOME INSURANCE

MODERN LIFE INSURANCE

CHAPTER 1

LIFE INSURANCE AND
THE AMERICAN ECONOMY

LIFE insurance is a business with far-reaching social and economic implications. Its first concern is with people's lives. It provides men and women with an institution through which they can systematically create financial security for their families and businesses. It also serves the economy as an important channel through which capital is made available to business and industry. It is a business that affects everyone, directly or indirectly. Life insurance is an important business which merits the study of all who would consider themselves skilled in business, economics, or finance. Fortunately, it is also an interesting business.

1. HUMAN LIFE VALUES

The insurance functions of life insurance companies deal with human life values. Unfortunately too many people tend to think of economic values solely in terms of tangibles: real estate, equipment, inventories. They do not consider the enormous value of the earning power of human lives. Few young or even middle-aged people own property values equal to anywhere near the value of their lives. For many people, the life value is simply what they can earn in future years.

Measure of Human Life Value. There are two sources of income: capital and labor or money at work and men at work. Money at work earns interest, rents, or dividends. Men at work earn wages, salaries, or commissions.

If, for example, the owner of the building which houses the campus drug store nets $300 a month from that operation, the building is said to be worth

1

$45,000 assuming a capitalization rate of 8%. If the building is completely destroyed by fire, lightning, or some other peril, the income is no longer earned and its value is destroyed.

An individual with earning power also has a definite economic value measurable in terms of dollars.

Adopting the customary age 65 as the terminal date of earning power,[1] a man's economic value may be said to be the present value of the total he may anticipate earning between his present age and age 65. For example, if a man earning $10,000 a year at age 50 lives to age 65, he will have earned a total of $150,000.[2] His actual life value, however, is less than $150,000 because (1) there is a chance that he might not live to age 65, and (2) a series of payments discounted in advance is never worth what they will total over a period of years. In other words, mortality and discount factors must be considered. Using a modern mortality table and 3% interest, the life value of a 50-year-old man earning $10,000 a year is about $112,000.[3] Life values figured in this manner often have been admitted in court as expert testimony in negligence cases involving liability suits for damages for permanent and total injury. If this man's earning power is cut off by death or disability, there can be said to be an economic loss, just as there is an economic loss when a building is destroyed by fire.

Life Insurance and Human Life Values.   With respect to human life values, life insurance has two functions: (1) to contribute toward its con-servation, and (2) to protect against financial losses resulting from its destruction.

Life Conservation. Life insurance companies are concerned not only with people's lives but also with things that affect them. Just as fire insurance companies are interested in fire prevention, so are life insurance companies interested in the prevention of accidents, diseases, and death.

Life insurance has fostered and still maintains medical research and

---

[1] While earning power does often continue past 65, selection of that age as its terminal date is not wholly theoretical. It is the common age of compulsory retirement set in the ever growing number of industrial and business pension plans, and it is the age when Social Security retirement benefits are started. Social Security encourages cessation of earned income at 65 by reducing benefits payable to those at that age who continue to earn more than a relatively small income. Further, while earning power may continue after 65, it is greatly reduced. The 1950 census returns showed that while median income from 55 to 64 was $2,553, that from 65 to 74 dropped to $1,379 and that after 75 dropped to $757. Actually, in the mass, earning power begins to drop after age 44. (*Statistical Abstract of the U.S.*, 1954, p. 118, Table 130.)

[2] Obviously, it may be more or may be less, depending on whether his income rises or falls between 50 and 65; however, illustrative assumptions can be made only on the basis of current figures.

[3] See Chapter 20 for a discussion of the method employed in reaching this figure. Society of Actuaries 1949 Annuity Table used.

health conservation activities toward the end of preserving human life value. The Life Insurance Medical Research Fund, co-operatively supported by many U.S. and Canadian companies is one example. It offers fellowships and grants-in-aid for research.

Life insurance companies have been active in the promotion of public health legislation, using their facilities for the distribution of information pertaining to the need for such legislation. The collection and dissemination of information regarding the extra accident and health hazard in certain occupations has tended to emphasize the need for corrective measures. A number of life insurance companies prepare and distribute to the public health booklets which are designed to promote life conservation.

Protection Against Financial Loss. It is through its services of providing protection against financial losses resulting from the destruction of human life values that life insurance is best known. This is how it should be for protection is its most important function, its *raison d'être*. Only a small part of the total value of human lives is protected by life insurance. Full insurance to value, however, will never be the case, nor should it be expected. Even the most avid life insurance fan recognizes that for the great majority of men, protection of the full value of their lives is financially impossible.[4] Nevertheless, based on the need for protection, it is clear that life values are inadequately covered. Furthermore, based on ability to pay, life insurance coverage falls far short of its potential. Even so, life insurance is one of the largest and most important industries in America.

2. SOCIAL AND ECONOMIC VALUES

In addition to contributing to the economy by preserving human life values and protecting against the financial consequences of their loss, life insurance also aids in financing business, industry, and government.

Financing Business and Industry. Expanding production is necessary to the maintenance of full employment and a healthy economy. A growing economy needs capital to finance new factories, machines, production and marketing research, materials, and labor. There was a stage in the historical development of the economy when the bulk of such financing could be done by individual financiers or by a small combination of them. Today the economy is too large and complex to depend on that type of financing for the major part of any necessary expansion. Instead, it must turn to the small saver; it must get its financing from millions of investors instead of a few. Thus it has looked more and more to public offering of corporate securities.

Life insurance companies, by investing funds that flow to them from

---

[4] See Chapters 2 and 15.

their many policyholders, have become a principal source of capital for the economy. They make available to industry the savings of millions who themselves never would or could invest directly in business. Further, by creative selling they encourage many to save who would not do so in any other form. Millions who have no other savings or investments of any kind have created sizable savings in the cash values of their life insurance. These savings have been put to work in American business and industry.

In effect, life insurance forms a huge investment pool of the combined savings of close to 100,000,000 Americans, a pool to which business and industry can turn for money to aid in expansion. Today this investment pool —the combined assets of the legal reserve companies of the country—amounts to close to $90,000,000,000. Approximately 44% of this total is invested in securities of business and industry.[5] To these funds should be added about 3% invested in commercial mortgages, many of which are a direct aid in the expansion of the facilities of production.

Each job in business or industry represents a given capital investment, say $10,000 on the average for the types of business and industry in which life insurance companies place their funds. Thus the money life insurance companies have invested in securities of business and industry creates close to 4,000,000 jobs. An annual investment of $450 is needed by American industry to maintain one job. The investments which life insurance companies make annually, therefore, are enough to maintain 10,000,000 jobs.

Other Financing.   In addition to supplying capital funds to business and industry, life insurance is an important source of financing in a number of other important economic activities. It has invested close to $10,000,000,000 in United States government securities and over $2,500,000,000 in securities of other governmental units. Its total investment in mortgages, residential, farm, and commercial, is well over $20,000,000,000.

How important a factor life insurance is in supplying capital funds can be illustrated with two examples: In 1953, life insurance companies increased their holdings of United States corporate bonds by $2,600,000,000, which was just about half of the year's increase in the long-term corporate bond debt. In that same year, for another example, companies increased their mortgage holdings by $2,100,000,000, which was about one fifth of the increase in the total mortgage indebtedness.

The investment departments of life insurance companies are always seeking the most favorable investment return available subject, of course, to the

---

[5] Approximate distribution of funds invested in securities of business and industry: railroad bonds, 12%; public utilities, 35%; industrial and miscellaneous bonds, 45%; stocks, 8%. It should be emphasized again that this is the approximate distribution and that the exact distribution varies from year to year.

standards of solvency which they must maintain. They have long been a major source of funds for those who seek to borrow for legitimate investment uses. After the speculative period in railroad financing had passed and there was a need for capital funds to spread rails over the country, life insurance funds were an important source of railroad capital. When the South experienced expansion in the late 1930's, life insurance funds flowed into that region at a faster rate than into other sections of the country. During World War II when there was a vastly increased need for financing the government, United States government securities were a large portion of life insurance company investments. When, in the postwar period, business and industry had a heavy demand for capital funds to be used in retooling for civilian production, corporate securities became a leading channel for new investment of life insurance funds. In this same period, when home building started on a record-breaking expansion, mortgage financing took the lead in life insurance company investing. As the Southwest and Pacific states began expansion in the late 1940's and early 1950's, life insurance capital increased its flow into that area.

Life insurance is one of the most important sources of capital funds for the economy, and the growth of the basic industries of the country has been aided substantially by the investment in them of funds paid in by policyholders.

Stabilization of Business.   In addition to the support life insurance gives to business and industry in America through its investment in their securities, it tends to stabilize business structure in three ways: (1) by reducing risk; (2) by establishing credit; and (3) by reducing the necessity of liquidation under unfavorable circumstances.

Small business units are predominate in the American economy: the sole proprietorship, the two- or three-man partnership, the small, close corporation, often called "the incorporated partnership." One of the major risks in the small business is the death of a principal or key figure in the enterprise. The risk of business liquidation after such a death is high.[6] Life insurance can be used to reduce and even eliminate this risk. By doing so, it not only stabilizes the business structure but also makes starting and investing in new business more attractive.

Life insurance also stabilizes a business by enhancing its credit standing. Policies on the lives of owners of a business are not only liquid capital themselves but also they increase the credit rating of the business. Particularly in the smaller business, suppliers are more willing to advance credit if they

---

[6] What these problems are and how life insurance solves them will be discussed in Chapter 18.

know that should the owner or key figure in that business die or become disabled, it will not be necessary to liquidate the business to obtain the cash to pay off the bills.

Social Contributions.   The economic contributions of life insurance and its social contributions are interwoven. Whatever life insurance does to stabilize business and industry and whatever it contributes to the expansion necessary to maintain full employment are social as well as economic contributions.

Life insurance also makes a number of other important contributions to social welfare. Foremost among these contributions is the prevention of economic want. Emergencies calling for more money than the individual has in current income are socially disturbing. Such emergencies arise in case of disability, old age, and death. Life insurance, by encouraging people to plan for these contingencies and to save systematically, serves in all these crises.

The prevention of economic want enables life insurance to contribute to the social organization of the nation by assisting in the maintenance of the family unit, the basis of the social structure. Life insurance tends to hold the family together in periods of financial emergency by providing it with a backlog of funds which make it less necessary for the family to scatter among relatives or appeal to charity for support. This is true, whatever the cause of the financial emergency: disability, death, or old age.

Finally, life insurance helps families plan for the education of their children. Many young men and women have attended college on the proceeds or cash values of life insurance.

3. SIZE AND GROWTH OF THE INDUSTRY

Helpful to an appreciation of the role life insurance plays in the American economy is an understanding of its size and growth.

Size.   In the aggregate, 100,000,000 people are paying over $10,000,-000 annually for some $375,000,000,000 of life insurance.[7] As a group, they have accumulated in savings over $75,000,000,000 through this institution. In addition, they are paying more than $3,000,000,000 a year for accident and sickness insurance.[8]

---

[7] Primary source of current statistics on life insurance is the *Life Insurance Fact Book* (New York: Institute of Life Insurance, annual). Statistics on the national economy will be found in the *Statistical Abstract of the U.S.* (Washington, D.C.: Department of Commerce, annual). These two works are the primary source of all statistics used in this chapter.

[8] This figure does not include the substantially more than $1,000,000,000 currently being paid to hospital service plans.

Four out of five American families own life insurance. On the average, insured families own about $9,500 of life insurance for which they pay about $255 a year in premiums and through which they have accumulated a savings of about $1,925. In addition, they are paying more than $75 a year for accident and sickness insurance.

Life insurance is the nation's most popular single savings media. Cash values in life insurance are almost three times the value of savings accounts in savings and loan associations, more than 2½ times the savings in mutual savings banks, more than 1½ times the savings in commercial banks, more than 25 times the value of Postal savings, and more than 1¼ times the redemption value of U.S. Savings Bonds.

The number of legal reserve life insurance companies in the United States is about 1,100.[9] These companies employ about 135,000 in their home offices and about 275,000 in their agency forces.

Growth. Some appreciation of the position of life insurance in the economy can be gained from a consideration of its growth over the 27-year period ending in 1955. Common measurements of the size of the life insurance business are amount of insurance "in force," assets, and income or receipts.

Rate of Growth. During the past 27 years, the total of life insurance in force has increased by about 265% and the assets of life insurance companies have grown by almost 419%.[10] The income or receipts of the life insurance business are made up of premiums paid plus investment and other income. In the past 27 years, total income has grown by about 223%. There has been about a 199% increase in premium income and about a 300% increase in investment and other income.[11]

The above percentages indicate the growth of life insurance in terms of current dollars and therefore reflect the substantial inflation which occurred during this period. The use of constant dollars shows the real growth. In terms of constant dollars, life insurance in force increased by about 134%, assets by about 232%, and premium income by about 91%.

Share of Growth. An analysis of the extent to which the life insurance industry has shared in the growth of the economy is necessary to complete the picture. During the same 27-year period that life insurance in force in-

---

[9] Every state in the union has at least one domiciled legal-reserve company and contrary to popular belief, home offices are not concentrated on the east coast. Texas leads in the number of domiciled companies with Louisiana second and South Carolina third.

[10] The much more rapid rate of growth of assets than that of insurance in force may seem a discrepancy. However, as it will be seen later assets must increase as policies grow older. Therefore, even during the great depression when the amount of insurance in force actually decreased, assets continued to increase.

[11] The greater rate of growth of investment and other income than of premium income is a reflection of the increase in assets.

creased by about 265%, the gross national product and national income [12] rose by about 270%. Disposable personal income [13] during this period rose by about 227% whereas premiums paid for life insurance advanced by about 199%. Savings [14] held by the people increased by about 412% whereas savings through life insurance increased by about 404%. In general, therefore, life insurance seems to have experienced a rate of growth neither markedly better nor worse than that of the economy at large.[15]

Pattern of Growth. The growth of life insurance has been more or less steady despite depression, war, and inflation with the consequence that life insurance premiums have absorbed more of the disposable personal income during the depression and less during inflation.[16] While the drop of the percentage of disposable personal income going into life insurance during the postwar inflation years often has been cited as evidence that life insurance has not grown as fast as the economy, the facts would seem to indicate instead, a degree of stability of growth which is matched by few other business institutions.

4. STABILITY OF LIFE INSURANCE

Since the social and economic organization is dynamic, the importance of an industry must be analyzed not only in relation to its contributions to a better life and its size and scope, but also in relation to its ability to adapt to social and economic change.

Perhaps the best answer as to whether or not life insurance can so adapt is the record of the past. It reveals that although there have been company failures, the industry as a whole has maintained an enviable record of stability.

Source of Stability. There are two great sources of the stability of life insurance: diversification of investments and its system of merchandising.

---

[12] Gross national product (often abbreviated GNP) is the sum of all private expenditures for consumption goods and services, gross private investments, and government expenditures. National income, another measure of economic growth, is the GNP less depreciation and indirect business taxes.

[13] Disposable personal income is the national income plus transfer payments less the sum of undistributed profits, corporate taxes, social security tax contributions, and personal taxes.

[14] Savings associations, mutual savings banks, time deposits in commercial banks, U.S. saving bonds, and postal savings.

[15] The growth of the accident and sickness insurance business has been almost phenomenal over the past several years. During the 15-year period, 1940–54, accident and sickness insurance premiums increased over 800%.

[16] The following ratios of premiums to disposable personal income indicates the fact that life insurance neither expands nor contracts at as fast a pace as does income.

| 1929–4.0 | 1937–5.3 | 1945–3.4 | 1953–3.6 |
| 1933–7.2 | 1941–4.3 | 1949–3.6 | 1955–3.7 |

Diversification of Investments. Life insurance applies the principle of diversification of investments not only in the number of different investments it holds but also in geographic distribution of those investments, their distribution by types of enterprise, by types of companies, by types of securities, by maturity dates, and by time of purchase.

First, investments of any given life insurance company are spread among industries and enterprises located in different sections of the country in order to minimize fluctuation or loss by localized depression.

Second, investments are distributed by type of enterprise. Not only do life insurance companies spread their investments among industrials, utilities, mortgages, real estate, and governments but also among different industries and different companies within an industry.

Third, life insurance investments are diversified in number. Thousands of different specific investment holdings are in the portfolios of even the relatively smaller companies.

Fourth, life insurance investments are diversified by date of purchase. Companies buy securities day in and day out, year in and year out. The cost of their investment portfolio is an average over good times and bad. Adverse investment conditions for any one year, or even for a period of several years, cannot do serious damage to a large portfolio.

Finally, life insurance investments are diversified by maturity date. In times of economic distress, investment maturities are available to help handle emergency calls for cash and thereby reduce the chance that other investments will have to be liquidated in depressed markets. As will be seen in the next section, diversified maturity dates, although giving an added margin, are not as important to the stability of life insurance as one would expect.

System of Merchandising. Both the basic nature of the product of life insurance and the method of merchandising it contribute to its stability, perhaps even more than its investment practices.

In the first place, life insurance is a continuing investment for the policyholder. It is not a one-time purchase. The vast bulk of policies is purchased on an annual (as contrasted to single) premium basis. The buyer undertakes a long-term obligation in his budget, and he is subject to some penalty if he drops the obligation: the penalty of loss of insurance protection. Therefore, he strives to keep up his premium deposits despite "hard times" for himself or for the economy.

In the second place, life insurance companies use an aggressive merchandising system. Through their agents, they forcefully solicit new business and strongly encourage existing policyholders to continue their deposits. The agent's income is directly dependent on the new policies he sells, and the compensation system under which he works penalizes him when policies are dropped.[17] Therefore, he puts time and effort into bringing in new business and conserving old.

While periods of economic depression markedly decrease the flow of new money into almost all other enterprises, the basic nature of the life insurance investment plus the activity of the agent keeps up the flow of money into life insurance. For instance, the premium income of life insurance in 1929, before the depression, was $3,350,367,354; while in 1933, in the depths of the depression, it was still $3,321,797,924. This continuous inflow of new money enables companies to meet cash calls in times of depression without the necessity of liquidating securities at distressed prices. Table 1 shows that during the worse years of the depression, despite the heavy demands for cash and loan values, the total income of the business each year was sufficient to meet all cash calls.

Table 1. Premium Income, Total Income, and Total Disbursements, 1930–37

Year	Premium Income	Total Income	Total Disbursements
1930	$3,524,326,635	$4,593,973,110	$3,198,537,056
1931	3,661,105,385	4,850,375,950	3,537,704,954
1932	3,504,255,574	4,653,395,656	3,997,698,360
1933	3,321,797,924	4,622,291,932	3,917,431,410
1934	3,520,984,136	4,785,984,654	3,661,718,746
1935	3,692,127,637	5,072,095,267	3,592,956,321
1936	3,683,487,169	5,180,225,071	3,518,026,585
1937	3,761,745,196	5,257,048,795	3,610,343,044

5. SUMMARY

The life insurance industry is one of the largest of all industries in America. Its present rate of growth is steady and in proportion to the growth of the economy.

The principal function of life insurance is to protect against the financial consequences resulting from the loss of human life values.

Both in the protection it offers and the benefits it pays out each year, the life insurance business is a socially and economically stabilizing influence. The assets of the life insurance companies support the basic business, industry, and services of the country and give each policyholder a vested

---

[17] For explanation of the basic compensation system used in life insurance, cf. Chapter 25. The agent is paid a commission for the sale of new policies and a "renewal" commission each year the policy remains in force. Sometimes these renewal commissions are for an initial period of years only, such as the first nine; increasingly, some type of renewal commission or service fee is being paid as long as the policy is in force. Therefore, when a policy is dropped, the agent loses whatever renewal commissions remain.

interest in the economy. The stability of life insurance offers safety and security to policyholders and their beneficiaries. Life insurance affects almost every living person in the country.

A business of such size and importance to the social and economic order is one which must be studied if a full understanding of the American economy is to be obtained.

Questions for Class Discussion

1. A seven-year-old boy was hit by an automobile. As a result of the injury, he was permanently and totally disabled. The driver of the car was sued for damages. You are called by the attorney for the plaintiff as an expert witness to testify as to value of this boy's life. Outline the nature of your testimony.
2. Loss prevention should be of as much concern to insurance companies as loss indemnification. Do life insurance companies have as great an incentive for loss prevention as do fire and casualty insurance companies? Is there anything that a life insurance company can do in the field of loss prevention that is not done? If so, why do you suppose it is ignored?
3. Why do people insure the value of their homes against loss by fire more adequately than they insure the value of their lives against loss by death?
4. The life insurance industry through its trade associations engages in and sponsors a great deal of investment research. Why? Describe at least three investment research projects in which you would expect to find life insurance companies interested.
5. Much is made of the economic contributions of life insurance to society in its role of financing business, agriculture, government, and real estate. Do other institutions fulfill the same functions? Why are life insurance companies so important as financial institutions?
6. Are there any economic contributions of life insurance to business and industry which cannot be performed by any other institution? Discuss.
7. Much is made of the many contributions of life insurance to social welfare. In what ways, if any, could life insurance make additional contributions to social welfare? Why would you think the contributions you suggest have been overlooked?
8. How do you account for the proved stability of life insurance? Is this stability an exclusive advantage of the life insurance industry? Discuss.
9. How do you account for (a) the growth of the life insurance industry over the past quarter of a century, and (b) the relatively wide fluctuation in the ratio between life insurance and the gross national product over the past quarter of a century?
10. In this textbook and in others, statistics are quoted here and there and on this and that. How accurate do you expect these statistics to be?

CHAPTER 2

THE NATURE AND
HANDLING OF RISK

INSURANCE is a device for reducing some of the risks inherent in the economy. It operates by combining a sufficient number of exposure units to make loss predictable. By definition, therefore, risk is a condition precedent to insurance. Consequently, an understanding of the nature and meaning of risk (and of certain matters closely related to it) is necessary to an understanding of insurance.

1. BASIC DEFINITIONS

Each field of knowledge has its own terminology. Insurance is no exception. Certain terms have several connotations outside the field and are subject to varying usage even within it. Such variations in usage may not be particularly confusing to one well acquainted with the field, but to the beginning student they can be not only a bother but also an unending source of misunderstanding.

It will help in the understanding of risk and its relation to life insurance if we differentiate among and define the terms *chance of loss, risk, peril, hazard,* and *loss.*[1]

Chance of Loss. Chance of loss is an expression of the probability that a loss will occur. It can be measured mathematically as a percentage of the possible number or amount of losses occurring from any given number or value of exposures to that loss. To put it another way, it is a fraction obtained

---

[1] While reference to common usage, trade usage, some other textbooks, and even accredited dictionaries might not reveal the exact definitions set forth here, we believe them sound in view of their purpose.

by dividing the probable number or amount of unfavorable events by the total number or value of possible events. To illustrate—

A coin has two sides. Tossed in the air, it will come down either "heads" or "tails." Assume the appearance of "tails" is an unfavorable event; then the probable number of unfavorable events is one, whereas the total number of possible events is two. As a percentage, the probability of an unfavorable event (tails) is 50%. As a fraction, it is 1/2. As a decimal, it is 0.5. As a bet, it is "even money": one to one.

As another example: [2] Assuming that the appearance of double ones, double sixes, or a one and two combination is an unfavorable event in the first throw of a pair of dice, then what is the chance of loss?

There are 36 possible combinations in a throw of a pair of dice, but only four of these combinations yield any of the "unfavorable" combinations producing two, three, or twelve. Thus, the probable number of unfavorable events is four, whereas the total number of possible events is 36. Consequently, the chance of loss in the first throw is four in 36—11.1% or 1/9.[3]

In illustrations based on tossed coins or thrown dice, it is simple to measure the chance of loss (which is the reason such illustrations were used). In them, the probability is based on logic—including mathematics as a form of logic. But what is the probability that a man now 21 will die before he reaches age 22—or what is the probability that he will die before reaching 65? What are the probabilities involved in loss by premature death, old age, accident, or sickness? It is not possible to measure these with logic. Instead, there must be statistical data—or what is called "empirical probability."

To determine the probable number of persons in any given group who will die at any age, statistics on a large number of lives have to be collected and formulated into tables—"tables of mortality." By observing the number of deaths out of a sizable group at a given age, the probability of death at that age can be ascertained. Thus, on the mortality table most widely used

---

[2] The use of this example is no suggestion that insurance and gambling are akin but rather that the throw of honest dice is a perfect example of the law of chance. Insurance is not gambling. In gambling, the risk is created by the transaction; in insurance, the risk is reduced by the transaction. For example, until a bet has been placed, there is no chance of losing on the throw of a pair of dice. But with respect to premature death, the risk is there until reduced by insurance. Thus gambling and insurance are opposites since one creates a risk whereas the other reduces it.

[3] Gamblers call it "odds," which would be expressed in this case as one to eight *for* or eight to one *against* loss on the first throw. In the game of "craps," the "house" loses if the gambler's first throw yields a seven or an 11 total. Eight different combinations produce seven or 11; thus the chance of the "house" losing on the first throw is eight in 36—22.2% or 2/9. In this case, the odds are seven to two for or two to seven against loss on the first throw.

in the United States at the present time,[4] the probable number of persons age 21 who will die before 22 is 2,382 out of 949,171, and the probable number dying before 65 is 371,289 out of 949,171 alive at 21; hence the probability of death during age 21 is the fraction 2,381/949,171 and during the 44-year period from 21 to 65, 371,289/949,171.

Statistical tables showing probabilities of death are called "mortality" tables; tables showing the probabilities of disability are called "morbidity" tables.

The principal reason for studying chance of loss in insurance is to establish a basis for premium computation. An accurate measurement of probability is essential to the establishment of a fair and equitable rate for insurance coverage.

Risk. Risk is uncertainty. In the field of insurance, it is the uncertainty of financial loss. If there is certainty that a loss *will* occur, there is no risk; if there is certainty that it will *not* occur, there is again no risk. Risk is a result of the fact that an individual cannot determine definitely what will happen to his property or person at any given time in the future.

Death is a certainty; therefore, the risk involved in a life insurance transaction is not *whether* the unfavorable event will occur, but *when* it will occur. From an economic standpoint, it may come too soon; i.e., during the productive years of life. Or, it may come too late; i.e., not until long after the ability to earn a living has ceased.

Accident and sickness are not certainties; therefore, the risk involved is not *when* the unfavorable event will occur, but *whether* it will occur. There is also uncertainty as to how long disability will last and whether it will be partial or total.

Risk exerts a retarding influence on economic activity. Insurance exists because people prefer a small, certain cost that can be budgeted (the insurance premium) to an uncertain but potentially large loss (the amount of the insurance) which cannot be budgeted.

Degree of Risk. The degree of accuracy with which a man is able to forecast the occurrence of loss is the basis by which degree of risk is measured. Assume the chance of an illness causing appreciable loss of time from employment in a given occupation to be one in 1,000. If an employer has only one employee, the degree of risk is uneconomically high even if the chance of loss is low. The employer is unable to predict (and, thus, unable to plan) for the contingency. His one employee, his entire staff, may be the one in 1,000 who becomes ill, or he may not. For him, the degree of risk is

---

[4] Commissioners' Standard Ordinary ("CSO"), reproduced in Chapter 20.

perfect (100% of his exposure), even if the chance of loss is low. Since there is no basis for predicting the outcome, uncertainty is complete.

Suppose, however, that the employer has 1,000 employees. His risk is reduced, because he can now predict that at any given time one employee probably will be sick. However, he still has no assurance that his actual losses will equal his expected loss. Sometimes, no employees will be sick; other times, two or three employees will be sick simultaneously. He is still uncertain; so there is still risk. If either none or two employees become ill, he has missed his calculation by 100%—but this represents only 0.1% of his exposure.

Suppose the employer has 100,000 people working for him. He can expect 100 to become ill. If as many as 10 more or 10 fewer actually are ill, he has missed his calculation by only 10% of his prediction, or 0.01% of his exposure. In other words, the larger the employee group, the more nearly predictable the incidence of illness among them. The risk is not entirely eliminated, however, for there is always the uncertainty that the losses will not take place as predicted; i.e., that there will be a deviation of experienced loss from the underlying probability of loss.

The degree of risk is measured by the probable variation of actual experience from expected experience. The lower the probable percentage of variation, the smaller is the degree of risk. As the number of exposures to a peril increases, the variation of actual from expected experience increases, but only as the square root of the number of exposures increases. Thus, when the number of exposures is increased, the number by which actual losses vary from expected losses also increases, but the *percentage* of variation *decreases.*

To illustrate with a simplified example:

Assume that the annual death rate from a given cause is one out of 100. If there is an exposure of 10,000 lives, the expected deaths will be 100 (the underlying probability). Actual deaths, however, would equal the underlying probability only by coincidence. Some years there would be more than 100; some years fewer. Assume the variation from the average over the past few years has been 50. This means the probable number of deaths each year will be between 50 and 150. The area of uncertainty is 100 cases, or 1% of the exposures.

Now if the number of exposures is increased one hundredfold to 1,000,-000, expected deaths will be 10,000. The probable variation of actual from expected deaths will also increase, but not one hundredfold. Instead, it will increase only tenfold, ten being the square root of 100. The probable number of variations from the underlying probability will increase to 500, and the probable number of deaths will lie between 9,500 and 10,500. The area of uncertainty is now 1,000 instead of 100; but whereas 100 was previously 1% of the number of exposures, 1,000 is only one tenth of 1% of the present 1,000,000 exposures.

The area of uncertainty (the degree of risk) grows relatively smaller as the number of exposures increases.

Chance of loss and *degree of risk* often are confused. It is not difficult to understand the difference between them when the extremes are viewed. For example:

Suppose there is either 0% chance of loss or 100% chance of loss. (Either there is no possibility the loss *will* occur or there is no possibility it will *not* occur.) These are the extremes in *chance of loss*. However, in *degree of risk*, both these extremes represent zero; i.e., either way, prediction is perfect. There is neither risk (uncertainty) nor degree of risk (inaccuracy of prediction).

If *degree of risk* and *chance of loss* were not separate concepts, there would then be the absurd situation of the greatest *chance of loss*, certainty, becoming the greatest *degree of risk*, uncertainty. The significant difference between the two concepts can be seen in the following illustration:

Assume two different groups of 1,000 exposure units to a given loss. Call them Group A and Group B. In Group A, the loss experience out of the 1,000 exposures in each of the past five years has been 2, 16, 10, 5, 7 for an average of 8 a year with an average deviation of 4.[5] In Group B, the loss experience has been 7, 8, 9, 7, 9, also for an average of 8, *but with an average deviation of only 4/5.*

Although the *chance of loss* in both groups is the same, there is a greater *degree of risk* in Group A, for here there is greater uncertainty over whether actual losses will be equal to expected. It is inability to predict the course of future events which introduces risk. As events become more predictable risk is reduced, irrespective of the chance of loss.[6]

Peril. A peril is anything which may cause a loss. Examples from the field of life and disability insurance are accident, sickness, premature death, and old age. Causes of loss (accident, sickness, premature death, old age) are often loosely called "risks." Correctly, *risk* is the uncertainty about the occurrence of a loss, whereas *peril* is the cause of the loss. A study of perils is im-

---

[5] The average or mean deviation is obtained by taking the sum of the deviations of the items from the arithmetic mean, without regard to + or − signs, and dividing by the number of items. The lower the average deviation, the less erratic the data.
[6] Chance of loss also can exert a retarding influence on economic activity. A large chance of loss will discourage business activity more than will a small chance of loss irrespective of the degree of risk involved.

portant to the understanding of life and disability insurance. Whereas life insurance policies usually are written to cover death from any cause, accident and sickness insurance often may restrict disability coverage to certain named causes, or to all causes of disability except those specifically excluded.[7]

Hazard. Hazard is a condition that increases the chance of loss arising from a peril. For instance:

An accident may be the ostensible cause of a permanent and total disability, but what was the cause of the accident? It may have been a faulty driver: careless driving, poor eyesight, liquor; or it may have been a faulty vehicle: bad brakes, poor lights, defective tires. It may be driving conditions: Winter brings frequent warnings from highway departments that "driving conditions are hazardous." These things are hazards and must not be confused with perils. Illness, for example, is a peril creating loss of income and adding medical expenses but it is also a hazard increasing the chance of loss by death.

Insurance companies recognize three types of hazard: *physical, moral,* and *morale.*

Physical hazard is an objective characteristic increasing the chance of loss from a given peril. For simple examples: coal mining and metal grinding are hazardous occupations because they increase the chance of illness by exposing workers to mineral dusts which may be inhaled. War and mountain climbing increase the chance of accident or death.

Moral hazard is a subjective characteristic of the insured which increases the probability of loss. It is found in the insured's habits, financial practices, or lack of integrity. In life and disability insurance, moral hazards are present in individuals of unsavory moral reputations, spendthrifts, alcoholics, dope addicts, and philanderers.[8]

Morale hazard like moral hazard is personal. Morale hazard arises out of indifference to loss. Possession of insurance may itself create a morale hazard. For instance, ownership of disability income insurance may result in a prolonged period of claimed disability since the incentive to get well may be reduced when insurance benefits are coming in. Possession of hospitalization insurance has definitely been associated with an increased incidence of hospitalization.[9] Life insurance produces a very small incidence of morale

---

[7] Exceptions are the suicide clause and the occasional aviation or war clauses found in life insurance policies. For a discussion of the limitations on perils in the A & S contract, see Chapter 11.

[8] A problem relating to moral hazard in disability insurance not found in life insurance is claim exaggeration. Cf. Chapter 11.

[9] The hazard is not wholly subjective here. Hospitalization insurance frequently results in more people taking advantage of "hospital-needed" diagnoses.

hazard, for rarely does an individual become careless of life simply because he is insured.

A study of hazards is important to the understanding of insurance. Insurance companies must review the hazards involved when an application for insurance is submitted. If the hazards are unusually large, the company must either charge a higher premium, restrict the coverage, or deny the insurance.[10]

Loss. Loss is a decline in or disappearance of values arising from a contingency.

The major types of losses against which one insures through a life insurance contract are unexpected expenses and interruption of income. Death *can* bring about loss of future income; it always brings about expense.

For the typical family, loss of income resulting from the death or retirement of its breadwinner is the more serious; however, expenses of last illness and burial also can be a problem in those families operating on a close budget.

For the wealthy family, death taxes and the cost of probating the estate could well be the more serious loss. Loss of income, although large, might be of only secondary importance, especially in view of the high tax bracket to which it was subject.

Accident and sickness also involve both expenses and income loss. Medical, surgical, and hospital expenses can run into large sums of money. Medical expense insurance can be used to reimburse at least part of these costs. Disability resulting from accident or sickness can also cause loss of income for lengthy periods, sometimes even permanently. The bulk of accident and sickness insurance purchased today is expense reimbursement. Most authorities, however, agree that income replacement insurance is more important. If there is income, bills usually can be paid in time; however, if income stops, even though the medical and hospital bills are paid by expense-reimbursement coverages, there is nothing for the everyday living costs for the disabled person and his family. Insurance companies are beginning to place more emphasis on the writing of disability income insurance.

Summary of Definitions. *Risk* is the uncertainty of financial loss. It must not be confused with *chance of loss*, which is the probable number of losses occurring from any given number of exposures. *Risk* must not be confused with *peril*, which is the cause of the loss. Still different is *hazard*, which is a condition that may increase the chance of loss. Finally, risk must not be confused with *loss* itself, which is the decline in or disappearance of values arising from a contingency.

---

[10] Cf. Chapter 19.

2. METHODS OF HANDLING RISK

There are four methods of handling risk:

1. Risk may be assumed and the burden of loss borne.
2. The hazard may be reduced.
3. Risk may be shifted.
4. Risk may be reduced by combination of exposures.

In each of the four methods, there are various ways risk may be assumed, shifted, or reduced.

Risk May Be Assumed.   An individual may assume the risk and bear the burden should a loss occur. Often it is good practice to assume risk. For example, both the frequency and the severity of accidental damage to railroad equipment could be reduced by prohibiting trains from operating above a speed of, say, 20 miles an hour. However, at that speed, rolling stock could make fewer trips, thus yielding less income per invested dollar. Consequently, railroads elect to move at faster speeds. They figure that the gross return from any given piece of rolling stock is increased sufficiently thereby to offset the increased accidental damage. Theoretically, railroads could increase speeds still further and thus further increase efficiency in utilization of equipment, even at the expense of a greater incidence of accidents. However, since not only property but also human lives are involved there comes a point at which the accident ratio is socially unacceptable. Therefore, both statute law and railroad regulations set speed and safety standards.

Although risk assumption is sometimes good business, frequently it is nothing more than the path of least resistance in meeting risk. Failure to take any action is automatic assumption of the risk.

Often when risk is assumed, there is an attempt to build a sinking fund to offset possible losses. Such use of sinking funds might prove unwise.

Specifically, it requires time to accumulate a sinking fund large enough to meet large losses. If the loss is one which comes on slowly at a predictable rate—depreciation, for example—a sinking fund is the proper device. The certainty of the date of the loss makes possible exact calculation of the rate of deposits needed. But if the loss is one the date or extent of which cannot be predicted in the individual case, then it is impossible to calculate the rate at which deposits to the sinking fund should be made. For example, a proposed $30,000 sinking fund to offset the loss of income to a family occasioned by the death or disability of its breadwinner may stand at only $5,000 when that death or disability occurs. Failure to understand the limitations of sinking funds as a risk-bearing device is a common cause of economic distress. This does not mean, of course, that it is wrong to build a contingency fund to insulate against the effects of a loss which is both uncertain and uninsurable. Thus a breadwinner who is uninsurable might find it desirable to build a contingency fund through stocks, bonds, real estate, or annuities in order to provide at least some financial protection for his family in case of his premature death or disability.[11]

The Hazard May Be Reduced. Measures may be taken to reduce the hazard; that is, to reduce the chance of loss. For instance, the development of wonder drugs has materially reduced the hazard of premature death or prolonged disability from certain diseases such as pneumonia. The development of more effective treatment for the diseases of infancy has reduced the death rate during those years.

Risk may also be handled by reducing the loss when it occurs. In this case, the risk (uncertainty) of loss is neither eliminated nor reduced, but its severity is checked. For example, while periodic medical examinations may not lessen the risk of cardiovascular disturbance, they can often catch the trouble in its initial stages and so lessen the severity of the affliction. Further, findings of such examinations may suggest medical treatment that will also reduce the hazard.

Risk May Be Shifted. One method of shifting risk is *hedging*. Hedging is a transaction involving the making of commitments on both sides of a risk so that whatever happens, the commitments compensate each other. The process is probably best illustrated by a betting transaction:

A loyal alumnus creates a financial risk for himself by betting $25 that his Alma Mater will win Saturday's homecoming game. As the day of the game approaches, he begins to think his judgment of his team's chances was more subjective than objective—more a matter of emotion than a study of the team's season record. So he decides to shift the risk to someone else. He bets $25 *against* his Alma Mater. Now, he can sit back and watch the game without worrying over his money because his commitments exactly offset each other. Whichever team wins, he will both win and lose $25, coming out even.

In legitimate business, hedging is constantly practiced in connection with such transactions as the buying and selling of wheat and other grains.[12]

---

[11] The use of a contingency fund to handle risk must not be confused with self-insurance. Self-insurance is possible only where there is a large number of comparable exposures to the same peril so that a definite loss ratio can be predicted. It follows, therefore, that it is impossible to self-insure one or two exposures. Self-insurance is nothing more than an insurance company operated by the self-insurer to insure his own exposures.

[12] There is a tendency to consider hedging as gambling and somewhat immoral—and the broker through whom a hedging transaction is made and the "futures" buyer who makes the transaction possible as elements somewhat deleterious in our economy. However, because of their essentiality to hedging, and because hedging shifts possible loss from a business it might seriously harm, the indication would seem to be that at least not all

The corporation provides another method of shifting risk. Through the corporation a part of the risk is shifted from owners to creditors. In the unincorporated business, the owners are the principal bearers of the risk that assets of the business will be insufficient to pay all claims against them. Because of limited liability in the corporation, this risk is shifted to the creditors.

Risk-shifting is not an uncommon practice in meeting the perils of premature death, disability, and old age. A man may refuse to buy life insurance and thus, automatically, shift the risk of premature death to his widow and children, or other members of society (taxpayers or private charity). He may refuse to insure against old age and shift the risk to his children. He may refuse to insure against disability and so shift the risk to relatives, friends, and charity. In the family society that characterizes our economy, most risks which are left uncovered by one member of the family are automatically shifted to other members—usually the more provident ones, sometimes merely the ones with least resistance.

Risk May Be Handled by Combination. The corporation is not only a device for limiting losses and shifting risks, but it is also helpful in reducing the burden of risk through combination. When the burden of the risk is divided among a number of people and the size of the investment required is reduced to the price of one or a few shares, each investor can put his money into several enterprises, thus diversifying his holdings. Diversification allows the individual investor to balance individual losses against individual gains, giving a measure of regularity to over-all results. This reduces the risk inherent in entrepreneurial investment.

Large-scale business as we know it in America today, and the high standard of living it produces, would be restricted without the corporate form of business organization; and large-scale business is, itself, a method of reducing risk. If a man has one cow and it dies, he loses his entire milk production. If he has a large herd, the loss of several cows will affect his total milk production only slightly—and in an amount he can predict and make allowances for in his budget. The principle can be illustrated in the field of insurance:

A large employer has less mortality risk in providing pensions for his employees than does a small employer. As has been explained, the greater the number of exposure units, the less the percentage of deviation from the underlying probability and the more predictable (and, hence, budgetable)

"speculation" is reprehensible but that some of it actually serves to stabilize our economic structure. Since the potential loss is created by competition, the speculation required to offset it can be eliminated only by eliminating that essential element of a free economy: competition.

the cost of the pensions. The small employer is able to secure the same advantage the large employer has by combining his employees with those of other employers in an insurance "pool" so that he achieves the same predictability of results as his large competitor.

This introduces another method of handling risk through combination: insurance.

An individual knows there is a possibility he may die (or become disabled) this year. Whether or not the possibility will become a reality is completely uncertain. However, if his risk were to be combined with that of many others the loss to the group becomes predictable within practical limits. The individual can then determine his share of the group loss and budget for it. Without insurance, budgeting for uncertain losses is impossible.

3. INSURANCE AS A METHOD OF RISK-BEARING

The meaning of "insurance" is often confused. It is sometimes used to designate a fund which is accumulated to meet uncertain losses. For example, a manufacturer of style goods adds to his prices early in the season to build up a fund to cover possible losses at the end of the season when he may have to reduce prices to clear his inventory.

A transfer of risk is sometimes spoken of as "insurance." An individual who contracts to indemnify another for an accidental loss is said to "insure" him.

However, not all preparations to handle uncertain losses are insurance, and to identify as insurance either an accumulation of a reserve or a transfer of risk is erroneous.

Definition of Insurance. An adequate definition of "insurance" must include both the building up of a fund or a transfer of risk *and* a combination of exposure units having the same common risk into an interrelated group.[13]

Insurance itself may be defined as a device for reducing risk by combining a sufficient number of exposure units to make their individual losses collectively predictable. The predicted loss is then shared proportionately by all those in the combination. This definition implies *both* that uncertainty is reduced and that losses are shared. These are the important aspects of insurance.

For the individual insured, insurance is simply a device that makes it

[13] One man with 1,000 buildings at different and widely scattered locations is in the same position from the standpoint of, say, fire insurance, as are 1,000 men with one building each similarly diversified. In the first case, we have a situation in which true self-insurance is possible; in the second, we have a situation in which only outside insurance will give adequate protection.

possible for him to substitute a small but certain cost (the premium) for an uncertain but potentially large loss (the amount of the insurance) under an arrangement whereby the few who suffer loss are compensated by the many who escape loss.

The Law of Large Numbers.   Insurance is based on mathematics; specifically, on that branch of higher mathematics known as "The Theory of Probabilities." In that branch of mathematics, insurance is concerned primarily with the "Law of Large Numbers" (or the "Law of Averages," as it is commonly called).

The Law of Large Numbers is based on the regularity of the occurrence of events. Therefore, what seems random occurrence in the individual happening seems so only because of an insufficient or incomplete knowledge of what may be expected to occur. For all practical purposes, the law may be stated thus:

> *The greater the number of exposures, the more closely will the actual results obtained approach the probable results expected from an infinite number of exposures.*[14]

As an example: The underlying probability at infinity is that half of all coins tossed into the air will fall "heads," and half "tails." The greater the number of tosses, the nearer the actual results will approach the underlying probability.

To put it another way: Happenings that in the individual appearance seem to be the result of pure chance occur with increasing regularity as the instances observed become more numerous. Driving a car, you turn a downtown corner and dent your fender against another car. To you, the event seems wholly unpredictable. Had you started from home a minute later, had you been delayed along the route a second more, had you pulled away from the last stop light less rapidly, there might have been no accident for you. It seems no formula could have predicted the accident.

Yet to the policeman on the corner where the accident took place, prediction is not nearly so impossible. He could tell you with a fair degree of

---

[14] *Absolute* certainty would be possible only if the number of exposures were to be carried to infinity and if there were no moral or morale hazard. There remains, therefore, in any combination or pool of insurable risks, a residual risk, which is the variation from the underlying probability that occurs because the combination, or pool, is smaller than infinity. This is commonly called the *deviation from average* and is much smaller than the degree of risk to which the individual is subject in regard to the same peril, because the combination more nearly approaches infinity than does the individual exposure. One of the factors determining the insurability of a peril is whether or not there are enough exposures to it to produce a combination of sufficient size to reduce the residual risk to a degree that will result in a deviation from average no larger than can be covered by an addition to the premium, which would not be so large as to price the coverage out of the market.

accuracy just how many drivers will be involved in an accident at that corner this week. If you should ask him to give you the statistics on a monthly basis, he could tell you even more accurately; and should you ask him on the basis of a year, the accuracy of his prediction would lead you to believe he has "second sight."

The policeman's accuracy in predicting the number of accidents increases, not because of the varying bases of times for which you asked him to predict, but because the greater the elapsed time, the greater the number of drivers exposed to the peril at that corner and, the *greater the number of exposures to a peril, the nearer the results approach the underlying probability.*

Just so, an insurance company, with statistics on millions of exposures, can tell you almost the exact number of people who will be killed, maimed, and injured in automobile accidents between now and next Sunday. Such accuracy, as in the case of the policeman on the corner, seems uncanny unless it is held in mind that *as the number of exposures increases, the nearer will be the actual results to the underlying probability.*

Thus, the Law of Large Numbers becomes the basis of insurance. Under the operation of this law, the impossibility of predicting a happening in an individual case gives way to demonstrable ability to do so when a successive number of exposures is considered. Applying these conclusions to life and disability insurance, we find, for example, that every year a certain number of accidents and illnesses take place and a certain number of deaths occur in each age group. If we isolate a small group of cases, we may find a wide variation between actual loss experience within that group and the expectation as determined by past experience for over-all exposure to the peril. But, given a large group of exposures, prediction becomes not guesswork but mathematical calculation.

We have noted [15] that inasmuch as the number of exposures never reaches infinity, there will always be a deviation from the average; that is, losses will not correspond exactly to the average loss as indicated by statistical evidence. Therefore, risk cannot be entirely eliminated through insurance, but it can be reduced to a manageable level. The insured eliminates his own risk entirely by shifting it to the insurer, where, through combination, the degree of the risk is reduced to the residual risk that the actual loss may not be equal to the predicted loss.

4. ESSENTIALS OF AN INSURABLE RISK

Not all risks are insurable. Certain tests must be met. The requisites of insurability are, broadly:

---

[15] Cf. Footnote 14.

1. There must be a large group of homogeneous exposure units.

2. The loss must be definite.

3. As far as the individual occurrence goes, the loss must be fortuitous and substantially beyond the control of the individual.

4. The potential loss must be large enough to cause economic hardship.

5. The cost of insuring must be economically feasible.

6. The chance of loss must be calculable.

7. The loss must not be likely to happen to the majority of insureds simultaneously.

A Large Group of Exposure Units. There must be a large number of exposure units to make possible the functioning of the Law of Large Numbers. A life insurer, for instance, cannot operate on the basis of 10 or 20 lives. The number of exposure units would be so small that the losses might greatly exceed the underlying probability. Insurance is not practical when the probable deviation from predictable loss is so large that premiums must be heavily loaded to take care of it. Losses must be predictable within a relatively narrow range.

The exposure units must be homogeneous; that is, be relatively alike. An insurance company which insured a heterogeneous collection of persons in an unknown combination of ages, states of health, and dangers of occupations could not predict what death losses would result. Predictions are possible only with groups consisting of known combinations as to age, health, and occupation. Therefore, insureds must be classified according to these characteristics. The rate of losses among a group of persons all of whom are age 22, in good health, and in nonhazardous occupations *can* be predicted; such a group is homogeneous. However, insurance classifications must be few enough in number so that there are a great many exposures in each of the classifications used. For example, age group classifications in life insurance are on the basis of full years rather than exact age down to the month. They are also limited in number of classifications as to health and occupation. Thus a category of retail sales managers, all with superior health and all age $42\frac{7}{12}$ years old, would be much too small to produce a reliably predictable loss ratio.[16]

Definite Loss. The loss must be clearly observable and difficult to feign. Death is almost impossible to feign, at least in most civilized countries. Disability, on the other hand, is more easily counterfeited. Consequently, dis-

---

[16] Insurers do not always seek applicants in every usable classification, however. Many restrict their operations to a given age range; others restrict their operations to what are called "standard occupations" and "normal" conditions of health.

ability income insurance is usually restricted both as to amounts and customers, and the moral hazard involved with each applicant must be carefully checked. However, more liberal coverage is generally available for disabilities arising from accidents than for disabilities arising from sicknesses, since accidental injury is usually more clearly ascertainable by an outsider.

A Fortuitous Loss. If there is certainty of loss, the peril is economically uninsurable. Depreciation, normal credit losses, and the like are not insurable. There is no uncertainty about their individual occurrence.[17] They should be handled by sinking funds or treated as a regular cost factor in pricing. Only fortuitious loss is insurable.

Death itself is not an insurable peril, because everyone is sure to die. In life insurance, however, the insurance is not against the peril of death but against the peril of untimely death—death which interrupts economic life. Permanent life insurance contracts (as contrasted to Term, which insures against death during a specified period only) contain ever increasing cash values payable to the insured on demand. At the ultimate age on the mortality table, these cash values equal the face values of the policies. Thus the inevitable death is not insured but is, in effect, handled through a sinking fund invested in life insurance cash values. Until such time as the cash values equal the face of the policy, the difference between those values and the face of the policy is covered by the insurance, in so far as the insured is concerned. In other words, the insurance, in effect, covers only the peril of unexpected death before the cash value equals the face value of the policy.[18] Cash values and face values of Whole Life policies currently issued are not equal until age 100, when the present mortality table assumes everyone is dead.[19]

Accident, sickness, and old age (the length of life beyond the earning span) are uncertainties. Not everyone experiences the losses they occasion.

---

[17] One of the reasons individual hospitalization insurance is proving unattractive to many insurers is that some of its coverages violate this test of insurability. As an example, it offers benefits for tonsillectomies among children, a surgical procedure so common among children as to be a virtual certainty in the mass exposure. As another example, it offers maternity benefits to young married couples where maternity is very likely to occur.

[18] The repeated use of "in effect" in this paragraph might be irritating but it is necessary since it is dealing in a convenient concept rather than an actuarial fact. Actually there are no individual reserves in a policy. Instead there are average reserves and correspondingly average "net at risks." Also the "net at risk" from the viewpoint of the insurance company is the difference between policy reserves and face amounts of insurance rather than the difference between cash values and face amounts of insurance. Cf. Chapter 23.

[19] On older tables, it is age 96 or less. On modern annuity tables it is more than 100.

Therefore, the frequency and duration of their occurrence is unexpected and, hence, insurable.[20]

Large Loss. The size of the potential loss must be large enough to represent a financial strain or economic hardship to the persons exposed to it. It costs money to operate an insurance company, and since net premiums must be "loaded" to cover the insured's share of this cost, the premiums for insuring small losses tend to be too high in relation to the amount of the exposure. For example, a life insurance policy with a face amount of $25 could be written for one year, but the cost of writing and administering the contract would tend to price it out of the market. At age 50, the actuarial cost of the coverage would be about 25 cents since the chance of loss during that year is about 1%.[21] The cost of issuing the policy and handling the records could easily amount to $4 (probably much more), bringing the total cost of the transaction to $4.25. In effect, such a contract if sold at cost would require a gross premium of 17% to cover a 1% chance of loss, not a very attractive arrangement. Better odds can be found at the race track.

On the other hand, the premium for a $1,000 one-year policy issued at age 50 is quoted in one rate book at $15.38. This represents a gross premium of slightly over 1.5% to cover a 1% chance of loss, certainly not a bad proposition for a man who cannot afford the loss.

If the potential loss is large enough to cause severe economic loss, insurance against it is worth the cost even though the premium has to be loaded for expenses. The determination of what constitutes a potential loss large enough to be economically insurable depends on each individual's circumstances. A $300 hospital bill might be ruinous to one man and, therefore, a

---

[20] On two qualifications (definiteness and accidental nature), disability comes near the borderline of uninsurability. Even such extremes as loss of limb or sight have occurred under circumstances which have at least given rise to doubt that they were accidental. And when is a man capable of earning and when not? Physical impairment can be observed and measured; but there are also psychological states that can render a man disabled but which are difficult of measurement. Assume you are a physician to whom a patient comes for certification of disability. The patient is unable to find employment; his family is literally starving: you know that unless he can obtain income from disability insurance, he will commit suicide in order to obtain funds for his family from his life insurance. Since a suicide drive is a psychopathic condition, can you say this man is *not* mentally unfit to earn a living and hence *not* disabled? From such situations arises the need for clear definitions of what should be considered disability for the purpose of the insurance and for restrictions and limitations on benefits that render disability financially unattractive while still protecting against economic catastrophe. Unfortunately, the result of these limitations and restrictions too often renders not only disability itself unattractive but also renders disability insurance unattractive in the eyes of some individuals who need what is in some ways this most important of personal insurances.

[21] This figure is based on the CSO table of mortality without the safety factor. Cf. Chapter 20.

loss against which he should insure. For another, a hospital bill under $3,000 might not be financially disturbing and, therefore, would be uneconomical to insure.

The size of the potential loss from disability or premature death is far greater than most people realize. The loss equals the value of a man's earning capacity over the period of disability or between the time of his death and the end of a normal earning span.

The hardship created when a man outlives his earning ability also can be severe. Therefore, the risks covered by death and disability insurance meet this test of insurability.

Economically Feasible Cost. It is not economically sound to insure against perils which produce a high chance of loss. Even though all other factors about them permit the calculation of a safe rate, such a rate is usually economically impractical. A life insurance rate could be calculated for a man age 98, but no one would be likely to pay it. The probability of death among a group of individuals age 98 (on the CSO mortality table) is about 72 out of each 100 alive. Disregarding interest calculations, the pure premium for $1,000 Term insurance at age 98 would be $720. When the cost of doing business is added to the actuarial cost the total premium comes close to, or is even in excess of, the face amount of the insurance, an obviously uneconomic rate.

The chance of major income loss from premature death (at most ages) or from disability is small enough to make the premium for insuring against each of them economic.

Although the amount of old age indemnification potentially necessary for any individual is extremely large, the cost of protection is within reach for three reasons: (1) The individual who starts his insurance early has a large number of years over which to prepare for the loss. (2) Some men will not reach retirement age. Their contributions toward a retirement insurance fund can be shared by those who live to retirement. (3) Of those who do reach retirement age, only a relative few will live long enough to require the maximum indemnification.[22]

The test of economic feasibility includes feasibility of the cost of rating and underwriting. For example, separating the good from the bad moral and morale hazard within certain occupations or social groups is so difficult that the whole group may be listed as uninsurable. This is especially true in the

---

[22] The constant increase in the average length of life is exerting an upward pressure on the cost of providing old age security, so that a point might be reached eventually where the cost of private insurance for old age would not be economically feasible at today's generally accepted retirement ages. Perhaps a new definition of "old age" is necessary—one that defines it in terms of significant inability to work. Cf. Footnote 24.

case of health insurance. The cost of the investigation necessary to determine the good risks in a group can be prohibitive.

Chance of Loss Must Be Calculable.   The history of an ample number of homogeneous exposure units must be available to give a reasonably clear picture of how frequently the risk produces' loss in mass exposure. The frequency is, of course, the measure of underlying probability of loss.

For some types of risks, the underlying probability may be determined by logic, as has been noted. Logic determines that the underlying probability of a flipped coin coming down "tails" is 50–50. No mass of experience is necessary to determine the probability. On the other hand, the probability of death at age 25 cannot be reasoned from logic. It can be determined only from past experience—a mortality table, for example, which is a report of the number of people dying out of a mass of exposures at any given age.

If the underlying probability cannot be determined either by logic or from history, it is not mathematically calculable, and the peril is uninsurable.[23] This is one of the reasons unemployment is not insurable commercially. The underlying probability can neither be calculated by logic nor determined from past history since it does not occur with predictable regularity. The chance of loss resulting from disability, however, is measurable when the peril is properly defined in the policy.[24]

Unlikely to Produce Loss to Majority Simultaneously.   If loss is highly likely to occur to the majority of the exposure units simultaneously, then the

---

[23] The tests of a large number of homogeneous exposure units and measure of probability may seem to be violated by "insurance" on the fingers of a pianist, voice of an opera star, anatomy of a burlesque queen, and the like. Known as "special risk" or "specialty" insurance, this is not true insurance. It involves transfer of risk from the insured to the insurer but not combination to reduce the individual risk to the residual risk of the mass. Two factors can make such coverage economically practical: (1) *Overcharge of premium,* there being no competitive or comparative rates and there being a tendency for the insured to overestimate the chance of loss and hence be willing to pay an uneconomic premium. (2) *Mass underwriting,* used as a substitute for mass exposure. The potential loss is parceled among a number of insurers, each taking a fragment small enough for him to handle without economic distress should the peril materialize. The position of each individual insurer ("underwriter") becomes that of a speculator, since, like the speculator, he has calculated his chance of loss subjectively rather than from objective logic or statistics. Sometimes on a new exposure a company must rely largely on guesswork. In the marine insurance field this is not at all uncommon. However, these transactions are not gambling, since, as we have seen, the risk in gambling is created by the transaction itself, whereas here it exists apart from the transaction and continues whether there is any transaction or not. The transaction is best called speculation, since speculators take on risks inherent in the economy.

[24] Were old age to be indemnified on a basis of the time at which it kills economic life in each particular case (rather than at a specific date uniform for a mass of exposure units), then the underwriting problems would be similar to those met in underwriting disability: When can earning power be said to have ceased for a given individual? Men can be found who are capable of keeping up the pace of business at 90. Others are wholly unable to do so when 25 or 30 years younger.

peril is generally uninsurable. Insurance operates on the principle of compensation of the few who suffer loss by the many who do not. If the *many* suffer the loss, then the *few* will be inadequate to compensate them—except at a premium that would violate the test of economic feasibility.

The chance of the perils of disability or death producing catastrophic losses is unlikely, assuming of course proper underwriting distribution. For protection against catastrophic exposures, life insurance companies, for example, insert war clauses in their policies during war emergencies.

Although the above characteristics are considered requisites for insurability, they are not always adhered to by companies in writing insurance contracts. For example, in the life and disability field, some coverages are written for low amounts, others are written when a high chance of loss exists, and still others when a chance of loss is not predictable. One large life insurance company in New York once drew up rate tables for unemployment insurance and tried to get permission in that state to write the coverage.

5. INSURABLE VALUE OF A LIFE

In the field of insurance, there are two methods of compensation for loss:

(1) *Indemnification for Actual Loss up to a Specified Maximum.* A fire insurance claim is paid on the basis of the actual cash value of the loss. The face value of the policy limits only the maximum payment.

(2) *Indemnification on the Basis of a Stated Value.* If a claim arises, payment is made, not on the basis of the actual cash value of the loss, but in an amount "stated" in the policy. Policies of this nature are sometimes held to violate one of the basic principles of insurance: indemnification without possibility of gain. However, if used properly, stated-value policies can be legitimate indemnification. In some cases, determination of the actual cash value of an object is practically impossible. A Rembrandt painting, for instance, has little intrinsic value in terms of paints and other materials. Its real value is what it will bring when offered for sale. The only way to determine its actual cash value would be to consummate a sale, which is impossible after it has been lost. It is best insured, therefore, for a stated value agreed upon by insured and insurer in advance.

A similar problem arises in determining the actual value of a human life if or when death or disability impairs it. How can it be done? Current earnings may be capitalized to life expectancy for some degree of estimate; but until life expectancy has been reached, there is no way of knowing whether current earnings will remain the same throughout life. Chances are that earnings will vary.

Actually, an *exact* determination of the economic value of a life is impossible. Therefore, actual cash value policies are impractical. Life insurance policies are written on a stated-value basis. It is agreed by the insured and the insurer that in the event of the death of the former, the latter will indemnify his beneficiaries for a stated amount—the face value of the policy. A stated-value form also is made the basis of payment in old age and many accident and sickness coverages, particularly disability income insurance. On the other hand, some medical and hospital expense coverages are based on the actual cash value method of indemnification.

While the stated-value indemnification basis of insuring solves for the insurer the problem of how much to pay on a contract, it does not solve the problem of how much insurance should be bought or written on a given life. For the company, the problem is one of avoiding overinsurance.[25] For the insured the problem is one of obtaining an adequate amount of insurance. If his dependents (including, broadly, all those who will suffer economic loss by his death or disability) are to be protected against loss, the insured must place an adequate value on his life. It is an established principle of law that there can be no fixed limits on the value of a man's life to himself.

The intrinsic value of the life of an individual is made up of the sum of his knowledge, ambition, perseverance, initiative, honesty, personality, and judgment. These qualities, being intangible and interacting, are difficult to appraise objectively. In common practice, therefore, the economic value of a man's life is measured by the objective standard of those who depend on it for financial support or gain. It can be measured by one or a combination of the following factors:

1. His contribution to the support of all those economically dependent on him.

2. That portion of his income which goes to charitable contributions.

3. That portion of the profits from a business which result from the contributions of his skill, labor, or management.

4. That amount by which his estate will be decreased by death taxes and other costs of dying, and by the process of transfer to his heirs.

5. That portion of his income that goes for the support of himself (as a measure of his economic value in the event of economic death by reason of old age).

Although the above factors are valid bases for determining a man's economic value, rarely can a given individual afford to insure the total amount of the value determined by them. One illustration alone will suffice:

---

[25] The insured is prevented from overvaluing his life by underwriting rules against overinsurance, considered a moral hazard even in life insurance.

Assume an individual age 39, whose current income is $400 a month net after taxes and personal expenses. If his life expectancy today is 30 years, then the present value of his earnings discounted at 2½% is $104,752. To protect this value with the cheapest form of life insurance (one-year Term) would require a monthly premium for the first year of about $90—an amount beyond the budget of a $400-a-month family.[26]

In the vast majority of cases, it is impossible to think in terms of full indemnity when planning a life insurance program. Instead, it becomes necessary for the individual to determine how much he needs to purchase in order to give his dependents (or himself at retirement) a minimum income for the minimum period they need to maintain themselves without undue financial distress. This amount is, of course, subject to the ability of the insured to pay premiums. Each man must determine for himself the maximum amount of premiums he can afford. The details of life insurance program planning are discussed in Chapter 15 of this text.

6. SUMMARY

Necessary to an understanding of any phase of insurance is an understanding of the basic principles on which the operation of insurance rests. First, certain definitions are necessary: (1) *Risk*—uncertainty. (2) *Degree of risk*—the accuracy with which a given loss can be predicted. (3) *Chance of loss*—the probable number of times in any given number of exposures that loss will occur. (4) *Peril*—that which can cause loss. (5) *Hazard*—that which increases the chance of loss. (6) *Loss*—a decline in or disappearance of values arising from a contingency.

Risk may be handled in four ways: (1) *assumed*; (2) *hazard reduced*; (3) *shifted*; and (4) *reduced*. One method of reducing risk is by combination in a group with the same exposure, which group is large enough to make the loss predictable with reasonable accuracy. The loss is then shared proportionately by all members of the group. Risk reduction and loss-sharing are the foundations on which insurance rests.

To be a subject for insurance, the peril must threaten a large and homogeneous group; it must produce a loss that is definite in time and place and which is accidental (as opposed to expected). Furthermore, such a peril must be capable of producing a loss large enough to be economically disturbing to the individual it threatens; yet the cost of insuring must be economically practical. The chance of loss from the peril must be calculable

---

[26] The difficulty involved in insuring old age on the basis of its full economic value is illustrated by the fact that it takes a premium of more than $100 a month from the age of 39 to age 65 for a man to provide a $200 a month life income so long as either he or his wife is alive *after* 65.

before it is insurable. The peril must not be likely to produce loss to the majority of insureds simultaneously.

Economic death, whether occasioned by disability, death, or old age, is an insurable peril; however, the amount of the loss is so difficult to determine that the coverage must be written on a stated-value rather than actual indemnification basis.

The economic value of a life is customarily determined by its value to those dependent on it for support or profit; however, because the value of a life to dependents is exceedingly great, the typical individual finds that he must set that value for his own case, not by the maximum potential, but by the minimum standard on which his family can get by without economic degradation—and on what he can get by in old age. What "economic degradation" may be in any given case is a matter for subjective determination by the individual insured.

Questions for Class Discussion

1. Risk leads to attempts to build up cash balances. Explain why this might be detrimental to the smooth and prosperous functioning of the economy.
2. What is the probability that a man age 30 with a wife 28 and two children seven and four all will be living 40 years from now? (Use CSO Table of Mortality reproduced in Chapter 20.)
3. Reduction of hazard or loss may reduce degree of risk, or it may increase it. Explain. If reduction of hazard or loss increases degree of risk, is the net result desirable?
4. Is it possible for there to be greater risk when the chance of loss is 1/10 than when it is 1/5? Explain your answer.
5. Could the death of an idle playboy cause economic loss to his family?
6. What are the ways of handling the risk of premature death? Old age? Disability? Which is the best method in each case?
7. Comment on the following statement: (a) Insurance reduces but does not eliminate risk. (b) Risk makes insurance both desirable and possible.
8. Life insurance companies usually do not underwrite the risk of death in the armed forces in wartime. What test of insurability would they be violating if they did? Why can the government insure this risk?
9. Distinguish among insurance, gambling, and speculation.
10. Is there more risk in the writing of life insurance or of disability insurance? Explain your answer.

CHAPTER 3

TERM AND ENDOWMENT CONTRACTS

ACTUARIALLY, there are three basic types of life insurance policies: *Term*, *Endowment*, and *Whole Life*. In addition, there is the Annuity contract, sometimes called "Life insurance in reverse." The purpose of this chapter is to discuss the nature and uses of Term and Endowment contracts.

1. TERM INSURANCE

Definition of Term Insurance. A Term policy is a contract which offers financial protection against the occurrence of death within the given period of time stated in the policy. It offers no protection or values in case of survival beyond the specified period.

Term insurance is comparable to most forms of property insurance contracts. For instance, an automobile insurance policy offers financial protection against the perils named in it for a period of one year. If these perils fail to cause a loss within that time, the policy expires without value. It may be renewed for another year, but it then becomes a new contract. Fire insurance is often written for periods of one, three, or five years. If fire does not occur, the policy expires without value at the end of that time. If the protection is to be continued, a new policy must be obtained or the old one must be renewed.

A policyholder who takes five-year Term insurance has protection against the financial consequences of death within that period but not beyond. If the policy is renewable, he may extend it for another term period at the rate applying at the new age; or he may, if it is not renewable, take a new policy, provided he is still an acceptable risk.[1]

The principal appeal of Term insurance is its low cost. A man age 25, for example, can purchase a $10,000 10-year Term policy for an annual gross premium of about $80. The cheapest form of permanent insurance would require a gross annual premium of more than $200.

A principal deterrent to the purchase of Term insurance is its lack of cash values available for emergency or retirement income.[2] Quite often an insurance buyer objects to the purchase of Term insurance because he does not want to "pay all those premiums and get nothing back." [3] In the above example, at the end of 10 years, the 10-year Term policy will expire without value whereas the permanent policy will have a cash value of $1220.[4] It should also be mentioned that some life insurance agents discourage the purchase of Term even in cases where it should be sold, since Term insurance yields them a lower commission. Some companies pay a lower rate of commission on Term insurance, and in every case the premium on Term is lower thus yielding fewer commission dollars.

Uses of Term Insurance. Term insurance will serve the policyholder adequately only when the protection need will expire simultaneously with the expiration of the term period. For example, a young mechanic borrows $10,000 to finance the purchase of machinery and tools to equip his shop. He feels certain that if he lives five years, he will be able to pay back the loan out of business profits. However, should he die before the end of that time, his family will have to bear the burden of the indebtedness. Therefore, his need is for a $10,000 Term insurance policy written for five years. If his death occurs while the loan is still outstanding, the proceeds of the insur-

---

[1] Some Term policies, however, may be changed to a permanent form of life insurance without medical examination or other underwriting scrutiny within a given time before the end of the term period. See discussion of Convertible Term later in this chapter.

[2] While the short term policy has no cash values, the long term policy is an exception. For example, in one typical company, a $1000 Term to age 65 issued at age 40 will have $7.39 in cash values in three years and $61.56 in ten years. In the 19th year, the cash value will be $78.66. After that, these values decrease. They will be $73.30 in the 20th year and will reach zero by the end of the 25th year. So even in long Term insurance while there may be some small value even this will disappear by the time retirement age is reached. The source and computation of cash values will be explained in Chapter 23 after certain technical matters necessary to their understanding have been covered.

[3] For some strange reason, he does not feel this way about his automobile insurance premiums. Perhaps it is because automobile insurance is sold as protection only, whereas life insurance is sold most often as a vehicle for accumulating a savings fund. Actually, the cash values of permanent life insurance policies are the by-product of the level premium system rather than the principal aim of life insurance. The emphases placed by agents on cash values has become another instance of the tail wagging the dog.

[4] All rates and values quoted in this chapter are based on participating policies, unless otherwise noted. For simplicity of illustration, it is assumed that all dividends are taken in cash. Rates and values vary slightly among companies.

ance will extinguish the debt and his family will be left an unencumbered estate. Frequently, lenders will request, sometimes even require, that their borrowers purchase this type of life insurance protection.

Other examples of life insurance needs for which Term insurance can be used advantageously can be cited:

A father who depends on his current earning power to finance his son's education can insure this earning power for the duration of the college period.

A business engaged in research in which one man is absolutely vital can insure its investment in this research by insuring the life of the key man for the duration of the project.

A young businessman embarking on a new adventure can insure his investment of time and money in the enterprise by insuring his life during the developmental stages of the business. It is usually several years before the new business will be of any value itself, apart from the owner.

A family man with a mortgage on his home may desire to insure his life for the decreasing amount of the mortgage for the period of its amortization so that in the event of his death he will be able to leave his family a home free of debt.[5]

These are by no means all the situations in which Term insurance may be used properly; they will, however, illustrate the point that Term insurance is to be used wherever there will be a loss if the policyholder dies before the end of a specified period, but where there will be no loss if he dies after that period.

Term insurance is also widely used by young people who have only a small amount of money to budget for insurance but who, on the other hand, have a large protection need. In such cases Term is used, not because of a temporary need, but because of a temporary financial condition. In many cases the policyholder plans to convert the Term into a permanent policy form—perhaps little by little—as he has more money available for premiums. For the same premium outlay, Term will provide more adequate, although temporary protection than will permanent policy forms.

Term insurance is attractive to students in professional fields, particularly those working toward one of the doctorates and, therefore, having a good

---

[5] Mortgage Redemption insurance is often written in the form of a permanent policy, especially when the policyholder needs more protection for his family than he has, aside from the Mortgage insurance. Under the permanent policy, as the amount of the mortgage reduces under monthly payment, the family's protection aside from the mortgage plan increases, since less of the insurance will be needed to pay off the mortgage at the death of the policyholder. "Mortgage Redemption" is the name of a plan rather than any particular policy form—the plan of paying off the mortgage in case of the death of the head of the family.

many years before they will be able to afford permanent insurance sufficient to cover their protection needs. In normal times, a young man starting out in a profession—medical, legal, or any type where his earnings depend upon building up a clientele—may have to get along for as many as ten or more years on an income too low to pay for adequate protection through permanent insurance. Such men will frequently obtain protection by using Term insurance as an emergency device.

College students planning marriage and facing military service might find Term insurance appropriate. They can obtain adequate protection in this way while postponing the purchase of permanent insurance until such time as they establish themselves permanently in civilian life.

Term insurance, if it is convertible,[6] will protect the policyholder's insurability for the minimum cost since, at the low Term rates, a large amount of insurance can be purchased for a small amount of money. This large amount of protection can be continued on a permanent basis later if the policyholder chooses, irrespective of changes in physical condition and occupational hazards.

Many established people need more death protection than they can afford to purchase on a permanent plan. They are people who are willing to sacrifice, in whole or in part, old age protection for themselves in order to obtain adequate premature death protection for their families. They look to Term insurance in such cases, not because it fits their need, but because it fits their pocketbooks. Term insurance gives the most for the premium dollar in premature death benefits but offers no protection against superannuation.

Limitations of Term Insurance. Every policy form has limitations. These limitations exist only when there is an attempt to use the policy to fulfill a need for which it is not designed. If Term insurance is used where the situation calls for permanent insurance, it has certain, clear-cut disadvantages. The disadvantages are:

(1) The need for life insurance protection may extend beyond the period of the policy. The policyholder may be uninsurable at the expiration of the term period and, therefore, unable to secure a new policy. For example, a five-year Term policy taken to insure a research chemist during a major project will expire before the project is completed if the chemist hits a snag and requires more time than the original five-year estimate. If the chemist loses his insurability during this period, insurance protection will be denied those who have heavily invested in the project.

(2) When Term insurance is used for a permanent and continuing need, the premium will increase at each renewal date and may become prohibitive

---

[6] That is, if may be changed to a permanent policy form without evidence of insurability.

in later years.[7] The table on page 39 shows the increased rate required at each renewal period of a five-year Term policy. For example, the rate at age 25 is $8.13 per thousand. The lowest-permium, permanent policy (Continuous-premium Whole Life) at that age and in the same company is quoted at $20.40—well over twice the rate of the five-year Term policy. It is easy, therefore, to see how a young man age 25 might be tempted to take Term insurance instead of continuous-premium Whole Life to fulfill his insurance needs. Assuming, however, that the portion of the insurable need which he is covering with Term insurance is a permanent one continuing throughout his life, he will find that his Term insurance at age 55 (which is, by the way, the last age at which this particular company will write five-year Term) will cost him $32.40 a thousand, or more than half again as much as the level premium he would still be paying had he bought continuous-premium Whole Life instead of five-year Term when he was age 25.

Should he reach 60, he would be unable to continue his Term insurance in this company. Assuming again that his need is a continuing one, such as the need for a burial fund, he would find not only that Term insurance would grow prohibitively expensive in the later years, but also that there would come a time when, despite the fact that he still needed protection, he would be unable to buy it. He might, of course, shift to a permanent policy form at that age if he is insurable. In the company used here for illustration, he would have to make that shift in his sixtieth year—the expiration date of the last five-year Term policy available to him.[8]

The annual cost of continuous-premium Whole Life at age 60 would be $76.12 per $1,000, almost four times the level premium at age 25. It should be pointed out, however, that a man age 60 would need less for death protection than would a man age 25.[9] Therefore, it might be possible for him to

---

[7] This is true unless the need decreases in size each year to the extent that the total premium can be kept reasonably low by reducing the face amount of the policy. If the amount of insurance needed decreases enough each year to offset the rising rate, the total premiums will not advance. For example, the $81.30 premium charged for $10,000 of five-year Term at age 25 will purchase roughly only $7,500 of five-year Term at age 35. If the need has been reduced by one fourth, then the premium can be kept level. However, few people own enough life insurance to feel justified in reducing their coverage as they advance in age except during those later years when the children are no longer dependent on parental support.

[8] Some companies will renew Term insurance beyond age 65, but the practice in the industry is for companies to set some upper age limit beyond which they will not renew Term insurance contracts.

[9] This would not be true if he had a large estate subject to heavy death and administration taxes. However, generally speaking, a man of 60 has only one dependent, his wife; and in all probability she will be at an age that requires less insurance for lifetime income than does a younger man's wife. For example, it takes slightly more than $71,000 insurance to provide a widow age 40 a life income of $250 a month whereas at age 65, this income can be provided with slightly less than $42,000 of insurance.

purchase adequate death protection at that age on a permanent policy basis without unduly increasing premium outlay by sharply decreasing his insurance coverage.

Annual Rates at Five-Year Intervals
Representative Five-Year Term, Par Basis

Age	Rate per $1,000
25	$ 8.13
30	9.23
35	10.91
40	13.47
45	17.36
50	20.03
55	32.40

(3) An important use of life insurance is to provide income for old age. Term insurance, having no cash values, cannot be used for this purpose. Some advocates of Term contend that life insurance should be used only to protect against the economic consequences of premature death and that other forms of saving and investment should be used to create values for old age. Statistical illustrations can be constructed to show that other forms of investment will build more for old age than will savings tied in with life insurance. In answer, those who advocate life insurance as a savings medium point out that there is a big difference between statistical compilations and actual fact; and they contend that while it is possible to show larger gains from investments, such illustrations must assume more "if's" than do savings through life insurance. Specifically, their argument is based on five observations.

1. The average person is unable to save over an extended period of years unless faced with some compulsion or penalty. A savings plan combined with life insurance compels a man to save at a time when he might skip a deposit under any other plan. The company sends the policyholder a premium reminder, the life insurance agent urges him to pay his premium, and the policyholder himself looks upon his life insurance premium deposits as an expense and budgets for them accordingly. The penalty for not paying the premium is the lapsation of the policy—something which "goes against the grain" of the average person.

2. Not only is there the inability on the part of the average person to save regularly each and every year, but also there is the inability to keep that which is saved. It is relatively easy on a man's conscience to draw savings from a savings account or to liquidate a government bond or corporate security to raise money to buy a temporary luxury. People, however,

are not so quick to cash in their life insurance policies. Many will not sur-render their policies before retirement for anything short of an emergency.[10] The result is that a retirement fund is more nearly certain to be there at age 65 if it is tied up with life insurance.

3. Savings placed in life insurance policies earn a fair rate of return. In order to earn more, a man must invest in properties or securities which re-quire not only investment skill to prevent loss, but also more time for man-agement than the average person has available aside from his regular em-ployment. There is no assurance that even keen investment skill can prevent losses during adverse market conditions. Cash values in a life insurance con-tract are unaffected by market conditions.

4. Interest and dividend returns on general investments are subject to federal income taxes in the year earned, whereas the annual interest incre-ments on life insurance policy values are not subject to the federal income tax until these values are paid to the policyholder during his lifetime. At this point, the taxable income is the excess of the amount collected under the policy over the total amount paid in premiums.[11] This tax treatment can be a real advantage to policyholders in high income tax brackets, because not only will their earned income drop upon retirement, but also their per-sonal income tax exemption will be doubled at 65. Thus if the policy values are paid out over the period of retirement, the amount subject to taxes in any one year will be small.[12]

5. The low interest rates available on high-grade investments suitable for retirement accounts make it imperative for the typical person to liquidate his capital in order to have an income high enough to finance his retirement. For example, a man who is fortunate enough to accumulate $30,000 by age 65 will be able to earn an investment income of only $75 a month from this fund, assuming a 3% return. This is hardly enough to provide for the cost of living even for a man content to sit at home on a rocking chair. The $75 a month needs to be increased by supplementing it with a part of the prin-cipal every month. The principal, however, must be liquidated systemati-cally through an annuity if an income is to be guaranteed as long as the annuitant lives. At age 65, $30,000 will buy an annuity of $189 a month.

---

[10] A theoretical advantage in buying Term and investing the difference in other forms of investments lies in the fact that in an emergency, savings can be withdrawn or securi-ties liquidated without lowering the amount of life insurance protection.

[11] Actually, only part of the premium paid represents an investment of principal. The rest is pure life insurance expenses such as would be a premium on Term insurance. Therefore, this formula, in effect, gives the policyholder a deduction for the premium paid for pure life insurance protection since the total premiums paid may be offset against the proceeds collected.

[12] Cf. Chapter 17 for a more detailed discussion of the role of taxation in life insurance planning.

If it is granted that liquidation of capital accumulations will be necessary for an adequate retirement income, there might be an advantage in making these accumulations through a life insurance contract. Currently, $30,000 accumulated in cash values in a life insurance policy can be liquidated as an annuity at age 65 under contract settlement provisions paying $203 a month—$14 more than could be purchased by a similar investment in a single-premium life annuity. In addition to paying more in annuity income, there may be another advantage of accumulating retirement funds through a life insurance policy. Annuity income rates are guaranteed in the life insurance contract. This might be an important guarantee, since mortality rates are decreasing. The effect of this decrease is a reduction in the amount of annuity income per $1000 of principal. These guarantees have proved valuable to those who purchased whole life insurance contracts over 30 years ago. Today, these policies can be cashed in at age 65 for annuity benefits that are much higher than could be purchased with the accumulated savings in annuity contracts sold today.

For example, a cash value of $30,000 in one of these old policies could be liquidated as an annuity of $236 a month—$47 more than the $30,000 would buy as a single-premium annuity at today's rates. This advantage, of course, assumes that the terminal fund will be $30,000 regardless of the type of investment medium used, an assumption which, more than likely, will not hold true. Investment losses and withdrawals might reduce the accumulations in speculative investments to a figure below the $30,000. Conversely, speculative gains might increase the figure to more than $30,000.

(4) Another disadvantage of Term insurance for the average person is its lack of cash values (except in the longer term policies, as previously mentioned). This lack of cash values means that, should there come a time when the policyholder is unable to meet his premium payments because of financial difficulties, his protection will expire. There are no cash values out of which to obtain a premium loan. This is true also in the case of all forms of property insurance; however, it is rarely that these forms cannot be renewed in subsequent years when the money again becomes available, the only danger being the occurrence of a loss in an unprotected year. In contrast, the insurability of a policyholder may change overnight. He may find that when money again becomes available, it will be impossible for him to obtain insurance.

Types of Term Policies. Term insurance is written in a variety of ways, each designed to meet a particular type of need. These variations among Term policies tend to offset some of the limitations of Term insurance. For example, long-term policies may offset the disadvantage of increasing insurance costs. Long-term policies, however, are considerably more expensive at younger ages. At age 25, Term to age 65 is about $14.44 a thousand as compared with $7.66 a thousand for one-year Term and $20.40 a thousand for continuous-premium Whole Life insurance. Renewable and convertible Term may offset the disadvantage of expiring protection. Briefly, Term policies may be classified as follows:

Straight Term policies are written for a specific number of years and automatically terminate at the end of the period. Most companies write five-year Term, ten-year Term, 15-year Term, and 20-year Term on a level premium basis.

Long-term policies, written by many companies, are of three general types: (1) *Term to Expectancy.* Such policies are written for a term of years extending from the date of issuance to the end of the policyholder's life expectancy. For example, Expectancy Term taken at age 20 will, according to the CSO mortality table, expire in 46.54 years, or at approximately age 66. (2) *Life Expectancy Term* is the same as Term to Expectancy except that it gives the insured an option of a conversion to a Whole Life plan, either for a drastically reduced amount of protection by continuing the premium payment at the expiration of the term period, or for the same amount of protection by paying an increased premium. Thus, for example, a man age 20 who buys a $10,000 Life Expectancy Term policy for an annual premium of $125 may at age 66 continue to pay this same premium and convert to $1,400 of continuous-premium Whole Life insurance; or he may pay a premium of $940 and continue the full $10,000 in force on a continuous-premium Whole Life basis. Of course, he could convert to an amount of insurance less than $10,000 and pay the appropriate premium or he could do nothing and allow his protection to terminate. (3) *Term to Age 65.* Under this plan, insurance expires at age 65. There are variations of the plan. Some companies may write Term insurance only to age 60, whereas others may write it to age 70.[13]

Renewable Term policies are those which may be renewed at expiration for an additional period without evidence of insurability. However, the renewal premium will be charged at the rate for the attained age at the time

---

[13] These three relatively common forms of long-term policies are not always known by the name used above. For example, one company calls its Life Expectancy policy, the "Emancipator" policy, while calling its Term to 65 "Select Economy" plan. One company even calls its Term to Expectancy policy a "Life Expectancy" policy. The terms as used in the above paragraph are adopted in this text because they are the most descriptive. Inquiry as to the exact provisions of any long-term policy will reveal at once its classification. The trade name given to the policy rarely will indicate its true nature; however, most insurance jurisdictions require that the exact nature of the policy be stated somewhere on the face, usually in a footnote line at the bottom.

of renewal. For example, a man 25 years old who takes out a $10,000 five-year renewable Term policy will pay an annual level premium of about $81 for five years. Then, if he renews the contract at age 30, he must pay an annual level premium of $91, which is the five-year Term rate at that age.

Most of the principal companies write some form of renewable Term insurance, although only a limited number will write *yearly* renewable Term on an individual policy basis; [14] that is, Term policies written for a period of one year and renewable at the end of each year up to an attained age, 60, for instance. More common are five-, ten-, 15-, or 20-year renewable Term. The period over which policies may be renewed is usually limited. Two common types of limitations are: (1) A limitation on the number of times renewals may be made. (2) A limitation on the age at which the insured may make his last renewal. Companies restrict the number of renewals in order to reduce adverse selection in later years. Policyholders in good health will be less likely to exercise their renewal privileges at advanced ages because of the higher rate, whereas those in poor health will be more inclined to continue their insurance in force as long as they are allowed to do so. The net result of unlimited renewal would be a higher mortality rate among policyholders and, consequently, an increase in cost.

Convertible Term gives the insured the right to convert to any permanent or Endowment form of insurance without evidence of insurability within a certain period of time before the expiration of the term of the contract. For example, a five-year Term policy may be convertible any time before maturity or, in some cases, any time within the first three years; a ten-year Term policy may be convertible any time before maturity, or, in some companies, any time within the first seven years. Term to 65 and Expectancy Term are usually convertible up to any time five years prior to their expiration date.

An example of a convertible Term policy is the National Service Life Insurance plan of World War II. National Service life insurance policies were all written on a five-year Term basis, with the privilege of conversion to a permanent plan at any time within five years, or within any longer period to which the privilege may be extended by the Veterans Administration or Congress.

The convertible Term plan is especially advantageous for a young man who is establishing a family but who is unable to afford the total premium required to give adequate protection under a permanent policy form. He can use a convertible Term policy which permits him to acquire a large amount of protection at a relatively small annual premium. Then, as his in-

---

[14] As contrasted to group insurance, for which cf. Chapter 13.

come increases, he can convert the Term insurance to a permanent contract.[15] For example, a young family man age 23 can purchase $20,000 15-year convertible Term for an annual premium of $165. He can convert this policy into a continuous-premium Whole Life at age 35 by increasing the annual premium $385, making a total premium of $550. By then, not only should he be able to afford the additional premium, but also he might want to start building a cash value for retirement while he still has time to accumulate a fund of reasonable size.[16]

Automatic convertible Term policies are those which are automatically converted into continuous-premium Whole Life or some other plan of permanent insurance at the end of a given number of years (usually one to five). They may also be converted earlier if the insured so elects. The automatic nature of the plan helps to meet the argument against the psychology of straight convertible Term insurance. The decision to convert is taken out of the hands of the often reluctant policyholder, and conversion is made for him by the company at a time agreed upon when the contract is issued.

A variation of the automatic convertible Term is the Modified Life policy to be discussed in Chapter 6.

Decreasing Term is another common form of Term insurance. Under this type of policy, the amount of insurance is reduced each year while the premium remains level throughout the period.

An important use of decreasing Term is to provide protection against the death of the breadwinner during the child dependency period, especially when the budget available demands strict economy in the use of insurance premiums. For example, in one prominent company an annual premium of about $120 gross at age 25 will buy $31,500 of convertible decreasing Term, decreasing $1,500 a year for 20 years. Dividends will decrease the net annual premium in later years. The policy will provide a monthly income of $158.75

---

[15] Often the best plan of insurance that can be recommended to the young man is convertible Term up to the full amount of his protection need and then a change to permanent policy forms as soon as his budget can stand the higher premiums. This recommendation is rarely made, however, because of the recognized fact that it is extremely difficult, psychologically, to get a policyholder to convert Term insurance. Moreover, there is always the danger that the young man holding Term will run into a year when he cannot meet the premiums and, unless he is using long-term policy forms under which there are cash values, he will have to lapse at least some part of his protection and then may be unable to obtain additional insurance when he is later able to pay the premium again.

[16] He might wish to make the conversions gradually over the period of the contract. For example, he can convert $5,000 at age 25 by paying an additional premium of $60. At age 30, by stepping up his premium $75 he can convert another $5,000. At age 35, he can convert the final $10,000 by increasing his annual premium $190. In this way, the increase in premiums is gradual with total premiums stepping up as follows: $165, $225, $300, and $490.

for 20 years if the insured dies during its first year. Should he die in subsequent years, the policy could be arranged to pay as follows, thus guaranteeing a fixed minimum income during the 20 year child dependency period.

Year of Death	Monthly Family Income
4th	$155.80 for 17 years
8th	152.45 for 13 years
12th	151.50 for 9 years
16th	157.40 for 5 years
20th	252.25 for 1 year

During the early years of the policy the cost of providing these benefits under the decreasing Term form is less than under the yearly renewable Term form. For example, to provide $31,500 protection at age 25 under yearly renewable Term would require an initial premium of about $210. A renewal of $30,000 at age 26 would require a premium of about $200.

Decreasing Term is written most often on a monthly decreasing basis and in combination with permanent policy forms under family income or mortgage protection plans. These special plans are discussed in Chapter 6.

Exclusive of Group insurance, of which over 90% is written on a Term plan, and of Industrial, in which no Term is written, less than 15% of all private life insurance in force in the United States is on a Term basis.

Statistics on Term are interesting. Contrary to what one would expect, level Term seems to be sold more often than average to high-income and high-age groups, and to executives, managers, proprietors, and professional workers.

2. ENDOWMENT INSURANCE

The Endowment policy offers insurance protection against death for a specified period of time. If the insured lives to the end of the Endowment period, the policy pays the face amount, either in a lump sum or, if elected by the insured, in installments. If he dies prior to endowment date, the face amount is paid to his beneficiary. Thus a $10,000, 20-year Endowment policy promises to pay $10,000 in event of the insured's death before the expiry of the 20th year, or $10,000 to the insured himself, if he survives the period.

The Endowment policy might be said to be a savings fund protected by Term insurance; that is, the policyholder decides that he wants to build up a certain fund of money at the end of a given number of years. In a sense, the insurance company establishes a savings fund for him to which he contributes regularly and on which interest is compounded annually. If he lives to the end of the term period, he will have accumulated the cash desired. However, the insurance company further agrees that if he dies prior to the end of that period and before the "savings fund" reaches the face value of the policy, it will complete the "savings fund" for him immediately out of the mortality fund and pass the full amount on to his beneficiaries at that time.

For example, suppose a man age 25 wants to accumulate a fund sufficient to put his newly born son through college 20 years from now. He figures that $5,000 will be the basic minimum necessary for this purpose.[17] He wants to be sure that this fund will be available whether he lives or dies. So he buys a 20-year Endowment insurance contract [18] for an annual net premium of about $220. By the time the father reaches age 38, he will have accumulated in his policy a savings fund of $2,165 (known in technical language as the cash surrender value). Should he die during the next year, this amount coupled with $2,835 insurance benefits would make up the $5,000 then payable to his son for later use in college. At the end of the 19th year, the policy is worth about $4,675. Death during the 20th year, therefore, would draw only $325 out of the mortality fund to make up the $5,000. Should he survive to age 45, the policy will have a value of $5,000, which is the full amount the father wants to accumulate for the education of his son. The policy becomes payable at that time, and there is no longer any death protection under it. During the 20 years the Endowment policy has provided a decreasing amount of insurance protection while the savings fund was gradually accumulated. The total deposits made amounted to $4,400. Interest on these deposits was enough to pay for the cost of the decreasing Term insurance and still leave a surplus of $600.[19]

Uses of Endowment.   Endowment insurance is used properly when the need for protection against premature death has been fairly well filled and there is a specific need for cash at a given time in the future. For example, an individual who needs to build a fund through annual saving to pay off a debt falling due at the end of 10, 20, or any given number of years might find an Endowment policy useful. A savings fund would be an excellent way to meet the debt, except that if the debtor dies before the fund equals the amount of the debt, his family would be faced with the problem of making up the difference at a time when the family needed every cent of its money.

---

[17] This assumes, of course, that present costs do not materially increase. Stop and think for a moment of the father who, back in 1937, estimated the prospective cost of a four-year college education for his then newly born son at $2,500, which was a liberal estimate based on 1937 prices.

[18] Don't jump to the conclusion that this is the policy he should buy. Defer your judgment until you have read Chapter 7.

[19] While this is a useful illustration to explain the concept of Endowment insurance, it is not technically correct as actuaries view it.

The Endowment policy also finds use as a vehicle for savings by those who find it difficult to save. Here the protection element is of little or no importance except that it provides the compulsion to make the regular deposits which otherwise might be "skipped." The protection value will be lost if the saver does not save regularly.

Endowment insurance is a vehicle for the accumulation of funds for a specific purpose. For example, an Endowment can be used to build a dowry for a daughter or a capital fund for a son to get a start in business. These, of course, are luxury uses of life insurance and should be ignored except by families whose protection needs are adequately covered.

Perhaps the most important use of Endowments is to provide retirement income. Endowments at age 60 and 65 are primarily intended to provide funds for old age. Purchased at relatively early ages, they offer a reasonably large amount of protection per premium dollar while accumulating a retirement fund which may be taken as cash or as an annuity income at age 65. For instance:

The participating premium rate per $1,000 of Endowment at 65 issued at age 25 in one rate book is $25.10. The rate for continuous-premium Whole Life in this same company and at that same age is $20.76. At age 65, the cash values of the Whole Life policy will provide a retirement income of about $4 monthly for life, per thousand of face value; while the Endowment at 65 contract will provide about $6.75. Approximately $125 a year invested in an Endowment at 65 contract will provide $5,000 of protection for dependents to age 65 and $33.75 a month retirement income for the insured after 65 (male). The same amount of money will pay for about $6,000 continuous-premium Whole Life, the cash values from which will provide the insured at 65 about $24 per month income at 65.[20]

A special form of the Endowment policy is Retirement Income Insurance, also called "Special Retirement Endowment," "Guaranteed Life Income," "Income Endowment," and many other names. The contract usually provides $10 a month retirement income per $1,000 of face value. Since under the life income option of one company writing the contract $1,000 provides only $6.75 a month, male, at 65, it is obvious that the policy must provide for values at age 65 in excess of the face of the contract in order to pay $10 per month per thousand of face value. In this particular rate book, the maturity value of the contract is $1,623 per thousand at 65. The premium, consequently, is much higher than Endowment at 65, being $33.19 at age 25,

[20] These retirement income figures are based on those quoted for male lives. The corresponding retirement figures for female lives are $29.00 for the Endowment and about $21.00 for the continuous-premium Whole Life policy. Women receive less life income per given amount of insurance since, on the average, they live longer than men.

almost $8 per $1,000 more. For female insureds, the same policy pays only $9.41 per thousand of face value at 65.[21] If the policy becomes a claim prior to retirement age, the face value or the cash value, whichever is the greater at that point, is paid. For example, if the man in the above illustration dies at age 55, his beneficiary will collect the cash value of the policy rather than its face, since by that time the cash value will exceed the face value by $36.00. If the insured dies at age 60, his estate will collect $1,312. On the other hand, if he dies at age 45, his estate will collect the $1,000 face value, for at that age the cash value of the policy is only $595.

Limitations of Endowments. The limitations of the Endowment form rise from its incorrect use. The temptation of a large sum of cash at the end of a relatively short period of time leads many people to purchase the plan when their real need is for premature death protection. Many individuals have reached the endowment age to find themselves in possession of several thousand dollars in cash, an amount wholly inadequate to offset their continuing death protection need.[22] Technically, the limitations of the Endowment are two: *expiring protection and low protection value.* Only when there is a limited and expiring premature death protection need plus a valid need for a cash fund at a given future date does the Endowment policy find its proper application.

Endowment policies often appeal to people as a way to "win, live or die." They forget that insurance is not a "bet." You never receive more than you pay for. An Endowment policy is, practically speaking, made up of two types of life insurance policies: Term and pure Endowment. When a man dies, he "wins" on the Term portion. When he lives, he "wins" on the endowment portion. Whichever happens, however, he pays for the portion of the policy on which he didn't collect: the Term, if he lives; the pure endowment, if he dies. If he dies, he would have been better off with pure Term insurance. If he lives, he would have been better off with a savings account, or a pure endowment, if it were available.

Endowment policies are more popular than Term insurance. Exclusive of Group life insurance, over 17% of all life insurance in force in the United

---

[21] Some companies adjust the difference between men and women by having separate premium rates in order to provide $10 per $1,000 for either sex. In the example quoted above, a $1,000 retirement income policy at age 65 for a female issued at age 25 would cost $36.13 annually or about $3 more than for males. A very few companies make no difference either in retirement payments or in premium rates.

[22] The policy, however, may include other than cash options; for instance, the insured may accept a paid-up policy at an *increased* amount in lieu of cash payment. The option also may allow the insured to accept a paid-up policy of the original face value plus a refund of the difference between the cash value of the new policy and the face value of the Endowment. Normally, either option will require that the policyholder be insurable.

States is written on the Endowment plan. Contrary to what might be expected, Endowment policies seem to be sold more often than average to low income groups and groups under age 30.

3. SUMMARY

Two types of life insurance contracts protect against premature death for specified periods only: Term and Endowment. Term differs from Endowment in that it pays no benefits to policyholders who live to the end of the term period. Endowments pay a surviving benefit.

Term insurance is subject to much abuse and criticism by critics who fail to see its sound uses. The line of attack on Term usually is that (1) it might expire before the need for insurance expires, (2) rates become prohibitive in later years, and (3) no cash values are accumulated for retirement. These attacks ignore the modifications of straight Term insurance. Renewable and convertible Term makes it possible for a young family man to purchase adequate protection when his need is greatest and his ability to pay is lowest. At a later date, the Term may be converted into Whole Life on a level premium basis and insurance protection is then guaranteed as long as it is needed. Cash values, which may be used for retirement or emergencies, will be building up.

Term insurance may well be used to cover temporary needs for insurance protection. It might also be used by low-income families unable to afford anything else. Finally, it can be used by those who, for one reason or another, prefer to make their saving outside of their life insurance.

People who prescribe Term insurance for every need and who sharply criticize all forms of permanent life insurance are called "Termites" by the life insurance business. "Termites" are to be condemned just as much as those who blindly criticize Term insurance and refuse to see any of its values.

As stated, Endowment insurance is more popular than Term but, perhaps, less useful in the majority of cases in which it is actually employed. Endowment forms provide a low amount of protection per premium dollar. They are best used, therefore, where protection needs are low in relation to a need for high cash values and a specified sum of money at a fixed future date.

Questions for Class Discussion

1. Several unkind statements often are made about Term insurance. Some are true, whereas others are off base. State and evaluate the arguments against Term insurance.

2. What are the various types of Term insurance that offset the limitations of straight Term?

3. Are there any limitations of straight Term which cannot be offset by some other form of Term?

4. Explain why long Term policies have cash values whereas short Term policies have no cash values.

5. Comment on the following statement: A man who owns a large amount of Term insurance and is saving money regularly elsewhere should convert some of his Term policies to Whole Life or Endowment insurance.

6. The Endowment insurance policy is the ideal insurance contract because you cannot lose with one. The policy pays off whether you live or die. It is the sure way of beating the company. Comment.

7. Describe a family situation which might call for the use of Term insurance; Endowment insurance.

8. Often the advice "Buy Term and invest the difference" is heard. What is this *difference* referred to in the advice?

9. What do you think about the advice referred to in the above question?

10. Although at any given age $10,000 of 20-year Endowment insurance costs more than $10,000 of 20-year Term insurance, it gives less life insurance protection. Is this statement true or false? Explain.

CHAPTER 4

THE WHOLE LIFE CONTRACT

AN UNFORTUNATE confusion in nomenclature exists in the use of the words "Whole life." Sometimes the term is used interchangeably with "Ordinary life." "Ordinary" has two very different connotations. It is applied to that class of insurance written for a minimum of $1,000 on an annual premium basis.[1] The word "Ordinary" is used to distinguish this type of insurance from Industrial insurance—a form of weekly-premium insurance usually of less than $500.[2] In an entirely different connotation, "Ordinary Life" is used to indicate that type of policy in which protection is furnished for the whole of life and upon which premiums are payable continuously throughout the lifetime of the insured. It is in its latter connotation that "Ordinary Life" is used interchangeably with "Whole Life."

Whole Life insurance is a broader term than Ordinary Life. It is insurance that furnishes protection for the whole of life regardless of how many years premiums are to be paid. Premiums may be paid over a limited period, such as 20 or 30 years, or they may be paid in one lump sum at the inception of the policy. When premiums are to be continuous throughout the lifetime of the insured, the policy is most commonly referred to as an "Ordinary Life" policy. In this sense, "Ordinary Life" is simply a type of Whole Life insurance and is not to be used to include all Whole Life forms. A more descriptive term for such a policy is "continuous-premium Whole Life," as contrasted to "limited-payment Whole Life" and "single-premium Whole Life."

[1] Premiums may be paid semiannually or quarterly by paying a small addition for handling and carrying charges.
[2] Cf. Chapter 12.

Uses of Whole Life. Of the several policy forms, Whole Life is perhaps the most adaptable to typical life insurance needs. Although some protection needs diminish as the individual grows older, no one ever outlives all need for protection against the financial loss occasioned by death. Death itself creates expenses, usually rather heavy. Consequently there is always a need for life insurance protection regardless of the age of the individual.

The Whole Life policy is further versatile in that it contains a savings element, the cash value, which permits the individual to protect simultaneously against the twin perils of premature death and of loss of income through old age. A Whole Life policy taken at a reasonably early age will have, at age 65, a substantial cash value per $1,000 of insurance. Most companies will permit the insured to withdraw this cash value in the form of periodic payments, if he so desires.[3] Some companies grant this income option in the policy. Others permit it by company practice.[4] A Whole Life policy, therefore, makes it possible for the insured to obtain a relatively high amount of protection against premature death per dollar of premium during his "family years" when he needs this type of protection most, and yet, automatically and at the same time, provide for his old age. Moreover, he will have a yearly increasing emergency fund on which he can draw for cash or a loan if necessary.[5]

Limitations of Whole Life. For the typical person, the limitations of the Whole Life policy are few. It does not offer exact protection for every need, yet it is the one policy which will provide reasonably satisfactory coverage for almost every need. In other words, whereas a Term or an Endowment policy might fit certain specialized needs of the insured better at any given moment, Whole Life insurance also will take care of that same need reasonably well while, at the same time, offering greater flexibility. If a need that originally called for Term or Endowment insurance is altered, such policies may no longer fit into the changed situation, whereas the Whole Life policy almost always will continue to serve the new needs reasonably well. It is the most flexible of all policies.

Perhaps the principal limitation of Whole Life insurance, when compared with Term insurance, is its higher annual premium. The primary insurance need for most families is income for the wife and children in the event of the premature death of the breadwinner. If only a very small

---

[3] Cf. Chapter 5 for a discussion of annuities.
[4] It should be held in mind that a contractual provision is a safer guarantee than "company practice."
[5] Remember, of course, that this latter advantage might well be a disadvantage, for in order to obtain the use of this emergency fund, the insured must either surrender his insurance or encumber it (although perhaps only temporarily) with a loan.

amount of money can be budgeted by the family for life insurance premiums, to buy Whole Life insurance would mean a sacrificing of vital death protection in order to build up cash values for emergency or retirement.[6]

Although the preceding paragraphs discuss the uses and limitations of Whole Life insurance, they do so only broadly. It is more realistic to discuss the uses and limitations of the various *types* of Whole Life policies, for their differences are significant. So, in the following discussion of the nature of each type of Whole Life insurance, consideration is given to their uses and limitations.

1. TYPES OF WHOLE LIFE POLICIES

Whole Life policies are classified according to the period over which premiums are paid. The more common among them are the continuous, limited, and single premium plans.

Continuous-Premium, Whole Life Policies. Continuous premium or "Straight Life" are contracts which provide death protection for the whole of life, with premiums payable continuously until death.[7] The insured pays the premiums at each due date as long as he lives; when he dies, the proceeds go to his beneficiaries. In Ordinary (as contrasted to Industrial), payment of the premium may be made on an annual, semiannual, or quarterly basis. In some instances, a company will permit monthly payment of Ordinary insurance premiums. Payment at intervals other than annually increases the cost of insurance slightly. For instance, the semiannual premium in one company is determined by multiplying the annual premium by 0.52. (The quarterly factor is 0.265 and the monthly factor, 0.092.)

There are three reasons for the higher fractional premiums: (a) If the full annual premium is not available at the beginning of the premium year, there will be a loss of interest to the company. The policyholder must make up this loss. (b) Also, and far more important, he must make up the extra expense involved in handling the premium more than once during the year: the mail room and bookkeeping costs, for example. Added together in the aggregate of thousands of premium payments, they will mount up to a substantial total. (c) Many companies do not call for the unpaid portion of the annual premium should a policyholder die after paying, say, only a semiannual premium. The loss of the other semiannual premium also must be considered in setting fractional premium rates. This latter reason does not

---

[6] The authors hasten to disavow that such a statement indicates they are "Termites." The Term advocate insists that Term is the only useful policy form. The authors seek to show only that Term has its uses and that it has advantages in proper application. Their endeavor is to show both proper and improper application of *all* policy forms.

[7] Or until the ultimate age in the mortality table on which the reserve is based.

apply to those companies which refund the unearned portion of the annual premium at death. For example, if death occurs one month after the annual premium is paid, the death claim is increased by some companies by 11/12 of the annual premium.

The continuous-premium Whole Life policy furnishes the maximum amount of *permanent* death protection at the lowest annual premium. For instance, at age 25, a gross premium of $20.40 will purchase $1,000 continuous-premium Whole Life insurance on a participating basis; at the same age and in the same company, that amount of money will purchase only $911 of Whole Life paid up at age 65; and only approximately $628 of 20-payment Whole Life. The continuous-premium Whole Life policy combines insurance and savings with a minimum sacrifice of protection, since the investment feature of the policy, while present, takes less of the premium dollar than in the case of any other permanent policy form.

The limitations of the continuous-premium Whole Life policy forms are few indeed. A common objection to these forms is that cash values available at age 65 for retirement income seem low when compared to those available in the Endowment at 65 or with Whole Life paid up at 65.

Early in life, every individual faces a twin peril, the peril of premature death and the peril of the destruction of earning power brought about by old age.[8] He has no way of knowing which of these perils may occur. The continuous-premium Whole Life policy gives him the fullest protection possible in one policy against both of them. If he lives past the period requiring large amounts of premature death protection, the indemnity offered by the continuous-premium Whole Life policy against old age is not as satisfactory as that afforded by a policy designed particularly for retirement. However, if he dies during the critical family years, the indemnity payable to his family will be far more satisfactory than it would have been under a policy designed principally for retirement. For example, with a $500 annual premium a man age 35 can purchase about $20,000 continuous-premium Whole Life whereas he can buy only slightly more than $14,000 Endowment at age 65. The cash value at age 65 of the $20,000 continuous-premium Whole Life will be just under $11,000. The value at age 65 of the Endowment, of course, is its face value of $14,000. Therefore, when in this case a policyholder selects a continuous-premium Whole Life instead of an Endowment at 65, he is getting approximately $6,000 more in premature death protection and giving up approximately $3,000 of old age protection—a fair and unselfish trade if premature death protection for his family is inadequate.

---

[8] Actually, he faces three perils, the third being the peril of disability. Cf. Chapter 11, "Accident and Sickness Insurance."

Another objection to the continuous-premium Whole Life policy is that premiums must be paid throughout life. Many people like the idea of a termination date on premium payments, especially since in late years they may find it difficult to pay premiums without undue hardship. This objection overlooks the fact that after the early policy years, the payment of premiums may be discontinued at any time without forfeiting the cash values which have been accumulated under the policy. If for any reason the insured can no longer pay premiums, he may, if he still needs the insurance, take either the paid-up values in the policy or its extended Term values. In either event, he may discontinue the payment of premiums while continuing in force all or part of his premature death protection. If, for example, an insured who owns a continuous-premium Whole Life policy taken at age 35 were to find at age 65 that he no longer could pay the premium, he could exercise his right to take the paid-up insurance values in the policy. In an illustrative policy this would amount to $705 per thousand of insurance in force. In other words, he could discontinue all premium payments on, say, a $10,000 policy, and still have life insurance protection in the amount of $7,050 for the rest of his life. If he needed more protection than $7,050, and were not in particularly good health, he might decide to take the extended Term option, which, without payment of premiums, would keep his policy in force at its full amount ($10,000) for approximately 14 years. Of course at the expiration of the 14 years, when he would be 79, there would be no insurance.

Actually, limitations of the continuous-premium Whole Life policy become apparent only when the contract is used to fill a need for which it is not designed. For instance, if it is applied to a temporary need for protection, it does not give as much face value per premium dollar as does one of the Term insurance forms. Limitations also will appear when the continuous-premium Whole Life policy is used to cover what is more of a retirement than premature death protection need. However, for the typical individual, whose need is primarily for protection for his family in case of his premature death and only secondarily for protection against old age, the continuous-premium Whole Life policy is almost ideal.

Continuous-premium Whole Life is the most popular single type of policy. Exclusive of group, about 32% of all life insurance in force is on this plan.

Limited-Payment Life Policies. Limited-payment policies are those on which the premiums are payable for a stated period: ten years, 20 years, 30 years; or until the insured reaches a given age, 60 or 65, for example. Several companies, instead of issuing a continuous-premium Whole Life policy, issue a policy paid up at age 85 which, for all practical purposes, is a continuous-premium plan. In all these plans, the insured pays a level annual premium during the premium-paying years. With the payment of the last premium, the policy is "paid up," and no more premiums will be required of him, despite the fact that the full amount of the policy will remain in force the rest of his life.

Technically, no Whole Life policy is ever "paid up." No more premiums need be paid by the insured, however, when the cash values in the policy have grown large enough to equal the net single premium for Whole Life insurance at that age. The high premiums of the limited-payment policy create reserve values of this size by the end of the premium-paying period. The interest on the reserve values (or better the invested assets offsetting the reserve) continues the policy in force. This interest (or part of it) in effect is the cost of the insurance to the policyholder for he could surrender his contract for cash and invest these funds himself and pocket the interest. The policy, therefore, theoretically is never "paid up" even though it may no longer represent any direct burden on the policyholder.

The limited-payment policy must not be confused with an Endowment policy. With the payment of the last premium, a limited-payment policy is fully *paid up*, but it is not *matured*. A matured policy is one under which the face value is paid either by reason of death or by reason of the survival of the insured to the end of a given period. A paid-up policy does not mature but simply relieves the insured from the direct payment of any more premiums.

As has already been illustrated, the limited-payment life policy offers less protection for the same premium dollar than does the continuous-premium form. The reason for this is obvious: Roughly, the shorter the premium-payment period, the larger must be each premium.[9]

Often it is suggested that limited-payment Whole Life policies are properly used in a life situation in which the most productive years are limited to a relatively short span of time. A baseball player, for instance, knows that his earning period as far as his profession goes will be limited to ten or 15 years. Therefore, it is argued, he may properly buy a ten-Pay or 15-Pay policy in order to adjust his premium payments to the most productive period of his life. For example, suppose a 21-year-old baseball player estimates he has 15 years of professional life ahead of him. He decides he can

---

[9] The participating rate in a representative company for 20-Pay Life at age 25 is $32.44 and for Ten-Pay Life, $54.42. Interest and mortality factors are important in distributing the premium among any given number of years, otherwise the cost of Ten-Pay would be exactly twice the cost of 20-Pay. See Chapter 20 for a technical and more accurate explanation of this point.

budget $1,000 a year for life insurance to protect against loss of this earning power by death. He reasons that it would be wise to have the policy fully paid at the end of his productive years so he buys $27,000 of 15-Pay Life. When he reaches age 36, the policy is paid up. But suppose that when he retires from baseball, he finds a high-paying job. He might be just as capable now of paying $1,000 a year for insurance as he has been over the past 15 years. But if he is uninsurable, he will be unable to purchase another policy.

Suppose, on the other hand, he had put this $1,000 a year into a continuous-premium Whole Life policy. He could have purchased about $58,000 of insurance, more than twice as much as under the 15-Pay plan. If circumstances are such that he cannot continue his premium payments at age 36, he can take a paid-up policy of about $23,000, only $4,000 less than the amount of insurance available under the 15-Pay Life plan with the same premium. If he can continue the premium, he may keep the full $58,000 in force as long as he wishes. The continuous-premium Whole Life is, therefore, more flexible. Just as important as its flexibility is the fact that it offers $31,000 more death protection during the crucial 15-year period when the family is growing up which is more than worth the possible sacrifice of $4,000 after that period expires.

If, on the other hand, this baseball player is among the fortunate few who are earning high salaries, he will be able to put more than $1,000 into life insurance. Suppose, then, he can channel $5,000 a year into premiums. Under the 15-Pay Life plan, this $5,000 would purchase $135,000 of life insurance—an amount which he considers adequate to settle his estate and protect his family. In this case, the 15-Pay would be an attractive policy, for it would build up large cash values. The interest earned each year during this period of accumulation will not be taxable, thereby resulting in an effective yield equivalent to (or better than, depending on the tax bracket of the insured) that on speculative investments. If at age 36 he continues to earn a high salary and is insurable, he can purchase more insurance on a high-premium plan. If he is not insurable, the present paid-up policy for $135,000 should be adequate if he does a competent job of estate planning.

The individual who plans to retire at age 65 and has arranged reasonable protection for his family in case of his premature death may properly use a limited-payment policy to provide the necessary cash to pay the cost of last illness, funeral, and death taxes. As a result, he will not be burdened with the obligation to pay premiums out of his retirement income.[10]

---

[10] Remember, too, that premiums on the continuous-premium Whole Life policy may be discontinued at age 65, at the expense of a reduced amount of insurance.

The limited-payment life policy is usable sometimes in special situations. For example, a father who wishes to make a gift of paid-up life insurance to his child may purchase the insurance on a limited-payment form so as to complete the payments before the policy is turned over to the child. Limited pay will also often prove useful in estate planning where income tax considerations are involved.

The limited-payment life policy also is useful for the person who wishes to accumulate more cash value per $1,000 of death benefit than is available under the continuous-premium Whole Life, but whose investable funds are insufficient to buy Endowment with its even higher cash accumulations. Like the Endowment at age 65, a Whole Life policy paid up at age 65 also is a popular investment type contract. Table 1 will show the difference in the amount of cash value accumulated in continuous-premium, limited-premium, and Endowment forms.

Table 1. Comparison of Rates and Values
Continuous Pay, Limited Pay, and Endowment
(Issue Age 25, Gross Par Rates)

Policy Form	Premium Rate Per $1,000	CASH VALUES PER $1,000 End of 10th Year	End of 20th Year
Continuous-Premium Whole Life	$20.40	$105.04	$261.11
Life Paid Up 65	22.20	122.88	304.39
20-Pay Life	32.50	224.68	551.37
20-Year Endowment	50.34	410.26	1,000.00

The larger investment element in limited-pay forms and the anticipation of completing premium payments at some time in the future, often lead to a misuse of these forms. If a man's need is primarily for protection for his family in case of his premature death—which is the basic need of most men— then the savings or investment factor should be a secondary consideration, if any consideration at all.

It must also be remembered that although the cash value for each $1,000 under a continuous-premium form is lower, it is possible to buy more units of protection with a given premium under continuous-premium Whole Life than is the case with the limited-pay or Endowment form. Thus with a given premium budget the difference in the total cash value that a policyholder has available at any given time will be less than the per-thousand differences shown in the above table. In truth, in the continuous-premium Whole Life policy, the total cash value available at the end of 20 years, assuming the same amount of premium is spent in each case, would not be too far below that obtained under a 20-Pay plan. For instance, the cash values per $1,000 at the end of 20 years according to Table 1 are about 2.1 times higher for 20-Pay life than for continuous-premium Whole Life. Actually however, per dollar of premium paid, the cash values of the 20-Pay plan are only 1.32 times higher.

Nevertheless the difference per $1,000 might tempt the buyer to take the 20-Pay Life when his premature death needs indicate he should take the continuous-premium. However, if he has $500 a year to spend for life insurance, he can buy approximately $29,000 continuous-premium but only $17,500 of 20-Pay Life, both on a nonpar basis. This means that if he dies before his family is grown, his dependents will receive $11,500 less under 20-Pay than under continuous-premium, a deficiency which might prove disastrous for them. For instance, $29,000 will provide a $200 a month income for approximately 14½ years whereas $17,500 will provide this income for only about eight years. Income for this extra 6½ years might well mean the difference between a child's finishing school and having to quit school and go to work without adequate education and training.

A significant factor in addition is that the continuous-premium Whole Life will provide higher retirement benefits at age 65. The reason, of course, is that premiums on the $17,000 20-Pay Life will be paid until 45 only, whereas premiums on the $29,000 continuous-premium Whole Life will continue beyond that time. At age 45, the cash value of the 20-Pay Life policy is about $9,650 whereas the cash value of the continuous-premium Whole Life is only about $8,200. From then on, the cash value of the continuous-premium Whole Life will gain on the 20-Pay by reason of the continued premium payments. By age 55, the cash value of the 20-Pay will be at $11,438 whereas the cash value of continuous-premium Whole Life will have grown to $12,940. At age 65, the 20-Pay policy will have only $13,225 available for retirement benefits. The continuous-premium Whole Life, however, will have a retirement fund of $17,583.

On the other hand, for the first 20 years the 20-Pay policy will have a higher total cash value than will the continuous-premium policy, which might make a difference in case of an emergency need for cash.

The decision as to which type of policy to buy depends, therefore, on whether the need of the buyer (and especially of his family) is more for cash values or more for protection against both the peril of living too long and the peril of dying too soon.

The limitations of limited-payment life policies are, therefore, those which arise from erroneous use. The greatest error in the use of these forms is made by people who should place the emphasis in their insurance program upon premature death protection rather than savings.

Limited-payment life policies are more popular than Term, but less popular than continuous-premium Whole Life. Exclusive of Group insurance, limited payment life accounts for about 28% of the life insurance in force. Contrary to what would be expected on the basis of insurance buying theory, limited-pay life policies are sold more often than average to low-income groups and to those under age 30.

Single-Premium Life Policies. These are contracts issued in exchange for the payment of the entire cost in advance through one lump sum premium. For example, a $20,000 participating single-premium Whole Life can be purchased at age 35 for about $10,575.[11] Once this premium is paid, no more premiums are required during the life of the policy.

Single-premium policies must not be confused with policies under which premiums have been discounted in advance. Many companies, by contractual agreement or as a matter of company practice, will accept a given number or amount of annual premiums in advance of their due date. The companies credit these advanced premium deposits with interest earned at each policy anniversary date. A minimum interest rate ranging between 2 and 2½% may be guaranteed. For example, the above $20,000 Whole Life contract can be purchased on the 20-Pay plan for an annual premium of about $780. The insured by depositing a lump sum of $13,109 with the company can discount these 20 annual premiums and in effect own a paid-up policy.[12]

Although both policies technically are "paid up," the two contracts are quite different. The 20-Pay contract with premiums discounted in advance requires $2,534 more in premiums than is required under the single-premium policy. The cost differential is justified by the higher death benefit payable under the prepaid 20-Pay Life during the first 20 years it is in force. As to death benefits, the two policies function in this manner:

When a single-premium policyholder dies, his beneficiary is paid only the face value of the contract. But upon the death of an insured whose premiums have been discounted, his beneficiary is paid the face of the policy plus a refund of unearned premiums. For example, if the insured dies at age 45, $20,000 will be paid under the single-premium policy whereas the discounted premium policy will pay about $27,198. This $27,198 figure includes the $20,000 of insurance plus the value of the ten unearned premiums of $780 discounted at 2% for nine years.[13]

---

[11] The rates and cash values quoted in this section are based on the rate manual of a prominent participating company. They vary slightly from company to company.

[12] Actually only 19 premiums are discounted since the first-year premium is paid in advance.

[13] Since one of the ten unearned premiums is due immediately, only nine are discounted.

The redemption values of the discounted policy also are higher during the first 20 years since the unearned premiums are refundable along with the cash values of the policy. For example, at the end of the tenth year the discounted policy has a cash value of $5,828 plus $7,196 of unearned premium or a total of $13,024. The single-premium policy has a cash value of only $11,027. At the end of the 19th year, the 20-Pay policy has a redemption value of $13,039 including $780 of advanced premiums. The cash value of the single-premium contract is $12,685.

At the 20th year when the premium deposit fund has been exhausted and all premiums are paid, the death benefits and cash values of the two contracts are identical. They both will pay $20,000 at death, and at the end of the year they will have a cash value of $13,061. From then on, the increases in cash values will be the same in the two contracts.

A tax advantage provides an incentive for discounting premiums. The interest earned by discounting premiums is not reportable as income under Federal tax laws. For people in high tax brackets, a 2 or 2½% compound interest is equivalent to a much higher effective rate of return on other investments.

At first blush, one would wonder why anyone would want to purchase life insurance on a single-premium basis. Admittedly, the idea of paying the entire premium in one lump sum would never occur to the typical man. Such a premium-paying arrangement would be neither desirable nor practical in most instances. Nevertheless, there are several legitimate uses for single-premium insurance. For example:

(a) Since life insurance has many attributes which qualify it as a desirable investment, the single-premium policy might be an attractive *investment medium* for some investors.[14]

(b) Single-premium Life insurance sometimes is a good place to put "windfall profits," which do not occur regularly and, therefore, do not justify an increase of the annual premium insurance budget. A lawyer, for instance, who collects an unexpected $2,000 fee or a life insurance man who closes a pension case yielding a $5,000 first-year commission could well afford in many cases to invest these funds in single-premium life insurance. In this way they maintain the fund's liquidity[15] while, at the same time, buying for themselves an investment with a guaranteed interest return, automatically compounded, which offers a chance of high speculative gains in case of premature death.

---

[14] Cf. Chapter 7 for a discussion of the investment features of life insurance.
[15] Except for the first few years when there is what is in effect a surrender charge.

(*c*) The single-premium plan sometimes is used to purchase life insurance to offset death taxes and the costs of distributing an estate. Annual-premium insurance also can be used for this purpose, but the single-premium plan immediately establishes the death-tax fund in full and requires no further deposit, sometimes an advantage in particular estate arrangements.[16] The purpose of single-premium insurance in this case is to put the maximum liquidity into an existing estate, and at the lowest cost. Funds for the payment of single premiums often are obtained through the conversion of other investments. Such changes in the character of investment accounts might well be warranted. One of the primary requisites of an investment earmarked to pay estate taxes is liquidity. Liquidity is defined as the ability of an asset to be converted into cash without delay and without loss in value. Life insurance more than meets this liquidity test, for not only does it automatically convert into cash at death when the cash is needed, but also it does so with an increase in value. Life insurance is always worth more at death than immediately preceding it.

(*d*) Single-premium life insurance also is used as a gift medium, particularly for children. At young ages large amounts of life insurance can be obtained for a relatively small investment. For instance, one company quotes a gross, participating, single-premium life rate of $323 per thousand at ages under six months. In other words, a paid-up life insurance estate can be purchased for an infant for just slightly more than 30¢ on the dollar. Moreover, such an estate will give him cash values for emergencies that might arise during his life and a small income in the form of policy dividends which he may either take in cash, leave on deposit with the company at interest, or use to buy paid-up additional insurance.[17]

Single-premium insurance has serious limitations when used by the typical individual in the typical life situation. The single premium for $1,000 of life insurance at age 25 would buy $30,000 or so of annual-premium insurance. Let it be repeated, again, that the need of the typical individual age 25 is for all the premature death protection he can possibly pay for, rather than for high cash values or even paid-up policies. In general, single premium is used validly only when premature death protection needs are already taken care of or where the money used consists of funds derived from a nonrecurring source. As an investment medium, its limitation is the same as other fixed value investments (bonds, mortgages, building and loan shares, etc.). It leaves the investor exposed to the perils of inflation. On the other hand, it offers excellent protection against deflation.

---

[16] Cf. Chapter 17.
[17] Cf. Chapter 10 for discussion of dividend options.

2. PREFERRED RISK AND "SPECIALS"

Since the early 1900's,[18] it has been a practice of some companies to issue "preferred risk" policies with reduced premiums. In recent years, however, there has been a greatly increased activity in this area; [19] moreover, whereas the earlier "specials" usually sought to reduce premiums by accepting only superior underwriting risks,[20] present trends are to apply the special premium principle to standard (average) and even to substandard lives.

The term "preferred risk" was more often applied to earlier policies because they sought to reduce the premium by reducing mortality. They were issued only on lives judged to be especially healthy.[21] However, since the newer, low-rate policies deal with larger packages of protection at lower rates rather than the principle of superior risk, the tendency is to call them "specials": "Five-Star Special," "Whole Life Special," "Business and Professional Men's Special," "$25,000 Special Whole Life," for example.

Nature of "Specials." The special policy most often is Whole Life (although the principle can be applied to any policy form), offered in a minimum amount, with or without special underwriting for superstandard risks, carrying a premium sharply reduced over a similar but not same form issued on the regular basis and, particularly, showing a very favorable net cost [22] at the usual periods selected for such illustrations: ten and 20 years. Below are illustrated the premiums on a Life Paid-up at 85 "special," issued only in $25,000 or larger policies, not requiring superstandard underwriting, participating basis, compared with a regular Life Paid-up at 85, participating, in a comparable company.[23]

Methods of Reducing Premium. In addition to superstandard underwriting, there are a number of methods by which reductions in premiums are achieved, one or several being used in connection with the same policy of any given company.

1. Requiring an annual premium, thus reducing collection costs.

---

[18] Metropolitan Life, for instance, began issuing a "preferred risk" policy in 1909.
[19] Speaking before the American Management Association on November 10, 1954, Robert E. Dineen, Vice President of Northwestern Mutual, reported that the use of "specials" nearly trebled between 1938 and 1954.
[20] The term "risk" is used here in its trade connotation and means "exposures." In this case superior underwriting risks means exposures in which the physical and other hazards are low so that chance of early death is less than average.
[21] Cf. Footnote 2, Chapter 19.
[22] Total premiums paid, minus total dividends, if any, minus cash value at the time selected for making the illustration.
[23] At the time this was written, no company issued a "regular" and a "special" in the same form; therefore, the comparisons used in the illustration must be as between companies issuing the same form rather than as between policies in the same company.

Table 2. Comparison of Rates per $1,000

(Life Paid-up at 85, $25,000 Minimum "Special," and Regular Life Paid-up at 85,
Participating Basis)

Age at issue	Special (Company A)	Regular (Company B)
25	$16.95	$20.59
35	22.97	27.57
45	33.59	38.83
55	50.70	57.95

2. Reduced commissions to agents, as much as 20% in the case of some "specials." [24]

3. Reduced gross premium on a participating plan, which reduction is brought about by a cut in the loading for expenses (the net cost, however, may not be reduced since the reduced premium may be reflected in reduced dividends).

4. Payment of a "surrender dividend," available only if the policy is terminated at the end of ten, 15, or 20 years but not payable if the policy is continued in force.[25] The termination or surrender dividend produces a particularly favorable net cost when the illustration is based on years in which the termination dividend is payable. Table 3 compares rates, cash values, and current dividends of a special Whole Life with termination dividends and a regular Whole Life, using comparable companies.

Table 3. Comparison of Rates, Cash Values, and Current Dividends

(Special Whole Life with Termination Dividend and Regular Whole Life, Issue Age 25)

End Policy Year	Rate per $1,000 Special $18.42	Rate per $1,000 Regular $20.24	Cash Value per $1,000 Special	Cash Value per $1,000 Regular	Dividend per $1,000 Special	Dividend per $1,000 Regular
1			$ 0	$ 3	$ 0	$2.12
2			9	21	1.13	2.36
3			22	39	1.38	2.59
5			51	67	1.87	3.15
10			126	140	3.07	4.34
20			287	299	5.71	7.23
Termination dividend					5.00	0

The termination dividend allows this "special" to show a lower net cost than the "regular" but the policy has to be terminated in order to achieve this advantage. Since many policies terminate before they are eligible for

---

[24] Reporting on a survey of 134 companies in mid-1955, the Life Insurance Agency Management Association stated that commission rates were reduced on specials by 42% of the $1,000,000,000 U.S. companies, 60% of the $150,000,000 to $1,000,000,000 companies, 65% of the under-$150,000,000 companies, and 7% of the Canadian companies.
[25] Critics call this a "bonus for lapsing."

termination dividends and many others stay in force long beyond the date upon which they become eligible, the cost of paying termination dividends is small.

5. Reduced cash values can be used as a method of helping to reduce premiums in "specials." That reduction will be noticed in the case of the "special" illustrated in the table above.

6. Reduced installments under settlement options also are sometimes found in "specials." For example, one company guarantees a life income of $5.86 per $1,000 at age 65 male on its "special," whereas a comparable company promises $6.32 on its "regular." At least one company guarantees no scale of installments at all for its "special," providing that if installment settlement is desired, payments will be made in amounts according to the tables in use at the time the policy proceeds or values are placed on options.

7. Reduced policy service also will help reduce premiums. If "fringe benefits"—right to convert to another form; right to receive cash values under options, for example—are eliminated from the contract and if, in addition, the company adopts a "tight" policy on special settlement agreements, permission to use options for contingent beneficiaries, and the like, costs of servicing the "special" can be reduced and, hence, the premium lowered.

8. A reduction in number of settlement options offered in the policy also may be used to help reduce the cost of handling the policy and, hence, the premium. For instance, where a regular policy of a "liberal" company may contain five or six different options of settlement, a "special" could reduce costs by including only two or three options—or none at all.

9. A large minimum policy often is required under the "special" plan. Most companies issuing "specials" today stress policy size as the big factor in reducing premiums. Many administration costs are incurred on a per policy basis; that is, there are few if any more clerical costs involved in handling a $100,000 policy than there are in issuing a $1,000 policy. To illustrate: If the unvarying administration costs per policy are $10 a year and the average policy is $5,000, then the net result of a percentage loading will be that a $1,000 policy pays $2 for the same service for which a $100,000 has to pay $200.[26] One company, which began issuing a $5,000 "special" in 1922, reports that its experience with that policy shows the difference in adminis-

---

[26] Actually, almost all companies do something about this disparity, whether they issue "specials" or not. Most companies, for instance, take the average size policy into consideration in dividend calculations and assess less administrative cost to plans having high average policies. Again, some companies take average size policy by age at issue into consideration. This method reduces cost for later ages, which are the bigger policy buyers. Proponents of specials charge these methods are insufficient to adjust the disparity. Cf. Chapter 23.

trative cost between a $1,000 policy and a $2,000 policy to be $1.75 per $1,000; between a $10,000 policy and a $1,000, $3.50 per $1,000; and between a $10,000 and a $100,000, 50¢ per $1,000.

The reduced premium for a larger policy is directly akin to the mercantile practice of "quantity discounts," and is a practice long used in life insurance in Great Britain and in Continental Europe, premiums being graded by size of policy.[27] Advocates of "specials" claim they produce greater equity among policyholders, since each pays more nearly what it actually costs to handle his policy.[28] Opponents, on the other hand, charge that "specials" lead to "price buying" without enough regard to whether the policy fits the insurance needs of the buyer. Specials usually are restricted to continuous-premium Whole Life or similar long-term premium forms. Also they tend to reduce service to policyholders, which, in the end, may be more important than the relatively few premium dollars saved by a "special" —particularly where that service is related to beneficiaries and trustee functions such as settlement options and agreements.[29]

3. SUMMARY

As contrasted to the limited protection offered in Term and Endowment insurances, Whole Life offers protection "until death do us part." Whole Life policies may be classified on the basis of the time over which premiums are paid. If premiums are payable "until death do us part," the policy is called *continuous-premium Whole Life,* Ordinary Life, or sometimes Straight Life. The most descriptive term is continuous-premium Whole Life, for it distinguishes this type of contract from the Limited Payment forms. Continuous-premium Whole Life is the most flexible of all insurance contracts. It offers the insured the opportunity to buy the maximum premature death protection

---

[27] Advocates of "specials" often point out that reduction of premiums in relation to policy size is a standard practice in fire and casualty lines. For instance, the premium for the first $10,000 is much more for a personal liability coverage than it is, say, for the second $10,000. This is not, however, a valid comparison. The reduction in the rate for the second $10,000 of casualty coverage comes from the fact that the chance of a claim involving the first $10,000, for instance, is far greater than the chance of a claim involving the second $10,000. The premium is reduced because of a lower chance of loss. In life insurance, the chance of loss on a $1,000 policy is exactly the same as on a $100,000 policy, except where there is a difference in underwriting standards as between the $1,000 applicant and the $100,000 one.

[28] One should not overlook the fact that in some situations it costs more to handle large policies. The big policies often require more expensive service involving trustee functions. Voluminous correspondence is more apt to be necessary with the $30,000 policy than with the $5,000 contract. Initial underwriting costs are higher, since more expensive underwriting activity is involved.

[29] Opponents of "specials" sometimes use the argument that they discriminate against the smaller buyer. Advocates point out that the same rate for the small buyer as the large buyer discriminates against the large. In other words, whatever discrimination there may be can work both ways.

while also building a fund for retirement. Its only limitation is that it sacrifices some premature death protection for a retirement fund. Obviously this is no disadvantage unless the policy is used by families which must cut premature death protection below minimum standards needed in order to afford the higher premiums required to build the retirement fund.

Limited-payment Life policies are those that require premium payments for a specified maximum number of years (most commonly 20 or 30) or until the insured reaches a given age (most commonly 60 or 65). The Limited-payment Life policy has the advantage of building up a savings fund at a faster pace but has the limitation of encouraging the insured to sacrifice necessary premature death protection in order to enjoy these greater living benefits.

Single-premium Life policies are contracts under which the entire premium is paid at their inception in one lump sum. It is principally an investment contract and offers holders of capital funds many investment advantages. Single-premium insurance is used as a gift medium. It also is used by men of wealth to achieve estate liquidity for meeting death taxes and other costs of dying. Although Single-premium Life insurance qualifies as a depository for capital accumulations and windfall incomes, it does not fit into the life insurance program of the typical family which seeks to achieve a balance between premature death protection and old age security through its life insurance, which must be purchased with carefully budgeted premium dollars.

In recent years there has been an increased activity among companies in issuing reduced-rate policies known as "specials." Formerly contracts with reduced premiums were called "preferred risk" contracts, since they were issued only to applicants who appeared to be superior underwriting risks. Today, these "discounts" have been extended upon other grounds.

In addition to or in place of restricting the contract to superior underwriting risks, companies can use various devices to reduce premiums: lower commission, less loading for expenses, surrender dividend, lower cash values, restricted settlement options, restricted service, and a large minimum policy. It is clear that a buyer of insurance must look to more than price in selecting an insurance contract. A "special" might do the job desired in a given program; but unless the policy, "special" or "regular," meets the need one would do well to look elsewhere.

Questions for Class Discussion

1. It has been said that in buying insurance one should apply the following rule: Buy as much premature death protection as you need and pay as much for

it as you can afford. Explain the reasoning behind this rule and indicate whether or not you agree with it.

2. A common objection to continuous-premium Whole Life is summed up in the statement, "I don't want to pay premiums all of my life." How would you counsel a young man who has just been sold a continuous-premium Whole Life?

3. It has been said, "When a young man age 25 buys a 20-Payment Life policy you can bet your last dollar that he has bought the wrong contract." Explain why you agree or disagree with this statement.

4. Under what set of circumstances would you recommend the purchase of a Limited-payment Life contract?

5. Is it true that actually no life insurance contract is ever paid up? Why or why not?

6. Mike Cassidy is faced with the decision whether to put his $2,000 inheritance into Single-premium Life insurance or United States Government bonds. What factors would you suggest that he weigh seriously in reaching a decision?

7. Assume that Mike Cassidy is considering a choice between Single-premium Life insurance and the common stock of a well-established corporation. What factors would you suggest he consider in reaching a decision?

8. James Moore is considering three $5,000 contracts: 20-Payment Whole Life, Term to age 65, and Single-premium Whole Life. From an underwriting standpoint, which would you expect would be (1) the most difficult to get, and (2) the least difficult to get?

9. Explain why you agree or disagree with the following statement: "The retirement values in a life insurance policy are a function of the kind of policy taken as well as of the amount of insurance taken."

10. B. J. Wright age 35 has been offered a $10,000 "special" Whole Life contract (continuous-premium Whole Life) for an annual premium of $235. Another company offered him its regular continuous-premium Whole Life for $276. What features relating to these two policies should Wright look into before reaching a decision as to which one to buy?

CHAPTER 5

THE ANNUITY POLICY

THE ANNUITY has become an important instrument in planning financial security for old age. The increasing emphasis placed by labor and management on industrial pensions has accounted for much of the growth in annuities over the past decade, and the special tax credits established for annuities in the 1954 tax law have stimulated the growth even more. Today, approximately 5,000,000 annuities are in force representing in the neighborhood of $2,000,000,000 of future annual income. Over half of this amount is provided under Group annuities.

1. THE NATURE OF ANNUITIES

The annuity has been called the "upside-down application of the life insurance principle." The description is apt. Whereas the purpose of a life insurance contract is the systematic accumulation of an estate, the purpose of an annuity contract is the scientific liquidation of an estate. One function is as important as the other since the family which improperly liquidates its estate may suffer eventually as much as the family which has no estate at all.

When a person purchases a life insurance contract, he agrees to pay the insurer a series of payments in return for which the insured will, at his death, pay his beneficiaries a specified capital sum. When he purchases an annuity contract, he pays the insurer a specified capital sum in return for a promise from the insurer to make him a series of payments as long as he lives.[1]

---

[1] This is, obviously, a simplification for the sake of illustration. The life insurance premium may be made in one payment as well as in a series; the contract may provide for payment of the lump sum at the end of an endowment period as well as at death; and the payment may be made in installments instead of a lump sum. The annuity premium may be paid in installments as well as in a lump sum; some types of annuities pay for a limited period, expiring regardless of whether the annuitant is still living; and some continue payments to a surviving beneficiary. See Section 2 on classification of annuities.

Like life insurance, the annuity is a risk-sharing plan based upon a group, the individual members of which are all the same age. Individually, these people could not draw upon principal without fear of outliving it. Under a risk-sharing plan, the funds of those who die early can be used to offset the excess withdrawn by those who live long after their principal is spent. While the insurance company does not know how long any one given individual member of the annuity group will live, it does know from the Law of Large Numbers, as applied to the experience of previous annuitants, approximately how many from that group will be alive at the end of each successive year. It can, therefore, plan to use the funds remaining out of the purchase price of those who have died early to continue payments to those who have lived "too long."

The amount to be paid the annuitant each year is calculated scientifically on the basis of mortality experience. Thus an immediate life annuity [2] will enable a man 65 to liquidate a $40,000 estate at the rate of $255 a month for life. In effect, each $255 payment includes interest on the unpaid "balance" plus a return of part of the principal. The annuity is, therefore, simply a method of assuring that a given sum of capital will be sufficient to provide an unchanging and regular dollar income to the annuitant as long as he lives.

It has been pointed out previously that two types of death threaten the financial security of every individual: physical death and economic death. Among the types of economic death is superannuation—that is, the inability of the individual, by reason of age, to earn a living.

The purpose of an annuity is to assure a person a fixed income he cannot outlive and which is well in excess of the income he could derive from investing the cost of the annuity in safe, interest-bearing or dividend-yielding securities.

The periodic income under the annuity is larger than that provided under direct investments because the annuity principle includes the consumption of some of the capital invested. The differential between the annuity income and income from direct investments is slight at young ages since at these ages the annuity payments are to last through the insured's life expectancy and only a small part of the capital can be consumed each year. At older ages, especially at the retirement ages of 60 to 70, the differential is more pronounced. For example, at age 40, $40,000 would purchase a life annuity of only $130 a month as contrasted to $255 a month it will purchase at 65. A conservative 3% investment would bring $100 a month. Whereas the differ-

---

[2] Annuity income can be elected on an annual, semiannual, quarterly, or monthly basis. An immediate annuity is one which starts paying income at the end of the first month, quarter, or whatever period has been selected.

ence of $155 a month between the annuity income and the straight invest-
ment income at age 65 may be large enough to warrant a sacrifice of the
principal sum, a difference of only $30 a month may provide insufficient
motivation.

2. ANNUITY CLASSIFICATIONS

Since there are many types of annuities, and since any given annuity may
be a combination of features from several types, a classification system becomes necessary to an orderly discussion. The classification of annuities
chart illustrates the system on which this discussion is based.

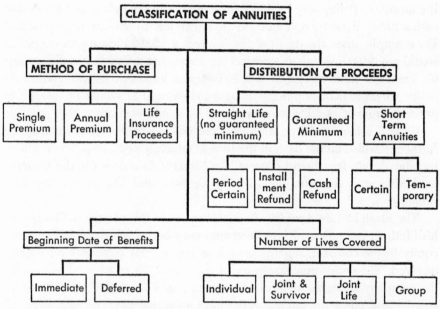

NOTE: These classifications are not mutually exclusive. For example, it is possible to have a Single Premium Deferred Joint and Last Survivorship Annuity with
a cash refund feature, etc.

Classification by Method of Purchase. Annuities may be classified according to method of purchase.

An annuity purchased by the payment of one lump sum is known as a
Single-premium Annuity. Once purchased, it requires no more deposits. For
example, a refund annuity [3] of $100 a month commencing at age 65 could
be purchased at age 55 by a woman for a single premium of $17,690. Were

---

[3] An annuity under which the company guarantees to pay the annuitant or his beneficiary
no less than the cost of the annuity: full refund of premium paid.

she to wait until age 65 to make the purchase the premium would be $23,430.

A deferred annuity purchased with an installment premium is known as an *Annual-premium Annuity*. In this case, premiums are paid periodically over the years prior to the date on which the annuity income begins. A refund life annuity of $100 a month commencing at age 65 could be purchased by a woman age 25 for annual premiums of $330. Were she to wait until age 50, the annual premiums would be $1,256. In either case the premiums are paid until age 65 when the annuity begins.

Finally, the annuity may be paid out of *life insurance proceeds* as an option of the policy contract. The cash value or the death proceeds of a life insurance policy may be distributed as an annuity in lieu of a lump sum cash settlement, under options contained in almost all life insurance policies.[4] For example, upon the death of the insured, a $20,000 life insurance policy would pay $100 a month as a refund life annuity to a female beneficiary age 65. The cash value at age 65 of a $30,000 continuous-premium Whole Life policy which had been purchased by a man at age 27 would be enough to provide him a refund life annuity of $100 a month at retirement.

Classification by Disposition of Proceeds. Second, annuities may be further classified on the basis of the time at which benefits stop. So classified, they break into four broad classes: The *Straight Life Annuity*, the *Guaranteed Minimum Annuity*, the *Annuity Certain*, and the *Temporary Life Annuity*.

The Straight Life Annuity offers an income to the annuitant throughout his lifetime, regardless of how long that may be. At his death, there is no equity in the contract, regardless of how few benefit payments have been received. The entire purchase price of the annuity is considered earned by the company upon the death of the annuitant. This is the purest form of annuity and offers the annuitant the largest income payment per dollar of purchase price. For example, a man age 65 could purchase a Straight Life Annuity paying about $160 monthly for $25,000. A refund annuity would yield only about $120 a month.

Psychologically, the Straight Life Annuity is difficult to sell and conducive to misunderstanding. Annuitants, and particularly their heirs, sometimes feel that the company has "confiscated" their premium if the total income received does not equal the purchase price. The misunderstanding arises out of failure to comprehend the operation of the insurance principle—failure to understand that some of the premiums of those who do not reach their life expectancy are used to pay incomes to those who live beyond their

---

[4] Cf. Chapter 10 for explanation of settlement options.

expectancy. The annuitant stands the chance of falling into either one of these classes. His heirs, therefore, have no legitimate objection if he happens to fall into the class that experiences early death.

Several types of guaranteed minimum annuities are available: *Life Annuity Certain, Installment Refund Life Annuity,* and *Cash Refund Life Annuity.*

A Life Annuity Certain promises to pay an income for life but guarantees a minimum number of payments. For example, a Life Annuity, Ten Years Certain, always will make 120 payments (if written on a monthly basis) irrespective of whether the annuitant lives or dies. If the annuitant dies, these payments will be made to his beneficiary. If the annuitant lives the payments will be made to him and will continue to be made until his death no matter how far off it may be. Thus, under such an annuity, if the annuitant himself were to die at the end of the eighth year, the monthly benefits would be continued to his beneficiary for two more years—or 24 months. But if the annuitant lives for 20 years, payments will continue for that length of time. Upon his death, all benefits and values terminate.

An Installment Refund Annuity agrees that, upon the death of the annuitant, the benefit payments will continue until benefits received equal the purchase price of the annuity. If the annuitant himself lives until the purchase price has been recovered, benefits continue only as long as he lives and then expire without remaining values.

For example, an immediate Installment Refund Annuity of $100 a month purchased by a woman age 50 would cost $30,700. Should the woman die at age 70, payments of $100 a month would continue to her beneficiary for five years and seven months—the length of time it would take to pay out the rest of the $30,700 purchase price.

A Cash Refund Annuity agrees upon death of the annuitant to return in cash the difference between benefits drawn and the purchase price paid by the annuitant. If the annuitant lives until he himself has drawn the purchase price, payments continue as long as he lives but cease without value upon his death.

If the Installment Refund Annuity illustrated above were a Cash Refund instead, then upon the death of the annuitant at age 70 the company would pay $6,700 in a lump sum rather than $100 a month for five years and seven months. When the refund is made in cash instead of installments, interest on the monthly decreasing principal not yet paid is sacrificed by the company. Therefore, the Cash Refund Annuity is more expensive than the Installment Refund.

Life Annuities Certain and Refund Annuities often carry cash values, equal, as a rule, to the discounted value of the unpaid, guaranteed installments or cash refund.

In the case of a relatively young annuitant, the difference between income payments on a Refund Annuity and a Straight Life Annuity is so small as to make the Straight Life Annuity seem uneconomical. For the capital sum of $10,000 a woman of 35 can purchase a monthly income of about $29.50 under an immediate Refund Annuity, while a Straight Life Annuity will offer her only a few cents over $30.00 a month. The difference is insignificant. On the other hand, a woman age 65 can purchase an income of about $46.30 a month with $10,000 through the same Refund Annuity whereas a Straight Life Annuity will yield her $56.10 a month for the same premium. The difference in this case is more significant.

The reason for the widening gap between incomes produced by Refund Annuities and Straight Life Annuities as ages advance is quite simple. The probability of an annuitant age 35 surviving a 20-year certain period is far greater than that of an annuitant age 65 so surviving. To put it another way, the older the annuitant is at the time the annuity commences, the less is the likelihood that he will outlive the period certain and consequently the more the company will have to charge as a differential to pay the refund or some portion of it.

When there are young dependents, a guaranteed minimum annuity is essential [5] unless there is adequate life insurance or other estate assets. A Straight Life Annuity completely liquidates the estate at the same time death liquidates the annuitant himself. Nothing is left behind to care for dependents. A properly arranged Refund Annuity or Life Annuity Certain for a parent leaves income to take care of the children should the parent die before such dependents achieve independence. For example, a ten-year certain life annuity for the parent of a ten-year-old son will gauarantee that an income will be available to support the child until he is 20 years old even if the parent should die in one or two years.

The Annuity Certain is a contract which provides the annuitant a given income for a specified number of years independent of his life or death. Upon the termination of these years, the payments cease. In no way is life expectancy a factor. This form of annuity is commonly used as a method of paying life insurance proceeds to a beneficiary. For example, instead of having the proceeds of a $10,000 life insurance policy paid to the beneficiary in a lump sum, the insured might direct that a series of 52 monthly pay-

---

[5] To put it more exactly, where there are young dependents, there is no place for an annuity of *any kind*, until and unless there is adequate life insurance to provide a new source of income when the head of the family dies, or unless the head of the family is uninsurable.

ments of $200 each be paid. In this way, he can assure his beneficiary an income over a fixed period of years, perhaps long enough to cover the critical child development period or to allow the widow to make a less abrupt adjustment to a lower standard of living.

The Temporary Life Annuity pays benefits only until a specified number of benefit payments have been made *or until prior death* of the annuitant. A woman age 50, with no present benefits from Social Security, might purchase a 15-year Temporary Life Annuity to provide her with income until age 65 when Social Security benefits start. Temporary Life Annuities are not widely sold.

Classification According to Beginning of Benefits. Annuities may be classified as to the time when benefits begin; that is, *Immediate Annuities* and *Deferred Annuities*.

The Immediate Annuity is purchased with a single, lump sum payment, and benefits begin at the end of the first income period. For instance, under the current rates of one company, a woman age 60 can purchase an Immediate Straight Life Annuity of $10 a month for a single premium of $2,164.50. Her monthly benefits will start one month after purchase. In the same company, the purchase price per $10 monthly income for an Immediate Cash Refund Annuity for a woman 60 is $2,680.97.[6]

Many companies writing Immediate Annuities establish a minimum age at which they will be written. These minimums range all the way from age one in some companies to age 45 in others. The most common minimums are 20 and 30, with a number of companies establishing a minimum limit at age ten. Sometimes a company will set a minimum age limit five years higher for women than for men. Actually there is good reason to restrict the age at which immediate annuities are written. As pointed out earlier, immediate annuities at young ages tend to be uneconomical. For example, a woman age 20 would pay about $3,492 for a nonpar Immediate Life Annuity (no refund) of $100 a year. For an Installment Refund Annuity in this same company she will pay about $3,577. A direct investment of either of these amounts at 3% would yield more than $100 a year. It would seem unwise, therefore, to liquidate capital in this instance when direct conservative investments would yield about the same periodic payment as would an annuity.

---

[6] Inasmuch as the life expectancy of women is considered to be five years more than that of men, the rates quoted here for a woman age 60 are the same as those for a man age 55. Some companies use a six-year differential. Other companies quote separate rate schedules for men and for women rather than rely on an age differential. For example, in one company a Participating Single-Premium Immediate Life Annuity of $100 a month age 60 male is $20,100; for female it is $22,740. The premium for male age 55 is $22,980. Thus the differential in this case is a little less than five years.

When written as a Straight Life Annuity, the Immediate Annuity is the simplest form of annuity contract. It provides for a regular payment throughout the lifetime of the annuitant, either annually, quarterly, or monthly. The first payment is made one year, three months, or one month after the date of purchase. Usually no proportionate payment is made for the fraction of a period from the date of the last regular payment to the date of death. There are no cash surrender values.

Under the Deferred Annuity the income does not begin until some period in the future, either a period elected in advance to correspond to the estimated end of the annuitant's income-producing period or at optional ages provided in the contract. The Deferred Annuity may be a Single-Premium Annuity or an Installment-Premium Annuity; that is, the purchase price may be paid in one lump sum or in a series of periodic (usually annual) payments over a period of years. Deferred Annuities also may be either Refund or Straight Life Annuities. Under the Straight Life Deferred Annuity, the annuity payments start at a specified date if the annuitant is alive at that time. The contract terminates without value upon the death of the annuitant, whenever that may occur, whether before or after the beginning of the income payments. If, in the case of the Annual-Premium, Straight Life, Deferred Annuity, the annuitant discontinues premium payments before maturity, he is given a paid-up Deferred Annuity of a reduced amount equal to the annuity values purchased by the premiums already paid plus accrued interest. Only a few companies write Annual-Premium, Straight Life, Deferred Annuities. These contracts are unpopular with both agents and buyers. As stated, the no-refund feature is conducive to misunderstanding. The buyer may feel "cheated" if, after paying premiums over a period of years, he gets no cash refund when he discontinues the plan.[7]

The Installment-premium Deferred Annuity frequently is called "Annual-premium Retirement Annuity." It is usually issued with a refund feature applicable during the accumulation period. If the annuitant discontinues premium payments, he may draw a cash value. While the refund feature almost al-

---

[7] From a sociological standpoint, it is regrettable that the no-refund feature of Straight Life Deferred Annuities is so misunderstood. If the premiums of those who die during the accumulation period could be used to provide retirement benefits for those who survive the period, the cost of providing old age security would be reduced substantially. The way retirement annuity contracts are presently constructed, the insurance feature is eliminated until the annuity payments commence. A man age 35 who buys a retirement annuity contract actually gets no insurance benefits by surviving to age 65. He gets only his contributions, plus interest, which are applied on an annuity at age 65. How much real insurance he gets after age 65 depends upon whether or not the refund feature is also included during the period of liquidation. From the standpoint of real insurance, current retirement annuity plans leave much to be desired, being a savings plan during the period of accumulation instead of insurance.

ways is included during the period of accumulation, it may or may not be included during the period of distribution. For example, an Annual-premium Deferred Annuity may be purchased with or without a refund feature during the accumulation period and with or without a refund feature during the liquidation period. Thus, a $100-a-month, nonparticipating Annual-premium Retirement Annuity taken by a woman at age 25, deferred to age 65, will cost about $225 annually if it has no refund after the benefits start but $270 if it provides for refund after 65.

Classification by Lives Involved. Annuities may be classified according to the number of lives involved in the contract. The usual annuity includes only one life, that is, annuity payments are contingent upon the life of only one person. Situations arise, however, when it is desirable to make annuity payments contingent upon more than one life.

The Joint-Life Annuity provides for payments throughout the joint lifetime of two people but ceases upon the first death. There are no benefits to the survivor. This annuity is valuable when there is an independent income sufficient to support one member of the family but insufficient for the support of two people. Since the annuity payments stop on the first rather than on the last death, they are cheaper than the Joint and Last-Survivorship Annuity. The market for this type of annuity is so limited that only a few have been written.

Joint and Last-Survivorship Annuities may be written as single-premium with the income payable until the death of the last survivor. Sometimes the contract will provide for a reduction in income payments upon the death of the first annuitant, say a one-third reduction, with two thirds of the previous income continuing to the survivor.

Joint and Last-Survivorship Annuities may be written as single-premium annuities. They also may be used as a method of receiving cash values or proceeds of life insurance policies. For example, a man age 65 with a wife age 63 could purchase, for a single premium of $23,000, an annuity which would pay $100 a month as long as either is alive. He also could use the proceeds of a $25,000 life insurance Endowment at Age 65 to provide an income of $119 a month to himself and his wife as long as either might live. If the contract provides for a reduction of the income by one third upon the death of one of the annuitants, then the policy will pay $139 a month during the joint lifetime of himself and his wife and $92 a month during the lifetime of the survivor. A few of the commercial insurance companies writing Joint and Last-Survivorship annuities will attach a refund clause to them, but most are written on a Straight Life basis.

Commonly, Joint and Last-Survivorship annuities are written on two lives—usually husband and wife—in order to guarantee income to both so long as either may live. This type of annuity option is commonly found among state and industrial pension plans.

Another form of annuity is the *Group Annuity*. Annuities are sold to employers for the purpose of funding retirement plans designed for employees. A discussion of group coverages is deferred to Chapter 14.

Several other types of annuities—or, more exactly, annuity combinations—may be found. In fact, there are at least several companies which will write any annuity combination anyone wants. However, the annuities discussed are those which are relatively standard in the business.

3. USES OF THE ANNUITY

The annuity has long been a favored investment in England and on the Continent, but in America it did not rise to general popularity until the depression of the 1930's. During that period of economic stress, there arose a need for a safe investment under a plan which would yield an unfailing and unchanging dollar income. The annuity was, in a certain sense, "rediscovered." Moreover, many individuals who had investments that formerly had provided them sufficient income found that depression losses had so reduced their capital that the income available from it was now insufficient to provide a decent living. A solution to their problem seemed to be the purchase of an annuity, combining systematic capital liquidation with interest earnings to yield a larger lifetime periodic income. For example, an investment of $30,000, paying an interest return of about $70 or $80 a month, could be transformed into a monthly lifetime income of $140 at age 60 by means of a life annuity. This additional income, of course, would be obtained at the expense of liquidating the investment; but it is assumed that a more comfortable income during the last years of life would be worth the sacrifice of an estate at death.

To Protect Against Lost Earning Power.   The primary purpose of the annuity is to protect against the contingency of outliving one's ability to earn a living; that is, to provide a guaranteed income for old age. The current high taxes and low investment yields make increasingly difficult the building up of a principal large enough to provide adequate investment income for retirement. For example, a woman age 68 can convert $8,250 into an annuity income of $600 a year, whereas a high-grade direct investment would rarely yield over $250 a year. Furthermore, when the principal is turned into an annuity, the annuitant is assured of a lifetime, guaranteed, fixed *dollar* income. Only inflation is capable of reducing the value of annuity income. This "inflation" objection to annuities is always prevalent in "boom" times, lying dormant in down cycles. Nevertheless it is a serious problem in connection with long-term financial planning.

Because of high taxes and low investment yields, most people today are faced with the necessity of building principal with the idea, not of preserving it intact to pass along to heirs, but of liquidating it systematically through annuities in order to obtain an adequate retirement income.

Table 1 shows the advantage of the annuity when compared with other conservative savings plans as a method of providing a retirement income. The table assumes that the investor will save $200 a year for a retirement income. It assumes, also, that the savings plan will provide a liberal 3% compound interest to age 65, *after allowances for income taxes and investment expenses and without any loss of principal or interest*. It further assumes a 3% *net* return after age 65. The table indicates that annuities under these assumptions provide, on the average, a retirement income almost twice that provided by funds invested in other conservative channels. The cost of this increased income is the liquidation of the principal at the death of the annuitant, as already pointed out.

Table 1. Income at Age 65

The Annuity vs. Other Conservative Savings Plans
(Assuming $200 is saved annually)

Age When Starting	Principal Created by Age 65	Interest Income on Principal after Age 65	Monthly Lifetime Income from Annuity * at Age 65
25	$15,533	$38.99	$68.10
30	12,455	31.14	55.50
35	9,801	24.50	44.35
40	7,511	18.78	34.45

* The income from $200 a year invested in an Annual-premium Retirement Annuity.

To Offset High Taxes. The annuity serves not only individuals with modest capital, but also, in many instances, it has a distinct income advantage for the man of wealth. Because of the federal tax structure, the Single-premium Annuity represents an unusual income-producing financial instrument to the wealthy man or woman. For example, assume that a man who has $25,000 of earned income a year and an equal income from investments has enough income tax exemptions and deductions so that his net taxable income is $40,000. Assume also that he is a widower and not head of a family as defined for income tax purposes.

If $25,000 of his income is from investments, it is reasonable to assume that he has an income-producing estate of at least $400,000. In addition to this, he has a large amount of nonincome-producing property: his home, automobile, place in the country, collections of art, and durable and semi-durable consumers' goods. Perhaps his total estate is valued at $600,000 for estate tax purposes.

Assume the net effective combined normal and surtax rate on an income from $38,000 to $44,000 is 62%.[8] So out of the upper $2,000 of his $40,000 total income, the man in our example must pay $1,240 to the government. He is allowed to keep only $760 for his own use. If this man is 60, approximately $30,000 will purchase a participating annuity paying a $2,000 guaranteed yearly income. Under the annuity income tax rule, he would report only $350 of each payment as the taxable portion of his annuity income each year.[9] The high-bracket tax rate applies to $350 instead of the full $2,000, reducing the total tax by $1,023 on the identical amount of income. In short, the annuity plan makes it possible for him to have $1,023 more of his income for his own use than if it were pure investment income. (Of course, part of his capital is being liquidated.)

Such a procedure reduces the value of the estate by $30,000, if the Straight Life Annuity is used. Although the purchase price of the annuity is $30,000, it actually costs the annuitant much less. Were the $30,000 left in

---

[8] This figure is not necessarily the current rate. Since tax rates change almost every session of Congress, it is impossible to use exact rates in a book. Our 62% figure is, therefore, merely an illustration. A good class problem would be to work out the illustration on the basis of current tax rates.

[9] In order to determine the amount of annuity income to be excluded from gross income reported for Federal income tax purposes, an exclusion ratio must be found for each individual contract. This exclusion ratio is applied to the total receipts under the contract for the taxable year of the recipient. The difference between the total receipts and the result of the computation is to be included in the gross taxable income of the recipient. The exclusion ratio is determined by dividing the investment in the contract at the annuity starting date by the expected return under the contract. This "expected return" is based on what the Treasury Department judges to be the life expectancy of the annuitant at the time the annuity begins. It is found by multiplying the annual return by a "multiple" obtained from tables established by Treasury regulation. The multiple for an Ordinary Life Annuity on one life, male, starting age 60, is 18.2 according to the tables in effect at the time of this writing [Table I, subparagraph (f), T.D. 6118, paragraph 1]. $2,000 annual income multiplied by 18.2 equals $36,400, which is, according to the Treasury, the "expected return" from the $30,000 annuity used in the above example (and if you don't believe it, argue with the Treasury, not the authors). The investment in the contract consists of the aggregate of premiums and other consideration paid less the aggregate of any amount or amounts received before the annuity starting date (dividends, for instance) to the extent that such amounts were excludable from the gross income of the recipient. Thus, if the investment in the above illustration is a net $30,000 and the expected return is $36,400, then the exclusion ratio is $30,000/$36,400 or 82.5% (82.47 rounded to the nearest tenth). The monthly payment is $166.66, of which 82.5%, or $137.49, is excluded. Thus, if 12 monthly payments are received during the year, the total to be excluded is $137.49 × 12, or $1,649.99. The annual exclusion is (rounded) $1,650, leaving $350 to be included in the gross taxable income of the annuitant.

the estate of this man, it would be taxed $9,600 upon his death.[10] So, in effect, he has purchased an annuity worth $30,000 for only $20,400. Tax laws do strange things to estate plans.[11]

To Liberate Funds for Immediate Use. The annuity also may be used when it is desirable to release a portion of capital for immediate use without reducing income. Thus the annuity is particularly valuable for making living gifts to philanthropic institutions. To illustrate, assume a retired elderly widower with $100,000 in capital investments which are giving him an average annual return after taxes of 3% or $3,000. Assume further that this is his only income and that he feels it will be impossible for him to get along on less than $3,000. The individual has, therefore, no capital which he can turn over to what may be a sincere philanthropic interest and the major object of his later life. By the purchase of a $50,000 Refund Annuity, he can guarantee his present $3,000-a-year income and can even increase it over 30% with a Straight Life Annuity. The substitution of an annuity income for a direct investment income will allow him to free $50,000 of his capital for a philanthropic contribution; moreover, his income will then be guaranteed for life and will be impossible to lose through default of investment. The one danger, however, is the possibility that inflation might make inroads on the purchasing power of this fixed income, as it will on any fixed income investment.

Although under an annuity his philanthropic interest will not receive as large a gift as it would were he to pass the total $100,000 to it at his death, it will receive the money earlier. Moreover, the annuitant will have the pleasure of seeing his money put to some social good while he is still alive. Most of all, the institution will be absolutely certain of receiving the money, which will not be the case if $100,000 is left to it as part of a will. Investment default might destroy the capital, and wills often are attacked by relatives. Outright gifts by the individual during his lifetime, however, rarely can be so contested.

Similarly, the annuity can release funds otherwise required for present support so they can be used for gifts to children or grandchildren before the death of the donor. The recipients then have the money while young, and the donor will have the satisfaction of seeing his heirs enjoy the money he has accumulated for them. Also, there may be tax advantages of making living gifts as distinguished from transfers at death.[12]

---

[10] Assuming the $600,000 gross estate is at least a $250,000 net taxable estate.

[11] Cf. Chapter 17.

[12] Gift tax rates are lower than those of estate tax, and there are some exemption advantages. Also, since the gift tax rates and the estate tax rates are progressive, a taxable gift takes property from the high estate tax bracket and places it in a lower gift tax bracket. See Chapter 17.

4. LIMITATIONS OF ANNUITIES

Expenditure of Capital. The most common objection to the annuity is that it "destroys" capital. However, this objection indicates a misunderstanding of the insurance principle. For example, the person who pays automobile or fire insurance premiums for 25 or 30 years at a total cost over the period of, perhaps, $3,000 would not think of saying that he has destroyed $3,000 of principal. He understands that the payments have been the cost of protection. This same thing is true in the case of the annuity. To say that the annuity destroys principal is the same as saying that property insurance destroys principal.

As we have seen, when an annuity is purchased, the annuitant joins with a large number of other individuals of the same age to create a fund which, measured actuarially, is large enough (together with interest to be earned on it) to pay every member of the group the life income agreed upon at the time of entry. Some in the group will live longer than others and receive more income than their total deposits; others will not live long enough to receive all their deposits; but the entire fund is used to guarantee that all annuitants will receive the given income for life. The premiums paid are the purchase price of that guarantee, not a destruction of capital.

However, whatever may be the situation technically, the fact remains that a man who lives off the income of $100,000 leaves the $100,000 for his heirs, whereas the man who invests the $100,000 in an annuity leaves nothing to his heirs (except as there may be some refund under the guaranteed minimum type of annuity). But, as indicated earlier, it is not necessary for a person to spend all his available capital to produce an income through annuities equal to that income yielded by the estate through direct conservative investments. Less than half the estate will often provide an equivalent income, especially at the older ages. The other half or more can be distributed to the heirs, who then can put it to work to build their own estates.

To many struggling heirs, a definite gift of $50,000 or $60,000 today is far more valuable than an unenforceable promise or hope of $100,000 at some unknown future date. How many young people able to raise $50,000 today would be willing to put it in a $100,000 single-premium life policy on their fathers? There would not be many, even though the $100,000 in life insurance proceeds are much more certain to be realized than the $100,000 general estate, which stands the chance of dissipation through investment losses.

Finally, except in the case of the very wealthy, an individual should not be concerned over conserving capital for his self-supporting heirs if, in order to do so, he must subsist on an income below that to which his thriftiness in saving over the years entitles him. Elderly people often pinch themselves financially in order to leave something to their heirs, without realizing that the heirs would much prefer that they enjoy their declining years with the higher income an annuity can offer. Again, the elderly often are so concerned over leaving something for heirs that they become a burden on those heirs for part of their support, merely to keep from spending their capital. More than one instance can be found of children who would be better off if their parents would purchase an adequate income through an annuity rather than depend on them for help. Parents can become a burden to the very people for whom they are conserving a relatively insignificant amount of capital.

Overemphasis on Retirement Values. The real limitations of the annuity arise out of its misuse or misapplication. Annuities insure against economic losses resulting from old age only. Without life insurance, they offer no protection against premature death.[13] Unfortunately, the high retirement values obtainable through annuities as contrasted to Whole Life insurance policies often attract family men who have inadequate life insurance protection. No insurable family man should purchase an annuity until he has adequate life insurance protection for his family.[14]

Peril of Inflation. In times of deflation (i.e., depression) the annuity is, and has proved, a haven for funds. Since the income from an annuity is fixed and guaranteed, a falling price structure increases its value. By the same token, a rising price structure (inflation) decreases its value. In periods of depression, the annuity is praised; in periods of inflation, it is criticized. The value of the annuity was emphasized in the years of depression prior to World War II; the drawbacks have been emphasized in the years of inflation after the close of World War II.

---

[13] Upon death of the annuitant, beneficiaries receive only whatever cash values the contracts may have had; these usually are only the savings of the annuitant, most often with, but sometimes without accumulated interest.

[14] This is a criticism of employee pension plans, too. Many a family man with an inadequate life insurance program is putting into an employee pension plan money he ought to be putting into life insurance protection for his family. This is true whether the plan is contributory or not. Through some queer lack of logic, people usually think of the employer's contribution to a pension plan as a "gift." Actually, in the final analysis, all contributions come out of the employee's pocket, since the money the employer puts into a pension plan is simply a deferred compensation expenditure chargeable to labor costs. However, since it is to be doubted that the average employee would put the extra money into insurance, or even savings, if it were paid to him as direct wages instead of deposited in a pension fund, it must be agreed that employee benefit plans are a definite social asset. Nevertheless, often the employer should be putting more of the money he is expending on employee benefit plans into life insurance on the employee in contrast to pensions. In other words, there is frequently an imbalance in employee benefit plans between premature death protection and old age pensions.

5. THE VARIABLE ANNUITY

The annuities discussed in the previous section are conventional annuities. They provide for periodic payments to the annuitant of a fixed number of dollars which remain the same throughout depression or inflation. The assets behind these annuities are invested for the most part in fixed dollar investments such as bonds and mortgages. A conventional annuity providing for a lifetime income of $200 a month will pay this amount regardless of general economic conditions. In contrast to the conventional fixed-dollar annuity is the variable annuity first issued by the College Retirement Equities Fund on July 1, 1952. Since that time, considerable interest has been developed in this type of annuity.

Nature of the Variable Annuity. The variable annuity provides the annuitant with lifetime income payments of a varying number of dollars fluctuating in accordance with investment results. The assets behind the variable annuity are invested principally in fluctuating dollar investments such as common stocks and other equity securities. The value of these assets at the time of disbursement determines the number of dollars the annuitant receives in each income period. Apart from the equity principle of investment, the variable annuity contains the same feature of the conventional annuity; i.e., the systematic liquidation of capital over the life time of the annuitant.

How the Variable Annuity Works. As in the annual premium conventional deferred annuity, during the period of accumulation a purchaser of an annual premium variable annuity agrees to pay a fixed dollar premium. For example, suppose the annuitant agrees to pay a premium of $100 a year. The $100 will be used to purchase units, the number of which depends upon the current value of the units in dollars. The first year the $100 might purchase 10 units, the second year it might purchase 9 units, the third year it might purchase 11 units, etc. By the time the annuitant has reached retirement age, he might have accumulated a total of 300 units. The liquidation of these 300 units will be based on the annuity principle. For example, according to the mortality tables the annuitant might be given an annuity of 25 units a year. The dollar value of these 25 units will depend upon fluctuation in the value of the assets in the equity annuity fund. The first year the annuitant might receive $500, the second year $520, the third year $495, etc. It is possible for the variable annuity contract to use the equity principle during the period of accumulation and the fixed dollar annuity during the period of liquidation. In such case at retirement the 300 units could be converted into fixed dollar investments and then liquidated as a conventional annuity paying a fixed number of dollars a year for life.

Why the Variable Annuity. The variable annuity is aimed at meeting two objectives: (1) To offer the annuitant some protection against rising price levels and (2) to give the annuitant an opportunity to share in the expected growth of the economy. Since 1900, the price level in this country has been rising on an average of 2% a year, and many economists see no reason to assume that this long run trend will not continue in the future. Deficit financing seems to have been accepted as an approach for checking downward trends in production and employment. Since both major political parties are committed to a policy of full employment, Federal budget deficits are likely to continue to exert inflationary pressures on the economy. Other "built-in" inflationary features are strong labor unions, parity farm prices, low interest rates and liberal financing. The variable annuity principle assumes that stock prices and the cost of living will move in the same direction thus giving the annuitant a fairly stable amount of purchasing power. Economic studies, however, indicate that changes in the value of common stocks and changes in the cost of living are not perfectly correlated. The stock market is much more volatile than are price levels. Therefore, even the most avid promoters of the equity annuity principle warn against committing all savings for retirement to variable annuities.

There are at least two drawbacks to the variable annuity, one economic and the other psychological.

The economic objection arises from the fact that the cost of living of any one individual will not necessarily fluctuate directly with the general price level. The general price level is based on averages, while the cost of living of any given person is based on his personal expenses, which may not contain in the same proportion each of the items used in averaging the cost of living. For instance, the housing cost of a person who purchases a home on a mortgage basis in times of lower prices will not rise exactly with the cost-of-living average, which figures in housing at the "going rate." Similarly, the cost of living of an individual who bought a home on a mortgage basis in times of high prices will not drop exactly with the cost-of-living average. Thus the variable annuity can never exactly keep pace with the price level. A variable annuitant with heavy fixed-dollar obligations acquired in times of high prices could be left with a serious deficit if his income fell directly with price averages.

The psychological objection to the variable annuity is displayed in the attitude of people toward the fluctuating dollar. A man who invests $1,000 and gets back $1,500 over a period when prices rise by more than 50%, is far less disturbed than if he had invested $1,000 and got back only $800 over a period when prices fell by 25%. In the latter case he would be better off economically; although he will be happier in the former case because he is better adjusted to it psychologically. Since the variable annuity is designed to provide more dollars for retirement income when prices are high at the risk of reducing the number of dollars when prices are low, it has to overcome this adverse psychological block.[15]

6. SUMMARY

The annuity is a true form of insurance since it takes advantage of the operation of the Law of Large Numbers and the pooling of risk to create certainty out of uncertainty. The uncertainty guarded against is the peril of living too long; that is, of outliving personal earning power and capital accumulations. Although there are many types of annuities and annuity combinations, each has its individual function.

The Immediate Annuity is the type to be purchased by the older individual who has a capital accumulation which is not sufficient to yield an investment income large enough to take care of basic retirement needs.

The Deferred Annuity may be either annual-premium or single-premium. The annual-premium Deferred Annuity is suited to an individual whose sole remaining need is protection against old age. The purchaser should have no need for additional premature death protection and must have a reasonably certain, regular income until the age the annuity benefits are to commence. The single-premium Deferred Annuity is best suited for the person with no additional protection need who has a large sum of capital to invest and who will not need annuity income until later. A frequent user of the single-premium, Deferred Annuity is the professional athlete whose earnings come in the form of large but irregular purses. It is also a form suitable for the professional man who picks up an unusually large fee that is not needed for current living expenses.

The Straight Life Annuity should be used when every dollar of the premium investment must go to build up an income which otherwise would be near or below subsistence levels.

A Refund Annuity of any type should be used only in cases in which the annuity income available is entirely adequate for the needs of the annuitant and the annuitant wishes the psychological satisfaction of "leaving something" for his or her heirs. It might also be properly applied when the annuity income is sufficient and the annuitant is in very poor health,[16]

---

[15] Some unions have had experience similar to what would happen under the variable annuity. They negotiated in their wage contracts a clause tying hourly rates to the Bureau of Labor Statistics' "cost-of-living" index at a time when the index was going up. Early in the 1950's, the index dropped, thus cutting wages. The unions then argued that the index must be wrong.

[16] It is questionable whether anyone in poor health should buy an annuity.

making the chance of his or her living very long unlikely. It must be used if there are dependent children to be supported from the annuity income, as in the case of an uninsurable family man. It should always be used at younger ages.

The Joint and Survivor Annuity is virtually imperative where there is no other income for the support of any one of two or more persons (most commonly a husband and wife) except the income from the annuity.

The Temporary Life Annuity is usable in the infrequent instances where some other source of income will become available at a certain date in the future, the interim income being supplied from the annuity.

Constantly, more and more people are reaching the age of retirement; at the same time, high taxes greatly reduce the number of dollars an individual can save; and low investment yields make it increasingly difficult for even the conservative and thrifty to build a competence for old age through direct investment. The annuity's scientific liquidation of principal and its combination with whatever investment return can be earned are the most effective, private-enterprise solutions to the dilemma.

Questions for Class Discussion

1. Life insurance policies pay off at death. Annuity contracts pay off until death. Since these contracts are the opposites, any developments or changes that will increase the cost of life insurance will decrease the cost of annuities. Is this statement true or false? Why?
2. Should a young woman 25 years old buy an immediate life annuity? An immediate refund annuity? Why?
3. Does a retirement annuity as customarily written provide for any real old age insurance during the period of accumulation (before age 65)? During the period after the annuity payments begin (after age 65)?
4. Under what set of family circumstances would you recommend each of the following: (1) Immediate Annuity, (2) Joint and Last-Survivorship Annuity, (3) Joint Annuity, (4) Temporary Life Annuity, and (5) Annuity Certain?
5. Under what set of conditions would you advise a young family man against the purchase of an annuity?
6. Why does an immediate annuity issued at age 65 yield a larger periodic income than a similar capital fund invested in direct conservative channels?
7. How is the equity annuity supposed to offset one of the principal drawbacks of conventional annuities? What are the major criticisms of the equity annuity?
8. Why do annuities cost more today than they did several decades ago? Why are they more popular today?
9. Would a capable investor ever seriously consider buying an annuity for himself?
10. Explain why a Cash Refund Annuity costs more than an Installment Refund Annuity.

CHAPTER 6

SPECIAL POLICY
COMBINATIONS

STRUCTURALLY there are only three types of life insurance policies: Term, Whole Life, and Endowment.[1] However, these basic forms can be combined in a variety of ways to produce what are called here special policy combinations.

Almost every life insurance company has several such combination policies in its rate book. Some are constructed to meet a particular type of life insurance situation. Others may be offered for competitive reasons, being specifically designed for sales appeal or to avoid comparison, or both. To attempt to discuss this latter type of special policy combination is beyond the scope of this book; there are literally hundreds of them. However, an understanding of them and their use in any given insurance situation involves breaking them into their component parts—which will always be some combination of Term, Whole Life, and Endowment, plus, occasionally, annuity elements.

This chapter discusses those special policy combinations which are more or less common, and are issued by a number of companies in a roughly standardized form.

1. SPECIAL ADULT POLICIES

Family Income. One of the most widely offered of the special policy combinations is "Family Income." First issued about 1930, it is designed to provide extra income during the family dependency period. Basically, it

[1] The Annuity is not, of course, life insurance but a reverse application of the life insurance principle.

consists of a monthly decreasing amount of Term which is at all times sufficient to pay a monthly income of a stated amount from the death of the
insured to a fixed future date. The primary purpose of Family Income is
stated in its name: to provide income during the years when the children
are growing up. The terminal date selected is intended to be the date on
which the last child in the family has reached an age of economic independence. The need for income to take care of dependent children is a constantly
decreasing one (as regards children already born) since a dependent child
moves constantly toward an age of independence; hence the application to
that need of decreasing insurance protection.

The number of income payments a beneficiary will receive under Family
Income depends entirely on the date of death of the insured. Assume that
on January 1, 1957, a man takes out Family Income on a 20-year plan. Under
this plan, his family has a guarantee of a fixed monthly income from the date
of his death until January 1, 1977, 20 years hence. If he dies in the month
of issue, his family will receive 240 monthly payments. If he does not die
until January 1, 1967, his family will receive only 120 monthly payments.
Should he die in December, 1976, the income payment would be made for
only one month since the expiry date is January 1 of the next year.

Family Income is available for varying terms of years, 5, 10, 15, and 20
being most common. However, a number of companies writing Family Income as a rider attachable to a permanent policy form offer these riders for
any number of years.

Family Income is available as (1) a simple, decreasing Term policy in
which case it is not a policy combination, or (2) a fixed combination of some
permanent policy form (usually continuous-premium Whole Life) and decreasing Term (in which case it is offered to the public as a "Family Income
policy") or, (3) a rider attachable to most permanent policy forms issued by
the same company and, sometimes, to long-duration Term forms such as
Term to 65.[2]

When Family Income is combined with a permanent policy form, either
in a fixed policy combination or as a rider, it is customary to state the
monthly income as a percentage of the face value of the permanent policy.
When it was originally introduced, it was common to make the monthly in-

---

[2] Here is a survey of the restrictions of 12 companies, showing typical forms to which
the rider is not attachable: Company A: Term. B: Term and Single Premium. C: 1-, 2-,
5-, and 10-year Term. D: Convertible initial and Renewable Term and policies with a
premium-paying period shorter than the family income period. E: 5-, 10-, 15-year Term
and Mortgage Redemption. F: Term. G: 5-, 7-, 10-year Term and policies with a
premium-paying period shorter than the family income period. H: Term. I: Term and
Modified Life. J: Juvenile. K: Reducing Term, 5-, 10-, 15-, 20-year Term. L: Multiple
Protection.

come 1% of the face; that is, a $1,000 policy paid $10 a month for the Family Income period. In recent years, there has been a trend toward 2%, 3%, and even 4%; that is, a $1,000 policy provides $20, $30, or $40 a month income for the family period. Actually, any percentage is possible since all that is necessary to increase the monthly income is to increase the amount of the decreasing Term, which provides most of the Family Income.

When Family Income is provided through a combination of Term and permanent insurance, the proceeds from the permanent policy are held at interest until the end of the Family Income period, at which time the proceeds become payable, either in a lump sum or under one of the settlement options. When this arrangement is used, the interest earnings on the basic policy are used to make up part of the monthly income, thus reducing the amount of decreasing Term necessary. For example, if the monthly interest guaranteed on a $10,000 basic form is $16.50, the amount of income that must be provided by the decreasing Term rider would be $83.50 if the contract is the customary $10 per month per $1,000 policy, or $283.50 if it is of the $30 per month per $1,000 variety.[3]

Under Family Income "policies" (as the combination of a rider with a basic policy often is called), many companies permit the insured to give the beneficiary the right to elect, upon death of the insured, to have the basic portion of the policy paid either in a lump sum or as additional monthly income. For example, if death occurs at the end of five years, a $10,000 policy with a 1% monthly income rider will pay the full $10,000 and reduce the monthly income to $83.50 if the beneficiary so elects. Or, instead of having the $10,000 paid as a lump sum benefit, the beneficiary is allowed to use the proceeds of the basic policy to provide an increase in the monthly income from, say, $100 to $149.91 by paying those proceeds out on a monthly basis for 15 years. The insured might also have the right to grant the beneficiary the privilege of electing to have the proceeds of both the permanent and the term insurance paid in a lump sum. For example, if the insured dies at the end of five years, the beneficiary may have the right to take a lump sum of $23,000 instead of the $100 a month for 15 years and $10,000 at the end of that time. Or, she may elect to have the $23,000 paid out as a monthly income of, say, $216 a month for ten years or on any other equivalent basis. If any of these options is taken, however, there will be no payment to the beneficiary at the end of the income period.

___

[3] If, under a 20-year Family Income policy paying $10 per $1,000, the insured dies at the end of the fifth policy year, it will take $13,000 of Term to provide the $83.50 a month for 15 years. But if the insured dies at the end of the fifteenth year, it will take only $5,000 of Term to provide the $83.50 for the remaining five years. Thus the Term decreases. The basic $10,000 policy, however, remains constant and is payable at the end of the 20-year period.

If the insured outlives the Family Income period, the pure Family Income policy (monthly decreasing Term with no basic policy) expires without value, except that it can usually be converted to a permanent form sometime prior to expiration. When converted, it is for the value of the Term still in force at that point, not the original amount of Term involved.

If the insured outlives the Family Income period in a combination permanent policy and Family Income rider, the Term portion expires and the premium for it ceases, but the permanent policy continues to maturity.[4]

Since the pure Family Income policy or the income rider is decreasing Term, it may be written for a yearly decreasing premium. Several companies have tried issuing it on that basis, but the decreasing premium seems to have little sales appeal. As a result, a level premium is almost invariably used.

Uses of Family Income. The pure Family Income policy (monthly decreasing Term only) offers the largest amount of premature death protection available per premium dollar, just as does all Term. In those common situations in which the number of dollars available for premiums is extremely limited but family obligations (usually because of young children) are high, it offers the best way to guarantee a family income during the period the children are growing up. Under the pure Family Income policy, the family income stops when the need for it expires; i.e., when the children are grown. It will be necessary to have other insurance if the widow is to be provided for beyond that time.

The pure Family Income policy also is useful as a mortgage insurance policy where the mortgage prohibits or sharply penalizes a "pay-off" prior to maturity. The monthly income from Family Income can be set to coincide with the duration of the mortgage in order to give the widow income to use in meeting those payments—15-year mortgage; 15-year Family Income, etc. In addition, as mentioned, some Family Income policies will agree to commute the value of the installments due at the death of the insured and pay it in a lump sum. Where the policy makes such provision, the beneficiary is able to decide at the time of the death of the insured whether to take the lump sum and pay off the mortgage (if prepayment will be accepted) or to meet the monthly payments as they fall due from the income provided by the policy.[5]

---

[4] For example, in one company the gross premium per $1,000 ten-year 1% monthly income insurance issued at age 30 is $25.89 for ten years and $23.79 thereafter. In another company, the gross premium is $27.36 for eight years and $24.01 thereafter. The permanent policy in these illustrations is continuous-premium Whole Life.

[5] In some policies, election to commute the Family Income monthly payments may be made only by the insured, or at least only if the insured has authorized such commutation at the choice of the beneficiary. Where the policy is to be used for mortgage retirement purposes, the situation regarding commutation should be checked by the insured at the time of purchase.

Rates for the pure Family Income policy are low. For instance, each $10 of monthly income on a 20-year, 16-pay, participating plan is $8.74 a year at age 25. The policy has no cash or loan values and is convertible to a permanent form for the amount of insurance still in force on the next policy anniversary date.

As stated, the pure Family Income policy expires without value if the insured outlives the Family Income period. Thus it leaves nothing for the widow after the children are grown. The basic principle of life insurance planning, as will be discussed in Chapter 15, is "first things first." If there must be a choice between providing income while the children are growing up and providing it for the widow after the children are grown, then logic seems on the side of providing the income while the children are growing. In this way, the widow will be able to stay home with her children during the years when they need her most. Also, she will be better able to keep them in school so that they can acquire the necessary education and skill to help support her after they reach the age of self-support and the insurance income has run out.[6]

A combination of the Family Income rider with a basic policy solves at least to some extent the problem of income for the widow after the children are grown. The face amount of the basic policy becomes payable when the Family Income ends, giving the widow cash or, if policy options allow, an installment income. For example, if the widow is age 45 when the Family Income payments stop, a $20,000 basic policy will provide her a life income of about $75 a month. Or, if she prefers, it will provide her about $105 a month for the next 20 years, until she reaches age 65 and Social Security becomes payable.

A 20-year Family Income rider for a $10 monthly income costs $3.71 on a participating basis at age 25 in the same company whose rate for pure Family Income was quoted above. In addition to the rate for the rider there is, of course, the rate for the basic policy to which it is attached: $20.96 a $1,000 for participating Whole Life in this company. The $3.71 rate for the rider and the $8.74 rate for the pure Family Income policy are not comparable. When the income is provided through a rider attached to a basic policy, the basic policy proceeds are being held at interest as illustrated and the amount of the interest earnings on it is used to make up part of the monthly income. Therefore, the rider is for a smaller amount of Term than

---

[6] This is not to imply that it is desirable economically, sociologically, or psychologically to have children take on the burden of supporting their mother the minute they graduate from, say, high school. However, if the choice is between that arrangement or a lack of income for an adequate family life while they are growing up, the former plan seems to be the lesser evil of the dilemma.

is the pure policy. In addition, the basic policy absorbs most of the expenses involved in writing and administering the policy. Where there is no basic policy to absorb these expenses, they must be added to the pure Family Income policy rate itself. Moreover, the rate for the pure Family Income policy is figured on the basis of 16 payments, although the contract runs for 20 years.

Limitations of the Family Income Policy. The pure policy, of course, expires without value; and neither it nor the rider in and of itself builds future values for retirement. However, since the primary concern of the overwhelming majority of policyholders is to be sure there will be income to take care of the family until it is grown, Family Income is one of the most useful special policies to be developed in half a century.

The traditional Family Income plan paying $10 per $1,000 of basic insurance can be misused in place of the pure Family Income policy (no basic policy).

To illustrate: Suppose a 25-year-old man with an infant child wants to provide an income of $250 a month from the date of his death until his child reaches age 20. This would require about $50,000 of life insurance costing about $1,000 a year on the continuous-premium Whole Life plan. On the other hand, the $250 monthly income can be provided with a $25,000, 20-year 1% Family Income policy for an annual premium of about $600. In comparison to $1,000 this would seem like a good buy and to the family that could budget $600 a year for insurance it would be worth serious consideration. Many families, however, do well to budget one third of that amount for insurance. For these families to use the typical 1% Family Income plan would necessitate a reduction in the amount of insurance to about $8,000, thus reducing the family income to $80 a month. If, however, the pure Family Income policy were purchased, a monthly family income of about $230 a month could be provided.

Of course, the pure Family Income policy can be misused in place of the traditional Family Income plan. If in the above case the family could afford the $600 annual premium, the traditional Family Income policy would be better for two reasons: (1) It would provide an income for the widow beyond the 20-year period, in this case, a life income of slightly under $100 a month if she were 45 years old at the time and (2) if the insured lived to age 65, it would provide him a life income of over $100 a month at that age. The pure Family Income policy will accomplish neither of these objectives.

The limitations of the Family Income policy are, again, the limitations of misuse.

One drawback of the Family Income policy is rigidity in case of subsequent additions to the family. If a man buys a 20-year Family Income policy when his first child is age one, the "program" will be disrupted by the birth of a subsequent child. The 20-year period will not be long enough to see the second child to maturity. However, no policy will cover this situation automatically. It will be necessary to purchase another 20-year policy— which will probably be needed anyway, since the additional child calls not only for a longer income period but, also, more income.

Companies writing Family Income insurance restrict the ages at which it will be written (20–55; 20–45, etc.), the types of policies upon which a Family Income agreement may be attached, and the amounts of insurance that may be written. The limitations vary among companies and depend upon a company's underwriting philosophy.

Family Maintenance Policy. Under the Family Maintenance policy (sometimes called Family Protection), if the insured dies within a given period, a monthly income of $10 for each $1,000 of face amount will be paid for a fixed period after the death of the insured, usually ten, 15, or 20 years. The face amount of the policy is paid at the end of the income period. If the insured lives until the expiration of the Family Protection period, the extra premium for the supplemental protection is dropped and the permanent policy remains in force for its face amount only.

The Family Maintenance policy is distinguished from the Family Income policy in that the income is provided for a period fixed *from the date of the insured's death.* For example, a man age 25 who takes a 20-year Family Income policy will leave his family an income of $10 per month per $1,000 face value for 15 years if he dies at age 30. On the other hand, if he had taken a 20-year Family Maintenance policy at age 25 instead he would have left his family an income of $10 per $1,000 of face value for 20 years.

The Family Maintenance policy is a combination of Whole Life or Endowment and Term. The Term usually may be converted without medical examination to a Whole Life policy [7] within a specified period of time from the date of issuance. Unlike the Family Income policy, the Term is not decreasing, but is level in amount. A 20-year Family Maintenance policy, for instance, is a Whole Life or Endowment contract plus a 20-year level Term rider. The Term insurance is for an amount which will yield an income for 20 years equal to a given percentage of the face of the basic contract, less the interest at which this face value will be held by the company. For example, a 1% 20-year Family Maintenance policy providing a $250 monthly income will combine $25,000 of Whole Life or Endowment insurance with

[7] At attained age or as of original date.

$41,400 of 20-year Term. The cost of the contract, using continuous-premium Whole Life as the basis, will be about $840 a year, compared to $600 for a Family Income contract.

As in Family Income insurance, the Family Maintenance policy may be written as a separate policy, or a rider may be added to an existing policy.

The uses of the Family Maintenance policy are much more restricted than those of the Family Income policy. For the most part, they are confined to special situations, peculiar to isolated, individual conditions. For instance, the insured might wish to make it possible for his widow to postpone as long as possible the election of the life income settlement option for the payment of the proceeds of his permanent life insurance policies. The longer she can delay the election of this option, the higher will be the life income she will receive. For instance, if a widow age 45 could postpone the election of a life income option for 20 years until she reaches 65, she could increase her monthly annuity income from her life insurance proceeds by $2.07 per $1,000. On $25,000, this would amount to more than $50 a month.

The principal *limitation* of the Family Maintenance contract is its use of level Term to meet a decreasing need for family protection. Therefore, in the majority of cases, Family Income is to be preferred over Family Maintenance.

Multiple Protection. Sometimes called "added protection," "additional protection," or some other special name coined by the issuing company. Multiple protection policies provide a specified amount of insurance until a given age or for some specified period, after which the amount is reduced. For example, one common form is $2,000 of insurance to age 60 or 65, and $1,000 thereafter. Another is $2,000 for ten or 20 years, and $1,000 thereafter. Multiple protection may be issued either as a policy or as a rider to be attached to some permanent policy form. The most common multiple policy is double protection, as illustrated above; however, triple and even quadruple protection policies and riders can be found.

In structure, the policy is a permanent policy form (usually continuous-premium Whole Life) plus an added amount of Term for the multiple protection period. For example, Double Protection to 65 is $1,000 of, say, continuous-premium Whole Life plus $1,000 of Term to 65. When multiple protection is written as a rider, the premium drops at the end of the additional protection period to that for the basic policy. When it is written as a single policy, the premium may drop at the end of the multiple protection period, or it may remain level throughout the life of the policy. For example, a $20,000 Double Protection policy can be purchased at age 25 in one company for an annual participating premium of about $345 until age 65, at which time coverage is reduced to $10,000 and the premium falls to about $206. In another company, this same policy can be purchased at age 25 for a level participating premium of about $308 which remains in force for the life of the policy and is not reduced when the insurance is cut. Both premium plans are actuarially equivalent.[8] Which premium plan is the more desirable depends upon one's budget and the need for building retirement protection. The higher initial premium plan will provide higher cash values for retirement, whereas the lower level premium plan might be more easily budgetable.

The use of the multiple protection policy is the same as that of the Family Maintenance form: extra protection during a period when it is needed—usually the family period. Whereas the Family Maintenance provides extra protection stated in terms of monthly income, the multiple protection plan states this additional protection in terms of extra face amount. In the Family Maintenance plan the extra protection must be taken at so much a month over a predetermined period,[9] whereas the extra protection in the multiple protection plan can be taken under whatever settlement option in the policy is deemed most advantageous in view of the income needs at the time of maturity. For this reason, multiple protection policies are more flexible than the Family Maintenance policy. The Double Protection package policy often is slightly cheaper than separate continuous-premium Whole Life and Term bought independently one of the other. The reason is that the expenses involved are loaded more heavily on the basic contract—expenses which the Term would have to bear if bought alone. In one company, the saving at age 25 is $1.82 per $1,000 nonpar. In another company, the saving is $2.01 per $1,000 nonpar. Therefore, if additional Term insurance is needed, Multiple Protection offers a way of getting it at less than usual market rates.

Limitations of the Multiple Protection policy arise mainly from the fact that it is quite easily misunderstood. Buyers often are attracted by the low premium—low in comparison to the same amount of face value in the form of continuous-premium Whole Life. They fail to understand (or remember in later years) that the premium is lower because the Whole Life policy provides the same amount of protection until death, whenever that may be, whereas the Multiple Protection policy reduces the amount of protection by

---

[8] In comparing the rate of one multiple protection policy with that of another, it is necessary to be especially careful to find out if the contracts are comparable. Not only do premium plans vary but so do the types of basic policies. Some might be Endowment at 85, whereas others might be continuous-premium Whole Life. In addition, some might provide the extra protection for a shorter period than others.

[9] Except as the policy may provide for commutation of either the income or the basic policy.

half or more at the end of some period, such as 20 years, or upon the attainment of some age, such as 65. Moreover, a Whole Life policy for a face amount equal to the original face amount of Multiple Protection will provide much higher cash values throughout the life of the policy. This may be particularly important if, at age 65, the policyholder wants to use cash values for retirement income.

A final limitation of the Multiple Protection policy is that it provides level Term rather than decreasing Term as provided in the Family Income policy. This in and of itself is not necessarily a disadvantage. It can be a disadvantage, however, when used by families that must struggle to meet the premiums required for the bare minimum amount of insurance necessary to bring the children to maturity. For this type of family, decreasing Term appears more realistic. Other things remaining the same, the need for insurance decreases gradually as the children grow older rather than decreasing all at once at some period 20 years or so in the future.

On the other hand, for the family that can afford the higher premium, level insurance has certain clear-cut advantages. As a person grows older, other things are not likely to remain the same. Any number of developments could cause a need for more insurance. He might have additional children. His income might increase and along with it his standard of living. This could cause him to re-evaluate the income needs of his family in event of his death. Also, as he grows older, he may accumulate property which could increase his death tax liability. Finally inflation might reduce the real value of his present insurance, creating a need for additional protection. Many families, therefore, might find that decreasing insurance is far from a realistic solution to their insurance problems.

Mortgage Protection. Any policy purchased with the primary purpose of retiring the mortgage in event of the death of the head of the family is "mortgage protection." Many companies, however, issue a special policy form under the name of "Mortgage Protection," "Mortgage Redemption," "Home Protector," or some such descriptive title. These policies are written on a yearly decreasing Term basis for the period of the mortgage. They are arranged so as to provide enough funds to retire the debt if the insured dies before the mortgage is paid off.[10] If the policyholder lives to pay off the mortgage himself, the policy expires without value.

The rate for the special Mortgage Protection policy is low. For instance, for a 20-year, 16-pay participating policy issued at age 25, one company

---

[10] As previously mentioned, since the Family Income policy is monthly decreasing Term, it can be used for mortgage redemption. However, yearly decreasing Term designed strictly for mortgage use reduces more exactly in the same amount that a mortgage reduces than does Family Income.

charges $6.01 per $1,000 of initial amount. The annual cost of protecting a reducing $16,000 20-year mortgage under this plan is $96.16, payable for 16 years. At any time the policyholder dies before the mortgage is paid off, the policy will pay approximately the amount necessary to retire the mortgage. For example, if the insured dies immediately, it will pay $16,000. If he dies in ten years, it will pay about $10,000. If death occurs at the end of 15 years, the policy will pay only about $5,600, but this will still be enough to pay off the debt and retire the mortgage.

A popular mortgage protection policy written by some companies combines reducing Term with continuous-premium Whole Life written on a level premium basis. The characteristics of this type of policy vary among companies. Some are written in units of $5,000 decreasing to $1,500 of permanent insurance at the end of the mortgage period. Others are written in $4,000 units decreasing to $1,000 permanent.[11] The purpose of the permanent insurance is to provide a margin for taxes, repairs, and upkeep. The policy is designed so that the sum payable at death always will be in excess of the mortgage in order to allow a margin for these expenses.

Uses of the Mortgage Protection policy are obvious. It is a special policy, designed for one purpose: to retire the mortgage upon the death of the breadwinner. Limitations of it are several: First, the mortgage might not allow prepayment.[12] This, of course, is no criticism of the policy itself but is, instead, a criticism of the settlement arrangements under the contract. The insured should check the provisions of his mortgage in regards to prepayment before buying mortgage insurance. If prepayment is not allowed, or is subject to a prohibitive penalty, the mortgagor should arrange to have his insurance policy settled on an income basis with the payments corresponding to the interval and amount of the mortgage payments. Further, the pure mortgage protection policy provides nothing for home maintenance. It is common to think that when the mortgage is paid off, one may live in a house "free." However, taxes, property insurance, and repairs continue—and usually amount to a substantial sum by the end of a year. These continuing expenses should be provided for elsewhere in the life insurance program, of course; but too often the Mortgage Protection policyholder thinks of that policy as providing his family a house "clear and free" in event of his death. Finally, the Mortgage Protection policy creates no permanent values; and while the policyholder might say he understands this at the time he pur-

---

[11] One company issues a plan that gives paid-up insurance at the end of the mortgage period for the amount of the premiums paid. This seems to be a contract designed to offer sales appeal rather than to meet any particular need.

[12] In other cases, where prepayments are allowed, a heavy penalty might be charged for the privilege.

chases the policy, too often as the years go by and the mortgage is finally paid off, he experiences a distinct shock to realize his insurance is gone, too.[13]

If a family man has reasonably adequate life insurance protection in other policy forms and a very limited additional number of dollars he can put into mortgage insurance premiums, the Mortgage Protection policy is his "best buy."

Modified Life. A Modified Life contract is a continuous-premium Whole Life contract under which premiums are redistributed in such a way that they are lower than average during the first three or five years and higher than average thereafter. The premium for a "Modified Five" [14] is generally constructed so that it doubles at the end of the first five years. For example, one company's rate at age 25 is $11.32 for the first five years and $22.64 thereafter. In another, it is $12.11 for the first five years and $24.22 thereafter. All companies, however, do not redistribute their premiums in this way. For example, a company may prefer to charge a little higher premium in the beginning so that the increase at the end of the five years will not be so large. As an example of this type of premium distribution, one company charges $13.31 for the first five years and $19.79 thereafter.

Variations also exist among the premium distribution formulae used with the "Modified Three." [15] One company charges $17.24 for the first three years and $20.28 thereafter; whereas another company charges $13.72 for the first three and $21.76 thereafter. The formula used by any company depends on its sales and underwriting philosophy.[16]

Dividend payments on participating Modified Life policies offset at least part of the increased premium. For example, the fifth-year dividend on a Modified Five purchased for $11.32 is $2.99. This dividend can be applied to the sixth-year premium, which jumps to $22.64. The third-year dividend on a typical Modified Three purchased for $17.24 is $3.67. This dividend will more than pay the $3.04 increase in the fourth-year premium.

Use of the Modified Life policy is particularly helpful to the young

---

[13] Actuarially, he has had full value for what premium dollars he has spent; but the point is human reactions, not actuarial values.

[14] That is, lower than the regular rate the first five years.

[15] That is, premium increasing after three years.

[16] The initial rate for Modified Life is higher than the initial rate for Convertible Term for the same period of time. However, the rate for Modified Life after the modified period will be lower than would be the rate on a continuous-premium Whole Life policy to which the Term would have to be converted for the same insuring effect as obtained under Modified Life. To illustrate: The gross Convertible Term rate at 25 in a typical company is about $8 per year per $1,000. If it is converted to continuous-premium Whole Life in three years, the rate per $1,000 will be about $24, compared to $21.76 for the Modified Life quoted above.

family man whose protection needs are high but whose income is insufficient at the present time to meet those needs with Straight Life insurance but whose financial situation is good enough that he can afford more than just Term insurance. Modified Life enables him to carry permanent life insurance at less than the rates for continuous-premium Whole Life for several years until his income increases. The same effect and a much lower initial rate could be obtained by the use of Convertible Term. Psychologically, however, the Modified Life is a better plan since it overcomes the difficulty most people experience when it comes to converting Term. Furthermore, the increase in rate at the end of the modified period is not as great as the increase required when Term is converted.

When a company does not write a Modified Life contract, it may offer as competition Automatically Convertible Term. The difference between the two policies is simply in rates. The Automatic Convertible Term will have a lower initial rate than the Modified Life, but will carry a higher rate at conversion. The choice between the two is basically a personal budget problem.

Limitations of the Modified Life policy arise chiefly from the fact that it is always difficult psychologically (and sometimes financially) for the policyholder to increase his premium when the modified coverage of the policy ceases and the premium advances. In the Modified Five cited as an example, even allowing for the dividends of $2.99 in the sixth policy year, the rate increases from $11.32 to $19.65, an increase of $8.33 per $1,000. On a $10,000 policy, this would be an increase of $83.30. Many policies are lapsed at the time the premium increases, indicating that the policy is often improperly sold or that the anticipated increase in income to meet the increase in rate did not materialize.

The other limitation of the policy is that cash values are smaller in the earlier years since they do not grow appreciably until the end of the initial three- or five-year period. For example, a comparison of cash values of a Modified Five and a continuous-premium Whole Life shows that, at the end of the tenth year, a Modified Five has a cash value of $90 per $1,000 face value if issued at age 25, whereas the continuous-premium Whole Life issued at the same age has a cash value of $131 per $1,000. This difference, however, decreases as the policies become older, so that by the time the insured reaches 65, the difference will be only $14 per thousand. The cash value of continuous-premium Whole Life at age 65 is $606, whereas the cash value of the Modified Five is $592.

In the final analysis, however, most policies are purchased not to be cashed out, but for death or old age protection. The death protection

afforded by the two policies is identical, and the difference in the retirement
protection is small; so the cash value limitation argument against Modified
Life is a weak one. Modified Life is a good policy for the young man who
wants permanent protection but cannot afford it immediately.

Graded-Premium Life.   A variation of the Modified Life is the Graded-
premium Life. In this contract, premiums advance each year for the first
few years (usually five) and then remain level throughout the life of the
policy. For example, in one company the rate for a Graded-premium Life
issued at age 25 is scheduled as follows: first year, $8.86; second year, $11.93;
third year, $15.12; fourth year, $18.42; fifth year and thereafter, $21.82. This
compares with a continuous premium of $20.41 if issued level premium at
age 25. The advantages and limitations of the Graded-premium Life are the
same as those of the Modified Life.

Guaranteed Investment Policy.   The "Guaranteed Investment" or "Coupon" policy occasionally is offered by nonparticipating companies in competition with participating companies. The contract combines a savings
feature with a life insurance policy. It has special appeal to prospects who
can pay higher premiums for a correspondingly greater, guaranteed return.
Most commonly, it is a variation of the 20- to 25-Pay Life policy, to which
are attached coupons, each redeemable in cash at the end of each policy
year. Usually the coupons compare favorably with dividends, because they
are designed to meet dividend competition; but they have a sales advantage
over dividends in the fact that they are guaranteed.

Commonly, the first coupon in such a policy is due at the end of the first
policy year, contingent upon the payment of the next annual premium. Each
coupon attached to the policy will be paid to the insured in cash upon surrender on its due date, provided the insured is then living and provided all
current premiums have been paid in full. Unused, matured coupons may be
payable on presentation, with compound interest for each full year after
their due date. In event of the death of the insured, matured coupons will
be paid the beneficiary in addition to the amount otherwise payable. A 20-
Payment Coupon policy issued at age 25 will require a nonpar premium of
about $36.27 per $1,000. This compares with $28.78 for 20-Pay Life in the
same company.

The Coupon policy places greater emphasis on savings than on protection. The rate per $1,000 for the Coupon policy is simply an amount suf-
ficient to buy the insurance values in the contract, plus a net amount which,
together with interest, will equal one guaranteed coupon at the end of that
year. The interest rate paid on the extra premium usually is in excess of
that obtainable through other comparable forms of investment. However,

if adequate life insurance protection is not owned, the funds used to purchase coupons could be used more advantageously to purchase additional life insurance, which, in the event of premature death, would far exceed the value of the coupons.

Return of Premium. A Return of Premium rider is issued by some companies. Typically, it will provide for the return of the total gross annual premium paid for the policy in the event of the death of the insured during the first 20 years. It is written in connection with policies issued at certain ages only, 18–50, for example. The Return of Premium rider does not increase the surrender or loan values of the basic contract and often is not issued with policies with annual premiums exceeding some maximum such as $200.

The cost of this rider is relatively low. For instance, at age 35 a Return of Premium rider for a continuous-premium Endowment at 85 amounts to only about $3.25 per $1,000. At the end of 20 years, when the rider expires, the premium will be reduced to the gross premium of the basic policy.

In structure, the Return of Premium is an amount of increasing Term insurance which is always equal to the total of premiums paid to that point. For example, during the first policy year the amount of Term insurance in the rider attached to a policy with an annual premium of $20 will need to be only $20; during the second policy year, $40; and so forth.

The rider has the benefit of increasing, at least slightly, the protection on a policyholder's life for a period of years, and that period often corresponds to the time during which he needs every bit of protection possible.

Miscellaneous Special Policies. Joint-Life policies are contracts written with more than one named insured. Most commonly, the Joint-Life policy is issued to two persons, with the face amount payable upon the occasion of the first death. Occasionally they may be issued payable upon the first death among several named insureds.

Last-Survivor life insurance policies can be considered as a variation of Joint-Life policies. They pay the face value upon the death of the last of two or more named insureds. The uses to which these two policies might be put are highly specialized, and they are not widely available.

Deferred Life policies agree to pay the face value only if the insured (usually a juvenile) survives a certain initial period. The value of such a policy is the preservation of the insurability of the policyholder, always a tenuous, overnight-changeable quality. The rate for such policies in the deferred years is extremely low in view of the fact that the contract usually guarantees, in the case of the death of the insured prior to the deferred date, only a return of premiums plus interest. The Deferred Life policy is, then, principally insurance against becoming uninsurable. It is not widely written in this country.

Reversionary or Survivorship Policy. The Reversionary or Survivorship policy (often called a survivorship annuity) has a named insured and a named beneficiary. If the beneficiary survives the insured, he or she receives the proceeds of the policy as a life income. However, if the insured outlives the beneficiary, the policy expires without cash values or other benefits.

This type of policy offers a young person an inexpensive way to provide an income for an older beneficiary. In effect, the Reversionary or Survivorship policy is decreasing Term insurance to the date of the death of the beneficiary. The rate is based upon both the age of the insured and the age of the beneficiary and is on a level-premium basis. When written with a young insured and an old beneficiary the cost is extremely low, since the beneficiary is likely to die before the insured. Under these conditions the policy would cost very little more than a short Term policy.

The Survivorship policy is not widely available.

2. JUVENILE POLICIES

Juvenile life insurance is insurance written on the lives of children, usually those under age 15. Ages classed as "Juvenile" vary from company to company, commonly running from zero through nine or zero through 14. There are a few cases of Juvenile policies running from zero to four and from zero to fifteen. In the last decade, Juvenile insurance has witnessed a wide growth in this country.

Most companies attempt to limit the issue of Juvenile policies to children of parents who belong to an economic status somewhat above average and only where the father is carrying considerable insurance on his own life.[17]

Because the insured under a Juvenile policy is a minor, control of the policy is conferred upon the beneficiary, either (1) by making the beneficiary the absolute owner of the policy, or (2) by use of a special provision conferring control on the beneficiary during his lifetime and on the insured at the death of the beneficiary or upon prior release by him. The special control provision is generally preferred.

Plans Available. Juvenile insurance is usually issued on one of the following plans: Life Paid up at 65; 20-Pay Life; 30-Pay Life; 20-year Endowment; Endowment at 85; 20-Pay Endowment at 85; Endowment at ages 16,

---

[17] The fact that close to one fourth of all weekly-premium insurance (insurance of small amounts designed for relatively low income families) is Juvenile insurance would not seem to indicate much success in limiting Juvenile insurance to above average income families.

17, 18, 19, 20, 21. Settlement options commonly are granted under all Juvenile policies at maturity.

Most commonly, insurance policies which are issued on the lives of Juveniles between the ages of 0 to 4 are written with graded death benefits. After the policy anniversary nearest to the insured's fifth birthday, the death benefit is equal to the ultimate face value. Table 1 shows a typical graded death benefit plan.

Table 1. Graded Death Benefits per $1,000 of Ultimate Face Value

Age at Issue, Nearest Birthday	1st Year	2nd Year	3rd Year	4th Year	5th Year
0	$ 100	$ 200	$ 400	$ 600	$ 800
1	200	400	600	800	1,000
2	400	600	800	1,000	
3	600	800	1,000		
4	800	1,000			
5	1,000				

For example, a policy for $5,000 ultimate face amount issued at age two will pay a death benefit in the first policy year of $2,000; in the second year, $3,000; in the third year, $4,000; and in the fourth and later years, $5,000. The premium for $5,000 Endowment at age 85, Graded Death Benefits, issued at age two is about $64 annually.

Policies issued on the lives of children five or more are issued at full benefits, and there is a trend toward issuing Juvenile with full benefits at one year or under.[18]

"Jumping Juvenile." A type of Juvenile policy which has been gaining in popularity in recent years is known in the trade as "Jumping Juvenile." It is called "Junior Estate Builder," "Junior Accumulator," "Guaranteed Estate," or some other name by the various companies issuing it. In its most common form, it is sold in "units" which provide $1,000 of protection to some age such as 21, automatically increasing to $5,000 at that time with no evidence of insurability and with no increase in premium. The continuous-premium Whole Life rate for this policy issued by one company on a participating basis is $45.12 at age one. If issued at age seven, the premium is $53.63. These premiums compare with $11.30 and $11.95 for level $1,000 of continuous-premium Whole Life at the ages indicated. Thus for $5,000 level protection, the premium would be $56.50 and $59.75 respectively. The cash

[18] Until relatively recently, New York prohibited issuance of graded benefit Juvenile, permitting only return of premiums under age five. The law has now been liberalized but contains restrictions on the amount of Juvenile at lower ages.

values on the Jumping Juvenile are higher than those on $5,000 level continuous-premium Whole Life. For example, at the end of 15 years, the respective cash values are $577.09 and $470.15. At the end of 20 years the cash values are $830.27 and $687.50. Beyond the 20th year, the difference in the cash values begins to narrow since the protection under the Jumping Juvenile increases to $5,000 without a corresponding increase in premium.

The basic policy is usually Endowment at 65, Life Paid Up at 65, or continuous-premium Whole Life. Its purpose is to protect the insurability of the child, provide protection for the parents against expenses resulting from the death of the child prior to 21, and give the young man or woman a larger amount of insurance coverage at the age when the need for it will be greater by reason of increased (or soon to be increased) responsibilities. The form has proved unusually attractive to parents.

Uses of Juvenile. Aside from the establishment of a fund to pay the cost of final illness and burial, the most common use of Juvenile insurance is to provide a college education. For that reason, there will usually be found in the rate book of any company issuing Juvenile a number of Endowment policies for various periods of years or to specified ages.

The Juvenile policy has the advantage of starting a permanent insurance program for a child at a low premium rate. For instance, a nonparticipating, continuous-premium Endowment at age 85 (for all practical purposes, a Whole Life policy) is $12 a $1,000 when taken under age six months, in contrast to $17.30 a $1,000 in the same company for an insured at age 25.

The Juvenile policy also makes it possible for an individual to have at least part of his life insurance policies paid up at a relatively early age. For example, a 20-pay Endowment at 85, issued when the insured is under six months, will cost $21.33 a $1,000 and will give the insured $1,000 of paid-up insurance before he reaches 21. Another advantage of Juvenile insurance is psychological. If a father encourages his child to pay part of the premiums out of a spending allowance, he may help develop a sense of financial responsibility the child may carry on through life. Some Juvenile insurance is purchased with this motive.

Perhaps the biggest advantage of Juvenile is that it makes certain the child will always have some life insurance even if he later becomes uninsurable.

Disadvantage of Juvenile. Juvenile insurance often absorbs premium dollars which should be used for protection on the life of a parent. As already pointed out, in theory most companies will not consider an application for Juvenile (except under special circumstances, such as the uninsurability of the father) unless a "substantial" amount of insurance is carried by that parent himself. However, the rate book of one very conservative company defines "substantial" as an amount "at least twice the ultimate amount of insurance in force and applied for on the lives of all of the father's children." This would seem to mean that a parent with only $2,000 in force on his own life could apply for and receive $1,000 on the life of a child. It is hard to conceive of any case in which $2,000 on the life of the father is adequate protection for his family. The death of a child will cause hardship in many families, and for at least that reason, there should be insurance on the life of the child; yet it does seem that the death of the child would cause far less hardship than would the death of the father.

The so-called College Fund Endowment policy is particularly dangerous. An Endowment at Age 18 on the life of a child under six months is $53.88 gross per $1,000 in a typical company. It would take a premium of over $400 a year to provide an $8,000 fund for college education, a sum that can take a large cut out of a family's insurance budget. When it is considered further that it takes almost $18,000 of life insurance to provide $100 a month income to a beneficiary for a period of 18 years (the time necessary to bring that same child from age zero to college), it can readily be seen how expensive it may be to invest money in Juvenile endowments for college purposes.

It is fine to provide a college education for a child, but it should be remembered that it takes money for a child to go through grade school and high school before he is eligible for college. The money for that should be provided through insurance before any investment is made in a policy to guarantee a college fund.

Payor Benefits.   The payor agreement provides that if the owner of a Juvenile policy (usually a parent) dies before the policy anniversary nearest a given age of the insured (usually 21), the company will waive subsequent premiums on the policy up to that age. Some payor agreements also provide for waiver of premium in case of permanent and total disability of the policy owner, or "Nominator." When the payor benefit is requested, a medical examination of the nominator, in addition to the one of the insured, is usually required. Certain underwriting rules relating to maximum and minimum ages of the payor, of the insured, and minimum age differences, may be applied. The cost of the benefit depends upon the age of the insured, age of the payor, and type of plan. For example, the cost of a payor benefit covering disability and death of the payor for a $1,000 Endowment at age 85 is about $2 when the insured is age two and the payor is 33. For an Endowment at age 18, the payor benefit would cost about $3.75.

3. SUMMARY

Special policy forms and combinations divide into two classes: (1) combinations which are more or less standard among all companies, the most typical example being the Family Income policy; (2) unique combinations, which are found only in the policy portfolio of one specific company or of a very limited number of companies, and which are usually designed either for salability or to prevent comparison of rates.

For the practical purposes of discussion, there might be added a third class of special policy combinations—those which are written with the supplemental contracts or riders which have been discussed. In this chapter, only the more common special policy combinations have been described.

Disadvantage of Special Policy Forms. The great disadvantage of special policy forms is that they are often entirely inflexible, covering effectively only one certain set of insurable circumstances; but because they are designed for salability and have many unique talking points, the agent will sometimes "push" them in cases in which the insurable needs of the prospect do not exactly fit the policy. In other words, with the special policy combination, there is a greater-than-usual risk that the need will be twisted to fit the policy rather than the policy selected to fit the need.

Advantages of Special Policy Forms. On the other hand, the special policy combination or form will usually fit more exactly than any of the standard policies the particular insurance need for which it was created. The more widespread that particular insurable need may be among the public, the less the danger that the policy will be misapplied. The Family Income policy, for instance, is an almost ideal combination for the man with a young family and a limited number of dollars he can put into life insurance. Since this is a very general life situation, the Family Income policy is rarely misapplied. In either buying or selling life insurance, the special policy combination must be studied carefully to make sure that its use in a particular situation is a result of the fact that is the most perfectly adapted life insurance "program" for the insurable situation and not just a sales package with "a lot of talking points."

The policies described in this chapter are often written under names different from those assigned herein. The names used here are those most commonly accepted.

Questions for Class Discussion

1. Compare and contrast the *traditional* Family Income policy with the *pure* Family Income policy. Develop a set of circumstances under which you would

recommend (1) the traditional Family Income, (2) the pure Family Income, and (3) neither type of Family Income policy.

2. How does the Family Maintenance policy differ from (1) Family Income and (2) Multiple Protection? Under what set of circumstances would you select the Family Maintenance policy to the exclusion of the other two?

3. J. B. Shure, aged 25, is offered the choice of two Double Protection contracts by the same company both on a participating basis. One carries a premium of $17.04 whereas the other carries a premium of $16.13. What could account for the difference in the premiums in the two contracts?

4. Mr. Shure is offered a Double Protection contract by another company for $15.33, participating. How can this company offer a rate which apparently is so much lower than either of the above rates?

5. What factors should be studied before recommending a mortgage redemption policy?

6. I. M. Young is presented two policies, one on automatic convertible Term, the other a Modified "Five." He asks you which he should buy. What should you tell him?

7. Under what family circumstances would you recommend the purchase of life insurance on children?

8. A proud parent is looking at two policies—one is a "Jumping Juvenile," which increases protection from $1,000 to $5,000 at age 21; whereas the other is a regular, continuous-premium Whole Life written for a level $5,000 throughout life. His child is one year old. How much would you expect the premium difference to be between these contracts? Which one would you recommend? Why?

9. Why was the return of premium rider developed? To whom would you recommend the rider?

10. Describe a life situation for which you would recommend the Survivorship policy. Why is the annual premium on this contract low for a given amount of insurance?

CHAPTER 7

THE "BEST" POLICY[1]

FREQUENTLY the authors are asked to give advice as to whether or not a particular policy is a good buy. Not too long before this chapter was written, one of the authors was approached by a student for advice. One of his fraternity brothers, who is working his way through engineering school by selling life insurance, had offered him a policy. The student had in hand a beautifully decorated proposal form filled out in somewhat illegible handwriting. "The agent," the naïve student reported, "said it was the best policy on the market. What about it?"

It took no more than an hour's study of the proposal form to deduce that this was a 20-pay modified convertible Endowment at 65 with triple protection to age 50, a 15-year Family Income rider, 19 guaranteed coupons, double indemnity in case of death by accidental means, $100 monthly indemnity for ten years and lifetime waiver of premiums in event of total and permanent disability, a return of cash value rider, and a $50 identification benefit.

"Whether or not this is the 'best' policy on the market would be difficult to say," the student was told. "I will say, however, that without a doubt it is the most nearly complete dictionary of life insurance terms I have ever encountered in one policy. However, before I can advise you as to its purchase, I will need to know whether you are (a) buying insurance or (b) collecting policies. If you are collecting policies, I urge you to buy this one because it is one of the rarest I have ever seen. I have no doubt but that in years to come, it will become a 'collectors' item.' On the other hand, if you are buying life insurance, then no one can look at a policy and tell you what policy is 'best.' He must, instead, look at you."

Determining the 'best' policy for any individual buyer starts, not with an

---
[1] This chapter is designed to serve as a summary of the preceding four chapters.

analysis of any given policy, but with an analysis of the buyer. It is necessary, first, to find out what the purchaser wants his insurance to do. Next, it is necessary to guide the buyer in reconsidering whether his decision on what he wants his insurance to do is actually what he needs to have done. Finally, it is necessary to find out how badly he wants to accomplish the objectives set up for his insurance. Oddly enough, it is not nearly as much the size of a man's income that determines how much he budgets for insurance premiums as the intensity of his desire to accomplish the desired objectives. The best illustration of this fact is found in the number of young family men who feel that a $40 *quarterly* life insurance premium would reduce them to starvation level but think nothing of putting that much *a month* into installment payments for an automobile. If it were the custom to display one's life insurance as obviously as it is to display one's car, many more men would find a way to meet the premiums for adequate amounts.[2]

1. MEANING OF THE TERM "BEST"

The term "best" has no meaning in and of itself. It has meaning only when it is used in comparisons. Therefore, there is no "best" policy in an absolute sense. A policy can be termed "best" only *when it is compared with other policies which could be applied to the same need.*

It is impossible to say what is the "best" policy until there is an answer to the question, " 'Best' for what need?" In purchasing or prescribing life insurance, it should be remembered that the higher the premium rate at any given age, the less premature death protection the policyholder is buying per premium dollar and the more he is putting into savings. If his need is temporary and wholly for premature death protection and not at all for savings, then Term is probably the "best" policy. If his need is largely for savings and only partly for premature death protection, then Endowment insurance is probably the "best" policy. If he wants to "split the middle," continuous-premium Whole Life is probably the "best" policy, for it provides a fairly large amount of premature death protection per premium dollar without wholly sacrificing savings. If a man's need is for income at retirement age

---

[2] Another of the authors was recently engaged in an argument with a young family man who contended "the government should do something about it" because it is impossible for a young family man to afford adequate income protection for his family. The author ascertained that this man was paying $900 a year in installments on an automobile for which he had no business use. At his age, that amount of money would purchase almost exactly $45,000 of continuous-premium Whole Life with a 20-year Family Income rider giving his family $450 a month income during the dependency of the children. Informed of this fact, his reply was, "But you just *have* to have an automobile. Everybody has one. Why, what would it look like if you didn't?" To the suggestion that if an automobile were that essential, perhaps "the government should do something about it," his reply was that *that* would be socialism.

without any death protection at all, then annuity is the "best" policy. If his need is entirely for savings and not at all for death protection or old age income, then life insurance is not indicated. Instead, the individual in question needs a savings account or an investment portfolio.

It is impossible to say what policy costs the most without knowing when the policyholder will die. The premature death insurance portion of one policy always costs the same as the equivalent insurance portion in any other policy. All are calculated on the same mortality table and at the same interest assumption—at least as far as any given company goes.[3]

The difference in premium rates among different policy forms is based on the extent of the investment element (cash value) in each form. The higher the investment element in a policy, the less is the premature death insurance purchased per premium dollar.

If a policyholder outlives his need for death protection, then the high-premium form has been the least expensive because less of each of his premium dollars has been spent for the premature death protection which was never used for that purpose.

If on the other hand a policyholder dies before he has outlived his protection need, then a Term policy would have been the least expensive. Virtually all the money his family would receive would be from pure insurance proceeds.

One other thing should be held in mind:

There may be said to be two types of investments: "current investments" and "terminal investments." Life insurance is a terminal investment. Its investment value is to be judged only in the light of what it does at maturity, at death, or at retirement age—not the current return it pays or its value at a cash-out point short of maturity, at death, or at retirement.[4] To compare life insurance with a current investment is to compare unlike things.

2. DETERMINING THE "BEST" POLICY

Most people buy life insurance for one or more of three basic reasons: to protect someone else against the economic effect of their premature death,

---

[3] Because of the possibility of adverse selection, death protection under a Term policy generally costs a little more than under a Whole Life or Endowment form.

[4] One of the fallacies of "net cost" illustrations is that they assume the policy is cashed out at a specified date, whereas a life insurance policy is designed to be kept in force to maturity at death or until retirement age. Only when it is so kept in force and only after the last dollar of benefits has been paid can its true net cost be determined. The fallacy in illustrations comparing the dollar advantage of buying a current investment with that of buying life insurance is that such comparisons are based on hindsight. They assume that the investor has lived or has died (depending on the illustration) at a given point, whereas any given investor at any given point in his life has no idea whether he will die in the next year or live to a ripe old age.

to provide cash or income for old age, or to utilize the semicompulsion features of the life insurance plan to build a savings account. In order to determine the best policy for any individual buyer, it is necessary to know which of the three reasons predominates in the given case. The best policy is the one which gives the policyholder what he finally decides he wants, regardless of whether the agent agrees that what the buyer wants is best for him.[5]

All of this means that in order to determine the best policy, it is necessary to know what each policy offers in the way of the three basic objectives for buying. Table 1 illustrates what a number of popular policy forms have to

Table 1. Death, Savings, and Retirement Values of Popular Policies Based on Annual Premium Outlay of $100 Issue Age 25, Unless Indicated Differently

(Typical Nonpar Rates Based on CSO 2½%)

Type of Policy	Death Protection	Savings (cash value) End of 20 yrs.	Cash Value at 65	Monthly Income at 65 (5 yrs. Certain and Life
Yearly renewable Term	Age 25: $14,881 40: 11,628 50: 6,506 60: 3,016	0	0	0
10-yr. renewable and convertible Term	Age 25: $10,070 35: 8,570 45: 5,921 55: 3,038	0	0	0
Convertible Term to 65	$8,547	$1,170	0	0
Continuous-premium Whole Life	6,333	1,678	$3,781	$24.61
Whole Life Paid up 65	5,701	1,755	4,294	27.99
Endowment at 65	4,854	1,820	4,854	31.60
Retirement Income at 65 (male)	3,364*	1,904	5,345	33.64
20-pay Life	3,686	2,035	2,779	18.09
20-yr. Endowment	2,168	2,168	0	0
Annual-premium deferred Annuity	Cash value equal to premiums paid during first 12 years, in excess thereafter.	2,315	6,460	42.05

* Or the cash value when it exceeds the face amount of insurance.

[5] For example, if the prospective insured has a wife and three children and refuses to budget more than $100 a year for insurance, Term might be the most sensible type of policy for him to buy. But if he wants to accumulate a savings fund for an emergency and is interested in having a large fund at age 65 with a minimum of death protection, then the best policy for these objectives is an Endowment at Age 65 or a retirement income policy.

offer for each of the three objectives. Since most people think of retiring at 65, that age is used in the table to illustrate retirement values. The 20-year point has been selected arbitrarily to illustrate savings values; although, of course, in a policy of more than 20 years' duration, the savings fund continues to grow beyond that point.

If Death Protection Needed. If death protection is the all-important reason for buying—to the complete exclusion of any considerations of savings or retirement [6]—then one of the Term forms may be the "best" policy. For example, in the above illustration $100 will purchase, at age 25, $14,881 yearly renewable Term, $10,070 ten-year renewable and convertible Term, and $8,547 convertible Term to Age 65. As time elapses, of course, the protection under all except the long Term will become less and less. All permanent or Endowment forms will give less insurance during the critical years.

Term is subject to two limitations. These limitations may or may not be important considerations in any given case. (1) Term insurance eventually expires, and no one can be certain that he will no longer have a protection need upon expiration or that in case the policy is not convertible he will be insurable and can replace the policy with a permanent form. (2) Term insurance has no cash values (except in long-term forms) upon which the policyholder can rely to meet premiums in an emergency. Since in many cases Term is used primarily because the buyer is pinched for premium dollars, the chances of his being unable to meet a premium due are greater than average.

It is possible, of course, to convert most Term forms. However, the human tendency is to put off conversion long after it could be afforded and to let the final conversion date expire.

A long-term form, such as Term to 65, overcomes some of the disadvantages of short-term forms. It does have cash values available for premium loans. Because it runs over the whole period of a man's normal working lifetime, he is more likely to find a time when he feels he has enough spare income to convert some (or all) of it to permanent insurance to take care of any continuing death protection needs in later life. However, Term to 65 offers only one of the functions of life insurance: protection against premature death. It does not build up values for retirement. Some type of Term, however, is the best policy if the only purpose for which the insurance is purchased is for protection against premature death.

If Need Is Savings. A need for death protection to the exclusion of sav-

---

[6] Death protection rarely is the sole reason for buying except in case of insurance purchased solely to cover a debt or where the number of dollars available for premiums is so small the buyer must ignore the other needs.

ings or retirement values is one extreme. The other extreme is a need for savings with little need for death protection or retirement values.[7] If this extreme exists, a relatively short-term Endowment policy may be the "best." The term of the Endowment policy should be made to correspond with the desired savings period. If, for example, the period is 20 years, then at age 25 a $100 annual premium will purchase $2,168 20-year death protection and a $2,168 savings account to be built up in 20 years should the insured survive the endowment period.

The Endowment policy is a convenient means of accumulating a fund which will be available to the policyholder at a fixed date in the future. As a method of saving, the Endowment form has two advantages over other methods of saving. (1) The policyholder has a definite savings schedule laid out for him and is reminded by premium notices to make these deposits. Further, he suffers some penalty—loss of the insurance protection—if he fails to adhere to the saving schedule. (2) In event of his death prior to maturity, his beneficiaries receive the face of the policy. This gives the savings plan a chance for speculative gain.

Endowment policies have some drawbacks:

In the first place, the protection element in them expires at a fixed date just as in the case of Term insurance. There is no way of knowing whether at the time of expiration all need for death protection will have passed.

In the second place, the attraction of a sizable sum of money at a specified date in the future too often leads the buyer into putting into the savings portion of the policy dollars that should be going into death protection. This is especially true in the case of young men who are lured into the purchase of Endowment policies by the appeal of high cash values.[8] It is often difficult for the young man with no dependents to see that he undoubtedly will have a family protection need within a few short years. He buys an Endowment form only to find that when he needs much more death protection than the policy affords, he is committed to as much premium as he can pay.[9] Theo-

---

[7] If there is actually *no* need for death protection, then *no* insurance policy is best, unless for some reason the prospective insured needs the so-called semicompulsion thrift feature which is so often argued to be an important psychological by-product of life insurance. An independent savings or investment fund would appear to be the best solution.

[8] And by the strange illusion that Endowment policies don't actually cost anything: "You get back more than you pay whether you live or die. You can't beat a deal like that."

[9] Agents are to blame as well as the buyer. Many consider it axiomatic that the young man cannot be sold protection and so talk an Endowment form to him as the line of least resistance. In other words, in such cases a conflict arises between salesmanship and professionalism. Professional principle demands that the prospect be brought to see what his true need is; but practical salesmanship foresees that resistance to the proper prescription may be so great that the prospect will wind up buying nothing if the agent keeps insisting that he buy something he doesn't want. At least the Endowment form will give him some of the death protection he needs. Such conflicts arise in all profes-

retically, he can convert his Endowment policy to a lower premium form, but such conversion almost always requires evidence of insurability, and insurability can disappear overnight.[10] A change in occupation as well as failing health can reduce the degree of insurability.

One of the limited-payment life forms also may be a good contract to use when emphasis is on a savings plan rather than on protection against death or old age. For example, on a 20-pay Life form, as indicated in Table 1, a $100 annual premium will buy only $3,686 of death protection and $2,779 of retirement protection as compared with $6,333 of death and $3,781 of old age protection under the continuous-premium form. But at the end of 20 years, $2,035 will have been accumulated in cash values under the 20-pay contract whereas only $1,678 will be available under the continuous-premium policy.

If Need Is Retirement Income. One of the most common reasons for savings is to build a fund for retirement. If the need is to provide for retirement income to the exclusion of death protection, then the best policy is an annual-premium, deferred annuity with neither death benefits nor cash values.[11] If the need is for some death protection but largely for retirement income protection then the Retirement Income policy is the best policy. If there is a moderate need for death protection but retirement values are still the predominant reason for buying, then the Endowment at 65 with the right to take the proceeds under income options might be best.

The various retirement forms have the same drawback as all Endowments: Too often they are taken before the policyholder's protection needs have actually crystallized. In the program of the average buyer, retirement income forms should be purchased last, after death protection needs are adequately covered.

If the Need Is for Both Death and Old Age Protection. If the need of the buyer is for relatively large amounts of death protection and reasonable retirement values as well—which is the need of most persons—then the continuous-premium Whole Life form is likely to be the best policy. If purchased prior to approximately age 40, the Whole Life form has a cash value

---

sional fields. The physician on occasion has to make a choice between insisting on treatment the patient resists to the point where the patient does nothing, or settling for less than the required treatment on the grounds that something is better than nothing at all.

[10] Substandard underwriting has developed to the point where there are statistically few people who are unable to get some form of coverage—but at a higher rate. The higher rate means that each premium dollar buys less insurance. It is a wise move to buy as much insurance as feasible when insurable at standard rates. The future insurability of any one person is unpredictable.

[11] If the deferred life annuity is written with death benefits and cash values equal to premiums paid then its rate is almost as high as for retirement income insurance, especially at older ages. Nevertheless this is the way most deferred annuities are written.

at retirement (65) of more than half of the face value. Table 2 shows the cash values and amount of income at age 65 for a $1,000 continuous-premium Whole Life and a limited-payment Whole Life according to various ages of entry.

Table 2. Cash and Life Income Values per $1,000 at Age 65
(CSO 2½%; Life Income Only, Male)

| Age of Purchase | Continuous Premium | | Paid Up at 65 | |
	Cash	Monthly Income	Cash	Monthly Income
20	$628	$4.21	$754	$5.05
25	607	4.07	754	5.05
30	580	3.89	754	5.05
35	547	3.66	754	5.05
40	505	3.38	754	5.05
45	452	3.03	754	5.05
50	382	2.56	754	5.05

The Life Paid-up at 65 policy, or any policy paid up before age 65 in the above company will have a cash value of $754 per $1,000 and pay $5.05 a month retirement income, regardless of the client's age at purchase.

If the insured wishes to combine in one contract retirement and premature death protection and yet build a sizable savings fund for emergency at a relatively fast pace, a 25- or 30-pay life might be the answer.

The choice between limited-pay and continuous-premium is, obviously, dependent on how predominant the retirement or cash value need is compared to the death protection need. The continuous-premium policy provides the most often desired balance between death protection and retirement needs. For that reason, it more nearly fits the need of the average buyer than does any other form.

3. INVESTMENT QUALITIES OF LIFE INSURANCE WHICH MAKE IT A GOOD SAVINGS MEDIUM

Safety of the dollar value of principal is an important requirement in the investment plans of most people.[12] No financial institution can boast of a better record than the institution of life insurance compiled during the past half century. Life insurance has earned for itself a reputation for dependable solvency which cannot be successfully challenged.

Liquidity also is a desirable investment quality. Emergencies arise which call for immediate cash. The cash values of life insurance are completely

[12] For a complete discussion of many of the points discussed below, see *Life Insurance As Investment* by Huebner and McCahan, D. Appleton-Century, 1933.

liquid, available to the policyholder within a few hours or a very few days. Moreover, cash values are known in advance for they are stated in the contract. It should be understood, however, that the liquidity of life insurance is of its cash and loan value, and not its face amount or even the money invested in the contract.

Avoidance of managerial care when investment is a side line often is desirable. With life insurance, there are no rents to collect, no repairs to look after, no markets to watch, no competition to worry about, no coupons to clip, and no watching to see if bonds are called before maturity.

Freedom from reinvestment is a valuable investment attribute. Reinvestment is conducive to loss of interest since there is almost always a time lag between the maturity of an investment and the reinvestment of the proceeds and between the receipt of interest or dividends and their reinvestment. Reinvestment also is conducive to dissipation of funds. When an investment matures, or dividends and interest are paid there may be a temptation to spend at least part of the maturity value rather than to reinvest it immediately. Further, reinvestment is managerial activity, which already has been labeled as undesirable in some investing plans.

A fair return is another requisite of a good investment and life insurance does yield a fair rate of return on that part of the premium which actually represents pure investment.[13]

It would appear at first glance that, to find the rate of return on a single-premium life insurance policy (for example), it would be necessary only to find at what rate the premium deposit accumulates at any point to the total of cash value plus dividends. However, such a procedure would not give the true rate of return. To find the true rate of return, the present value of the nonpar cost of the decreasing amount of insurance at risk each year [14] for the period under consideration must be subtracted from the single premium. The remainder is the effective amount invested in the contract. Once the equivalent investment deposit and the cash value at the end of any given year plus any accumulated dividends are found, then by mathematical formula and interpolation it is possible to calculate the actual rate of return for any given period. For example, what would be the rate of investment return on a $20,000 single-premium policy issued at age 35 if the policyholder keeps it in force for 15 years?

The nonparticipating single premium for the amount of the decreasing

---

[13] Actuaries would rise up in horror at the suggestion that any part of the premium actually represents pure investment; nevertheless it is a convenient concept.
[14] Face value less cash value (or single premium during earlier years when it is larger than cash value) each year multiplied by the term rates at each successive age.

Term insurance involved for the 15-year period would amount to $1,104.[15] In order to determine the actual amount invested in the policy,[16] this amount is subtracted from the single premium of $10,575 giving a net investment of $9,471. The value of the investment [17] at the end of 15 years is $13,569.[18] The $9,471 net investment will accumulate to $13,569 in 15 years at an interest rate of 2.425% compounded annually. If the contract were held another 15 years until the insured reaches age 65 (30 years) the rate of return would be 2.978%.

Protection from creditors' claims sometimes is an investment considera-tion. In many states,[19] this protection under certain conditions is accorded to proceeds and often to cash values of life insurance policies by law. Also in many states, the payment of life insurance proceeds may be arranged in such a way as to protect against not only the creditors of the insured, but also against creditors of the beneficiaries.

Favorable tax treatment is a definite investment consideration, and life insurance stands in a favorable position in this regard. Interest credited to the funds on deposit by the policyholder (the cash value) are not taxed in the year earned. How the gain is taxed otherwise is indicated in Table 3. In most other investments the interest is subject to the federal income tax in the year earned at the rate applying to the tax bracket into which it falls.

Table 3. Taxation of Interest Accretions on Life Insurance *

Nature of Benefits **	Income Tax Status
Death Benefits	Nontaxable
Endowment proceeds or policy cash values	Taxable only for the amount proceeds or cash values received exceed net premiums paid.

* Cf. Chapter 17 for a more complete discussion of this subject.
** Taxation of installment proceeds under settlement options is discussed in Chapter 17.

Facility of estate settlement might be a quality desired in an investment. If so, life insurance merits serious consideration. A life insurance estate made payable to named beneficiaries can be settled directly without the time and expense involved in the probate of a will. It can also be made payable to the beneficiary as a life income, giving her the benefit of the investment services of skilled technicians and planned settlements without the expenses involved

---

[15] Figured by applying a nonpar yearly renewable Term rate for the amount at risk (face of policy — cash values or invested premium if higher) at each successive age over the 15-year period, and discounting them to the present at 2½%. The final result involved 45 separate computations.
[16] The premium paid less the cost of the actual insurance involved.
[17] The cash value plus dividends accumulated at 3%.
[18] Rounded off to even dollars.
[19] Cf. Chapter 8.

in the creation and administration of a trust. Finally, a beneficiary under a life insurance policy, unlike a devisee under a will or testament, is not subject to the risk of delay or loss resulting from contention. Especially where major philanthropic interests are involved, relatives have been known to attack wills.

4. SUMMARY

The "best" policy is not to be determined by a study of policies themselves. It can be determined only by the objectives of the prospective buyer. The best policy for him is the policy which is best suited to his objectives. His objectives are, theoretically, his *needs*; practically, they are his *wants*. What a man wants is not always what he needs. While the professional principle of life insurance selling calls for doing everything possible to see that a man buys the right kind of insurance to fill important needs, it sometimes comes to a choice between letting him fill his wants or go altogether uninsured.

When the agent meets with a prospect who wants what he wants even though it is not what he needs, the agent has the choice of refusing to be a party to any other than the most effective "prescription," leaving the prospect uninsured,[20] or of giving him a less effective prescription on the theory that a partially effective medication is better than no medication at all.

Most people buy life insurance to fill one of three needs: [21] income for dependents in case of death; income for old age; savings. Income for old age and savings are closely related.

If the cash value in a life insurance policy can be called "savings," then all life insurance policies except Term and Annuities are made up of a combination of savings and pure insurance. Finding the "best" policy for any need is, therefore, a matter of choosing the one which has most nearly the exact combination of savings and insurance the need requires.

The only way for a buyer to select the "best" policy is for him to make an honest, objective appraisal of his needs—or of the exact combination of savings and protection which constitutes his need. Because self-analysis

---

[20] And there are agents who *will* refuse to sell other than the most effective policy for the need. For instance, the authors know one agent who keeps the equivalent of a full year's income in liquid savings just so he will never be forced by his own financial need into taking an application for other than the "best" policy for the case. Some of his colleagues consider his attitude the height of professionalism; others label it "bull-headedness."

[21] There are other reasons for purchasing life insurance aside from these three basic uses. Some of them will be mentioned in Chapters 15, 17, and 18. Among them are insurance for gift purposes, business insurance, estate plans, etc. However, here we are talking about the primary family needs.

tends to subjectivity, he will be wise to seek an outside check of his self-evaluation.

The man who is sick can ask the advice of friends—and he often does. If he is wise, however, he asks the advice of an expert: the physician. A man who is seeking a diagnosis of his insurance needs can ask his friends—and often does. If he is wise, he asks the advice of an expert: a competent agent.[22]

There are no "good" and "bad" policies, per se. Every policy—even the remarkable combination used to open this chapter—has its use. Any policy can be used incorrectly. It is a "good" policy when it is used for the right need. It is a "bad" policy when used where it does not apply. The "best" policy is determined by a study of the economic situation of a man, not by a study of policy rates, values, and provisions.

The man who learns to study his needs first and policies second is on the way to intelligent life insurance buying.

Questions for Class Discussion

1. For what type of insurance situation would you recommend renewable Term insurance?
2. Explain why no one policy can be called the best policy.
3. Why do you suppose that Endowment insurance is so often improperly used?
4. For what type of insurance situation would you recommend 20-pay Life?
5. Life insurance is often proposed for those whose sole buying motive is a vehicle for saving money. Should these people buy life insurance?
6. Should a person who owns a 20-year Endowment change this policy to a continuous-premium Whole Life if he feels that the latter now is the best policy for him?
7. What information do you need in order to prescribe the best policy for your neighbor?
8. Do you think most people buy the best policy? Why or why not?
9. If, after careful study, you decide upon the policy that is best for you, and your life insurance agent says his company does not write that policy and instead offers you one which he thinks is best for you, what should you do? If you are the agent and are asked for a type of policy that your company does not write, what should you do?
10. Do insurance buyers' wants and needs always coincide? Explain your answer.

---

[22] By the time you finish this course, you will have no difficulty in distinguishing a competent agent from the one who is trying to bluff his way into a sale.

CHAPTER 8

ESSENTIAL ASPECTS
OF INSURANCE LAW

THE SUBJECT of insurance law covers a vast array of topics. Typical of these are contract law, construction and interpretation of insurance contracts, insurable interest, doctrines of warranty, representation and concealment, the law of agency, waiver and estoppel, rights of creditors and beneficiaries, and the regulation of insurance companies. This and the next two chapters are concerned primarily with all these topics except regulation. A discussion of the regulation of insurance companies is deferred until Chapter 27.

The discussion in these chapters is not intended as a comprehensive survey of insurance law; instead it is directed to the general student of life insurance. It is designed primarily to provide the legal background fundamental to a practical, everyday understanding of policies and the rights and obligations of parties to them.

This and the next two chapters should be considered as a unit. In several instances it will be found that a point treated briefly in this chapter is discussed further in one of the others, where its development is deemed more logical from an organizational standpoint.

1. THE POLICY AS A CONTRACT

The life insurance policy is a legal contract. As such, it is, in general, subject to the law of contracts;[1] although general contract law is often so

[1] While some few states have contract codes, these codes are only general rules. Much depends on their interpretation. The "law of contracts" is found chiefly in what is known as "Case" or "Decisional" law, which is made when an appellate court renders a decision. Such decisions have the force of law since they will generally be followed by other courts in rendering decisions.

modified in its application to life insurance as to be almost unrecognizable.[2]

Since an insurance policy is a contract, the making of it and the binding of parties to it are subject to the fulfillment of the requisites of a contract: (1) There must be an offer. (2) The offer must be accepted. (3) There must be a valuable consideration. (4) The parties to the contract must have legal capacity to make a contract. (5) The contract must not be against public policy. A discussion of each of these conditions as it applies to or operates in the case of the life insurance policy contract follows.

Offer.   In the making of a life insurance contract, an offer may be made by either (1) the insurance company or (2) the applicant.

An application submitted without the payment of the first premium is not an offer but rather an invitation to the company to make an offer. In such a case, the company makes the offer by issuing the policy.

If, however, the application is accompanied by the payment of the first premium, the offer is made by the applicant. If a policy other than the one applied for in the application is issued [3] then the issuance of the altered policy becomes a counter offer by the company.

Usually when the application is accompanied by the payment of the first premium, the company makes a counter offer by issuing the applicant a conditional receipt.[4] The counter offer is a conditional offer to insure the applicant if he meets the requirements of insurability established by the company under the plan, at the premium, and for the amount requested.

Acceptance.   An offer may be accepted either (1) by payment of the first premium or (2) by issuing or delivering the policy. If the offer is made by the company, the applicant accepts it by paying the first premium. If the offer is made by the applicant, the company accepts it by delivering the policy.

Although in a few jurisdictions unreasonable delay on the part of the company in processing applications accompanied by the first premium has been held to constitute acceptance, in the majority of jurisdictions it is

---

[2] Woodruff, in his *Selection of Cases on the Law of Insurance* (1924) inserted the following significant statement in his preface: "What do they know of the law of insurance who only the law of contract know?" He goes on to say that general contract law has "in various instances been badly warped if not broken in order that insurance law may accommodate itself to the 'actuality of facts.'"

[3] This situation will occur, for instance, in the case of applicants who because of conditions of health or occupation are not insurable at standard rates. The company may issue the policy with a larger premium than quoted, or it may issue another type of policy.

[4] The *conditional* receipt often is referred to as a *binding* receipt. It is binding, however, only *if* certain conditions are met. The use of the word "if" completely destroys the meaning of the term "binding." See 63 Yale L. J. No. 4, *Comment, Life Insurance Receipts: The Mystery of the Non-Binding Binder.*

treated as a rejection of the offer.[5] Some companies state on their conditional receipt that a delay of 60 days, for example, in issuing the policy may be construed as rejection.

Effective Date of the Contract. A few words are now necessary to clarify the position of the parties relating to offer, acceptance, and the effective date of the contract.

When the premium is not paid with the application the contract is not bound until the policy is issued and the agent has delivered it and has accepted the first premium, all while the applicant is still in good health.

When the premium is paid with the application and a conditional receipt is issued, the effective date of the contract depends upon the provisions of the conditional receipt. Three types of receipts are used. The most common form makes the insurance effective as of the date of the application or medical examination whichever is the later, provided the applicant is found insurable as of that time. Under this form, any claim arising after this date will be paid even though the application papers may not yet have reached the home office, if the facts on the application and the results of the medical are such that the company would have accepted the application had the applicant lived. Cases of claims being paid even though no policy has been issued are by no means rare. Also under this type of conditional receipt, if the health of the applicant changes after the medical examination or if other changes in insurability occur, the policy will be issued if the applicant were insurable at the time of application or medical examination.

A second type of conditional receipt used by a number of companies is the approval form which provides coverage beginning with the date the application is approved by the company at its home office. This form of receipt does not offer the insured any protection for the period running from the date of the application until it is approved by the company. The only advantage this type of receipt has over no receipt at all is protection for the period from the approval of the risk to the delivery of the policy.

A third type of receipt is the unconditional binding receipt. According to a recent survey of company practices, only two companies, one in Canada and the other in Ohio, issue a truly binding receipt. Under its terms, the company binds the insurance from the date of the application until the policy is issued or the application is rejected. The companies put a time limit on the binder, 31 days for one company and 45 days for the other.

When the premium is paid with the application but no conditional re-

---

[5] Some courts, while not holding an unreasonable delay as an acceptance, have held the company liable in tort for negligent delay in acting upon the application.

ceipt issued, the contract is not in force until the policy is issued and delivered to the applicant.[6]

Whether the issuance of the policy or its actual or constructive delivery to the applicant constitutes acceptance depends largely on the agreement between the insurer and insured. Delivery of a policy is not necessary to its validity or enforceability unless there is an agreement between the contracting parties requiring that delivery be made. However, most life insurance contracts specify delivery as a condition precedent. Whether this delivery must be actual or constructive depends largely on the wording of the application. Unless, however, the application makes it absolutely clear that actual delivery is required, the general rule of case law [7] is that constructive delivery is enough. Actual delivery involves the physical transfer of the policy from the insurer into the possession of the insured. If the application says that the agent shall not deliver the policy to the applicant unless he is in good health and has paid the first premium, actual delivery is required. Constructive delivery is usually considered to have been effected if the company has intentionally and unconditionally given up control over the policy and placed it in the control of someone acting for the policyholder, including the company's own agent. Thus it might be held that a policy placed in the mail to the agent by the company has been constructively delivered.

Mere possession of a policy does not establish delivery if all conditions have not been filled. For instance, a policy might be left with the applicant for inspection; [8] but his possession of it does not establish delivery if the premium has not been paid. On the other hand, the policyholder does not have to produce the policy to prove it was delivered. The general rule of delivery is that it is not who has actual possession of the policy but who has the right to possession.

Interesting questions arise with respect to applications without conditional receipts and those with conditional receipts that have been antedated to gain advantage of lower rates. If the application has one date, the policy

---

[6] The applicant in this case may withdraw his offer any time before acceptance and has a legally enforceable right to a refund of the premium. Under the conditional offer plan, the applicant is not legally entitled to a refund of premium should he change his mind before the policy is issued, although in practice companies may grant this refund.

[7] There are decisions to the contrary, holding that delivery is a condition precedent to putting the contract into force and cannot be met by constructive delivery. Conflicting decisions are to be found on every point in this discussion.

[8] This is commonly done; but it is usual to require a receipt from the applicant which shows the policy has been handed to him for inspection only and not as legal delivery. Such a receipt is probably not a legal necessity if it can be clearly shown he has not fulfilled all of the conditions precedent, but it is a wise precaution and will prevent misunderstanding with the beneficiary should something happen to the applicant before he pays the premium.

another, and delivery is made on still another, which date governs the (1) due date of subsequent premiums (2) incontestable period and (3) suicide period? The policy becomes effective when the offer has been accepted. This will be the actual or constructive delivery date of the contract after the full first premium is paid. The policy, however, is not dated as of the delivery date but instead is dated commonly as of the date of the application. Sometimes it is dated as of the time the policy is actually written. In either case it is a date which is earlier than the delivery date. The courts generally have held that the policy date determines the date on which premiums are due even though this means less than one full year's protection for the first premium unless, of course, the conditional receipt was given at the time of application. As for the suicide and incontestable clauses, the operative date also is held to be the date on the policy even though it is earlier than the date actual protection began. If the date on the policy is later than its actual issue date, the operative date begins when the protection begins. Of course, if the clauses themselves state the operative date, then this date is usually held to cover.

Consideration. The consideration given by the insured for the promises of the company are the statements made in the application and the payment of the full first premium, or in the event of quarterly or semi-annual premiums, the first premium installment. Although agents of some companies are empowered to accept notes, it is customary to require that the premium be paid in cash. Even so, it is relatively common for agents to accept notes for the first premium. Unless the agent is empowered by his company to do so, however, the note constitutes a personal loan from him to the applicant. Under these conditions, the first premium is construed to be a cash payment. More is said on the subject of consideration in Chapter 9.

Legal Capacity. For a valid agreement to be effected, the parties involved must have the legal capacity to enter into a contract. If the company is organized and empowered to solicit business under the insurance code and complies with the code in issuing the contract, its capacity to contract is clear.

With respect to the legal capacity of the insured to contract, two problems arise: minors and the mentally incompetent. In the absence of contrary state statutes, contracts made by minors are voidable except for the reasonable value of necessaries.[9] In the interest of public policy, marriage contracts are made an exception.

---

[9] A distinction should be made between the terms *void* and *voidable*. An agreement which is prohibited by law and therefore is not held to be a valid contract is called void. If a contract is held to be valid but one party has the right to rescind the contract on the grounds of incompetency, fraud, or duress, the contract is called voidable.

Legal majority is 21 in most states. In some states, females have the power to enter into contracts at 18. A large number of states have special statutes giving minors over anywhere from 14½ to 16 the capacity to make a life insurance contract. In New York, for instance, a minor over 14½ (insurance age 15) may apply for insurance on his own life. This is in recognition of the fact that, although life insurance is not a necessity, it has important values to the insured and his family. Strictly speaking, a minor is capable of entering into a contract and it is not illegal to make a contract with a minor, although the contract may be held unenforceable if the minor decides to repudiate it at a later date. The insurer, however, is bound by the contract so long as the minor wishes to continue it in force. If the minor repudiates his contract in those states which do not have the special statutes mentioned above, the law will allow him a refund of *all* premiums paid, although a *few* courts will allow a deduction for cost of protection received. The practice of issuing an insurance contract on the application of a minor is relatively frequent despite the danger of repudiation. However, there is no question of legal capacity involved in the case of insurance on a minor if the application for it is made by a competent adult.

Insanity or mental incompetency [10] precludes the making of a valid insurance contract if a guardian has been appointed. If no guardian has been appointed, a contract made by the insane or incompetent is voidable and is handled in the same manner as are contracts made by minors.

A person who is too intoxicated to understand the nature of the contract he is about to make [11] also does not have the legal capacity to contract. He may repudiate the contract when he becomes sober. A full enforcement of this principle might reduce the "club room" sales of life insurance policies.

It should be pointed out that there are only two parties to a life insurance contract, the insurer and the insured. While it is common to think of the insured as the person on whose life the policy is issued, this is not always the case. Where the beneficiary applies for the policy and retains all incidences of ownership, that beneficiary is, technically, the insured. This means that the person on whose life the policy is issued (the *cestui que vie*) is not a party to the contract and has no rights in it.

Public Policy.   To be valid, a contract must be for a legal purpose and not contrary to public policy. Although in the early history of the life insurance business some courts did hold a life insurance policy to be a con-

---

[10] The standard of mental competency is very low and includes all but the feeble-minded.
[11] The ability to understand the nature of the transaction in which a person is about to enter is interpreted very broadly; otherwise most life insurance policies made by the soberest of men would be voidable.

tract for illegal purposes,[12] today no such question is involved. There are several instances in which an insurance contract will be held to be against public policy. The first of these involves the question of insurable interest.

(1) *Insurable Interest.* The applicant for life insurance must have an insurable interest in the life of the person on whose life the policy is to be written. Without insurable interest, an insurance policy becomes a gambling contract and as such is unenforceable at law. In the majority of cases, the person on whom the insurance is to be issued and the applicant are one and the same. If he is, insurable interest is held to exist without question or to be immaterial to the contract.[13] Also, the court places no restrictions on the amount of insurance he is allowed to buy. The only limits are those imposed by the practicalities of each situation, which depend upon prudent underwriting.[14] Further, he has the right to name anyone he wishes as his beneficiary.[15] This latter right is guaranteed by statutes in some states and is established by court decisions in others.

However, if the application for the insurance is made by a party other than the *cestui que vie* and the applicant is to be the beneficiary under the policy, he must have an insurable interest in that life. An insurable interest is a reasonable expectation of financial benefit from the continued life of the person whose life is covered or an expectation of loss if the insurant dies. For instance, a parent has a clear insurable interest in the life of a minor child, since he is entitled to the services and earnings of that child. A person also has a clear insurable interest in the life of his or her spouse—the wife because of her husband's legal obligation to support her and the husband because of the value of his wife's services. Actually, the relationship between husband and wife carries a sufficient presumption of insurable interest without requiring proof of close financial ties. To a lesser extent, courts have

---

[12] During the Elizabethan period, life insurance was widely used as a gambling device. By the end of the seventeenth century, several countries had outlawed life insurance but later amended their laws to allow life insurance where a pecuniary interest existed.

[13] Vance, in his work on Insurance Law, argues that the insurant does not have an insurable interest in his own life since in effect he does not live to suffer a financial loss by his death. He concludes that the better reasoning is that insurable interest is not material when a person insures his own life. Patterson in his *Essentials of Insurance Law* agrees with this contention.

[14] An application for amounts of life insurance in apparent excess of the applicant's ability to pay will be looked upon with suspicion by an underwriting department as a possible indication of moral hazard.

[15] Until 1953, when a law was passed in Texas giving a statutory insurable interest to any beneficiary appointed by any person of legal age upon whose life the insurance was written, a beneficiary in that state had to have an insurable interest. Regardless of the legal rights possessed by the insured, however, the naming of an unrelated beneficiary for other than a valuable consideration will be looked upon with suspicion by a company's underwriting department as a possible indication of moral hazard and by its legal department as a possible source of litigation over the payment of proceeds.

held close ties of blood or marriage sufficient to establish insurable interest, such as ties between brother and sister, parent and child, and even grandparent and grandchild. The court decisions in these cases seem to have based the insurable interest either on a presumptive financial relationship or *love and affection*. In the latter cases, the resulting loss is construed to be an emotional one rather than a pecuniary one. These latter decisions, however, are in the minority since the majority rule is that in the absence of a pecuniary interest, *love and affection*, even when backed by family ties, do not establish an insurable interest.

There are a number of clear-cut examples of insurable interest that do not involve family relationships. A creditor has an insurable interest in the life of a debtor. A business has an insurable interest in the life of a key employee or part owner. A surety has an insurable interest in the life of his principal.[16] Anyone being supported by another has an insurable interest in that person's life, and a woman has an insurable interest in the life of her fiancé. These last two illustrations point up the general rule that insurable interest need not be based on an obligation legally enforceable by law or even on a moral obligation. Only a factual expectation is required.

A general rule is that even though an insurable interest exists, one person may not insure the life of another without his consent. As a matter of practice, insurance companies generally require the insurant to sign the application for the policy. New York has a specific statute which rules void all life, accident, and disability policies which are procured without the consent of the insured. Certain specific exceptions are made. For example, a wife may take insurance on her husband's life without his consent; [17] an employer does not have to obtain the consent of his employees in establishing a Group insurance program for them; a father does not have to secure the consent of his minor child in the majority of cases.[18] The *consent* rule is a precautionary measure against the moral hazard. Even though an insurable interest does exist, one person may be worth more dead than alive to another if there is sufficient insurance. Such a situation would place the insured in a precarious position and might not be overly conducive to longevity.

It is generally held that the insurable interest need exist only at the time of the application. The courts generally do not inquire into the status of the interest as of the time the policy becomes a claim. Thus a business can

---

[16] That is, someone who has guaranteed the performance of another has an insurable interest in the life of the person for whose nonperformance he will be liable.

[17] This is an exception to the New York statute. In other jurisdictions courts may require consent.

[18] Some states place statutory limits on the amount of life insurance which a parent may take on a minor child.

continue a life insurance policy on the life of a key man or part owner who is no longer associated with the firm or company. A creditor may continue a policy on a debtor after the debt has been paid off.[19]

The amount of insurable interest is not a matter of concern for the courts. If insurable interest exists at all, it is generally held to be for the full amount of the insurance. It is invariably held that the life insurance contract is not a contract of indemnity. The beneficiary does not have to establish the amount of his loss. It is presumed to be the amount of the policy. The one exception is the case of insurance by the creditor upon the life of a debtor. The courts generally require a reasonable relationship between the amount of the insurance and the indebtedness. A creditor cannot insure the life of a debtor for, say, $5,000 when the debt is only $150. Such a transaction would be viewed as a gambling contract against public policy. Courts, however, have upheld policies for as much as $6,500 when the debt was only $1,000. The amount of the allowable discrepancy between the insurance and the debt is a matter for the court to decide in each disputed case. The courts have generally been liberal in interpreting what is or is not reasonable. The amount of insurance in any event should be enough to repay the premiums, and, perhaps, interest thereon, as well as the debt.

(2) *Enemy Aliens.* A contract with an enemy alien is held to be against public policy and hence void. There is no question on that point. However, questions do arise when a contract has been made with an alien friend who later becomes an enemy, as in case of war. Usually the situation makes it impossible for the alien or the company, or both, to carry out the terms of the contract. The disposition of life insurance contracts made under such conditions has been subject to diverse court decisions. In general, it has been held that the policy terminates and the reserve as of the date of failure to comply with its terms (usually to pay the premium) becomes payable to the owner of the policy. The nonforfeiture provisions apply just as in the case of any other lapse. In some cases it has been held that the policy is suspended but may be reinstated later.

(3) *When the Beneficiary Murders the Insured.* Payment of the proceeds of the policy to a person who has murdered the insured is considered against public policy. Where the purpose of the murder was simply to collect the insurance, there is no question that the court will not allow the beneficiary to collect. A man is not entitled to profit by his own wrongdoing. If the motive of the murder was not to collect the insurance, but, for example, to

---

[19] Some courts have held that, in a debtor-creditor relationship, an insurable interest is required at the time of the death of the insured since for this purpose life insurance is a contract of indemnity. This is a minority view.

gain revenge, again the courts will deny the murdering beneficiary the right to collect the insurance. But if the beneficiary should kill the insured in self-defense, or while insane, the courts will award him or her the proceeds of the policy.

Homicides are not always murders; they may be manslaughters—that is, they may represent the unlawful killing of a human being without malice expressed or implied. The attitude of the courts in manslaughter cases is not unanimous as in murder cases, although the general view is that the beneficiary may collect the life insurance proceeds if he commits involuntary manslaughter.[20]

When the murdering beneficiary is not allowed to collect the proceeds of the life insurance policy, the proceeds are paid to the estate of the insured. Where the murdering beneficiary is also an heir to the estate of the insured, some courts have held that the beneficiary may receive all the estate to which he is entitled under the will or laws of descent. Other courts have ruled that the estate is to be divided among the innocent heirs. This latter ruling seems more in line with the spirit of the law.

Finally, when the insurer can prove that the policy was taken with murder in mind, it can have the policy voided upon the grounds of concealment. Premiums paid are usually refunded to the estate of the murderer, his heirs, or as otherwise directed by the court.

(4) *When the Cestui Que Vie Is Executed for a Crime.* Although some courts on the grounds of public policy have denied the right of a beneficiary to collect the proceeds of a life insurance policy, if the *cestui que vie* has been executed for a crime, the general rule is to allow recovery. In most states, a constitutional provision requires that no conviction be allowed to work a forfeiture of the estate of the convicted party. On the basis of these provisions which most courts hold as expressing a public policy, life insurance policies are not held to be defeated if the *cestui que vie* meets his death by execution for a crime; it is felt that the innocent parties (the beneficiaries) should not be penalized for the crime of another (the *cestui que vie*).

Distinguishing Characteristics of Policy Contracts. Although requiring the same elements as all contracts, the insurance contract has a number of distinguishing characteristics. It is a contract of *utmost* good faith, a *unilateral* contract, a *conditional* contract, *a valued contract,* a contract of *adhesion,* and an *aleatory* contract.

---

[20] Several states have statutes which prevent a beneficiary from collecting proceeds of insurance policies if he unlawfully kills the insurant. Patterson suggests, however, that the courts might interpret such statutes to apply to murders only. Cf. Patterson, *Essentials of Insurance Law* New York: McGraw-Hill Book Co., 1935, p. 136.

Utmost Good Faith (uberrimae fidei). Most contracts are good faith contracts. In the insurance contract, however, each party has the right to depend on the utmost good faith of the other party regarding the nature of the risk to be assumed. Neither "buyer beware" nor "seller beware" has any place in insurance dealings. A level of good faith above that in the usual commercial transaction is required. It is upon this principle that doctrines of warranties, representation, and concealment are based.

A life insurance company does not have to insure all applicants. It can and does select among them. In the process of selection, the company relies in part on information furnished by the applicant. If this information is false or incomplete, the company may be in a position to void the contract by resorting in legal action to the doctrines of *warranties, representation,* or *concealment.*

A warranty in insurance law is a statement or condition incorporated in the contract relating to the risk, which the insured presents as true and upon which it is assumed that the insurer relied in issuing the contract. Marine insurance, the first branch of insurance to develop commercially, evolved the doctrine of warranty as it applies to insurance. The Marine underwriter was usually called upon to underwrite a hull and cargo which he had no chance to inspect. In fact, it might be lying in a port 10,000 miles away. Therefore, he had to depend entirely upon the word of the person seeking the insurance. Hence all information in the application for the insurance was warranted to be absolutely exact. If it turned out to be untrue in any particular, the insurance was void whether the misstatement was intentional or unintentional, material to the loss or immaterial. Literally, if the captain's wife were warranted to be a redhead and she turned out to be a blonde, the policy could be voided. The strict warranty rule still prevails in marine insurance. Thus the materiality of all statements is established in advance by contract and thereby is taken out of the hands of judicial interpretation.

The doctrine of warranties carried over into the field of life insurance in its early days. Answers to questions upon application for coverage had to be literally true, and the policy could be avoided for any misstatement, intentional or unintentional, regardless of whether in the opinion of the courts the questions were material or immaterial.

However necessary in the marine field, it early became apparent that the doctrine of warranty was too harsh for life insurance. Public opinion, enlightened companies, and, finally, legislation were factors in outlawing the application of the doctrine of warranty to life insurance. The effect is to revert to the common law of misrepresentation and concealment. This makes it necessary once again to rely upon a jury or the court [21] rather than upon a contractual arrangement for the determination of materiality of the misrepresented or concealed fact.

Strictly speaking, a representation in insurance is a statement made to the insurer by the insured or his representative before the contract is made as an inducement to the formation of the contract. It is neither attached to nor made a part of the contract, for then it would become a warranty. However, in the case of life insurance state statutes usually declare that representations cannot be used as defense against claims unless they are written and attached to the policy. In states having such statutes the apparently irreconcilable is reconciled by the passage of a simple statute which declares that in the absence of fraud all warranties in a life insurance contract are to be interpreted as representations. Some states prohibit avoidance unless the misrepresentation increases the hazard.

In general, the doctrine of representations holds that a policy is voidable by the insurer in the event of a misrepresentation of a fact which is material to the risk; that is, which would have led the company to deny the insurance or ask for better terms had it had a correct statement of the matter on the application. The general rule is that the policy is voidable even though the misrepresentation is made innocently with no intention to deceive. It must be held in mind, however, that an honest statement of *opinion*, even though it proves in error, cannot be cause to rescind a contract.[22] Whether a statement is to be interpreted as one of opinion or fact is up to the court, based on the evidence before it.

The general rule is that a fraudulent misrepresentation of an *immaterial* fact will not provide sufficient grounds for avoidance. The purpose of the doctrine of representation is not to punish a dishonest insured but to protect the insurer. If the insurer is not harmed he should not be allowed to void the contract under this doctrine.

Uniquely among contracts, life insurance and a growing number of A & S insurance contracts contain clauses rendering them incontestable after a specified period of years—one, two, or three. If the misrepresentation is not discovered by the company prior to the expiration of the period of incontestability, it cannot be used to avoid the policy or as a defense against a

---

[21] The jury, if evidence is conflicting; the court, if it is not.

[22] A very few states restrict misrepresentation even beyond the question of materiality, for they require through statute that before a contract may be avoided, the loss itself must result from the fact misrepresented. In these jurisdictions, death by an automobile accident may require payment of the proceeds of a life insurance policy even though the insured misrepresented his health.

claim. The incontestable clause and its ramifications are discussed more fully in the next chapter.

Concealment also may be grounds for rescission. A concealment is the failure to disclose a material fact; that is, remaining silent when there is an obligation to speak. In life insurance, in order to void a policy, a concealment must be both *material* and *intentional*. It is often difficult to determine the difference between an intentional and an innocent concealment. The test of fraud (intentional deception) is applicable only to facts which are obviously material. For an insured to be guilty of concealment, he must (1) know the concealed fact before he signs the application or (2) after he signs the application but before the policy is issued.

It is the duty of the applicant to reveal in full all details or information about questions on the application. A partial answer is concealment. Assume that the application asks if the applicant has ever had pain in the chest, and although he has one now, he says "no." He would be guilty of a misrepresentation. Assume on the other hand that the application asks if he has consulted a physician in the past four years and if so for what purpose, and that he reports that he consulted one for a common cold but fails to report he has consulted one about the pain in his chest. He would be guilty of concealment.

The applicant has no responsibility to reveal information not asked for on the application, since it is assumed that if it is not asked for it is not important, nor does the applicant have a responsibility to reveal information that can be presumed to be known to the company. Further, if a question on the application is not answered and the policy is issued anyway, the company will be deemed to have waived the requirement for an answer.[23]

In conclusion, it might be pointed out that while courts seem inclined to lean over backwards in interpreting the doctrines of warranty, representation, and concealment in favor of the policyholder, they are also inclined to take a serious view of palpable fraud. The best advice to the applicant for a life insurance policy is not to rely on the penchant of courts, and espe-

---

[23] A waiver is generally defined as the intentional relinquishment of a known right. Thus, the company has a right to demand an answer to the question not answered. If it does not, it has intentionally departed from the right to ask for the answer. Closely related to waiver is "estoppel." Estoppel comes about when one party to a contract, by his action or inaction, induces the other to change his position to the disadvantage of the first party. Whereas one court might hold that failure to demand an answer to an unanswered question constituted *waiver* of the right to make the demand, another might hold the company was *estopped* from demanding the answer. Waiver and estoppel are alternative methods of being placed in the same situation. Whether a given result is reached by waiver or estoppel, the result is essentially the same. The dividing line between the two concepts is decidedly blurred.

cially juries, for deciding in favor of the individual as against the "soulless corporation," but to answer each question with a clear conscience and reveal any information that he thinks might make a difference.

Unilateral Contract. In the field of contracts, a distinction is drawn between *bilateral* and *unilateral* contracts. In the bilateral contract, each party to the contract makes promises to the other, each in consideration of the promises of the other. In the unilateral contract, only one of the contracting parties makes legally enforceable promises. A life insurance policy contract is a unilateral contract.[24] Only the insurer makes any promises. The insured does not even promise to pay premiums. It is impossible for him to be held for breach of contract. Payment of premiums is merely a condition for the continuation of the promise of the insurer in its present form. Not only can the insurer not force the policyholder to pay premiums, but he cannot even void the contract if premiums are not paid. The contract remains in effect as to the nonforfeiture provisions and the right to reinstate.[25] On the other hand, the insurer is forced to accept premium payments from the insured, and to keep the contract in force in accordance with its terms.

Conditional Contract. The obligations or promises of the insured as set forth in the policy contract are conditional; that is, they are conditioned on the performance of certain acts by the insured. For example, they are conditioned on periodic payment of a stipulated premium, furnishing proofs of death or disability, and the like. Performance on the company's part is also conditioned upon death resulting from causes other than certain specific ones like suicide (within the suicide period), war, or some types of aviation.[26]

A Valued Contract. Most fire and casualty insurance contracts are contracts of indemnity; that is, they agree to pay only to the extent of the loss the insured has suffered. For instance, a $10,000 fire insurance policy will not pay $10,000 for every fire. It will pay only the actual cash value of the damage suffered up to a maximum of $10,000. The Accident and Sickness policy may have some indemnity provisions; for instance, it may agree to pay the cost of medical or hospital care, or of surgical procedure up to a maximum limit; but if the actual cost is not the maximum limit, then it will pay only the actual cost. In other provisions, accidental death, dismemberment, loss-

---

[24] Exceptions are sometimes found in assessment contracts.

[25] Cf. Chapter 9.

[26] Such restrictions were once much more common. In the earlier days of life insurance in America, policies were often filled with restrictions regarding travel abroad, travel below or above certain latitudes, travel in Indian country, etc. The present-day policy has dropped almost all such prohibitions, the latest, airplane travel, gradually being dropped from more and more policies. Special restrictions such as war clauses come and go, depending on the imminence of war or nearness to a past war.

of-time benefits, for example, it is not a contract of indemnity but one of stated value.

The life insurance policy, however, is never a contract of indemnity. It is an agreement to pay a given sum of money upon the occurrence of a stated contingency (death or survival in case of Endowment). It may also pay additional amounts in event of disability or of death by accidental means, but these, too, are stated values, not indemnities. They do not depend on the actual cash value of the loss.

Furthermore, the usual physical damage property insurance contract calls for subrogation to the insurer of any rights or claims he may have against anyone else for indemnification for that same loss.[27] The doctrine of subrogation does not apply in the case of the life insurance contract.

Contract of Adhesion. In the case of some contracts, both parties to it may bargain for the terms. In the case of life and disability insurance contracts, no such bargaining is possible.[28] The terms are stipulated by the insurer and must be accepted or rejected *in toto* by the applicant.[29]

Actually, as will become apparent in the next chapter, insurance companies do not have complete control over the terms of the contract either. As in a marriage contract, neither party is the sole master of the conditions. Standard provisions, reduction of warranties to representations, and entire contract statutes have seriously restricted the insurer in dawing up contracts.[30]

Nevertheless, in life and Accident and Sickness insurance the insurer draws his own contract within the limits of the law. Therefore, since the in-

---

[27] To illustrate: If an automobile on which there is collision coverage is struck by another automobile, the insurer will be obligated to indemnify the owner of the struck car for the loss. When the owner accepts that indemnification from his insurance company, he hands over to it (subrogates) his right to sue the owner of the car which struck him. If the collision company elects to prosecute the claim, and if it subsequently collects, it retains the sum collected up to the amount it paid, turning the excess, if any, over to the policyholder. However, if the passenger in the death seat is killed, his life insurance company is not entitled to subrogation rights against the careless driver. The estate of the deceased may collect both from his insurance company and from the guilty party (or the liability insurance company involved).

[28] There is, sometimes, a chance for a limited amount of bargaining in a large A & S Group case or in the case of a manuscript policy covering a special A & S risk. For a discussion of special risk or "specialty" policies, cf. Chapter 11.

[29] Except as some riders and supplemental agreements may be accepted or rejected without affecting the basic coverage. However, in such cases the rider or supplemental agreement must be accepted or rejected *in toto* with no bargaining for its terms. It may not, of course, be possible to reject the rider and still have the basic policy issued, as in the case of a waiver of a pre-existing condition of health in an A & S policy or a rider on a life insurance policy excluding the war risk.

[30] On occasions when the question as to whether an insurance policy is a contract or a statute (especially with respect to standard policies and provisions) has been put up to the courts, the resulting discussion has generally led to opposed results.

sured cannot bargain for the terms of the contract, courts hold to the principle that in the case of ambiguity in contract terms, the policy will be strongly construed against the insurer. It is his responsibility to make the terms clear.[31]

Aleatory Contract. Most contracts are commutative, that is, each party gives up in property or services equivalent monetary values. In the sale of a secondhand textbook,[32] for example, the buyer gets the book and the seller gets its equivalent value in cash. In an aleatory contract, there is no mutual exchange of monetary values. The company might pay out far more to any one policyholder than it receives from him. Likewise a policyholder might pay out more than he receives from the company. There is an element of chance.

Aleatory contracts may be of several types: gambling, speculative, and insurance. A *gambling* contract is illegal. It creates the risk from which the chance of gain or loss stems. The *speculative* contract is legal. It shifts an existing economic risk from those less prepared to assume it to those more prepared (or willing) to do so. The *insurance* contract, also legal, reduces the risk in society by taking advantage of the predictability made possible through the Law of Large Numbers.[33]

In Summary. An insurance policy is a legal contract. As such it is subject to the general law of contracts, atlhough in some aspects the law of contracts is so altered when applied to insurance as to be somewhat unrecognizable. For a policy to be valid, it must meet the essentials of all contracts: There must be an offer, acceptance, consideration, and mutual assent.[34] The agreement must be made between parties legally capable of contracting. The objective must not be for an illegal purpose, and must not be against public policy. Finally, a life insurance contract has certain special characteristics, most important among which, perhaps, are its unilateral nature and the fact that it is a contract of adhesion.

2. CREDITORS' RIGHTS IN LIFE INSURANCE

The primary purpose of life insurance is the protection of the dependent family in the event of the death of the insured. If insurance benefits were limited to those who survive a solvent insured, protection for beneficiaries might in some cases be lacking when most needed. Accordingly, the states

[31] There is a moot question in the case of statutory provisions as to whether ambiguities should be interpreted against the companies since the consuming public was in theory represented by the insurance commissioner in the drawing up of the statutory provisions.
[32] Which may or may not be a used book.
[33] Cf. Chapter 2 for an elaboration of this point.
[34] Mutual assent in a policy contract is evidenced by the application signed by the insured and the written policy issued by the insurer.

have enacted statutory provisions exempting the proceeds of life insurance policies from the claims of creditors of the insured. In the words of a New York court, these exemption laws were enacted for

> . . . the humane purpose of preserving to the unfortunate or improvident debtor or his family the means of obtaining a livelihood, and preventing them from becoming a charge upon the public.[35]

The laws vary from state to state.

The rights of creditors in life insurance therefore depend largely upon state statutes, which not only are different in themselves but also are subject to even further variation by the effect of court decisions. Although the exact rights of a creditor in any state can be ascertained only by a close study of the laws and court decisions in the state involved, a general summary may be given under five headings: (1) Rights of the *cestui que vie's* creditors in the proceeds of the policy. (2) Rights of the beneficiary's creditors in the proceeds. (3) Rights of the insured's (*cestui que vie*) creditors in the cash values. (4) Rights of the beneficiary's creditors in the cash values. (5) Rights where state statutes do not apply.

Rights of the Insured's Creditors in the Proceeds. The rights of a creditor of the insured in the proceeds of a life insurance policy are usually severely restricted.

All the proceeds may be exempt, or, in some states, only the proceeds up to a maximum amount are exempt. In some states, the statutes observe the purpose implied in the above court opinion and limit their protection to proceeds payable to the insured's wife or children. Others protect all policies payable to married women. Some include policies payable to any dependent relative. A number of statutes exempt proceeds payable to any beneficiary, other than one who is himself the insured, without regard to relationship or dependency.[36]

Proceeds paid to a trustee for the benefit of a given beneficiary rather than directly to that beneficiary have the same protection from the claims of creditors as if paid directly. This rule is well established by both case and statutory law.

The rights of creditors in disability benefits payable to the insured are usually not restricted by exemption laws in the same manner as are life insurance proceeds. However, a number of states do exempt such benefits up to a certain limit, such limit being, with variations, either a fixed total amount monthly or a maximum annual premium paid for the benefits.

---

[35] Crossman Co. *v.* Ranch, *263 N.Y. 264, 188 NE, 748.*
[36] Such broad exemption would seem a perversion of the original purpose of such exemptions and be not a protection of dependents but merely a means of avoiding the just claims of creditors. These broad exemptions have been widely criticized.

Creditors' rights in annuities also are usually not limited by the exemption laws applying to proceeds if the purchaser is the annuitant. In the absence of some specific statutory provision, an ordinary annuity may be reached by the creditors of the annuitant. It has also been ruled [37] that a trustee in bankrutpcy can reach the annuity income payable to an insured from the cash values of a life policy. A few states exempt annuity income even where the annuitant purchases the policy himself; this exemption may, however, be limited to a given amount. Where a person purchases an annuity for someone else, a number of states exempt proceeds from creditors' claims.

Rights of the Creditors of the Beneficiary in the Proceeds. Generally, the statutes exempt the proceeds from the claims of the insured's creditors only, although in a few states the law extends to the claims of the beneficiary's creditors as well. If the statute does not extend to the beneficiary's creditors, the insured may make this protection possible by including in the policy settlement agreement a *spendthrift trust clause* [38] which states that the benefits payable to any beneficiary hereunder after the death of the insured shall not be assignable nor transferable nor subject to commutation or incumbrance, nor to any legal process, execution, garnishment, or attachment proceeding. To take advantage of the clause, policy proceeds have to be made payable to the beneficiary under one of the installment settlement options, and usually the payment arrangement has to be set up by the insured. The funds so held by the company for distribution are not attachable under the spendthrift trust clause. This clause protects only the money being held by the company. As soon as the beneficiary receives the money, it may be available to her creditors.

More than half the states have statutes recognizing spendthrift trusts. These statutes were enacted either because the courts were not recognizing spendthrift trusts or because the courts were recognizing them and there was a desire to put certain restrictions on these arrangements. Some statutes were enacted solely to clarify the situation.

In the majority of those states where no statutes exist, courts have upheld spendthrift trust clauses when used. This leaves only a few states where these clauses are held to be against public policy and are disallowed. In these states, one way to protect the proceeds from the claims of the bene-

---

[37] In re Schaeffer, *U.S.D.C. 189, Fed. 187.*

[38] Reference to the term *trust* in the exemption statutes and court decisions is a careless use of nomenclature since no trust actually is involved. The funds used to pay the principal and interest under life insurance settlement options are mingled with the general assets of the insurer and the relationship between the insurance company and the beneficiary is one of debtor-creditor only.

ficiary is to create a discretionary trust and make the trustee the beneficiary under the policy. Under the discretionary trust, the corpus of the trust cannot be encumbered. The beneficiary is entitled to collect from the trust only that amount periodically that the trustee in his own discretion cares to give him.

Rights of the Creditors of the Insured in the Cash Values. In most states, the wording of the laws granting exemption from creditors' claims are broad enough to exempt cash values as well as proceeds. Where the statutes are not clear on the subject, court opinion has been divided. Usually the use of the term "proceeds" in the statute without the addition of "avails" or "cash values" is held to restrict the protection to death proceeds only. Some courts, however, have held that whatever protection is afforded against the claims of the creditors of the insured in the proceeds extends also to the cash values. Actually much depends upon the language of the statute involved.

Rights of the Creditors of the Beneficiary in the Cash Values. Most state statutes do not provide for protection against the claims of the creditors of the beneficiary. As for cash values, they do not create much of a problem since the beneficiary does not have an absolute vested right in these values unless named irrevocably. Even then, many courts hold that the beneficiary cannot cash in the policy without the consent of the insured. When this is the case, the beneficiary's creditors have no rights since it is impossible for the creditors to exercise more rights in the debtor's property than the debtor himself can exercise.

Rights of the Creditor When No State Statutes Apply. Where the policy is not protected by state statutes, the rights of creditors in the proceeds or cash values of life insurance are governed either by common law or by federal statutes. Federal statutes governing are those applying to "GI" insurance and those relating to bankruptcy.

Under common law, creditor's rights in life insurance proceeds and cash values depend upon how the beneficiary is named in the policy. If the insured or his estate is designated beneficiary, the proceeds of the policy are considered a part of the general assets of his estate, and as such can be reached to satisfy a judgment obtained by the creditor against the insured. The availability of cash values to meet claims of creditors is not too clear but the general rule is that a policy containing a cash value can be attached before maturity. Whether or not the creditors can collect the cash value of the policy appears to depend upon the policy provisions. These provisions are of two broad types. If delivery of the policy to the company for cancellation is all that is required as a condition of payment, the courts usually will allow creditors to obtain the cash values by effecting the delivery. If the right to have the cash values paid is an option to be exercised by the insured, the insurer is under no obligation to pay these values until the insured elects the option. The attaching creditors cannot make the election for him.

If the beneficiary is a third party, the proceeds of the policy paid to the beneficiary upon the death of the insured are held to belong to the beneficiary and may not be reached by the insured's creditors. The proceeds, however, are subject to the claims of the beneficiary's creditors. The cash values of the policy also are held to be judgment proof on the principle that the beneficiary's right cannot be defeated by the insured's creditors. It appears to make no difference whether the vesting in the beneficiary is absolute, conditional, or qualified. The rule generally is followed in cases involving both irrevocable and revocable beneficiary designations for if the insured has reserved the right to change the beneficiary, the courts ordinarily will not require him to do so to satisfy a creditor's judgment. As for the creditors of the beneficiary, the cash values of a policy may be reached only if the beneficiary has been named irrevocably and has an absolute and unconditional vested interest.

Under a federal statute designed to protect veterans benefits, the values of government life insurance are protected from the claims of creditors. This protection extends to the values before and after maturity of the policy and apply to the creditors of both the insured and beneficiary.

When an insured becomes bankrupt, the Federal Bankruptcy Act applies. Two provisions of this Act affect the handling of life insurance. Section 6 of the Act states:

> This Act shall not affect the allowance to bankrupts of the exemptions which are prescribed by the state laws in force at the time of the filing of the petition in bankruptcy. . . .[39]

As a result, only policies which do not come under state exemption statutes are subject to bankruptcy proceedings. For these policies, section 70a governs. Under this section, the trustee takes over the property of the bankrupt including the property which the bankrupt could have transferred or which could have been levied upon. Since policies payable to a third party without the right to change the beneficiary cannot be transferred by the insured, the trustee will not have the right to take them over. The trustee,

---

[39] Although this provision does not mention life insurance, it was established in Holden v. Stratton, 198 U.S. 202 (1905) that policies exempt under state law are excluded from the bankruptcy irrespective of section 70a, explained below.

however, is entitled to the *net* cash values of all policies under which the insured has reserved the right to change the beneficiary.[40]

A surrender of life insurance policies to obtain the cash values, however, might cause the insured and his beneficiary undue hardship. The policy might be an unusually favorable one with preferred settlement options, or the insured might no longer be insurable. Recognizing a possible hardship, section 70a adds:

> When any bankrupt who is a natural person shall have any insurance policy which has a cash surrender value . . . . . . he may, within 30 days after the cash surrender value has been ascertained and stated to the trustee . . . . . . pay or secure to the trustee the sum so ascertained and stated and continue such policy free from the claims of the creditors. . . .

Under this provision, the insured can continue the policy in force by paying over its cash surrender value to the trustee. A possible source of funds for use in complying with this provision, of course, is a loan secured by the cash values of the policy.

Right of Government as Income Tax Creditor. In order to understand the right of the government as an income tax creditor of the insured, a distinction must be made between cash values and death proceeds. The laws exempting cash values from claims of the insured's creditors do not ordinarily exempt them from the government's claim for tax liabilities.[41] Policies with an irrevocable beneficiary designation or which have been assigned to the beneficiary are exempt from such a claim because the property rights belong to the beneficiary, not the tax-liable insured. However, if the designation or assignment has been made with intent to defraud the government, the beneficiary may be held liable for the insured's tax up to the extent of the cash value. Death proceeds, however, are not subject to the government's claim for tax, except that the government can hold the beneficiary liable (if he or she is a transferee) to the extent of the cash value of the policy at the time of the insured's death minus any loan outstanding against the policy.[42] If the estate of the insured is the beneficiary under the policy, then of course the policy proceeds like all other estate assets are subject to the Federal government's tax claims.

---

[40] The trustees are entitled only to the *net* cash values. If the insured had already borrowed these values under the policy loan provision or if a failure to pay premiums has placed the policy under the extended term non-forfeiture option, there are no *net* values available for the trustee.

[41] Cf. Cannon *v.* Nicholas, *U.S.C.C.A.*, *80F.* (*2nd*) 934 and U.S. *v.* Steele, *U.S.D.C.N.Y.*, 9/7/39. Except that by Treasury ruling the cash surrender values of War Risk insurance policies are not subject to distraint proceedings for the collection of delinquent federal income taxes. Cf. *GCM*, *IRB–XV–7–7957*.

[42] That is, where there has been a transfer in fraud of creditors.

Two Exceptions. There are two broad exceptions to the established rules in this section. Creditors of the insured may attach the proceeds or cash values of a life insurance contract regardless of how the policy is set up if (1) the premiums are paid from embezzled funds, or (2) premiums are paid while the insured is insolvent and in fraud of creditors. The burden of proof, of course, is on the creditor and its establishment is not easy.

In the event that life insurance is purchased with embezzled funds and thereafter becomes a claim, the general rule seems to be that the victim of the embezzlement is entitled to recover that part of the proceeds of the policy which has been purchased by these funds, that is the percentage of the proceeds which equals the percentage that the embezzled funds bears to the total premiums paid. Contrary opinion requires simply a return of the embezzled funds with interest.

An insolvent debtor can pay premiums for a reasonable amount of life insurance to protect his family without prejudicing the insurance to the rights of his creditors. This is the law in the absence of fraudulent intent. If fraud is established, the creditors may recover from the proceeds of the policy up to the extent of the premiums paid plus interest.

The Illinois Statute. To this point the discussion of necessity has been general. For a quick reference to the laws of any given state, see the *Digest of Insurance Exemption Laws,* published by Insurance Research and Review in its *Advanced Underwriting Service* [43] or look directly into the state statutes involved.

The following is a digest from the service of the Illinois law for illustrative purposes both for life insurance exemptions and spendthrift trusts.

> LIFE INSURANCE: The statute provides that all proceeds payable because of the death of the insured, and the aggregate cash value of any or all life and endowment policies and annuity contracts payable to a wife or husband of the insured, or to a child, parent or other person dependent upon the insured, whether or not the right to change the beneficiary is reserved, and whether or not the insured or his estate is a contingent beneficiary, shall be exempt from execution, attachment, garnishment or other process for the debts and liabilities of the insured, except as to premiums paid in fraud of creditors.

> SPENDTHRIFT TRUSTS: Statute provides that any domestic life company may hold the proceeds of any policy issued by it with such exemptions from claims of creditors of beneficiaries other than the policyholder as shall have been agreed to in writing by such company and the policyholder. The same rule applies to a foreign or alien company when authorized by its charter or laws of its domicile.

---

[43] Address: 123 West North Street, Indianapolis, Indiana.

3. POWER OF AGENCY

Life and Accident and Sickness insurance operate through a system of agents. Companies grant to selected individuals the power of agency. The power of agency is much broader than the power of attorney: the power of attorney is power to act *for* the company in legal matters, but the power of agency is the power to act *as* the company for one or more specific purposes or for all purposes. In the eyes of the law, an agent is the company. His knowledge is presumed to be the company's knowledge, and the company's knowledge is presumed to be his knowledge.[44]

Types of Agents. Two types of agents may be distinguished: general agents and special agents. A general agent is empowered to act as the company in all matters. A special agent is empowered to act in certain matters only.

Unfortunately, there is a confusion in the use of terms in the insurance business as between the legal designation of the types of agents and the common usage of the designation. It is common to use the term "general agent" to describe an agent who is empowered to appoint subagents in a given territory. Actually, he is only a special agent, since he is authorized by his agency contract to act for the company in certain matters only: appointment of subagents in his territory, solicitation of new business, collection of premiums, and related matters. He cannot bind the company on, say, change of contractual provisions, and other functions reserved for executive officers. These executive officers are the real and only true *general agents* of the company. What is commonly called a "general agent" in the life and A & S insurance business is actually a "special agent"; while the man who is usually called an "agent" is, actually, a "subagent." [45]

In a discussion of the legal aspects of agency from the point of view of life insurance, four matters need consideration: presumption of agency; apparent agency; limitation of powers of agency; and responsibility of the principal for acts of agents.

Presumption of Agency. If a company has supplied an individual with forms and other materials which make it logical for anyone to presume that such individual is an agent of the company, it is likely that a court would hold that there is a presumption of agency. Under these conditions

---

[44] This sentence is a very broad generalization to which there are many exceptions. For a collection of interesting cases on agency in life and Accident and Sickness insurance, see Barry Oakes, *Principal, Agent, and The Public*, Conference on Insurance, University of Chicago Law School, Conference Series Number 14, 1954.

[45] A "subagent" who has the authority to appoint other "subagents" often is called a "district agent."

the company is bound by the acts of this individual to the extent that it would be bound by the acts of any other agent who has the express authority that is presumed in this case. For instance, if a former agent is allowed to retain materials which could lead the public to assume he is still an agent, he will probably be held to have a presumptive power of agency.

On the other hand, there is no reason to assume that a man is an agent for a company merely because he represents himself as an agent. He must be so equipped or so presented by the company as to raise a reasonable presumption on the part of the public that he is so empowered.

Apparent Agency.   The authority of the insurance agent is set forth in his agency contract. For the soliciting agent, that authority usually includes soliciting and taking applications for new business, arranging medical examinations, and accepting renewal premiums in exchange for renewal receipts properly signed by the company. It usually specifically excludes the right to make, alter, or discharge any contract; to waive any forfeiture; to waive payment in cash; to extend the time of payment for any premium or to accept payment of past-due premium; to approve evidence of good health; or to accept any money due the company other than premiums, as described.

In addition to the express authority granted by the company to the agent by contract, the agent is held in common law to have certain implied authority. For example, any authority which the public may reasonably assume that an agent has is implied so long as the public has not been notified to the contrary. This is the doctrine of apparent agency and it arises from the fact that it is unreasonable to expect the public to scrutinize the actual agency contract before dealing with the agent.

The doctrine of apparent agency, however, does not mean that the public can assume that an agent has the power to do whatever he does. For the presumption to exist there must be an action or lack of action on the part of the company (1) that gives the impression that its agent has the authority in question or (2) that fails to correct the impression that an agent does not actually have the express authority for the disputed act. For instance, it is well-established practice in the business for an agent to accept premium money. If a company were for some inconceivable reason to deny this power to an agent, it almost certainly would be held that he had the power under the doctrine of apparent agency, assuming, of course, that the third party did not know of this restriction. On the other hand it is not a common practice among companies to empower soliciting agents to commit the company to a mortgage loan. Therefore, the action of an agent in so committing the company would not likely be held within the scope of apparent agency.

Again, while the agent's contract expressly states that he does not have authority to accept a past-due premium, it likely would be held that the agent had that power if he has done so frequently in the past without protest from the company, since the policyholder from whom he had accepted past-due premiums had the right to assume such acceptance was within the scope of his apparent agency.

Limitations on Power of Agency. Limitations of the power of agency must be properly communicated to the public. Announcements of such limitations contained in application forms and in the policy meet this requirement.[46] Policies contain a provision to the effect that only certain designated officers of the company have the power to make or modify any contract of insurance, or to extend the time for paying a premium, and that the company shall not be bound by any promise or representation "heretofore or hereafter given by any agent or person other than the above." [47] This clause serves as proper communication to the public of the limitations on the power of both special agents and company officers. Company officers not named obviously do not have the powers.[48]

Responsibility of Principal. Since an agent is the principal within the scope of his power of agency, granted and apparent, the company is responsible for his acts. In fact, in the eyes of the law the acts of the agent and the acts of the company are one and the same. Further, limitations on the agent's authority must be in conformity with the general rules of law. A company cannot disclaim responsibility for any actions of the agent which are reasonable and necessary in the pursuit of his duties as an agent. To a limited extent, the company is even responsible for the misstatements and misrepresentations of its agents, even if fraudulent in nature. In the event of misrepresentations or fraudulent promises on the part of the agent, the applicant can demand and receive a refund of premiums paid. Usually, however, the

---

[46] The requirement can also be met by oral or written communication not a part of the policy or the application.

[47] Oddly enough this clause does not always give the company the protection it desires. For example, in West v. National Casualty Company, 112 N.E. 115, the court accepted the principle that the agent can waive the clause which restricts his power to alter or modify the policy. The theory is that an agent operating within his actual or apparent authority may waive any clause beneficial to the insurer since he is the insurer. Thus the agent can waive the clause which prohibits him from waiving clauses and, after that, waive whatever clause he wishes that is in the company's favor. However, when the restrictions are put in the application, the insured is on notice before the contract becomes effective, thus largely negating the situation which occurred in this particular case.

[48] In general, any limitation on the powers of general agents (that is, company officers) contained in the company's charter is effective. A charter is assumed to be public knowledge. However, restrictions in the bylaws would not be effective—unless properly communicated—because bylaws are not public knowledge. In general, the public has the right to assume, unless otherwise notified, that general agents (company officers) have all powers necessary to carry out the contracts of the company.

company cannot be forced to live up to these misrepresentations or fraudulent promises.

As has been stated, the knowledge of the agent is assumed to be the knowledge of the company. Therefore, if the agent knows a material fact about the application, the applicant has a right to presume that he has given that information to the company. The fact that the agent may have failed to communicate the information to the company is no defense for the company. For instance, assume that in answer to a question on the application, the applicant gives information to the agent that the agent knows would cause the company to "rate up" or reject the application.[49] Assume further that the agent fails to record the answer or the adverse part of it. Should the company discover the information after the policy is issued, it cannot invoke the doctrines of concealment or misrepresentation to avoid the policy since legally the company had that information when it was given to the agent.

The responsibility of the company, when an agent erroneously interprets a policy clause or provision to an applicant or policyholder, depends on the clause or provision involved. If it is ambiguous in wording, it will probably be held that the agent's interpretation is valid. If, on the other hand, the wording is clear so that any reasonable person could see by reading it that the agent was misinterpreting the clause, the company would probably not be held to the misinterpretation.

When making the medical examination, the examining physician is the agent of the company. His concealment of or failure to report any facts found by him or revealed to him by the applicant is the responsibility of the company.

Brokers as Agents. In most jurisdictions, there is a difference between the relationship among insured, broker, and company and that existing among insured, agent, and company. Generally speaking, the broker is the agent of the *insured*, not of the *company*. Technically, the insured, or prospective insured, empowers the broker to act for him as his agent in obtaining insurance. Consequently, the actions of the broker are not held to be binding upon the company. In insurance law there are exceptions, however. In some states, there are statutes which make anyone who solicits insurance for persons other than himself the agent of the insurer on all policies arising out of the solicitation. Some states make the broker the agent of the company only for delivering the policy and collecting the premium. Therefore, it becomes necessary to look to state law to determine whether or not a statutory agency has been created out of the operations of the broker. If so,

---

[49] Cf. Chapter 19.

it becomes necessary to examine the statutes further to determine whether the agency is created for all or just some of the broker's operations.

4. SUMMARY

The life insurance policy is a legal contract and, as such, it is subject to the general law of contracts, with a number of variations. To be a valid contract, it must possess the requisites of a contract: offer, acceptance, consideration, capacity to contract, and legal purpose. It has a number of distinguishing characteristics which affect the laws of contract as applied to it: It is a contract of utmost good faith, a unilateral contract, a conditional contract, a valued contract, a contract of adhesion, and an aleatory contract.

An insurance policy is held to be against public policy unless there is an insurable interest. An insurable interest may be defined briefly as a pecuniary interest in the continued life of the *cestui que vie* (who is the person whose life is insured). Mere family relationship alone is not always sufficient to establish insurable interest. On the other hand, support by the insurant does constitute insurable interest even if there is no family relationship involved and support is not a legal obligation. Insurable interest need exist only at the time the designation is made.

Statements on an application are, in absence of fraud, representations and not warranties; that is, they are approximations to the best of the knowledge and belief of the applicant and are not warranted to be exact in detail. In general, an unintentional misrepresentation is cause for avoiding the policy if it is material; that is, if the company would not have issued the policy at the rate charged had it known the correct details.

Concealment may be cause for voiding the policy, also. However, the applicant is not required to volunteer information not asked for on the application or which may be presumed to be knowledge of the company. Concealment exists only if the applicant is asked a question and does not answer or answers only partially. Concealment must be both intentional and of a material fact to avoid the policy.

The life insurance policy may be said to be "sheltered property" when it comes to the rights of creditors. While the rights of creditors in policy proceeds vary from state to state, they are almost always severely restricted. Further, the policyowner may usually specify in settlement agreements that the beneficiary shall have no power to encumber, alienate, or assign the unpaid portion of any proceeds being settled on an installment basis.

In many states, the wording of the law exempting proceeds is broad enough to extend to cash values. Where the law is not clear, court decisions are diverse.

State exemption statutes are particularly useful in the event of the bankruptcy of the insured since, in the absence of bankruptcy, the insured seems to have rather effective protection under common law.

Life insurance companies are corporations. The corporation is a legal "person" but not an actual person. Therefore, it must operate through actual persons who are designated as "agents." An agent is a natural person who is empowered to act as the corporation. In most corporations, the general agents of the corporation are its executive officers, or those executive officers designated by the charter.

In addition to general agents, the life insurance corporation transacts much of its business with policyholders and applicants through a system of special and subagents. Its special agents are empowered to act for it in certain matters relating to the solicitation of new insurance and servicing of old. Such special agents may delegate certain of their powers to subagents.

Unfortunately for the clarity of the discussion of agency, it is the custom to call special agents (who have the authority to designate subagents for soliciting and servicing policyholders) "general agents," and to call subagents "agents." [50]

The authority of an agent is set forth in his agency contract. However, it is broadened by the doctrine of "apparent agency." This doctrine holds that if it is reasonably for the public to assume that an agent has certain powers, he is legally held to have them. There must be a reason for the assumption.

An agent is not merely a *representative* of the company; he *is* the company, in so far as his agency powers are concerned. Therefore, his actions are binding upon the company. Since his knowledge also is presumed to be the knowledge of the company, information imparted to him is, legally, imparted to the company.

No brief statement such as contained in this chapter can be more than a general review, subject to infinite contrary decisions and varying discursions. In the first place, the various jurisdictions which make up the United States and its districts and territories vary in their statutes relating to any part of the subject. To add to the confusion, various courts of the same jurisdiction will not always react in the same way. For almost every statement made in this chapter, at least one contrary court decision could be found.

Questions for Class Discussion

1. Two years before applying for the policy, the insured had consulted a physician, and was told he had no heart condition. The insured failed to report

---

[50] In fact, some companies insist on calling subagents "special agents," which confuses the matter even further.

these consultations on the application. The insured died seven months after the policy was issued. Is the company liable?

2. The insured told the agent that his wife was to undergo an operation. The agent told the insured that the policy would cover the insured's impending operation. The policy, however, excluded surgical benefits if the illness originated within 90 days. The insured's wife underwent the operation 104 days after the effective date of the policy. Is the operation covered?

3. In October, 1947, the insured applied for the policy upon his life, and he was examined by the company's physician. The physician discovered that the insured had abnormal blood pressure, resulting from the presence of one or more specific diseases, not identified by that symptom alone. The application showed that the insured had undergone a chlorecystectomy and an appendectomy. The company refused to issue the regular policy, but agreed to issue the policy as a substandard risk, and a higher premium was charged. The application provided that no contract should be effective until delivered to the insured during good health, and the company later denied liability on the ground that the insured was not in good health at the time the policy was delivered. Is the company liable?

4. The insured married Bill Waco Smith during the early part of 1950. At that time she was 19 years old. About a month later, application was made for the policy sued on, and at the same time applications were made to other companies, until a total of $7,000 was issued. In each instance, Mr. Smith applied for the insurance, although he was accompanied by his wife. The first premiums were paid by him. The insured died on April 3, 1950, as a result of being poisoned by her husband. He was convicted and sentenced to life imprisonment. Is the company liable on the policy?

5. Under a policy issued to the insured, the proceeds were payable to his wife, and the secondary beneficiaries were her daughter by a previous marriage and a child of the present marriage. Marital discord developed, and a divorce action was filed. While it was pending, the insured's wife telephoned and invited him over to her house for a conference—after making sure they would be alone. An argument developed and she testified that he struck her and she then shot and killed him—with a gun she had ready. The court ruled that she did not kill him in self-defense and the killing was not justified, and she should not benefit from her act. She contended that under the community laws of California, one half of the proceeds of the policy belonged to her, and she brought suit as administratrix of her husband's estate for the recovery of the remainder. How should this case be settled?

6. The insured and beneficiary were in a saloon when the company's agent complained about business being poor. In jest, the insured stated that he would be glad to take out a policy and name his companion as the beneficiary if the companion would pay the premium. His companion accepted the offer, and the insured signed the application for $1,000. He stated that his health was good and that he was 36 years of age. He died four months later, and the company then learned that he had been examined in a local hospital a month after the policy was issued and was found to be suffering from heart disease. He died as a result of coronary occlusion a little over three months

after the policy was issued. The death certificate gave his age as 38. Can the beneficiary collect under the policy?

7. The insurance company reduced payment of disability benefits after the insured became 60 years of age, relying upon the provision that all indemnities payable under the policy would automatically be reduced 50% after the insured became 60 years old. The insured became totally disabled about three months before the age limit, and the company commenced payment of benefits. After the 60th birthday, the company reduced the benefits one half. The insured construed the age limit provision to mean that the benefits would be reduced in the event of disability occurring after the insured became 60 years of age. Therefore he sued for recovery of full benefits. How should the case be decided?

8. The policy was issued on May 14, 1951, and, at that time, the insured was up and around the house, cooking, cleaning, performing her household duties, and caring for her husband and two children. The company denied liability because she was not in good health at the time the policy was issued but was, in fact, suffering from cancer. She died October 15, 1951. The family physician testified that the insured consulted him about female trouble several weeks prior to April 8, 1950. On that date, he did a biopsy and submitted it to a pathologist. After receiving the report from the pathologist that cancer was present, he did a total hysterectomy. After the operation she underwent radium treatment and deep therapy. However, an edema showed up two or three months prior to her death and she was under constant medical care thereafter. Her physician testified that she had cancer at all times and was never free of it. He stated further that he told her after the radium treatment that she was all right "because she was an individual who couldn't be told the facts." He didn't recall whether he had told her husband the truth. Is the company liable?

9. At the time of his death the insured was insolvent, and he owed income taxes in excess of the amount due on his insurance policy—$12,597.70. His insurance policy was payable to his widow as beneficiary, and the United States brought an action to recover the unpaid income taxes from the widow to the extent of the policy proceeds. An Illinois statute exempts insurance proceeds payable to the widow from claims of creditors. Is the Government entitled to recovery?

10. A wife shot her husband in a Southern state. In spite of the fact that common law prohibits a criminal from benefiting financially from her crime, the widow collected a substantial part of her husband's insurance proceeds. How is this possible?

CHAPTER 9

GENERAL POLICY
PROVISIONS

I T I S perhaps a tribute to the insurance business and the regulation of it that an insurance contract can be called the nation's least read best seller. Almost everybody believes in life insurance and the majority of people buy it; yet few policyholders ever read a life insurance contract all the way through with any attempt to understand its various provisions. This is sometimes unfortunate, for policyholders frequently have the most garbled impression of what any particular policy promises.

A life insurance policy is a legal contract, its validity as such having been established in the United States since 1815.[1] As a contract, it contains provisions setting forth the rights and duties of the policyholder and the company. Although it is necessary to look beyond the policy into statutes or court decisions for the interpretation and full effect of policy provisions, these provisions nevertheless are the basis of the agreement between the company and the policyholder (and the beneficiary, estate, heirs, or assigns of the policyholder, as a matter of fact).

1. STATUTORY LAW RELATING TO POLICY CONTRACT

The provisions of the policy contract are closely related to statutory law, since most state insurance codes provide for (1) a set of mandatory provisions, (2) prohibited provisions, and (3) permissible provisions.

Mandatory Provisions. While in life insurance there are no "standard

---

[1] Lord v. Ball, 12 *Mass.* 115 (1815).

151

policies"[2] such as may be found in fire insurance, almost all states require the inclusion of certain mandatory provisions in every policy contract issued in their jurisdiction. The law sets forth the substance of these provisions, which form the minimum requirement. Other provisions, or other wording of the mandatory provisions, if more favorable to the policyholder, may be substituted. If a mandatory provision is left out of a policy, the courts will interpret the contract as though it contained the provision.

With some variation among the states, mandatory provisions usually cover (1) grace period; (2) incontestable clause; (3) policy is entire contract; (4) misstatement of age; (5) policy dividend distribution; (6) option to be applied in event of premium default; (7) loans and table of loan values; (8) tables of installment payments where options are available; (9) reinstatement; (10) dividend options; (11) valuation of nonforfeiture provisions; (12) deferment of loan and cash value payment.

Each of these provisions is discussed later in the chapter.

The fact that there is no standard policy in life insurance, plus the fact that mandatory provisions do not specify the exact wording of the provision but only the minimum it may provide, leave room for companies to draw up policy contracts more liberal than the law requires. Competition, therefore, produces some variations among policy forms and provisions.

Prohibited Provisions. In addition to requiring specific minimum provisions, the laws also prohibit the inclusion of certain other clauses. Examples of prohibited provisions are (1) forfeiture because of failure to repay a loan while indebtedness under a policy is less than its cash value; (2) limiting the time in which an action in law or equity may be commenced to fewer than two years after the cause of the action; (3) backdating a policy for more than a specific period (commonly, six months) before the original application was made; (4) requiring warranties in the application; (5) providing that the rights and obligations of the policy shall be governed by the laws of a state other than that in which the policy was issued; (6) excluding or restricting liability for death caused in a specified manner except certain permissible exclusions; (7) a provision for any mode of settlement at matu-

---

[2] Standard policies were attempted in New York following the Armstrong investigation in 1906. Four other states passed similar legislation in 1907. Standard policies were abandoned in 1909. (For a discussion of reasons, cf. Krueger and Waggoner, eds., *The Life Insurance Policy Contract*, Boston, Little, Brown & Co., 1953 p. 339 f.) In lieu of the standard policy, New York adopted a set of provisions required in substance. These provisions are the basis of the mandatory or "standard" provisions now required in almost all states. They should not be confused with the 1912 Standard Provisions for A & S policies or the Uniform Provisions for A & S policies discussed in Chapter 11.

rity of less value than the amount insured by the policy;[3] (8) assessable clause (New York). If a prohibited provision is inserted in a contract, the courts will interpret the policy as though the provision did not appear.

Permissible Provisions. The law requires the inclusion of certain provisions, it prohibits the inclusion of certain others, and it allows but does not require another set of provisions. These permissible provisions apply to the exclusion of coverage in event of (1) death from military service in wartime; (2) death within five years as a result of war while traveling outside the United States, its possessions, or Canada; (3) suicide in fewer than two years; (4) death resulting from certain types of aviation; (5) death resulting from certain hazardous occupations if it occurs within two years of the date of the policy; or (6) death while the insured is a resident of a foreign country if it occurs within two years of the date of the policy.

Generally speaking, the provisions of a life insurance policy contract may be classified under the headings of Insuring Agreement, General Provisions, Nonforfeiture Options, Settlement Options, and—in the case of participating policies—Dividend Options. This chapter will consider the Insuring and General provisions. Nonforfeiture, Settlement, and Dividend provisions will be discussed in Chapter 10.

2. INSURING CLAUSE AND CONSIDERATION

The Insuring agreement and the Consideration clause are usually found on the face of the contract as the opening statement.

The Insuring clause agrees to pay immediately upon receipt at the home office of due proof of the death of the named insured the sum of X dollars, provided premiums have been duly paid, the policy is in force, and is then surrendered or properly released. The agreement is subject to all the conditions, benefits, and privileges described in the policy pages which are made a part of the contract.

The Insuring clause varies slightly according to the type of policy. The clause as detailed above applies to Whole Life contracts.

The Consideration clause declares that the legal consideration for the policy is the application, which is attached to and is a part of the policy contract, plus payment of the first premium or its first installment. Payment of subsequent premiums is a condition precedent to the company's promise to continue the policy in force.

---

[3] The latter restriction would prohibit a company from calling a policy paying $100 a month for ten years a $12,000 policy. It must express the face in terms of its commuted value.

In addition to identifying information about the applicant and information designed to reveal the nature of the hazard,[4] the application has the following clause dealing with consideration.

> AGREEMENTS: Information in this application (including statements of Proposed Insured in Part II hereof)[5] is given to obtain this insurance and is true and complete to the best of my knowledge and belief. The policy may limit the Company's liability for death from certain hazards of aviation, and, if it does, I elect to accept a policy with such limitations. The conditional receipt form originally attached to and bearing the same number as this application is the only receipt authorized for any payment made herewith. Except as otherwise provided in such receipt form, the Company shall incure no obligation because of this application unless and until a policy is delivered to the applicant and the first premium thereon is paid in full while the health and other conditions affecting insurability of the Proposed Insured are as described in this application.

There is a great deal of confusion in the law as to what constitutes payment of the premium. Does it have to be in cash? Can it be by check? Will a promissory note be sufficient? If the agent has authority from his company to deal in premium notes, then the cash payment clause is waived and a promissory note is adequate consideration for a binding receipt. Unless the note contains the stipulation that the policy will be repudiated if the note is not honored at maturity, the premium is considered paid and the company's action is limited to its rights on the note. The policy is now independent of the whole transaction. A check is customarily considered as cash and therefore it fulfills the cash payment condition. What if the check is no good? If the company agrees to accept the check as absolute payment rather than conditional payment, then acceptance of a check for the full first premium binds the contract even if the check is no good. In this case the insurer has the right only to court action for recovery of the value of the check. Most checks, however, are accepted as conditional payment. In these cases, the courts rule that the debt is unpaid if the check is not honored. Thus, the first full premium is not considered paid, and the contract is not in force. Companies usually include a condition in the contract to the effect that "no check or bank draft accepted in exchange for this receipt shall be considered as cash unless payment is received upon presentation to the proper bank."

3. GENERAL PROVISIONS

The general provisions of the policy usually consist of the statutory provisions named plus various permissible and miscellaneous provisions. Each

---

[4] Cf. Chapter 19 for discussion of the application.
[5] Part II is the medical section.

of these will be discussed briefly [6] here in approximately the order in which they are found in the customary life insurance policy.

Ownership Clause. The person in whom the ownership privileges of the policy are to be vested is set forth. This may or may not be the named insured. In some cases it might be the beneficiary or an assignee. Ownership privileges are the right to receive cash values, loans, dividends (if any), and other benefits accruing under the policy. The clause also includes the right to exercise all options and privileges described in the policy, and to negotiate with the company on all matters relating to any change in, amendment to, or cancellation of the policy.

Entire Contract. The policy and the attached application shall constitute the entire contract between the company and the insured or policy owner. This clause is statutory in most states, and its purpose is to prevent the company from making its bylaws, charter, or any other instrument not in the contract a part of the policy. At one time, the practice of making the charter and bylaws of the company a part of the insuring contract was prevalent. This worked a hardship on the policyholder. In the first place, the policyholder rarely knew what was in the company bylaws and charter. In the second place, a change in these instruments would change his contract of insurance, probably without his knowledge.

Actually, the policy, application, and amendments are not the entire contract, despite the statement to that effect in every policy. Statutory law is also a part of every contract, as is judicial or case law. The policyholder and company cannot waive the benefits of the law even by mutual agreement. The matter is further complicated by the fact that although it is clear that the law is a part of every policy contract, under the existing system of state-by-state regulation and varying common law interpretations, it is not always clear which is the governing law. Consider the following situation: The policy has been issued in one state by a company domiciled in another. The policyholder has moved to a third state. He has several cobeneficiaries who reside in still different states. Laws often vary from state to state, and court decisions may vary by jurisdictions. Which law applies has been the subject of conflicting court decisions in the past. A distinction has to be made between the law governing the validity of the contract and the law governing the performance of the contract. As to questions of validity, most courts have held that the law of the place in which the contract is made

---

[6] It is beyond the scope of this book to give a definitive analysis of each provision or to go into the various case law ramifications. These details are interesting and in fact sometimes amusing but have educational value only for those specializing in the law. If interested and time is available, see Krueger and Waggoner, *op. cit.*

governs.[7] As to disputes in performance, the majority of courts have held that the jurisdiction is in the place of performance, which is usually the home office of the company.

There are still other factors which sometimes make it necessary to look beyond the policy despite the "entire contract" clause: often, as mentioned, the conditional receipt, issued with the policy when settlement is made, contains provisions that are actually a part of the agreement between the policyholder and company; the law of most states does not require that an application for reinstatement of the policy after lapse be attached to the policy, yet such an application is usually held to be a part of the contract inasmuch as the company can contest settlement if there has been misrepresentation in connection with reinstatement; riders are a part of the contract if attached to it and made a part of it by reference, but courts have held that such riders need not be signed by both the policyholder and the company to be effective; a few courts have held that even advertising material is a part of the policy contract, although the decision is not general. Some courts have held that the "entire contract" requirement does not preclude the use of subsequent agreements, since the requirement and provision refer only to the contract at the time it is first issued.

In other words, while the "entire contract" clause does prevent the company from making charter or bylaws a part of the contract, it does not in every case prevent the necessity for looking outside the policy for the whole contract.[8]

Premium Payment. The policy acknowledges receipt of the first premium and states the date on which subsequent premiums will be due. In Ordinary policies, the basic period of premium payment is usually annually; however, the policyholder may, upon agreement with the company, pay semiannually, quarterly, or sometimes monthly. Premiums are payable at the home office, agency office, or to an agent in exchange for a receipt signed and countersigned by a cashier and, usually, the company registrar.

If the premium is paid on other than an annual basis, the fractional premium is, technically, an installment payment. Since it is the custom to calculate premiums on the assumption that a full year's premium will have been paid for the policy year in which death occurs, unpaid installments can be properly deducted from maturity values. However, the practice of reducing policy proceeds by the amount of the unpaid installments for the

---

[7] This usually is the state in which the policy actually is delivered by the agent to the insured. Some courts hold that the governing jurisdiction depends upon the intent of the parties.

[8] For an interesting discussion of this point, see *Trends in Life Insurance*, Daniel J. Reidy in The Insurance Lecture Series, University of Connecticut, Spring, 1953.

rest of the year is subject to public misunderstanding. Therefore, it has become the predominant practice to waive unpaid fractional premiums due after the date of death. Moreover, some companies make a provision for refund of a proportionate amount of any premium paid beyond the date of death, whether the premium is paid annually or fractionally. The effect of these practices is to increase the cost of insurance. The added expense of premium refunds can be handled by loading the premium for it.[9]

Some companies incorporate a premium deposit provision in the contract under which money to be used for future premiums may be deposited in advance, at interest, and credit to premium payment as premiums fall due. According to company practice or contract provision, the fund may or may not be withdrawable, a minimum rate of interest may or may not be guaranteed, and the deposit fund upon death of the insured may or may not become a part of the policy proceeds to be distributed under one of the settlement options to be discussed in the next chapter.

Grace Period. Most states require companies to include in their policies a "period of grace" after the premium-due date during which the policy remains in full force even though the premium has not been paid. The period is usually stated as "one month," "one month but not fewer than 31 days," or merely "31 days." The law usually permits a provision for an interest charge for any portion of the grace period used, but few if any policies include this charge. If death occurs during the grace period before the premium has been paid, the amount of the premium due is deducted from the proceeds.

A relatively few states require the sending of premium notices,[10] usually not less than 15 days nor more than 45 days before premiums are due. The typical law in these few states prohibits the company's lapsing a policy within one year after default if it fails to comply with the notice provision. Therefore, in such states failure to give premium notice has the effect of extending the grace period to one year.

The effect of the grace period is give a month's free protection to those who eventually lapse their policies. The cost of such protection must be

---

[9] If the practice is to waive fractional premiums, the loading can be either restricted to these premiums (the more equitable way) or it can become a part of the gross annual premium. If the practice is to refund the premium for the rest of the period, the gross annual premium will have to be loaded to handle this additional cost. Actually, an instantaneous premium rate may be figured, which is different from loading the premium additionally. The practice of refunding premiums and loading all policies for the cost seems to be the most equitable way of handling the problem of unpaid fractional premiums.

[10] A second premium notice is not required. Companies formerly made a practice of sending a second notice but, in the interest of economy, they have generally discontinued this plan.

made up by the policyholders who pay their premiums—and the interest lost on payments that arrive at the end of the grace period must be offset in effect by an additional loading on all policies. The effect is to penalize the prompt premium payer. General use of the grace period provision came in about the turn of the century as part of the over-all liberalization of the policy contract, but may have been dictated more by competition than any true need for liberalization.

Reinstatement. If premium payment is not made within the grace period, the policy lapses.[11] However, half the states require provision for and almost every policy in the other states make provision for reinstatement within a stated period after such lapse. In those states requiring a reinstatement provision, the period is three years; however, the policy may make more liberal provision, and periods up to five or more years are found.[12] Reinstatement clauses were voluntarily inserted into policies by a number of insurance companies long before they were required to do so. These clauses were first used during the period before nonforfeiture provisions were introduced into the contract. They were designed to meet in part the inequity of complete forfeiture of defaulting policyholders.

Reinstatement means that the policy is revived and the relationship of the policyholder and the company goes back to the status existing before the lapse. It is not a new policy but a revival of the old one. Reinstatement usually [13] requires evidence of insurability satisfactory to the company and payment of all premiums in arrears with interest thereon at a specified rate. Naturally, the policy must not already have been surrendered to the company for cash.

Evidence of insurability, in cases of reinstatement, is required to prevent selection against the company.[14] If the policy lapse has been recent, the company usually requires only a statement from the policyholder certifying that he is in good health. Otherwise a medical examination may be requested. Insurability means not only good health but also good habits. If

---

[11] Except that if the policy contains provision for and the policyholder has elected to take advantage of an automatic premium loan, the loan value in the policy will be used to pay the premium or any portion of it for which it is sufficient. If there is no automatic premium loan provision, then any cash value may be used to keep the policy in force on one of the nonforfeiture values, usually extended-term insurance. See Chapter 10.

[12] A survey of policies reveals some containing provisions which place no time limits at all on reinstatement privileges.

[13] Unconditional acceptance of a past-due premium, intentional or otherwise, will effect reinstatement without any of the requirements set forth by the reinstatement provision.

[14] Selection against the company means that people who suddenly find their health impaired reinstate their policies if they are allowed to do so. Those in good health will not reinstate so readily. Thus, there is selection against the company.

the policyholder no longer meets underwriting standards, his policy will not be reinstated.

A reinstated policy usually reopens the clause dealing with incontestability.[15] The policy may be contested at any time after reinstatement during the number of years of contestability provided in the contract. However, the majority opinion holds that reinstatement does not reopen the suicide clause. There seems no basis in logic for the difference between the treatment of the incontestible and the suicide clauses.

There are two basic reasons for reinstating an old policy rather than taking a new one. First, many old policies have more liberal settlement options, or they may have other desired provisions which are no longer available. Second, the policyholder eliminates the acquisition cost, which he would have to pay all over again were he to take a new policy. Reinstating old policies rather than purchasing new ones is usually the more economical way of re-establishing a given amount of insurance unless there are other unusual circumstances.

Incontestability. The incontestability clause in a life insurance policy makes it impossible for the company after a period of time (usually two years) to contest any statements made in the application or any concealment of material facts in order to avoid payment of the proceeds. The clause is usually a simple statement announcing that except for nonpayment of premium the policy is incontestable after a specified period of time. The clause means that, after the contestable period, the company cannot seek to set aside the policy on the grounds that it was obtained by misrepresentation.

The incontestable clause as found in policy contracts is an anomaly among contract provisions. The law of contracts holds that fraud vitiates any contract, that a contract involving fraud is void from its inception. Further, the law usually holds that an agreement to disregard fraud is a violation of public policy and hence void.[16] Yet the incontestable clause, which is an agreement to disregard fraud in the life insurance contract after a specified period, has been in use since the 1860's, is required by many states, and has

---

[15] Among contrary opinions are two theories: (1) Fraud in the application for reinstatement vitiates that application and therefore leaves the policy as it was: lapsed. It follows, therefore, according to this view, that reinstatement is not a contract but instead waiver of a lapse. This view, however, has been held by only a few courts. (2) Many more courts have held that reinstatement does not reopen the incontestable clause in the original policy but does subject the reinstated policy to contestability based on the reinstatement agreement which is of itself a new contract governed by all the common law principles relating to fraud.

[16] When the clause makes the policy incontestable from the beginning, the courts will usually honor it in cases of simple misrepresentations but not in cases of fraud.

been held to apply in the most flagrant cases of fraud. Although there is social and economic justification for incontestablity in life insurance, there is no generally accepted legal explanation for the incontestable provision or for the decisions upholding it.[17] It is a clause peculiar to life insurance contracts.[18]

The incontestable clause is designed to protect the policyholder and beneficiary against any attempt to set the policy aside; it does not, however, prevent a claim from being contested on the grounds that it is excluded from coverage under the terms of the contract. A defense against a claim is a suit to enforce contract provisions, not to set the contract aside. Similarly, it does not prohibit suits over construction of the policy or over its terms; nor does it bar a defense that the policy never went into force.

Since the incontestable clause is a provision of the contract, it has no force until there is a contract. If the contract legally never goes in effect, the clause is not operative. For example, if an impersonator makes the application and takes the physical examination, or answers the health statements, the policy can be set aside even after the contestable period since it is held that there was never mutual assent, as required for a valid contract, and that no contract ever existed.

The incontestable clause is for the protection of the insured and beneficiary only. Thus if there should be a fraudulent conspiracy among the insured, beneficiary, and medical examiner, the policy could not be set aside after the contestable period, nor could the company recover damages from the insured or beneficiary. However, damages could be assessed against the examiner since he is not a party to the contract.

As the clause itself is an anomaly among contract provisions, so is the inclusion of the wording, "except for nonpayment of premiums." The incon-

---

[17] Horne and Mansfield in *The Life Insurance Contract*, Life Office Management Association, 1938, refer to the usual incontestable clause with a waiting period as "something in the nature of a private contractual 'statute of limitations' to modify the statutory limitation." The authors quote the decision in Clements v. Life Ins. Co. of Va., *155 N.C. 57, 70 S.E. 1076 (1911)*, to the effect that the "courts will not aid those who sleep on their rights, but only those who are vigilant." A legal right must be asserted within a proper time or not at all.

[18] Lest this discussion create a one-sided impression, it should be pointed out that while it is true that the courts have interpreted factual situations which appear to be fraudulent in such a way that they are considered misrepresentations within the effect of the incontestable clause, no court has, to the knowledge of the authors, construed a set of facts as fraudulent and then stated that once the contestable period has run, the company may not defend against a claim which would be against public policy. It is true that there is a line of cases, which Horne and Mansfield apparently had in mind in their statement quoted in Footnote 17, that construes the incontestable clause as a statute of limitations. In such cases, where fraud can be read into the situation, the normal operation of a statute of limitations will terminate the right of the aggrieved party to defend. This line of cases is not the majority.

testable clause prevents setting aside the policy as of the beginning of the contract. Nonpayment of premiums does not set aside the policy from the beginning. The lapsing insured still has rights under the policy: reinstatement and nonforfeiture, for example. The wording seems to be a remnant of earlier days when some policies provided that in the event the premium was not paid, the policy would become void, thus avoiding the policy from its beginning. The inclusion of the wording is now so well established that its omission might be looked upon by some courts as something different and, therefore, subject to new rules of interpretation.

As has been pointed out, a defense against a claim on the grounds that it is improper or not covered is not, actually, a suit to avoid the policy but to enforce the conditions of the contract. Enough courts, however, have mistakenly held otherwise in the case of the disability and double indemnity provisions, that the usual wording of some incontestable clauses has been altered to state an exception in the case of those provisions. Such a clause might read:

> This policy shall be incontestable after two years from its date except for nonpayment of premiums and except for the restrictions and provisions applying to the double indemnity and disability benefits provided.

Other policies will seek to meet the situation by providing, in the riders adding disability and double indemnity, that the other provisions of the policy do not apply to those riders.

The majority court opinion in early cases held that if the insured dies during the contestable period, the period continued to run. The reasoning seemed to be that since the clause is for the protection of the beneficiary as well as the insured, all terms of it should apply to the beneficiary too.

This interpretation led some companies to change the wording of the incontestable clause on new policies to read that the policy should be incontestable after having been in force for a given period. This attempt to prevent beneficiaries from obtaining the protection of the incontestable clause by withholding claim until the expiry of two years did not work out according to expectations. Courts then held that the policy was still "in force" after the death of the insured since it was running for the benefit of the beneficiary. Therefore, some companies have changed the clause to provide that the policy shall be incontestable after having been in force for the period specified during the lifetime of the insured. This wording has been held by virtually all courts to mean that upon the death of the insured during the contestable period, the policy can never become incontestable. This latter wording is the most common among incontestable clauses,[19] and has been adopted as part of the required policy provision laws in a number of states.

The practice of allowing parties to a life insurance contract to fix by stipulation the length of time after which fraud can be used as a defense is justified. The impracticability of assembling evidence and witnesses many years after issuance of the policy is clear. Defense against fraud is especially difficult if it must be made by a beneficiary after the death of an insured accused of the fraud. The incontestable clause is particularly valuable to the beneficiary in preventing delayed settlement resulting from long and tedious court action.

Misstatement of Age. Most state laws require that all policies include a provision that if the age of the insured has been misstated, the amount of the insurance will be such as the premiums actually paid would have purchased if the age had been correctly stated. For example, if a person age 30 gives his age as 25 and purchases a $10,000 nonpar Whole Life policy for $165.60, he will have not $10,000 of insurance when his real age becomes apparent, but approximately $8,670 of coverage. The rate at age 30 is $19.10 as distinguished from $16.56 at age 25 in a given company. At $19.10 per $1,000, $165.60 will purchase $8,670 of insurance.

Adjustment of the proceeds by reason of misstatement of age is not blocked by the incontestable clause. The adjustment is not a contest of the policy but an operation of a policy provision.

Suicide. Almost every policy contains a provision excluding suicide, "while sane or insane," from coverage and limiting liability of the company to a return of the premiums paid on the contract. The exclusion runs for a limited period, such as one or two years. The clause is a result of (1) conflicting court decisions regarding the right of the beneficiary in absence of such a clause to recover in the case of suicide of the insured, and (2) the development of an attitude that while other insureds should be protected against the higher cost which would result if claims were paid on policies purchased in contemplation of self-destruction, protection against this contingency should not work harm upon the innocent beneficiary.[20]

---

[19] Companies have not always included the phrase, "during the lifetime of the insured," in the incontestable clause. When included, it is a legal remedy, and any contest over the situation must be tried by jury. Juries tend toward decisions adverse to insurance companies. If omitted, the matter becomes one of a suit in equity.

[20] Some courts have held, in the absence of suicide clauses, that inasmuch as the charge for insurance is based on mortality statistics which include deaths from all causes, coverage of suicide is not an undue cost burden on other policyholders. Cf., for one example, Campbell v. Supreme Conclave, I.O.H., 66 N.J.L. 274, 49 Atl. 550, 54 L.R.A. 576 (Ct. Err. & App. 1901). The limited duration exclusion of the modern suicide clause theoretically protects against the fraud involved in taking out a policy in contemplation of suicide while adhering to the theory that all deaths should be covered in absence of fraud.

The limited period of exclusion is deemed proper and valid protection against the fraud involved in taking out a policy in contemplation of suicide, while allowing recovery after that period can be considered protection of the innocent beneficiary. The majority opinion of the courts today is that "suicide while sane or insane" can be properly excluded from coverage for a given period of years as in the standard suicide clause if the contract so provides and if there is no state statutory prohibition against the suicide defense.[21]

Inasmuch as suicide is an exclusion of coverage by terms of the contract, most courts hold that it is not affected by the incontestable clause. Denial of claim on the grounds of suicide under the suicide exclusion is not a contest of the policy but a suit to enforce policy provisions. Such conflicts arise only where the suicide exclusion runs longer than the contestable period.[22] Since the type of incontestable clause now most widely used ceases running on the death of the insured, there is little possibility of conflict of this nature arising where the suicide period is less than or equal to the incontestable period.

Since the majority of court opinion holds that a reinstated policy is not a new policy but the old policy restored to its former condition, it follows that the usual suicide clause, running from the date of issue of the policy, is not renewed or extended by reinstatement of a policy under the reinstatement clause. The suicide clause runs from the original date of issue, not date of reinstatement.

Where the claim involves life insurance coverage, the burden of proof is on the defendant (the insurance company) to establish the insured's suicide within the exclusion clause. Because of the instinct of self-preservation, where there is doubt the court always assumes that the death is unintentional rather than intentional. While the plaintiff has the benefit of the legalistic assumption that a sane man will not commit suicide, the assumption stands only until evidence is introduced to prove suicide.

Loan Values. The general provisions usually declare that, at any time while the policy is in force, the company will lend to the policy owner, at a specified rate (usually 5% or 6%) on the security of the cash value of the policy. Accrued interest at the effective rate is considered payable at the same time as premiums are payable, or, if no further premiums are due, at the end of each policy year. If the interest is not paid when due, it is usually added to the principal. If the entire policy indebtedness then outstanding

---

[21] A Missouri statute (*Mo. Rev. Stat. Ann. paragraph 5851*) makes the suicide defense available only where it can be shown the insured took out the policy in contemplation of self-destruction.

[22] This might be the case in Virginia, for example, where a two-year suicide period is allowed, but only a one-year contestable period.

is within the limit of the maximum cash value available, the policy remains in force. If it is not, nonpayment of interest renders the policy null and void at the expiration of the grace period, after notice has been mailed to the last known address of the insured. Loans may be paid off at any time while the policy is in force. Loans will not be made on policies which have been put on the extended term option.[23]

A policy loan does not have the same legal effect as other loans for it specifies no date for repayment. Courts have held policy loans to be advances of funds which are ultimately payable to the policyholder or at his direction either as cash values, matured endowment, or death benefits. The estate of the insured, therefore, is not liable for an unpaid policy loan. The recourse of the company is to deduct any unpaid balance from the policy proceeds, or from the face amount of a matured endowment. For example, if an insured dies with a $3,000 policy loan outstanding on a $15,000 policy, the company will pay $12,000 to the beneficiary. The beneficiary cannot recover the other $3,000 from the insured's general estate, since the loan is not a legal obligation of this estate.

In the case of an irrevocable beneficiary designation, the beneficiary must join in the request for the loan and in the loan agreement. In Juvenile policies, the applicant, who is usually the parent, has the sole right to execute any policy loan agreements until the child reaches majority. If the law gives a juvenile the right to contract for life insurance in his own name at an age prior to legal majority,[24] the juvenile is then the owner of the policy and may exercise any borrowing rights contained in it. Where a juvenile or mental incompetent has a court-appointed guardian, the guardian may exercise the borrowing privilege under court approval. However, it has been held that if the insurer has no notice of mental incompetency, then a loan made upon application of the policy owner is made in good faith. The exclusive right of an assignee to borrow on the policy is clearly set forth in the standard assignment forms developed by the American Bankers' Association and the Association of Life Insurance Legal Counsel, which have been accepted by the companies.

When the company makes a loan, the policy is assigned to it. However, it has been held unnecessary for the company to have physical possession of the policy since it can prove assignment through the separate loan agreement, which in addition to the policy provision itself also sets forth the terms of the loan. Should the insured subsequently borrow on the policy from another lender, representing to the lender that the policy is unencum-

---

[23] One of the nonforfeiture options. Cf. Chapter 10.
[24] As in New York, where a juvenile has the power to contract for insurance at age 15.

bered, the insured is guilty of a criminal act. The lender probably would be held to have been negligent in making the loan since no assignment is binding on the company until the company is notified. If the lender had duly notified the company in advance of the loan, he would have learned of the existing policy loan. No lender who would do otherwise could be considered prudent.

The status of loan values where the insured is in bankruptcy is unclear. The United States Supreme Court has refused to review a federal appellate court decision [25] to the effect that the insurer must pay a trustee in bankruptcy the cash values of a bankrupt's policies even though it had already loaned the money to the bankrupt without knowing of his status.

If at the time a loan is made an unpaid premium is due or past due, the company has no right or obligation to deduct the amount of that premium from the loan value. In fact, since the policy loan provision states that the maximum cash value will be available on demand,[26] and since payment of a premium is a voluntary act, most courts hold that the premium could not be deducted without the consent of the insured.

Through the use of an automatic premium loan provision a policyholder can guarantee his policy against lapse if he fails to pay a specific premium so long as the policy has sufficient loan value to cover the payment. The automatic premium loan states that if the policyholder fails to pay a premium, the company will automatically pay that premium by drawing on the loan value of the policy at the agreed-upon rate of interest. A few states require that an automatic premium loan provision be put into the policy, but few United States companies include automatic premium loan provisions in their contracts unless the clause is specifically requested by the insured. Some companies endorse an automatic premium loan provision on the policy, and still others, will under no conditions write automatic premium loan clauses except in the states in which they are required to do so. Automatic premium loan provisions are the rule with Canadian companies. Where the provision is available, the policyholder should insist upon it in his contract,[27] for it is not difficult to overlook the payment of a premium by accident, especially now that companies send only one premium reminder. However, the automatic premium loan provision must not be abused by constant reliance upon it. It should be treated simply as protection against an oversight in paying the premium.

The loan privilege in the life insurance contract is a valuable provision,

---

[25] Lake v. N.Y. Life, et al.

[26] Subject to the provisions of the Delay clause, to be discussed.

[27] Many agents make it a practice to have the clause inserted for all applicants without asking the applicant.

for it enables a policyholder to draw upon cash values to meet a temporary financial reverse without forcing him to lose his insurance. If the policyholder has become uninsurable, the loan privilege is even more important to him. The danger of the loan privilege is that it may be abused. When a policyholder borrows on a policy, he must remember that he is borrowing on his family's future financial security.

The question is often raised, "Why do you charge me 5% to borrow my own money?"

When a policyholder borrows on the security of his policy, he is not borrowing his own money, but money which belongs to all policyholders as a group and money which must be invested at interest in order to support the premium and dividend structure of the company. The policyholder's equity in the company still continues to earn interest for him even though he has taken the money out by a loan.

"Then why do you charge me 5% to borrow while you are paying me only 2½% on my reserves?" [28]

The net return on a policy loan is less than 5%. It costs money to make and service policy loans, much more money than it costs to handle the average investment in the company's portfolio.

Policy loans make up a sizable share of a company's investments. Even in good times, policyholder loans constitute 3% or 4% of all assets held by life insurance companies. In 1932, 18.34% of assets were in policy loans. Like lapse ratios, and for the same reasons, policy loans fluctuate with economic conditions.

Assignment. A number of circumstances might arise in which the insured might wish to assign his life insurance to another party, or to use his policy as collateral for a loan or to secure other indebtedness. Under such circumstances he would want to assign it to the lender or other creditor. He might wish to sell his policy for value; for example, if he becomes seriously ill and needs cash he might wish to sell the policy to someone else rather than take the cash value from the insurance company. A life insurance policy on a man in bad health has a speculative value in excess of its cash value. A sale of the policy would involve an absolute assignment of it to the purchaser. Contrary to the rule in fire insurance where the contract is personal in nature, the owner of a life insurance policy has the right to assign it without consent of the insurer as long as the assignment does not defeat the vested rights of others, such as, for example, an irrevocable beneficiary. The right of assignment in life insurance is so well established that no permissive

---

[28] The term "my reserves" here is used in its loose and popular connotation rather than in the actuarial sense.

clause is necessary in the policy. Instead, the assignment clause in the contract is concerned only with protecting the company against double liability.

The typical assignment clause declares (1) that the company shall not be bound by any assignment until notice (usually in the form of the original or a duplicate of the assignment document) has been filed with the company, (2) that the assignment shall be subject to any indebtedness to the company (thus giving the company a prior right over any assignee), and (3) that the company accepts no responsibility for the validity of the assignment.

This clause does not mean that an assignment of which the company has no notice is void. It means, instead, that the company shall have no obligation to an unrecorded assignee if it pays out cash values or proceeds before the assignee presents a claim. In the case of a contested assignment after a policy has become a death claim, the company would seek to pay the proceeds into court, thus discharging its contractual obligation and allowing the distribution of the proceeds to be decided by legal process.

Several problems can arise in connection with an assignment:

1. A situation can develop where more than one assignment has been given, the second having been made before the company was notified of the first. The general rule is that the assignee first in point of date of assignment has the prior assignment,[29] but an exception is made to this rule if the assignee fails to take proper precautions to protect his rights. Controversies over the priority of assignments, however, are not matters in which the insurer needs to be arbitrator. As mentioned above, the practice of the companies is to pay the proceeds into court in case of disputes, and let the court decide which assignee has the prior claim.

2. The beneficiary might not be revoked before the assignment is made.[30] Where the beneficiary is revocable, in absence of revocation the courts generally have held that the assignee has the prior claim on the grounds that a revocable beneficiary has no present interest but only a future expectation. Therefore, if the assignee has established his interest at any time before the proceeds have been paid to the beneficiary, the assignee is entitled to recover. Also, assignment itself has been held to be notice of

---

[29] This is the so-called "American Rule." The "English Rule" is that the first assignee to give notice to the debtor prevails. Some American courts have adhered to the English rule.

[30] If the policy contains the following clause (as some do), then no problem is created by failure to change the beneficiary. "Whenever an assignment is executed by an owner of a policy who has the reserved right to change the beneficiary, the effect of such assignment shall be to destroy the rights of any named beneficiary in favor of the assignee." Cf. *Assignments of Life Insurance Policies* by Robert Dechert in the *The Beneficiary in Life Insurance*, Philadelphia, University of Pennsylvania Press, 1948, p. 28.

intention to change the beneficiary and has been interpreted by courts as a change.[31] On the other hand, if the beneficiary is irrevocable, then his or her compliance in the assignment must be obtained before there can be a valid assignment.

In using a life insurance policy as collateral for a loan, conditional assignment is to be preferred to a change of beneficiary. If the beneficiary is changed to the lender, he then has the right to collect the full amount of the proceeds; if assignment is made, his right can be restricted to his interest "as it may appear." For example, assume a lender wishes to protect a $1,000 loan should the insured die prior to repayment. It would seem at first glance that the simplest arrangement, in view of the confusion which exists over the rights of the beneficiary in assignments, would be to change the beneficiary on the policy to the creditor. But if the loan should be partially repaid before the death of the insured, then the contingent beneficiary will have to depend on the creditor for a refund of the difference between the proceeds and the amount still owed. This might involve the expense and delay of litigation. Proof that the change in beneficiary was to secure the debt might not be so easily obtained where family relationships are involved. On the other hand, an assignment of the policy proceeds to the creditor as his interest may appear would automatically pay the beneficiary the difference between the $1,000 proceeds and the amount of the debt still outstanding at the time of the death of the insured. Even here, however, where family relationships are involved, there might be litigation over the interest of the assignee at the time of the insured's death.

3. The assignee has failed to follow the assignment procedure set forth in the policy. Most courts, again, will hold that the failure can defeat the assignee's claim. The company can, however, if it wishes, waive the notice requirement and pay the proceeds to the assignee or it can ignore the assignment and pay the proceeds to the named beneficiary.

4. The assignment has been made by an incompetent policy owner. The general rule is that unless the company has been notified of that incompetency, it has no liability for having accepted the assignment. The company takes care of these situations by including a statement in the assignment

---

[31] Since in the past there has been a body of decision upholding the revocable beneficiary's rights over those of the assignee where the beneficiary did not consent to or acknowledge the assignment, it would be a wise precaution for the assignee to obtain evidence of the consent of the named beneficiary at the time of the assignment. It might even be better for the assignee to request that the beneficiary be changed to the insured's estate before the assignment is made. While this protection is not necessary under majority opinion, courts do have a way of springing unhappy surprises.

clause to the effect that the insurer accepts no responsibility for the validity of any assignment.[32]

5. The policy might have been assigned to someone who does not have an insurable interest. The United States Supreme Court held in the case of Warnock v. Davis [33] that since a lack of insurable interest will invalidate a policy taken out on the life of the insured, it should likewise invalidate an assignment of such a policy to a third party. However, in a later case, Grigsby v. Russell,[34] the court held that a policy could be assigned and sold like property, justifying the apparent discrepancy between the two cases by saying that the transfer in the Warnock-Davis case was a wagering contract while it was not in the second case.

Perhaps no more accurate a principle relating to assignments can be formulated than the one stated by the Circuit Court of Appeals of Maryland in its opinion rendered in the case of Rittler v. Smith: [35]

> It is the settled law in this state that a life insurance policy is but a chose [36] in action for the payment of money and may be assigned as such . . . if it be a bona fide business transaction and not a mere device for covering a gaming contract.

In other words, assignment can be made to someone who has no insurable interest provided the assignment is a bona fide business transaction (as for valuable consideration, for instance) and not a mere cover for a gambling adventure. Obviously, the "rule" is so general that except in the most obvious cases of either bona fide business transaction or of "gambling transaction," the validity of any assignment to a third party who has no insurable interest depends on a particular court's definitions of these two types of transactions. There are, of course, exceptions to this rule, for in some states the courts have ruled that in every case the assignee must have an insurable interest.[37]

Kinds of Assignments. An assignment may be made for a consideration. A voluntary assignment is one made without consideration. It is valid if made in good faith; however, it will not be considered to have been made in good faith if the assignment is made to avoid the question of insurable interest

---

[32] If the company were to accept any responsibility for the validity of assignments, such acceptance might be held to lend weight to the assignment, whereas the company should have no standing as a judge of such validities.

[33] *104 U. S. 775* (1881).

[34] A. H. Grigsby, Petitioner, v. R. L. Russell and Lillie Burchard, Administrators of John Burchard, Deceased. *222 U. S. 149* (1911).

[35] *70 Md. 261* (1889).

[36] A piece of personal property.

[37] These states include Alabama, Kansas, Kentucky, Missouri, Pennsylvania, and Texas.

or to defraud creditors. The absolute assignment gives the assignee all rights under the policy, both before and at its maturity. The collateral assignment is designed to serve as security for a debt and restricts the rights of the assignee to the amount of the debt, plus premiums paid on the policy, and interest. Creditors prefer the broader absolute assignment since they feel that the collateral assignment unduly restricts their actions with respect to the policy. A compromise has resulted in the development of the American Bankers' Association's standard assignment form, which gives the assignee the rights he needs for complete freedom and security while at the same time it protects the assignor's interest. This assignment form was prepared by the American Bankers' Association and the Association of Life Insurance Counsel. It gives the assignee bank "all claims, options, privileges, rights, titles, and interest" in the policy and all riders or supplemental contracts in connection with it, including:

1. The right to collect the proceeds.
2. The right to surrender the policy.
3. The right to borrow on the policy.
4. The right to receive dividends.
5. The right to exercise the nonforfeiture rights.

Under the ABA form, the assignee agrees, however, that it will repay to the beneficiary the difference between the proceeds collected and the unpaid balance of the debt, that it will not surrender or borrow on the policy unless there has been default in the loan or in the payment of premiums by the assignor—and then not until after giving the assignor 20 days' notice, and that it will not prevent the assignor from changing the beneficiary or from the election of any optional form of settlement or from collecting disability benefits so long as such collection does not reduce the amount of insurance.

Delay Clause. Especially since the cash-value "runs" of the depression of the 1930's it has been customary to include in many policies a clause declaring that the company has the right to defer the payment of a cash value or the making of a cash loan for a period not exceeding six months from the date of application for that cash value or loan, except when it is for the purpose of paying renewal premiums on policies in the company. The deferment clause sometimes applies also to withdrawal of proceeds retained at interest or commutation of guaranteed payments under settlement options. Although the clause itself is often mandatory, its use is elective. This is in line with a similar provision regarding bank accounts that was introduced as a result of experiences during the early 1930's when bank depositors and insurance policyholders demanded deposits or cash values, not because they were needed, but simply because they were afraid they could not obtain them.[38]

Beneficiary Clause. All Ordinary policies, and, today, almost all Industrial policies and Group insurance certificates allow the insured to name a beneficiary, that is, a person who is to receive the proceeds of the policy at his death. In fact, he may usually name several successive beneficiaries in the order in which they are to take priority should the primary beneficiary not survive the insured. These are known as "contingent" or "secondary," "tertiary," etc, beneficiaries.

If the insured has reserved the right to change the beneficiary, he may at any time the policy is not assigned make such a change without the beneficiary's or beneficiaries' permission upon conforming with the procedure for such change as set forth in the clause. This procedure is, in general, written notice to the company, to be effective only if endorsed on the policy.[39]

If the beneficiary has been named without reserving the right to change, the designation is called "irrevocable" and the person so named, "irrevocable beneficiary." An irrevocable beneficiary can be changed only with his or her written consent. Further, an irrevocable beneficiary must consent to any assignment before the assignment will be accepted by the company.

An irrevocable beneficiary designation may be absolute or reversionary. Under an *absolute* designation, the cash values in the policy will be in the beneficiary's estate if he should predecease the insured. Some opinions hold that the absolute beneficiary also has the right to exercise all the policy privileges without the consent of the insured. Others hold that the exercise of these rights must be joined in by the insured because the insured has not given up all incidents of ownership by naming an irrevocable beneficiary. The absolute beneficiary designation is not common.

A *revisionary* designation specifies that, upon the death of the last bene-

---

[38] A story illustrative of the unreason of those times is that of an acquaintance of the authors who tells how, after having seen three banks in which he carried deposits close in 1932, he called at the branch office of a life insurance company in which he carried relatively substantial coverage. "If I'd want a couple of thousand dollars of loan value," he quotes himself as asking, "how long would it take you to get it for me?" The cashier studied the policies for a minute or two and rubbed his chin. "Oh, 48 . . . 72 hours," he said. Our friend's reply was, "Thanks. I'll let you know if I need it"; and he walked out and never went back. He says himself that if the cashier had hesitated in naming the amount of time, he would have applied for a loan or cash immediately.

[39] A number of court cases, however, have held that compliance with the procedure for change has effected a change even though not yet physically endorsed on the policy at the time of the death of the insured. These cases have usually involved situations in which adequate written notice had been dispatched to the company but had not yet been received at the time of death, or cases in which the insured was unable to deliver the policy because of circumstances beyond his control, such as an estranged wife or relative having physical possession of the policy without irrevocable beneficiary right, ownership rights, or assignment.

ficiary, all rights in the policy revert to the insured. The exercise of any rights under the policy requires the joint action of both insured and beneficiary. If the contract does not state the nature of the disposition should the irrevocable beneficiary die before the insured, the majority of courts hold that the rights of the beneficiary pass to his or her heirs. Some courts, however, hold that where the beneficiary is a donee (that is, not a creditor or purchaser for value), his rights terminate with his death and revert to the insured. This seems more in line with the intentions of the insured.

If, however, the beneficiary is revocable, then he or she has no vested rights until the death of the insured, and the policyholder may exercise any ownership rights in the policy without the beneficiary's consent.[40]

Although the rights of the revocably beneficiary become fixed upon the death of the insured, they do not necessarily become so upon the maturity of an endowment. Sometimes the policy contains a provision that the beneficiary may be changed only prior to the maturity of the policy; but without such a provision, the beneficiary is changeable after maturity of an endowment as long as all proceeds have not been paid.

Cases arise in which the beneficiary, after the death of the insured, wishes to name a beneficiary to receive any unpaid proceeds remaining upon the death of the first beneficiary. If this "beneficiary's beneficiary" is named irrevocably, there is no problem. However, if he is named on a revocable basis, there is controversy over whether or not the designation is testamentary in character—that is, in the nature of a will rather than a beneficiary designation. Not enough litigation has involved the question to state a "majority opinion"; although a number of able writers on the subject have held it is not testamentary in nature and New York has passed legislation to the effect that the rights of such a secondary beneficiary are not to be voided on the grounds of noncompliance with the laws on wills and intestacies.

If no beneficiary is named in the policy, the proceeds are paid to the insured's estate, and their distribution becomes a matter of his will, or, if he has no will, of the laws of descent.

It has been pointed out [41] that while almost all other provisions of the life insurance policy are not subject to change by the insured, the beneficiary clause is the one provision he writes himself. It is his instruction for the

---

[40] Horne and Mansfield in *The Life Insurance Contract*, Life Office Management Association, 1938, point out on pages 125–126 several interesting cases in which courts have held a revocable designation to be the same as an irrevocable one. For example, delivery of the policy to the insured's wife in consideration of marriage gave her a vested interest which the insured could not defeat by naming another beneficiary.

[41] Robert Dochert, "Beneficiary Clauses and Their Legal Implications," Krueger and Waggoner, eds., *op. cit.*, p. 82.

disposition of the property (the proceeds). In that sense, it corresponds to a will, *but only in that sense.* A beneficiary designation is not a testamentary distribution of property. It is distribution by contract. It does not have to be drawn or witnessed with the formalities required for a will, and it does not have to be admitted to probate. In paying the proceeds, the company is not, in a legal sense, distributing the insured's property but is merely paying a stated amount of its own funds not traceable to anything received from the policyholder and, usually, in excess of the amounts of money paid by that policyholder.[42]

The designation of beneficiary should be drawn so that there can be no doubt as to the exact person intended. For instance, proceeds might go to the "wrong" wife where there is both a wife and an ex-wife and the beneficiary designation was merely "wife" without indicating her name. The same situation could (and has) arise when the beneficiary was designated as "Mrs. H. M. Case" rather than by her given name.[43] The accepted practice is to designate a spouse by her given name, followed by her relationship with the insured, such as "Myra Jones, wife of the insured." "Wife of the insured" is held to be merely a description of the status of Myra Jones at the time of designation and not of any subsequent wife.

Extreme care should be taken when children are designated as beneficiaries. If the children are designated by name with no qualification, those born after the designation was made might be excluded. The general rule, however, is that a class designation such as "children of the insured" includes all children at the time of death. Perhaps an even clearer designation is "children who survive the insured," for this usually is considered to include a posthumous child. This type of designation usually will be held to include also adopted children, although a safer designation in such cases is to state, "children of the insured, including those legally adopted" or some such wording acceptable to the insurance company. The designation, "my children," will exclude those of a spouse by a previous marriage, while "Myra Jones, wife of the insured, and our children" or "children of the union" will exclude all children of either spouse by a previous marriage.

These examples of the effect of various wordings indicate the necessity for careful consideration of the beneficiary designation.

---

[42] This may seem a contradiction since it is obvious that, in an actuarial sense, there is a direct connection between the premiums paid by the policyholder and the amount of proceeds paid; but here reference is made in terms of the legal agreement involved. The company did not make any agreement to take money from the policyholder and later pay it back to his heirs. It simply made a contract with him that in consideration of the payment of the premium, it would pay a specified sum to his beneficiary at death.

[43] Day *v* Case 43, Hun 79 (1887).

In designating children as beneficiaries, the legal principle that life insurance proceeds, like any other money, cannot be paid directly to a legal infant should not be overlooked. Since a minor is legally incompetent to accept payments, he is also legally incompetent to issue receipts for them. To pay funds to a minor might subject the company to double payment. At majority, the beneficiary might bring suit to recover proceeds for which the company had no valid receipts. So where there are minor beneficiaries, a guardian might have to be appointed.[44] The proceeds may be held by the company, accumulated at interest until the majority of the child, and distributed at that time. While most companies will agree to this settlement plan, money left to an orphaned child in most instances is needed currently for support and education and cannot be left on deposit with the company.[45]

A problem also arises when the insured and primary beneficiary die in a common accident with no evidence as to which died first. The burden of proof that the beneficiary outlived the insured usually is on the representative of that beneficiary since the great majority of states have adopted the Uniform Simultaneous Death law. The law provides that if there is no evidence as to whether the insured or beneficiary died first, the presumption shall be that the insured survived the beneficiary. The proceeds would, then, go to the secondary beneficiary or, in the absence of any, to the estate of the insured. If the beneficiary clearly survived the insured and died shortly thereafter, the proceeds would go to the beneficiary's estate. This may or may not be desirable in a given case. If it is not, then a common-disaster clause can be used to provide that, upon the death of the insured, the proceeds shall be held at interest for a specified period and then paid to the primary beneficiary at the end of that period, if surviving, otherwise to the secondary beneficiary (or whatever other distribution is desirable in the particular case).

In most cases, the rights of the beneficiary are superior to those of general creditors, including the reimbursement of anyone who has voluntarily paid premiums on the policy.

Numerous questions can arise over the exercise of ownership rights in a policy, most of which can be avoided by the growing practice of including

---

[44] A surviving parent is not automatically the guardian of the estate of a minor. To act in that capacity, he or she must be legally appointed guardian by the court. Pennsylvania has a statute that allows the insured to designate a guardian in a life insurance policy to receive funds for a minor beneficiary.

[45] A number of states permit waiver of guardianship and allow payments to be made payable to someone else for the benefit of the minor. The amount of such payments is limited, usually less than $500. New York permits an 18-year-old beneficiary legally to receive from a life insurance company and to give a binding receipt for up to $2,000 a year, payable by reason of death.

an ownership clause in policies. Such a clause specifically names the person in whom the rights to exercise any policy privileges shall be vested. If the policy contains no such clause, the statement can be included in the beneficiary designation itself.

Beneficiary designations have become exceedingly complex, but the complexity is steadily reducing litigation involving them until, today, such cases are insignificant.

4. MISCELLANEOUS PROVISIONS

In addition to the above provisions, a number of others will be found in most policies. These are:

Policy Change. The policy may contain a provision to the effect that the insured may at any time change the policy to one of another form. The provision may specify the forms to which the policy may be changed. Usually change to forms requiring higher reserve liabilities and consequently higher premiums may be made without evidence of insurability; change to forms requiring lower reserve liabilities and lower premiums is subject to evidence of insurability [46] because of the possibility of adverse selection.

Policy Year. A typical clause reads, "The policy year referred to herein is the year beginning on the —— of ——, 19–, or any anniversary thereof." Its purpose is to define clearly the actual meaning of the term, "policy year," so that it will be clear when this term is referred to elsewhere in the policy.

Basis of Computation. A provision in the policy sets forth the basis of reserve calculation, which in Ordinary policies [47] issued today is the 1941 CSO table with an interest assumption ranging between 2% and 3%, commonly 2½%. Additional benefits in event of accidental death or permanent and total disability are excluded from the computation. The basis of the cash value calculation also may be set forth.

Modifications and Agreements. Any modification or changes in the policy and all agreements in connection with it must be endorsed on or attached to the policy in writing, and over the signature of a specified officer or officers, such as the president, vice president, secretary, assistant secretary, treasurer, or assistant treasurer. No other person has authority to make changes and agreements, to waive provisions, or to extend the time for premium payment. Some modification clauses also declare specifically that no agent has authority to make changes, waivers, or the like.

---

[46] Change to a lower reserve form means the company will be increasing the amount at risk; that is, there will be an increase in pure insurance which is defined as the difference between the face of the policy and the reserve liability charged against that policy. Hence, the insured with a health problem indicating a shortened life expectancy will be inclined to shift to a form giving him more pure insurance per premium dollar.

[47] As distinguished from Industrial insurance. See Chapter 12.

The purpose of the clause is, of course, to clarify both to the policy-holder and to the courts just who has authority to alter a printed policy.

Representations and Warranties. All statements in the application shall be deemed representations and not warranties unless there is fraud involved; and it is provided that no statement may be used to contest the policy or a claim unless it is in writing on the application attached to the policy.

5. RESTRICTION OF CERTAIN HAZARDS

Two exclusions or restrictions [48] occasionally found in policies seem to merit separate discussion. One relates to aviation and the other to war.

Aviation Restriction. Restriction of coverage in case of death from avia-tion is universal in double indemnity provisions, occasionally found in dis-ability provisions, but now only rarely encountered in the life insurance policy itself, except in wartime. Such wartime restrictions usually are dropped retroactively upon cessation of hostilities.

While at one time it was common in life insurance to exclude liability in all cases involving death from aviation, the increased activity in aviation over the years and its excellent safety record have resulted in the liberaliza-tion of the provision. In other words, historical developments have seen an *exclusion* change into a *restriction* and the current trend is toward the elimi-nation of substantially all restrictions. Among the types of restrictions still occasionally found are:

1. Exclusion of all aviation deaths except those of fare-paying passengers on regularly scheduled airlines. The exception to the exclusion has been gen-erally extended to passengers on nonscheduled airlines as well since the ex-perience has been favorable in this phase of aviation.

2. Exclusion of deaths in military aircraft only.[49]

3. Exclusion of pilots, crew members, or student pilots (and, sometimes, anyone who has any duties in connection with the aircraft or the flight). The extra rate for pilots and crew members on commercial airlines has been either eliminated completely or substantially reduced in the last few years.

---

[48] Actually, they are restrictions more than exclusions since they do cover *some* types of deaths from the so-called excluded hazards.

[49] James T. Phillips, Vice President in charge of Underwriting, New York Life Insurance Company, has this to say about military aviation: "A comparison of trends in the ex-perience as between civilian and military aviation brings out a fundamental difference which is of paramount importance in underwriting aviation risks. In civilian aviation, safety of personnel is the all-important factor and we can expect scientific advances to be directed toward making civilian flying safer in the future. Although safety is important in military flying, it must take second place to combat efficiency so that many tech-nological developments in military aviation are likely to increase the military aviation hazard." *Insurance Lecture Series,* University of Connecticut, 1953, p. 67.

Extra rates for private pilots also are being reduced and in some cases eliminated.

4. Aviation death while on military maneuvers.

It should be pointed out that almost all these restrictions can be eliminated if the insured is willing to pay an extra premium. The exclusion clauses are used only when the applicant is unwilling to pay the extra cost or where the type of aviation in which he is engaged is subject to a hazard on which the company has insufficient statistics to compute a rate.

While there was considerable litigation over the validity of aviation exclusions when they were first used, all jurisdictions now permit at least some restriction. The question of whether exclusions in the restriction were in conflict with the incontestable clause has arisen, but this point now seems clearly settled. Just as in the case of the suicide exclusion, denial of a claim for an excluded hazard is not a contest of the policy but enforcement of a policy provision. Litigation involving military aviation deaths has been undertaken on the grounds that aviation exclusions were meant to exclude only civil aviation. Courts, as a rule, have not gone along with this line of reasoning. On the other hand, the aviation exclusion was held not to apply in cases where the insured was killed by gunfire while in flight under the interpretation that the immediate cause of the death was gunfire, not aviation. The doctrine of proximate cause, however, has been invoked to exclude deaths resulting indirectly from flying, such as drowning after a plane crash.

Some states seek to limit the extent of restrictions, such as requiring that at least fare-paying passengers on civil aircraft be covered. However, attempts of states to outlaw all restrictions or to limit them severely can result in the denial of insurance in that jurisdiction to anyone participating in aviation.[50]

War Restriction. In wartime, companies usually insert restrictions in their contracts, generally referred to as "war clauses." These restrictions are usually contained in policies written during periods of impending war, and especially in those policies issued to young men of draft age. The clauses generally provide for a return of premium with interest or a refund equal to the reserve valuation of the policy in event death occurs under conditions excluded in the policy.

War-caused death is a hazard not calculated in rating life insurance policies. Premiums are based on a mortality table that covers peacetime

---

[50] This happened in Nebraska after State *ex rel.* Republic National Life *v.* Smrha, *138 Neb. 484*, 293, N.W. 373 (1940). It was necessary to pass legislation permitting exclusion of certain aviation hazards in order to alleviate the situation.

death only. There is no way to calculate the added risk of warfare until after a war is over. Each war to date has created its own mortality rate. Further, issuance of policies without a war exclusion in time of war would result in drastic antiselection: those going into military service would be inclined to buy larger policies than they would have purchased in peacetime.[51]

War clauses usually are cancelled at the end of the hostilities.

Courts universally recognize that it is impossible for a private insurer to assume the added hazard of war at ordinary rates. Therefore, virtually no legal questions arise over the validity of war clauses.

In general, there are two types of war clauses, usually known as the "status" type and the "result" type. One is a "while" clause whereas the other is an "if" clause. Under the "status" clause, liability of the company for the death of the insured is excluded *while* the insured is in military service, regardless of the cause of his death. Often this clause is liberalized to exclude only death outside the home area, as defined in the clause. The home area is usually defined as the 48 states, District of Columbia, and Canada. Under the "result" clause, liability is excluded *if* the death is a result of war. Under the status clause, the cause of death does not matter; under the result clause, it is all-important.

Double indemnity and disability riders or clauses are usually terminated or suspended by war.

Both types of clauses have given rise to endless litigation—so endless it is impossible even to summarize here.[52] The principal type of litigation, however seems to have been over whether the wording of the clause makes it a "status" clause or a "result" clause. These cases arise, for example, when a soldier is killed in a tavern brawl or dies as a result of a common civilian disease. Unless the wording is so clear as to make the clause unquestionably a "status" clause, the courts tend to bend over backward to interpret it as a "result" clause.

---

[51] After both World Wars I and II, many companies found they could have covered the war hazard without extra premium and, therefore, paid war death claims retroactively despite the war exclusion clauses. The practice of paying war-incurred death has been debated on actuarial grounds. The fact that companies found that they could have covered the hazard, however, does not mean they would have been able to do so had they issued policies without the exclusion. The exclusion tended to restrict the amount at risk to a figure small enough so that the effect of war deaths did not disturb over-all mortality experience. Had policies been issued without the restriction, antiselection might have increased the proportion of insurance on military personnel to the degree that mortality might have jumped to the point where it could have had a serious affect. The advantage of the war clause, then, seems to be in controlling adverse selection.

[52] For such a summary and citations, cf. Krueger and Waggoner, eds., *op. cit.*, Chapter 18.

Another type of litigation involves the time when a person might be said to be in military service. When the term "active service" is used, courts have excluded the period of training. In one amusing decision (amusing to us but not to the insurance company involved) a court held that the words "while on duty as a soldier" did not include a sailor who died of appendicitis while in the service. The court made a definite distinction between a soldier and a sailor, which distinction the men of the services have always insisted exists as a matter of pride in their own superior branch (whichever that might be). This decision indicates the importance of carefully spelling out to the courts just what the war clause intends to exclude. Implied intention means little to a court eager to protect the family of the serviceman.

In addition to litigation over the interpretation of the clause and the nature of the death is that over the existence of war itself. This problem arises in the time interval between enemy attack, as at Pearl Harbor, and actual declaration of war by the Congress; between the end of actual hostilities and the declaration of the end of the war; and in such situations as the Korean conflict. The status of the last, whether "war" or not, is still being litigated at the time of this writing, and decisions each way are announced regularly.

6. SUMMARY AND CONCLUSIONS

The life insurance policy is a legal document setting forth the rights and obligations of the policyholder, beneficiary, and company. It is a rather unique contract in that all its provisions, except one, set forth the obligations of one party to the contract—the insurer. The one condition the policy imposes on the insured is the periodic payment of premiums, and even if he defaults in his part of the contract, he cannot be held liable for its performance.

Some of the provisions of a life insurance policy are required by law. An exact list of them varies by states. Only the substance of the required provisions is set forth; the wording is left to the insurer, and any variation of the required provision that makes the policy more liberal to the policyholder is allowed. In life insurance there are no standard policy forms as there are, for example, in fire insurance.

Provisions often required by state law are incontestability, loan value, grace period, reinstatement, policy ownership, misstatement of age, policy to constitute the entire contract, annual participation of surplus, nonforfeiture values, table of settlement values when offered.[53] For the most part, these required provisions are for the protection of the policyholder.

---

[53] See Chapter 10.

In addition to required provisions, most states prescribe a set of "permissive" provisions, that is, provisions that need not but may be included. For the most part, these are for the protection of the insurer. Examples are suicide exclusion, assignment, travel and residential exclusions, policy modifications, payment of premiums, consideration, aviation, and war exclusions.

Some provisions are required, some are permitted, and some merely clarify the position of the parties. Examples of this last type of clause are the beneficiary clauses, statement of reserve and cash value calculations, policy year, and the like.

The interpretation of the provisions of a policy and the litigation over their interpretation and application fill volumes of law reports. The attempt in this chapter has not been to provide an exhaustive analysis or a guide to citations, but merely a summary of the major trends of interpretation and case law. For every statement made, a contrary opinion or court decision could be found, but the discussion has sought to follow the majority opinion.

In addition to the provisions discussed in this chapter are those policy provisions relating to the various policy options. These are discussed in the following chapter.

Questions for Class Discussion

1. The policy issued to the insured excluded death resulting from operating any kind of aircraft. The insured was a captain in the United States Air Force, and was on duty as the pilot of a military fighter plane on a reconnaissance flight over southeastern Korea. He was shot down and died as the result of enemy gunfire. Is the company liable?

2. The insured's policy was issued on June 22, 1951, but provided that its effective date was March 14, 1951, to give the insured the benefit of lower premium rate. It provided that the company would be liable only for return of premiums paid if the insured should commit suicide within "one year from the date of issue of this policy." The insured committed suicide on May 23, 1952, and the company denied liability for the face of the policy and admitted liability only for the return of premiums paid. The beneficiary sued for recovery of the face of policy. What should be the verdict?

3. The husband and wife each applied for "Commercial Whole Life" policies, the husband paid the premium on the wife's policy, and the wife paid the premium on her husband's policy. Each policy provided that the payor of the premium was the absolute owner of the policy. The premium on the husband's policy was increased from $1,767.80 (as determined by the agent) to $1,808.60, which was not satisfactory to the applicants, and both policies were refused. Action was brought by the husband and the wife to recover the premiums paid with the applications. Can the premiums be recovered?

4. The annual premium, due on May 4, 1950, was not paid and the policy lapsed. Thereafter, the agent called on the beneficiary several times in an

effort to have the policy renewed, but the beneficiary informed him he did not have the funds available. The record showed that he owned property at that time valued at $75,000. After the policy lapsed, the insured consulted the family doctor and was referred to a specialist who diagnosed the trouble as cancer. She underwent an operation on September 7, and went home on September 10. Seven months later she died as a result of cancer. Three days after his mother returned from the hospital, the plaintiff, who was the beneficiary, told the insurance agent that he was ready to have the policy reinstated. The beneficiary could not read or write, but he answered the questions in the reinstatement application and the agent filled in the blanks with the information given him by the insured. The beneficiary's wife signed the insured's name to the application. The plaintiff testified that he did not know of the insured's illness or her hospitalization. Can the beneficiary collect?

5. After the issuance of the policy, the insured had had an operation by which over half of his stomach was removed. Thereafter, he permitted his insurance policy to lapse. In applying for the reinstatement, negative answers were made to the questions inquiring if he had consulted a physician within the last five years or had had a surgical operation or had been hospitalized. The agent testified that he asked the insured the questions in the application for reinstatement, and that he inserted the answers as given by the insured; that the insured took the application, appeared to read it over, and then signed it. Is the company liable for payment of policy face?

6. The policy was issued on August 28 and the insured died in the following May. He was taking a bath, and death may have resulted from a severe bruise on the head or from water in the lungs. The jury found that death was accidental. However, the company contended that the policy was null and void from inception because the insured had concealed a baseball injury which had caused him to have dizzy spells for some time thereafter. The beneficiary testified that the insured had told the soliciting agent (who was also the staff manager in charge of men for the company) about the injury; that he had been struck upon the head while playing baseball, and after that time he had had dizzy spells; that he had consulted doctors and had been hospitalized; however, he had shortly before that time been examined for employment by a physician and had been passed with a favorable report. The beneficiary testified that the soliciting agent told the insured there was no need to mention that if he had had no trouble recently. The agent testified that he did not recall the conversation and that his memory was "hazy." The company argued that the agent's testimony should not have been admitted since the contract provided that no agent had authority to make any concessions or vary the terms of the policy. At the time the application was signed, the insured also signed an authorization permitting the company to secure any information concerning past medical attendance or advice or hospitalization. Is the company liable?

7. Some of the provisions of the typical life insurance policy are designed to protect the company whereas others are designed to protect the insured. Classify the provisions according to the parties protected.

8. John Jones has a $1,000 continuous-premium Whole Life policy. His tenth

annual premium is due on July 1. He fails to pay the premium and dies on July 15, how much does his beneficiary collect? Suppose he dies on August 15, how much does his beneficiary collect?

9. How do you account for the fact that the life insurance contract has been liberalized over the ages?

10. If you were a banker to whom a life insurance policyholder is applying for a loan, would you rather have the policy assigned to the bank or have the bank named as the beneficiary of the policy?

CHAPTER 10

POLICY OPTIONS

IN ADDITION to the general provisions of the life insurance contract discussed in Chapter 9, the policy also contains certain other provisions offering the policyholder several choices: (1) in case of lapse or surrender of his policy, (2) in method of receiving or applying policy dividends, and (3) in method of payment of proceeds. The purpose of this chapter is to discuss the options usually available under each of these three headings.

1. NONFORFEITURE OPTIONS

No level-premium permanent policy form which has been in force more than a minimum amount of time (generally one to three years) can expire without value. From almost the beginning of level-premium insurance, introduced in England by Old Equitable in 1762, at least some companies have recognized the fact that under a level-premium plan of insurance the policyholder who surrenders his policy before maturity has contributed more than his share of premiums and deserves some type of refund.

Under a natural premium plan of insurance, the premium automatically increases each year as mortality rates increase with age. The level premium is a plan whereby the annual premiums are distributed evenly over the period during which they are paid. This means that the policyholder must pay more than the actual cost of insurance in the earlier years of the policy. For example, the natural premium at age 20, nonpar, would be about $6.15 per $1,000, whereas the level premium for continuous-premium Whole Life would be about $14.65.[1] Non-forfeiture values arise from these initially high premiums and the investment return on them.[2]

Early attempts at making refunds of premiums in event of termination

---

[1] See Chapter 21 for an actuarial explanation of the level premium plan of insurance.
[2] For a more detailed and exact explanation of the nature and source of non-forfeiture values, see Chapter 23.

often were confined merely to a statement that the company would give consideration to a refund in case of surrender or would "purchase back" the policy for an "equitable consideration." In 1851, the Scottish Widows' Fund and Equitable Assurance Company of Edinburgh added contract surrender values to its policies. By 1861, most United States companies had established rules for granting nonforfeiture values, and some included them in the policy as a contractual right. In 1861, Elizur Wright, member of the first Board of Insurance Commissioners of Massachusetts, effected the passage of a state law requiring extended insurance as a nonforfeiture value; and most companies began to adopt definite forms of nonforfeiture values even when not subject to Massachusetts law. After the Armstrong investigation in New York (1905), states not yet having nonforfeiture laws generally adopted them.

Life insurance policies today provide for two or more nonforfeiture values, any one of which may be elected by the policyholder within (usually) 60 days after the due date of any premium in default; and if no such election is made, then a stated form of paid-up benefit becomes effective.

The three most common forms of nonforfeiture options found in policies are (1) cash value; (2) extended Term insurance; (3) reduced paid-up insurance. Since in a sense the cash value is the basis of the other two options, it will be discussed first.

Cash Value. If the policyholder surrenders his policy before maturity, the company has collected from him more than was necessary to meet the cost of his policy during the time it was in force. Therefore, he should be entitled to a refund of the overpayments.[3]

Prior to the passage of the Standard Non-Forfeiture Valuation laws,[4] completed in most states prior to 1948, the accepted method of determining the amount of the cash value was to use the legal reserve required in any given policy, minus a "surrender charge" of not more than $25 for each $1,000 of insurance. The purpose of the surrender charge was to enable the company to recover that part of the cost of issuing the policy which had been paid out of surplus.[5] Cash surrender value usually was offered only

---

[3] The premium computation formula, however, does not contemplate a refund of the so-called overcharge in addition to the face value, payable at death. Cf. Chapter 20 for further explanation.

[4] More commonly referred to in the business as the "Guertin Laws."

[5] Acquisition costs (commission to the agent, medical fee, investigation fee, all the clerical costs involved in underwriting and issuing a new policy) take so much of the first-year premium that the net amount remaining for the company is substantially less than that needed to finance the legal reserve required for the policy without decreasing surplus. The resulting decrease in surplus is restored from future renewal premiums, which are greater than the amount required to offset year-by-year additions to legal reserves.

after the expiration of the first three policy years, and the surrender charge usually diminished and disappeared entirely after the policy had been in force for a minimum number of years, depending on the basis of valuation.

The reserve-less-surrender-charge method of fixing surrender values was subject to several criticisms. It was inequitable since it depended upon the reserve basis used by the company for solvency purposes rather than upon the actual funds contributed by the policyholder prior to withdrawal. The surrender charge itself was misunderstood and was often interpreted as a penalty for discontinuing the contract rather than as a charge for high first-year costs which otherwise would be recovered from future premiums. These criticisms, along with the desire to substitute sound actuarial principles for heretofore crude empirical standards for surrender values, led to the development and passage of the Standard Non-Forfeiture law.

Under the Standard Non-Forfeiture law, there is no fixed relationship between the cash surrender value and the reserve, and no surrender charge as such. Instead, the minimum value required is determined according to a formula. This formula fixes the maximum first-year expenses that may be charged against each type of policy at each age for purposes of determining the nonforfeiture value. This first-year expense is then amortized over the premium-paying period of the policy by taking a level amount from the expense loading in the gross premium each year.[6]

The Standard Non-Forfeiture law does not require that a surrender value be given after any specified arbitrary period of time but instead requires that such value be given at whatever time and for whatever amount such value is produced by the formula. Thus one policy at one age may produce a surrender value at the end of the first policy year, whereas another will not show such values for several years.[7] The result is greater equity in nonforfeiture values than under the reserve-less-surrender charge method of computing them.

Cash values in permanent policy forms increase yearly. Short-Term policy forms have no cash values. Long-Term forms may have cash values; but these values will increase up to a point, thereafter declining to zero on

---

[6] The formula for Standard Non-Forfeiture valuation develops an "adjusted premium" which is the net level premium for any given policy plus an amount sufficient to amortize the first-year expenses within the policy premium-paying period. If all this fails to make sense to you, wait until you have studied Chapter 23, and then try it again.
[7] The Non-Forfeiture law does not specify a cash value but only some form of paid-up insurance benefit, the form of which is to be left up to the company. This paid-up benefit is to be automatic if none of the options is elected within 60 days after the due date of the premium in default.

the expiry date of the policy.[8] In Table 1 are typical examples of cash values on several policy anniversaries for selected ages of issue.

Table 1. Continuous-Premium Whole Life ($10,000 Minimum)
Cash Value per $1,000 of Face, CSO 2½%, Participating

End Policy Year	AGE AT ISSUE		
	20	30	40
1	$ 0	$ 0	$ 0
2	0	2	12
3	7	19	34
5	33	52	77
10	103	141	189
20	248	322	407
At age 65	628	580	505

20-Year Endowment
Cash Value per $1,000 of Face, CSO 2½%, Participating

End Policy Year	AGE AT ISSUE		
	20	30	40
1	$ 11	$ 11	$ 11
2	52	52	52
3	94	94	94
5	182	182	181
10	423	421	418
20	1,000	1,000	1,000

20-Pay Life
Cash Value per $1,000 of Face, CSO 2½%, Participating

End Policy Year	AGE AT ISSUE		
	20	30	40
1	$ 0	$ 0	$ 1
2	14	23	32
3	37	50	64
5	84	106	129
10	211	257	304
20	503	603	705
At age 65	754	754	754

Life insurance policies with cash values are one way of creating emergency funds. These values may be withdrawn in cash, taken as a policy loan, or used as collateral for a bank loan. However, drawing on other types of savings, if available, may often be more advantageous. Taking the values in a life insurance policy in cash necessitates terminating the contract, which it may not be possible to replace later and which will always have to be

---

[8] Cf. Chapter 3.

replaced at a higher rate. Taking the values as a loan means paying the insurance company a higher rate of interest than the company is crediting to the policyholder under the reserve. While bank loan rates in times of free credit may be a point or two lower than the rate for policy loans, they will still be higher than the amount being credited the policyholder under the policy. On the other hand, the cost of using funds from other saving media is the loss of interest they would have earned if not withdrawn. Since the interest rate on most such media used by the average person is usually very low (only 1% or 2% on bank savings accounts, for instance, as compared with 4% to 5% on policy or bank loans), the cost of emergency funds drawn from sources other than life insurance cash values will usually prove less.[9]

Perhaps the more important use of life insurance cash values is as a vehicle for building a retirement fund which can be paid to the insured as an annuity upon retirement. Sometimes the option to take cash values as an annuity is written into the policy, whereas at other times these options are granted as "company practice." A knowledge of life insurance cash values is essential in the development of a sound family life insurance program.[10]

When reference is made to the "savings"[11] or "investment" element in a life insurance policy, the cash values actually are what is meant.

Paid-up for a Reduced Amount. Reduced, paid-up insurance is the nonforfeiture value used by some companies as automatic if no option is elected by the insured within 60 days after the due date of the defaulted premium. If in these companies the policyholder fails to pay his premium and makes no overtures to the company about the disposal of his policy, the company automatically applies the paid-up reduced amount option.[12] A defaulting policyholder, of course, may elect this option himself if he wishes.

In the case of the paid-up reduced amount nonforfeiture value, the company applies the cash value available under the policy at the time of lapse to the purchase of whatever amount of fully paid-up insurance it will

---

[9] This is not intended as an argument against life insurance but as an argument for keeping life insurance policies unencumbered and building one's primary emergency reserves through savings media other than life insurance. Life insurance is not designed to be used as a banking account.

[10] Cf. Chapter 16.

[11] New York law prohibits referring to a cash value as "savings," a sound technical but hair-splitting practical distinction.

[12] It is not widely understood by policyholders that even if they do nothing after lapsing a premium, some value will continue in force for some time after that lapse—provided there was a paid-up value under the nonforfeiture valuation formula at the time of lapse. Cases are not uncommon of beneficiaries who discovered long after the death of the insured that the old policy on which premiums had not been paid for years was still in force for some value at the death of the policyholder. The beneficiary should never discard a lapsed policy found among the effects of the deceased but instead should check with the company to see if it still has value.

buy at the net, single-premium rate[13] on the same plan as that of the
original policy. Thus the paid-up insurance under a Whole Life policy will
be, of course, Whole Life, and will be Endowment under that type of contract. The examples in Table 2 show the amounts of paid-up insurance available at the end of given policy years based on several ages of entry on three
policy plans.

Table 2. Special Continuous-Premium Whole Life ($10,000 Minimum)

Paid-Up Values per $1,000 of Face, CSO 2½%, Participating

End of policy year	AGE AT ISSUE			
	20	30	40	50
1	$ 0	$ 0	$ 0	$ 0
2	0	5	23	42
3	20	44	64	84
5	89	141	140	168
10	249	281	315	360
20	494	535	578	621

20-Pay Life

Paid-Up Values per $1,000 of Face, CSO 2½%, Participating

End of policy year	AGE AT ISSUE			
	20	30	40	50
1	$ 0	$ 0	$ 2	$ 10
2	40	54	62	68
3	103	114	121	124
5	225	233	234	233
10	510	512	505	490
20	1,000	1,000	1,000	1,000

20-Year Endowment

Paid-Up Values per $1,000 of Face, CSO 2½%, Participating

End of policy year	AGE AT ISSUE			
	20	30	40	50
1	$ 18	$ 18	$ 17	$ 17
2	80	80	78	77
3	142	141	138	134
5	261	260	254	246
10	539	535	526	508
19	960	959	957	950

The paid-up option should be elected when the policyholder's need for
insurance protection has decreased but will continue to exist until the maturity date of the policy. For instance, at age 65, financial protection against

---

[13] While this is hardly an actuarial explanation, it serves the useful function of clarifying
the concept.

death is still needed for at least final expenses. If the policyholder has in force more death protection at retirement than he feels will be needed to pay the cost of dying (last illness, funeral expenses, taxes, etc.), he can convert some of the insurance to the reduced paid-up insurance option, making it unnecessary to continue premium payments and allowing him to spend his entire retirement income for the cost of living. At the same time, he will have insurance protection for the rest of his life. For illustration, assume that a policyholder at age 65 (or any other age, for that matter) has $50,000 of life insurance in force and no dependents and wishes to take the cash values of this insurance as a retirement income. He wants to be sure, however, that upon his death there will be money for final expenses. If his paid-up insurance values are approximately $500 per $1,000, he can establish a $2,500 final expense fund by putting $5,000 of his $50,000 of insurance on the paid-up option, leaving him $45,000 to convert into a retirement income.[14]

Another use of the reduced paid-up option is to keep a continuous-premium Whole Life in force on a paid-up basis when the family need expires or when disposable income decreases.

Extended Term. The extended Term option is more commonly used as the automatic option in the event that the lapsing policyholder fails to elect one of the other two nonforfeiture provision within the required time. Under this option, the company in effect, converts the net cash value of the policy into single-premium Term insurance for the full face of the policy for a period as long as it will purchase. "Net cash value" means that any policy loans are deducted from and dividends added to the cash values as listed in the policy.

In the case of Endowment policies, if the cash value will extend the Term beyond the maturity date, the amount of net cash value in excess of that needed to continue the face amount to maturity will be used to purchase pure Endowment; that is, Endowment without life contingency. In other words, if an Endowment policy with five years to run is placed on an extended Term option, it will be handled as follows: First, assume the cash value of this particular policy is $567.41 and that the amount required for a net single premium for a Term policy for five years at the age of surrender is only $54.63. The $512.78 remainder would be used to purchase a pure Endowment. The amount of five-year pure Endowment that can be purchased at this age with a net single premium of $512.78 is $963.47. If under this option the insured dies within five years, his beneficiary will collect

---

[14] Which would give him approximately $150 a month on a life only basis, a proper option if he had no dependents, as assumed in the illustration.

$1,000 (the amount of the extended Term insurance); however, if he lives for five years, he will collect $963.47 (the amount of the pure Endowment).

Under extended Term, the full amount of the policy remains in force for a limited period of time instead of (as in the reduced amount option) a reduced amount of insurance remaining in force for the full policy period.

Table 3 shows the length of time each of several policies will remain in force at full value, assuming given ages of issue, if these policies are put on the extended Term option at the end of the policy years indicated.

When there is a loan outstanding against an extended Term policy, it is deducted both from the face of the policy and from the cash value. This means that a smaller amount of insurance is extended for a period shorter than would be the case had there been no loan. Were the loan deducted from the cash value only, the policy would be extended for even a shorter period.

Assume a $10,000 policy issued at age 25 which has been in force 20 years on the continuous-premium Whole Life basis. Assume further that the policy has a loan outstanding against it for $1,000, and that the policyholder decides to discontinue premium payments, forget the loan, and put the insurance on the extended Term nonforfeiture option. A 20-year-old continuous-premium Whole Life policy of $10,000 issued at age 25 in a typical company has a cash value of about $2,840. When this policy is placed on the extended Term basis, the loan is subtracted from both the face value and the cash value of the policy. Thus, this policy will extend $9,000 for as many years as $1,840 will provide at the net single premium for Term insurance at the attained age (45).

At first glance it might seem unfair to subtract the amount of the loan from both the face value and cash value of the policy. On closer examination, however, the logic of this procedure becomes apparent. To allow more insurance would result in adverse selection, making it profitable for everyone to borrow heavily on his policy when he reaches his deathbed, and then surrender it for extended Term insurance for its full amount. The effect would be to increase the insurance, contrary to all good underwriting practices. Suppose that shortly after he borrows the $1,000, the insured in the above case decides to cash in his policy. He will be entitled to collect only $1,840, since he already has received $1,000. Suppose, instead of cashing in the policy, he dies shortly after getting the loan. His beneficiaries will collect only $9,000, since the face of the policy as well as its cash value is encumbered by the loan. If he neither dies nor cashes in his policy but instead surrenders it in exchange for an extended Term contract, his present in-

Table 3. Special Continuous-Premium Whole Life ($10,000 Minimum)

Extended Term Durations per $1,000 of Face, CSO 2½%, Participating

End of Policy	AGE AT ISSUE					
	20		30		40	
Year	Years	Days	Years	Days	Years	Days
1		0		0		0
2		0		192	1	265
3	2	242	4	187	4	132
5	10	308	10	28	8	9
10	21	273	17	86	12	260
20	25	303	19	244	14	20
At age 65	17	172	15	215	13	43

20-Pay Life

Extended Term Durations per $1,000 of Face, CSO 2½%, Participating

End of Policy	AGE AT ISSUE					
	20		30		40	
Year	Years	Days	Years	Days	Years	Days
1		0		0		57
2	5	162	5	247	4	142
3	13	2	10	287	7	258
5	23	36	17	278	12	130
10	34	209	26	177	18	277
20	Paid up		Paid up		Paid up	

20-Year Endowment

Extended Term Durations and Pure Endowment ° per $1,000 of Face
CSO 2½%, Participating

	AGE AT ISSUE								
	20			30			40		
End of policy			Pure Endow-			Pure Endow-			Pure Endow-
Year	Years	Days	ment	Years	Days	ment	Years	Days	ment
1	4	164	$ 0	2	351	$ 0	1	251	$ 0
2	18	0	1	11	259	0	6	299	0
3	17	0	71	17	0	11	10	248	0
5	15	0	207	15	0	158	15	0	30
10	10	0	515	10	0	489	10	0	423
19	1	0	960	1	0	958	1	0	956

° The amount of endowment to which the insured will be entitled in addition to the extended Term. Under the extended Term option, the amount of death protection remains the same as long as the extended Term runs, but the amount of endowment payable is reduced.

surance (in this case $9,000) is continued for the period purchased by the remaining cash value (in this case $1,840).

When a policyholder no longer can continue premium payments and yet wishes to keep insurance in force, he must chose between reduced paid-up insurance and full extended Term insurance. If the policyholder is in good health and needs permanent protection, obviously he will select reduced paid-up insurance. This is true especially if the policy has a large cash value, since the larger the cash value, the smaller will be the reduction in the amount of insurance. If, on the other hand, the policyholder is in poor health or has a temporary insurance need, he will be inclined to select the extended Term option. A factor that is sometimes considered to favor reduced paid-up insurance, however, is that under the participating policy plan it continues to pay dividends. Dividends are not customary under the extended Term option.

When any one of the nonforfeiture options is used, the original policy cannot be reinstated without satisfactory proof of insurability, and then only during the reinstatement period. Most policies cannot be reinstated at all if they have been surrendered for their cash value. To reinstate an old policy or to purchase a new one, the policyholder must prove insurability either through a medical examination or through the health statement taken with nonmedical policies. Hence, if the reason for default is a temporary inability to meet premium payments, the nonforfeiture options should not be used if there is a great need for insurance protection and a reasonable expectation of recurring ability to pay. Instead, the loan value should be used to pay premiums until the temporary financial embarrassment has passed. If one of the paid-up insurance nonforfeiture options is selected, the policyholder might not be able to pass an examination or qualify for standard insurance, should he wish to reinstate later. If the cash value option is selected, the policyholder might never be able to replace his policy with one as good as the one surrendered. For these reasons, the automatic premium loan provision should be considered.

2. DIVIDEND OPTIONS

Life insurance policies may be issued on either a participating or a nonparticipating plan. Under the participating plan, policyholders are entitled to policy dividends. These dividends, on the average, reflect the difference between the premium charged for the policy and its actual cost as experienced by the company. Under the nonparticipating plan, policies are written for a premium lower than the gross premium on participating insurance. In general, participating plans are written by mutual companies and nonparticipating by stock companies. However, stock companies can and do issue participating plans, and some mutuals issue nonparticipating plans.[15]

Nature of Dividends. Dividends distributed to participating policy-

---

[15] For a more complete discussion and analysis of participating and nonparticipating plans, as well as of mutual and stock companies, cf. Chapter 24.

holders are not profits in a commercial sense but, instead, are a return of an overcharge of premium.[16] That portion of the company's surplus which is not deemed necessary to strengthen contingency reserves may be distributed among individual policyholders.[17] The method of calculating dividends is rarely if ever stated in the policy contract. Instead, the policy makes some such statement as, "This policy, on each anniversary while in force, except as extended Term insurance, shall participate in the divisible surplus of the company, but payment of the first dividend shall be contingent upon and proportionate to the premiums due and paid for the second policy year. *The company will annually determine the dividends of such surplus apportionable to this policy.*" [18]

The dividend clause often includes a provision for the payment of dividends for the fraction of the policy year in which the policyholder dies. The practice on post-mortem dividends varies from full payment of the current year's dividend to a pro rata share. No fractional dividends, however, are paid upon surrender of the policy.

Participating policies offer the policyholder the choice of several methods of receiving these annual [19] refunds. The common dividend options are (1) pay in cash, (2) apply toward the payment of the premium, (3) leave to accumulate with interest credited annually at a guaranteed minimum rate of interest, (4) use to buy paid-up additions to the policy, (5) use to convert a Whole Life policy to an Endowment (or shorten the endowment period), and (6) use to pay up the policy in fewer than the contract years. The automatic option varies among companies, being cash in some companies, the accumulation option in others and the paid-up addition option in still others.

---

[16] See Chapter 17 for a discussion of tax laws relating to policy dividends.
[17] Cf. Chapter 23 for a discussion of the source of surplus and the problems involved in its apportionment.
[18] Italics ours.
[19] Annual distribution of policy dividends is required by the laws of many states, particularly New York, where the system of deferred dividends popular in the late nineteenth and very early twentieth century led to abuses castigated by the Armstrong Committee. Cf. Chapter 26. Even where not required, the practice of annual policy dividends is usually followed. However, dividends paid over longer periods, quinquennial, for example, are not unknown and have their sincere advocates. Also, as discussed in Chapter 4, surrender dividends are paid by some companies on "specials." Under the laws of New York and those of a number of other states, dividends are not restricted exclusively to *regular* annual payments. Extra dividends at reasonable intervals or dividends on policy terminations are allowed. Extra and terminal dividends, however, are carefully supervised by the insurance regulatory departments of the states in order to prevent a disproportionate amount of funds from being used for these types of dividends. In general, these special dividends must not be too large in comparison with the regular annual dividends apportioned on the policies in preceding years, otherwise they will be declared inequitable.

In Cash. If no optional method of receiving or applying dividends is indicated by the policyholder, either in his application or at some time in the future, dividends will sometimes be paid in cash.[20] This form of settlement, however, is the most rarely used in the case of annual premium policies, since to pay the full premium and receive back the company's check for the dividend becomes simply a process of taking from one pocket and putting into the other. However, in cases in which the policy is paid up, dividends are often taken in cash.

Apply Toward Payment of Premiums. The application of policy dividends to pay part of the premiums is the most common method of using dividends.[21] Usually the company's premium notice will show the gross premium, the amount of dividend for the period just passed, and the net premium due, that is, the gross premium minus the dividend. It is necessary merely for the policyholder to send his check for the net premium, which, together with the dividend, will take care of the premium due for that period.

Accumulate at Interest. If the policyholder so indicates, dividends credited to the policy will be retained by the company and accumulated at the guaranteed rate of interest specified in the policy, compounded annually.[22] If, however, the company should earn more than the guaranteed rate of interest, the earned rate will be credited. Should it earn less than the guaranteed rate, it must, nevertheless, pay the contractual rate. For example, today most companies guaranteeing 2% or 2½% on dividend accumulation are paying 3%.[23] Other companies are paying only 2½% except on those older policies that guarantee higher interest rates.

Companies may include a contract provision automatically applying accumulated dividends at the expiry of any grace period to the settlement of any arrears in premium or interest, if the accumulated dividends are sufficient for that purpose. If the dividend accumulations are insufficient to meet the full annual premium, they may be used automatically to pay the corresponding quarterly or semiannual premium but never to pay a fraction of these premiums.

If the dividends are not withdrawn (and are insufficient to pay a full quarterly premium), they may be applied to increase the period of time for which the policy will be continued in force for its full, face amount under the extended Term insurance nonforfeiture provisions.

The contract also usually provides that dividend accumulations may be

---

[20] About 20% of all dividends are paid in cash.
[21] Over 40% of all dividends are used to pay premiums.
[22] Approximately 25% of all dividends are left to accumulate at interest.
[23] Some, especially Canadian companies, are paying even more than 3%.

withdrawn at any time provided they have not been applied under a non-forfeiture option.

Practice in the application of dividend accumulation varies from contract to contract. In general, however, it is a reasonably well-established principle that a company will not allow a policy to lapse while it has in its possession dividends sufficient to pay the premium. This has been held the obligation of the company even in cases in which the policy provided that "no premiums shall be construed as paid, either wholly or in part, by reason of dividends remaining with the company under the accumulation option." [24]

If dividend accumulations are neither withdrawn, used for premium payments, nor applied under a nonforfeiture option, they will be included in the cash settlement made at the time the policy matures as a death or Endowment claim or upon the surrender of the policy.

Dividends left to accumulate can amount to a rather sizable sum over a period of time. For example, although present dividend and interest scales are not guaranteed, in one representative company, dividends left to accumulate under a $10,000 continuous-premium Whole Life policy issued today at age 35 would, at age 65, add $3,936 to the $5,468 guaranteed cash values in the policy. In terms of retirement income, the dividend accumulations would increase the monthly life income from $33.70 to $57.90, male, 120 months certain. Dividend accumulations, therefore, can substantially increase the retirement values in an insurance program.

Paid-up Additions. The policy contract usually provides that, upon the election of the policyholder, sums credited as dividends may be applied to the purchase of additional participating insurance, usually referred to as "dividend additions." [25] Providing insurance at net, single-premium rates, these options represent the least expensive way a policyholder can purchase insurance since no charge is added to the rate for expenses.[26] For example, the gross rate at age 28 for a $1,000 single-premium Whole Life policy in one representative company is $466.58, over 46% of the face of the policy. In this same company, a policy dividend of $1 at age 28 will buy $2.51 of paid-up insurance. The effective rate here is only about 40% of the amount of insurance since it is the net rather than the gross rate. These paid-up additions are generally eligible for future dividends along with the original contract.

Table 4 indicates the amount of paid-up insurance purchased in a repre-

---

[24] Cf. Indianapolis Life v. Powell, *104 S.W.* (*2d*) 157 (*Tex. Civ. App. 1937*).

[25] About 15% of the dividends are used to add insurance.

[26] "Net rate" used here means gross rate less cost of operation and should not be confused with the same term used to designate gross rate less dividend.

sentative company by a cash dividend of $1.00 at the ages given for Whole Life and for Endowment at Age 65.[27]

Table 4. Amount of Paid-up Insurance Purchased
by a Cash Dividend of $1.00
(Whole Life and Endowment)

Attained Age	Whole Life	Endowment at Age 65
20	$2.95	$2.58
25	2.67	2.32
30	2.42	2.09
35	2.19	1.88
40	1.99	1.70
45	1.81	1.53
50	1.66	1.38
55	1.53	1.25
60	1.42	1.12

Over a period of years, paid-up additions can produce a substantial amount of insurance. For example, if dividends on a $20,000 continuous-premium Whole Life policy issued at age 45 were used to buy paid-up additions, by age 65 the amount of paid-up insurance purchased by the insured under one company's present dividend scale would amount to $4,840.

Companies usually provide that the paid-up additions may be surrendered at any time for a cash surrender value equal to the full reserve value thereof, which will always equal or exceed the original cash dividends.

Occasionally companies require evidence of insurability if the paid-up option is elected after the policy has been in force for a period of time. The justification, of course, is the elimination of adverse selection in the use of the option.

Accelerative Endowment Option. Dividends may be used in one of two ways to shorten an endowment period or to convert a Whole Life policy into an Endowment. Under one plan, dividends are accumulated at interest until their total value plus the policy cash value equals the face value of the policy. At this point the company, at the insured's option, will pay the face amount to the insured as a matured endowment. For example, the $20,000 continuous-premium Whole Life policy issued at age 45 could mature as an Endowment at age 75 if dividends were left to accumulate at interest. At age 75, the cash value of the policy plus the value of the accumulated dividends equals $20,000. If the policyholder under this plan dies before age 75, his estate collects both the policy face and the accumulated dividends.

A less common plan is to apply the dividends directly to the cash value

---

[27] These rates are those of one company. Rates of other companies vary slightly.

of the policy in the year in which they are paid. Cash values accumulate faster under this plan for two reasons: (1) cash values are increased by the amount of the dividends themselves, and (2) with higher cash values there is, in effect, actually less insurance at risk.[28] This means that a greater proportion of the future premiums collected can be used to build the cash value and less will go to pay the cost of insurance. The ultimate effect is that the cash value will equal the face of the policy more quickly, and the policy will endow even earlier than under the "accumulated-at-interest" plan. This plan, known as the accelerative endowment, differs from the accumulated-at-interest plan in that at prior death, only the face value of the policy is paid.

Paid-up Policy Option. Dividends may be accumulated until they, when added to the cash value already in the policy, equal the net single premium for a paid-up policy at the attained age. The above $20,000 continuous-premium Whole Life policy issued at age 45 could be paid up at age 69 if the paid-up option were exercised at that time. If the insured dies before age 69, his estate collects the face of the policy plus the dividends. At age 69, the cash value of the policy plus dividend accumulations equals $15,812, the net single premium for a $20,000 Whole Life policy at that age. The policy could be paid up even earlier if the insured elects the paid-up option when the policy is issued. In this case, the dividends are credited directly to cash values rather than accumulated separately at interest. In this event, if the insured dies early, his estate collects only the face amount of the insurance. This latter variation operates the same as the similar variation discussed in connection with the accelerative endowment.

The application of either of these optional methods of paying up the policy saves the policyholder loading costs allocated to the remaining premiums, which no longer have to be paid.[29]

Which Dividend Option to Select. The problem of selecting a dividend option is by no means simple. No cut and dried answer is possible, although several guideposts may be established.

If the policyholder is operating on a tight budget, perhaps the only choice he has is to take his dividends in cash or use them to pay premiums. If on the other hand he can afford to select one of the other options, he has to make a choice among paid-up additions, accumulations-at-interest, or

---

[28] Amount at risk has been defined here as the face of the policy less its cash value.

[29] Occasionally policy contracts provide other optional methods of receiving dividends. Examples of these are the additional annual-premium insurance option and the Yearly Renewable Term option. The use of these options when allowed requires evidence of insurability unless selected at the time the policy is issued (in which case insurability is automatic).

accelerative payments. If he feels that it is more important that he increase his death protection than his retirement protection, paid-up additions is the proper choice, assuming, of course, the Term insurance option is not available. Paid-up additions will increase both death and retirement protection but will increase death protection more.

If the need for retirement protection is greater, then the accelerative Endowment option is the proper choice. Under this option there is no increase in death protection whatsoever, as the dividends are used to increase cash values solely. Only the face of the policy will be paid upon death of the insured.

The accumulations-at-interest option seems to stand between the accelerative option and the paid-up additions option. It offers more death protection but less retirement protection than accelerated endowment and more retirement protection but less death protection than paid-up additions.

Since interest credited under dividend accumulations subject to withdrawal is taxable in the year credited, paid-up additions or the accelerative option might offer the best possibilities where a tax problem is involved.

The cash value of paid-up additions will almost equal the value of dividend accumulations. Thus the insured can have the benefit of increased protection through the years and then cash in his additions at 65, if he so desires, and have almost the same amount of cash as if he had left the dividends to accumulate.

At age 65 on the continuous-premium Whole Life policy of one company, for an illustration of the above point, the cash value of the accumulations based on a 20-year extension of its current dividend scale would be $3,035.80 for a $10,000 policy issued at age 45. The cash value of paid-up additions would be $2,950.60, or just 2.9% less. When it is held in mind that the interest on dividends left to accumulate is includible for income tax in the year credited, whereas the interest rate credited on additions is not, the net value of the additions is almost always in excess of that of the accumulations, in spite of the fact that the former had also provided what, solely from the point of view of this comparison, can be considered as "free" insurance.

3. OPTIONAL METHODS OF SETTLEMENT

The purpose of life insurance is to leave an income to take care of beneficiaries, upon the death of the insured, or to take care of the insured himself in old age. It is not the basic purpose of insurance to leave a capital fund [30] to be taken care of by the beneficiary or insured. In keeping with this

---

[30] Except to retire a mortgage or immediate debts, or to clear an estate. Cf. Chapter 16.

thought, life insurance companies have developed a number of income options which are now included in most life insurance policies. These options may be elected either by the insured or by the beneficiary. The insured's election naturally takes precedence unless a choice to change is left to the beneficiary.

The proceeds of the policy at maturity are paid to the beneficiary or policyholder in a lump sum, unless some other plan of settlement agreement is chosen.[31] The policy contract of one company states the matter thus:

(a) *By Insured.* The Insured shall have the right, with the privilege of change before this Policy becomes payable, to elect payment of the net proceeds payable by reason of the death of the Insured under one or more of the Settlement Options described below.

If this Policy provides for maturity as an endowment or for surrender for cash, upon such maturity or surrender one or more of the Settlement Options shall then be available for payment of the net proceeds to the Insured as Direct Beneficiary. The Insured may, with the privilege of change, designate one or more Contingent Beneficiaries under the election.

(b) *By Direct Beneficiary.* If no election is in force when this Policy becomes payable by reason of the death of the Insured, a Direct Beneficiary, in lieu of payment in one sum, may then make the election, except that Option E [32] may be elected only by two Direct Beneficiaries. Upon any such election, the interest of any Contingent Beneficiary designated by the Insured shall terminate. The Direct Beneficiary may then, with the privilege of change, designate one or more Contingent Beneficiaries under such election.

(c) *Limitation as to Availability.* Except with the consent of the Company, the Settlement Options shall not be available to any Direct or Contingent Beneficiary not a natural person taking benefit in his or her own right, or to any assignee.

If the net proceeds of this Policy shall be less than $1,000, or if the performance of an election would result in periodical payments less than $10, the Company may deem the election ineffective and pay the proceeds or the then commuted value in one sum.

(d) *Endorsement.* No election, designation, direction, revocation, or change shall be effective unless duly made in writing and until filed at the Home Office accompanied by this Policy for endorsement.

The most common optional modes of settlement offered by policy contracts are as follows: [33]

---

[31] Except in Family Income or Family Maintenance policies where the insuring clause agrees to pay, not cash, but an income of so much a month for a stated period or to a stated date.

[32] Joint and Last Survivorship.

[33] About 28% of the aggregate Ordinary and Group death benefits, matured Endowments, and cash surrender values in a typical year are now settled on an income basis. This figure compares with 10% in 1930 and indicates improved insurance planning.

Interest Only. Under the interest-only option, sometimes called the "deposit option" because it resembles money on deposit in a bank, the company holds all or a part of the proceeds or cash values and pays the beneficiary or the insured a contractually guaranteed rate of interest or a higher rate as may be determined annually by the company in view of its earnings. The policyholder may provide, if he wishes, that no part of the principal sum shall ever be withdrawn by the primary beneficiary, being payable to a secondary beneficiary or to the estate of either the beneficiary or policyholder [34] upon death of the primary beneficiary.

The policyholder may, on the other hand, direct that the proceeds be held at interest with the right of the beneficiary to withdraw in whole or in part. For example, a policyholder might direct that proceeds from a $20,000 policy be held at interest only, with the guaranteed or earned interest payments payable to his widow as long as she shall live, but granting her the right to withdraw principal amounts not to exceed $500 in any one year. A important use of the interest-only settlement with the privilege of partial withdrawal is to provide an emergency fund for the widow which she may use in case there are unexpected expenses beyond her income for the year. The withdrawal of any part of the principal sum will, of course, reduce subsequent interest payments. The policy might provide for the withdrawal of the full $20,000.

Another use of the interest-only option with right of full withdrawal is to create an estate clearance fund which will be needed soon after but not immediately upon the death of the insured. The interest-only option is better than the lump sum settlement for this purpose, since the fund will earn interest until it is actually needed. The policyholder also could direct that at his death the policy proceeds shall be held at interest until named children have reached a specified age.

Many varied uses of the interest-only option can be worked out. In the main, this option may be used economically when the proceeds either are very large or very small. In the case of $200,000 of insurance, the 2% interest option will yield $4,000, a sufficient income especially if there is Social Security or other estate income. If the proceeds are very small, the income which would be available at young ages under the life income option would be insufficient to support the beneficiary. For example, a $25,000 policy at

---

[34] Many companies hesitate to agree to pay any remaining proceeds back to the estate of the policyholder, as contrasted to payment to the estate of the last surviving beneficiary. Payment to the estate of the insured may necessitate reopening that estate a half a century or more after the policyholder's death. Moreover, it can be a factor in disqualifying the proceeds for the federal estate tax marital deduction. State laws on perpetuities may also be involved.

2% interest would yield an income of but $500 a year. At 3% it would yield only $750 a year. Neither income is enough to maintain even a subsistence standard of living. The beneficiary may find it better in this case to select the interest-only option and thereby preserve the principal. If she can work for several years to supplement the interest income, she can later convert the insurance proceeds into a life income at an age when such income will be enough to maintain at least a minimum living standard. If this is not possible, she can select now one of the shorter period options to be discussed.

The interest-only option is used also in insurance planning when there is reason to defer the payment of the policy proceeds to a later date. A common period for deferral is to the end of the widow's social security dependency income. As soon as the youngest child reaches age 18, the widow's social security income terminates until she reaches age 65. A $10,000 policy purchased to replace this social security income may be held at interest after the insured's death until it is needed. Some few companies will agree to hold the interest payments, too, and accumulate them at compound interest until needed; but most companies require the beneficiary to take the interest payments in cash. Many of these companies, however, will accumulate the interest during the period of the minority of a beneficiary. Such accumulations often are made under policies purchased to provide a college education fund.

Another reason for deferral is to take advantage of higher interest guarantees on older policies. Many policies issued before the middle thirties guarantee 3% to 3½%. Policies issued in the middle forties guarantee 2½% to 3%. Policies issued today guarantee only 2% to 2½%.[35] Newer policies should be used to meet the need for income over the first few years and older policies deferred for use in providing the income thereafter. These older policies are placed on the interest-only option until they are ready for liquidation under one of the other options.

The older policies not only carry higher interest guarantees but also assume mortality experience more favorable to the annuitant. Thus the newer policies would be better for fixed period income needs whereas the older policies would be preferable for providing lifetime income. The face value of the policy could be kept intact under the interest-only option until the newer policies are liquidated and then be placed on a lifetime income

---

[35] Whereas many companies guarantee only 2 or 2½%, they are paying higher rates in practice—some over 3%. Some companies make a differential between the guaranteed rate and the rate paid as applied to options which allow withdrawal privileges and those which do not allow them. Nonwithdrawal options in these cases pay higher rates of interest.

option. In this way, the beneficiary can obtain the greatest value from these guarantees. Unfortunately, however, some companies do not allow a beneficiary to use the interest-only option for a number of years and then change to a lifetime income option at guaranteed rates. In these companies, such changes can be made only at the lower rates then current.

Installment for Fixed Period. Under the installment for fixed period option—sometimes called "Installment Certain" or the "time option"—the proceeds are retained by the company and paid in equal installments over a specified number of months or years.

The fixed installment option provides that the proceeds will be held by the company and paid in equal annual, semiannual, quarterly, or monthly installments, including both principal and interest, for a definite number of years irrespective of whether or not the primary beneficiary lives out that period of years. Upon the death of the primary beneficiary, the payments either are continued to a secondary beneficiary or their commuted value is paid to the beneficiary's estate.

Under the fixed installment option, the length of the income period selected determines the amount of each installment. Interest computations on proceeds as yet unpaid are based on a rate specified in the policy, with excess interest being allowed when earned. Because under this option the principal sum is gradually paid out along with interest, the amount of each guaranteed installment is increased only by the excess interest earnings on the remaining principal. The actual amount paid in each installment under participating options, therefore, might well decrease gradually as the principal decreases, even though the total rate of interest paid remains unchanged.

The use of a limited option as contrasted to installments for life is recommended when it is desirable to have the proceeds of a policy paid out in a relatively short period of years to cover a particular need, and when the proceeds, if paid under a lifetime installment option, would be insufficient in amount. For instance, few would argue that it might be desirable to provide a widow with an income of $300 a month for life. If, however, a $20,000 policy will provide her, say, a lifetime income of only $60 a month, it will be better to pay the proceeds out under the limited installment option. In this way, the insurance will provide an income sufficient to permit her to maintain her family and educate the children even though that income terminates before her death. The children may be in a position to take care of themselves and their mother when the fixed period expires.

Specifically, a widow age 35 will receive about $60 a month guaranteed from $20,000 on a 10-year Certain and Life thereafter option. Under the limited installment option at 2%, she will receive a guarantee of slightly over $180 per month for ten years. If there is Social Security to supplement the $180, it may be adequate to support the children until they reach maturity. It is generally considered sound insurance planning to spread the insurance income thick enough to cover minimum living expenses over a short period of time rather than to spread it too thin over a long period of time to be of any real help. Table 5 shows the amounts of monthly income per $1,000 of proceeds which limited installment options will pay for different numbers of years at various interest assumptions.

Table 5. Guaranteed Installments of Principal and Interest per $1,000 of Proceeds

No. of Years Payable	Monthly 2%	Monthly 2¼%	Monthly 2½%	Monthly 3%
5	$17.49	$17.60	$17.70	$17.91
10	9.18	9.29	9.39	9.61
15	6.42	6.53	6.64	6.87
20	5.04	5.16	5.27	5.51
25	4.22	4.34	4.46	4.71
30	3.68	3.80	3.93	4.18

The time option was first used by company practice in 1867. About 1889, companies began including the option by rider. Soon thereafter, companies began to include the option in the body of the policy. Today these options are almost universally granted.

Installments in Fixed Amounts. The installments in fixed amounts option—often called "amount option"—provides for the payment of an unvarying annual, semiannual, quarterly, or monthly installment of a predetermined amount until the proceeds and the interest thereon are exhausted. The desired size of each installment determines the length of the income period, in contrast to the fixed period installment option, where the length of the period selected determines the amount of the income.

Since the fixed amount option provides for installments in definite sums, any excess earnings apportioned on the unpaid principal will lengthen the income period rather than increase the size of the payment. Any fractional amount of the proceeds and interest remaining at the end of the income period will be paid with the last full installment.

The advantage of this option is that the income is exactly the same each month until all proceeds with interest are exhausted. The beneficiary can budget with more assurance and exactness. Of course, unless adequate provision is made for continuing the desired income for a long enough period, there is danger that the proceeds may be used up just at a time when a continuation of the income is essential. Again, as in the case of the limited installments option, it is frequently better to be certain that the beneficiary will have a specified and adequate income for a limited period than a smaller income for life.

Table 6 illustrates the guaranteed length of time for which a given monthly income will be provided by various amounts of proceeds at 2% under this option.[36]

Table 6. Length of Time Various Incomes Are Provided by Various Amounts of Proceeds—2% (Amount Option)

Monthly Income Desired	AMOUNTS OF PROCEEDS						
	$1,000		$3,000		$5,000		$10,000	
	Years	Months	Years	Months	Years	Months	Years	Months
$ 50	1	8	5	3	9	1	20	2
60	1	4	4	4	7	5	16	2
70	1	2	3	8	6	3	13	6
80	1	0	3	2	5	5	11	7
90	0	11	2	10	4	10	10	2
100	0	10	2	6	4	4	9	1

One additional point should be kept in mind in deciding whether to select the amount option or the time option. Some policies mature at death with a loan outstanding against them. In such cases, the time option would reduce the amount of each periodic payment, whereas the amount option would reduce the number of period payments. This fixed amount option is one of the newer options, making its first appearance in 1901. It did not become rather generally used until the twenties and thirties.

Life Income.   Under the life income option, the proceeds of the policy are retained by the company and paid in equal annual, semiannual, quarterly, or monthly installments for as long as the payee lives. Much more often, the option guarantees payments for a minimum number of years, usually ten or 20. At the death of the payee, the present value [37] of any unpaid guaranteed installments will be paid in one sum to the executors or administrators of the payee or payments will be continued to, or commuted for, any named contingent beneficiary. There are then two life income options: those payable for life only, and those payable for a fixed number of years (or guaranteeing a fixed minimum amount of dollar payments) and life thereafter. This latter variation will be recognized at once as a type of refund annuity.

The life income options bring to the payee the advantages of the annuity

[36] Occasionally a company will guarantee higher interest rates under fixed period and fixed amount options than it will under the interest-only option.
[37] Usually commuted on the basis of 2% to 2½% compound interest per annum.

discussed in Chapter 5. If the periodic income available under the life income option is sufficient, then it is the most valuable of all settlement options, for it provides the insured or his beneficiary a given income for life.[38]

Table 7 gives the guaranteed monthly incomes payable for $1,000 of face value under the life income option for life only and for ten and 20 years certain using a 2% interest assumption.[39]

Table 7. Monthly Income per $1,000 at Various Ages Under a Life Income Option *

Age **		Life Only	10 Years Certain and Life	20 Years Certain and Life
Male	Female			
	20	$2.51	$2.50	$2.49
20		2.64	2.63	2.62
	30	2.79	2.78	2.76
30		2.98	2.97	2.93
	40	3.22	3.20	3.13
40		3.51	3.47	3.37
	50	3.87	3.81	3.63
50		4.33	4.23	3.92
	60	4.91	4.73	4.22
60		5.68	5.34	4.50
	70	6.68	6.04	4.74
70		8.02	6.82	4.91

* 1937 Standard Annuity Table, 2%, rated down one year.
** Male takes female rate five years older.

The problem involved in choosing between various certain periods and life only options are no different from those discussed in the chapter on annuities. Where the beneficiary has dependents, or has not yet reached retirement age, it is wise to select a period certain. The length of the period to be selected depends upon the length of the period of the dependency involved. A glance at Table 7 will reveal that a life-only option does not become very attractive for a woman until beyond age 60; a period-certain

---

[38] Do not be confused by the term "the insured or his beneficiary." The option is used by the insured to provide himself a retirement income with the cash values of a Whole Life policy or the proceeds of an Endowment. The option is used by the beneficiary (whether selected by the insured or beneficiary) to provide her with a lifetime survival income upon death of the insured.

[39] Some companies guarantee 2½%. To see the difference that 1/2% makes, the following figures indicate incomes at 2½%:

Life Only

Age	Female	Age	Female
25	$2.91	50	$4.08
30	3.05	55	4.51
35	3.23	60	5.07
40	3.45	65	5.80
45	3.73	70	6.75

feature also might prove profitable for an entirely different reason. A common practice of some companies is to pay dividends for excess interest earned during the guaranteed period but dispense with participation after the guaranteed period expires. Thus, if dividends are paid, the actual periodic payments received during the guaranteed period might be greater than those under the life only option.[40]

Joint and Survivorship. Some contracts include as an option the privilege of having the cash values or proceeds distributed as an income payable until the death of the last survivor of two persons. The option may or may not offer a minimum number of guaranteed payments and most often is selected when cash values in a Whole Life policy or proceeds of an Endowment policy are taken as a retirement income for a husband and wife. The joint and survivorship option guarantees income to a man and his wife as long as either shall live, whereas the use of the regular life income option would provide a retirement income only so long as the policyholder himself lives or for the guaranteed period, if that be longer. The joint and last survivor option also is used when it is desirable to provide a lifetime income for two beneficiaries, a mother and father, for example. The amount of each payment under the option is based on the ages of both beneficiaries. Some options provide for a decrease in the income upon the first death to about 2/3 of the joint income.

Table 8. Special Joint and Survivor Settlement
Monthly Installments per $1,000 of Proceeds

Male Age	Female Age	LIFE ANNUITY AS LONG AS EITHER LIVES Joint and Survivor Income	LIFE ANNUITY REDUCED TO 2/3 AT FIRST DEATH Joint Income	Income to Survivor
60	56	4.12	4.75	3.17
60	57	4.17	4.81	3.21
60	58	4.23	4.87	3.25
60	59	4.29	4.94	3.29
60	60	4.34	5.00	3.33
60	61	4.40	5.07	3.38
60	62	4.46	5.14	3.43
65	61	4.60	5.38	3.59
65	62	4.67	5.46	3.64
65	63	4.75	5.54	3.69
65	64	4.82	5.63	3.75
65	65	4.90	5.72	3.81
65	66	4.97	5.80	3.87
65	67	5.05	5.89	3.93

[40] Some companies allow no participating dividends under any type of life income option, whereas others allow participation under all life income options for the full life of the option.

Table 8 shows the monthly installments per $1,000 of proceeds payable under the joint and last survivorship option in a given company.

The option was first issued in 1901 as a special agreement. Now many companies will include the option by rider and some include it in the contract. It is the least popular of all the options.

Other Options. Most life insurance companies will, in addition to the optional modes of settlement offered in the contract, permit the election by the policyholder in advance of his death, or by the beneficiary thereafter, of any reasonable and sound mode of settlement. Many companies will, further, write special settlement agreements which they will attach to and make a part of the policy contract.[41] In other words, it is possible to use a life insurance policy not only as protection and investment, but also as what is, in effect, a trust. For example, some companies will write a remarriage clause in the option agreement under which the funds will be paid to the primary beneficiary (in this case the widow) as long as she does not remarry. Upon proof of her remarriage, the funds go to the secondary beneficiary. Notification and burden of proof of remarriage usually are on the contingent beneficiary or guardian.[42] A number of companies include a clause which makes payments for education contingent upon submission of a certificate of attendance at a college or university.

Advantages of Settlement Options. Among the most important provisions of the life insurance contract are those dealing with settlement options. It is through the selection of the proper options that better insurance programs are built. The use of income options rather than lump settlements has several advantages. (1) It demonstrates the importance of adequate insurance coverage by stressing the amounts of life insurance necessary to fill specific needs. (2) It enables the policyholder to leave an assured income to take care of his family rather than a principal sum to be taken care of by

---

[41] At the present time, it is the practice of some companies to provide in special settlement agreements that the options selected under them shall be the options, not in the policy, but those in use by the company at the time the option goes into effect. A number of observers question the ethics of this provision on the grounds that (a) it denies the policy the certainty which is one of the values of life insurance and (b) breaches the contract in effect if not in law. The authors have, on occasion, discussed this practice with company legal counsel and found that in at least some instances, counsel of companies following the practice doubt not only the ethics of it but also the legality. Remarked one counsel: "This is a practice forced on me by the actuarial department on the basis of so-called 'actuarial principles'; but I have never been able to get them to give me dollars and cents figures on the potential loss involved in standing by the options in the policy, and I dread the day I may be called upon to defend the provision in suit."

[42] Often the guardian and the primary beneficiary are the same so that such a clause might be ineffective. It is questionable, however, whether or not a remarriage clause is in the best interest of society.

his family. The fund is managed by the insurance company and not exposed to the hazards of investment by inexperienced hands. (3) It applies the annuity principle of liquidation and thus provides the largest possible return commensurate with the degree of safety afforded. (4) It enables the assured to take advantage of certain quasi trust services of life insurance companies. (5) It offers certain tax advantages which are explained in Chapter 17.

The actual use of settlement options in life insurance programming is discussed in Chapters 15 and 16.

4. SUMMARY

Life insurance policies contain three groups of options which are open to the insured (and his beneficiary): nonforfeiture options, dividend options, and settlement options.

The nonforfeiture options are cash, paid-up insurance of reduced amounts, and extended Term insurance. Dividend options include cash or offset against premium, paid-up additions, accumulation at interest, and accelerative Endowments. Settlement options include interest only, fixed period, fixed amounts, life income, and joint and last survivorship. If no settlement option is selected, the policy proceeds are usually paid in cash.

In order to get the most from his insurance, it is imperative that the insured study all his options and make the best possible selections in keeping with his objectives.

Questions for Class Discussion

1. Your uncle has a $20,000 continuous-premium Whole Life policy which has been in force for 30 years. He no longer wants to pay the premiums on the policy. What information would you need in order to be able to advise him in his choice of options?

2. When there is indebtedness outstanding and a policy is put on the extended Term nonforfeiture option, how do you explain the logic behind subtracting the debt from both the face value and the cash value of the policy?

3. Your roommate tells you he is going to purchase a $25,000 continuous-premium Whole Life policy and surrender it for its cash value in about 30 years. Would you say he is buying the wrong policy since he does not plan to hold it to maturity?

4. Assume that a friend of yours buys a $30,000 continuous-premium Whole Life policy at age 35. How much monthly income will it pay him at age 65 if he takes part of the nonforfeiture value as a paid-up policy for $5,000 and the rest as a retirement income?

5. Describe the circumstances under which you would recommend the selection

of each of the following dividend options: (1) cash, (2) paid-up additions, (3) accumulation-at-interest, and (4) accelerative Endowment.

6. Explain why a policy will mature earlier under the accelerative Endowment plan than is possible under the accumulation-at-interest plan of dividend application.

7. What factors should be taken into consideration in making a selection between the fixed amount and the fixed period options?

8. Describe as many situations as you can under which you would recommend the use of the interest-only option.

9. Why do some companies guarantee higher interest rates under some options than under others? Why do some companies guarantee higher interest rates for settlement options than other companies?

10. Under what circumstances would you recommend each of the following methods of settlement of a life insurance contract? (1) Life income 20 years certain. (2) Life income no years certain. (3) Joint and last survivorship income. (4) Lump sum.

CHAPTER 11

ACCIDENT AND
SICKNESS INSURANCE

LIFE insurance is designed to offset the loss of earning power caused by death or old age. Disability is an even more frequent peril to earning power. Death and old age can occur but once in a lifetime, whereas disability may occur several times. In fact, statistics indicate that on the average an individual suffers some important degree of disability from injury or sickness seven times during his life.

Insurance against income losses and expense resulting from injury or illness is called "Accident and Health," "Accident and Sickness," or "Disability" insurance. Disability insurance is probably the most descriptive of the nature and function of the coverage; however, the industry seems to favor the term, "Accident and Sickness," or "A & S."

One cannot claim to be well versed in life insurance without at least some knowledge of Accident and Sickness coverages, since both deal largely with insuring income, and life insurance companies write about 80% of the Accident and Sickness insurance premium volume in the United States.[1]

1. THE NEED FOR ACCIDENT AND SICKNESS INSURANCE

Injury and sickness can cause two types of financial losses: (1) Loss of income resulting from the inability to work, and (2) expenses of medical, hospital, and nursing care.[2]

---

[1] Life insurance companies write about 50% of all individual A & S premiums and about 90% of the group coverage; and more and more life insurance companies are moving into the A & S business.

[2] In these costs may be included the price of the "wonder drugs" so widely used today.

210

Statistics show that accidents cause almost ten million injuries and 100,000 deaths a year. Of those injured, 500,000 will suffer some degree of permanent disability. The sickness toll is even greater.[3] The Census Bureau has estimated that four million people a day between the ages of 14 and 64 are too ill to work. An individual's chances of having at least some type of illness over a 12-month period are four out of five. On the average, a typical family will have three illnesses a year requiring medical attention.

Annually, according to the American Medical Association, over 17,000,000 persons are admitted to hospitals and the number is increasing. The daily hospital census in the United States is approximately 1,500,000. Every third family averages a hospital admission each 12 months; and an individual's chances of being hospitalized in the same period of time are one in nine.

Medical treatment is even more frequent than hospitalization. One person out of 50 each year has medical bills totalling at least 25% of his annual income and one out of 100 has bills totaling 50% or more of his income. The national medical bill is estimated at over $6,000,000,000 a year and is steadily rising.

The annual wage loss in the country from accident alone is estimated at more than $2,500,000, and the loss from sickness is said to be three times that amount.

2. TYPES OF COVERAGE AVAILABLE

Although accident and sickness coverages vary widely, they may be classified into a relatively few broad, basic types.

Accident Coverages. Insurance against loss from accident only is the grandfather of all disability coverages. Accident insurance is still widely sold under separate policies and as a part of contracts covering both accident and sickness. Indemnities may be limited to lump sums or may also include a series of periodic payments to offset loss of time (income). In general, accident policies provide for the payment of fixed, scheduled amounts for accidental death and dismemberment, and for certain fractures and dislocations. The fixed, scheduled benefits for fractures and dislocations may be optional; that is, if the policy also covers loss of time, the insured at the time of the injury may elect these benefits in lieu of the loss of time indemnities. In addition to these specific lump sum benefits and weekly income benefits for loss of time, accident policies may also offer indemnities, up to a maximum, for the actual cost of hospitalization, medical, nursing, and surgical care. Certain "fringe" benefits may also be offered; for example,

---

[3] Of all working days lost from disability, sickness accounts for 90%, whereas accident accounts for only 10%.

double (or even triple) indemnity for certain uncommon causes of injury, such as hurricanes or tornadoes, lightning, or the explosion of a steam boiler.[4]

Sickness Coverages. Sickness coverages have developed more slowly than have those for Accident,[5] largely because of the lack of reliable morbidity statistics and because of the greater moral hazard involved.[6] Sickness coverage is never sold separately from Accident coverage; although some companies will issue a separate Sickness policy if the applicant already owns an Accident policy in that same company.[7]

With the exception of death, dismemberment, dislocation, and fracture benefits, the types of indemnities available under Sickness coverages are the same as those under Accident insurance.[8] Surgical benefits usually are included which allow a specified maximum for each of several types of operations "scheduled" in the policy.

Hospitalization Coverage. Policies are available which cover only the cost of hospitalization and, to a varying extent, the medical care incidental to such hospitalization. This type of coverage is the baby among the important Accident and Sickness coverages, although by number of insureds it is by far the most popular.[9]

Hospitalization policies cover two basic items: daily charge for room and board (and the floor nursing and routine services that go with it), and

[4] Double indemnity benefits also extend to the insured who is injured while a passenger in and upon a public conveyance provided by a common carrier for passenger service, or while a passenger in a passenger elevator car.
[5] Cf. Chapter 26, "Development of Life Insurance."
[6] Disability is not as definite and observable in sickness cases as in accident cases.
[7] Sickness insurance is not sold separately from Accident insurance for underwriting reasons. A request for Sickness coverage alone seems to be a red flag in underwriting. Underwriters immediately suspect that the person has some condition which he knows will soon result in a claim. Further, the public tends to overestimate the chance of loss involved in the Accident hazard as compared to the Sickness hazard—whereas the chance in the latter is far greater than in the former. Therefore, if a man does not want accident coverage (which he thinks of as a big hazard) but does want Sickness coverage, the indication is that he may have a claim in his hat. Another reason (which companies probably would not admit) is that Accident insurance is a reasonably profitable coverage. Sickness insurance is a touchy one. It can be a source of severe loss. Therefore, if the company is going to undertake the hazard which might cause them loss, it wants it balanced by undertaking the same amount of risk, simultaneously, which will be sure to make them a profit. The problem of underwriting Health insurance historically has been a tough one and the writing of it broke many of the early companies that tried it.
[8] Sickness benefits never include death. Death from sickness is considered "natural" and can be covered only by life insurance. There are no indemnities for dismemberments, fractures, dislocations, sprains, etc., because sickness does not produce that type of disability.
[9] About 100,000,000 people have some form of hospitalization insurance. Next in line is surgical coverage with 85,000,000 insureds.

the charges for special services such as operating room, laboratory, X rays, and drugs.

The basic form of the surgical expense policy, which may be purchased with or independently of hospitalization insurance, is a schedule of specified maximums that will be paid for various listed operations. The most expensive type of operation usually carries the highest maximum with others "scaled down." A typical schedule will list from 35 to 40 operations or types of operations, ranging from a maximum of, say, $200 for cutting into the cranial cavity, removal of a portion of the vertebrae, or removal of a lung or kidney, down to, perhaps, $10 for suturing wounds. Schedules vary in maximum amounts and in the proportions among the various operations listed. Most schedules also contain provision for unscheduled operations.

Medical Expense Coverages.   Medical expense coverage is of several types. It may be written to pay irrespective of disability or it may restrict coverage to expenses when the policyholder is disabled. An even more restrictive plan limits coverage to nonsurgical medical treatment only while the insured is hospitalized.

Three types of limitations are common in medical expense policies: (1) exclusion of the first few treatments (physician's calls) (2) a limit on the benefit per call; (3) an aggregate benefit that will be paid for medical treatment. Medical indemnity for house calls is usually higher than for office calls. -

Benefits may be added to most medical insurance plans to pay costs of diagnostic procedures not covered by hospitalization insurance. Amounts payable may be limited in a schedule for each of several types of diagnostic procedures involved, or they may be limited in aggregate amount.

A & S policies may include blanket expense coverage under which costs of accidents only as distinguished from illness will be reimbursed on a non-scheduled basis up to a maximum aggregate. Blanket coverage for sickness is available through Limited policies; that is, policies covering expenses for certain specified diseases only, such as scarlet fever, spinal meningitis, tetanus, diptheria, *et alia*. Expenses are covered on a blanket basis up to a specified maximum such as $5,000, $7,500, or $10,000.

Major Medical or "Catastrophe" Coverage.   "Catastrophe" medical is a relatively new coverage. It provides virtually blanket protection for medical and hospital expenses up to a given maximum but excludes coverage on the first several hundred dollars of expenses. This exclusion technically is known as a deductible, and most commonly is $250 or $500. The most common maximum limits of coverage are $2,500, $5,000, $7,500, and $10,000.

Usually the maximum applies to any one accident or disease. A new accident or disease, or the recurrence of an old one after a stated interval of time, is eligible for the maximum.[10]

A "coinsurance" feature,[11] under which the insurer pays only a certain percentage (usually 75% or 80%) of the excess above the deductible, is not uncommon in major medical contracts. The co-insurance provision is an attempt to hold down the medical and hospital bills.[12]

A variation of Major Medical plans is the Major Hospital Expense policy covering only those charges for medical treatment incurred after an initial period of hospitalization. The hospitalization requirement is considered by some authorities to be additional protection against unnecessary medical treatment.[13]

3. CLASSES OF ACCIDENT AND SICKNESS COVERAGE

Accident and Sickness insurance may be further classified as to merchandising methods or market appeal. Any system of classification has its overlappings and, at some point, must be wholly arbitrary; however, the following is a common classification system of Accident and Sickness policies:

1. Commercial
2. Industrial
3. Noncancellable, Guaranteed Renewable
4. Limited
5. Special Risk (or "Specialty")
6. Fraternal
7. Life Insurance Riders
8. Wholesale (or "Employee" or "Franchise")
9. Group
10. Blanket

Commercial. The term "Commercial" originally was intended to designate coverages sold primarily to white-collar workers in commerce and business as contrasted to the blue-collar workers in industrial plants. Distin-

---

[10] Except that in some plans in which coverage continues beyond age 60 or 65 (which are the usual termination ages), the policy provides that coverage will expire when the maximum has been paid on an aggregate basis after the stated age.

[11] Not to be confused with co-insurance as used in property insurance.

[12] Statistics indicate that medical and hospital charges vary in direct proportion both to the amount covered by insurance and to the income of the insured.

[13] If precautions against unnecessary and prolonged medical treatment and hospitalization seem to reflect on the medical profession, the reflection is not without support among medical men themselves who have publicly deplored unnecessary hospital admissions, unnecessary use of diagnostic and treatment aids, and unnecessarily long stay in hospital when the patient is covered by hospitalization insurance. Hospital staffs have been accused by members of the medical profession of ordering every laboratory test available in lieu of reliance on "the art of physical diagnosis." Cf. *Accident & Sickness Insurance,* David McCahan, ed., Philadelphia, University of Pennsylvania Press, 1954, p. 61 f.

guishing features of commercial insurance today do not include the color of the insured's collar. Commercial policies are usually issued for larger Principal and Capital [14] sums as well as for higher weekly indemnities than are Industrial policies. Premiums are payable annually, although they may be budgeted into semiannual or quarterly premiums by the addition of a small handling and carrying charge.

Commercial policies may offer the entire range of benefits for accidents alone or for accident and sickness combined.

Principal and Capital sums usually are written from $1,000 to $30,000 and income indemnities for total disability usually run from $10 a week on up and are payable over a period of a few weeks up to a lifetime.[15] Income indemnities for partial disability as a result of accident are commonly 50% of those for total disability and run for a more limited period, usually from 30 to 180 days. Partial disability from sickness is difficult to determine.[16] As a result, many Commercial policies make no provision for it. Others seek to define it in much the same way as partial disability from accident: "inability to perform some but not all" of the duties of the insured's regular occupation. Often benefits are payable for partial disability only when it follows a period of total disability. Hospitalization benefits usually are expressed in terms of a maximum per diem ($7, $10, or more) and are payable for a specified period (30, 60, 90 days, for instance).[17]

Optional (or "elective") indemnities for accidental injuries, consisting of stated amounts for certain fractures, dislocations, and sprains, are contained in most Commercial policies. The original idea of these stated indemnities was that they were to be elected in lieu of loss-of-time benefits for the kind

---

[14] The "Principal Sum" is the amount payable as a result of accidental death. The "Capital Sum" is the amount payable for "complete" dismemberment (loss of two limbs or both eyes).

[15] Sickness benefits usually are paid for shorter durations. For example, total disability from accident may result in benefits for lifetime while, in the same policy, those for sickness will be limited to not more than ten years. However, policies paying lifetime benefits for accident often will sometimes offer lifetime benefits for confining illness through a rider attached to the policy in those cases where underwriting evaluation of the risk indicates an unusually good physical and moral hazard. Usually benefits beyond the first few years require house confinement.

[16] Since disability from sickness is more difficult to define than disability from accident, it has been common in Commercial policies to require house confinement and treatment therein by a physician as a proof of total disability from sickness. However, since the house-confinement provision has caused much public misunderstanding, there is a tendency today to eliminate the requirement and to define total disability from sickness as a condition which prevents the insured from performing *any* of the duties pertaining to his regular employment.

[17] Some policies provide for a percentage increase in the loss-of-time benefit for hospital expenses instead of a per diem allowance. In connection with accidents only some policies pay the actual cost of hospitalization, medical care, etc., up to a specified maximum such as $500.

of injury that might not cause sufficient disability to be compensated fully under the policy definitions. Now, Commercial policies sometimes make the "optional indemnities" the minimum that will be paid for such injuries, and provide loss-of-time benefits also if the disability falls within the policy definition.

Surgical schedules often are found in Commercial policies ,and occasionally nursing fees are included in the sickness coverage.

Commercial policies are renewable at the end of the policy term only at the option of the insurer and often may be canceled by the insurer at any time.[18]

Not all Commercial policies contain every provision discussed in these pages. For instance, a policy may be limited to Capital and Principal sum alone; or it may provide loss-of-time indemnities without Capital and Principal sum. And do not be disturbed if you find benefits not included here.[19]

Industrial.   Industrial policies are sold on a weekly or monthly premium basis [20] with collections to be made by the agent at the policyholder's home or place of work.

Industrial policies usually are cancellable and renewable only at the option of the company, although noncancellable, guaranteed renewable Industrial policies are available.

The differences between Industrial and Commercial seem to be narrowing today, with the difference in method of paying premiums being in some cases the one big remaining distinction.

Noncancellable, Guaranteed Renewable.   Policies which cannot be cancelled except for nonpayment of premium and which are renewable at the option of the insured up to a given age (usually 60 or 65) are called "Non-

---

[18] Such cancellation or failure to renew is without prejudice to claims existing prior to cancellation. For instance, an insured might be permanently disabled at, say, age 25, by accident or some such crippling illness as polio. The company might cancel the policy the very hour it learns of the accident or illness (unlikely, but good enough for purpose of illustration); however, it would have to pay benefits for the duration of the disability or for the number of years promised in the contract. The cancellation clause often is misunderstood. Good companies do not insert these clauses for use as escape traps when the insured's health fades. They are put in chiefly as "stop-loss" protection against moral hazard. Studies show that cancellations or renewal refusals amount to as little as one half of one per cent of all contracts, and these figures include some few companies that are notorious in the use of both the cancellation clause and the right to deny renewal.

[19] All kinds of "frill" benefits are available. For example, there may be an indemnification benefit for the cost of putting a person injured away from home in communication with or in the hands of relatives.

[20] When the primary basis of premium payment is monthly, the policy is sometimes called "Intermediate" or "Semi-Industrial." Sometimes premiums in Commercial policies also are payable monthly. The privilege of converting the annual to a monthly premium is granted in Commercial policies by requiring the payment of an additional charge.

can." The abbreviation may be looked upon as undignified by the English purist and as nondescriptive by those of an actuarial mind. The fact nevertheless remains that the term is commonly used and needs to be recognized.

Since it is possible to issue a policy that is noncancellable, yet not guaranteed renewable, some confusion may easily be found in the use of the term "Noncan." Some companies and their agents have offered to the public as Noncan a policy which is not guaranteed renewable, with resulting disappointment on the part of some of the buyers. This type of policy is but slightly different from the cancellable Commercial policy. Failure to allow renewal is just about as effective an underwriting procedure as cancellation.

Inasmuch as over the years the term "noncancellable" has come to mean to the public and to most insurance men a policy which not only omits the cancellation clause *but also* gives the insured the right to renew at his option, it is generally considered misleading to refer to a policy which omits only the cancellation clause as Noncan. The term is correctly and ethically applied only when it refers to a policy which is both noncancellable and guaranteed renewable.

The types of benefits offered in Noncan policies are no different from those offered in Commercial policies and, except for more conservative limits, the range of benefits is comparable.[21] Since rates, as well as renewals, are guaranteed in Noncan, underwriters feel that they need to be more conservative.[22] They are not too eager to commit themselves for high limits years in advance since they have no way of knowing what the loss frequency and loss severity rates will be in the distant future. Moreover, it is difficult to underwrite the moral hazard over a long period of time. An unpredictable change in the circumstances of a risk can easily transform it into a moral hazard.

Noncan policies may offer benefits for the same duration as those found in Commercial policies. Generally, however, the benefits are for shorter

---

[21] The emphasis in Noncan usually is on loss-of-time benefits.

[22] Experiments in writing Noncan *without* guaranteed rates are being watched with interest in the industry as this is written. Since the rate is not guaranteed, the insurer can charge whatever loss experience indicates is a fair rate for any class or age group at any given time. In this way, the insurer is not unalterably committed to the original rate for the life of the policy regardless of changes in morbidity experience. A guaranteed rate must be "loaded" to allow for increased morbidity. Thus Noncan without guaranteed rates can be sold initially for less than policies with guaranteed rates. The "open rate," however, still gives the insured the guarantee that his coverage will continue as long as he desires (up to the maximum age). Although sound actuarially, there is still a question of whether or not this type of coverage is marketable. It might prove to be a source of policyholder misunderstanding if rates have to be increased sharply at some future time.

periods, and they do not offer benefits for sickness lasting longer than ten years.[23]

Limited. Limited policies are those covering only specifically named accidents or diseases. Examples are the "dread diseases" contract already mentioned and the "Travel Ticket," "Newspaper," and automobile accident policies. "Travel Ticket," once sold as an extra stub on a railway ticket, is now commonly sold over the ticket counter or, especially in airports, from vending machines. The coverage is limited to accidents occurring while a passenger on a common carrier on which the insured has purchased a ticket, and for the one trip alone. "Newspaper" policies, issued in conjunction with a newspaper subscription, are usually limited to a small list of accidents. Both types commonly contain a Principal and a Capital sum for death and dismemberment and a limited measure of expense reimbursement. Automobile accident policies cover accidents suffered while an occupant of a passenger automobile and, in some cases, as a pedestrian.

Although sold at relatively low premium rates, Limited policies are a source of public misunderstanding. The public, always hunting "bargains," is inclined to buy these policies without understanding that they do not pay for all accidents, not even for many of the more common ones. For that reason, Limited policies are usually surprinted on the face in red with some such warning as, *"This is a limited policy. Read its provisions carefully."*

Special Risk (or "Specialty").[24] Special Risk coverage offers the customary benefits or any combination of them found in orthodox Accident and Sickness policies but usually features higher limits and underwrites hazards not written in orthodox policies. Some examples are war hazards in this country and abroad; risks covering the nonappearance of an actor or other performer because of accident or sickness (written for the benefit of the employer, not the performer); loss of license by a commercial pilot because of disability; accident to amateur or professional athletes; human guinea pigs in scientific experiments; atomic and hydrogen bomb experiments; etc. Any list of perils underwritten by Special Risk is limited only by the imagination. The Special Risk underwriter never refuses to consider a case because of the unusual nature of the hazard.

Special Risk underwriting and rating is subjective; that is, it depends not upon statistics of past experience, but upon the judgment of the underwriter. Since a distribution of many like exposures is impossible under Special Risk

---

[23] At least the authors do not know any that will. However, with the growth of competition such a policy will probably come.

[24] One prominent Special Risk carrier further divides coverage into "Aviation" and "Special Risk." In effect, it establishes any special risk having to do with aviation peril as a separate classification.

insurance, underwriters substitute for it a spread of insurers (mass underwriting) through reinsurance.

Fraternal. Some fraternal organizations offer accident and sickness benefits to members, usually on a restricted basis.[25] It is common for certificates of fraternal coverage to exclude a long list of diseases and disabilities and to pay reduced benefits for still other diseases. Medical expense coverage is rarely found except on a need (charity) basis.

Life Insurance Riders. Life insurance riders offering accident or disability protection are not usually classified along with other accident and sickness coverages. Since they are written as a part of life insurance policies rather than separately, they are often by-passed in discussions of Accident and Sickness insurance. There is no reason to exclude them from this discussion. These riders are:

(1) *Double Indemnity for Death by Accidental Means.* A life insurance policy for a small additional premium may carry a rider agreeing to pay an additional amount equal to the face of the policy if death is the result of *accidental means* occurring before the end of the policy year nearest the insured's sixty-fifth birthday and within 90 days after the accident. Usually the extra premium for the rider is payable only during the regular premium-paying period, but not beyond the policy anniversary nearest the insured's sixty-fifth birthday. The provision does not apply to Paid-up or Extended Term insurance or to additions to the policy paid for by dividends from participating policies. It does not affect the regular cash values of the policy.

(2) *Waiver of Premium.* For a small extra premium [26] it is common to attach to a Life policy a rider providing that in the event the insured becomes permanently and totally disabled before age 60 (in some companies 65), premiums will be waived for the duration of the disability beyond a specified period, usually six months.[27] The Waiver of Premium benefit usually is not written for married women.[28] Since the gross premiums, rather

---

[25] Note the term "usually." Some larger fraternals offer coverages in every way comparable with regular insurance companies. See Chapter 26. In fact, these fraternals actually have pioneered a number of the coverages now considered standard. The discussion in the above paragraph refers principally to the hundreds of small fraternal societies to whom insurance coverage is only an incidental service.

[26] For the company, the chance of loss involved in the case of Waiver of Premium riders is relatively small (although the loss itself can be costly to the individual). For this reason, rates are extremely low. For instance: On a participating Ordinary Life policy with one company, disability waiver at age 25 male is $1.20 per $1,000 additional premium per year. On a 20-Pay Life policy in the same company at the same age, it is $1.02 a $1,000. On an Endowment at 65, it is $1.30 per $1,000. The premium charge for women is often more than the male rate for the same plan and age.

[27] The maximum age limit for women generally is five years lower than that for men, and the rate for women often is much higher than that for men.

[28] The Waiver of Premium rider issued to single women may contain a clause which terminates the coverage in event that the insured marries.

than the net premiums, are waived by the company, the disabled policy-holder continues to receive a full dividend on participating policies. The policyholder's relations with the company with respect to nonforfeiture values, death benefits, maturity values, and dividends are the same as though he had continued to pay premiums from his own pocket.

When there is no Disability Income insurance, Waiver of Premium in some cases has been used to provide the disabled policyholder with needed cash. The Waiver keeps the policy in force and continues to build its cash values. These cash values may be drawn upon by the policyholder for loans. As the policy values increase the loan may be increased.

(3) *Disability Income.* Disability income riders agree to pay a monthly income, equal usually to one half of 1% to 1% of the face of the policy, in the event that the insured becomes permanently and totally disabled. This income is paid for the duration of the disability,[29] beyond a specified period—again, usually six months.

Disability income riders are written to cover only *total* and *permanent* disability. *Total disability* is defined as any disability which will render the insured incapable of engaging in *any* work for pay or for profit. Although this is a strict definition, courts require reasonableness in its application. The strictness of the definition is designed to protect the company in border-line cases so as to keep the rate as low as possible. Certain disabilities are considered total by their nature. Among these are the loss of sight in both eyes or the loss of the use of both arms or both legs, or of one arm plus one leg. *Permanent disability* is defined as any disability continuing longer than a period specified in the rider, commonly six months. Accordingly, the loss of both arms is not considered permanent until after the waiting period.[30]

Disability income coverage under life insurance riders generally terminates at age 55.[31] Any disability which develops subsequent to age 55 is ruled out. One who is disabled before that age, however, continues to re-

---

[29] It may seem contradictory to provide that benefits for a *permanent* disability will be paid *for the duration of the disability,* since it would appear that, by definition, the duration of a permanent disability is for the life of the policyholder. However, legal cases have held that there need be only a "reasonable assumption" that disability is permanent for it to be so classed. Hence, a disability may be deemed legally "permanent" and yet recovery may eventually be effected. Consider also the implication in the following true story: During the days of the "Great Depression," a company was pressing a customer for payment of an account. Finally, the customer wrote asking for an extension of time. He explained, "I expect any time to start drawing permanent disability benefits, temporarily." The story is not a mere joke. This very type of "temporarily permanent" disability, certified by many physicians and upheld by many courts during the depression, broke the back of the disability income and Noncan disability insurance business for a generation.

[30] Ridiculous as it seems, this is nevertheless true.

[31] A few companies still write age 60 as the limit.

ceive his payments. As a rule, disability clauses are issued only on applicants under 50. Some companies have a limit of 45, whereas others will write applicants as old as 55. A maximum limit on income benefits is established by insurance companies.

When a Disability Income rider is attached to an Endowment policy, the disability income ceases at the maturity date of the Endowment. Formerly, the contracts provided for disability income until death of the insured, irrespective of the endowment date. Usually women are not granted the monthly income disability rider.[32]

Disability benefits are not payable for disability beginning after a policy is on an Extended Term or Paid-up insurance basis.[33]

4. THE A & S POLICY

For convenience of discussion the A & S policy will be divided into three sets of provisions: (1) Individual Policy Provisions; (2) Uniform Provisions; and (3) the Application. Since the A & S application is attached to and becomes a part of the usual policy contracts, it should be considered a part of the policy provisions.

Individual Policy Provisions

As in life insurance, there is no standard contract in A & S insurance. Certain provisions relating to what might be called the operating conditions of the policy are prescribed by law in all insurance jurisdictions, but all other policy provisions are up to the insurer. These unprescribed provisions are considered under this first heading. They include the Insuring Clause; Benefit Clauses and schedules; and Exclusions, Limitations, and Reductions.

Insuring Clause. Not only do insuring clauses vary as to their wording but also they have been subject to varying and sometimes conflicting interpretations by courts. Fortunately, however, these clauses have been somewhat simplified during the past few years. The following is representative of the type of wording widely used today:

> [The Company] does hereby insure the person named, hereinafter called the Insured, against loss resulting from accidental bodily injury sustained while this policy is in force, directly or independently of all other causes, or for sickness originating more than —— days after the policy date, pro-

[32] When they are, they commonly pay a higher premium. See Chapter 19.
[33] In addition to the above classes of A & S policies, there are additional ones: Wholesale, Group, and Blanket. These will be discussed in Chapter 13. Several other classes of A & S are sometimes recognized by various authorities. For example, Workmen's Compensation insurance offers accident, sickness, death, and dismemberment coverage and various medical benefit indemnities are also commonly offered in connection with liability insurance policies.

vided that in either case total disability commences while this policy is in force . . .

It is important to note that the insuring clause specifies that the accident or sickness must begin during the policy term. In other words, pre-existing conditions are excluded. This is customary with individual A & S policies. Group policies, however, ordinarily waive pre-existing conditions since compulsion, which is a part of Group underwriting, reduces the possibility of antiselection.[34]

As a precautionary measure to assure that claims for sickness are for conditions originating within the term of the policy, many insuring clauses insert a "probationary" period. Typical is a provision that the disease must be contracted after the policy has been in force for 14 days.[35]

As to accidents, note that the clause refers to "accidental bodily injury." Many older policies and some few current Limited policies require that the injury must result from *accidental means*. The difference in the wording is important in theory, although in practice courts do not recognize as much difference as the underwriters intend. Many courts have discarded the distinction altogether. Actually, however, not all "accidental bodily injuries" result from "accidental means." Only those bodily injuries which result from an act that is unforeseen, unexpected, or unusual result from accidental means. An injury, although itself unexpected or unforeseen, but nevertheless following from ordinary means, voluntarily employed, in a way which is not unusual or unexpected, cannot be considered as resulting from accidental means. For instance, a student undertakes to carry his trunk up a flight of stairs. In the process, he strains his back. He has suffered an *accidental bodily injury* but this injury is not a result of *accidental means*. A strained back is a possible if not probable consequence of carrying a heavy object up a flight of stairs. Legally, a prudent man is held capable of anticipating the possible consequences of any voluntary action he undertakes. If on the other hand the student while carrying the trunk trips over a number two iron (which happened to be on the top step) and falls, breaking his arm, the injury has resulted from *accidental means*. Tripping over a golf club is not a foreseeable consequence of carrying a trunk up a flight of steps.

The distinction between *accidental bodily injury* and *accidental means*

---

[34] In Group insurance, all eligible employees are automatically covered under a noncontributory plan; and under a contributory plan, 75% must participate for the coverage to be effective. Thus an average of health conditions is ordinarily obtained. A worse than average selection of risk is less likely to occur when Group insurance covers pre-existing conditions than it is if individual policies covered such conditions.
[35] The number of days varies from policy to policy.

is difficult to apply. For that very reason, the *accidental means* wording is used less and less all the time.[36]

Note the phrase *"directly or independently of all other causes."* Companies insert this phrase in the hope that it will effectively eliminate pre-existing conditions, such as abnormalities or diseases, as loss causes and restrict recovery only to those injuries caused exclusively by accidents. For example, according to the wording of the contract, if a man who is waiting at the curb for traffic to pass suffers a sudden dizziness and falls in front of an oncoming taxi, the dizziness is the immediate cause of any injuries sustained and they have not resulted "directly and independently of all other causes." It would seem clear that such injuries would not be compensable under the accident coverage of a policy. In cases where a disease following an accident causes death or disability, courts allow recovery if it can be shown that the injury set in motion the chain of circumstances resulting in the loss, regardless of a contributing or concurrent disease. For instance, if a young man suffers pneumonia following an automobile accident in which he was involved, it is possible that the contract will be held to cover for the resulting disability loss if it can be shown that the disease is the direct result of the accident. The recovery would be based on the *doctrine of proximate cause*, which can be defined as follows:

> In the event of the concurrence of several causes, the loss will be deemed to have been caused by the dominating peril so long as there exists an unbroken chain of cause and effect between the peril and the loss, whether or not the peril is active at the consummation of the loss.

Formerly, some insuring clauses in A & S policies specified that the injury must be a result of "external and violent" means, sometimes adding, "leaving visible wounds or contusions." Although now virtually extinct in A & S contracts, this wording is still common in Double Indemnity riders used with life insurance policies. Court interpretation of the term "violent," however, is liberal. It seems that the size of the force operating on the body is unimportant. The court considers all force violent, including the bite of a tiny insect. The "visible wound or contusion" clause nevertheless is strictly interpreted by the court so that for the beneficiary to collect under a Double Indemnity clause, the insured must have been in an accident sufficiently violent to have abrasions, bruises, or cuts on his corpse. An exception is made in the contract in the case of accidental drowning or of internal injury revealed by autopsy.

---

[36] It is still used in the Double Indemnity riders written in connection with life insurance policies.

Benefit Provisions. The kind and range of benefits offered in Accident and Sickness policies have already been discussed. It is necessary now to consider definitions found in the benefit provisions.

(1) *Nature of Dismemberment.* "Loss" of limbs is defined as "actual severance through or above the wrist or ankle joints" and "loss" of sight is defined as "entire and irrecoverable loss." [37]

(2) *Nature of Total Disability.* Four definitions of total disability are common today in Accident and Sickness policies.

A. Inability to engage in *any* occupation for wages, gain, or profit.[38]

B. Inability to perform any and every duty pertaining to one's *own* occupation.

C. Inability to engage in any and every duty pertaining to one's own occupation for a specified period (one, two, or three years, for instance) and inability thereafter to engage in *any* occupation for wages or profit.

D. Total loss of business time.

Actually, what constitutes Total Disability has been determined more by court decision than by the wording of contract provisions. Most courts adhere to one of three rules, referred to as the *Middle Rule*, the *Liberal Rule*, and the *Common Care and Prudence Rule*.

The Middle Rule holds that the inability of the insured just to carry on his usual occupation is not enough to establish total disability. Instead, the insured must be unable to perform any and every duty pertaining to the entire range of gainful pursuits in the light of his age. However, mere fanciful ability to engage in an occupation wholly beyond the insured's normal capacities will not preclude recovery. In other words, an insured should not be allowed to recover total disability indemnities if he can earn a reasonable living even though not able to continue in his former occupation.

The Liberal Rule holds that general or occupational total disability exists if the insured is unable to continue the duties of his *own* occupation. Ability to perform the duties of some other occupation does not preclude recovery even though earnings from it could be substantial.

The Common Care and Prudence Rule holds that the insured is totally disabled if work would increase or aggrevate his disability, endanger his life, impair his health, threaten imminently to shorten his life, or cause him pain or inconvenience.

While courts generally have recognized the distinction made in policies between occupational ("his occupation") and general ("any occupation")

---

[37] It will be recalled that, in the definition of total disability in the life insurance disability rider, reference is made to loss of *use* of arms or legs, or one of each. It does not require severance.

[38] This is the definition customary in life insurance disability riders.

disability in clauses combining them both, they have almost completely ignored any other distinctions. They have held to one of the three rules discussed—different jurisdictions holding to one or another of the three. So seemingly impossible is it for a carrier to write a definition of total disability that courts will recognize, that some companies have given up defining it and rely entirely on case law.[39]

(3) *Definition of Partial Disability.* Partial disability is usually defined as "inability to perform some but not all" of the duties required by the insured's regular occupation, or "inability to perform any major duty" of his regular occupation. Thus a typist with a broken hand would be partially disabled, but a receptionist whose main duty is meeting the public and making appointments but who does occasonal typing as a "fill-in" job might not be held to be partially disabled by the same injury.

(4) *Nature of Confining Illness.* While the trend seems to be toward defining the nature of total disability from sickness in the same terminology as total disability from injury, some policies require house confinement (and regular medical attendance) as a condition. In such cases, a hospital and, usually, a sanatorium are included in the definition of "house." House confinement usually is not considered to have been violated if the insured goes to the office of a physician or to a hospital for examination authorized by the physician, or if he takes a walk or does other things outside the house under the direction of his doctor if such activity normally is considered to have therapeutic value.

(5) *Nonconfining Sickness Definition.* Some policies do not require house confinement as a condition of total disability from sickness as long as the insured is unable to perform any of the duties of his occupation. Other policies, particularly those offering long-term or lifetime sickness benefits, may not require house confinement for total disability for the first several years, but will require confinement after that period. In some policies, partial disability will be defined in terms of nonconfining sickness: *"Disease which shall continuously prevent the insured from performing every duty relating to his regular occupation but shall not require house confinement."*

Limitations, Exclusions, and Exemptions. Whereas a Life insurance policy usually covers *all* deaths (except suicide within an initial period stated, or war and certain aviation perils), an Accident and Sickness policy covers only *some* accidents and *some* sicknesses. Each policy contains cer-

---

[39] It should not be assumed that the liberalized interpretation is a "victory" of the courts over "villainous insurance companies." Every restrictive word dropped increases the coverage which, in turn, increases the premium required.

tain Limitations, Exclusions, Exemptions, and Reductions. The following list is fairly complete.[40]

Accident exclusions

1. War or act of war, declared or undeclared.
2. Accident suffered while in the armed forces.
3. Suicide, sane or insane, and intentionally self-inflicted injuries.
4. Aviation accidents, except those of a passenger plane on a regularly scheduled passenger trip over an established line. (The trend is to include aviation except as a pilot, crew member, or when giving or receiving instruction, or performing duties aboard or requiring descent from an aircraft.)
5. Injuries contributed to by bodily or mental infirmity, hernia, ptomaines, bacterial infection, disease, medical or surgical treatment (except infection resulting from an injury, as blood poisoning from a wound).

Sickness exclusions

1. Pre-existing conditions.
2. Disability which does not begin during the term for which premiums have been paid.
3. Sickness suffered while in the armed forces.[41]
4. Sickness for any period during which the insured is not under the care of a legally qualified physician, surgeon, osteopath, other than himself (and sometimes, "not related to him by blood or marriage").
5. Sickness for any period for which indemnity is payable on account of accidental injury.
6. Pregnancy, childbirth, or miscarriage.
7. Illness incurred in the torrid zone (or, in some policies, outside the United States and Canada).
8. Disability from mental illness or venereal disease, or both.

Not all of these exclusions will be found in every policy, and some others not listed will be found occasionally.

Standard and Uniform Provisions

Standard Provisions. About 1909, state legislatures began to study the problem of unduly restrictive claim practices and other abuses in the A & S business. In order to offset much of this criticism, the National Association of Insurance Commissioners (then the Convention) drew up a group of standard provisions for Accident and Sickness policies. By 1911 this set of

---

[40] In addition to the accident exclusions listed below, the Double Indemnity rider used with Life insurance may exclude death from poison or inhalation of gas, riot, insurrection; or as a result of a law violation by the insured. The life insurance disability rider also may exclude law violations.

[41] Inasmuch as there is neither loss of income nor cost of treatment if accident or sickness is suffered in the armed forces, it works no hardship on the insured to exclude the payment of these insurance benefits.

provisions, with some state-by-state variation, was put into law in all jurisdictions; and the requirement was made that any A & S policy issued in the jurisdiction must contain this set of provisions exactly as worded in the law. Fifteen of the provisions were mandatory except in Group insurance, policies of co-operative insurers, and A & S riders on Life policies. In addition, the law set up five optional provisions which had to be used (one or more) if the policy mentioned any subject or subjects covered by these provisions.

Although no longer incorporated into new policies, many older policies still contain the standard provisions. Therefore they are of more than historical importance. The subjects formerly included in the standard provisions are now handled through the Uniform provisions, which are discussed in the next section.[42]

Uniform Provisions. In 1950, the National Association of Insurance Commissioners approved and recommended for adoption in all insurance jurisdictions a set of "Uniform Individual Accident & Sickness Policy Provisions." This set of provisions replaces the "Standard Provisions," which had become less "standard" with the passing years. Developments in the business had made some of the old standard provisions less applicable and these changes had been reflected in variations and amendments in the laws of the various states.

The "Uniform Provisions," however, cover the same general area as the "Standard Provisions," [43] but in somewhat different order and with changes adapting them to modern A & S insurance. There are 12 mandatory provisions and 11 optional ones. Moreover, the law establishes certain regulations involving policy conditions not embodied in the policy provisions themselves. The law does not apply to Workmen's Compensation, Reinsurance, Blanket insurance, or Group coverages. Disability riders on Life policies also do not come under the Uniform provisions law. The following is a brief resume of the content of each provision, preceded by its number and title as given in the model law.

The Mandatory Provisions

(1) *Entire Contract; Changes.* The policy and endorsements constitute the entire contract. Changes are valid only if endorsed on the policy by executive officer of company. Agent cannot waive any provisions.

(2) *Time Limit on Certain Defenses.*

---

[42] The standard provisions are not listed here but may be found by referring to a policy specimen form containing them. They are eliminated from the discussion since they are somewhat like the Uniform provisions.

[43] And they cover it in what is perhaps the most atrocious concoction of legalistic jargon ever inflicted on the public. For grammatical construction, those who wrote it would fail a freshman composition course in any accredited college or university.

a. In absence of fraud, no misstatement on the application shall void the policy or be used to deny claim after the policy has been in force three years.[44]

b. After three years, the policy shall be incontestable on the grounds of pre-existing condition.

(3) *Grace Period.* A grace period shall be granted for payment of premiums. (*The period must be not less than seven days for Weekly Premium, ten days for monthly premiums, and 31 for all others.*)

(4) *Reinstatement.* Reinstatement is effected without application if premium is accepted by the company. If reinstatement application is required and a conditional receipt is given with such application, reinstatement is automatic if the application is not refused 45 days from the date of receipt. A reinstated policy will cover only injuries occurring after date of reinstatement, and sickness which begins ten days after such date. The reinstatement premium cannot be applied retroactively for more than a period of 60 days prior to the date of reinstatement. (The last provision may be omitted from policies which are guaranteed renewable to at least 50 or for five years after age 44.)

(5) *Notice of Claim.* Written notice of loss or commencement of a claim must be given within 20 days of such loss or as soon thereafter as is reasonably possible. Notice to company or agent with information sufficient to identify the insured shall be sufficient. In case of loss-of-time benefits payable for at least two years, notice of continuation of the disability is required every six months, except for legal incapacity.

(6) *Claim Forms.* Claim forms shall be supplied the insured within 15 days of the receipt of notice of claim. If claimant does not receive such forms within 15 days, he will be considered as complying with proof of loss provision (number 7) if he submits written proof of the occurrence, character, and extent of the loss.

(7) *Proof of Loss.* The insured must furnish proof of loss for loss-of-time benefits within 90 days after the termination of the period for which the insurer is liable, and for any other loss within 90 days after date of such loss. In case it is not reasonably possible to furnish such proof in 90 days, it must be filed as soon as possible but in no event later than one year unless the insured is legally incapacitated.

(8) *Time of Payment of Claims.* Claims for specific losses will be paid immediately upon proof. Claims for loss-of-time benefits will be paid at periods specified in the policy but never less frequently than monthly.

(9) *Payment of Claims.* Death benefits will be paid to the beneficiary if designated, otherwise to the insured's estate. All other benefits are payable to the insured. This provision may also include the following:

a. Up to $1,000 of any indemnity payable to the insured's estate or to a minor insured or beneficiary [45] may be paid to any relative by blood or marriage deemed by the company to be equitably entitled to it.

---

[44] *Optional clause for policies renewable to at least 50 or for at least five years after 44.* After policy has been in force three years (excluding any period of disability), it shall become incontestable as to statements in the application.

[45] Or beneficiary otherwise incompetent to give a valid release.

b. At the option of the insured, indemnities for medical, surgical, and nursing services may be paid directly to hospital or person rendering the service.

(10) *Physical Examination and Autopsy.* The insurer shall have the right to examine the insured during pendancy of a claim and to perform an autopsy where it is not forbidden by law.

(11) *Legal Actions.* No legal action to collect a claim shall be started sooner than 60 days or later than three years after the time proof of loss is required to be furnished.

(12) *Change of Beneficiary.* Consent of the beneficiary is not necessary to any changes in the policy unless the beneficiary has been named irrevocably. (*Reference to irrevocable beneficiary may be omitted.*)

The Optional Provisions

If the policy covers any subject contained in one of the following optional provisions, then it must use the substance of the provision as set forth in the law. A similar provision which, in the opinion of the state insurance commissioner, is more favorable to the policyholder than the statutory provision may be used instead. Optional provisions numbers (1), (2), and (9) are the ones most commonly used.

(1) *Change of Occupation.* If the insured changes his occupation to one more hazardous or is injured or becomes ill while doing anything pertaining to a more hazardous occupation *for compensation,* benefits will be reduced to those that the premium would have purchased for that occupation, subject to the limits fixed by the company for such more hazardous occupation. If he changes to a less hazardous occupation, he may apply for a rate decrease.

(2) *Misstatement of Age.* If age is misstated, benefits will be those which the premium would have purchased at the correct age.

(3) *Other Insurance with the Same Insurer.* One of the following provisions may be used.

a. If the insured has other policies in force with the company aggregating more than a specified maximum, the excess shall be void and the premium for it will be refunded to him or to his estate.

b. If the insured has more than one like policy with the same company, he or his beneficiary may elect which shall be paid, and the premium for the others will be returned.

(4) *Insurance with Other Insurers.* If the insured has duplicating coverage on a service or expense-incurred basis [46] with other insurers and fails to notify this insurer, the company's liability shall be the pro-rata proportion that the company's indemnities bear to total indemnities under all policies.[47]

---

[46] "Service basis" policies are those which pay the hospital, physician, or nurse for services performed, such as Blue Cross and other prepaid hospital or medical care plans.
[47] For example, a policyholder who has two policies, each paying $200 for a specified accident, would receive only $100 from the prorating policy because its prorata proportion to all indemnities covering the same accident is one half. Premiums for the benefits not payable are returned.

The policy may define the nature of duplicating coverage.[48] If it does not, the provision will not be construed to cover Group, automobile medical payment coverage, coverage provided by hospital or medical service organizations, union welfare plans, employer or employee benefit organizations, third-party coverage, or benefits required by any compulsory benefit statute (such as Workmen's Compensation).

(5) *Insurance with Other Insurers (Covering other than expense-incurred benefits)*. This provision extends the pro rata other insurance clause applying to expense-incurred benefits to loss-of-time benefits. A company may use one, the other, or both, for that reason the optional provisions include two separate clauses.

(6) *Relation of Earnings to Insurance*. If the loss-of-time benefits under all policies owned by the insured exceed either his monthly pay at the time of disability or his monthly average for the past two years, whichever is greater, the liability of the company shall be for the proportionate amount of such benefits as the amount of the monthly earnings bears to the total amount of monthly benefits.[49] Premiums for the portion not paid will be returned. A minimum monthly benefit, however, is established. The provision also permits specifying the nature of "other coverages" and declares than in the absence of such specification, the provision shall not be construed to include the same kinds of coverage listed under provision (4). This provision may be used only in a noncancellable policy.

(7) *Unpaid Premiums*. Unpaid premiums may be deducted from claim payments.

(8) *Cancellation*. The insurer may cancel on five days notice and refund the unearned premium pro rata. After the initial policy term, the insured may cancel, effective upon receipt of notice by the company, and receive the unearned premium calculated on a short-rate basis.[50] Cancellation shall be without prejudice to claims arising prior thereto.

(9) *Conformity with State Statutes*. Any provision of the policy which, on its effective date, is in conflict with statutes of the state in which the insured resides at time of issue is automatically amended to meet the minimum state requirements.

(10) *Illegal Occupation*. Liability is denied if the loss resulted from the insured committing or attempting to commit a felony or engaging in an illegal occupation.

(11) *Intoxicants and Narcotics*. Liability is denied for any loss resulting from intoxication or drugs unless administered on the advice of a physician.

---

[48] Such definition is subject to the approval of the state insurance department.

[49] Assume an insured has two policies containing the above clause, each providing loss-of-time benefits of $200 a month, or a total of $400. At the time of disability, he was earning only $200 a month, and the average of his monthly earnings for the two years preceding was $185. Since he is currently earning only half as much as the total coverage written, each policy will pay only half the $200 monthly benefit promised. (How the framers of the model bill could parlay the explanation of this, as they did, into a 500-word provision containing only four sentences, one of which is 250 words long, is a feat that has the authors baffled.)

[50] The short rate provides less than a pro rata refund.

Other Requirements of the Uniform Provisions Act

(1) The entire monetary and other considerations must be expressed in the policy.

(2) Effective and termination dates must be expressed.

(3) The policy must cover only one person, although it may be amended to include a spouse and dependent children under 19.

(4) The type used in the policy must be at least 10-point [51] and must not give undue prominence to any portion of the text.

(5) Exceptions and reductions that are general shall be grouped under a descriptive head.

(6) Only rates, classes of risks, and a short-rate table may be made a part of the policy although not printed therein.

(7) A policy in violation of the Act shall be construed as though it conformed to the Act.

(8) No policy provision can restrict or modify the provisions of the Act.

(9) Statements on the application shall be binding only if the application is attached to and made a part of the policy; and if the insured requests a copy of a reinstatement application and does not receive it in 15 days, no statements on it shall bind the insured.

(10) Only the applicant can alter statements on the application.

(11) False statements on the application bar recovery only if material to the risk.

(12) Supplying claim forms, acknowledgment of notice of claim, and investigation of a claim are not waiver of defense against the claim.

(13) The policy will remain in force for any part of a policy term that goes beyond the age limit, and acceptance of a new premium after that term keeps the policy in force, subject to any cancellation provisions in the policy.

(14) If a misstatement of age leads the company to accept premiums beyond the age limit, liability is limited to a refund of premiums.

(15) The Act does not apply to Workmen's Compensation, Reinsurance, Blanket or Group, Life policy riders, or Annuity riders covering permanent and total disability.

The insurer, with the approval of the commissioner, may omit or modify any provision inapplicable to or inconsistent with the coverage provided in the policy.

---

[51] Ten-point is the size of the type used in the body of this book. It is one point larger than the type in which this summary of the Uniform Provisions is set, and is two to four points larger than most newspaper type. Furthermore, the old Standard Provisions—in effect for some 35 years before the introduction of the Uniform Provisions—went so far as to require that Exceptions, Exclusions, and Reductions had to be set in bold-face type. Thus the old canard about "the fine print" is nothing more than a "gimmick"; and it is noteworthy that critics of "gimmicks" in A & S policies often fall back on the use of a "gimmick" in their criticism.

The Application

The application which forms a part of the policy asks for the usual personal information for purposes of identification; it also asks for a description of the type of plan for which the application is made and the name of the beneficiary of the insurance. Moreover, the application searches for information about other insurance, declined applications, and the health and accident history of the applicant. For use in the underwriting of loss-of-time benefits, the application sometimes asks about the applicant's monthly earnings.

The applicant is requested to sign the application and it is on the basis of these questions that the policy is issued. In signing, the applicant signs a statement that he has read the answers and that they are correct [52] and agrees that recovery shall be barred if misstatements material to the risk are made with intent to deceive. [53]

The application usually states that the insurance will not take effect until there has been settlement for the premium and the policy has been issued as applied for. As with life insurance contracts, the policy goes in force on the date of the application if the first premium is paid with the application and the insured is an acceptable risk; otherwise, it does not go into force until the first premium is paid on delivery while the insured is in good health. If the settlement is partial, the policy will remain in force for a pro rata fraction of the original period.

Attached to the application is an authorization to any physician to give medical information concerning the applicant to the company or its representative. Medical examinations, however, are almost always required for noncancellable policies. They are sometimes required for broader coverage Commercial policies or may be requested if the facts of health history need clarification or checking for underwriting reasons.

---

[52] In view of the importance of the statements on the application, the applicant himself should fill it out. As a practical matter, however, since the applicant is unacquainted with the form and the form must be filled in so it can be photostated, it is universally the practice for the agent to ask the applicant for the answers and then write them on the form himself. Some applicants do, but no applicant *should* ever sign the application without reading the questions and the answers filled in by the agent. The authors wish to explain that this advice is no reflection on the integrity of agents. Anyone who has ever dictated to a stenographer knows the mistakes that can creep into the transcriptions of even the best shorthand operator.

[53] It is remarkable what a "poor memory" many applicants have when it comes to health history; and it is interesting how many applicants who obtained the policy by fraudulent concealment of details of poor health history will cry "fraud" at the insurer when claim is denied.

5. STATE AND SOCIAL INSURANCE COVERAGES

In addition to Accident and Sickness coverage supplied by commercial insurance carriers in the Life, Monoline, and Casualty fields, such coverages are offered in restricted form through state and social insurance plans.

State insurance is defined here as coverage provided by a carrier set up by a government, whether federal or state, and whether required by law or not.

Social insurance is defined for the purposes of this discussion as insurance required by law, whether issued by a state carrier or not. Several states [54] require employers to provide nonoccupational disability insurance for employees on a contributory basis. In Rhode Island the coverage must be placed with a state carrier; in the other states commercial insurers compete with state carriers for the business.

In 1946, the Railroad Unemployment Insurance Act of 1938 was amended to include cash benefits for any kind of disability injury or illness whether work-connected or not. The program is state insurance administered by the Railroad Retirement Board, an independent agency of the Federal Government.

Every state in the United States and every province of Canada has Workmen's Compensation laws based on the principle that industrial accidents and disease are a part of the cost of production and should be compensated regardless of who was at fault. These acts set up scales of benefits payable for death and for each type of injury. In about half of the jurisdictions, Workmen's Compensation insurance is compulsory. In the other half, insurance is optional but the liability of the employer is not eliminated. If he elects not to come under the act, he automatically waives certain common-law defenses, and his liability is theoretically unlimited instead of prescribed by schedule. A few states have monopolistic state funds; most states allow the employer to insure with private carriers.

6. HOSPITAL CO-OPERATIVE PLANS

Co-operative A & S insurance plans are set up by employees' associations, employers, unions, consumer groups, student groups, hospitals, medical associations, and medical clinics. They are frequently termed "nonprofit" plans because they are usually organized under laws exempting them from certain taxes imposed on commercial insurance companies. Chief among these plans in size and extent of operations are Blue Cross and Blue Shield.

[54] California, New York, New Jersey, and Rhode Island. Bills for similar social insurance in other states are being introduced constantly.

Blue Cross. The "Blue Cross Plan" is a name commonly applied to any of the various hospital service plans offered in different localities and loosely co-ordinated at the top by the Blue Cross Commission. The Commission, however, has little authority except to establish suggested standards and provide guidance to those individual plans which recognize it.[55]

Blue Cross is a system of providing hospital service and care as opposed to paying direct cash reimbursement or indemnity benefits to the insured. Hospitals agree to provide Blue Cross enrollees with given types of services at predetermined contract prices. The hospital is then reimbursed by the plan to the extent that the services used are covered by, and expenses incurred are within the limits of, the plan.[56] Blue Cross plans are usually established on a Group basis, although individual enrollments are sometimes permitted and community enrollments have been tried.

Blue Cross policies vary considerably from one hospital association to another, and even within a given association there may be some variety as to depth and breadth of coverage. Rates for identical coverage will vary by locality since hospital costs differ by locality. Blue Cross plans usually limit hospital accommodations to semiprivate rooms, since the current practice among hospitals is to charge the private-room patient more for all services, drugs, and dressings than is charged the ward or semiprivate patient. However, Blue Cross plans will make a per diem allowance on a private room.

The Blue Cross enrollee must go to a hospital co-operating with the plan in order to have expenses covered up to the policy maximum. However, when he must be hospitalized in a nonplan hospital, he is allowed a stated dollar per diem.

Blue Shield. "Blue Shield" is the general designation of the Association Medical Care Plans offered as a "running mate" with Blue Cross. A Blue Shield plan may be either a group practice plan or a medical prepayment plan. Under the group practice plan, the enrollee selects his physician from a list of those participating in the plan, and medical care of given types and up to scheduled maximums is supplied. Under the medical prepayment plans, fees within certain limits and up to specified aggregate amounts are paid to any physician or surgeon selected by the subscriber. Blue Shield plans sometimes provide that fees up to aggregate maximums over a given period will be paid in full for those subscribers who earn less than a given wage level. For subscribers earning above those levels the physician may charge an additional fee.

---

[55] Contrary to common public impression, the Blue Cross plan is not one plan on a national basis but is composed of a host of plans independent of one another using only the common name "Blue Cross."

[56] Limits are usually in terms of number of days of service rather than dollar amounts.

Such arrangements have not proved entirely satisfactory. Often the wage level set for full payment is unrealistically low; or the additional fee the physician charges above the minimum wage level is so great as to lead the subscriber to question whether his premium has really bought anything.

7. SUMMARY

Protection against expenses and loss of income resulting from accidents and sickness is one of the most essential of all insurance needs. The American public has only recently been awakened to this fact. As a result, the Accident and Sickness insurance business is growing by leaps and bounds.

The prospective purchaser of Accident and Sickness insurance is faced with a great array of policy forms. One researcher found 300 different contracts, no two of which were identical. Fortunately, however, most policies may be classified by coverage offered into several basic categories. In addition, policy forms available to individuals may be classified into commercial, industrial, noncancellable, and limited. There are also special risk contracts and disability riders on Life policies.

Commercial policies generally are restricted to insureds who are in business and professional work presenting virtually no occupational hazard. Typical of the occupations included in these classes (A through D in one classification manual) are bank clerks, college teachers, college students, professional billiard players, chefs, nurses, college athletic coaches, barbers, and insurance salesmen. Most of the personal accident and sickness insurance sold is of this type. Benefits generally are liberal, and the policies contain relatively few restrictions and exclusions.

Commercial policies cover every conceivable combination of benefits to suit the needs and whims of the buyer. The typical, liberal, broad-form policy will cover accidental death and dismemberment, double indemnity for death resulting from any of several types of accidents, medical expenses for accidents, weekly indemnity for total or partial disability caused by accident or sickness, hospital and nursing costs, and a specified surgical indemnity schedule. For example, a policy might provide:

$5,000 for accidental death and dismemberment with certain dismemberments graded downward to $1,250.

$25 weekly for total disability, lifetime for accident, starting immediately; one year with two weeks waiting period for sickness.

$10 weekly for partial disability, 26 weeks maximum, *accident only.*

$500 blanket for physician's or surgeon's fees, hospital charges, nurses' fees, *accident only.*

$12.50 weekly for hospital and nursing cost for a period not exceeding 20 weeks, *sickness only.*

$100 maximum surgical indemnity schedule, *sickness only.*

The cost of this policy varies as between companies and occupational classifications. Illustrative of premiums for the above policy is $67 annually for a college teacher (Class A) and $92 for a college athletic coach (Class D). These are illustrative premiums only. Any variations from them should not be considered evidence of extortion or philanthrophy on the part of the company quoting them. The above benefits, of course, may be substantially increased by payment of a higher premium.

Some companies term as *semicommercial policies* those issued to occupational classes E through H. Typical of these classes are filling station attendants, taxi drivers, private detectives, boxing instructors, R.F.D. mail carriers, and window-cleaning janitors. Semicommercial policies usually carry scheduled rather than blanket medical provisions and provide a lower scale for all benefits than does the typical commercial policy. For sickness benefits they often require house confinement. Sometimes they provide for one half of the regular benefit for total disability not house-confining. The rates for semicommercial policies are considerably higher than those for commercial policies. Semicommercial risks written to exclude occupational accidents usually can be written at Class A commercial rates.

Industrial policies are weekly premium policies. In types of coverage, they no longer vary markedly from Commercial.

Noncancellable policies are those contracts which grant the insured the right to renew to a specified age, usually 65. They are more expensive, require higher underwriting standards, may have longer waiting periods for sickness benefits, and usually are more restrictive as to limit of benefits than are commercial policies. Noncancellable disability income coverage is far behind the market for commercial policies.

Limited policies [57] are those contracts which restrict coverage to certain accidents or diseases such as automobile accident policies, travel and ticket policies, newspaper policies, and special disease contracts. The cost of these policies is in keeping with their severe restrictions.

Special risk policies are those that cover the unusual hazards where the chance of loss is not statistically measurable. Each case is written on its own merits and the policy is tailor-made. Examples of special risks are accidents in connection with participation in races, athletic events, and experimental projects.

Life insurance riders include waiver-of-premium benefits and monthly income benefits for permanent and total disability. They also include double indemnity benefits for death resulting from accidental means.

---

[57] All insurance policies are limited. There is no such policy as an all-risk contract, although the market is flooded with such policies in name.

An important development in disability insurance is *major medical,* sometimes called catastrophe insurance. This type of contract is written with a deductible amount of from $200 on up and with a fixed maximum benefit. It frequently requires the insured to share in the loss over and above the deductible. This is called a coinsurance requirement. This type of policy is well worth consideration; it represents true insurance, as it eliminates small losses. A $5,000 policy with $200 deductible would cost a man under 50 only about $32 a year (illustrative only). A $500 deductible would reduce the cost to $20.

Hospital care insurance is available on a service basis from co-operative hospital organizations, the most common of which is widely known as "Blue Cross." Medical expense coverage is available through the Blue Cross running mate, "Blue Shield." Although these organizations compete with commercial insurance carriers for the hospitalization and medical expense insurance market, they do not write disability income coverages. This market is left to private carriers, except in those states where a state fund competes for the nonoccupational disability income market for required coverage.

Although the Accident and Sickness insurance business is strictly regulated and the policies issued contain a number of mandatory and optional provisions, the buyer needs to be careful in choosing his coverage wisely.

Questions for Class Discussion

1. Which are more indicative of the need for disability insurance, the statistics on the *severity* or those on the *frequency* of accident and illness?
2. Twenty per cent of the illnesses account for more than 50% of the medical bills of the country. Does this statistic offer any suggestion to the prospective buyer of medical care insurance?
3. How do you account for the rapid increase over the past years in the amount of Accident and Sickness insurance written in this country? Why has hospitalization insurance grown faster than disability income coverage?
4. In an attempt to discourage government disability insurance, there is a tendency for industry spokesmen to quote figures showing how many people are covered by private insurance. Do these figures give a complete picture of the status of disability protection in this country?
5. Are the benefits payable usually more liberal under accident insurance or under sickness insurance?
6. In commenting on catastrophe medical insurance, one authority stated that there is a question "whether the primary purpose of any kind of health insurance plan is to cover financial losses essentially or, on the other hand, to encourage early diagnosis and care, and by such preventive measures reduce the ultimate volume of sickness and its attendant costs." Comment on this observation.
7. Can a person obtain comprehensive disability insurance protection from Blue

Cross plans? What would you consider to be a comprehensive disability insurance plan for yourself?

8. Even though states require uniform provisions how can you account for the variety of Accident and Sickness contracts?

9. A friend of yours asks if the disability insurance policy offered to him by the American Flag Insurance Company is a good policy. What would you need to know about him, the policy, and the company to give him an answer?

CHAPTER 12

INDUSTRIAL LIFE
INSURANCE

BROADLY speaking, there are three branches of the life insurance business: Ordinary, Industrial, and Group. Up to this point, the discussion has been concerned chiefly with the Ordinary branch; that is, with insurance purchased by individuals in face amounts, usually, of $1,000 or more, and paid for at the office of the company on an annual, semiannual, quarterly, or, occasionally, monthly basis. This chapter is concerned with the Industrial branch of the business.

1. DEFINITION

A precise definition of Industrial insurance is difficult inasmuch as it means different things to different companies, especially in the area of monthly-premium policies.

Industrial insurance is insurance issued in small amounts, usually in less than $500 face amount with premiums collected at frequent intervals. The most common premium interval is weekly, although monthly premium Industrial is also written.[1] Industrial premiums are expected to be paid to an

---

[1] Recently, some of the largest Industrial writers have begun to issue monthly premium Ordinary in amounts of less than $1,000 of face value. Thus some monthly premium business that formerly went to the Industrial branch now goes to the Ordinary. Inasmuch as the three traditionally largest Industrial companies, Metropolitan, Prudential, and John Hancock, in that order for many years, have begun issuing monthly premium Ordinary in amounts of less than $1,000, the apparent rate of growth of Industrial will probably be affected. Also, the switch to the Ordinary columns of much of the new monthly premium business has resulted in these three companies losing their leading ranking as the one-two-three leaders in the production of new Industrial insurance.

agent who calls at the door rather than to the company office, as in the case of Ordinary.

While there has been some tendency in recent years toward pricing and proposing Industrial insurance in terms of face amount, as is done in the case of Ordinary, traditionally the quotations in rate manuals have been in terms of amount of weekly (or monthly) premium. The sale is of a five-cent-a-week, ten-cent-a-week, etc., policy as contrasted to the Ordinary practice of selling a $1,000, $2,000 policy, etc.

The term "Industrial" originally developed from the fact that the insurance historically was intended to be sold to workers in industry—hourly wage workers, primarily. Today the term is somewhat confusing. There is a tendency among laymen to think that Industrial insurance refers to coverage purchased by the employer for employees—in other words, to confuse it with Group insurance. Further, while the bulk of Industrial may be in force on the lives of industrial workers, many an Industrial policy will be found in the insurance portfolio of commercial employees and professional personnel. For many people, Industrial was their introduction to life insurance —a policy purchased on them by their parents or by themselves when still very young. In many a neighborhood of incomes far above the lower levels, the Industrial agent is thought of as "our insurance man."

Since the term "Industrial insurance" is a misnomer, some writers prefer to call it "Weekly Premium" insurance. With the growth of monthly premium Industrial, this term is also a misnomer. The authors, therefore, have chosen to stay with the old term "Industrial" on the stagnant ultraconservative theory that "what was good enough for old Grandad is good enough for us."

2. STATISTICS ON INDUSTRIAL INSURANCE

Over 110,000,000 Industrial policies are in force in the United States, amounting to a total of about $40,000,000,000. Industrial life insurance comprises well over 10% of the total of all life insurance in force in this country. The average size Industrial policy is about $350.

The ownership distribution of Industrial is far different from that of Ordinary and Group. Men own only about one third of all Industrial life insurance in contrast to their ownership of about 80% of Ordinary and 88% of Group. Women own close to one half of Industrial, while about one fifth is on the lives of children.

Annually, Industrial insurance pays approximately $730,000,000 to policyholders and their beneficiaries, which is about one seventh of the total annual life insurance benefit payments in the United States.

Thus Industrial insurance plays an important role in America's life insurance picture. Actually, the dollar figures do not tell the whole story. In terms of policyholders, about two out of every three are Industrial, and about one out of every three persons in the country is covered by an Industrial policy. Far more people have contact with life insurance, and know about the protection it offers firsthand, through the Industrial branch of the business than through the Ordinary; and yet the Industrial branch is a far more recent development than the Ordinary.

3. ORIGINS AND DEVELOPMENT OF INDUSTRIAL

Although the life insurance industry in the United States and in America in general has progressed far beyond the development of life insurance in England, it is in England that the prototypes of most American life insurance policies and practices are found. This is as true of Industrial insurance as of Ordinary insurance.

Eighteenth and Nineteenth Century England. Industrial insurance originated in England. In the latter part of the eighteenth century and throughout the nineteenth century, the term "Industrial Insurance" was commonly used to designate the insurance feature of the Friendly Societies [2] as well as insurance issued by commercial companies with a face value less than £20 on any one life.

The development of the factory system during the eighteenth and nineteenth centuries created a need for insurance protection heretofore filled by the craft society. In addition to the craft societies, or guilds, the customs of rural helpfulness had succeeded up to that time in providing a degree of protection against sickness and death. However, neither the craft guilds nor rural customs provided adequately for members of an industrial community, which was neither rural nor craft organized.

As industrialization grew in English communities of the eighteenth and nineteenth centuries, and as the protection afforded by the craft guilds and by rural custom proved to be inadequate, local burial societies were formed. These societies used little, if any, actuarial science. [3] They were continuously in trouble, and, as a result, were superseded by larger societies known as "central" or "general" societies, which eventually established branches known as "affiliated" societies. These sought to take care of the insurance needs of industrial workers and miners. They made it a practice to collect

---

[2] Cf. Chapter 26.
[3] Premiums were not scientifically calculated nor were adequate reserves maintained.

premiums by personal solicitation on weekly or other regular but short-term bases.

In time, the general societies were themselves plagued with abuses, insolvencies, and dishonesty. The result was parliamentary investigation. For instance, in August, 1853, a parliamentary "Select Committee on Assurance Associations" made an exhaustive report, pointing out Industrial insurance abuses but strongly recommending further expansion of the system on a sound basis as the only solution to the insurance needs of the industrial workingman. The committee's recommendation was an indirect invitation to the strong companies of England to extend insurance to the lower income groups on a basis which these groups could afford. It thus set in motion the development of modern Industrial insurance.

First Companies.   The first British Industrial company was the *Industrial General,* founded in 1849. It remained in business for only a short time, being replaced by the *British Industry,* which was eventually taken over by the *Prudential of England.*

Modern Industrial life insurance business dates from the year 1854, when the Prudential of England decided that the time was ripe for a reputable Ordinary company to enter the Industrial field. In that year, it inaugurated a system of issuing life insurance policies for ages 10–60 inclusive in amounts smaller than available from Ordinary companies; and it adjusted face amounts to the size of the fixed weekly premium to be collected. For instance, a penny a week at age 20 purchased £8 10s.

The first Industrial policy was issued by Prudential of England on November 13, 1854, and the first claim was paid by the company on January 4, 1855. These dates are generally considered to be the first "issue" and "claim" dates in the history of modern Industrial insurance.

The Prudential of England tried hard to put Industrial insurance on a sound basis and made a painstaking effort to establish adequate mortality tables, but progress was slow and beset by sharp competition and criticism. An infant mortality table was, nevertheless, developed in 1856. Soon afterwards, policies were issued to age seven (in contrast to the previous minimum age of ten). It was two years later, 1858, when the issuance of Industrial insurance on the lives of infants began.

Industrial Life Insurance in the United States.   The introduction of Industrial insurance in the United States was made by the namesake of the Prudential of England, the Prudential Life Insurance Company of America, organized in Newark, New Jersey, in 1875, as the "Prudential Friendly Society." The Metropolitan and the John Hancock followed the Prudential four years later.

At the introduction of the business in the United States, policies were closely patterned after those issued in England. Premiums were payable on a weekly basis and collected by company representatives at the homes of policyholders. Policies were issued for 5¢, 10¢, 15¢, and upward, the face value always depending upon the premium at age of issue. The result was odd amounts of insurance.

For many years, the only insurance available on the lives of children was that obtainable through Industrial companies.

4. INDUSTRIAL POLICY CONTRACTS

While Industrial insurance differs only slightly from Ordinary in types of policies issued there are some significant differences between the two in policy provisions.

Types of Contracts.   Industrial offers many of the same types of policies found in the Ordinary branch of the business. The range is narrower but the present tendency is toward an increase in the number of forms. Whole Life paid up at 65 or 75 is more common than Whole Life paid up at 85 or continuous-premium Whole Life. Twenty-pay Life is also a common form. Twenty-year Endowment policies were once popular for children; however, in view of the decline in interest rates in the past two decades, many companies have stopped issuing short-term Endowments on a weekly premium basis, offering them, instead, on the less expensive monthly premium plan, both Industrial and Ordinary.

The scarcity of continuous-premium Whole Life and especially Term forms might be considered unfortunate since in theory, at least, the purchasers of Industrial are those who cannot afford the premiums on policies of $1,000 or more. One principle of insurance buying [4] is that when dollars available for life insurance premiums are extremely scarce, they should be used to purchase as much premature death protection as possible unless there are extenuating circumstances which would rule this principle inapplicable. Obviously the Limited-Payment and Endowment plans common in Industrial insurance do not buy as much face value per premium dollar as could be purchased under one of the Term plans.

Industrial insurers probably would argue that there are extenuating circumstances which would rule out the above principle. They would say that for a large number of people weekly premium life insurance is the only form of savings the policyholder has and that a Term form would eliminate this important savings feature. Actually, the Endowment form was introduced in 1892 and sold mainly as a savings plan. They also suggest that the

[4] Acceptable to almost everyone.

psychology of the Industrial buyer is such that he would not buy any insurance which fails to offer any "living benefits." Finally, they would recall that for the most part Industrial policies first issued in the United States were continuous-premium Whole Life. Limited-Payment policies were introduced later because it was found that the burden of continuous payments in late years was too heavy for the typical Industrial policyholder of that time.

As to the two sides of this argument, the conflict seems to be between what a man should do as against what he will do.

Policy Provisions. In general, the principles involved in and the provisions of the Industrial policy are similar to if not identical with those of the Ordinary contract. However, there are a number of important differences, most of them a result of the special nature of the business, the small size of policies, and the type of risks covered.

Because of the small amounts of insurance involved, the Industrial policy cannot economically offer some of the options found in Ordinary insurance. On the other hand, these small amounts make it possible to offer a greater degree of liberality in some provisions of Industrial than can be offered in Ordinary. The following are the major differences usually found:

Cash Values. The Industrial policy usually must be in force a longer time before cash and paid-up values become available. Although the period may be as short as three years in some companies, five years is more common.

Loan Values. Loan values generally are not provided in Industrial policies. Since the face value is small, the loan value would be small also, and therefore the cost of servicing policy loans would be disproportionate to the money involved. Assignment to a bank is usually permitted, however, thus making it possible for the Industrial policy to be used as collateral.

Assignment. Assignment of the Industrial policy is usually prohibited, as described above, except to banks as collateral for a loan.

Optional Settlements. Again because of the small amounts of insurance involved, Industrial policies usually do not provide for options of settlement. Sometimes such options are found in Industrial policies issued for a face value of $500 or more.

Dividend Options. Participating Industrial policy dividends usually begin not later than the fifth year on weekly premium policies and not later than the end of three years on monthly premium contracts. It is uncommon to find dividend options. Dividends generally are paid on one basis only, usually as paid-up additional amounts of insurance.

Nonforfeiture Provisions. Extended Term insurance is available as early as six weeks in policies of some companies and after six months, as in Ordinary, in many. After three years of premium payment, the Industrial policy usually gives the insured the other nonforfeiture options: a paid-up policy for a reduced amount or cash. Ordinary policies usually offers these options at the end of two years.[5]

Contestability. Industrial policies are contestable for only one year, becoming incontestable thereafter if the policyholder is living. A two-year contestable period is customary in Ordinary. Further, the only basis for contesting an Industrial policy is the failure of the insured to report on the application form treatment received for a serious physical condition within the two years prior to the application.[6]

Suicide. Since the amount of insurance involved in an Industrial policy is small, it is not deemed necessary to include the usual suicide waiver clause found in Ordinary.

Reinstatement. The Industrial reinstatement clause is more liberal than that found in Ordinary, and company practice in reinstatement is even more liberal than the actual terms of the clause. Industrial policies that have been in force more than five years and are not more than six months in arrears [7] may usually be reinstated without evidence of insurability. Premiums in arrears usually may be made a lien against the policy. This relieves the policyholder of the burden of paying cash at the time of reinstatement.

Change of Plan. Usually the Industrial policy contains a provision allowing the insured to change from the more expensive weekly premium plan to the less expensive monthly premium plan. Some companies also will allow a change from Industrial policies to Ordinary policies. The technical procedure in such a change is to shift the reserves from the Industrial policies to the account of an Ordinary policy issued in an amount equal to the total of the converted Industrial policies. The premium rate for the new Ordinary policy will be established on the basis of an age of issue which would have produced the amount of reserve established as of the present date.

Beneficiary Designation. Originally, Industrial policies did not provide for the designation of a named beneficiary. Instead, the policy was payable

---

[5] Since values are so small in Industrial policies, the choice of nonforfeiture provisions is withheld until the end of the third year because the expense of paying them—in contrast to granting Extended Term—would be disproportionate to the values received.
[6] The applicant is not expected to judge the seriousness of a condition for which he has been treated but only to report all treatment. Assume that he fails to report a visit to his physician ten months before application. If it turned out this treatment was for a common cold, it would hardly justify contest; however, if it turned out to be for, say, a malignancy, the failure would be grounds for contest.
[7] In exact terminology, a policy is "in arrears" when it is behind on premium payments but not yet past the grace period. Thus if the grace period is four weeks on a weekly premium policy and three weeks' premiums are unpaid, it is three weeks in arrears. (Grace is usually four weeks on weekly premium and 31 days on monthly premium Industrial.)

to anyone who appeared to the company to be entitled to the proceeds, especially as evidenced by possession of the policy or by proof of having paid the funeral expenses. The New York law now prohibits this type of beneficiary arrangement unless the beneficiary fails to surrender the policy and submit proof of death within the period stated in the contract.[8] In most policies issued today, a beneficiary may be designated just as in Ordinary insurance. However, the Industrial policy in contrast to Ordinary insurance contains a "facility of payment" clause. The following is an example of this clause.

> Such insurance shall be paid to the beneficiary, if any, last named in this policy, provided such beneficiary shall (1) Be of age and legally competent and (2) Surrender this policy with due proofs of death within thirty days after the date of such death; otherwise the company may make payment to the insured's estate or to any connection of the insured by blood, adoption, or marriage, appearing to the company to be equitably entitled to it by reason of having incurred expense on the behalf of the insured for maintenance, medical attention, or burial.

Note that the clause provides that if the beneficiary is a legal infant, or legally incompetent, the company may pay the proceeds to any relative of the insured who appears to be equitably entitled to them. The clause avoids the cost and delay involved in the appointment of an administrator or guardian.

In addition to the differences in similar clauses between Industrial and Ordinary, described above, the Industrial policy usually contains a number of provisions not customarily found in Ordinary:

Death by Accidental Means and Dismemberment. Double indemnity for death resulting from accidental means, available as a policy rider in most Ordinary contracts, is included in all Industrial policies and is automatically charged for in the premium. Also included is a dismemberment provision. Loss of two limbs or total loss of sight carries a lump sum benefit equal to the face of the policy, and the death benefit will be endorsed as paid up— payable whenever he dies without the payment of any further premiums during his lifetime. Loss of one limb or one eye carries a benefit equal to one half the face value and also makes the policy paid up.[9]

"Money-back" Option. The Industrial policy contains a clause allowing the insured to surrender the policy within the first few weeks (commonly two) and receive a refund of all premiums paid; that is, he is not charged

---

[8] "Which," according to the law, "shall not be more than 30 days."
[9] A payor benefit, under which premiums payable until the child reaches age 21 or so are waived in event of the death of the father, is available for an additional premium, as in Ordinary juvenile policies.

for the cost of the insurance protection he has received during the "approval" period.

Premium Reduction. Many Industrial policies provide that if the insured pays the premiums directly to a company office rather than to the house-to-house agent, he will be entitled to a reduction of, say, 10%. Some companies allow the policyholder who pays the premium directly by means of a money order to deduct the cost of the money order.

Difference in Underwriting Practices. Several underwriting practices differ as between Industrial and Ordinary:

No Medical Examination. Industrial policies do not usually require a medical examination. A medical examination is sometimes required at older ages, if the amount applied for warrants it, or if the application reveals a need for it. Even when required, the Industrial medical is usually both less intensive and less extensive than that given in Ordinary insurance.

Range of Standard. Many applicants who would be accepted for Ordinary only at substandard rates qualify for Industrial at standard rates.

Application Not Part of Policy. It is not customary to make the Industrial application a part of the policy.

Insuring Age. Age for the purpose of determining the rate of an Ordinary policy is age *nearest* [10] birthday. For Industrial, it is age *next* birthday. Thus for Ordinary, the applicant is age as of last birthday for six months; while for Industrial, he is age as of his next birthday one day after passing a birth date.

5. PREMIUM PAYMENT AND COLLECTION

Industrial Field Organization. The differences between premium payment and collection methods of the Industrial and the Ordinary branch of the life insurance business are so extensive as to create a noticeable difference in field organization. The Industrial field is divided into districts organized on a geographical basis. In less populous areas, each may cover several small towns; in large cities, each may cover only one neighborhood. The objective is to form a district which will require the smallest amount of traveling time, and hence maintain the highest possible ratio of collections per field hour. A manager is placed in charge of each district. His title is usually "district manager." He corresponds to an Ordinary branch manager. He supervises the work of the assistant managers, sometimes called "superintendents," and agents. The assistant managers help the manager in the selec-

---

[10] The authors contend that since one can be between only two birthdays at any given age, the term should be, "age *nearer* birthday." However, when it comes to trade argot, the better part of valor is to ride with the tide.

tion and training of men, help the men in canvassing for new business and conserving the business already on the books, settle death claims, and check agents' account books. The assistant manager is usually paid a salary, plus an overriding commission on the new business written by his men, plus an allowance for persistency of new business and the conservation of old business.

The Industrial life insurance agent, commonly called a "debit man," is charged primarily with the duty of collecting premiums on the "route" assigned him, even though the Industrial policy contract carefully specifies that the premium is payable at the Home Office and that it only *may* be paid to the agent. Secondarily it is the duty of the Industrial agent to sell new Industrial policies and Ordinary policies,[11] on which he receives a commission. He must also service the policyholders on his debit as new developments in family situations occur or as claims arise.

Each new Industrial policyholder receives not only his policy, but also a receipt book, and it is the duty of the Industrial agent to sign this book each time he collects the premiums. He, in turn, has a "debit book" in which are recorded the names and addresses of policyholders and the amount they owe per week. This is the agent's account book, which should correspond always to the receipts in the policyholder's receipt book. "Spot" checks by inspectors at a regular interval audit the agent's accounting.

A "debit" is the sum total of the premiums an agent is required to collect each week. A debit may consist of as many as 1,000 or even more policyholders. The debit book changes each week as surrenders and claims are deducted and new business and revivals are added. The debit work of the agent is expected to be completed by Thursday morning so that the rest of the week can be spent canvassing for new Industrial and Ordinary business. In most agencies, the policies written by an agent outside his own territory are transferred to the agent in whose territory they are written, in order to hold down the collection cost, which would be increased if an agent were to start collecting in geographical areas not in the line of his regular debit route. Usually an agent receives as many new policyholders by the transfer system as he loses, so there is little objection to the plan.

6. COST OF INDUSTRIAL INSURANCE

There is much misunderstanding about the cost of Industrial insurance. This form of insurance has been more widely criticized and maligned than

---

[11] Between one third and one half of all Ordinary is sold by combination agents—those who sell both weekly premium and Ordinary policies—according to Eldon Stevenson, Jr., speaking before the Life Insurers Conference, Colorado Springs, May 19, 1955.

any other branch of the industry.[12] Because the cost is demonstrably higher to the policyholder, critics have implied that companies make excessively large amounts of money on Industrial policies at the expense of the lower income groups for which they are primarily written. Actually the high cost of Industrial insurance can be explained on grounds other than excessive profits.

Premium Comparisons. Although because of differing policy contracts it is difficult to compare rates exactly, it is nevertheless true that Industrial premium rates are higher than Ordinary premium rates. The special study of Industrial insurance conducted by the New York State Insurance Department in 1937 presented gross premium comparisons between Industrial and Ordinary life insurance, as shown in the accompanying table. Spot checks indicate that the ensuing years have not greatly altered the comparative status.

Gross Annual Premiums per $1,000 of Face Value

Plan of Insurance	Age	Industrial	Ordinary
Continuous-premium	20	$23.01	$19.20
	30	31.71	24.48
	40	44.83	33.48
20-Pay Life	20	33.77	29.64
	30	43.33	35.16
	40	54.17	43.99
20-year Endowment	20	60.47	49.44
	30	63.41	51.12
	40	68.42	54.60

These differences, however, are illusionary for two reasons: (1) The Industrial premium includes dismemberment disability benefits and double indemnity benefits for deaths arising from accidental means, as described previously; Ordinary premiums quoted do not include them. The comparison cannot be validated by the simple addition of the disability and double indemnity rates to the Ordinary rate since the disability clause attachable to the Ordinary policy is much more liberal than that included in the Industrial contract. (2) Dividend rates affecting net premiums vary between Ordinary and Industrial insurance so that comparative gross rates do not tell the true story. For example, in one major participating Industrial writer the Industrial rate for a 20-payment Life issued at age 25 is about 19% higher than the same contract issued as Ordinary. In a major Nonpar writer, the difference between these two contracts is almost 28%.[13] Comparisons made at other ages and with other types of contracts will show different figures. These com-

---

[12] See *Investigation of Concentration of Economic Power, Temporary National Economic Committee,* Monograph 28, 1940, and Monograph 28A, 1941.
[13] The cash values of these Industrial policies, however, will be close to 9% higher than the cash value of the Ordinary contract at the end of 20 years.

parisons given here are intended only to show that comparisons on the basis of *gross* rates show results entirely different from those based on *net* rates. Comparisons made with Nonpar contracts tend to be somewhat more accurate since they eliminate one more variable, the dividend.[14]

The 28% differential quoted above, however, is not to be taken as a naked statement that Industrial insurance costs 28% more than Ordinary insurance. In fact, the New York State Insurance Department's study of Industrial insurance previously mentioned indicated that on the average Industrial was 15% more expensive than Ordinary, and that two thirds of this difference could be wiped out by paying premiums at the office of the company, leaving Industrial only 5% more expensive than Ordinary. The differences, of course, vary widely among companies.

Cause of Higher Premium. The higher premium rates of Industrial insurance result from three factors: (1) higher mortality costs, (2) higher cost of administration, and (3) higher lapse rates.

(1) *Higher Mortality Cost.* In the past, the mortality of Industrial policyholders has been much higher than that of Ordinary, especially at the younger ages. A recent study reports [15] that Industrial mortality is half again as high at ages 16 to 40, but only 14% higher at all ages combined. Current Industrial death rates are about on a par with those of the general population of the United States.

Two reasons for the difference in the Industrial and Ordinary mortality rates are: (*a*) Industrial is sold to lower-income groups whose living standards and health conditions have not, in the past, been equal to those of the average Ordinary buyer. The difference in the standards of the two groups, however, gradually is becoming less pronounced and this is one of the reasons why Industrial mortality rates are decreasing faster than those of Ordinary. (*b*) Medical selection is the exception in the Industrial case, and the range of "standard" is greater than in Ordinary, as already mentioned.

(2) *Higher Administration Cost.* The administration cost of Industrial is higher than for Ordinary. (*a*) Since the amount of insurance per policy is much smaller, the fixed costs involved in issuing a policy naturally will be higher for each dollar of insurance. (*b*) It costs money to handle a premium. Whereas the Ordinary premium may be handled once, twice, or four times a year, the Industrial premium will be handled 52 times. The expense

---

[14] See Chapter 24 for a discussion of the variable factors to consider in comparing the costs of various insurance contracts.

[15] H. A. Lachner, "Recent Trends in Industrial Life Insurance," *Insurance Lecture Series,* Storrs, Conn., School of Business Administration, University of Connecticut, 1954, p. 46. However, the Industrial death rate has been improving faster than the Ordinary so that mortality rates of the two forms are tending to converge.

of door-to-door collection also adds to the handling costs. A study of the costs of one large Industrial writer indicates that about 90% of the excess of Industrial over Ordinary costs is due to the additional service of collecting premiums in small amounts, at frequent intervals, and at the door. Operating expenses from 1939 to 1943 took 19.5¢ of the premium and investment income dollar in the Industrial branch, while taking only 11.3¢ in the Ordinary. Distribution expenses accounted for almost the entire 8.2¢ difference. In Ordinary insurance, field expenses accounted for 7.3¢ of each dollar; in Industrial insurance, these expenses took 15.4¢.[16] Another study indicated that the expense charge on weekly premium policies collected at the door exceeded that for monthly premium Ordinary by about 13%.[17]

(3) *Lapse Rate.* The lapse rate of Industrial insurance is higher than that of Ordinary. The higher rate is partly due to the greater frequency of premium payment. Each time a premium falls due, the policyholder is faced with the question, to pay or not to pay. Whether to yield to the temptation to use the money for present needs or to continue the insurance in force for the future protection of himself and his family has to be decided.[18] In the case of the Ordinary policy, he faces that decision once, twice, or four times a year. In the case of the weekly premium policy, he faces it 52 times a year. Obviously, the more times he is faced with the decision, the greater is the chance that the demon temptation will win over noble intentions.

A factor that is probably even more important is the fact that the type of people who purchase Industrial—again on the average—are more quickly affected by adverse financial fluctuations. Unexpected expenses or the temporary loss of income to which the hourly wage worker is more subject than the salaried man quickly affect the Industrial policyholder's ability and decision to keep up his policy.[19]

Three other factors are important in causing the higher lapse ratio among Industrial policyholders:

(1) *Improper Selling.* If a policyholder is not properly sold in the beginning, he is always a potential "lapser." Industrial insurance has undergone

---

[16] Malvin Davis, *Industrial Life Insurance*, New York, McGraw-Hill Book Co., 1944, p. 138.

[17] H. A. Lachner, *op. cit.*, p. 52.

[18] According to one great life insurance enthusiast, this question involves a serious moral principle. Speaking at the 1914 meetings of the National Association of Life Underwriters in Cincinnati, Professor S. S. Huebner is reported to have said that the proper education in life insurance would lead one to believe that a person has committed a crime if he dies without life insurance. Of the poor departed one, it should be said: "He did not die, he absconded." Cf. R. Carlyle Buley, *A Study in the History of Life Insurance*, New York, Appleton-Century-Crofts, Inc., 1953, p. 442.

[19] Labor is now making progress on its drive for the guaranteed annual wage so that eventually this factor may become of lesser importance.

serious criticism for high-pressure selling. A person who is pressured into buying something he cannot afford, for a need he does not understand, is a likely prospect for lapsation. Much of the high-pressure selling used by agents is caused by the pressure these agents get from their managers to meet quotas that are set too high. Spokesmen for Industrial insurance argue that cases of high-pressure selling are the exception rather than the rule. Be that as it may, high-pressure selling can cause lapsation, and lapsation is expensive—especially if it occurs during the early months that the policy is in force.

(2) *Improper Servicing.* This arises out of the lack of adequate training facilities for agents and from the high rate of turnover among agents.[20] Many companies, however, are making an effort to select and train their agents scientifically in order to improve the service available to policyholders. One way they have done this is by revising their agents' compensation systems in order to give more compensation for business which continues in force. The result has been to reduce the over-all lapse rate of Industrial insurance, since the agent gains by concentrating on quality business.

(3) *The Psychology of Industrial Policyholders.* This is a factor in lapsation. The Industrial buyer is less often accustomed to budgeting and less inclined to carry through with any plan that calls for a strict budget.[21]

Despite these inherent lapsation factors, the lapse rate of Industrial has not been too markedly greater than that for Ordinary. For instance, Lachner reports [22] that in the Metropolitan Life, largest of the Industrial insurers from the standpoint of business in force, the Industrial lapse rate in a recent year as compared with Ordinary was as follows:

Comparative Lapse Rates

Weekly Premium	Monthly Premium Industrial	Monthly Debit Ordinary	Ordinary
3.36%	3.08%	2.72%	2.52% [23]

[20] The better Industrial writers will resent this point. They will point out—and correctly—that their selection, training, and supervision plans are more careful than those of most Ordinary companies and that a high percentage of their agents hold the CLU designation, generally considered to be a mark of the professionally trained underwriter. However, we are speaking here in terms of averages. It is probable that while the major portion of Industrial is written by agents of companies with well trained field forces, these companies do not have the majority of agents by number.

[21] The difference between the inability of the Industrial policyholder to plan and budget and the inability of the Ordinary policyholder to do so is entirely a matter of degree. By and large, most people are negligent in budgeting and in carrying through on long-term plans.

[22] Lachner, *op. cit.*, p. 51.

[23] The Institute of Life Insurance reports a lapse ratio of 3.2% on Ordinary for a group of companies writing 80% of the business.

These ratios express the relationship between the number of policies lapsed or surrendered less reinstatements to the mean number of policies of that class in force during the year.

Lachner reports substantial reductions in the lapsation of Industrial policies within six months after issue. From 30% in the mid-thirties, it has dropped to under 8%.

In all probability, the lapse ratio among Industrial policyholders would show a positive correlation with the records of arrears in installment payments on household goods, regularity of deposits in savings pass books, and contributions to Christmas Savings accounts.

7. INTERMEDIATE INSURANCE

"Intermediate," like "Industrial," means different things in different companies. At their origin about 1890, Intermediate policies were in amounts of $500 or more with provisions for quarterly or more frequent premium payments. In general today (but not invariably) Intermediate insurance is composed of policies of between $500 and $1,000. They are written on an annual, semiannual, or quarterly premium basis, and are sometimes offered on a monthly basis, with door-to-door collection.[24] Since collection costs are lower, even when the policy is collected as frequently as monthly, somewhat more liberal benefits at standard rates can be allowed in Intermediate policies.

Intermediate policies form a relatively important part of the business of most Industrial companies. Policyholders applying for more than $499 of Industrial are encouraged to take monthly premium, "Debit Ordinary" instead. Although some companies write Intermediate up to a maximum of $3,000, most prefer not to write it in an amount over $1,000.

When the amount of an Intermediate policy is $500 or more, rates are more favorable than for Industrial. Some companies also issue Ordinary down to amounts of $500 if paid quarterly or less frequently.

8. SOCIAL SERVICE OF INDUSTRIAL

Some of the larger companies in the Industrial branch have been active in the health and welfare fields. Their activity in this field is not based on the assumption that the average Industrial buyer can profit more than the Ordinary buyer from health, sanitation, and safety education but that he is difficult to reach through the usual educational channels. The Industrial

---

[24] In some companies, the term "Intermediate" is applied to policies of $1,000 or more issued to persons ineligible for standard rates. The more common name for such policies is "Substandard"; although "Intermediate" may be less insulting to the policyholder. "Intermediate" has so many differing uses that the term alone connotes little until details are given.

agent, therefore, is used as the medium through which health information is distributed to Industrial buyers. Literally billions of leaflets and pamphlets have been thus distributed.[25] There can be no question but that some of the gain in mortality rates shown in Industrial insurance has been a result of the efforts of Industrial insurers and their agents in distributing health information in general and acquainting Industrial policyholders in particular with the many important health discoveries and disease treatments of the past 40 years.

One of the major Industrial companies discontinued[26] only within the past few years a "visiting nurse" system it maintained for Industrial policyholders without direct charge. The system resulted in over 100,000,000 calls by nurses on policyholders during the years it was in effect.

9. APPRAISAL OF INDUSTRIAL INSURANCE

Industrial insurance, admittedly expensive and viciously criticized at times in the past, nevertheless, has grown to tremendous proportions since its beginning. Today the amount of Industrial insurance in force is equal to 20% of the amount of Ordinary and over 10% of the total of all insurance in force in the United States.

Through industrial insurance, countless thousands of working people throughout America have received at least some small amount of money upon the death of a member of the family, to pay the cost of burial. Others have received cash from maturing Endowments, and still others have drawn on cash values to help out during times of emergencies. For many Industrial policyholders, life insurance represents the only form of savings. Industrial life insurance is filling a gap in available insurance protection, and no substitute tried to date has done as effective a job.

Savings Banks Life Insurance,[27] founded for the purpose of providing inexpensive insurance to low-income families, has never succeeded in blanketing the citizens of the states in which it is written to the degree that Industrial insurance has, with all its expensive door-to-door collector-salesmen. No critic of Industrial insurance has ever been able to suggest any better private enterprise alternative. Commissioner Sumner T. Pike of the

---

[25] Metropolitan alone has distributed about a billion and a half such pamphlets in the past 40 years. They have gone not only to Industrial policyholders but also to schools and the general public. The company has also carried on a long-term program of national advertising promoting health and safety.

[26] Reasons given for its discontinuance: (1) increasing health knowledge on the part of policyholders; (2) growth of other agencies, so that it came to be used by only a relatively small number of policyholders; and (3) increased cost of the service resulting from general rise in the price structure of the nation. Cf. Lachner, *op. cit.*, p. 54.

[27] Cf. Chapter 24.

Securities and Exchange Commission, one of the most bitter critics of Industrial insurance before the Temporary National Economic Committee (1938–1940), could think of no alternative other than federal grants for last illness and burial, or the sale of life insurance through the Post Office.

Post Office selling was tried in England and failed. It was tried in Japan and met with a reasonable degree of success. There is, however, no way of comparing the success of Post Office selling of small amounts of life insurance in Japan with what might have been accomplished there using the methods such as those employed by Industrial insurers in the United States.[28] Reference to the experience of the savings banks in Massachusetts, Connecticut, and New York, and to the Wisconsin State Life Fund [29] indicates that low-rate insurance sold by Post Offices in this country might not meet with any particular degree of success. Moreover, it would be naïve to assume that the quality of selling through the Post Office would be as good as, much less better than, that of Industrial agents. Buyers themselves, unfortunately, cannot be expected to have enough knowledge to decide for themselves what to buy.

As for federal grants for last illness and burial, the question resolves itself into one of political philosophy and a subject for the field of social insurance rather than a life insurance text.[30]

The proportion of Industrial insurance to total insurance has been dropping in recent years; but the drop has been a result of faster increases of other branches rather than a lack of growth of Industrial. Actually, Industrial has shown substantial growth, well over 50% more being in force today than at the end of World War II. It would have shown even more growth had not the three largest Industrial companies begun within recent years to issue monthly premium Ordinary in amounts of less than $1,000. At least one large Industrial company is even issuing weekly premium Ordinary.

The rate of growth of Industrial has been slower than that of the total of insurance in force for several reasons in addition to the reporting system of the three companies mentioned:

(1) Since World War II, all incomes have risen, but the lower income levels have risen even more markedly. Millions who, before the war, would have purchased Industrial have moved into income brackets justifying the purchase of Ordinary. Moreover, in view of high prices, the amounts of coverage offered by Industrial seem even more inadequate to buyers. People

---

[28] It must not be assumed, however, that the quantity of Industrial insurance sold is a measure of the quality of its selling.

[29] Cf. Chapter 24.

[30] See Domenico Gagliardo, *American Social Insurance*, New York, Harper & Brothers, 1955.

who formerly purchased Intermediate policies of $500 or $600 can now buy Ordinary policies of $1,000 without materially increasing their effective coverage.

(2) Social Security has cut into the market for Industrial insurance. Even for the purpose of providing a burial fund, the motivation in the past for the purchase of much Industrial, Social Security offers lump sum death payments equal to or greater than many of the Industrial policies once purchased for that purpose. In order to compete with Social Security, the combination agent has had to talk in terms of the larger amounts of insurance available through Ordinary, thus contributing to the rate of growth of Ordinary at the expense of Industrial.[31]

(3) The amazing spread of Group life insurance since the end of World War II has had its effect on the field of Industrial. It is in the highly industrialized areas that Industrial has lagged most. For instance, very little Industrial insurance is written in the New York City area compared to the population. Millions of hourly wage and lower salaried workers who would, in the past, have had nothing without Industrial insurance are now covered by Group at their places of employment at no cost or a very small cost to themselves. Some Group plans even cover dependents. Once again, to compete with Group, the combination agent must talk in terms of the larger amounts of Ordinary.

How much these factors will affect the growth of Industrial in the future remains to be seen. A downturn in the economy could make the amounts of insurance customary in Industrial more attractive again. Further, such a downturn could check the spread of Group. Employers operating on close margins or even at a loss would be less likely to add the cost of Group insurance to their operations. Unions might lessen their demands for Group if it came to a choice between insurance and maintaining the wage level.

On the other hand, continued prosperity will continue the spread of Group insurance and increase its benefits. Some states now prohibit the writing of Group on dependents of workers.[32] If all such restrictions were removed, it seems inevitable that the effect on Industrial would be drastic.

The continued expansion of Social Security, which also seems inevitable,[33]

---

[31] A development not without favorable social benefit.

[32] To some extent, these restrictions have been fostered or maintained by agents' organizations. They see in Group a threat to the agency system, which system, they contend (with some good arguments on their side), has been responsible for the high degree of development of insurance protection in North America and which is essential to the continued growth of insurance in force.

[33] "Inevitable" since both major political parties seem to favor it or to "adopt" it, at least, as a vote-getting or vote-saving device. Actually, it seems as though a national election and a new Social Security bill are becoming almost synonymous.

cannot fail to have an adverse effect on the growth of Industrial. It is common to point out that, since the inception of Industrial, there has been a very substantial increase in this form of insurance and that, therefore, Social Security has not seriously affected it. How much greater the rate of increase would have been in view of the great increase in national income and increase in population had there been no invasion of the field by Social Security is a matter of speculation. In the past several years, increases in Industrial have not kept pace with the growth of the economy.

However, it seems unlikely that the place Industrial fills will ever be superseded by other forms of coverage, either private or social insurance. There will always be people who, for one reason or another, need to buy "in smaller packages."

Further, neither Group nor Social Security offers the degree of personal service available through the weekly premium agent, who, because of his weekly calls at the home, tends to become not only an insurance consultant but also a general financial advisor, and a counsel on all family problems.[34] Neither the Group nor Social Security representative is in person at the door when the baby is born, when the young man or woman is married, when the grandfather is laid to rest—there to congratulate, advise, and console and to urge thrift and protection throughout the years.[35]

Before leaving Industrial insurance, one more point should be made in the interest of the buyer. If one can afford the premiums for Ordinary and does not need the budget compulsion of the weekly premium plan, then he should buy Ordinary. For example, a weekly premium of 30 cents at age 25 will purchase from one prominent Nonpar Industrial writer a $500 Endowment at age 65. These premiums amount to $15.60 a year. For less than one dollar a year more ($16.56), $1,000 Nonpar continuous-premium Whole Life can be purchased from an Ordinary writer at age 25. The $1,000 Ordinary will have a cash value at age 65 of $597. Thus, 96 cents a year more will buy $500 additional death protection to age 65, and $97 more cash value at age 65 if Ordinary rather than Industrial is purchased.[36]

10. SUMMARY AND CONCLUSIONS

While a precise definition of Industrial insurance is difficult because it is applied to different types of policies by different companies, in general

---

[34] Whether or not he is a qualified advisor on all family financial, psychological, and social problems is another question. Advice given by "untrained" experts often is worse than no advice at all, especially in the unusual case where it is followed.

[35] For some people, this is a real advantage of Group and Social Security.

[36] This is simply one comparison. Comparisons made between other companies, other ages, or other policies will yield different results.

it is insurance issued in small amounts, usually less than $500 face value, and collected at frequent intervals, most commonly weekly, by an agent calling at the door.

In general, the Industrial branch of the business offers about the same choice of policy forms as found in the Ordinary branch, although over-all there are probably not quite as many different Industrial forms as there are Ordinary. Term insurance in particular is not offered except perhaps as a part of policy combinations involving Whole Life or Endowment.

Most of the provisions of the Industrial policy are similar to if not identical with those in the Ordinary form. However, a number of differences are found. Some of the more noticeable differences frequently (but not always) encountered are these: Lack of loan values, options of settlement, and dividend options; fewer nonforfeiture provisions; earlier incontestability and more restricted grounds for contest; no suicide waiver; more liberal reinstatement provisions; death by accidental means and dismemberment benefits written as part of the policy rather than as a rider as in Ordinary.

Some underwriting differences are also noticeable in Industrial: Medical examinations of applicants are unusual. A wider range of physical and occupational condition is considered "standard." The application is not made a part of the policy. Insuring age is *next* birthday.

The cost of Industrial insurance is higher than that of Ordinary, but not as much higher as some critics have implied. This higher cost is a result of higher Industrial mortality, higher lapse rate, and higher administration cost. Industrial mortality runs about 14% higher at all ages combined than does Ordinary. The difference is greater, however, at younger ages. The lapse rate is higher, but, again, not as much so as often implied, and experience is improving. For instance, one large company reports that, in a recent year, its over-all weekly-premium lapse rate was 3.36% as compared to 2.52% for Ordinary. The lapse rate in the first six months has been greatly improved since the mid-1930's, when it ran at 30%. Today it is slightly under 8%. Administration cost is the biggest of the three factors accounting for the higher cost of Industrial. A study by one company showed that 90% of the excess in cost of Industrial over Ordinary is a result of the necessity of collecting premiums in small amounts, at frequent intervals, at the door.

"Intermediate" policies are, generally speaking, a class of business standing halfway between Industrial and Ordinary. The term is applied to so many types of business by different companies that, used without any explanation, it is almost meaningless. The most common application of the term is to policies issued for amounts of $500 to $1,000 face value. However, some companies issue "Intermediate" as high as $3,000 and some issue Ordinary as low as $500 if the premium is to be paid quarterly or less frequently. The Intermediate premium is lower than the Industrial.

In addition to spreading the benefits of insurance to millions of people who would never buy Ordinary, Industrial companies have contributed much to health, safety, and welfare activities. They have engaged extensively in health and safety education through distribution of pamphlets and leaflets to policyholders and schools and have even supplied nursing service to policyholders without direct charge.

The comparative role of Industrial among the three branches of insurance may decline, but its continued existence and steady growth seem assured.

Questions for Class Discussion

1. Explain why the term *Industrial* is a misnomer for the type of insurance it designates.
2. Among Industrial policyholders are many people who could afford Ordinary insurance. Does this necessarily mean that Industrial insurance is improperly sold?
3. How do you account for the fact that Industrial insurance is not written on a term basis? Is this good or bad?
4. In some ways Industrial policies are more liberal than Ordinary policies and in other ways they are less liberal. How do you account for the fact that these two classes of insurance policies are not identical in their contractual provisions?
5. Why do you suppose that the sale of Industrial insurance has not kept pace with the average rate of growth of life insurance in force in this country?
6. The New York Life Insurance Company is the largest "Ordinary" life insurance company in the world. Why do you suppose it does not write Industrial insurance?
7. Explain how the job of an Industrial agent differs from that of an Ordinary agent? Which job would you prefer? Why?
8. It is said that Industrial insurance is the most profitable line of insurance that the companies can write. Explain the reasons for this conception. To what extent is it true?
9. Industrial insurance often is severely criticized. Some critics feel it should be outlawed. Can you build a defense for Industrial insurance? If so, what would this defense be? If not, why not?
10. What do you suspect the critics of Industrial insurance would say in rebuttal to each of the points you made in defense of it in Question 9? Do you have answers for the rebuttal? If you made no defense for Industrial insurance in Question 9, what do you suspect the advocates of Industrial insurance would say in rebuttal to your reasons for not defending it? Do you have an answer for the rebuttal?

CHAPTER 13

GROUP LIFE AND
DISABILITY INSURANCE

THE FIRST standard definition of Group insurance was drawn up by the National Association of Insurance Commissioners in 1918, and subsequently adopted by many states. Although amended since that time in ways to be described later, it is still a good description of the basic and distinguishing features of Group life insurance. The following is a reproduction of this definition:

> Group life insurance is hereby declared to be that form of life insurance covering not less than 50 employees with or without medical examination, written under a policy issued to the employer, the premium on which is to be paid by the employer or by the employer and employees jointly and insuring only all of his employees, or all of any class or classes thereof determined by conditions pertaining to the employment, for amounts of insurance based upon some plan which will preclude individual selection, for the benefit of persons other than the employer; provided, however, that when the premium is to be paid by the employer and employee jointly and the benefits of the policy are offered to all eligible employees, not less than 75% of such employees shall be so insured.

1. HISTORY AND DEVELOPMENT OF GROUP

The meteoric rise of Group insurance in this country is one of the phenomena of the insurance business. The first policy was written in 1911 by the Equitable Life Assurance Society of New York on the lives of about 125 employees of the Pantasote Leather Company. At the beginning of the next year, the Equitable formed a Group department, and in July, 1912, it wrote $5,946,564 on the lives of 2,912 employees of Montgomery Ward and Co., a

260

case so large that it brought Group insurance immediately to the attention of the American public.

From that start less than 50 years ago, Group insurance has grown and prospered so that today over $100,000,000,000 is in force covering the lives of close to 50,000,000 people. Actually, at the present time, about half the country's working force has Group life insurance coverage averaging over $3,000 per person. Between $450,000,000 and $500,000,000 a year are paid out in benefits under Group life policies. Today, Group represents close to 30% of all life insurance in force in the United States, and the amount is climbing so fast that the figure quoted may be entirely out of line by the time this chapter is off the press.

Phenomenal as has been the growth of Group life insurance, its current growth is not as marked as that of Group Accident and Sickness insurance.

Several types of Group A & S coverages are available. The oldest is Group hospital expense, first written in December, 1929, on 1,500 school-teachers by the Baylor University Hospital, Dallas. Today, over 35,000,000 persons are insured against the expense of hospital care, and more are being added in staggering numbers each year.

In 1938, the first Group surgical expense plan was written. This coverage has proved equally as popular as Group hospital coverage so that the numbers insured are about the same under both types of plans. Group medical expense insurance was introduced in the 1940's; today over 15,000,000 are covered under such plans. Group major medical was introduced in 1950. The popularity of this form is growing so rapidly that it is useless to quote figures on it; such figures inevitably will be completely out of date by the time this appears in print.

At the close of World War II, the total Group A & S premium in the United States was about $200,000,000. At the present time, it is pushing toward $2,000,000,000. Based on the trend to date, it is not illogical to assume that within the next quarter of a century Group may become the dominant form of life and A & S insurance in this country.[1]

2. NATURE OF GROUP INSURANCE

As previously stated, the basic nature of Group insurance is summarized in the original definition drawn by the National Association of Insurance

---

[1] Whether the rise in the importance of Group insurance is good or bad is subject to violent argument within the industry. The acquaintance of the authors with the business and men associated with it—the adequacy of which acquaintanceship is beyond their subjective ability to judge—leads them to suspect that if the "gloves" of public relations were removed, the "sides" of the argument would be preponderantly the field forces of the business (the agents) worried about major increases vs. the home offices (the companies) viewing the rise as a major accomplishment.

Commissioners. This definition, however, has been subject to several revisions. While the definition has not been adopted by every state, it does serve as the basic standard operating procedure of Group today. The important changes in the Commissioners' current definition from the original are these:

(1) The minimum size of groups eligible for Group insurance has been reduced to 25, and in some states to as low as ten.

(2) Eligible groups have been broadened from employees of one employer to include (a) debtors of a creditor whose indebtedness is repayable in installments; (b) members of a labor union; (c) employees of more than one employer when grouped under a trustee; (d) employees of two or more labor unions grouped under a trustee.

(3) Directors of a corporation, partners in a partnership, or a proprietor in a sole proprietorship are not eligible for coverage in a Group plan unless they are *bona fide* employees or actively engaged in the conduct of the business.

(4) The maximum amount that can be issued on any one life under Group Term is $20,000.[2] This limitation does not apply to Group Permanent plans.

(5) When Group is issued to trustees of one or more employers or unions, there must be 100 persons insured under the plan and not fewer than five persons per unit.

(6) If the plan is established by members of an employers' association consisting of fewer than 600 members, at least 60% of the employer members whose employees who are not already covered for Group life insurance must participate.

(7) In the case of an employers' association Group, the coverage on the employees of any individual employer may not be terminated by the company if the employer drops out of the association.

The Commissioners' definition has been broadened by state law in many cases. For instance, the New York law in 1949 made two additional types of groups eligible:

(1) An association of civil service employees.

(2) One or more units of state troopers, state police, or policemen's benevolent associations.

Statutory Regulation. The model Group law of the National Association of Insurance Commissioners,[3] makes mandatory the following provisions in Group policies:

---

[2] While all the provisions of the standard definition are subject to state-by-state variation, this one is, perhaps, subject to the most variation. Some states have no individual limit at all.

[3] Not adopted in all states.

(1) Grace period of 31 days.

(2) Incontestability after two years.

(3) Application shall be attached to the policy.

(4) Statements made by the policyholder (employer or trustee) and participants shall be representations.

(5) Conditions under which the company may require *evidence of insurability*. For example, companies usually require under a contributory plan that an employee must make application for insurance within 31 days after becoming eligible or he will become subject to medical examination upon application for membership.

(6) Misstatement of age and how it is to be adjusted. Unlike ordinary insurance, the premium will be adjusted to the full protection accorded the employee by the benefit formula in use if the age of an employee has been misstated. This seems to be a more equitable arrangement than adjusting the insurance to the premium as in the case of ordinary insurance, because employees are entitled to the full amount of insurance arranged for them under the Group formula. Age should have nothing to do with the amount of insurance available. The cost of insurance to the employee under a contributory group plan does not vary with his age.

(7) Facility of payment clause in event there is no living named beneficiary. This clause allows the company to pay up to $250 of the proceeds to any person who appears equitably entitled to such payment by reason of having paid the expenses of final illness or burial in behalf of the insured.

(8) Certificates of participation shall be issued to each employee covered. The certificate states the insurance benefits, the beneficiary, and the rights and conditions of the insured in case of termination of employment or of the group contract. These rights are:

(*a*) If employment is terminated the insured may elect within 45 days and without medical examination to take an individual policy on any plan but Term for the same amount for which he was covered under the Group contract at the premium applying at his attained age.

(*b*) If the master policy is terminated an employee who has been covered for at least five years may take an individual policy on any plan except Term for an amount not exceeding the smaller of *either* the amount terminated less the amount of any new or reinstated Group coverage effected within 45 days *or* $2,000.

(*c*) In case the insured dies after termination of employment or of the master contract but within the period during which he had the right to take an individual policy, he shall be covered under the Group policy even though no application for the individual policy had yet been made.

Contributions. A Group plan may be either contributory or noncontributory. It is *contributory* if the employee pays any part of ("contributes toward") the premium. It is *noncontributory* if the employer pays all the premium. Originally the noncontributory plan was used almost always. It is much simpler in operation. All employees of the eligible class are covered. The task of selling the idea of coverage to 75% of those eligible as is necessary in the contributory plan is eliminated. Further, there is no problem of apportioning the cost among classes of employees. Record-keeping is much simpler because the employer does not have to collect money from participants, record the collections, hold the money until premium-due date, and handle all the other details involved. Also, the employer has more control over the plan when he is financing its full cost. Finally, the entire cost of a noncontributory plan is a deductible business expense under income tax regulations. Under the contributory plan, employees are not allowed to deduct their contributions from their personal incomes for tax purposes.

The depression of the 1930's seems to have been a major factor in the introduction of the contributory plan. Faced with narrow margins of profit or even actual operating losses, employers turned to the less expensive contributory plan. Throughout the 1930's the contributory form was predominant.

At the present time, however, the pendulum seems to have swung back once again to the noncontributory plan. In the first place, throughout the 1940's and into the 1950's the economy has been on the upswing. Narrow profit margins and the widespread losses of operation during the depression no longer are the rule. Furthermore, inasmuch as Group premiums paid by an employer are deductible and inasmuch as taxes on employers have been high, employers have been willing to assume the full expense. In many cases, premiums on Group insurance are being paid with 50-cent or even smaller dollars since, if these dollars were retained as profits, 50 cents or more would have to be paid in taxes. In the third place, during the period of the wage freezes of World War II and the Korean conflict, unions became aware of insurance as a "fringe" benefit for which they could bargain. As a measure for controlling inflation, they were restrained from bargaining for increased wages.

In most cases, unions tend to favor the noncontributory plan.

Regardless of whether the plan is contributory or noncontributory, the employer is responsible for the payment of premiums. Under contributory plans, it is customary for the employer to withhold a proportionate share of the employee's contribution from each of his paychecks.

Underwriting. In Group insurance, the basis of underwriting is the group covered, in contrast to individual insurance where the basis of under-writing is each individual insured.[4] The Group underwriter is not interested in any one individual who is participating in the plan, but in whether or not the composition of the group is such that can be insured.

The industrial classification of the group, the attitude and financial status of the employer, ages of the employees, their length of service, their distribu-tion by sex, race, and nationality—even the physical condition of the place of employment [5] (sanitation, type of structure, safety precautions, fire exits, etc.)—all can have a bearing on the underwriting evaluation of a group. Agency relations and competition, however, tend to make some of these fac-tors more theoretical than actual.

Since in Group the underwriting unit is the group, not the individuals in it, the health of any one given individual is of no consequence except as it may affect the "average." Thus Group requires no medical examination of individuals to be covered.[6] Even individuals with impairments or conditions that would require heavy extra rating in an individual plan, or who would be completely uninsurable under an individual plan, can be included. In the A & S Group, pre-existing conditions can be covered for the same reason. They will be offset by the extra-healthy individuals who are included under the plan. Group operates on the theory that if the group is selected, there will be no need to select the individuals, and the average of the group expe-rience will approximate that of a similar number of individually selected risks. It is customary underwriting practice today, however, to load the premiums if 25% of the employees are overage; i.e., 60 or more.

The group covered under the master contract is, as far as the individuals in it go, a random group since under a noncontributory plan all eligible members are covered, and under a contributory plan 75% must be covered. This eliminates much of the choice on the part of the individual participant and is the essential aspect in Group underwriting. Where persons to be insured are allowed to decide whether or not to take the coverage, as in individual policies, there will be, on the average, a tendency for the poor risks to take the insurance and the very good risks to reject it. This, as has been explained, is called "antiselection" or "adverse selection." Given an opportunity, the public will select against the company, giving it proportion-

---

[4] See Chapter 19 for a discussion of underwriting and risk selection.

[5] A group of employees, all or many of whom are under one roof, constitute a potential catastrophe hazard; so the hazard is important to Group underwriting. If it is extra-hazardous, it may call for an extra premium.

[6] As the Commissioners' definition states, Group may require a medical examination. In actual practice it rarely does. Life insurance medical examinations today cost around $7.50. Thus the elimination of the examination in Group is a distinct saving and one of the factors reducing the rate for Group in comparison to that for Ordinary.

ately more poor risks than good risks. Although this is true to a substantial degree in life insurance, it is even more true in A & S.

Two additional factors help offset the coverage in employee groups of impaired risks and pre-existing conditions:

(1) A group of employees is to a certain extent actually preselected. Employers hesitate to hire people in poor health. Some even require a medical examination as a condition of employment. The percentage of impaired risks and pre-existing conditions, therefore, is held down in the case of new employees.

(2) There is some tendency for employees whose health deteriorates to drop out of employment and thus out of the group. In the case of Group A & S, they are thereby eliminated from coverage.[7] In the case of Group life, although an individual is entitled to take an individual policy without examination, the over-all rate of such "conversions" is small.

As indicated, Group insurance may be issued to groups other than employee groups. It may be issued to creditors, unions, trustees of an association of employers, associations of two or more unions, and in some states, even to associations of such persons as medical associations, insurance agents' associations, hog-raisers associations, et alia. The enabling laws for insurance on these groups specify that the group shall have been formed prior to seeking the coverage and shall have a legitimate purpose other than that of obtaining insurance.

In the case of employer associations and, to a large extent, unions, the same two factors indicated above which tend to reduce the number of impaired risks also are applicable. They do not apply, however, in the case of creditors and of associations. In the case of creditor Group, there is no element of preselection. However, since creditor Group covers persons buying on installments for the period over which they are in debt, individual participants are insured for relatively short periods of time so that the lack of preselection apparently is unimportant. The past experience of creditor Group seems to bear out this fact. What effect the lack of preselection has

---

[7] Group A & S policies containing a provision for "conversion" to individual coverage without examination upon termination of employment are the subject of current experimentation. Just recently, one large life company and one casualty company presented reports on their experence with conversions of Group hospital-surgical plans to a joint meeting of the Bureau of A & H–H & A Conference. It is probable that provision for "conversion" will become common in A & S policies. Both companies reporting allowed conversion to cancellable forms only, thus giving them an added margin of safety since they could, technically, withdraw from a particularly bad risk. One of the companies reported that its records for three years showed only one cancellation by the company among all converted policies. It would be interesting to know, however, how many, if any, of the applications for conversions were accepted that would not have been accepted as new applicants.

in the case of associations is a matter of debate in the business. Some underwriters contend that insuring association members is bad underwriting practice, while others will defend the practice equally as vehemently. No conclusive evidence on either side is available.

3. GROUP LIFE INSURANCE

Group life insurance generally is written on a one-year Term basis. One-year Term is a popular plan because it is low in cost, and rate adjustments necessitated by a changing group are simple. Also, since one-year Term involves no reserves arising out of level premiums, there are no accumulated cash values to be adjusted as the group personnel changes.

The Master Policy. For convenience of discussion, the holder of the master contract in the Group case is referred to here as the "employer" and the participating individuals as "employees." The insurer is referred to as the company. However, wherever the term "employer" is used, the terms "trustee," "creditor," or "association" could be substituted; and wherever the term "employee" is used, the terms "union members," "debtors," or "association members," could be substituted.

Only one policy contract is issued in the Group case, the master contract issued to the employer. The individuals whose lives are insured are not policyholders; they are participants in the plan. The evidence of insurance given them is not an insurance policy but a "certificate of participation," or, as most Group men prefer to call it, "certificate of insurance."

Policy Provisions. The insuring provisions and contract terms of Group insurance are contained only in the master policy. Most states require a set of standard provisions either identical with or very close to the set recommended by the National Association of Insurance Commissioners. The following provisions, in addition to the ones already discussed, usually are found in Group life contracts:

(1) *Temporary Suspension of Employment.* The policy usually provides that in the case of sickness or temporary layoff, the insurance may be continued for some such period as three months.

(2) *Clerical Errors of Employer.* A clerical error on the part of the employer, such as failing to notify the company that an employee has become eligible for coverage, shall not deprive the employee of such coverage.

(3) *Disability.* Commonly, the Group policy provides that if an employee becomes totally disabled prior to age 60 and remains disabled to the time of his death, the amount of insurance on his life at the time of disability will remain in force. This is, in effect, a waiver of premium clause. Annual notice of the continuation of the disability is required. For a small

extra premium, the contract can be written to mature if total and permanent disability occurs before age 60. In this case, the proceeds of the policy become payable, usually on a five-year installment basis, as a disability claim rather than a death claim.[8]

(4) *Installment Settlement of Proceeds.* The Group policy usually permits the employee or his beneficiary to elect an installment settlement of policy proceeds. Commonly, the policy provides for only short-term fixed amount installments of, say, one to five years. However, if the amount of the insurance is reasonably large, the company usually will make available some of the options customarily offered in ordinary policies.

(5) *Retired Employees.* Group policies may provide for the continuation of coverage on retired employees. In such cases, the amount of insurance may be reduced. It is customary for the employer to pay the entire cost of postretirement protection even if the plan is contributory for active employees.

(6) *"The Formula."* The "formula" in Group insurance is the schedule of benefits payable. In fact, it is sometimes called "The Schedule." According to the Commissioners' definition, the formula must be based upon some plan that precludes individual selection. The amount of coverage for each individual must be established by a predetermined rule and not by his own choice. This is, of course, to eliminate adverse selection.

Five methods of determining the amount of insurance on the lives of individual participants are in general use:

(a) A flat amount for everyone, such as $2,000 for each covered employee.

(b) The employee's salary or salary bracket, either an amount equal to, say, one year's salary or $1,000 for employees earning under $3,000 a year, $2,000 for those earning $3,000 to $5,000, etc. The wage brackets and amount of coverage for each are, of course, established by the employer.

(c) Based on the employee's job classification; for instance, $2,000 for employees with no supervisory capacity; $5,000 for department heads, $10,000 for officers, etc.—again, the classifications used and amounts for each being the choice of the employer.

(d) Length of service; for example, $1,000 for employees with less than five years' service, $2,000 for those with from five to ten, etc.

(e) A combination of any of the above methods; for instance, $1,000 for

---

[8] This latter provision was commonly included in predepression policies without extra premium. Policies issued during, roughly, the depression period provided for the payment of the amount covered if death occurred within one year after the termination of employment if the termination was caused by total disability and occurred before age 65. The disability had to be continuous until death, however.

nonsupervisory employees with less than five years of service, increasing to $2,000 at the end of five years; $2,000 for department heads with less than five years of service, increasing to $4,000 after five years, etc.

Use of the employee's salary or salary brackets to determine the amount of insurance is probably the most common method. In a number of plans established through collective bargaining, a flat amount per employee is used with no variation among employees.

(7) *Classes of Employees Covered.* A Group plan does not have to cover *all* employees of the employer (or 75% of them, if contributory). It may cover only certain classes. However, any class must be determined by conditions of employment.[9] For instance, an employer might decide to cover only hourly wage workers; or only salaried workers. A college might decide to cover only the teaching and not the clerical and maintenance staffs. It might further restrict the coverage to only those members of the teaching staff who hold the rank of assistant professor or higher.

When an employee in an excluded classification moves into an eligible classification, he becomes eligible for the coverage just as though he were a new employee. If an employee should move from a covered class to an ineligible one, his coverage would terminate just as though he had left the employment of the employer. His conversion rights would be the same.

It is customary in most plans to require a probationary period of service, say 60 days or three months, as a condition of eligibility. The waiting period avoids the clerical work involved in handling cases of temporary or transient employees.

Employees who become eligible for coverage under a noncontributory plan automatically are covered without any action on their part. Those who become eligible under a contributory plan must make a written request to the employer (in the form of an "enrollment" card) within a stated time after becoming eligible—31 days, for instance. If they wish to enroll in the plan after the period expires, they may be required to furnish evidence of insurability at their own expense.

(8) *Alterations of Policy.* As is typical of all life insurance policies, the group contract declares that no agent shall have the right to alter or amend the policy, to accept premiums in arrears or extend the due date, to waive any required proof of claim or extend the date such proof is due. No change in the policy is valid unless approved by an officer of the company (and the specific officers authorized to make changes may be specified) and evidenced by an endorsement or amendment signed by the officer.

---

[9] A class based on desire for the coverage rather than on conditions of employment obviously would lead to adverse selection.

(9) *Beneficiaries.* The employee shall have the right to change his beneficiary at any time by filing written notice of the change with the company and having it endorsed on his certificate. Should the employee die before the actual endorsement is made, the change is effective as of the date of the notice. The company, however, shall not be held liable if the proceeds had already been paid before the notice was received.

(10) *Assignment.* Since employee certificates are not insurance policies, they are not assignable, and benefits are not assignable prior to a loss. Benefits, of course, are assignable after a loss.

(11) *Register of Participants.* The policy requires the employer to keep a record or register which at all times shows the names of participating employees, the amount for which each is covered, the date of entry into the plan, and the time and amounts of any increases or decreases in coverage.

(12) *Due Date, Computation, and Payment of Premium.* (a) Premiums usually may be paid monthly, quarterly, semiannually, or annually, and the time and frequency of payment may be changed upon the written request of the employer. (b) Premiums are payable in advance. (c) The company will compute an average rate, using the initial schedule of benefits and the employee data supplied by the employer. (d) At any renewal date, or whenever the terms of the policy are changed, the employer or the company may request a recomputation of the rate to reflect any new schedule of benefits or any major change in the age distribution of employees. (e) The initial premium and the premium on any renewal date shall be the average rate per $1,000 applied to the total amount of insurance (in terms of thousands) in force on all employees, regardless of the age of each participant. (f) Any premium adjustments involving the return of unearned premiums to the employer shall be limited to the 12-month period immediately preceding the date evidence is received by the company that such adjustments should be made. Since premiums are paid in advance, a refund is due when the number of employees is reduced. (g) If premiums are not paid by the end of the grace period, coverage shall cease. The employer, however, will be liable to the company for the pro rata amount of the premium for the grace period or for that part of the period consumed prior to the date the company received notice that the employer intends to discontinue the plan.

(13) *Policy Dividends and Nonpar Adjustments.* If the policy is participating, dividends will be paid in cash to the employer or, on his written request, applied on the next premium. If the plan is nonparticipating, provision is made for a retroactive adjustment of the premium if actual experience indicates one is merited. An employer usually is entitled to an adjust-

ment if the total of claims paid plus a "retention" percentage is less than the premiums collected. The "retention" percentage is based on the amount the company estimates is necessary for administration costs, contingency reserves, insurance costs,[10] and a margin for profit. Should dividends or adjustments exceed the amounts contributed by the employer in a contributory plan, the excess must be used for the benefit of the employees: refunded to them, used to enable them to skip contributions for a period, or applied to buy additional insurance or benefits.

(14) *Renewal.* When the plan of insurance is one-year Term, the policy contains a provision permitting the employer to renew the contract at the end of the policy year and at the end of each subsequent year, contingent upon (*a*) payment of premiums, (*b*) 75% participation in contributory cases and 100% in noncontributory cases, and (*c*) the minimum number required by the policy (or statute) for a group.

The Certificate of Participation. The master policy requires the company to issue to the employer for delivery to each employee an individual certificate stating the insurance to which the employee is entitled, to whom benefits are payable, and summarizing the provisions of the policy affecting the employee.

Surrender of the certificate is a condition precedent to the payment of a death claim or the exercise of any rights under the policy.

The certificate itself certifies that under a Group policy, identified by policy number, the employee is entitled to benefits named subject to the provisions of the master policy; and it identifies the beneficiary. It then gives a summary of the policy provisions affecting the employee, such as:

(1) Authority of agents

(2) Cessation of insurance

(3) Conversion privilege

(4) Disability benefit

(5) Change of beneficiary and facility of payment

(6) The formula or schedule

It also usually contains space for endorsement of any change of beneficiary.

Determining the Rate. The problems involved in rate-making for Group are much the same as for Ordinary.[11] The premium will depend on (*a*) the

---

[10] The insurance cost is to pay for bad experience on other groups; i.e., to pay some of the claims in other groups when these claims exceed the premiums collected from those groups. There is always the possibility that the claims in any group will exceed premiums collected. Rates must be loaded with an insurance charge to offset this contingency. The larger the group, the smaller is the percentage loaded in the retention limit for the insurance charge.

[11] See Chapters 20 and 21 for a discussion of rate-making principles.

total amount of life insurance involved; (*b*) the disability benefits offered; (*c*) the plan of insurance; (*d*) the ages of the members of the group; (*e*) the type of industry involved; [12] (*f*) the race of group members. Some industries are more hazardous than others, and some races have a higher rate of mortality.

If the plan is contributory, a flat amount per thousand is established as the employees' contribution. New York law sets the maximum at 60¢ per month per $1,000, and this is the amount usually adopted. It may be less, of course, at the choice of the employer.

The rate quoted is a weighted average reflecting the composition of the group. The average is computed as follows:

(1) The rate at the attained age of each employee is multiplied by the number of $1,000 for which he will be eligible.

(2) To find the total premium for the group, add the premiums found for each member.

(3) Divide the total premium by the amount of insurance (in thousands) involved in the group. This gives the average rate, which is the rate charged for the policy. It also will be the rate used for adjustments involving new entrants, and terminations regardless of the ages of such entering or terminating employees. It will be used until recalculated in conformity with the provisions of the policy.

It might seem at first glance that an easier way to arrive at the average rate would be to average all ages involved. This method would give an erroneous result. Actually, it is impossible to average ages for insurance because the death rate varies at each age. As ages increase, the mortality costs increase at a faster pace. The death rate at age 50 is more than twice that at age 25. It would be possible to average ages for Group insurance premiums only if the death rates and ages increased at the same pace. Table 1 will clarify the problem.

In this case, the average age is 35, and the average mortality rate for the group is 5.36. To use the death rate at age 35 (4.59) for rate-making

Table 1

Number of Employees	Age	Total Age	Death Rate	Total Death Rate
10	25	250	2.88	28.8
10	35	350	4.59	45.9
10	45	450	8.61	86.1
				160.8

Average mortality rate for this group: 160.8 ÷ 30 = 5.36

[12] In general, rates are determined by the nature of the industry, not by the job classifications of individuals in the group.

would understate expected mortality experience, for the actual "average" of the death rate for the group (5.36) is a factor falling halfway between the mortality rates at age 37 and 38. Thus it is erroneous to average the ages of the group for use in premium calculations. It is necessary, instead, to calculate the rate for each age in the group before an average rate can be found.

If the group requires an extra rating (that is, if it is "substandard"), an amount is added to the total premium which represents the estimated difference between tabular and expected mortality for the year (in the case of Group Term). If only part of the group is subject to the extra hazard (as, for instance, an organization with two plants, only one of which is engaged in extra-hazardous work), the cost of the extra premium is, nevertheless, distributed over the entire group. The average rate is always the same for each member of the group regardless of his age or the job he performs.

The initial rate is usually guaranteed for the first year—sometimes longer —and subsequent increases cannot be applied retroactively.

In adjusting the average rate, the company takes into account its experience with the particular group and with all other groups, the latter factor being one of the elements taken into consideration when setting the retention percentage.

In contributory plans, each employee contributes a flat amount per thousand regardless of his age. The effect is that a young man will be paying a higher percentage of the cost of his insurance than will an older man. Actually, at ages under about 40, the customary 60 cents a month per $1,000 ($7.20 a year) employee's contribution will more than pay the cost of his insurance. Beyond about age 40, the cost of insurance is greater than his contribution. There is at least some equity in having the employer pay more of the cost of the insurance for the older employees who, on the average, will have rendered more years of service.

Comparative Cost of Group Life Insurance.   Group is the least expensive form of life insurance because:

(1) Group insurance is written without medical examination, eliminating that fee, which otherwise must be added to cost.

(2) Less sales solicitation and a lower commission scale on identical policy forms make acquisition costs lower than those paid for Ordinary policies. Commissions are paid on a sliding scale, the percentage decreasing as the total amount of insurance increases.

(3) Much of the service rendered to individual policyholders by the insurance company is rendered, instead, by the employer, thus reducing the insurer's cost of administration.

(4) Mortality experience is more favorable, in spite of the fact that there is no medical selection. Table 2 indicates the superior mortality experience of Group insurance.[13]

Table 2. Death Rate per 1,000

Age	Group	Ordinary
23	1.70	2.35
33	2.38	2.83
43	4.85	5.86
53	11.66	12.95
63	26.50	30.11
73	64.72	69.93

One reason for better mortality in Group insurance is that death following extended illness often does not affect a Group contract. Persons who suffer from a long illness before death are in the majority of cases not employed at the time of their death. Second, being employable, group policyholders are preselected.

The mortality cost among converted Group certificates, however, is higher than among the regular Ordinary policyholders. Those in bad health are more inclined to convert their policies, while those in good health may not take advantage of the conversion privilege.[14] The adverse selection resulting from the conversion privilege is charged against the Group contract by assessing a charge of so many dollars per thousand of converted insurance. Although the cost of conversion is charged against the Group business, this charge is not reflected in mortality costs.

Table 3 will give some indication of the cost differences in Group and Ordinary insurance when both are issued on a yearly renewable Term basis.

Table 3. Non-par Yearly Renewable Term *
RATE PER $1,000

Age	Group	Ordinary
20	$ 4.09	$ 6.71
30	4.66	6.98
40	6.54	8.79
50	13.57	14.39
60	27.55	30.41

* Note that rates at ages 20, 30, and 40 are less than the $7.20 these people would have to pay under a contributory plan calling for the usual 60¢ a month per employee. Note also that the cost of insurance at 20 and 30 is less even at Ordinary rates than the 60 cents.

---

[13] Comparative net cost factors, Valentine Howell, *Life Insurance: Trends and Problems*, edited by David McCahan, Philadelphia, University of Pennsylvania Press, 1943, p. 129.
[14] Often employees who are uninsurable fail to convert their policies. Sometimes the reason is ignorance or lack of interest; but many times, it is the inability to pay the premium for permanent insurance. Were it possible to convert to Term forms, chances are that a greater percentage of Group would be converted.

The cost of Group Term insurance in the typical case usually runs about 1% of the total amount insured.

Group Permanent. While the vast majority of Group life insurance is written as one-year Term, some Group Contracts are written as "Group Permanent." Group Permanent, however, is increasing in importance and according to some observers it seems destined to play a prominent role in the future.[15] Under the Group Permanent plan, at least part of the coverage is placed on permanent level-premium policy forms. Such plans most commonly are used where Group life insurance is designed to protect against both premature death and old age. They also are used where the employer wishes to give the employee a postretirement life insurance program which will require no premium payments after retirement. Two major types of Group Permanent are written:

(1) *The Unit-Purchase Plan.* A unit of paid-up Whole Life or Retirement Income insurance is purchased annually during the period the employee is covered under the plan. The employee may be eligible for Group Permanent after a certain number of years of service, after a given age, or after meeting a standard involving a combination of both tests. The unit purchased may be set up on a sliding scale, increasing each year, or it may be uniform. Group Permanent usually is combined with Group Term. In some plans the amount of Group Term purchased on each employee may decrease as the amount of permanent increases so that the total amount of insurance in force on his life remains constant.[16] In some plans, the employers' contributions may be used to buy Group Term while those of the employee are used to purchase Group Permanent. When this is the case, the additional amount of paid-up Permanent purchased decreases each year since its rate goes up as the employee's age advances.

In the usual case, Group Term is terminated when the employee resigns, is fired, or retires. The terminated Term insurance, of course, is subject to conversion at the attained age. The Group Permanent remains in force since it is paid-up insurance. Instead of retaining the Permanent insurance, however, the ex-employee may have the option of taking that portion of its cash surrender value which has been purchased by his own, but not by the employer's, contributions to the premium. Cash surrender values, however, are not allowed while the employee remains under the plan.

The first unit-purchase Group Permanent plan was written in 1941. When the plans are contributory, the usual employee contribution rate is $1.30

---

[15] See especially a paper delivered to the Society of Actuaries by Robert G. Espie at the Western Springs meeting, June, 1955.
[16] That is, assuming that the employee does not shift from one benefit class to another.

monthly for each $1,000 of insurance. Instead of a flat rate for each employee, some plans call for a contribution rate which varies with the age of the employee at the outset but remains level throughout the period of coverage. The plans commonly provide postretirement life insurance protection equal to about 1/3 to 1/2 of the amount of preretirement protection. Special arrangements involving a continuation of Term insurance often are made for employees who are within 20 years of retirement when the plan is installed, since they will not have had time to build an adequate amount of Group Permanent.

(2) *The Level-Premium Plan.* Under the level-premium plan of Group Permanent, Whole Life, Endowment, or Retirement Income may be used. Level premiums are payable for life or to retirement age, depending on the type of policy to be used. On termination of employment, the employee may take the cash value of the permanent plan, the paid-up value, or continue the entire amount of the coverage in force by paying the full premium direct to the company instead of through the employer.

Group Credit Insurance. Group Credit insurance, used by a creditor to cover the lives of his debtors, has shown an amazing growth during the past ten years.[17] From an insignificant amount in force as late as a decade ago, the total now outstanding is in the neighborhood of $10,000,000,000 written under well over 18,000,000 master policies.

Under creditor insurance, the proceeds are used to cancel the outstanding balance on debt, relieving the estate of the insured of the liability.[18]

Wholesale Insurance. Wholesale insurance is an adaptation of some of the principles of Group insurance to groups which are too small to qualify for Group coverage. Wholesale is used also in some large groups where the required percentage of participation cannot be obtained under a contributory plan.

"Wholesale" is also called "Employee insurance"; and currently at least one state prohibits the use of the term "Wholesale." [19]

Under "Wholesale," individual policies are issued to each person in the group, and individual underwriting is allowed. Physical examinations may be required, although in practice they are usually waived in favor of a statement of health. The employer, while not applying for the insurance, signs an agreement with the company to pay the premiums. The plan may be contributory or noncontributory, but in either case the employer is re-

---

[17] Creditor insurance often is used by vendors to cover vendees buying under the installment plan.

[18] The premium in Group Credit insurance may be paid either by the borrower (or debtor) or by the creditor (or vendor).

[19] "Wholesale" is still the common name for this type of plan in the life insurance field.

sponsible for the payment of the premium, and (if the plan is contributory) for its collection from employees.

Wholesale is written under conditions designed to eliminate as much adverse selection as possible. The amount for which the employee is insured is not left up to him but is set by a predetermined schedule.

As in the case of Group, the usual plan of insurance is one-year Term, and the method of arriving at the rate is the same as in Group. The insured names his own beneficiary and has possession and control of the policy (instead of having only a certificate of participation). The contract usually carries the "conversion" privilege. Because of the smaller size of the group covered and a consequent higher administration cost, the premium for Wholesale is somewhat higher than for Group.

In practical effect, Group and Wholesale are the same. In fact, many an employer or employee will say he has "Group insurance" when, in fact, the plan is Wholesale.

Since the reduction in the number of participants required under Group went into effect, Wholesale has found less application than formerly.

Group Annuities. Annuities as well as life and A & S insurance may be sold on a group basis. However, discussion of Group Annuities is more properly the subject of the ensuing chapter on insurance in pension plans.

4. GROUP A & S INSURANCE

Most of what has been said of the theory of Group life insurance also applies to Group Accident and Sickness insurance. The two forms of Group coverages are much alike except for contractual provisions and types of coverages available.

The Group A & S Contract. The number of similarities between Group A & S and Group life contracts is greater than the number of differences. The differences result principally from the nature of the perils covered. Just as the Group life contract differs in some ways from the Ordinary life policy, so does the Group A & S contract differ in some ways from the individual A & S policy. Mention should be made of the principal points of difference.

(1) Many Group A & S policies provide benefits only for nonoccupational accidents and illness. Occupational disabilities are left to the coverage provided under the Workmen's Compensation laws. For an extra premium, occupational injuries can be covered under Group A & S. Since the benefit structure under Workmen's Compensation laws often is very low, it is considered desirable to include occupational coverage in the Group plan, especially in those industries where the added cost for this coverage is nominal.

(2) The A & S insurer reserves the right to refuse renewal of the Group policy on any renewal date, in contrast to Group life insurance, which is renewable at the option of the insured (the employer). The right to refuse a renewal applies only to the master contract. No individual participant may be canceled or denied renewal *except* by termination of the entire Group.

(3) Termination of the master contract or of an individual certificate is without effect on prior disability, just as in the case of terminations of individual policies. Moreover, a period is allowed after termination during which claims developing out of conditions existing at the time of termination are covered. For example, Group hospital and surgical benefits usually are payable for three months after termination if the claims are the result of a condition existing when the contract was terminated but which did not require hospitalization or an operation at that time. Pregnancies in progress at termination are covered; and any maternity benefits applicable are paid if incurred within nine months after termination even if pregnancy was not known to be in progress at the time the contract or certificate expired.[20]

(4) The Standard or Uniform Provisions, required by law to be contained in individual contracts, are not required in Group contracts. These provisions are for the most part details relating to the presentation of claims. Provisions in Group policies on claim handling usually are so much more liberal than the Standard or Uniform provisions that the use of these provisions actually would be restrictive. Other provisions similar to those set forth in the Standard or Uniform Provisions which are protective to the policyholder, however, are required in Group policies.

Clauses prorating benefits for other insurance, change of occupation, misstatement of age, and time limit on legal action are examples of other individual policy restrictions omitted in Group.

Greater liberality in Group provisions is possible for several reasons. The two most important are: (a) The benefits payable are relatively smaller than those under individual policies and are for shorter periods. (b) The rate under Group coverage may be adjusted up or down periodically. The employer, therefore, has an interest in preventing claim abuse and improving his loss experience.

(5) The insuring clause for loss-of-time benefits is more liberal in Group than in many individual policies. In Group contracts, disability is defined in terms of the employee's *own* occupation rather than in terms of *any* occupation. The usual definition is the inability to perform any and every duty

---

[20] This is true in substantially all group A & S plans covering maternity.

of the insured's own occupation. However, there is currently a trend toward an even more simple definition, requiring only that the insured employee be unable to perform his regular work.

Types of Coverage. Group insurance can cover virtually all insurable accident and sickness perils in any combination. The following are the most frequent coverages and ranges of benefits:

(1) *Accident and Sickness Coverages.* Principal and capital sums often are made available for accidental death and dismemberment benefits. Weekly or monthly indemnities also usually are included in event of disability as defined in the policy. Income benefits resulting from accidents may begin with the first day of disability, whereas a short waiting period, seven days being typical, is required for sickness benefits. Benefits usually are payable for 13, 26, or 52 weeks, except that benefits for disability from pregnancy will be more limited, six weeks for example. Accidental death and dismemberment sometimes are written alone, without loss-of-time benefits, and usually pay for occupational as well as nonoccupational injuries.

(2) *Hospitalization.* Hospital room and board may be covered for a flat per diem up to a maximum number of days, such as 31 or 70; while miscellaneous or "special" hospital expenses are covered either (a) on an "unallocated" basis up to a maximum of 10 to 15 or more times the daily room and board, or (b) on an "allocated" basis; that is, with the maximum for each type of service set forth in a schedule. When the unallocated basis is used, it is common to allow a substantially greater limit beyond the fixed multiple of room allowance, but with a coinsurance factor under which the insurer pays three fourths and the insured pays one fourth. A maximum amount or time limit is established on these extras. The purpose of the growing liberality in hospital extras is to help offset the cost of the "wonder drugs," which is to the benefit of the insurer since, while expensive, they shorten hospital stay. Maternity benefits may be added up to a maximum of about ten times the daily room benefit, or a flat amount regardless of the duration of hospitalization.

(3) *Surgical.* Indemnities for surgical procedures are written, usually as set forth in a schedule of maximums for each procedure.

(4) *Medical Expense.* Three types of medical expense coverage are usually available: (a) "In-Hospital," covering medical attendance other than surgical up to a per call maximum and a maximum total either in dollars or in duration of time. (b) "Medical expense" covering physician's calls while in the hospital or while totally disabled, on the same basis as above. (c) "Comprehensive medical expense," covering physician's calls at so much per call and an aggregate dollar or time total regardless of the nature

of the disability. Usually the first two or three calls are excluded. Maternity calls also are usually excluded, especially after diagnosis.

These four types of coverages are the ones which currently are the most popular in Group A & S plans. In addition to these coverages, several more are available and are used to a much lesser degree.

(5) *Diagnostic.* Expenses up to a specified maximum for the cost of X-ray examination or any microscopic or other laboratory tests or analyses.

(6) *Catastrophe (or Major Medical or Major Hospital).* Virtual blanket coverage for expenses between a deductible and an aggregate maximum, often written with a coinsurance feature under which the insured pays 20% or 25% of the covered expenses. Group forms of this coverage are the same, in general, as described in Chapter 11.

Where state laws permit, dependents of the insured also may be covered under a Group plan. Exceptions are accidental death, dismemberment, and loss-of-time benefits. They are not available in dependents' Group.

Blanket. Blanket coverage may be considered a separate classification or a phase of Group insurance. It is similar to Group in that it covers a number of people in one policy as contrasted to one individual per policy. It is unlike Group in that the individuals covered are not specified and may change constantly.

Blanket coverage may be written on all passengers of a common carrier, for example. Under this form of insurance, anyone aboard the carrier at the time of an accident is covered. It is issued on spectators at a sporting event; to an institution of learning, covering all pupils; to volunteer fire, ambulance, and first-aid groups; to campers at a camp; to members of an athletic team; and, in general, to any association of persons having a common denominator other than the insurance coverage itself.

Wholesale (or "Franchise" or "Employee"). Wholesale A & S insurance is relatively new, so much so that no one of the names given in the paragraph heading has yet come to be used exclusively.[21]

Wholesale A & S insurance is so much like Wholesale life insurance that all that need be said about it at this point is that it is available.

5. REASONS FOR USING GROUP

Four reasons for establishing a Group insurance plan in any given business or industry call for a brief discussion. They are industrial relations, social obligation, the demand of unions, and the desire of the employer or key men to obtain their own personal insurance at low rates.

---

[21] "Franchise" usually is the choice of Casualty and monoline A & S business. "Wholesale" usually is the choice of the life insurance business since this form of A & S is the same in general nature as that class of mass-sold life insurance called "Wholesale."

Industrial Relations. Much is made of the industrial relations aspects of Group insurance by writers and salesmen. Group plans are said to attract better employees, reduce employee turnover, and improve morale and efficiency.

The value of Group insurance in attracting and holding employees is at least open to question.

First, it may seem logical to argue that the worker will accept that job giving him the greater insurance benefits if all other working conditions as between two available jobs are equal. However, particularly in the case of life insurance, anyone who deals with prospective buyers knows there is a lack of logic in the thinking of many people about the need for and ownership of life insurance. To a lesser degree, the same is true in the case of A & S insurance.

Second, the value of any condition of employment depends on contrast. If two jobs offer the same conditions, that condition is no factor in influencing a person in the choice of or encouraging a person to remain on a job. Today, Group insurance is so widespread in business and industry that it offers no contrast. Whichever job he chooses, the employee will usually be covered by Group; and almost any other job to which he might shift also will be covered. It is possible that the lack of a Group plan might prove a disadvantage in obtaining employees and holding them, but under today's conditions it would appear that the existence of a plan has little effect in obtaining or holding employees.

It seems more likely that there is validity to the claim that Group improves morale and hence efficiency. In the first place, it may have some effect on morale by giving the employee a feeling that the employer has at least some degree of concern over his welfare off the job. This is probably more true in the small business than in the large, for in large business the employer is so remote from his employees that all conditions of employment are largely impersonal.

Group will help raise morale and efficiency by reducing the financial worries of employees. The effect of Group life in this respect is probably slight. However illogical it may be, few healthy people worry much about dying or the effect of their death on their dependents—except when forced to do so by the life insurance agent; in Group, the agent-policyholder relationship found in individual policies is virtually nil. However, people are conscious of the costs of accidents, sickness, and hospitalization. Death comes only once to an employee and he has not yet experienced it, whereas he has probably experienced the cost of disability many times. Further, there is constant publicity about the costs of medical and hospital care which keeps the employee reminded of the potential financial crisis he faces. Group A & S will lessen his worry about possible loss. If his dependents are covered by the plan, disability in the family will not cause him the financial worry it otherwise would and hence it will help to keep up his efficiency on the job.

Social Obligation. Throughout the twentieth century there has been a growing philosophy that the employer has an obligation to his employees over and beyond wages. In fact, failure to take such responsibility would, today, be considered the worst kind of public relations.

Since the employer feels an obligation to "do something" for sick or injured employees or for dependents of deceased employees, he faces a potential monetary loss (expense). This loss is unpredictable both as to time of occurrence and as to amount; therefore, it is a proper subject for insurance. The employer through Group insurance can protect himself against this potential loss. If he does not insure it, he stands to pay a large, uncertain loss out of pocket. The possibility of this potential loss often is an important factor in the employer's decision to install a Group plan.

Demand of Unions. In recent years, Group insurance has moved into the scope of collective bargaining. Employee financial security is of vital concern to the unions. The unions recognize that Group insurance is an effective way of providing this security. There seems little question but that the direct demand of unions for Group insurance has been one of the principal reasons for establishing Group insurance plans. Either the union makes a direct demand on the employer to establish a plan, or the employer establishes it in anticipation of union demands. Employers often feel that they have better control over plans established independent of unions and that they enjoy a greater advantage in employee relations by initiating the plan themselves. The employer, however, cannot establish a plan independent of the union if the union chooses to bargain for it. Group insurance is subject to collective bargaining and the union has a legal right to insist on having a part in the formulation of a Group insurance program. Often the union insists upon exercising this right in order to lead its members to feel that the union is gaining advantages for them which they might not otherwise have gained. Sometimes by the bargaining process the union does achieve a more favorable plan for its members.

"Get It Wholesale." There is no question but that some Group plans are established because the employer in a smaller business or the executives in a larger one look at Group insurance as a way to get life insurance at less than the individual policy rate. Even where there is a statutory limit on the amount of Group coverage that can be written on an individual life, the limit usually allows a substantial amount of insurance and the premium saving, therefore, also is substantial. Premiums paid by the employer for Group insurance are deductible as a business expense. This further reduces the effective cost of this type of insurance. In a large business, where ownership and management are divorced, executives find it easy to sell themselves on life insurance when the premiums are to be paid out of corporate funds. Stockholders rarely object. The owner-manager in the small business may be just as much intrigued with the tax savings involved and the low cost of group coverage on his own life as he is with the needs of his employees.

The "get it wholesale" appeal to the employer himself must be put down as a frequent reason for establishing a Group insurance plan.

In summary, it can be said that there are business, social, and selfish reasons for establishing Group insurance in any given business or industry; and, finally, Group coverage has become so widespread today that the business which is without it stands out as an oddity and is likely to suffer in its employee and public relations.

6. AN APPRAISAL OF GROUP INSURANCE

The amount of Group insurance in force is influenced by economic conditions. It increases by leaps and bounds when the economy is on the upgrade, and decreases during periods of major unemployment. However, Group insurance has become so much a part of the employment picture in the United States [22] that even the severest economic depression could have no more than a temporary effect upon it.

As mentioned,[23] Group life insurance has already begun to replace Industrial insurance as the form of protection most often owned by lower income groups. Group also is having an effect on the Ordinary life insurance business. It is one of the factors leading to an increase in the size of the average Ordinary policy. Group insurance tends to take care of the demand for the smaller policy. The effect of Group on the Ordinary business, however, has been less significant than its effect on Industrial because Group plans, by and large, have not to date offered the large amounts of insurance available under Ordinary.

In the life field, both Industrial and Ordinary were well developed before Group appeared on the scene. In the A & S field, great strides were not made until the 1950's, when the Group plan of writing insurance already was

---

[22] Group business in Canada has not increased as sharply as in the U.S. In a recent year in which new Group writings in the U.S. increased 84% over the preceding year, they fell 30% in Canada.

[23] See Chapter 12.

well established and booming. It is possible that Group A & S will prevent individual A & S—both Industrial and Commercial—from ever developing to the ranking positions individual contracts have achieved and still hold in the life business.

Group and the Agency System. While technically Group insurance is sold under the agency system, it probably would be more practical to describe the marketing of Group as a channel which utilizes services of the agency system merely because that system is there and traditional.

Agents are used to initiate Group cases, but details more often are handled by salaried Group representatives. There is little agent-client relationship between either employer and agent or employees and agent, at least in comparison to the degree that such relationship exists in the Ordinary and Industrial branches of the business. In the small or medium-size Group case, an enterprising agent sometimes makes capital of his potential service to individual employees as a means of making sales contact with them and servicing all their insurance; but by and large, the individual agent is squeezed into a minor role.

Moreover, some companies will write Group "around" the agent; that is, they will write it direct and pay no commissions. This trend was given much impetus in 1954 by the federal employees' case in which $6,700,000,000 of Group life was placed in force on 1,700,000 federal workers with payment of only a token commission. Unions have been bargaining for Group written direct without commissions and probably will, in the future, demand that larger cases be so written.

Group does not, therefore, foster the spread or development of the agency system.

Whether it will weaken the agency system depends upon the future growth and spread of Group and, particularly, on statutory limitations on the amount of Group life that can be written on an individual life, on the spread of Group written where there is no employer-employee relationship, and the prohibitions on dependents' Group life.

Some individual agents and most agents' associations are active in fostering or protecting legislation which keeps Group from expanding further into dependents' coverage, high individual limits, and association fields. Many individual agents, however, either see no threat or are oblivious to it; so the agents' ranks are not unanimous in their view of the possible effect of Group insurance on their markets. For the most part, companies have no fears at all about the expansion of Group into any area that can be underwritten, although they are sometimes restrained in their pronouncements on the subject as a matter of relations with their agency forces.

Group and Social Insurance. Some advocates of Group contend that Group retards the growth of social insurance. They argue, with logic, that the demand for social insurance coverage arises from people who have inadequate private coverage and that the best way to decrease the demand for social insurance is to see that everybody has private insurance. Group, they say, offers the means of spreading private protection to all people.

On the other hand is the argument that one of the advantages private insurance holds over social insurance is the service of the agent. The individual agent services Group and existing social insurance such as Social Security, National Service Life Insurance ("NSLI"), and veterans' benefits. He does this in the course of his work in counseling people on their insurance needs, in programming coverages for them, and in helping settle claims. It is often an individual insurance agent who obtains the papers necessary for death and A & S claims for all the personal coverages in effect, individual, Group, and social insurance.

If Group should crowd the individual agent out of the picture, or even seriously reduce his ranks, the service of private insurance would be cut off or restricted to the extent that except on ideological grounds private insurance would offer no advantages over social insurance.

When Group is sold to protect the employer against the cost of his moral obligation to employees and is sold as a basic floor of coverage for individual participants, few observers have any argument with it. However, there is much argument over the validity and advisability of selling Group where there is no employer-employee relationship and in amounts that attempt to make Group a substitute for an individually prescribed and tailored life insurance program.

Group has been likened to a company car: a big saving while a man has it, but what becomes of it when he changes jobs?

7. MANAGEMENT DECISIONS IN ESTABLISHING GROUP PLANS

The employer who decides to install a Group plan must make several decisions before the plan can be formulated.

Contributory vs. Noncontributory. The contributory plan makes it possible for the employer to offer higher limits of coverage without a correspondingly higher premium outlay on the part of the employer. Some Group men argue that the contributory plan makes the employee more conscious of his insurance and consequently the employee-relations value of the plan is more effective. On the other hand, the noncontributory plan is much simpler to administer, is more often demanded by unions, and at least originally, some Group men insist, impresses the employee more, because he looks upon it as a "gift." Under the contributory plan, the employee tends to think that he is paying for what he gets. Often he overlooks or discounts the extent of the employer's contribution, which sometimes is much greater than his own. In fact, many employees under a contributory plan do not even understand that the employer is paying any part of the cost at all.[24] Perhaps the net effect from an employee-relations standpoint is the same whether the plan is contributory or noncontributory. The decision rests on conditions peculiar to the case, whether or not collective bargaining is involved, and the philosophy of management.

Eligibility. A decision must be made as to whether to insure all employees or to set up standards of eligibility. As mentioned, it is common to exclude all employees with less than a specified minimum period of service in order to exclude temporary and transient employees. It is permissible to limit coverage to only certain departments, the wage roll only, the salary roll only, or any other group as long as there is no adverse selection.

Types of Coverage. Under a Group life plan, there is little decision involved in type of coverage. The employer needs to decide only on whether the plan is to be Group Term exclusively or whether some Group Permanent is to be included. In the case of Group A & S, there are many decisions to be made: Should the plan include only hospitalization and surgical benefits (the most widespread coverage in Group A & S)? Should it include loss-of-time coverage (perhaps the most important, since bills can be paid if income continues)? Should it contain provision for medical reimbursement, diagnostic expense, etc.?

The Formula or Schedule. To some extent, the types of coverage purchased will depend on how much the employer feels he can budget for Group premiums. The budget is even more important, however, in setting the schedule of benefits. Employers usually like to provide life insurance benefits equal to at least one year's income, although there are many cases where much less than this amount is provided. In the case of A & S, a decision often will have to be made whether to offer a wide range of coverages with low limits or to offer only a few coverages with more adequate limits. From the standpoint of the basic principle of Group—to provide a floor of protection—it might seem better to spread the premium money over all pos-

---

[24] This is largely the fault of employers, who rather generally fail to "merchandise" their Group plans by planned continual publicity. One excellent way to keep employees reminded of their Group insurance is to give each individual employee a statement, annually, of how much money the employer has paid in premiums for insurance benefits for that employee.

sible coverages in order to give the employee some help with any kind of medical bill. However, any Group plan will come in for more criticism from employees if it pays what they consider an inadequate amount than if it pays no amount at all. The psychology of the employee in regard to the matter seems to be that if there is no coverage at all for a contingency that befalls them, it is just "tough luck"; but that inadequate coverage for that contingency is a "cheap plan."

Company to Buy From. Group plans largely are "price merchandise." A Group buyer will usually "shop" far more extensively than will an individual buyer. Further, he will often get "bids" from a number of companies. The individual buyer is influenced heavily by the agent, from whom he expects future service. In Group plans, the agent often is of far less importance. Even though an agent may solicit the case, details of setting up and servicing the plan usually will be handled by salaried Group representatives who may change from time to time. In the larger case, the details for the employer (once the plan is established) usually are handled by a member of his clerical staff. Hence, the agent-client relationship has far less influence on the purchase of Group than on the sale of individual policies.

If the employer already has some coverages and is adding more, he usually will want to purchase it from the same company. Placing all Group coverages in one company reduces administrative detail. Moreover, the more insurance an employer has with a given company, the better is his bargaining position on rates, service, and claims. The higher combined premium is likely to give him a lower retention limit.

The reputation of the company for promptness in handling claims and other details of service also will have a bearing—probably more bearing after the plan is installed than before. Most employers assume, unless they have convincing evidence to the contrary—perhaps from another employer— that service from any substantial company will be about the same as that from another. However, after the plan is installed they may become dissatisfied with the service and decide to switch the plan to a different company.

A major factor in choice of company in most cases is cost. Costs of identical plans tend to vary among companies, especially after the first year. One of the factors in the rate is the retention limit—the amount of the premium retained by the company for contingencies and expenses. In the larger Group case, bargaining over the size of the retention assumes an important role in the choice of the carrier. Competition is sharp. The size of the retention a company feels it must have is a matter of variables which a company can interpret in a number of ways. The buyer tries to drive down the retention rate,[25] usually buying from the company which guarantees the lowest one.

One other device sometimes used in competitive bidding in Group insurance is the level commission plan. The agent will request that his commission be loaded in the quoted rate as a level commission rather than as a high first-year commission. This will produce a lower first year rate and will give the agent a competitive advantage with the strictly price buyer.

8. SUMMARY AND CONCLUSIONS

Group insurance is a plan for covering a large number of people under one master policy issued to employer, union, or association trustees. The employer is the policyowner, and all contractual relationships are between him and the company.[26] The individuals covered under the insurance are third parties to the contract. Individual participants in the plan are not issued policies but certificates of participation which summarize the provisions and coverage of the master policy but refer to it for contractual terms.

Rules for Group are such that individuals have as little choice in the plan as possible. As a result, antiselection is reduced to a point that need not be considered in underwriting. The underwriting unit is not each individual covered but the composition and character of the whole group as a unit. For that reason, risks unacceptable on an individual policy basis can be insured under a Group plan.

Group is lower in cost and more liberal in provisions than is the individual policy. It is lower in cost because (a) the employer takes over many of the administrative duties; (b) commission scales are lower; (c) medical examinations are eliminated; and (d) in the case of Group A & S, the employer has an interest in weeding out false or padded claims in order to control his net premium outlay.

Group probably has some value in employee relations and employee morale and efficiency, although the effect is probably less than advertisements and sales presentations would make it appear. Group does protect the employer himself against the unbudgetable cost of discharging what has come to be considered his social or moral obligation for the welfare of his employees.

---

[25] In fact, he frequently succeeds in driving it down to a level that makes many observers of the Group business raise their eyebrows.

[26] If the policy is with a mutual company, only the employer has a vote for directors. The covered employees, not being policyholders, have no vote.

Questions For Class Discussion

1. If you were a life insurance agent, would you like to see the use of group insurance expand? Why or why not?
2. What arguments could you use in a sales presentation for group insurance?
3. What opportunities for employment do you suspect exist in the group insurance field? Do any appeal to you?
4. If you were an employer, which type of group plan would you take: Term or Endowment?
5. Why do you suspect the laws for eligible groups have become more and more lenient?
6. In establishing a group insurance program, what are the decisions that need to be made by management?
7. If you were an insurance consultant for a business firm, how would you go about recommending the company in which they should place their insurance?
8. Although many of the provisions of the group contract are similar to those of the Ordinary contract, there are some differences. How do you account for these differences?
9. When you become employed upon graduation and are invited into a contributory group life plan, is it to your advantage to accept the invitation? Discuss.
10. Do you think the group principle could be extended to property and liability insurance, fire and automobile, for example?

CHAPTER 14

INSURANCE IN
PENSION PLANS

THE ECONOMIC problem of the aged in the United States today is not only significant but also it is growing. According to the 1950 census 12.4% of the population in this country was 65 or over. Population projections [1] indicate that at the next census the percentage will be from 13.6 to 16.1. Estimated figures for 1975 suggest 16% to 20.5% and the forecasters predict that by the year 2000 from 19% to 29.3% of Americans will be beyond retirement age. How to provide economic care for these aged is a significant question.

In a basically agricultural economy of small independent farmers who earn their living off the land, the aged can be retained in the family group without too great a family burden. Usually old people are able to contribute enough labor or other services to "pay their way."

In a business economy of small proprietors, it is customary for business owners upon reaching retirement to pass their interests to their families. In return, the families provide the income necessary for support of those retired. Here, as in the agricultural economy, the aged can usually render services to the business sufficient to "pay their way."

In an economy such as that which exists in the United States today where industrialization, urbanization, big business, and big agriculture are predominant, economic care of the aged often is beyond the financial capacity

[1] Cf. the following: *Retirement Security in a Free Society*, New York, National Association of Manufacturers, 1954); *Actuarial Study No. 24*, Washington, Federal Security Agency, Social Security Administration, 1946); Census Bureau projections of 1947 and 1950; projections of National Resources Planning Board, 1943; National Resources Committee, 1937; and Committee on Economic Security, 1934.

of the family. In addition, not only is the tradition of the family "caring for its own" breaking down but so also is its will to do so.

Since efficient and competitive enterprise generally has no place for the superannuated employee, it is often impossible for him to provide income in his old age on a "pay-as-you-go" basis. Therefore the job of taking care of the superannuated worker and his dependents today seems to fall on (a) the workers' individual ability and effort to amass a competency during his working years, (b) the government, (c) the employer, or (d) some combination of these three.

(a) To many, self-reliance for old age income seems to be the only real American way. However, today's low investment yields make the problem of amassing a competence out of one's own earnings a difficult one—difficult not only in absolute terms but difficult also in terms of the things that must be foregone during productive years. It is not human nature to give up present things freely for future benefits. Furthermore, mass marketing methods now in vogue do not encourage thrift. The American economy is geared to mass production. To maintain full employment, goods have to be sold so that they do not pile up in the warehouses and lead to a curtailment of production. To sell these goods, distributors resort to powerful advertising and other sales promotion methods. One of the most effective methods has been the development of installment selling with "nothing or little down" and "easy" monthly payments. With effective advertising and sales presentations making man dissatisfied with what he has and with installment selling under the easy payment plans making it possible for men to buy the things that are supposed to make him happy, there is no wonder that man finds it difficult to save. Actually, instead of saving a part of present income for future use, the tendency is to spend part of the expected future income for present use.

What have low investment yields to do with the problem? When 6% compound interest was available on savings,[2] about $244 put away each year over a working lifetime—say ages 25 to 65—would build a fund which, at the same 6%, would pay $200 a month. During those days price levels were such that $200 a month provided more than enough for a comfortable retirement. Today, when people can hardly expect to earn over 2½% compound on savings, building a fund that will pay $200 a month at 65 requires an annual saving of about $1,236—and it is not easy now to live on $200 a month.

Income taxes also take a higher toll today. This means that in the above illustration more than $1,236 a year will have to be deposited to provide

---

[2] Today 6% is so unrealistic that it was necessary for the authors to look through four books of tables before finding one that included a 6% basis.

$200 a month at retirement. In the 6% days, either there were no income taxes at all, or the rate and amount subject to that rate were relatively small.

The annuity offers a more feasible method of funding retirement, but even here the cost is more than the average person can meet through accumulations. It takes about $32,000 to purchase a single-premium, immediate, life annuity of $200 a month at age 65, male, and about $37,500, female. Few indeed are the people who can save about $35,000 out of income even over a working lifetime of 40 years.[3] At 2½%, this would require a saving of about $450 a year during this period.

Inflation is another important economic consideration. The government is committed to a policy of maximum employment consistent with private enterprise. A high level of investment is essential to the maintenance of full employment.[4] A falling price level discourages investment. A rising price level encourages investment. A number of distinguished economists argue that a healthy economy depends upon a gently rising price level. Based on historical observation, it is not unrealistic to expect price levels to rise on the average of approximately 2% a year over a working lifetime. Thus the young man who plans his retirement income on the basis of current price levels may find that planned income amount grossly inadequate when he reaches old age.

High wages often accompany high prices. With the progressive income tax rate, however, the worker retains only a part of the increase in wages, although all of it represents a cost to the employer. Higher wages, therefore, in themselves might not be a solution. This factor makes it difficult for even the higher-paid executive to plan for his own retirement and still maintain the standard of living expected of him.

In summary, note three major factors that make it difficult, if not impossible for the typical person to provide for his own old age: low interest rates, high taxes, and inflation. A logical question at this juncture is why are interest rates low, taxes high, and future inflation almost a foregone conclusion. The answer begins and ends with government economic policy. In between is a discussion of the causes and nature of this policy, a subject which is omitted here as beyond the scope of this book.[5]

---

[3] Perhaps it would be better to put it, "Few are the people who *will* save" those amounts.
[4] Any major decrease in private investment spending will have to be offset by government spending if the level of employment is to be maintained. Although government economic policy is directed toward the maintenance of private investment spending, it does not preclude heavy increases in deficit-financed government spending should such a program become necessary for the continuation of economic prosperity.
[5] Interested students can review the pertinent discussions in any standard up-to-date textbook in the Principles of Economics.

(*b*) This leads to a discussion of the next method of providing for old age security: government retirement programs, or as they are more commonly called, Social Security. Because of the difficulty the individual faces in accumulating a competency by direct savings, such difficulty being partly the result of government fiscal policy, the government has found it both economically desirable and politically expedient to enter the old age funding picture. The result is the retirement benefit system under the Social Security Act.[6] The original purpose of Social Security was to provide only the floor upon which the balance of an adequate retirement income could be built by the individual. At best, its responsibiilty seems to have been to provide only a subsistence-level income. There are those who question whether the subsequent liberalization of the act has held to its original principle—or that, if it has held to its original concept, it will continue to do so. At any rate one can reasonably expect Social Security benefits to continue to increase at least in accordance with price levels, otherwise Social Security will fail to do its job.

The financing of the Federal old age and survivors' benefit program is on a basis of taxation.[7] Increases in Social Security benefits increase the tax burden.[8] With the possibility that, in less than 50 years, somewhere around one quarter of the population will be in age brackets now eligible for Federal old age benefits, the question of how high the tax will have to go is a pertinent one.

(*c*) The third method of handling the problem of old age financing is for the employer to assume some of the burden. Some will argue that the burden is never assumed by the employer because the funds used by the employer to finance retirement benefits are a part of labor cost, which could otherwise have been paid out in wages.[9] The government also co-operates by giving employers certain tax benefits under approved pension plans. The tax aspects of pensions are discussed later.

Spurred by the rise in the social philosophy of employer responsibility for the welfare of employees and by the demands of organized labor, employers have been entering the field of old age financing with great rapidity.

---

[6] Old age assistance on a needs basis also is available from the various states, subsidized under the federal Social Security Act.

[7] See Chapter 24 for a brief discussion of Social Security funding.

[8] There is a tendency to overlook the fact that "deductions" from pay checks for Social Security are another tax, and that the deduction from the worker's pay is only half of the total tax. The employer pays the other half.

[9] This reasoning does not include the fact that the employer expects to gain certain additional advantages through granting his employees a pension—advantages which he might not gain by paying out the funds in the form of direct wages.

In 1951, there were approximately 17,000 qualified [10] pension and profit-sharing retirement plans in the United States. Today the estimated number approaches 30,000.

1. TYPES OF PENSION PLANS

Broadly speaking, there are two types of pension plans: *funded* and *unfunded*.

Funded vs. Unfunded Plans. The unfunded plan is hardly any plan at all. It is simply a matter of paying the employee a stipend out of the current earnings of the company, and is sometimes referred to as the "supplementary payroll" plan. By and large, such plans have not proved a solution to the retirement problem because (*a*) they are mostly discretionary,[11] and (*b*) they are paid out of current income. Of the two weaknesses, the latter is probably the more serious. The current income of any business fluctuates, and there may come a time, or times, in the life of the business when current income is insufficient to continue the stipends. Further, businesses are subject to mortalities just as are human beings. The result is that the unfunded plan offers the retired worker no assurance of continued security.

It was the financing of pension plans out of current income that lead to what might be considered the first crisis in pension planning. Salaries and wages rose during the industrial boom created by World War I. Since most pension plans are based at least in part on the income of the worker, pension plans paid out of current income were strained to meet the cost of benefits to workers who retired at peak salaries.

Shortly following the war came the industrial depression, cutting down the amount of money the employer could pay for pensions out of current income without seriously endangering the solvency of his business. It was at that time that widespread attention was first given to the use of acturarial and investment principles in pension planning.

The funded pension plan is an attempt to handle pension obligations over the years during which they accrue rather than to charge them against current income in the years during which they are paid. One of the oldest funding devices is the balance sheet reserve. Under this plan, accrued pension

---

[10] That is, qualified with the Treasury Department for tax deductibility of the employer's contributions.

[11] That is, the employer decides whom he will pension, and for how much at the time the pension payment commences. In practice, of course, retirement ages and incomes by classes of employees do tend to become established under a discretionary plan, but any individual employee short of retirement age has no contractual assurance that he himself will receive anything, when, or how much. Thus he has no sound basis for personal financial planning. Unfortunately for labor-business relations, some pension plans are still of this type, giving to the employee both the impression of insecurity and of employer paternalism, if not outright charity.

obligations are carried as a liability or surplus reserve on the balance sheet. To it the employer credits, from time to time, sums of money which he feels may be sufficient to pay the retirement benefits which have been established through formal schedule or informal custom.

This type of balance sheet reserve is the weakest of all methods of funding. Actually it is a most crude method of funding pension plans, for it does not earmark *specific* assets for pension financing. It is only slightly removed from the unfunded plans which pay benefits from current earnings. The only difference in the two plans is in cost accounting. Under the informal plan the pension cost is charged as an expense in the year paid whereas in the so-called balance sheet funded plan the cost of pensions is charged as a reserve to the year in which the liability is incurred. The balance sheet plan gives the illusion of sufficient funds to pay benefits without the necessity of drawing on current income, and also creates a difficult tax problem since the tax deduction might have to be taken in the year the benefit is paid rather than in the year in which the accrual of pension benefits is charged.

Two prerequisites of sound pension funding are (a) conservative estimates of the future cost of benefits based on sound actuarial data, and (b) the actual deposit of funds into a separate account to be used to pay pension benefits.

Methods of Funding. Broadly, there are two methods of funding: (a) the uninsured plan; and (b) the insured plan. Of these methods, only the insured plan in every case meets the above two prerequisites of sound pension funding. The uninsured plan calls for the actual deposit of funds but does not guarantee that conservative estimates based on sound mortality and interest assumptions have been made of the costs of future benefits. There might be a tendency in self-administered plans to underestimate the amount needed to fund benefits because, in the early years after the establishment of the plan, demands on the fund are light. Many cases are on record where both interest and mortality have been overestimated leaving the fund actuarially unsound.

Under the uninsured plan, a trust for the benefit of the employees is established.[12] Into this fund, the employer pays either (a) regular amounts based on estimates of the amounts needed to pay all benefits or (b) irregular amounts, as in the case of profit-sharing trusts. The trustee invests the money, accumulates the earnings, and distributes the benefits to eligible employees. This is called the "Self-Administered Trusteed Plan."

A number of arguments often are suggested in favor of a self-administered pension plan. These arguments, of course, can be applied soundly only

---

[12] The trust must be created without the possibility of reversion to the employer if contributions to it are to qualify for tax deductibility.

to those corporations large enough to self-insure the pension risk. The advantages are (1) greater economy of operation, (2) greater flexibility in establishing and administering the formula, (3) possibility of more profitable investment experience since there is more investment freedom.[13] It must be remembered, however, that while certain advantages of self-administered plans are always possible, they are by no means assured as are the advantages of the insured plans.[14]

While some trusteed plans will provide that the funds shall be invested in immediate annuities at the time an employee retires, by and large, the self-administered trusteed plan does not use insurance. Therefore, inasmuch as the subject of this text is insurance and the area of this chapter is insurance in pensions, the mechanics of the self-administered plan will not be detailed.[15]

2. TYPES OF INSURED PLANS

Insured pension plans may be classified broadly into two groups: those using Group policy contracts and those using individual policy contracts. Under each general classification are two or more types of plans, each of which will be discussed.

Group Annuities. Like a Group life or A & S plan, a Group annuity plan consists basically of a contract between the employer and the insurance company for the purchase of deferred retirement annuities for each of the employees participating in the plan. All actuarial, administrative, and investment services are handled by the insurance company, in contrast to the self-administered trusteed plan where these services are performed by the trustee. The plan may be either contributory or noncontributory. If the plan is contributory, usually a specified percentage of the number of employees, customarily 75%, will be required to participate and there is a provision that the plan may be canceled as to future purchase of annuities if participation falls below the requirement.

It should be stressed, however, that participation in the case of the

---

[13] For a critical appraisal of the freedom allowed in self-administered pension plans see *Labor Law and Industrial Relations* by Charles W. Anrod, Chicago, Institute of Social and Industrial Relations, Loyola University.

[14] For an interesting and informative discussion of the attitude of an insurance company spokesman on the relative advantages of the two funding methods see *The Advantages of the Insured over Uninsured Pension Plans* by Stephan Hansen, Director of Group Insurance, The Great West Life Assurance Company, Winnipeg, Canada.

[15] For a brief but comprehensive discussion, cf. Dan M. McGill, *Fundamentals of Private Pensions*, Homewood, Ill., Richard D. Irwin, Inc., 1955, pp. 113 ff.; or *Handbook for Pension Planning* (various eds.), Washington, Bureau of National Affairs, 1949, pp. 138 ff.

Group annuity plan is not for underwriting purposes,[16] as in the Group life plan. Instead it is to effect the administration economies that are responsible for the lower rates of Group annuities as contrasted to individual annuities. Also, unlike Group life, state statutes do not set the minimum number of lives that must be covered under the plan.[17] As a matter of underwriting practice, however, individual companies usually set a minimum on the number of lives. The most common limit is 25, although many companies are reducing their requirements to ten. As a rule, companies also have a minimum annual premium requirement, making a special administrative charge on cases falling below either a minimum aggregate annual premium or a minimum premium per participant.

Again as in Group life, the master contract is issued to the employer, with certificates of participation given to the individuals under the plan. These individuals hold the status of third-party beneficiaries.

The first modern Group annuity contract was issued on Christmas Day, 1921. Termed "Group pension plan" at that time,[18] it called for the employer to purchase annually for each employee a single-premium deferred annuity of $10 a year. Retirement age was 65, at which time the employee would collect a lifetime income equal to the sum of the annuities purchased for his account. Thus an employee who retired with 20 years of service under the plan would receive an annuity of $200 a year.

This *unit-purchase* plan is the basic Group annuity plan; although today a number of variations have been made in it.

More common than the purchase of annuities of like amounts for each participant is the purchase of annuities varying in amounts according to a schedule of salary brackets. For instance, one amount will be purchased annually for employees earning $2,000 to $3,000; another, for employees earning $3,000 to $4,000, etc. Since each unit of the single-premium, deferred annuity is purchased annually, the total of the annuities at retirement reflects

[16] There could be some adverse selection in the case of failure of employees in poor health to join the plan, but the effect of this in the mass is likely to be insignificant.

[17] A number of states at one time sought to apply the statutory definition of Group life to Group annuities. Currently, all such administrative rulings have been rescinded except that the New York law has been interpreted to require a minimum of two lives.

[18] The name was changed from "annuity" because of the disrepute into which the term "pension" later fell as a result of unfavorable experience with nonactuarial pensions. One of the worst of such experiences from a public relations standpoint was that of Morgan & Company, a packing firm which merged with Armour & Company in 1923. Morgan had established a pension plan in 1909, limiting its maximum liability to $500,000. At the time of the merger, 600 employees had already retired under the plan, and actuaries calculated that over $7,000,000 would be necessary to pay the promised benefits. A member of the Morgan family voluntarily contributed $500,000 to the fund, but that succeeded in postponing the debacle by only 14 months, at the end of which time all benefits ceased leaving 600 old people "high and dry." The disaster received nationwide newspaper attention.

both the number of years of service of the employee and his salary experience over these years.

Obviously, since years under the plan play a large part in determining the size of the annuity received by the employee, the employee near retirement when the plan is installed will not receive benefits commensurate with his services. A separate formula often is established for past-service benefits, calling for, perhaps, 50% lower benefits than those paid for future service. Since the cost of past-service annuities on old employees may be substantial, their purchase is often spread over a period of years. The Bureau of Internal Revenue, of course, has fixed a formula for determining the *minimum* number of years over which the cost of funding past-service benefits may be deducted.[19] Purpose of the regulation is to prevent companies from taking excessive deductions in high profit years.

In most cases, some employees will be close to retirement age. Their cases can be handled either by (a) excluding them from the Group annuity plan and handling their pensions on the "supplementary payroll" pension plan, or (b) by buying immediate annuities on their lives.

The original Group annuity plan mentioned earlier provided for the full vesting of each deferred annuity unit in the employee as purchased; that is, he became the owner of that annuity regardless of future service with the company. Today it is more common in Group annuity plans to withhold vesting until the end of a given period of service—maybe ten years; maybe 20. Any period is possible. A popular arrangement is progressive vesting; that is, say 10% a year beginning with the fifth or tenth year so that the plan is fully vested in 15 or 20 years. The reason for denying immediate vesting is to eliminate the liability of the employer for pension benefits for people who have not rendered the company substantial service. The longer the waiting period required for vesting, the lower will be the probable cost to the employer. Further, withholding vesting may be a factor in reducing employee turnover.[20]

An employee's rights in the annuities in event of termination of employment depend on whether or not the annuities purchased for him are vested.

---

[19] Contribution to a qualified pension plan may be deducted up to 5% of the compensation otherwise paid to participating employees, *plus* contributions in excess of 5% where actuarially necessary to fund past and current service credits distributed as a level amount *over the remaining future service of each employee.* An alternative provision allows annual deductions for the normal cost of the plan, *plus* a sum not exceeding 10% of the cost of past-service or other supplementary credits as of the date the participants are included in the plan.

[20] While the authors doubt the efficacy of Group insurance in reducing employee turnover, they believe pension plans may have a very real effect, particularly in the case of the employee who has a number of years of service with his company and thus has built up substantial values he stands to forfeit by changing jobs.

If the plan is noncontributory and not yet vested, he receives nothing. If it is vested, the employee keeps the paid-up annuities already purchased for him. If the plan is contributory but not vested, his contributions—but not those of his employer—are returned to him. The plan may provide that these contributions be returned with or without interest. The usual rate of interest, where allowed, is 2% compounded annually. If the plan is contributory and vested at the time of termination, the employee may withdraw his own contributions in cash and retain the paid-up annuities purchased by the vested portion of the employer's contributions. Or, if he wishes, he can leave his own contributions in the plan to provide paid-up annuities along with those purchased by the employer's contributions. If he elects to keep the paid-up annuities, he still retains the right to withdraw his own contributions in cash at any time prior to his normal (65) retirement age. Some contracts give the employee a vested interest only if the employee uses his own contribution for a paid-up annuity. If the employee later cashes out his annuity, he forfeits his interest in the paid-up annuity based on the employer's contribution.

Usually the plan forbids the employee to withdraw his contributions prior to termination of employment.

In case of death before retirement, any contributory premiums are returned to the estate or designated beneficiary of the employee. Usually the returned money is credited with interest.[21] Optional modes of settlement are usually allowed to the beneficiary. It is not common to grant death benefits out of the employer's contributions, those contributions usually being used to purchase a straight, no refund annuity.

In case of death after retirement, the annuity may or may not pay a refund. In its "pure" form, the unit purchase deferred Group annuity plan provides neither death benefits nor loan privileges. As stated, the employer's contributions usually are used to purchase life annuities without refund. The purchase of refund annuities would materially increase the cost of the plan. The cost superiority of "pure" annuities carrying no refund features is illustrated in Table 1.

Note the tremendous saving in the cost of the life annuity granting no return if death occurs before age 65 contrasted to those that pay death benefits before retirement. Therefore, in the interest of providing the largest retirement income possible there are usually no death benefits if the plan is noncontributory. If it is contributory, the customary procedure is to use the employee's contributions to purchase modified refund annuities. In that case,

---

[21] Under a plan which does not credit interest, the retirement benefits will be slightly higher, or the cost will be slightly lower for the same benefits.

Table 1. Single Premiums for Annuities of $10 Monthly

Commencing at Age 65—Male Lives Only—Nonparticipating Contracts

	AGE AT ISSUE		
	25	35	45
1. No return on death before age 65. Annuity payments for life only.	$414	$541	$722
2. Return of Single Premium (or cash value if greater) on death before age 65. Annuity payments for life only.	534	701	919
3. Return of Single Premium (or cash value if greater) on death before age 65. Annuity payments guaranteed for ten years and life.	580	761	998

the employee's beneficiary or his estate receives the difference between the accumulated value of his contributions and the total of the benefits he has received.

While early Group annuity plans contained provision for income in event of disability, today it is rare to find such provisions,[22] except that the annuity may provide for early retirement at whatever rate of benefits the annuities already purchased will pay at that age.

When employment is terminated by other than retirement, death, or ill health, nonvested annuities purchased with the employer's contributions are canceled and a credit of their values is made to the account of the employers to be applied toward the premiums for future annuities to be purchased under the plan. Unless the amount of the canceled annuities is very large, the only evidence of good health required will be a statement from the employer that he believes the terminating employee to be in good physical condition. If the amount of the annuity is large, the company may require a medical examination of the terminating employee or may hold up the credit (paying interest on it meanwhile), for, say, five years.[23]

Credits to the employer can be used only to buy future annuities for employees. Tax laws prevent them from being used in the interest of the

---

[22] The removal from Group annuities of disability provisions, other than early retirement, was occasioned by the same factors which, during the adverse loss experience of the 1930's, led most companies to drop their disability income riders on life policies. Inasmuch as the trend of the 1950's has been again toward offering such riders on life policies, it is not illogical to assume that they might appear again in retirement annuity contracts.

[23] Costs under the plan are based on the assumption that premiums paid for those who die before retirement will be used to help pay the benefits of those who outlive the mortality assumptions—just as in the case of any annuity benefits. Therefore, to make credits to the employer on account of the termination of an employee before retirement who is in ill health would be similar in effect to adverse selection and will upset cost calculations.

employer. The company usually reserves the right to modify the terms of the Group annuity contract. Any modification or change in the contract is without prejudice to annuities already purchased.

As far as the insured is concerned, the plan may be discontinued at any time.[24] Notice to the company or failure to pay a premium effects discontinuance. Annuities already purchased, however, remain in force. The discontinuance applies only to the purchase of future annuities.

There are four conditions under which the insurer may discontinue the plan: (1) Nonpayment of premiums. (2) A drop in the number of eligible employees below the minimum required. (3) A drop in the participation percentage in a contributory plan below the required percentage. (4) Refusal of the employer to consent to new conditions imposed under the terms permitting contract modifications.

Rates. Rates for practically all plans since 1939 have been based on the 1937 Standard Annuity Table. Currently companies are rating the table down one or two years; i.e., assuming the annuitant is one or two years younger than actual age, thus producing a lower rate of mortality than the tabular rate.[25] Female ages are usually set back five years from male,[26] thus increasing the annuity premium required of them.[27]

The interest assumption for Group annuity rates is commonly 2% or 2¼%. The loading factor is usually 5% to 8% of gross premium, allowing 2½% or 3%, on the average, for administration expenses and the rest for a contingency reserve, which reserve is required by law in some states. Loading not actually

---

[24] The Bureau of Internal Revenue places restrictions or penalties on discontinuance of such plans. These restrictions are designed to prevent employee benefit plans from being used as tax avoidance schemes. Also, if the plan is a part of a union collective bargaining agreement, discontinuance will be restricted by that agreement.

[25] With the increase in the average length of life effected in recent years, an annuity table based on past experience is likely to overstate the death rate. Since the longer an annuitant lives, the more money the company pays out, a lowered death rate increases the cost of an annuity. Assuming the annuitant is younger than he is sets the rate higher to offset the increased cost of his longer life. Since Group annuities are rated after the first year on the basis of actual experience for the year passed, it does not make too much difference if an out-of-date table is used.

[26] See the 1937 Standard Annuity Table.

[27] It is interesting to note that while companies take cognizance of the greater average length of life of women in setting rates for annuities, they have not usually done so in setting rates for life insurance, where their greater average length of life should, theoretically, lower the premium. An alleged reason is that the average policy on women has been smaller than on men so that acquisition and administration costs have eaten up the mortality savings. However, just at the time this is being written, a major reinsurer has announced premium scales that rate women down three years as compared to men and are 15 to 16% lower than for men. This does not mean that life insurance rates on women will be reduced by such an amount across the board. It is the larger policies which are reinsured, and on larger policies certain fixed acquisition costs, such as much of the home office clerical work involved, are proportionately lower.

used is returned in dividends; and excess reserves are released as credits to the employer.

It was once the practice to guarantee Group annuity rates for the life of the contract. The contract usually provided, however, that rates could be changed on or after the fifth anniversary of the contract but such rate changes would not apply to future annuities purchased for employees who were enrolled in the plan prior to the date of change.[28] Since 1935 the general practice has been to guarantee the initial rates for premiums received during the first five contract years only, with changes thereafter applying to everyone under the plan.[29] After the first five years, rates may be changed annually.[30]

Rate guarantees and conditions for purchases of annuities for past service credits are the same as those applying to the purchase of annuities for future service credits. Only past-credit annuities purchased during the initial guarantee period take the initial rates.[31]

Deposit Administration Plan. One objection of the employer to the Group Annuity plan is the lack of flexibility in the handling of its costs. The employer's contributions in the Group Annuity are used annually to buy deferred, single-premium annuities. Employers have been inclined to look with favor on the self-administered plan, where the financing is more flexible and the funds are not actually committed on behalf of any one employee until he reaches retirement age. The "deposit administration" variation of the Group Annuity plan was developed by the insurance companies to offer the employer some of the advantages of the self-administered plan while still offering him an insured plan.

Under the deposit administration plan or DA plan as it is commonly called, the periodic contributions of the employer are not allocated to the purchase of annuities for a particular employee until he is ready to retire.

---

[28] At least one prominent company still guarantees the rates through the lifetime of existing employees and reserves the right to change only the rates on new employees. In other words, any rate changes made by this company are effective only on employees placed under the plan subsequent to the rate change.

[29] Obviously, the rate changes cannot apply retroactively to annuities already purchased.

[30] Cf. Footnote 28.

[31] If the employer wishes to spread the purchase of annuities for past service over more than the initial rate guarantee period, all past-service annuities may be purchased immediately by means of a loan from the insurer, to be repaid in annual installments over a period of years. If an employee for whom past-service annuities have been purchased under the loan dies, retires because of ill health, or terminates with a vested interest, loan payments for his past credits must be continued until completed. In case of termination for other reasons, the employer receives a refund of the original single premium for the past-service annuity with interest, minus a surrender charge and the present value of that part of the loan which has not been repaid.

Instead, employer's contributions are accumulated as a deposit with the insurance company. If employees contribute, their contributions are held in individual accounts. As each employee becomes eligible for retirement, the funds necessary to purchase single-premium annuities are taken from the general employer account, added to the individual employee account (if any), and used to purchase a single-premium immediate annuity of a size sufficient to provide the benefits scheduled under the retirement plan. The annual deposit required of the employer will be the amount the actuary estimates will be needed to adequately fund the plan. The insurance company, however, does not guarantee the adequacy of the fund. The retirement benefit, however, is guaranteed once a conversion is made into an annuity.

The DA plan gives greater flexibility than the Group Deferred annuity in the selection of the retirement age and in the establishment of a relationship of benefits to final average salary. No "normal" retirement age is necessary in the deposit administration plan. Instead, an assumed distribution of retirements may be used, based on past experience. That is, the employer, surveying past retirement ages, determines how many employees may be expected to retire at different ages—or in different age brackets. This past distribution may then be used as the assumption for future distribution and may give effect to a weighted average age at retirement that might reflect probable experience, and, hence, costs, more accurately than the assumption of a "normal" retirement age of 65, as is common under the usual Group Annuity plan. Further, the deposit administration plan, postponing purchase of any annuities to actual retirement age instead of purchasing them annually, permits benefits to be based on final average salary, a figure not determinable until actual retirement is effected.

There being no purchase of annuities until actual retirement, there are no credits to the employer for terminations. Allowance may be made for estimated terminations in measuring the size of the deposit the employer is required to make into the fund each year to meet the established schedule of benefits.

The insurance company usually guarantees a minimum rate of interest and the maximum percentage charged for administration on all funds deposited during the first five years. Annuity premium rates enter the picture only at the time of the retirement of any individual employee, and these are usually guaranteed for the first five years also.

Under the DA plan, actuarial calculations must be made for terminations, salary increases, early and late retirements, etc. The employer is free to hire independent actuarial consultation, or the insurance company will furnish the service. This freedom to use independent actuarial services [32] is one of the attractions of the plan. Employers often feel insurance company standards are too rigid and require higher deposits than are actually necessary.[33]

Next to the Group Deferred Annuity, the DA plan is the most popular type of insured pension arrangement.

Immediate Participation Guarantee. Another variation of the Group annuity developed to meet the competition of the self-administered plan is the Immediate Participation Guarantee plan, first written in 1950. Sometimes called the "Pension Administration Plan" or "Direct-Rated Deposit Administration Plan," it seeks to combine the flexibility of Self-Administered Trusteed plans with the guarantees of insured plans.

Group annuities and Deposit Administration plans remove from the control of the employer the deposits made to fund benefits. Further, the employer's participation in any cost savings is deferred through the operation of the dividend formula. Finally, these plans involve the creation of contingency reserves. In competition, advocates of the self-administered plan point out that their plan enables the employer to keep the funds in his business, reflects immediately any gains in cost factors, and obviates contingency reserves. Instead of having a contingency reserve for losses, such losses are made up by additional contributions to the plan if and as needed. The Immediate Participation Guarantee plan ("IPG") seeks to achieve for the employer these "advantages" of the self-administered plan.

IPG is usually nonparticipating and written only on large groups consisting of 2,000 or more members. As in Deposit Administration, a fund is established into which employer contributions for the cost of benefits are deposited. This fund is credited annually with the actual net rate of interest earned by the insurance company. No minimum rate is guaranteed as in Deposit Administration. The fund is charged annually with actual administration expenses and charged or credited with variations of experiences from assumed mortality. Since there is no contingency fund, the plan is not guaranteed against investment loss; hence, the fund is adjusted annually for capital gains and losses.

Under some plans, all benefit payments are charged directly to the fund as made. Under other plans, upon the retirement of an employee, the fund is debited with the gross single premium for an annuity equal to the amount

---

[32] Usually any standard that can be justified on the basis of the employer's past experience will be acceptable to the insurance company.
[33] Also, the independent pension consultant, who often originates a pension case, more often will suggest deposit administration since it might mean the continuation of his services on a retainer's fee for as long as the plan is in effect, or for as long as he is available, whichever is shorter.

necessary to pay the scheduled benefits. At the end of the year, all outstanding annuities are canceled (an accounting transaction), and any excess of the single premium over the amount paid in benefits is returned to the fund. The fund is then debited for a new annuity for the next year, the rate being at the attained age of the retired employee but on the schedule of rates prevailing at the time of his retirement.

In other words, everything is handled on an immediate basis, thus giving the employer immediate participation in all cost factors.[34] This is the characteristic that gives the plan its name. In exchange for this immediate participation, the employer sacrifices many of the guarantees of the conventionally insured plan, and some of those of Deposit Administration.

In effect, the IPG plan resembles the self-administered trusteed plan with the insurance company performing the functions of the trustee. One important difference, however, is that once an employee has retired, the insurance company takes over the guarantee of his future benefits instead of leaving this function to the fund. It is in this connection that the combination of the flexibility of the self-administered plan plus some of the guarantees of the Group annuity plan is achieved through IPG.

In IPG, the employer is more or less free to make any contribution-rate assumptions he considers reasonable. The insurance company merely sets a minimum and maximum rate of annual contributions. The employer alone is responsible for any deficits which develop in the plan. The one requirement the company has is that the fund at all times be large enough to pay the benefits promised for employees already retired. Should it shrink to that minimum, the contract provides that annuities will be purchased for them, and the plan will revert to a conventional Group annuity. What happens to those under the plan but not yet retired is up to the employer.

In general, IPG annuities are purchased at the rates in effect at the time each employee retires. Some plans guarantee that all money deposited in the plan during an initial period of, say, five years, plus all interest earned on

---

[34] Such as mortality improvement, interest earned on funds left with the company, administration expense, turnover. In the self-administered and IPG plans (and, to some extent, in Deposit Administration), the employer always thinks of this participation in terms of potential gain. Advocates of "immediate participation" will usually illustrate these potential gains in contrast to the conventionally insured plans. Rarely, however, is equal stress given to the potential losses (or increased expenses, to put it another way). "Immediate participation" applies not only to gains but also to losses. This is not intended as criticism of "immediate participation" plans but only of the sales arguments frequently used for them. It should be remembered, also, that the informal, "pay-as-you-go" plan, now generally in disrepute, also gives "immediate participation." The cycle of enthusiasm in any type of "immediate participation" plan, especially the self-administered, follows closely the economic cycles of investment experience. When investment earnings are high, enthusiasm in "immediate participation" is high; when they go down, enthusiasm wanes and employers become more aware of the value of guarantees.

that money, can be applied to the purchase of annuities at a scale of guaranteed rates. Or, there may be a rate guarantee for all annuities purchased during an initial period, such as ten years.[35] After the expiration of any initial period of rate guarantee, rates for annuities for newly retiring employees are adjusted annually.[36]

An IPG plan may be discontinued either by the insurance company or by the employer. If the plan is discontinued, the following alternatives for handling money already deposited are available:

(1) The fund could continue to operate until such time as the amount in it drops to the minimum required, whereupon it would come under the provisions for automatic discontinuance and revert to a closed annuity contract.

(2) The difference between the amount required to buy annuities on those already retired and the total amount in the fund could be used at the time of discontinuance to buy deferred, paid-up annuities on those not yet retired to the extent of the funds available.

IPG contracts sometimes provide that the employer may transfer the IPG funds to another funding agency upon payment of a surrender charge.

Group Permanent. As explained in Chapter 13, Group life insurance can be written wholly or partially in the form of permanent policies as contrasted to the customary one-year Term contract. Such a plan is called "Group Permanent," and it may be used as a retirement plan as well as a life insurance plan. The Group Permanent contract may be the entire retirement plan. All premiums for the plan are paid directly to the insurance company, not through a fund, and all benefits are paid by the company. Termination costs are higher than under a Group annuity plan, and administration is more complicated. The statutory minimums for size of group and participation, as set by varying state laws, must be met. The general characteristics of the Group permanent plan were discussed in Chapter 13 and need not be repeated here.[37]

The policy most commonly used in Group permanent plans is the Retirement Income contract providing $10 of monthly income at retirement age for each $1,000 face amount of insurance. Since the retirement income

[35] Obviously, few plans will purchase many annuities during the early years of operation; therefore, this latter is less of a guarantee than the one which allows all money deposited during a given period of years to be used at any time in the future to purchase annuities at initially guaranteed rates.

[36] Remember that this rate adjustment affects only the initial annuity purchased for any employee. If the plan of canceling all outstanding annuities at the end of each year is used, such canceled annuities are replaced by annuities at the same rates that prevailed when the initial annuity for the retired worker was purchased.

[37] Cf. Chapter 13.

policy eventually builds a cash value in excess of its face value,[38] use of this policy to fund a retirement plan increases the death benefit available at later ages. This higher death benefit increases the cost of the plan by about 3% of gross premiums, which additional cost can be eliminated by providing a level benefit. When a level death benefit is desired, any type of policy which develops a cash value can be used. However, if the benefit schedule is based on $10 per $1,000 of insurance and other than a retirement income policy form is used, it will be necessary to supplement the retirement benefit from the insurance with other funds at retirement.[39] This extra amount may be handled on a deposit administration plan, and most Group permanent master contracts make provision for such a fund. Alternatives are to supply the additional benefit out of the employer's current income or to accumulate the extra amount needed in a trust, in which case the plan becomes a "combination": combination of insured and self-administered.

Under the "combination plan" benefits are essentially the same as under a Group permanent plan. Death benefits before retirement are always the face value of the insurance. If the plan is contributory, it is customary to apply all the employee's contribution to the premium on the insurance. The employer's contributions are used to complete the premiums and to build the trust fund. Withdrawal benefits to the employee on termination depend on vesting provisions. They may include all or part of the cash values of the insurance. It is not common, however, for the employer's contributions to the trust fund to vest in the employee.

Contributions to the trusteed fund are the responsibility of the employer. Companies will furnish actuarial tables showing the amount which should be in the fund at the end of each year at the assumed rate of mortality and interest. However, the employer is not bound to follow the table. He may employ an outside consultant to set the rate of contributions or he may use guesswork. What he does in this connection is of no concern to the insurance company, whose only responsibility is to supply the life insurance and whatever annuities the cash values of the life insurance policies will provide at retirement age.

It is common in combination plans to have the trustee handle all money, paying the life insurance premiums as well as managing the trust fund. This arrangement is called a "Pension Trust."

The Group permanent plan is best adapted to a benefit schedule which provides a retirement income based on a flat percentage of salary, disre-

---

[38] Cf. Chapter 3.
[39] This is true because no other policy form will pay a retirement income at age 65 of $10 per $1,000 of insurance. The $1,000 Endowment of age 65 pays less than two thirds of the required amount.

garding length of service. Salary usually is considered in terms of brackets with so many units of, commonly, $10 a month [40] of retirement benefit purchased on a level premium basis for each salary bracket. Insurance adjustments resulting from changes in salary sufficient to change brackets are made on contract anniversaries, except that short duration coverages for salary increases in the immediate ten years before retirement age may be provided.

Usually the employee may elect any one of the standard annuity settlement options available from life insurance companies in lieu of the customary life income option, if election is made before retirement date.

Years of service may be given weight in the benefit schedule by use of a unit of benefit for each year of service rather than a flat percentage of earnings. However, the death benefits resulting under such a plan are less attractive.[41]

The Group permanent plan will have a normal retirement date as in the case of the Group annuity. The selected date is the earliest date for retirement with "full" benefits. If the plan permits early retirement, the cash value built up for the employee as of retirement date can be used to purchase an immediate annuity of whatever size it will buy at the attained age of the employee. In the case of late retirement, the usual plan is to start retirement benefits at the normal age even if the employee remains at work. The employee might be allowed to defer his retirement by taking the interest-only option, to be converted later to a life income for a higher amount upon actual retirement. While the procedure of delaying the start of the benefits and crediting the employer with the benefits not paid can be worked out in Group permanent as in the Group annuity, the former plan is not so well adapted to the arrangement because of the large death benefits payable upon death before retirement.

In case of death before retirement, the employee receives the face value of the insurance on his life. If the plan is based on a Retirement Income contract, the cash value may be more than the face value. In that case, the cash value is paid exactly the same as in the case of an individual Retirement Income Insurance policy. Usually the standard forms of settlement options are available to the beneficiary.[42]

In case of death after retirement, the benefit payable to a beneficiary

---

[40] Some companies offer plans that provide other than $10 units—anywhere from $20 per $1,000 of face value down to $7.50 per $1,000.

[41] Death benefits under this plan would increase each year. This is contrary to insurance theory that usually the greatest amount of death protection is needed for the young man with a growing family.

[42] Cash settlement is not common.

varies according to the type of annuity income selected. If a life annuity has been used (the usual basic provision of a plan), there is no refund. If an annuity certain has been elected, the remaining certain payments will be made. If a joint and last survivor annuity or a contingent annuity [43] is elected, payments continue at the same rate or at a reduced rate during the lifetime of the second person.[44]

In event of termination of employment prior to vesting, under noncontributory plans the cash value [45] is credited to the employer to be used for future premiums. If the plan is contributory, the employee's withdrawal value is equal to the cash value less a surrender charge on the amount of insurance purchased by his contributions. The surrender charge allocates a portion of administration costs to the terminated benefits. In more liberal plans, the employee's withdrawal value prior to vesting may be his contributions plus interest. The coverage may be converted without evidence of insurability to an individual policy of the same type on termination of employment, with the employee assuming the full premium. His withdrawal value may be used to provide paid-up benefits or to add to the reserve under the new policy which will have the effect of keeping his premium under that required at his attained age.

The Group permanent contract, like Group Annuities, may be discontinued by the employer at any time by nonpayment of premium. It may be discontinued by the insurance company if the number of participants or the percentage of participation drops below the required minimums.

Premiums in Group permanent plans are level for each unit of purchase. Usually the initial rate structure is guaranteed for a period of from three to five years. Thereafter, rates may be adjusted, but only as to new entrants into the plan or additional units for those already covered.

Generally, rates are somewhat higher than for the Group annuity but lower than for individual policies. The lower cost is a result of elimination of the medical examination and savings on acquisition and administration costs.

Dividends are payable under participating contracts and experience credits are granted under nonpar contracts. Each Group permanent master contract is considered individually for purposes of dividends and experience credits; thereby each case pays net what its own deviations from the basic assumptions require.

---

[43] In which the other person (usually wife) is not a joint annuitant but a beneficiary whose benefits are contingent on the death of the annuitant.

[44] Death benefits for the various kinds of annuity options are the same as those for the corresponding annuity, described in Chapter 5.

[45] Unlike the cash value of an individual policy, however, that of Group permanent is based on the full level reserve.

Individual Contract Pension Trust. In addition to the various Group insurance and annuity plans for funding the benefits to be paid under a retirement plan, individual life insurance or annuity policies are used. Under the plan, a corporate or individual trustee is set up [46] who applies for the policies, holds possession and title to the individual policies, collects the money to pay the premiums and, sometimes, receives benefits for payment to the employee or his beneficiary. It is more common, however, for the benefits to be paid direct to the individual.

The individual contract pension trust is most widely used by small groups, too small to qualify for a Group plan.[47] Most companies have maximum limits on the size of the group they will take under such a plan, 200 being an example of a liberal limit.

Several types of policies may be used under this plan as under the Group permanent plan; however, again as under the Group permanent plan, the most common life insurance contract is the Retirement Income policy, and the most common annuity contract is the retirement annuity.[48] Which is used in any given case depends on whether a life insurance feature is desired in the plan prior to retirement.

Evidence of insurability is required for retirement insurance policies, usually a medical examination, although a health statement may be substituted if the company writes nonmedical.

Since most companies will not issue individual retirement contracts to run less than ten years, it may be necessary to provide when the plan is established that employees age 55 to 60 will retire on the tenth anniversary of the installation of the plan.

One difficulty encountered where retirement insurance policies are used is the uninsurable individual. The solution is the purchase of a retirement annuity for him, foregoing the insurance protection.

If the individual pension trust is discontinued:

(1) Cash values can be used to purchase paid-up deferred annuities.

(2) The employee can take over full premium payments or the policy can be reduced in size if he wishes to pay a smaller premium.

(3) The cash value of the policies can be made available to employees.

In case of termination before vesting, the employee receives his own contributions plus a nominal rate of compound interest and the employer's

---

[46] In order first to qualify the plan for tax deduction to the employer, and also for administrative convenience.

[47] The individual contract pension trust also is used often by agents of companies which have not entered the Group field. At various company meetings, agents of one prominent nongroup company seem to have fun exchanging stories about the truckload and bushel basket deliveries they have made of individual contracts for pension trust cases.

[48] For descriptions of these two policies, cf. Chapters 3 and 5, respectively.

contributions are credited to the trust. If the plan provides for vesting and any part of the benefits is vested at the time of termination, the employee receives both his own contributions and the appropriate part of the employer's contributions.

The benefit formula is usually set by salary brackets, as in the case of Group plans. Under most plans, the pension benefit is a certain percentage of attained salary regardless of age or length of service. In effect, this automatically takes care of past service benefits. If more exact past service credit is desired, the individual policy can be adjusted to any size that equitably reflects the desired credit.

Under the annuity plan, in event of death before retirement, the cash values accumulated by both the employer's and employee's contributions are paid the beneficiary. In the case of retirement insurance, the beneficiary collects the face value of the insurance or the cash value, whichever is higher. Usually the annuity will provide a death benefit in the event death occurs within a given period of years after retirement. Under the retirement insurance plan, the annuity option will, likewise, usually have a period certain. Of course technically any type of annuity payment, life, certain, or refund can be used.

The cost of an individual contract pension trust is somewhat higher than a Group permanent plan using the same type of policy. Acquisition and administration costs are higher because separate policies are issued instead of a master policy and certificates. As in all individual contracts, the rates applying are those in effect at the time each policy is issued and are guaranteed for the life of the contract. Dividends are earned on the same basis as on any individual policies but are credited to the trust and are used to reduce premiums. This is true even in contributory plans.[49] Dividends reflect company-wide experience rather than just the experience of the individual plan, as in Group insurance.

3. SPECIAL PLANS

Two types of special pension plans are: (1) deferred profit-sharing and (2) equity or "variable" annuity.

Deferred Profit-Sharing. It is possible to fund a pension plan through profit-sharing with the employees. The plan has appeal to some employers

---

[49] To qualify for tax deduction, a pension plan must provide "definitely determinable" benefits at retirement. Since dividends are not guaranteed in amount, their use to purchase paid-up units of retirement benefit would make exact retirement benefits undeterminable. Contributory plans in nonprofit organizations are able to use dividends to purchase paid-up additions without penalty because of the tax-exempt nature of the corporation.

because (1) it gives employees a direct interest in the earnings of the firm and therefore some feel that it tends to promote efficiency, and (2) it does not impose a fixed cost on the employer. The second appeal seems to have more influence in the establishment of a profit-sharing pension whereas the first appeal seems to have more influence in the establishment of a cash distribution profit-sharing plan. Reduced to a simple description, the deferred profit-sharing plan receives each year a percentage of company profits based on a predetermined profit-sharing formula. These payments are held in trust for distribution to employees at retirement or earlier in event of death or disability. As in the case of the conventional retirement plan, insurance need not be used. If it is used, it can be employed in either of two ways:

(1) All funds can be accumulated and invested by the trustee. At the retirement of each individual, funds to his credit can be used to purchase immediate annuities for whatever amount of benefit the available money will provide.

(2) A benefit formula can be set up. The share of profits paid into the plan each year can be used to buy as much insurance annuities as possible up to the amount necessary to provide the benefits in the formula. If the profit money is insufficient, the employees can make up the difference on a contributory basis.

The first of these uses is the more common.

As can be seen, the big disadvantage of the profit-sharing pension plan is that either the amount of the benefit is unpredictable and varying or the cost to the employee is unpredictable and varying.

To reduce the effect of the undesirable feature of profit-sharing pensions, a basic pension trust plan can be set up to gaurantee a minimum retirement benefit, known in amount and cost. Then a profit-sharing trust can be established to provide additional benefits, the amount of which depends on the size of the profit-sharing fund accumulated over the years.

Equity or "Variable" Annuities.[50]   The traditional annuity—like all forms of insurance—is based on fixed-return investments of guaranteed maturity value, largely bonds and mortgages. As discussed in Chapter 5, when the purchasing power of the dollar drops (prices go up), the effective return on the traditional annuity also drops.[51] The variable annuity is based on investments (largely common stocks) which are guaranteed neither as to

---

[50] As this is written, the form of "annuity" being discussed is so new that the name for it is not yet fixed. Early called "equity annuity," it now seems to be more often termed "variable annuity."

[51] On the other hand, as prices go down, the effective return of the traditional annuity goes up.

income nor liquidation value. As the purchasing power of the dollar drops (prices go up), the income from and price of some common stocks are likely to increase.[52] Thus the return from the variable annuity varies in number of dollars but, theoretically, tends to be more constant in terms of purchasing power. The appeal of the variable annuity in retirement plans is to provide the retired worker a dollar which will do as much for him when he is ready to spend it as he did for it when he acquired it.

The benefits and conditions of payment under the variable annuity plan of funding retirement income may follow the pattern for any annuity plan previously discussed. However, since the plan adjusts automatically for gains and losses, there are no dividends or rate credits. Benefits in the plan are defined in terms of shares in the fund or units of benefits instead of dollars of contribution or retirement income. The value of a share or unit in the plan will change from year to year in proportion to the over-all change in the value of the investments behind it.

The equity or variable annuity was introduced by the Teachers Insurance and Annuity Association under a separate organization called the College Retirement Equities Fund. Known as "CREF," this organization sells the variable annuity either on a group or individual basis to college staffs only. The equity annuity is available to industry in general only on a self-administered basis. Insured plans are not written as an equity annuity. Existing legislation does not permit it. However, seeing in it a medium for meeting the competition of self-administered plans, several life insurance companies —among them one of the largest—are seeking legislation to permit its writing. The plan has serious opposition from within the life insurance business, however.[53]

4. MANAGEMENT DECISIONS IN PENSION PLANNING

Any number of reasons may impel management to install a pension plan for its employees. It may wish to reduce labor turnover, increase employee efficiency, improve employee morale, meet union demands, or insure what it considers the social responsibility of business to take care of its superannuated employees. Whatever the motivating factor or factors, manage-

---

[52] Whether or not the return on the variable annuity decreases in terms of purchasing power when prices decrease depends upon the relationship between the decline in the dollar income paid under the variable annuity and the price level. Only if the dollar income declines faster than prices will the purchasing power of the variable annuity decline.

[53] For a discussion of the attitude of different interested parties on the equity annuity, cf. R. I. Mehr and C. W. Anrod, *Current Problems in Pension Planning,* University of Illinois Bureau of Business Management, 1953.

ment needs to make several decisions before its pension program can be designed.

Contributory vs. Noncontributory. As in Group life and disability insurance, the employer must consider whether he wants his plan contributory or noncontributory. Some pension planning experts favor contributory plans for the following reasons:

(1) Employee contributions make a more adequate pension possible with a given employer contribution.

(2) The employee is likely to be more interested in the plan and to understand it better and appreciate it more if he is asked to contribute to it.

(3) Employers feel that contributory pensions are less paternalistic. Employees tend to rebel against paternalism in industry.

(4) Employee contribution is the American way, as exemplified in the contributory feature of the Social Security Act.

Other employers favor noncontributory plans because:

(1) Tax laws favor noncontributory pensions. The employer can deduct his contribution for income tax purposes. The employee does not have that privilege. A pension plan involving a $100 contribution by the employer means more than a $100 pay increase to the employee. If the employee is in a 20% income tax bracket, it means an increase of $125, for the employer can pay with $100 what it would take an employee $125 to pay. The difference is correspondingly greater as employees enter higher tax brackets.

(2) Employers have more freedom in selecting the plan and specifying the benefits.

(3) Employees might counteract with additional wage demands were they asked to contribute toward a pension.

(4) Contributory plans often discriminate against the young employee, and many may not join the plan.

Eligibility. Another decision relates to eligibility requirements. An employer does not have to cover all employees to qualify his pension plan for tax deduction. He may cover, for example, only salaried workers, or only wage earners, or he may exclude young employees and old employees as classes. A waiting period not to exceed five years is allowed as a prerequisite to eligibility.

In general the Commissioner of Internal Revenue will exercise discretion in approving plans that appear permanent and are set up in good faith. The employer must set up his eligibility requirements in this light. The plan must not be discriminatory in favor of officers, stockholders, supervisory employees, or high-salaried employees.

A major problem of eligibility is determining how to provide for employees who are near or past retirement age. Each company must determine its own course, based upon the number of such employees and its financial condition. Many methods of handling the problem are available, running all the way from complete exclusion of employees already at retirement age to granting them full benefits. Where benefits are paid to employees who are near or past retirement age at the time a plan is installed, the benefits often are paid out of current earnings. They are not funded and may not even be formalized.

Fixing the Retirement Age. The selection of a retirement age is another decision that has to be made. All employees do not become old at the same age; nevertheless, a workable retirement plan must select the retirement age in advance. The most common retirement age is 65, selected to conform to the Social Security retirement age. An age less than 65 might be too expensive. For example, the cost of retiring employees at age 60 is close to 50% more than the cost at 65. If the cost of retirement continues to rise, there may be a time when companies will at least consider 70 as the age of retirement. There is some thinking in that direction today.

Many companies have set up minimum and maximum retirement ages, giving employees the option of selecting the year within that range in which they wish to retire.

Benefit Formulas. An important problem in pension planning is the determination of the size of benefits to be paid to employees upon retirement. In arriving at the benefit structure, the employer must make certain that the benefits are adequate on the one hand, and on the other that they are within his ability to pay.

Benefits are usually designed to supplement Social Security payments to a livable level. The amount of benefits may be based on average earnings, or they may have such bases as final earnings, average earnings over past five years, average earnings in highest ten years, or any other logical combination. It is generally considered that a pension, to be adequate, should supplement Social Security benefits up to a minimum of 50% of average earnings, at least in the case of lower income workers. It is also generally considered desirable to give some weight in the pension formula to years of service.

There are three widely accepted methods of setting pension benefits.

(1) Years of service method, under which credits toward the amount of the pension are given for both past and future service. Usually the amount of the credit for past service is smaller than that for service after the installation of the plan, it being one of the functions of a pension plan to hold employees in the future. Some such formula as that shown may be used.

PERCENTAGE CREDIT PER YEAR OF SERVICE

Annual Earnings	Past Service Credit	Future Service Credit
1st $4,200	0.5%	1.0%
All over 4,200	1.0%	1.25%

Larger credits often are allowed on earnings over $4,200 annually because these earnings are not covered by Social Security.

(2) Flat percentage method, under which a flat percentage, say, for example, 35% or 40%, of either average or final salary is provided to all employees completing a minimum number of years of service by age 65. This method attaches no reward to years of service beyond the minimum.

(3) The money purchase method, under which a percentage of the worker's pay is set aside by the employer and often matched by the employee. At retirement age, this money is available for a pension. Past-service benefits and minimum pensions often supplement payments to older workers. Many plans have minimums, and a few have maximums.

Vesting. Another decision to be made deals with the requirements for vesting. After how many years of service should a discharged or resigning employee receive any benefits from the employer's contribution to the pension plan? There are several advantages of early vesting which often outweigh the cost disadvantage.

(1) Better employee relations, since disgruntled employees can leave without losing anything.

(2) Increased interest in the plan among younger employees. A plan under which they must work for years before they own anything in it has little present reality.

(3) Fairness of the plan, since many people will change jobs at least once or twice in a lifetime.

(4) Greater ease in qualifying the plan for tax deduction under the Internal Revenue Code. Vesting is not required for qualifications, but technicalities make it desirable. If a plan discriminates in favor of employees who are officers, owners, supervisors, or highly paid workers, or if it is not for the exclusive benefit of employees and their beneficiaries, then it will not meet the requirements of the Bureau of Internal Revenue for tax exemption. Failure to vest interest may lead to a violation of one of these principles.

Funding. A final decision deals with funding. Should the plan be self-administered or insured? If insured, should it be under a Group annuity, deposit administration, Immediate Participating Group, Group permanent, or individual policies under a pension trust? Each of these funding methods has its uses and limitations. The employer must select the one that best fits his need.

5. SUMMARY

The economic problem of the aged in the economy is becoming increasingly acute. Not only is the percentage of aged to total population increasing, but also it is more difficult for the average man to prepare for retirement today than it was a generation or so ago. High income taxes leave less margin for saving out of current earnings, and low investment yields reduce the amount that savings can earn. As a result, building a competency for old age out of individual earnings has become extremely difficult. Inflationary trends add to the difficulties.

One solution to the problem is government participation in old age pensions. The philosophy of the Social Security Act, however, has been to provide only a basic minimum, enough for subsistence level existence. Americans want more than this for their old age.[54]

Another solution is for the employer to participate in funding retirement. At the present time, the employer has entered into pension funding to a large degree, and all indications are that he will go into it even further as years go by. His participation is fostered both by the government through tax favoritism granted to funds used to establish retirement plans for the benefit of employees, and by Union activity.

Retirement plans established by employers may be funded or unfunded; that is, benefits may be paid on a pay-as-you-go basis or on a basis which calls for the building up of a fund actuarially computed to be sufficient to meet the promised benefits as they fall due.

Funded plans may be self-administered, or they may depend on insurance contracts. Insured pension plans may be either on a Group basis or on a basis of individual policies. Each plan has variations.

Group Plans. Several types of Group plans can be distinguished:

(1) *Deferred Group Annuities.* A Group annuity, consisting of a master contract and certificates of participation, is purchased. Under the plan, paidup deferred annuities are purchased annually for each participant. At retirement, the employee receives the aggregate income from all annuities purchased for him over the years covered.

(2) *Deposit Administration Plan.* The DA plan is a variation of the Group annuity. The contributions to the plan are not used to purchase de-

---

[54] How far the government should go in providing income for the aged is a question of political philosophy. If this sounds like a "quisling" statement, it is meant to be. The authors are not prepared to discuss—in this text, at least—the political aspects of the problem.

ferred annuities annually but are accumulated in a common fund for the retirement of each covered employee. When an employee reaches retirement age money accumulated in his behalf is used to purchase a single-premium, immediate annuity.

(3) *Immediate Participation Guarantee Plan.* A fund is established into which contributions are made to pay the cost of retirement benefits. The fund is credited annually with the actual interest earned by the insurance company, is charged annually with actual administration expenses and mortality variations, and adjusted annually for capital gains and losses. Benefit payments may be charged directly to the fund, or the fund may be debited annually for the cost of annuities for retired employees. In this latter case, all outstanding annuities are canceled at the end of the year, money not used is returned to the fund, and new annuities are purchased. The result is that the employer participates immediately in all gains (and losses) from any facet of the plan instead of waiting for the operation of a dividend formula, as he must under the Group annuity plan.

Group Permanent. Group permanent may be used as a retirement plan. Any life insurance policy written for a duration at least equal to the normal retirement age established in the plan (usually 65) may be used, but the most common plan is the Retirement Income contract paying $10 a month retirement income at age 65 per $1,000 of face value. Since such a policy develops a cash value in excess of face value, it is slightly more expensive than other policy forms. However, no other policy form pays a monthly retirement income of $10 per $1,000 at age 65. Therefore, if some other form is used to fund a $10 per $1,000 formula, a side fund may be established to supplement the retirement benefits. Such a side fund may be handled by the insurance company on a deposit administration basis, or it may be handled on a self-administered basis. How the fund is handled is no concern of the insurance company, which is obligated to provide only the guarantees in the insurance contract. If an insurance contract is used to fund part of the benefits and a self-administered fund is used to supplement it, the plan is called a "combination" plan.

Individual Contract Pension Trust. Where the group to be covered by the pension plan is too small for a Group plan or the percentage of participation in a contributory plan is below the minimum required for Group by either the company or the statutes, the plan may be funded by individual insurance or annuity policies. In this case, each employee is insured on an individual basis with all the usual requirements of individual underwriting. Any policy written for a period equal at least to retirement age is usable, but the common plans employed are the Retirement Income policy and the retirement (annual premium deferred) annuity. A trustee is established to receive all funds for premiums, to apply for the insurance, and to hold and own the policies. The trust may receive the benefits and pay them to employees, but, more commonly, benefits are paid directly to the employee or his beneficiary.

Profit-Sharing. Retirement pensions can be funded by a profit-sharing plan. A percentage of profits determined by the profit-sharing formula is deposited in a fund each year. The portion of the fund credited to each employee may be used (1) to pay pension benefits on a self-administered basis; (2) purchase deferred annuities annually or meet premiums on retirement insurance contracts, with the employee making up any deficit between the money available from the fund and the total premium necessary; (3) purchase immediate annuities at the employee's retirement age; (4) purchase benefits supplemental to a basic pension plan; or (5) to fund future benefits with past-service benefits funded on another basis.

Variable Annuities. The variable annuity is an annuity based on equity investments in contrast to fixed-return investments. The income from it is expected to vary with the rise and fall of the purchasing power of the dollar, thus theoretically giving the annuitant not a fixed-dollar return, but a return keyed to the cost of living. In other details of handling, the pension plan based on a variable annuity is the same as one based on a fixed-return annuity.

There is no question but that employer participation in retirement financing is of growing importance, economically and socially. Because insurance offers guarantees and administrative help, the insurance plans play a major role in the field of industrial pensions.

Questions for Class Discussion

1. What do you think is the best solution to the problem of old age security in this country?
2. How do you account for the vast increase in the number of industrial pensions in this country?
3. If you were advising management on establishing a pension plan, would you recommend a self-administered plan or an insured plan?
4. If, in establishing a pension plan, you find that you have a large number of employees near retirement age, what can you do to handle this problem without increasing the cost of the pension to a prohibitive level?
5. How would you recommend handling the problem of vesting in a pension plan?
6. Suppose an employer wishes to establish a pension for his employees but does not want a fixed cost. What would you suggest?

7. Under what circumstances would you recommend a Deposit Administration plan rather than a unit purchase Group annuity?
8. Do you think a pension should be made dependent on a profit-sharing plan? Discuss.
9. Would you recommend the use of the equity annuity in a pension plan? What do you suspect to be the attitude of labor toward such a plan?
10. Discuss the decisions which management must make in establishing a pension plan and indicate how you would go about making these decisions.

CHAPTER 15

PROGRAMMING INCOME
INSURANCE: NEEDS

ONE OF THE most frequently asked questions is "How much insurance should I own?" The best answer is an adaptation of Abraham Lincoln's reputed reply to the query, "How long should a man's legs be?" Lincoln's response was "Long enough to reach the ground."

Just so, the answer to the question, "How much insurance should I own?" is, "Enough to cover your needs," subject, of course, to the ability to pay premiums. Since most people can use more insurance than their budgets will afford, an intelligent job of insurance buying requires economy in use of dollars available for premiums.

Intelligent insurance buying (or selling) involves the process of programming, for actually this process is the only valid way of finding out how much and what kinds of insurance a man should own. Programming involves several steps. First it consists of analyzing needs; deciding how to cover these needs adequately (tempering wants with ability to pay); and then determining how far present assets,[1] including insurance, go toward filling these needs. From this analysis, the gaps in coverage can be ascertained. The next step is to determine how much and what kinds of insurance are necessary to fill this gap. The final step involves making recommendations on distribution of policy proceeds, proper designation of beneficiaries, and consideration of the various policy safeguards available, such as provision for common disaster, spendthrift clause, automatic premium loan, and the like.

---

[1] Where there is any significant amount of general property to be taken into account, the process becomes one called "Estate Planning" (to be discussed in Chapter 17).

It should be noted that the title of this chapter is *not* "Programming *Life* Insurance," but, "Programming *Income* Insurance." It has been demonstrated previously that three perils can interrupt the flow of income: death, old age, and disability. An income insurance program is, therefore, a three-legged stool. To try to base it on two legs—death and old age, as is the case when programming is confined to life insurance holdings alone—is to leave the program in precarious balance.[2] This discussion of programming, handling death, old age, and disability needs concurrently will come as a shock to the confirmed life insurance man but is the only sound concept of programming if there is any real meaning to those clauses calling for complete service to clients in the codes of ethics of such organizations as the National Association of Life Underwriters, American Society of Chartered Life Underwriters, and International Association of Accident & Health Underwriters.[3]

1. DETERMINING NEEDS

The first step in programming income insurance is to determine needs. This can be done only on an individual basis. No one set of needs is universally applicable to all policyholders any more than is one set of symp-

[2] This is a concept that is difficult for the experienced life insurance agent to understand, unless he represents one of the life companies that has been in the A & S business for some time. The typical life agent thinks of writing A & S as something apart and different from his regular line of work. If he takes disability into consideration in programming, he often thinks he has served his client adequately by arranging waiver of premium—or by selling a small, loss-of-time policy as an afterthought. The established life insurance agent still is a long way from understanding *income* insurance programming; and the training procedures of even the largest life companies now in the A & S field—with some very few exceptions—do little to show agents the need for programming death, old age, and disability needs *simultaneously*. The reaction of the typical life insurance agent to disability insurance programming along with life insurance is amazing. He regards A & S as no more than an inferior sideline, even if he does not completely refuse—as many do—to have anything to do with it. When cases are called to his attention in which individuals with adequate life insurance programs were seriously hurt through lack of adequate disability insurance, his attitude is either that it was all "an act of God" over which he had no control or the rationalization, "Well, why didn't some A & S agent sell him?" Many life insurance agents do not like to sell A & S insurance because they do not like to be "bothered with" frequent claims. Some do not write it because they do not care to take the time to learn the business. Many of these rationalize their ignorance with the statement: "Selling A & S could ruin the good public relations I have built up over the years since there is so much claim chiseling in the A & S business." While instances of chronic claim chiseling do exist, they are the practice of only a handful of companies out of the hundreds writing A & S. No life agent should have any trouble finding a completely ethical A & S company. If he is placing his business in such a company and still has claim trouble, it is for one of two reasons: (1) He is doing a poor selling job, allowing the client to expect more than the policy promises and failing to point out all exclusions at the time the policy is sold; or (2) he may be dealing with the wrong kind of clients. Instead of the company chiseling on claims, the clients may be chiseling on the company—a not uncommon situation in the A & S business.

[3] Which codes call for professional standards of service.

toms universally applicable to every sick man. Likewise, no one arrangement of income insurance policies can be said to fit the "average" buyer any more than one medical prescription can be said to be the cure for all physical disorders. Programming, like medical treatment, is entirely an individual thing.

The first step in any discussion of programming is to list and then describe insurance needs. There are a number of uses for insurance. Some of them represent needs, whereas others represent only wants or whims. The interest here is in those basic needs which are not only the most common and widespread, but also the most important to the greatest number of buyers.

The following is a list of seven basic insurance needs listed in the order considered by the authors to represent their usual importance to the typical family man.

1. Cash needs
2. Readjustment income
3. Family-period income
4. Life income for widow
5. Educational fund
6. Wife insurance
7. Retirement income

Cash Needs. A "Clean-up" or "Clearance Fund" is the first cash need. A man may be completely free from debt before he dies, but his death can create expenses that could plunge his estate deeply into debt. The act of dying costs money. To put it callously and somewhat crudely but nevertheless practically, it will cost money to dispose of the body and for a place to put it. These two costs are inescapable. They are by no means, however, the only possible costs involved.

Few deaths are instantaneous. Usually there are unpaid bills for medical services, hospital services, nursing care, and other such items which can mount to large sums. In cases of serious illness no one thinks about economizing or cutting corners on anything that might help: specialists, treatments, transfusions, operations, oxygen tents, special foods, medicines, anything to keep the patient alive.

Included in the total Clearance bill will be outstanding current bills. Few people pay cash day by day. Almost everyone runs at least partly on credit: a charge account at the grocery or drugstore, accounts at department stores, a gasoline credit card, a club account, the utility company services. . . . For the thrifty man, living well within his means, these bills may total merely in the tens of dollars; for a good many people, they will run into the hundreds. In cases where there are major obligations outstanding—loans at the bank, an automobile on installments, a mortgage—they may run into thousands.

Finally, if there is any estate other than life insurance left to named beneficiaries, expenses of probate and administration become involved.

The Clearance fund need of the individual does not have to be met by life insurance; but since no man knows when he will die, unless he uses life insurance, he will have to maintain liquid assets equal to whatever cash amount he estimates will be needed at death. Thus, if it is assumed that $2,000 will be necessary to take care of Clearance expenses, then without life insurance the individual will have to have $2,000 in liquid assets on hand today, and keep them on hand throughout his future lifetime—a rather large order for the average man. Moreover, under this method, the "Clean-up" bill will be paid with 100% dollars, that is, a $2,000 Clearance bill will cost $2,000. On the other hand, if life insurance is used, there is a chance that the $2,000 Clearance bill will be paid with less than $2,000. The total cost of a life insurance Clearance fund will be the total of premiums paid plus interest. How much that will amount to depends on the policy used, as illustrated in Table 1.

Table 1. Effective Cost per $1,000 of Clean-up Expense Insurance Assuming Death at End of Year Indicated

(All policy forms, representative nonpar. Issue age assumed: 25)

PREMIUMS PAID INCLUDING INTEREST FOREGONE *

Year of Death	Single Premium Life	20-Pay Life	Continuous-Premium Life
1	$408	$25.50	$17.34
2	416	51.51	35.03
3	424	78.04	53.07
4	433	105.10	71.47
5	442	132.70	90.24
10	488	279.22	189.87
15	538	440.98	299.87
20	594	619.58	421.32
25	656	684.07	555.41
30	725	755.26	703.45
40	883	920.66	1,047.37

* Two per cent interest *net after taxes* is assumed, a fair assumption for a safe and liquid investment.

Life insurance is the most logical way to pay Clean-up expenses. The act of dying creates the need for the money; and life insurance proceeds, maturing because of death, furnish the cash to offset death expenses. An asset which has a higher value at liquidation (in this case death) than it has during life is especially valuable for Clean-up expenses.

One difficulty involved in programming life insurance for final expenses is that death is not usually instantaneous but often comes after protracted illness which runs up medical and hospital bills. While reasonably accurate estimates can be made of the size of other final expenses, possible medical and hospital bills are a matter of pure guesswork. If they cause the need for cash to exceed the amount of life insurance assigned for Clean-up expenses, the rest of the program may be upset. The family will have to dip into policies intended for other uses. The result is that often, in an attempt to "play it safe," more life insurance is assigned to the Clean-up fund than is needed. While it is true that money left after final bills are paid is not lost, it is also true that if the excess money had not been assigned to the Clean-up fund, it might have been arranged more profitably in the program.

The solution to this problem of planning is medical expense insurance, using the term in the broadest sense to include all insurable expenses of illness: physician, surgeon, hospital, nurse, drugs, etc. Since such insurance, subject to its maximum, automatically adjusts itself in size of benefits to the size of the bills incurred, the guesswork regarding how much should be allotted for medical expenses in the Clean-up fund is reduced.

Since medical insurance should be part of the insurance program of every family, no special medical policy for Clean-up purposes is necessary. The same policy that handles medical expenses in case of recovery will pay these expenses in case of death. The need for medical insurance to solve the big problem of Clean-up—how much to allot for final medical bills—should not be overlooked.

Mortgage insurance is the second cash need most common among life insurance buyers. In most family budgets, mortgage payments (or the monthly rent) are the largest single item, running 25% and sometimes even more of monthly income. Therefore, if mortgage payments can be eliminated or even reduced, a much smaller income will suffice to keep the family together.

Perhaps the best arrangement is to provide for sufficient proceeds to pay off the balance on the mortgage, if prepayment is acceptable under the terms of the mortgage contract involved.[4]

Even when the mortgage is paid off, the reduction in housing outlay effected, of course, is not the full amount of the previous monthly payments. Under the type of mortgage widely used today, monthly payments include

---

[4] As pointed out in Chapter 6, too often neither the agent recommending and placing the mortgage insurance nor the mortgagor takes the trouble to check this point. As a result, families sometimes find themselves with cash on hand to pay off the mortgage but a mortgage contract which prohibits prepayment to maturity. Also, some mortgages will penalize prepayment, especially in the early years of the mortgage. If the contract in question does have a penalty provision, then the amount of mortgage insurance should be increased to cover it.

not only principal and interest but also taxes and even insurance. These charges still will have to be met after the mortgage is retired. Therefore, not only cash to pay off the mortgage but also an additional amount of mortgage insurance should be provided to be paid out as monthly income to meet taxes and insurance.

Mortgage insurance is an inexpensive way to increase the income of a widow. For example, at age 25, $61 a year will purchase a $10,000 mortgage policy on the yearly-decreasing Term plan covering a 20-year mortgage. Assume that the payments of principal and 5% interest on the mortgage are $75 a month. If the insured dies within the first year, family expenses would be reduced $75 a month if the mortgage were paid off with the proceeds of the policy. If, on the other hand, the $10,000 were settled under a 20-year time option, the policy would pay a monthly income of only $51.58 (assuming 2¼% interest). The family income, therefore, is increased $23.42 a month if the policy proceeds are used to retire the mortgage.[5]

The need for mortgage insurance is not adequately covered by death insurance alone. The family economic situation will be just as bad (sometimes worse) in case the breadwinner becomes disabled. The situation which gives rise to the need is created by loss of income and what causes the loss—death or disability—makes little difference in the financial effect on the family. Therefore, mortgage disability insurance is as necessary as is mortgage life insurance.

If the mortgage does not allow prepayment or if the insured is disabled, mortgage insurance should be in the form of monthly income payments rather than a lump sum.

An Emergency Fund is a third cash need. The best the average man can do with his insurance program is to provide a minimum livable income for his family in the event of his premature death. Such minimums offer no leeway in case of emergencies which take extra cash. While it is true that when one has a guaranteed income he can obtain credit to pay unexpected bills, repayment of the loan even in small monthly payments may prove an extreme hardship for the family.

In the larger insurance program where there is a sizable margin between subsistence and the income payments provided, the need for emergency cash can be taken care of by reserving for the widow the right to withdraw at any time some of the proceeds being held by the company.[6]

---

[5] The reason is, of course, that the interest on the unpaid portion of the mortgage is twice as much as the interest on the unpaid portion of the proceeds held by the company while making the 20-year installment payments.

[6] Also, this right of withdrawal will be instrumental in qualifying the life insurance proceeds for the Federal Estate Tax, Marital Deduction.

If there is danger that the beneficiary may withdraw funds needlessly, a maximum can be set on the amount of withdrawals at any one time, during any period of time, or in the aggregate. For instance, the right to withdraw might be limited to not more than $200 in any one year with the number of withdrawals limited to five.

In the smaller insurance programs, where a withdrawal of part of the proceeds would reduce the insurance income to a level below subsistence, the problem of extra cash for emergencies is better handled by a special emergency fund. For instance, assume that the minimum income to the wife for life is only $75 a month. Withdrawal of $1,000 of the proceeds for an emergency (even if allowed by the company) would reduce a life income which commenced at age 50 by about $4 a month—a serious cut on a $75-a-month income. On the other hand, if there is an emergency fund consisting of the proceeds from a $1,000 policy, the emergency can be met without infringing on the $75-a-month income.[7]

The emergency fund also provides a safeguard against the effects of inflation. Often a program provides (or a beneficiary elects) an installment income which is adequate for living expenses at the time chosen, only to find that prices rise to an extent that this income is no longer sufficient. For instance, a widow with one or two children and a house clear of debt might have found $150 a month entirely adequate in the late 1930's, only to discover a few years later as prices rose that this income was worth little more than half of its original purchasing power. If there is an emergency fund, the widow could draw upon it by putting it on one of the income options to supplement her $150 a month. This would ease the situation.[8]

One of the big emergency needs for funds is illness, especially when it requires hospitalization or surgical treatment. As in the case of Clean-up, it

---

[7] If the company will hold as low as $1,000 at the interest option with the right of withdrawal, then this is the option to use for an emergency fund. Since most companies will not accept as low as $1,000 on an interest-only option, then the proceeds should be taken in a lump sum and deposited in a bank to be held for emergencies.

[8] It is hardly possible that any emergency fund set up under a program calling for $150 a month income would be sufficient to double that income, but it would help. For instance, such a program would probably call for no more than a $2,500 emergency fund at best. This amount would provide about $22.50 a month additional income if put on a ten-year fixed installment basis. Nevertheless, $172.50 would be better than $150. Furthermore, the basic principle of programming is to cover first needs first. Providing income until children reach self-sufficiency (or an age at which they can do at least part-time work to supplement the family income) has a high priority among needs. Thus the children may be nearer the age at which they can help out when the effect of the inflation is felt. If this is true, the emergency fund can be spread over fewer years with a resulting increase in the monthly benefits. As an example, if only five years of increase income are needed, $2,500 will pay almost $45 a month. In larger programs, larger emergency funds can be established to handle the inflation threat more adequately.

is impossible to estimate how much might be needed in the emergency fund for medical bills. Rather than tie up money in an emergency fund to meet the unbudgetable expenses of medical care, it is much simpler and more economical to provide for these costs by arranging for enough family income to pay premiums on medical care insurance. In this way these so-called unbudgetable emergency expenses become budgetable. In working out the family's insurance program, therefore, instead of adding, say, $1,000 to the emergency fund to pay possible medical expenses, it might be better to put a $1,000 policy on a 20-year installment option yielding approximately $60 a year. This additional income would pay the premium on an amount of hospitalization, surgical, and medical expense insurance for the widow and children that would provide benefits, if required, far in excess of $1,000 in total bills over the 20-year period.

Actually, as long as insurance is available, laying aside cash in an emergency fund to meet possible medical bills is economically unsound. Insurance programming requires close budgeting and medical care insurance helps make this possible.

There may be additional cash needs at death if the insured has a sizable bank or policy loan. In such a case, the amount of the loan can be covered with Term insurance.

In summary, it might be emphasized that it is well not to underestimate cash needs. Until a person has seen firsthand how much final expenses can amount to, it is hard for him to realize how high they can run.[9]

Readjustment Income. After cash needs have been taken into consideration, attention must next be directed toward income needs, the most important of which is the Readjustment Income. Since only few breadwinners, if any, can afford an income replacement program that will permit a family to continue the same standard of living, loss of earned income means family expenditures will have to be cut—usually drastically. However, for the family to reduce expenditures to a sharply lower level the very instant earned income is interrupted is almost impossible. It takes time to cut living expenses. Acquired buying habits must be replaced. Study must be given to the question of how expenditures can be cut with the least harm to living standards. It may be necessary to dispose of the home and find a less expensive place to live. A change in food habits to less expensive diets might be necessary. The entertainment and recreation budget will have to

[9] One of the authors has seen family experience in which the amount provided in the Clean-up fund was a $250 Industrial policy and the actual costs to be settled (a cancer case), just short of $10,000. However, this case doesn't prove a need for $10,000 life insurance assigned to Clean-up but for inclusion of medical expense insurance as a part of programming for final bills.

be sliced. The necessity of cutting these expenses all at once can cause panic that might easily result in a sacrifice of possessions and holdings that, under calmer circumstances, could be liquidated more advantageously. Finally, an immediate reduction in the standard of living with, perhaps, the urgency of the mother seeking early employment, can be devastating to family morale—especially coming on top of the death, shocking accident, or dreaded illness which caused the loss of income.

A family left without earned income might be compared to a family stranded on the top floor of a building without stairway or elevator. A forced jump from the top floor to ground level may seriously injure the family. The Readjustment Income provides a stairway to bring the family down safely. For example, if earned income net after taxes is $600 a month, an income insurance program that can provide only $200 a month in the event of death or disability results in a "long jump" for the family should the insured contingency occur. The distance will be covered with less chance of financial and psychological injury to the family if income can be dropped by stages—say to $400 the first year, $300 the second, and reaching the $200 level the third. This will give the family time to make an orderly readjustment both in expenditures and in life generally.

In many cases, Cash Needs and Readjustment Income will represent the only program a family can afford, particularly in the earlier family years when earnings are relatively low. Such a program means the family will have to earn its own way after the first few years. The readjustment income, however, will give the family time for reorganization. For example, the wife or widow, if she must become the breadwinner, will have the opportunity to take a commercial college or refresher course in order to prepare herself for a remunerative and responsible position.

It takes very little additional life insurance to provide a readjustment period income. Table 2 shows the amount of life insurance required to provide $100, $200, and $300 a month for one, two, and three years.

Table 2. Amount of Life Insurance Required to Provide a Monthly Readjustment Income (2½%)

Years	$100 a Month	$200 a Month	$300 a Month
1	$1,187	$2,374	$3,560
2	2,344	4,688	7,032
3	3,473	6,946	10,420

To provide the readjustment income as suggested in the above family situation calling for a gradual step down from an earned income of $600 a month to an eventual insured income of $200 a month would require only

$3531 of additional insurance. This amount will pay the desired extra $200 a month for one year and the extra $100 a month for the second year.[10]

The amount of disability income necessary to provide the readjustment income is expressed in terms of the desired income rather than, as in life insurance, in terms of principal amount.

If an income insurance program can be arranged that will provide an income not too far below that provided by earned income, a readjustment income is unnecessary. Situations such as this are common among families that are fortunate enough to enjoy a moderate investment income.

Family Period Income. When Cash Needs and Readjustment Income have been taken care of, the next step in the average income insurance program is to provide income for as many of the child-rearing years as possible. The younger the child, the more important is his mother's full-time care. If his mother must work to replace the income shut off by the death or disability of his father, the child has, in effect, lost both parents. Therefore, the ideal insurance program furnishes a livable income for the family until the youngest child can become self-sufficient, usually age 18. It may be contended that it is not ideal for a child to have to work full time as soon as he reaches 18; but the fact remains that by that time, most children are through high school and are at least capable of full-time work.[11] If the family feels it can afford enough insurance to provide a family income beyond the youngest child's eighteenth birthday, there is no reason to do otherwise if it can be done without sacrificing other important income needs to be discussed later.

Life insurance income for the family period can be developed by stages as the insured's income increases. For example, it could be constructed in blocks of five years each. Table 3 shows the amounts of life insurance necessary to provide various monthly incomes for subsequent five-year periods and for a total of 20 years.

If there is more than one child, the income can be reduced as each child reaches self-sufficiency. For example, assume a family with three children, ages 13, eight, and three. Assume further that the self-sufficiency age is 18 and that after the death of the father, each child is to receive $50 a month until he is 18 and that the mother is to receive $50 a month as long as she has a child under 18 in her care. In insurance planning, it must be assumed

---

[10] $2,344 plus $1,187 totals $3,531—$100 for two years plus $100 for one year. This amount of insurance can be purchased at age 25 on a Term plan, if necessary, for about $22 a year, less than $2.00 a month.

[11] The fact is, the majority of children still go to work rather than to college upon the completion of their secondary education. This is not to suggest, however, that college is not worth while, although for some its value is certainly debatable.

Table 3. Amounts to Provide Monthly Incomes Shown
for Subsequent Five-Year Periods (2½%)
and for a Total of 20 Years

Monthly Income	First 5 Years Will Require	Second 5 Years Will Require	Third 5 Years Will Require	Fourth 5 Years Will Require	Total Required for 20 Years
$100	$ 5,650	$ 4,994	$ 4,414	$ 3,901	$18,959
150	8,475	7,491	6,621	5,851	28,438
200	11,300	9,988	8,828	7,802	37,918

that death will occur tonight, so the following amounts of insurance will be necessary to fulfill the wishes of the father:

Face amount needed at beginning of the first 5 years	$11,300
Face amount needed at beginning of the second 5 years	7,491
Face amount needed at beginning of the third 5 years	4,414
Total needed to pay $50 per child per month until he is 18, plus $50 for the mother until last child is 18	$23,205

If this $23,205 of life insurance were paid out as a level income over the 15-year period, it would provide only about $160 a month—which would be $40 a month short of the amount planned for the first five years. Such an arrangement might force the oldest child to seek employment earlier while allowing the youngest child to have the advantages of $60 a month over the planned minimum. The result would be inequality of opportunity for the children, to say nothing of the hardship to the whole family during the first five years, a time when the oldest child is least able to supplement the family income.

In order to make sure that life insurance proceeds will be paid out in the manner planned in the insurance program, the insured must be careful and deliberate in the selection of his settlement options. In the above case, rather than have the entire proceeds settled on a level 15-year income basis, a part of the insurance should be settled on a five-year income basis; another part on a ten-year settlement option, and the remainder placed on a 15-year income option. In this way a decreasing amount will be paid each five years as desired.[12]

If the family income period is for more than a few years, as it is likely to be, arranging disability insurance for the family period will call for a combination of A & S insurance and disability income riders on life insurance.

---

[12] A discussion of the kind of insurance to be used (decreasing Term, continuous-premium Whole Life, Endowment, etc.) has been purposely omitted here since the kind of policy to use is a function of a combination of a number of needs rather than of one need. The right kind of policy to use will be discussed in the next chapter.

While long-duration income benefits for disability arising from accident are widely available in A & S insurance, coverage for more than the first few years of sickness is rare. Even when available, sickness benefits often require house confinement after the first few years.

Most disability income riders on life insurance require a six-month waiting period. Therefore, they need to be supplemented by A & S coverage.[13] However, if a Readjustment Period disability income has been arranged, then this income will more than cover the life rider waiting period, with the life rider providing the continuing income in event of long-term disability from either sickness or accident.

Lifetime Income. Planning for a lifetime income after the child-rearing period presents more of a problem in event of death than it does in event of disability. The need for lifetime disability income can be covered adequately for a reasonable premium outlay through disability income riders on life insurance policies. However, the need for a lifetime income for the widow upon death of the insured requires large amounts of life insurance as indicated by Table 4.

Table 4. Amounts of Proceeds Required to Provide a Woman with Each $100 a Month of Lifetime Income, No Period Certain

(1937 Standard Annuity Table, 2%, rated down one year *)

Age Income Starts	Proceeds Required	Age Income Starts	Proceeds Required
25	$37,880	45	$28,490
30	35,840	50	25,840
35	33,560	55	23,090
40	31,060	60	20,370

* Company practice might rate the table down more and set interest assumptions a little higher.

Fortunately, the need for lifetime income is less imperative than for the less expensive income needs previously mentioned. If children can go to work, they can always support a widowed mother or help her support herself. They can also help support a disabled father. However, most people find the idea of full dependency on their children at any time in life repugnant. The responsibility of supporting parents creates a hardship on the children that can be crippling to their economic and even emotional lives. Receipt of such support places the parent or parents in an uncomfortable role. Even if it is not possible to arrange for complete economic sufficiency,

[13] Group A & S benefits providing income benefits up to 26 weeks or more are gradually becoming the pattern in American industry. These benefits, however, like those in Group life, often are inadequate and have to be supplemented by additional coverage written on an individual basis.

provision for at least some income will lighten the burden on the children and give the parents a feeling of some independence. There is a difference between living *with* children and living *off* children. A grandmother who can buy the grandchildren an occasional gift and who can take the family out to dinner now and then seems far less of a burden than one to whom even pin-money must be supplied. It is surprising how much an income as small as $60 a month can add to the personality of a mother-in-law. This income might even be enough with a moderate amount of financial help from the children to allow her to have her own separate apartment, perhaps at less financial expense to the children than the cost of her complete support in their own homes, and certainly at less wear and tear on their emotions.

As said, the financial problem of providing lifetime income in event of disability is not as great as that of providing life income in event of death. Table 5 compares the participating premium outlay required to purchase enough life insurance to provide $100 a month with the cost of providing $100 monthly disability income through a life insurance policy rider. In the case of the life insurance illustration, assume the husband and wife are the same age.

Table 5. Amount of Annual Premium Needed to Provide $100 a Month Lifetime Income (10 Years Certain) from Life Insurance Proceeds Compared to to That Required to Pay $100 a Month Disability Income Under a Life Insurance Disability Income Rider

Age of Issue and Age Income from Life Insurance Begins for a Female	Annual Premium for Required Life Insurance *	Annual Premium for Required Disability Income Rider **
25	$313.14	$ 45.70
30	329.92	52.10
35	383.36	60.60
40	436.20	73.10
45	516.88	93.10
50	636.22	134.80

* Figured on the basis of five-year renewable Term insurance to reflect actual cost of insurance. Disability income rider will be placed on the permanent insurance contracts in the program or on multiple protection plans.
** Figured on the basis of $10 monthly disability income per $1,000 of continuous-premium Whole Life and includes Waiver of Premium. Matures face amount of contract as Endowment at age 65 in event of disability before age 55.

The drawback of the disability income rider is that it can be purchased only in combination with life insurance. The rider used in the above table provides $10 a month disability income for each $1,000 of face value of life insurance and, usually, the rider cannot be attached to Term insurance. Thus it is necessary to have $10,000 of permanent life insurance for each $100 of monthly disability income needed.[14] Where it is not possible to purchase enough permanent life insurance to provide the needed disability income protection then it will be necessary to purchase other forms of A & S insurance.

Educational Fund.   Whether in order of importance the need for a college education fund for the children should come before or after the life income for the widow depends on the philosophy of the individual insurance buyer. Those who argue for providing college income at the expense of other needs rely on the theory that the more education a child has, the greater will be his earning power and the better able he will be to assume the financial burdens of the family. Statistically, this may be true.[15] For any given child, it may not be. It depends on his aptitudes and general intelligence. The argument also assumes that the children will be willing to support their mother and that their mother will feel easy about accepting their help.

On the other hand, there are those who will argue that if the child is relieved of the financial burden of supporting his mother, he will be in a better position to try to earn his way through college and to build a more normal life for himself after he finishes his education.

About all that can be said of these opposing arguments is that the importance of the college education fund among life insurance needs depends on the circumstances, thinking, and over-all philosophy of each individual family and the vocational interests and abilities displayed by their children. It might be added, however, that with the exception of retirement insurance, life insurance agents find the least buying resistance in the sale of college education insurance.

It is somewhat common to build college funds for children through the purchase of Juvenile Endowments. The underlying motive for their purchase is to guarantee that funds will be available for college whether the father lives or dies. The motive in itself is a valid one, but there is grave danger in using Juvenile Endowments unless there is already adequate life insurance to fill the more primary insurance needs of the family: clean-up, mortgage or home maintenance, readjustment, child-rearing period, and life income for the widow. The prospective college freshman first has to finish grade school and high school. A college fund will do little good if sufficient funds

---

[14] Some companies will issue only $5.00 a month disability income per $1,000 of life insurance. In these companies $20,000 of permanent life insurance will be needed to buy $100 a month disability income. Many companies do not issue the rider at all.

[15] Although statistical studies on the increased earning power effected by a college education show widely varying figures, there seems little doubt that higher education is profitable—*if the student is capable of absorbing it,* or if it will be of value in the vocation he plans to follow. There are, of course, many profitable vocations in which income will be increased more by spending the same four years in gaining practical experience.

are not provided to finance the secondary education.[16] Juvenile Endowments are generally uneconomical. They consume premium dollars which usually can be used better for additional insurance on the breadwinner. Table 6 shows the participating annual premium at various ages of issue for a Juvenile Endowment at age 18 and the amount of participating continuous-premium Whole Life and 20-year Term (both with Waiver of Premium) the same premium would buy on the life of the father at different ages of issue.

Table 6. The Premium for a $1,000 Child's Endowment at 18 with Payor Benefits * and the Amount of Continuous-Premium Whole Life and 20-Year Term (both with Waiver of Premium) That Can Be Purchased on the Life of the Father with the Premium on the Juvenile Endowment
(Participating Basis)

Age of Child At Issue	Premium per $1,000 of Juvenile Endowment Insurance	Assumed Age of Parent	Amount of Continuous-Premium Whole Life (Waiver of Premium Included) That Could Be Purchased on the Life of the Father with the Premium for the $1,000 Juvenile Endowment	Amount of 20-Year Term (Waiver of Premium Included) That Could Be Purchased on the Life of the Father with the Premium for the $1,000 Juvenile Endowment
0	$59.95	25	$2,956	$6,595
1	63.59	26	3,054	6,722
2	67.85	27	3,174	6,902
3	72.62	28	3,304	7,120
4	78.05	29	3,452	7,384
5	84.33	30	3,624	7,687

* Provides waiver of premiums if parent dies or becomes disabled before maturity of the policy.

The Juvenile Endowment with payor benefits including waiver of premiums in the event of either death or disability of the premium payor may be a good way to meet college income needs if the more important family life insurance needs have been met. In the average family's life insurance program, however, it is almost impossible to budget for the relatively high premiums of Juvenile Endowment.

A more economical method of providing for a college fund is through life insurance on the head of the family. Under this arrangement, enough life insurance is included in the program to pay not only the Clean-up and other prior needs, but also to finance the college education of the children. This plan automatically provides funds for college education only in case of the death of the father. It provides no funds in case of survival. The plan presupposes that in case the father lives, he will be in a position to finance

---

[16] An illustration of the danger of college Endowments was well depicted in a cartoon from an insurance journal. A girl of approximately 18 is shown scrubbing the kitchen floor. In the other room, her employer is saying to a caller: "She's a jewel, but she's leaving to go to Vassar when her educational policy endows this fall."

the college education of his children out of current earnings—a College Income insurance plan, not a College Income savings plan. A family cannot afford to save for a college education at the expense of an adequate family insurance program.

Tables 7 and 8 show how much less expensive it is to guarantee a college education in event of the death of the parent with 20-year Term insurance than with Juvenile Endowment at age 18.

Table 7. Comparison of Annual Cost of Providing $100 a Month, Ten Months a Year for Four Years with Juvenile Endowment at 18 Including Death and Disability Payor Benefits, and with 20-Year Term Insurance on Life of Parent (Waiver of Premium Included) at Various Ages of Issue
(Participating)

Age of Parent	Age of Child	Juvenile Endowment Age 18	20-Year Term on Life of Parent
25	0	$221.69	$40.92
26	1	235.95	42.34
27	2	252.11	43.83
28	3	270.18	45.47
29	4	290.66	47.19
30	5	314.12	49.10

Table 8. Comparison of Annual Cost of Providing $200 a Semester for Four Years to Pay Tuition with Juvenile Endowment at 18 Including Payor Benefits and with 20-Year Term Insurance on Life of Parent at Various Ages of Issue

Age of Parent	Age of Child	Juvenile Endowment Age 18	20-Year Term on Life of Parent
25	0	$ 89.00	$16.43
26	1	94.72	17.00
27	2	101.21	17.59
28	3	108.47	18.25
29	4	116.69	18.94
30	5	126.11	19.71

The reduced cost is at the expense of the endowment benefit. The endowment benefit, however, would be at the expense of family protection.

Instead of 20-year Term, the college education fund might be provided by use of one of the Whole Life forms. For example, it takes about $5,350 of death benefits to provide a college education fund of $100 a month for ten months and $200 a semester, over a four-year period. If the father lives until his children reach age 18, the cash value of the Whole Life policy can be used for the college fund. If taken at age 30, the cash value of a $5,350 continuous-premium Whole Life policy at the end of 15 years would provide one fourth of the needed income. The cash value of a 20-Pay Life for the same amount would yield almost one half of the needed income. If the child-rearing period income (which would no longer be needed) is provided by a Whole Life policy, its cash values also can be used to supplement the college income need, if necessary. As will be seen later, however, these cash values probably are earmarked for retirement income.

Providing a college income in event of disability is more difficult than in event of death. It is not possible to arrange a disability income policy or rider that will pay only during the college years.[17] If the Juvenile Endowment is used to build a college fund, then waiver of premium in event of disability of the payor will assure college income. If Whole Life policies on the life of the parent are used, waiver of premium will insure the cash values for use when the child is ready for college. The only other plan would be excess disability income. If disability occurred a number of years in advance of the time the children are ready for college, the excess income could be accumulated in the bank until needed. If disability comes late, then it might be possible for the parent to borrow the necessary funds for his child's education on the security of this guaranteed future income, assuming, of course, that his life insurance policies, containing waiver of premium, will offer additional security in event of death.

Wife Insurance. The need for insurance on wives is widely neglected because it is so little recognized.[18] Income insurance is thought of in terms of replacement of *earned* income, and with typical egotism, the male considers himself as the only member of the family contributing to earned income. While the wife in a family may not be bringing in a check each pay period,

---

[17] There seems to be no actuarial reason why a delayed-benefit disability income policy could not be devised to pay income over a four-year period starting at a future date coinciding with the time the child would be ready for college. No such policy is available at the present time (at least to the knowledge of the authors) because there is no demand for it. Programming disability insurance is in such a rudimentary stage at the present time that the need for that type of policy is hardly recognized.

[18] One of the authors has been harping on this subject for over a decade and has written articles on it which have been reproduced in sales-idea services and company magazines—with the same general effect as a pebble dropped in the middle of the Atlantic Ocean. Agents commonly ignore the need or relegate it to the position of needs they bring up only if they have covered every other need they can think of, including many purely luxury needs or pure whims of far less importance in family financial planning. Moreover, companies discourage wife coverage by often making unavailable for women policy forms that would be best adapted to the need, such as Family Income. The combination agent (who writes both Weekly Premium insurance and Ordinary) recognizes the need far more than the average Ordinary agent because he is closer to his family clients by reason of his regular collection calls on them. Companies writing disability income insurance make it completely impossible to cover the need for protecting the family against the disability of the wife by refusing a nonworking woman any form of disability income coverage. Reproached, they ask, "How can you determine whether a nonworking woman is actually disabled or just wants a rest?" The question is a good one; but until someone devises a definition of disability that will weed out the malingerers, an economically vital coverage is being denied families which desperately need it.

she is providing services that, in the event of her death or disability, can be replaced only by a substantial addition to the family budget. Moreover, the income value of the wife's services is both income and Social Security tax free whereas the cost of domestic servants is not only subject to Social Security taxation but, also, it is not a fully deductible expense for income tax purposes.[19] Therefore, the economic contribution made by the wife to her family is more valuable income-wise than it appears on the surface. To be more specific, Table 9 shows how much would have to be earned at various income levels to offset the additional cost of an $1,800-a-year housekeeper.[20]

Table 9. Amount That Must Be Earned Before Taxes to Pay a Housekeeper $1,800 a Year

(Includes amount necessary to pay Social Security taxes on her wages rounded to nearest dollars)

Net taxable income	Amount to earn before taxes
$ 2,000	$2,313
4,000	2,376
6,000	2,644
10,000	3,006

Thus a life insurance policy on the wife paying $1,800 a year for the services of a housekeeper is equivalent to an increase in the gross income of the widower of from $2,313 on up, depending on his income tax bracket.[21]

Retirement Income. Loss of income can result from superannuation as well as from disability and death. So great a peril is old age that it has been made the subject of social insurance; that is, it is in some measure compulsory in America to provide for a retirement income.

To anyone under, perhaps, 45, superannuation seems very distant. Just as it is hard to visualize the horror of a train wreck killing 500 people in far-off China, so it is difficult for the individual of 20 or even 30 to visualize

---

[19] One of the authors, being a bachelor living in his own home, knows the economic value of the services of an intelligent home manager. In order to find time to write this book he must hire intelligent domestic servants to keep his house and yard in order. He must earn far more than dollar for dollar since his earnings, being those of a bachelor, are subject to a heavy income tax rate whereas the cost of the domestic help is not deductible. The whole thing seems to him like a losing proposition.

[20] The tabular figures would be somewhat affected by the fact that a widower who must hire help to care for dependents in order to be gainfully employed is allowed to deduct part of the cost of such help from taxable income. Whether this deduction will offset the loss in tax savings resulting from the inability to report a split income is certainly questionable.

[21] The death of the wife can cause additional losses: (1) Clean-up expenses and (2) loss-of-income tax savings from the split income provision of Federal Tax law. The disability of the wife can cause heavy medical bills which might be taxen into consideration in the planning of medical expense insurance.

the horror of the inability to earn a living at far-off 65. When the train wreck comes to one's own locality, however, his attitude toward it is much different. Unfortunately, when old ages comes to one's own back yard, it is too late to do anything about it. The cure for dependency at 65 is best started at 25.

Too many people when approached on the subject of systematically planning for old age casually say: *"I won't live that long; or if I do, I'll have enough in the bank."*

Men do live; and women, too: Table 10 shows to what extent.

Table 10. Expectation of Life and the Chance of Living to 65

Based on the 1949 Annuity Table (without projection *) compiled by the Society of Actuaries

Age	Age to Which a Man May Expect to Live	Number Out of 1,000 in Each of Ages Shown Who May Expect to Live to Age 65
20	74.23	776
25	74.41	779
30	74.61	782
35	74.85	787
40	75.15	793
45	75.57	803

* The above table does not take into consideration probable improvements in mortality rates over the future as reflected in the past. If future expectation were considered (1949 Projected Table) the expectations would be 77.68, 77.82, 77.94, 78.12, and 78.39 respectively. The chance of reaching age 65 also would be higher; for example, at age 20 it would be 862 instead of 776 out of 1,000.

Men do live. More than 75% of those at age 20 will attain and pass age 65. The chances of living to retirement are even better at older ages. Moreover, having reached retirement age, the chances of living for a period of years sufficient to consume a large amount of capital are good.

The man who lives to 65 can expect to live to age 80—15 more years.[22] If his cost of living in addition to Social Security is as little as $100 a month, he will in those years use up $14,858. If he has $14,858 at age 65 in the bank earning 2%, it would seem that he could reasonably anticipate drawing $100 a month from principal and interest for the rest of his life. However, should he outlive his age 65 expectancy, he can just as reasonably expect to live about 6¾ more years, during which time he will need an additional $5,100. Men age 80 have a life expectancy of 6.74 years, to be exact. Each year that a man lives, his probable year of death advances. If he survives his age 80 expectancy and reaches age 86¾, then he may expect to live about 4¼ more years, during which time he will spent another $4,391. As far as the

---

[22] 1949 Society of Actuaries Annuity Table (without projection).

annuity table goes, this process will continue through age 109½. Consequently, to be statistically certain of not outliving his capital when consumed at the rate of $100 a month, a man age 65 should have enough to last through age 109½, or $31,805, an amount a little beyond the accumulation ability of the average man under today's conditions.[23]

Methods of Protecting Old Age Income. In general, there are seven sources from which the individual who has outlived his earning power can draw money for retirement: (1) charity, (2) Social Security, (3) employer pension, (4) capital, (5) investment income, (6) life insurance, and (7) annuities. Each of these may be discussed briefly.

(1) *Charity.* Charity may come from one of two sources, public or private. The former type includes all institutional charitable sources and all types of township, county, state, dominion, or federal "relief," relief being defined as a stipend based on need rather than vested right. The latter type, private charity, includes any contributions of friends and relatives, especially children.

Aside from the fact that there is no guarantee of future charity, the tradition and principle of independence are so ingrained in the American conscience that few are ever content with charity as a solution to the problem of outliving earning power. No one in planning for financial security has a place for charitable receipts in his plans. Charity is for the man who has had no plan.

(2) *Social Security.* Although Social Security provides an income in old age, it does not supply what the average individual looks upon as enough for reasonable comfort. Social Security provides the base upon which an individual may build his own retirement plan.

(3) *Employer Pensions.* Industrial pensions in many instances supply reasonably comfortable old age income, and an increasing number of people are being covered under private pension plans. However, the mobility of American labor does much to negate the security granted by industrial pensions as many such pensions are now set up.[24]

---

[23] The life expectancy of women is slightly higher. For example, a woman age 65 may be expected to live to age 84. At 83 she may expect to live to about 87½. Annuity tables for women, however, also go only to age 109 at which age (like men), she has a life expectancy of 1/2 year.

[24] Both the number of employer pension plans and the benefits payable by them vary with the ebb and flow of business conditions, and the number of workers covered varies with the ebb and flow of employment. Few pension plans offer adequate vested interest in the employer's contributions to the fund, those being usually forfeitable with severance of employment except after a number of years.

The result is that the average employee starts in under an employer pension plan, works a few years, and is laid off or changes jobs, forfeiting what the employer has put into the plan for him and probably dissipating the withdrawn accumulation of his own

(4) *Capital.* Expenditure of capital is an unsatisfactory solution to the problem of old age income because of the large amounts required and because an individual may liquidate his capital before he himself is liquidated.

As has been demonstrated, a man who intends to live off capital at the rate of $100 a month after age 65 must have $31,805 to be actuarially safe. The accumulation of $31,805 over a 40-year working lifetime [25] requires an annual saving of about $460.[26] This is a larger amount than the average man can save each and every year with never a withdrawal or the loss of a day's interest or a penny of capital over a 40-year working lifetime.

(5) *Investment Earnings.* As a source of old age income investment earnings eliminate the problem of outliving capital but pose the same problem in regard to accumulation. At 2½% interest, it takes about $48,000 to produce an income of $100 a month. Over 40 years, the accumulation of $48,000 requires a regular annual saving of approximately $695 at 2½% compound interest, net after taxes. The problem of accumulation is, then, the problem under the Investment Income plan of providing for old age. How many young people age 25 are already saving the necessary $57.92 a month at the 2½% compound interest net after taxes assumed during the period of accumulation?

(6) *Life Insurance.* A more practical solution to the problem of supplying old age income may be found with life insurance. A premium of $695 a year at age 25 will buy about $24,800 nonpar Retirement Income insurance, which will pay $248 a month for life (120 months certain), starting at age 65. To guarantee an income of $100 a month to himself, the individual would have to save, not $695 a year for 40 years, as under the Investment Income plan, but only about $280—a far more feasible saving and one more likely to be carried through in view of the persuasion of premium notices

---

contributions. If the new employer has a plan, the employee must start in "from scratch," probably only to repeat the withdrawing process a few years later, so that even if he reaches retirement age while under some employer plan, he has come under it too late to receive much from it. It is possible that business and industry at large should give consideration to the widespread use of a type of employee pension plan which will (1) not so easily forfeit the employer's contribution, and (2) be transferrable: that is, under which the major portion of such benefits as have been accumulated under one employer will be transferred with the employee when he goes to a new employer, thus making it unnecessary for the worker to start over when he changes jobs.

[25] A 40-year working lifetime assumes the beginning of full-time employment at age 25. While this is undoubtedly later than the average starting age for the general population, it is approximately the starting age for most persons who complete the education required for the kind of a job which will give them any chance at all to build a retirement fund out of capital.

[26] Assuming 2½% compounded annually *net after taxes*, a fair assumption in view of today's rate of return on long-term investments of sufficient safety to justify use in a retirement income plan.

and the psychology of "giving up something" if the premium is lapsed and the policy forfeited. Included in the $100 a month life insurance retirement plan is $10,000 protection in case of premature death.

Policy forms other than Retirement insurance contracts can be used, as will be discussed later.

(7) *Annuities.* If premature death protection is not needed, annuities offer a slightly less expensive source of retirement income. The Annuity is, of course, specifically constructed for the purpose of replacing earning power lost as a result of superannuation. If capital accumulation has been relied on throughout the working years, and the total is insufficient either to last long enough if drawn upon or to earn the income required at a safe rate of interest, the Annuity will (1) guarantee against capital being exhausted too soon and (2) provide a larger monthly payment than any reasonable interest earning. For example, $48,000 at 2½% interest will provide $100 a month. Invested in a single-premium Life Annuity, it will provide at age 65 about $315 a month, somewhat less for a woman. To put it another way: if the capital accumulation plan has been used to age 65, and there is not the $48,000 available to yield $100 a month at 2½%, about $14,640 will provide the desired income if a straight life Annuity is used. An installment refund Annuity of $100 a month will require single premium of about $18,800.

At a starting age of 25, an annual-premium deferred Annuity will yield a lifetime income of about $40.70 a month, ten years certain starting at age 65, per $100 of annual premium. Thus the creation of an income of $100 a month through an annual-premium deferred Annuity for a man at 65 will take a yearly saving starting at age 25 of about $246 a year as against $695 in a capital accumulation and investment income plan where 2½% compounded annually is assumed.

It is better for the average person to use the annual-premium Annuity plan rather than to try to save the money elsewhere for liquidation through a single-premium Annuity because (1) of the greater compulsion to make the saving regularly, (2) of the greater compulsion to keep what is saved, (3) of the guarantee that the cost of the annuity will not go up in the years between the age at which savings are started and the time the single-premium Annuity is purchased 40 years later.

If in planning an insurance program for a family, Whole Life insurance policies are used to cover the premature death needs, the cash values of these policies usually will create, automatically, sufficient retirement income protection for the policyholder if he outlives the need for death protection. For example, a young man who has enough continuous-premium Whole Life insurance to provide, in case of his death, a life income of $150 a month for his 30-year-old wife, will also have for his own retirement, should he live to age 65, well over $100 a month. The cash values of his protection policies will provide this retirement income despite the fact that he has purchased the policy offering the lowest old age income per $1,000 of permanent life insurance.

The primary insurance need of the man with dependents is income for these dependents. If he takes care of that adequately with permanent insurance, retirement income will take care of itself.

The needs just discussed are the common needs of the average family, considered in the usual order of their importance. It is well to hold in mind, however, that income insurance needs are purely personal and differ in some degree in each case.

2. OTHER NEEDS

The needs which have been discussed up to this point are what are usually considered basic needs. In addition, there are a number of other needs or, more properly, uses (sometimes whims) which can be satisfied by life insurance. These can be considered only by the few families which have basic needs adequately covered.

"Head-Start Fund." An attractive story can be made of the advantages of buying life insurance on a child at an early age. The purchase, so the story goes, will give a boy a definite financial head start in life in at least two ways: (1) by creating backlog cash values which may be useful in starting him in his business career; (2) by allowing him to take care of his own family needs in the future at a smaller total premium outlay. As an illustration of both of these advantages, note the comparison in Table 11.

Table 11. Comparison of Rates and Values Purchasable with $100 Annual Premium at Age 10 and Age 25

Age of Issue	Type of Policy (Nonpar)	Face Value	Loan Value at Age 35	Monthly Income Value at 65
10	C-P Whole Life	$8,250	$2,250	$34.00
25	C-P Whole Life	6,000	858	22.75

Travel Fund. Endowment policies are attractive to some families as a means of providing money for extensive travel at some future time. There is a financial disadvantage, however, in using the Endowment for this purpose if the savings period is short. Generally, short-term Endowments do not show as large a gain over the Endowment period as could be earned through even a low-yielding savings account. The Endowment policy plan for accumulating a travel fund (or any such special fund) offers two advantages over other methods of accumulation. (1) It provides an amount of life insurance protection to be used to supplement other needs until the policy matures. (2) It offers a greater degree of compulsion on the saver to carry his savings plan through to completion.

Dowry for a Daughter. The Endowment can be used to provide a dowry for a daughter. Dowries are not a common practice in the United States, but few are the young couples who could not use one in the early years of their marriage, especially in furnishing or building their home. Advantages of using the Endowment policy for this purpose are exactly the same as those discussed under the travel fund need.

While the daughter is still dependent on the parent, the dowry policy will serve as Clean-up protection for the parental family unit, a family need, as has been seen. The Clean-up use nevertheless would be solely a by-product of the dowry use. A family that can afford the luxury of building a dowry for the daughter could well afford the expense of burial from regular income.

A "Special Dates" Fund. Another luxury use of life insurance is to provide a "special dates," or "anniversary," or "Christmas" fund. A relatively small policy included in the program of the head of the family or of the mother (or of both) will provide the money to buy the requisite gifts on birthdays, anniversaries or, most commonly, at Christmas. A $1,000 policy will provide a woman age 35 a single payment of about $40 annually for 20 years certain and life thereafter. This payment may be arranged for December of each year, for example, and may help make Christmas a little more enjoyable for a fatherless family.

Gifts and Bequests. Charitable instincts are not confined to the wealthy. Many men and women of modest means are as much impelled to philanthropy as the million-dollar giver; yet to the person of modest means, what he can give or leave may seem so small as to be unworthy and insignificant. For such a person, life insurance offers a chance to make the gift he never hoped to give—a living gift through endowment insurance or a bequest through life insurance.

For instance, the $2,500 that may seem like a small bequest will, at age 40, purchase about $5,000 nonpar, single-premium Life insurance, or $3,700 nonpar, single-premium, 20-year Endowment.

Still more satisfying are the gifts which can be arranged through annual-premium Life or Endowment policies. The $100 a year that seems to the man or woman of 40 an insignificant gift—hardly philanthropy—can be turned into a bequest of almost $4,000 through use of a nonpar, continuous-premium Whole Life policy.

It is also possible for groups of individuals—a number of alumni, a Sunday School class, a civic club—to arrange a substantial endowment for a charitable, civic, or educational organization by the use of contributions in the form of annual premiums on life insurance on a given member of the group. The charitable institution is named beneficiary. Ten men about age 35, each of whom would hardly consider himself a philanthropist if he could afford to spend no more than $45 or $50 a year for charitable gifts, could arrange a combined gift or endowment of $20,000 or more through the use of continuous-premium Whole Life insurance on the life of one of them.[27]

High income tax rates and high living costs leave fewer free dollars to save, especially after paying today's high living costs. Low interest yields retard the growth of savings. High estate tax rates reduce the proportion of the accumulation which can be passed to heirs. Thus it has become increasingly more difficult to build family fortunes, with the result that the number of large donors to philanthropic causes and institutions is dropping constantly.

Yet our country looks to philanthropy-supported institutions to supply many of the public's needs and much of its culture.

Without the privately endowed college, for instance, there would be insufficient higher educational facilities in America. Without private money, our library facilities would lag, many phases of social work would be cut off, and churches would be without support. The necessity has arisen, therefore, for replacing the single, $1,000,000 gift with 1,000 gifts of $1,000. Philanthropy can no longer depend upon superwealth but must draw from men and women of modest means. Life insurance offers to them—and to philanthropy—a chance to make the insignificant gift grow in size and become the kind of gift an individual feels is worth giving.

Other Luxury Needs. Innumerable other luxury uses could be named for life insurance in a family group and still more might be peculiar to a particular family and its likes. There is insurance for grandchildren, insurance to build a fund to give a daughter a memorable wedding, insurance to help a son set himself up in business, insurance to accumulate a fund to buy a lake cottage, insurance to provide for a daughter's old age—the list is almost inexhaustible. The danger is that since most of these luxury needs have a high degree of sentimental appeal, too frequently they are filled while basic family needs are ignored.

---

[27] Sometimes individuals take out life insurance policies for their own use, but make the dividends payable to some philanthropic institution. This results in a painless method of giving.

SUMMARY

The summary of this chapter will be deferred to the end of programming discussion, which is continued in Chapter 16.

Questions for Class Discussion

The questions for this chapter are deferred until the end of Chapter 16, which is a continuation of the present discussion.

CHAPTER 16

PROGRAMMING INCOME
INSURANCE: TOOLS
AND TECHNIQUES

NOW THAT the nature of income insurance needs has been established in the foregoing chapter, attention can be turned to the actual process of programming income insurance to cover them.

1. THE TOOLS OF PROGRAMMING

The purpose of programming is to meet needs; the tools of programming are the settlement options. While the nature of settlement options was described in Chapter 10, a brief review and elaboration of their basic uses [1] is necessary as an introduction to the process of programming.

To repeat: Life insurance policies provide for the payment of a stated sum of money upon the death of the insured.[2] Almost all policies,[3] however, provide that at the election of the insured while alive, or at the choice of the

---

[1] The various uses of each option are somewhat a matter of opinion among different authorities of equal standing. Undoubtedly, therefore, there will be some disagreement with some of the uses suggested here.

[2] There are some exceptions, such as the Family Maintenance and Family Income policies, which call for the payment of an income for a stated period or until a stated date.

[3] Group is often an exception, providing only for cash payments. Many Group policies, however, permit the payment of proceeds on a period certain basis of relatively short duration, such as five years; and most Group-writing companies will place larger amounts of proceeds on longer term, fixed-period bases and on some other options on request. Such requests are usually considered on an individual basis; so that the available options on Group contracts vary.

beneficiary at the time of settlement, the lump sum of the proceeds will be retained by the company and paid out on any one of the following optional modes of settlement:

Interest Only. The proceeds of the policy may be left with the company at interest. Under this settlement, the company pays a guaranteed rate of interest as a monthly, quarterly, semiannual, or annual income as desired, except that most companies have some limitation on the minimum amount they will pay in any one installment, such as $10, for an example. If, therefore, the interest paid monthly would amount to less than the minimum, then quarterly payments must be elected; if quarterly are smaller than the minimum, then semiannual must be elected; and so on. Usually the beneficiary may retain the right to withdraw "in whole or in part," or the insured may have elected in advance of death that only a certain amount may be withdrawn in any one year.

Proceeds left at interest only are almost exactly comparable in effect to money deposited in a bank savings account. Common situations in which the interest option can be effectively employed are these:

When Cash or Income Is Not Needed at Once. If the program is such that adequate income has been provided for various needs and there is still a sum over and above the amount required for immediate use, selection of the interest option will guard against dissipation of these excess funds.

Deferred Needs. Certain policies may have been arranged to provide cash or income at given future dates, such as during the years the children are in college. The proceeds to fill these needs can be left at interest only until the children are ready for college.

When Uncertain Amounts Are Required. The amount that will be necessary to settle final expenses is never known exactly. Many agents recommend, therefore, that estate settlement funds be left at interest only with the right of withdrawal. Under such a settlement plan, excess amounts are less likely to be dissipated. Moreover, since all bills will not be payable at once, the money will earn interest until it is paid out. For example, inheritance and estate taxes are not due immediately. Neither are unpaid income taxes. Therefore, funds programmed to pay these taxes should be left at interest and allowed to earn as much as they can until the taxes are due.

Emergency Fund. The Emergency Fund should be left at interest only since it is not to be used until an unforeseen emergency arises. In the meantime it should be earning interest. If paid in cash, theoretically it could be deposited in a savings account and earn interest. However: (a) many savings accounts do not pay as much interest as is usually paid by an insurance company under the interest-only option,[4] (*b*) the easy accessibility of bank savings subjects the emergency fund to withdrawal for purposes not wholly emergency in nature.

As a Hedge in Connection with Social Security. Social Security will provide a fairly substantial survivorship income in event of the death of a covered worker if he leaves children under age 18. However, the exact amount the family will receive from Social Security is uncertain. It is dependent on the continued life of the children and upon the children's marital status. If a child dies or marries before age 18, his Social Security income terminates. If that child is the only one under age 18, income to the widow also terminates. As a hedge, therefore, life insurance proceeds may be left at interest, giving the widow the right to withdraw up to a given amount each year to offset any loss of Social Security payments. The use of life insurance for this purpose is closely akin to the Emergency Fund, of course, and may be considered a part of that fund.

In Event of Common Disaster. Many policies have a "common disaster" clause which provides that if the insured and his wife die simultaneously (usually defined as within 15 to 30 days of each other or some similar, short period), the proceeds will not be paid to the widow and, thus, will avoid being tied up in her estate.[5] If a policy does not contain a common disaster clause, the same result can be accomplished by leaving the proceeds of the policy at interest only, giving the beneficiary the right either to withdraw in whole or in part, or to elect any option in the policy. Included in this settlement arrangement also is the stipulation that the funds do not legally pass to the beneficiary until actually claimed and paid either in cash or by a settlement direction. In some cases, the short time limit available in the common disaster clause may be considered too short.[6] If so, the above interest-only arrangement might prove more effective in accomplishing the desired objectives.

Life Income. If lifetime income is required, the younger beneficiary does not receive a great deal less from the interest-only option than from the life

---

[4] It must be remembered that the insurance companies under participating options pay excess interest above the rate guaranteed under the policy if additional interest is earned.

[5] In some cases, the heirs of the insured and those of the beneficiary will not be identical, particularly in the case of a childless couple. If there is no arrangement for common disaster, it might be held that the beneficiary survived the insured, and, as a consequence, the life insurance proceeds have become vested in her. The proceeds would then pass through her estate to her heirs, whereas the insured might have preferred to have his own heirs enjoy the benefits of his life insurance.

[6] Suppose the clause provides that in event of the death of the beneficiary within five days of the insured, the proceeds shall not have passed to her. If the beneficiary survives six days instead of five, the insured will have not avoided the situation which he had hoped to avoid through the use of the common disaster clause.

annuity option. The advantage of preserving the principal might be well worth the differential. Generally speaking, if the beneficiary for whom life income is needed is under age 45 or 50, it will be better to use the interest option until that time, giving her the right to change to the annuity option then, if desired.

In using the interest-only option, at least three rules should be followed: (1) Life insurance proceeds should not be tied up so tightly that in event of an emergency need they cannot be drawn upon. (2) The beneficiary should not be left an inadequate income from interest in an attempt to preserve principal.[7] (3) As among several policies, the right ones should be selected for the interest option. All policies owned should be checked so that (other things being equal) the ones with the highest interest guarantees are used. Also policies which pay less interest under the interest-only withdrawal option than they pay under other options generally should not be used to meet the interest-only needs.

Fixed Period Option. The fixed period option provides for equal payments over a specified period of time. When selected for the beneficiary by the insured, it should be chosen with extreme caution. Although election of, say, the ten years' time option may be justified at the time the election is made, it may be wholly unrealistic by the time the policy matures. Suppose, for example, the option is selected for the Readjustment Fund. This may be a useful income arrangement when there are dependent children, but if the children are grown, by the time the policy matures, the widow might be far better off if the proceeds were paid to her as a life income. Again, Educational funds often are arranged to pay proceeds over a fixed period of four years, starting on a given date. Suppose, however, that on that date the son is in the Armed Forces or the daughter is already married. If the fixed period option has been elected, the proceeds will have to be paid out over the four designated years, regardless of how ridiculous is the arrangement.[8]

---

[7] This is particularly important in view of the fact that increases in living costs may make an income that seemed reasonably adequate at the time it was selected inadequate in later years. A decline in the purchasing power of a fixed dollar income might have to be offset by drawing on principal or by shifting to an income option paying higher periodic benefits; hence the right to withdraw should be included, and the right to elect another option should also be granted in a special settlement agreement, if the company is willing to do so.

[8] The argument that the insured can change the election if his situation changes at any time prior to his death is insufficient. What an insured can do and what he will do often are not the same thing. (a) He may die before he realizes that the fixed period option is incorrect for the new situation. (b) Insureds simply do not review their programs often enough to keep them always up to date. If life insurance agents would more often accept the responsibility of initiating an annual review of the programs of his clients, then the risk of dying with antiquated life insurance settlement options would be substantially reduced.

The fixed period option does have some uses:

Where the Amount Is Small. Limited amounts of proceeds may be put on either the fixed period or the fixed amount option. Two factors should be considered in making the choice: (a) The possibility of an outstanding loan against the policy at death of the insured. (b) Whether or not the policy is participating.

If there is a loan outstanding, it will reduce the amount of each benefit check under the fixed period option. Under the fixed amount option, it will reduce the duration of benefits.

If the policy is participating, dividends will increase the amount of each benefit check under the fixed period option. Under the fixed amount option, they will increase the duration of benefits.

Therefore, whether to put a small amount of proceeds under the fixed period or fixed amount option depends on the relative importance of *time* and *amount* in the particular case at hand.

Where the Exact Years of Required Income Are Known. The period of years extending between the time the last child reaches age 18 until the widow becomes 65 is known as the Social Security Blackout Period. During these years the widow is ineligible for Social Security benefits. Life insurance proceeds payable on a fixed period option may be used to replace the loss of Social Security income during this "blackout" period. Cognizance should be taken, however, of the possibility that Social Security income might be interrupted before the child's eighteenth birthday if he should die or marry before that age.

If unusual situations peculiar to a nontypical program should present special reasons for using fixed period options, they should always be analyzed carefully to determine whether some other option would serve the purpose better.

Specified Amount Option. Under the amount option, policy proceeds are paid out in installments of a fixed amount until the principal (and interest credited to it) are exhausted. The option, also called "principal and interest to exhaustion," is probably the most used option in programming. It is efficient in most small programs, although, in larger programs, interest only with the right to withdraw is more flexible.

One of the greatest advantages of this option is to provide variable amounts of income from the same policy. For instance, it takes more money to finance a year of high school than a year of grade school. The college years require even more. An educational plan might be arranged under the fixed amount option whereby an extra $10 a month (over and beyond the basic family income) is paid during grade school, $25 during high school, and $75 during college. The option also is useful for the Readjustment Income plan, which specifies decreasing amounts of income for several years—say $400 a month the first year, $300 the second, and $200 thereafter.

The specified amount option is particularly useful in co-ordinating life insurance proceeds with Social Security. Benefits under Social Security decrease as each child reaches age 18. If the family plans call for college, there may be a need to replace the loss in Social Security income by increasing the amount of each income installment provided under a life insurance policy.[9] The fixed amount option is the only option under which it is possible to arrange a settlement plan requiring an increase in income at some time in the future.

The principal drawback in the use of the fixed amount option is rigidity. If in the future income needs happen to be greater than is anticipated when the program is drawn up, additional withdrawals as under the interest option are not possible.

If, in using the amount option, several policies are involved in making up a given amount of income, the policies should be arranged to pay *concurrently* and not *consecutively*. The reason is obvious. If two policies are arranged to pay consecutively and one is lapsed or impaired by a loan, there will be a gap either between the cessation of payments from one and the beginning of the payments from the other, or after the end of the payments from the latter.

Life Income Option. As the name indicates, the life income option provides income for the life of the payee. In fact, it is often called "the annuity option," since in effect—if not purely technically—the proceeds [10] of the policy are used by the company to buy a single-premium annuity on the life of the policyholder or beneficiary. The annuity income, however, usually is greater than the policyholder or beneficiary could purchase separately with the same amount of money. Purchase of the annuity separately would re-

---

[9] This is not a "flaw" in Social Security but a recognition of the fact that at age 18 a child is capable of earning a living without continuing his education. The purpose of Social Security is to provide minimum needs; hence it provides income until the age at which the average child finishes high school. Perhaps it would be helpful if it would also pay income for four more years of education; but if so, by projection of the same type of reasoning, it would be just as logical to extend it for a few more years while the young college graduate is getting a start in a business or profession—and so on ad infinitum.

[10] Or the cash or endowment value, when the income is to be paid the policyholder. Some companies will allow endowment proceeds to be put on options payable to other than the insured.

quire payment of acquisition costs, whereas all such costs have already been
paid on the life insurance policy before it is converted into an annuity.[11]

Virtually all policies offer life income on a basis of ten or 20 years certain.
In addition, five- and 15-year periods are frequently offered as guaranteed
minimums. Straight life incomes, that is, with no minimum number of payments guaranteed, also are available. Finally, it is becoming more common
to find joint and survivorship life income options included in the contracts.[12]

The use of the life income option is practical only when (1) there is a
large amount of insurance, and (2) the beneficiary is not too young. Table 1
compares the amount of income available to a female beneficiary on a ten-
year certain and life thereafter 2½% option with the amount available under
the interest-only option.

Table 1. Comparison of Monthly Income per $1,000 of Proceeds to a Female from Life Income Option and Interest Option
(Interest Assumption 2½%)

Age	Life Income Option	Interest Option
20	$2.81	$2.08
25	2.93	2.08
30	3.08	2.08
35	3.26	2.08
40	3.48	2.08
50	4.09	2.08
60	5.01	2.08

When the amount of insurance is small and the recipient of the income
is relatively young, the best arrangement for lifetime income calls for the
use of two options with an automatic change provision. The policy should
be placed on the interest-only option with a provision that at a specified age
(45 or 50) automatic change will be made to the life income option. In this
way, it is possible to take advantage of the higher income differential at
the later age.

Actually, the life income option is rarely useful in the average life insurance program. The usual program does not include enough life insurance
to make a life income option practical. To leave a widow a meager life

[11] "Thus, to advise a beneficiary or policyowner to cash in a policy to purchase an
annuity is little short of dishonesty. This is especially true in the case of older policies,
as the options available in policies issued some years ago are far more liberal than those
in current policies." Hugh S. Bell, C.L.U., *Up the Ladder to Bigger Sales*, Indianapolis,
The Rough Notes Co., 1953, p. 55.
[12] As a matter of company practice, most companies will allow the choice of a joint and
survivor income—and of other certain-period life incomes—even though not written in the
policy. However, often they will require that if an option not guaranteed in the policy
is selected, the benefit tables in use by the company at the time the payments begin will
be the tables used in computing benefits.

income that forces her to go to work and "farm out" the children is not much better than no income at all. The end result is the same: The children are deprived of a full-time mother. When there is an inadequate amount of life insurance to do a complete job, as is the usual case, it is far better to cover some needs adequately rather than cover all needs only scantily.

The greatest use of the life income option in the average program is for the insured's own retirement benefits.

2. THE PROCESS OF PROGRAMMING

The process of programming income insurance consists of the following steps:

1. Determining the nature of each income insurance need.

2. Determining how much income should be provided for each of these needs, tempered by what can be afforded.

3. Determining how far the following present and expected future assets can go in meeting the goals: life insurance already owned, estimated Social Security benefits, employer-provided Group Life and Disability insurance and pension benefits, and the general estate.[13]

4. Determining the gaps between the estimated income needs and the amount currently available to meet these needs.

5. Recommending the kinds and amount of additional insurance to fill as many of the gaps in needs as can be afforded, deciding which needs to cover only partially and if necessary, which needs to leave completely uncovered.

6. Selecting and putting into effect all settlement options and safeguards necessary to the efficient functioning of the program.

To discuss each of these steps briefly:

Determining Needs. As was said, needs in any given case are individual. Discovering which needs exist is a process of applying the basic list discussed in Chapter 15 to the case at hand. Some will fit; others will not. For instance, the needs of a single man might well be confined to Clean-up and Retirement; but this cannot be stated as a rule. He might have dependent parents or other relatives, in which case he would have premature death protection as well as Clean-up and Retirement needs. A childless couple may have only cash needs, readjustment income, income for the widow for life, wife insurance, and retirement. A widower will not need wife insurance.

Two general rules can be stated with reference to determining needs:

(1) *Keep First Needs First.* Some needs have more appeal than others.

---

[13] As mentioned, if the general estate is at all significant, the case becomes one of estate planning, to be discussed in the next chapter, rather than simple programming.

A notorious example is the educational endowment. It is not at all uncommon for parents to buy high-premium educational endowment policies while leaving the need for grade or high school income inadequately covered. Obtaining a college degree is a fetish in America. The so-called "living needs," such as income for retirement, always seem to have great market appeal. For example, people are quicker to purchase high-premium policies to build up cash values than they are to buy low-premium policies offering principally death protection. This is true, often at the expense of adequate premature death protection.

Another fad is to insure the lives of children for more than Clean-up expenses while the father's protection is inadequate. The motivation often is "I want to do the things for my children that my parents never were able to do for me." Clear and unemotional thinking on the subject will dictate that the best way to protect the children is to increase the insurance on the life of the father. After all, what has a dead parent done for his child if he has bought $2,000 of life insurance on his child at the expense of almost $2,000 of insurance on his own life?

(2) *Look Ahead.* A young, unmarried man may today have no need for income for a wife and children, but what are the possibilities of need for it in the future? To the young, unmarried man, retirement income has far more appeal than income for a family that does not yet exist. The result is that many a young man has "loaded up" on high-premium retirement insurance before he is married, only to find that in a very few years his need for protection is vastly greater—or, at least, more pressing—than his need for retirement funds. At this time, however, too many of his available premium dollars are going into the retirement fund. A sound program not only covers today's needs but also provides flexibility for future needs.

Determining Amounts. Far more difficult than determining needs is determining the amount of cash or income necessary to fill them. Obviously, most people would like to fill the needs so completely that neither death nor disability would materially reduce the family standard of living. The cost of full coverage at any income range is virtually impossible. For instance, Table 2 shows the amount of life insurance required and its annual cost on a yearly renewable Term basis to provide for the continuation of the predeath income to the widow for the rest of her life. The ages of the insured and widow are assumed to be 25. Each additional year the insured lives will not only bring about a reduction in the amount of insurance needed but also an increase in the rate for each $1,000 of insurance purchased. For purposes of making a comparison Table 2 shows the cost also at assumed ages of 45 for the widow and the insured. Note that the increase in premium rate from age 25 to 45 was greater than the decrease in amount of insurance required, as reflected in a higher premium charge at age 45.

Table 2. Amounts and Cost of Continuing Given Incomes

(Life Income, No Refund; Assuming Insured and Beneficiary Age 25; and 45; Nonparticipating Rates on Yearly Renewable Term Basis.)

| | AMOUNT OF INSURANCE REQUIRED | | PREMIUM REQUIRED | |
| | Insured and Beneficiary | Insured and Beneficiary | Insured and Beneficiary | Insured and Beneficiary |
Annual Income	Age 25	Age 45	Age 25	Age 45
$ 2,400	$ 69,910	$ 54,720	$ 470	$ 605
3,600	104,865	82,079	705	908
4,800	139,819	109,439	940	1,210
6,000	174,774	136,799	1,174	1,513
12,000	349,548	273,599	2,349	3,026

In other words, to continue the present income of a family after the death of the breadwinner would require a premium outlay of just about 20% of earned income if both the insured and his wife were age 25. If they were both age 45 it would take over 25%. These figures indicate the cost of providing for continuation of income in the event of death only. The cost of a full replacement of income at age 65 and a full replacement of income in the event of permanent and total disability [14] would add another 25% if taken at age 25. Thus the cost of full coverage would be close to 50% of annual, tax free income—far beyond what even the most insurance-conscious family would ever consider spending for insurance. The problem of income insurance planning, therefore, is not to get full coverage but, instead, to do the best possible job of covering exposures with the amount of insurance that can be afforded. The process of determining the amount of income to be provided boils down to the problem of deciding the minimum amount of income on which a family can get along. In practice, the agent finds that his job in evaluating needs in programming is to be forever driving down the amounts of cash or income the prospect insists are necessary. Many agents will approach the problem of determining how much income to assign to each need by first getting a commitment from the family on how much can be budgeted a month for insurance and then making that amount cover as many needs as possible without spreading the insurance too thin.

Subtracting Present Coverage. After the minimum amounts have been determined, the next step in the programming process is to subtract from the total insurance needed whatever insurance (and other assets) is already owned.

---

[14] Subject to maximum disability income in which companies will participate.

An important asset in the estate of the average family man today is Social Security. Potential Social Security benefits for dependents or for retirement total tens of thousands of dollars.[15]

Another important asset in the average programming case is Group insurance and company pension plans. Employee security plans are widespread and are continuing to grow in importance. Even self-employed professional men often have some Group insurance and sometimes pension benefits through an association group.

Other types of benefits often encountered are veterans' benefits, railroad and civil service benefits, and teachers' retirement plans. In addition to these, one or more life insurance policies usually are already in force.

In the process of programming, it is essential to determine at the start the exact nature and extent of all earning assets and sources of emergency income. Since this discussion is confined to simple programming, income from general property and investments is not considered. Simple programming, by definition, is not a process in which general property or assets play a significant part. In starting the simple programming case, however, it is necessary to check for other property and for the possibility of substantial inheritances, since their existence in any significant degree will change the case from simple programming to one of estate planning.

Recommending Additional Insurance. Just as amounts of income to be provided in the average program must be a compromise between wants and ability to pay, so the choice of policies to fill gaps in coverage often is a compromise between the best policy for the purpose and the policy the insured can afford. For example, while a permanent policy form is more desirable than Term for most uses, because the former provides for both premature death protection and protection against old age (through cash values), the premium necessary to fill all needs on a permanent policy basis may be too great. It must then be decided whether to cover as many of the needs as possible with permanent insurance, leaving others unfilled, or to forego the emergency and old age protection afforded by cash values and cover the entire program with Term. The decision here is largely a matter of programming philosophy and, to some extent, the character of the insured. For instance, if the insured has a strong sense of responsibility, an ability to plan ahead, and a facility for handling his money, then convertible Term might be the recommendation. On the other hand, if he cannot handle his

---

[15] The amount of Social Security benefits, being a matter of legislation rather than contract, is changed so frequently that there is little point (and some danger) in quoting exact figures in a book. The reader has no way of knowing from the book itself whether the figures quoted are current or not. Up-to-date figures are available free in pamphlet form from any local Social Security office.

money, if he is frequently "broke," then it might be better to forego some of the protection now and use permanent insurance. The cash values of the permanent insurance can be drawn upon to pay premiums if he is "broke" when they come due. With Term, he might lapse the policy, whereas with permanent insurance, what he has—even though inadequate—might be kept in force. If so, he will be better off with something less than adequate premature death protection than with no premature death protection at all.

Fitting Needs and Selecting Options. The process of fitting uncovered needs and selecting options is best illustrated by a case example. The following is an illustrative example, deliberately "padded" to bring out as many facets of programming as possible and yet avoid extreme technicalities beyond the scope of this discussion. Some points may seem unreal for an average case but are included for illustration. Further, it should be remembered that both programming philosophies and the characters of policyholders differ; so ideas on the exact way to handle any given situation will vary. The attempt here is not to set up exact rules, but to illustrate a process. There could be as many different ideas on the exact way to handle any given program as there are people offering a solution.

3. A PROGRAM ILLUSTRATION

The program assumes the following facts:

Father
   Age   30
   Occupational classification   Best
   Income (gross before taxes) $6,500
         (net after federal and state taxes)   5,800
   Obligations
      Mortgage, 20-year, now 5 years old.
      Original amount   10,000
      Balance due   9,000
   Present coverages [16]
      Social security for family   200 mo.
      Social Security retirement   80 mo.
      Noncontributory group Life   5,000

---

[16] As previously explained, Social Security benefits are a matter of legislation and subject to frequent change; therefore, figures used here are to be considered as illustrative only. It seems unquestionable to the authors that Social Security benefits will soon include disability income, and that the retirement age for women will be reduced to some such age as 62. These and other changes would alter the exact recommendations made here; however, the attempt here is to illustrate a process which remains the same regardless of changes in Social Security benefits or provisions—and, for that matter, regardless of future changes in life insurance rates and, perhaps, even cash values and income settlement benefits.

Noncontributory pension plan | An amount enough to supplement Social Security to a total of $150 a month

20-Pay Life policy, taken at age 22, with Waiver of Premium | 2,500

$5,000 continuous-premium Whole Life with 1% Family Income rider, 20-year basis taken at age 25 | 50 a month and 5,000 proceeds at end of income period

Term to 65 taken at age 27 with Waiver of Premium | 5,000

Hospitalization policy | 8 per diem room rate

Mother
Age | 28
Present insurance, Industrial, taken age 11 | $592
Hospitalization (share of family policy) | 8 per diem room rate

Son
Age | 5
Present insurance, E. 18, taken age 2 with payor benefit Death and Disability | $1,000
Hospitalization (share of family policy) | 8 per diem room rate

Daughter
Age | 3
Present insurance, E. 18, taken age 0 with payor benefit Death and Disability | $1,000
Hospitalization (share of family policy) | 8 per diem room rate

Husband and wife agree that the family could get along on approximately $250 a month, especially since most of it would be tax free, if the husband could no longer earn a living. They would like to be able to keep the house. The husband feels that in the event of his death $2,000, plus the $325.50 lump sum benefit he estimates he would receive from Social Security, would be enough, barring protracted illness prior to death, to pay final expenses, balances on appliances purchased on time, and, perhaps, leave at least a few hundred dollars for emergencies. He feels it would be better to dispose of the family car. To hold on to it would require a large sum to complete the payments and a higher income to take care of gasoline, insurance, taxes, and general repairs. He further assumes that in event of his death, his family would receive the maximum under Social Security.[17]

---

[17] Actually, some would consider this a somewhat dangerous assumption. If his income has ever been below the maximum counted for Social Security or ever drops below it in the future, his family might receive less than the maximum. There is little possibility,

Present Situation in Event of Death. In view of the income needs of the family and the assumptions based on things as they are today, the family's present coverages might be distributed as follows:

From date of death until the son reaches age 18–$265.63 a month
    $200 from Social Security
     50 from Family Income rider
     15.63 from 2½% interest on $5,000 Term and $2,500 20-pay life held for later distribution

Since the income need determined is met with Social Security and the Family Income rider, the better plan would be for the $15.63 to be accumulated at interest and distributed at the end of the Family Income period when it will be needed more. However, if the companies involved will not allow such accumulation, the interest will have to be distributed as current income.[18] In this case, the mortgage situation, to be discussed in a moment, makes the extra income useful.

From the date son reaches 18 until daughter reaches 18–$250.28 a month
    $162.80 from Social Security (reduced when son attained 18)
      21.85 from son's $1,000 Endowment at 18, paid out in equal installments for four years
      50.00 from Family Income rider
      15.63 interest on $5,000 Term and $2,500 20-Pay

While enrollment of the boy in college will increase rather than decrease the need for income, it is assumed that the decrease in income at this point can be made up by (*a*) refinancing the house and reducing the payments on the mortgage (the mortgage is almost paid off) and (*b*) having the son earn part of his way through college.[19]

---

however, that Social Security benefits will be lowered in the future—although it must be admitted that a strong possibility exists that they will be *increased*. However, as a practical matter, some assumption must be made in programming with Social Security. Just as in the programming of life insurance proceeds, the assumption is made that no policies will ever be lapsed or will be impaired by loans at the time they mature. Further, no program is a static thing. All programs should be reviewed frequently and if the assumptions upon which they are based are changed these changes should be considered in bringing the program up to date.

[18] Many companies will allow the insured to provide for the accumulation of interest under the interest option during the minority of a beneficiary. A few companies allowing interest accumulations do not restrict it to minority, but allow it for a specified period, at which time the increased amount is to be applied under another option.

[19] There is always the possibility of a G.I. Bill to take care of college expenses. This, of course, will defer these expenses while the son serves his duty in the armed forces.

From the time the daughter reaches 18 until the son finishes college—$250.00
a month

$ 21.85   from son's Endowment at 18
    21.85   from daughter's Endowment at 18
    22.50   from 20-Pay Life principal and interest to exhaustion. (Will last
            about 10 years)
   183.80   from $5,000 Term and from $5,000 basic policy to which Family
            Income rider was attached, both on principal and interest to ex-
            haustion. (Will last close to 5 years)

The Family Income policy purchased by the father when the son was born has now expired. Social Security benefits also are terminated until the widow reaches age 65. The girl is now ready to enter college. It is assumed that she will be able to do part-time work and in that way help pay the extra expenses college enrollment will bring about. Also, since the children are grown, the mother can seek full-time employment.[20]

From the time the son is graduated until the daughter's graduation—$228.15
a month

$ 21.85   from daughter's Endowment at 18
    22.50   from 20-Pay Life
   183.80   from $5,000 Term and from $5,000 basic policy to which Family
            Income was attached, both on principal and interest to exhaustion

The son is now completely independent of the family's income; the girl should be able to find some part-time or summer employment; and the mother is free to work. Therefore, the reduced income should be enough. If there is any deficit, the boy could contribute something from his earnings.

For a period of slightly under one year after girl graduates—$206.30 a month
    $183.80   from the Term and the basic policy to which the Family Income
              rider was attached
      22.50   from the 20-Pay Life policy

This income will end in less than a year after the girl finishes college, for at this time the proceeds of the Term and permanent portion of the Family Income policy will be exhausted. Although this income is for a brief period it will give the mother a "breathing spell" during which to decide what adjustments she will make now that virtually all her income will soon be gone.

Until widow is about 53—$22.50 a month
    $22.50   from the 20-Pay Life policy

[20] She could, of course, seek full-time employment earlier, but under present Social Security laws she would stand to lose some of her Social Security benefits. Also, if at all possible, it is best to keep the mother at home while the children are growing up.

If for any reason the mother cannot support herself, this small monthly income will give her spending money and thereby make her that much less of a financial burden on her children during their early years out of college, which in all probability will be their least productive period.

From widow's age 53 to age 65—$0
From widow's age 65 for life—$81.40 a month
    $81.40 from Social Security

This program takes all the present life insurance with the exception of the $5,000 Group life insurance policy; $2,000 of the Group is put into the Clean-up fund. At least a few hundred dollars of the fund will be left over to establish an emergency fund if final medical and hospital expenses are not too great.

Now comes the problem of the mortgage, on which he owes $9,000 at this time. At least one of two things could have been done: (1) $9,000 could have been taken from insurance proceeds to retire the mortgage. This, however, would have the effect of increasing the net income of the family during the 15 years that the mortgage has left to run, and these are 15 years during which the family's income is most adequate by the standards set up by the family itself. The income during those years is made up almost wholly of Social Security and fixed payments from the Family Income plan. Neither can be lowered to offset the savings effected by paying off the mortgage. On the other hand, a reduction of insurance proceeds by $9,000 to pay off the mortgage would drastically reduce the income during the years after the Family Income payments are exhausted and the Social Security payments are interrupted.

Hence, under this particular program, it would seem better [21] to let the mortgage stand, using the rest of the $3,000 of Group either to prepay part of the mortgage so as to reduce the monthly payments, if allowable, or to be paid out as additional income during the 15 years remaining under the mortgage. The installments could be used to help meet the mortgage payments as they fall due. The $3,000 paid over a 15-year period (assuming the Group insurer would allow the option) would add about $20 a month to the family's income, thus helping to reduce the effective burden of the mortgage payments.

As between prepaying a part of the mortgage and taking an income option, the former is preferable. While interest will be paid under the settlement option, the amount paid on the mortgage is undoubtedly greater, even

---

[21] And the authors admit this is a matter of judgment to which there can be dissent.

after all income tax considerations. Under the terms of the mortgage, however, prepayment may not be allowed.

Present Situation in Event of Disability. It was decided by the family that a monthly income of $250 is the minimum necessary to maintain the family unit should earned income be destroyed. While present insurance provides the desired income during the child-raising period in event of death, it provides nothing whatsoever in event of disability; and Social Security provides nothing as this is written. Hospitalization insurance is available providing benefits up to $8 a day, plus surgical and miscellaneous benefits.

Present Situation at Retirement. If the insured lives to age 65, his retirement income situation will be as follows:

From husband's age 65 for next two years—$177.00 a month
   $150 a month from Social Security and company pension, which pension
          is an arrangement to supplement whatever Social Security he receives up to $150
    27 from cash values in the basic policy to which the Family Income
          rider is attached and the 20-Pay Life policy, paid out on a joint and
          2/3 survivor option (if available)

The income from the life insurance does not include all cash values available, since a Clean-up fund is still needed. Therefore, $1,000 of the 20-Pay Life policy is retained, since it is fully paid up.

From wife's age 65 as long as both live—$231.30
   $150.00 a month to husband from Social Security and company pension
    54.30 a month to wife from Social Security
    27.00 from life insurance

For husband's life if wife dies before he is 65—$182.06
   $150.00 a month from Social Security and company pension
    32.06 from life insurance cash values on life income only (no period
          certain) basis since there is no need for the joint and 2/3 option

For wife's life if husband predeceases her before he is 65—$81.40
   $81.40 from Social Security

This figure assumes that the husband's life insurance proceeds have been exhausted by the time the widow is 65. Should he die shortly before age 65, her income might be supplemented by a substantial amount of life insurance proceeds.

For wife's life if husband predeceases her after she is 65—$99.40
   $81.40 from Social Security
    18.00 from the joint and 2/3 survivor option in insurance proceeds

Family's Present Protection Picture. Wife: $592 Clean-up. Each child: $1,000 Clean-up or Educational fund. Disability: $8 a day hospital benefit for each, plus surgical and miscellaneous benefits in policy.

Weaknesses in Present Picture. It will be far easier to spot the weaknesses in the family's present income protection picture if the major points of the program outlined above are charted, as they are on the next page. Once it is so visualized, these weaknesses become immediatealy apparent:

PRESENT PROTECTION PICTURE

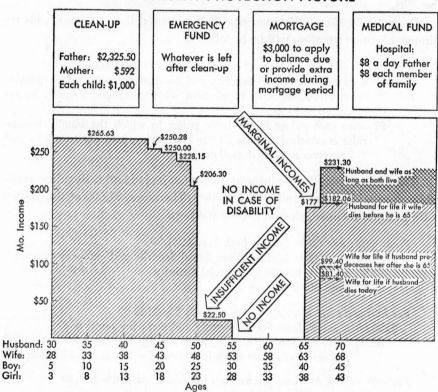

CLEAN-UP	EMERGENCY FUND	MORTGAGE	MEDICAL FUND
Father: $2,325.50 Mother: $592 Each child: $1,000	Whatever is left after clean-up	$3,000 to apply to balance due or provide extra income during mortgage period	Hospital: $8 a day Father $8 each member of family

Disability. The most glaring defects in the program are inadequate protection against major medical expenses and lack of disability income insurance. Depending on its exact provisions and the limitation on hospital stay, the present hospitalization policy would probably pay not more than a maximum of several hundred dollars. With a $6,500 income, the family probably could pay these relatively small hospital bills out of pocket without undue distress. This hospitalization insurance hardly seems necessary, but they have no protection against the bills that might run beyond what they can pay without help, bills that should be handled by insurance.

Clean-up. Under today's price structure, $2,000 is not an adequate Clean-up fund, especially if there is a protracted illness or accident that requires expensive medical care before death.

Life Income to Widow. From virtually the time the second child finishes college until the widow is 65, she is without income. While in planning the program with the present insurance it has been assumed that she could go to work at that time or the children could support her, (*a*) she will then be 48, and employment for older women is not easy to find even in the best of times; (*b*) it is certainly not desirable to place upon children just starting out on their own careers the burden of supporting a widowed mother. This is especially true when one of the children is a girl who may be married and would, therefore, have to ask her husband to contribute to his mother-in-law's support. Such an arrangement does not assist in making marriage a success.

Widow's Income after 65. The $81.40 income provided entirely from Social Security certainly is not one most 30-year-old men in the $6,500 income class would consider enough for their own subsistence, let alone adequate for their wives.

Retirement. The husband's retirement picture is weak. After he is 65, it will require him and his wife to live on $177 a month for the first two years. This income is enough for subsistence, but it certainly will not provide a comfortable two years, especially since the lean years will come immediately after he has been accustomed to a much higher earned income.

Family Protection. Although the amount available for Clean-up on both the children is reasonably adequate, the policy assumes that their death will not be preceded by heavy medical expenses. The amount for Clean-up on the wife is inadequate. Furthermore, the educational endowments on the children are absorbing a disproportionate amount of premium money for the amount of protection they provide, and are far from adequate for a college fund.

Minimum Recommendations.[22] (1) Drop the present hospitalization

---

[22] It is on "recommendations" that authorities differ widely. Rarely will any two of the most competent insurance agents agree exactly on recommendations in programming cases such as the one set up here. In fact, a good project for the reader would be to work out and defend a different set of recommendations—and even a different arrangement in the program of the present insurance. If such a project is undertaken, the chances are good that there will be as many different recommendations as there are people engaged in it. The authors agree on the program set forth here, although they realize that, at best, they have reached an unstable agreement.

policy which is costing $89 a year, and take in its place a major medical policy with $500 deductible and $5,000 maximum and no coinsurance.[23]

The major medical policy will take care of heavy medical expenses of the insured and his family in the event of serious accidents or illness. It can also lessen the burden on the life insurance program by paying the large medical and hospital bills often preceding death. This reduces the necessity for adding more life insurance for the Clean-up funds of the mother and children. Further, since the policy suggested continues benefits after age 65, it also solves the problem of emergency and Clean-up after retirement. Heavy medical expenses in old age before death are common. A paid-up policy of $1,000 is being retained on the husband after 65. Insurance of $592 on the wife also is continued. With major medical insurance, these sums should be enough in the usual situation which does not involve estate taxes and other such expenses.

Finally, the major medical policy strengthens the father's Clean-up fund. Unless he has heavy debts outstanding, $1,000 will pay final bills other than medical, now insured. This would make it possible to release $1,000 of the present Clean-up fund to be used more effectively elsewhere. Or, the $1,000 could be held as an emergency fund.

(2) Provide disability income insurance. The first consideration is the mortgage. In event of the disability of the wage earner, there will be no income to continue payments on the mortgage. A mortgage disability insurance policy in the amount of the monthly payments should be arranged. Since the first payment would not be due until a month following disability, a policy with a 30-day waiting period is recommended. If the mortgage payments are equal to $100 a month including taxes and property insurance, a disability income policy of $100 a month would be necessary. In addition to the mortgage income policy, additional disability income coverage of $150 a month is necessary to bring the total disability income up to the $250

[23] If a policy with coinsurance is used, the recommendation to drop the basic hospitalization policy might need to be reconsidered. Under a $5,000 maximum, $500 deductible major medical with 75% coinsurance, for instance, a medical bill of $5,000 would cost the family $1,625 (which cost would be the $500 deductible plus 25% of the remaining $4,500, the insured's share under the coinsurance clause). With coinsurance, it might be considered necessary to retain the basic policy to pay some part of the $1,625 potential. Also, the policy suggested here applies the deductible only to the *total* medical bills of the entire family in case of common accident or illness; whereas many policies apply it to the bills of *each individual* in case of common illness if not in case of common accident. As this is written, major medical is in its formative stage. Some underwriters feel it is safe to omit the coinsurance clause and apply the deductible only once; some contend it is not safe to do so from an underwriting standpoint. Neither school of thought has, at this stage, enough statistical evidence to convince the other. In recommending the policy above, the authors are not taking the "no coinsurance" side of the underwriting argument but are merely accepting policies as they are and making the recommendation that best fits the illustrative case.

income agreed upon by the family as the minimum needed. In addition, another $100 a month with payments limited to 12 months should be purchased for a disability readjustment income plan. Statistically, few disabilities last over a year, and it will be difficult for the family to cut its expenditures to $250 the first year, perhaps more difficult in the case of disability than in the case of death. When the head of a family dies, it is obvious to everyone that income has stopped permanently. The family knows it will be necessary to cut expenditures to the bone at once. In the case of most disabilities, the family for at least the first year keeps expecting the wage earner to recover and postpones cutting expenditures. If he does not recover after a year, the family by that time will realize the necessity of cutting down expenditures. The extra $100 above minimum requirements for at least the first year will help in this readjustment.

(3) Provide income for widow from 48 to 65. Even a small income will be better than none at all. It will prevent her from becoming a full burden on the children if she cannot find a suitable job. A small income can change her from an old woman to an elderly lady. It can do a great deal for her pride.

The above are the minimum recommendations in the case illustrated. By no means do they cover all the weaknesses in the program—the retirement situation, for instance. However, the retirement need would seem secondary to the death and disability need at this point in the family's growth. Further, no additional mortgage life insurance is recommended. The income payments during the mortgage period are adequate to handle the periodic payments. Certainly it would be well to pay off the mortgage and thereby save the interest; but the recommendations above seem to be more important at this point.

The family's present premium outlay is as follows: [24]

$5,000 Group, noncontributory	$ 0
Company pension plan, noncontributory	0
20-Pay Life	68.50
$5,000 Family Income plan	100.15
$5,000 Term to 65	51.65
$ 592 Weekly Premium on wife @ 20¢ a week	10.40
$1,000 E. 18 on son (with payor benefit)	62.03
$1,000 E. 18 on daughter (with payor benefit)	54.38
Hospitalization policy	89.10
	$436.21

[24] All rates used in this program illustration are nonpar, selected because they approximate net par rates and therefore, give a truer picture of actual cash outlay. Also nonpar rates make it possible to avoid the complications of dividend assumptions. In addition to the premiums above will be the payroll deduction of the Social Security tax.

The Policies to Select. The policies to select must be determined not only by what is adapted to the need, but also by what the family can afford. After careful consideration of its budget, the family decides it can afford an additional $7 a week, or $364 a year.

The Major Medical Need. The policy to use for medical expenses has been indicated. It will cover the family for $70 a year. This represents a net saving of $19 a year over the present hospitalization insurance.

Mortgage Disability Policy. Recommended here is a commercial policy [25] for $100 a month with a 30-day waiting period, lifetime for accident and three years for sickness, house confinement not required. A longer period for sickness benefits might be desirable, but cost is a factor. This policy will cost approximately $30 annually.

Family Period Disability Need. While the $100 a month policy suggested above will pay the mortgage, other family expenses will continue. To take care of them, $150 a month commercial, with a seven-day waiting period [26] and lifetime accident and sickness benefits is suggested. It is true that sickness benefits after the first two years under this policy will require house confinement, but even with that restriction, the degree of protection afforded seems worth the slight increase in premium as compared with the mortgage policy, which offers no coverage for disabling illness after three years. It is written without principal sum. This policy will cost about $79.50 a year.[27]

Readjustment Disability Need. The recommendation for the readjustment disability income need is another commercial policy (no principal sum) paying $100 a month for disability from sickness or accident, limited

[25] Noncan advocates will roundly condemn any suggestion of a commercial policy, but similar coverage on a noncan basis would cost twice as much and necessitate cutting down on other badly needed coverage. The authors agree that it would be ideal if every disability program could be made up of noncan coverage and every life program made up of permanent policy forms. However, as previously stated, it is necessary in the average program to temper what is desirable by what can be afforded. Cf. Chapter 11 for a review of the different classes of A & S insurance.

[26] The waiting period is chosen on the assumption that the employer will continue wages for the first week of disability. Probably in the case of an employee in the $6,500 bracket wages would be continued for longer. In that case, a longer waiting period would cut the cost slightly.

[27] Perhaps the next step in this program, when the insured's income has risen to some extent is to change this to a noncan policy so he will have his basic protection in a permanent policy form. However, the noncan probably will not pay lifetime benefits for sickness. Also, if the insured ever buys enough permanent life insurance, he can purchase disability income riders for these contracts paying $5 or $10 per month per $1,000 of insurance. The number of life companies issuing these riders is in the minority. They pay only in the event of permanent and total disability and require, generally, a six-month waiting period. The cost in one company at age 30, written on a continuous-premium Whole Life policy, is $5.21 per each $10 of monthly income. In another company, it is $3.20 per each $5 of monthly income. Waiver of premium is included in both illustrations.

to one year. It will cost about $44.00 a year. (The higher cost of this policy than of the mortgage policy for the same amount is largely because of the shorter waiting period.)

At this point, the recommendations have taken $223.50 of the $364 the family says it can budget, leaving $140.50 plus the $19 saved on hospitalization, or a total of $159.50 to use in filling the income needs of the widow.[28]

Income for Widow after Children Are Grown. The decision to be made is whether to use the $159.50 of remaining premium budget to buy a permanent policy form or to buy Term. A permanent policy would purchase less income protection for the widow. On the lowest premium permanent policy form, continuous-premium Whole Life,[29] $159.50 will purchase approximately $9,300. Distributed as a monthly income over the 17 years between 48 and 65, $9,300 of insurance will pay the widow approximately $55. This amount of income will probably be insufficient for her to live independently; although it will enable her to pay much of her way if she lives with the children.

The permanent policy has two advantages: (1) it will strengthen the retirement program which is at present weak, and (2) it will increase, through the use of cash values, the fund available for emergency needs. However, with reasonably adequate disability coverage, the need for such emergency money is not too urgent.

On the other hand, the Term policy will provide much more income for the 17 years and can be converted to a permanent form if and when the insured's income increases. The $159.50 available for premiums will purchase about $22,000 ten-year Term with waiver of premium (important, since much of the present program would be lost if disability prevented premiums from being paid, there being waiver of premium on only $7,500 of the present insurance). Distributed over the 17 years following the widow's age 48, the $22,000 of proceeds would pay her around $126 a month.

The proceeds of this policy will be left at interest with the company until the widow reaches age 48. The interest, at 2½%, amounts to $45.83 a month or $550 a year, will have to be withdrawn when due. This additional income

---

[28] The confirmed life insurance man who has never sold A & S or never studied the need will be shocked at using up so much of the premium money for disability needs rather than using all of it to give the widow income from 47 to 65. However, he would also agree that the first thing in programming is to get the family through the child-rearing period. By building up the disability income protection, concentration has been on doing just that. A nice income for the widow 19 years away will not be of much help to a family that loses its income during the child-rearing period because the father is disabled.

[29] If the husband's income prospects are particularly bright, a Modified policy might be used. Another suggestion is a deferred survivorship policy, which represents the way one of the authors has handled this problem in his own program. However, since this policy is relatively rare it is not a good one to suggest in an illustration such as this.

will be welcomed during the college years when incomes are dropping. However, during the child-rearing period it will increase the income well above the $250 minimum set by the family.

In view of the fact that $250 is a "tight" budget for a family of three, it may well be that the family will want to use the extra $45.83 for current expenses. However, in view of the fact that the family has decided that $250 is enough, it seems that a better plan would be to postpone the use of the additional $550 a year until the widow reaches age 48; the widow's income at that age being now only $126 could stand an increase without exceeding minimum limits. Unfortunately most companies will not allow proceeds to be accumulated at interest until the end of a specified period with the increased amount to be under another option.[30] Fortunately, however, several companies can be found that will allow accumulations for a given period.[31] If the insurance is with one of these companies, the payment to the widow at age 48 will be increased in proportion to the value of the interest accumulations. If the insurance is with one of the companies that will not allow proceeds to accumulate at interest, then the beneficiary could take the annual $550 check and deposit it in a savings bank for safekeeping and interest accumulation until the widow is 48. Money in savings accounts, however, is so accessible that it has a way of being dissipated.

A sure but expensive method of transferring the interest income from the years when it is less needed to the years when it is badly needed is for the widow to buy an Endowment policy on herself, the endowment period selected being the number of years remaining until she reaches age 48.[32] For instance, if she were to become a widow next year, a 20-year Endowment would mature at exactly age 48, and her $550 a year interest income would purchase about $11,600. At 48 she could take the proceeds of the policy on a 17-year basis and thus add $66.34 to the monthly income during the years to age 65, bringing the total up to $192.50 a month, a much more satisfactory level of income. The amount of additional income will be less, of course, if the insured dies five years from now, because $550 a year will buy less insurance under a 15-year Endowment plan and with the widow five years older.[33]

---

[30] An exception is made during the minority of a beneficiary, as previously explained.
[31] Cf. current edition, *Settlement Options,* a Flitcraft publication.
[32] This will have to be approximate since Endowments are not usually available for odd periods of years. Also the use of Endowments is not recommended if there are only a few years left to run. Short-term Endowments tend to be uneconomical.
[33] Chances are that inasmuch as this recommendation cannot be effected in the program today, but must depend on the widow's action in the event of her husband's death, it will never be followed. The interest income will simply be used currently.

The Endowment plan as a vehicle for accumulating the periodic interest payments is particularly useful when life insurance on the widow is desirable to add additional funds for the children if she should die while they are still dependent. However, if insurance on the life of the mother is not a primary consideration, a conventional saving plan, which eliminates the cost of the insurance, will give her more cash at the end of the period. For example, the deposits of $550 a year will increase to $11,600 in 20 years under the Endowment plan. Under a straight savings plan paying 2% net after taxes, compounded annually, the same annual deposits will accumulate to $13,630.65 since there are no insurance costs to be met.

Program with the Recommendations. If the recommendation to purchase Term and use the interest from it (in event of the father's death) to buy Endowment on the mother is followed, plus the disability insurance recommendations, the program will be set up as follows:

Cash available in event of death

$1,325.50 in case of death of father, $1,000 from Group and $325.50 from Social Security (assuming he receives the maximum)

592.00 in case of death of mother, from Industrial policy

1,000.00 in case of death of each child, from their Endowment at age 18 policies

5,000.00 maximum for last illness, from major medical

Emergency Fund

$1,000.00 from Group (Held at interest with right to withdraw, this will provide about $20 a year to help meet the premium on the major medical, which is to be continued on the rest of the family in event of death of the father.)

5,000.00 maximum for medical expenses from major medical (This is a maximum for each separate accident or sickness as long as the policy is in force.)

Mortgage Fund

$3,000.00 from Group, to be used to reduce the principal, if possible, or supplement income to meet payments during dependency period if mortgage does not allow prepayment. If necessary to reduce principal even more, the $1,000 Emergency Fund can be used, but the Emergency Fund will then be weak because (a) there will be nothing from which to draw if expense of illness up to major medical deductible is too much to pay out of income, and (b) emergencies other than illness can arise: house repairs as one example.

100.00 a month to meet mortgage payments in case of disability of father—lifetime accident; 3 years' sickness

From date of death or disability until son is 18
$265.63 a month in event of death
    $200.00 from Social Security
      50.00 from Family Income rider
      15.63 from 2½% interest on $5,000 Term and $2,500 20-Pay
          life being held for later distribution
  250.00 a month in event of disability of father for one year
  150.00 a month thereafter (plus any benefits from Social Security that
      may be added by legislation passed after this writing: and also
      plus the $100 a month to cover the mortgage payments, which
      is, however, shown under "Mortgage Fund")

From date son reaches 18 until daughter is 18
$250.28 a month in event of death
    $162.80 from Social Security
      50.00 from Family Income rider
      21.85 from son's $1,000 Endowment at 18
      15.63 from $5,000 Term and $2,500 20-Pay being held at
          interest
  250.00 a month in event of disability for one year
  150.00 a month thereafter (plus mortgage payments, as noted)

From date daughter reaches 18 until son finishes college
$250.00 a month in event of death
    $ 21.85 from son's E. 18
      21.85 from daughter's E. 18
      22.50 from 20-Pay Life, principal and interest to exhaustion
    183.80 from $5,000 Term and $5,000 continuous-premium
          Whole Life to which Family Income rider was at-
          tached, both principal and interest to exhaustion
  250.00 a month first year in event of disability
  150.00 a month thereafter (plus mortgage payments)

From date son graduates until daughter's graduation
$228.15 in event of death
    $ 21.85 from daughter's E. 18
      22.50 from 20-Pay Life
    183.80 from Term and continuous-premium Whole Life
$250.00 a month first year of any disability
  150.00 a month thereafter (plus mortgage payments)

For a period of slightly under one year after girl graduates
$206.30 a month in event of death
    $183.80 from Term and Whole Life
      22.50 from 20-Pay Life
  250.00 a month for first year of any disability
  150.00 a month thereafter (plus mortgage payments)

Until widow is 53
$214.84 a month in event of death
 $ 22.50 from 20-Pay Life
  126.00 from $22,000 Term
   66.34 from Endowment purchased with interest on the Term
    held until this time
 250.00 a month for first year of any disability
 150.00 a month thereafter (plus mortgage payments)

Until widow is 65
$192.34 a month from Term and Endowment proceeds
 250.00 a month for first year of any disability
 150.00 a month thereafter (plus mortgage payments)

The retirement picture remains, for the time being, exactly the same as before. However, the insured would be expected to convert the Term, purchased now because the protection need is more immediate than the retirement. The cash values of that converted Term would add to the retirement picture. Presumably also, as the insured's income increases, he will review the program with his agent and make additions to it that will strengthen it throughout as rapidly as possible. A program can be set up only on the basis of needs as they appear and income available at the time the program is being worked out. Changing needs and changing income call for regular changes in the program.

The new program is visualized in the accompanying chart.

One possible additional recommendation might be made. Many agents would hesitate to make it for fear it would be interpreted as "twisting"; [34] but in this case it might be a sound one to consider. The two educational policies on the children are providing only $1,000 Clean-up protection (deemed enough in view of the addition of the major medical) and not anything like an adequate college fund. Nevertheless, they are costing $116.41 a year. The same amount of continuous-premium Whole Life could be purchased on each child for a combined premium of about $20 a year, including waiver of premium in case of disability or death of the father. This would release close to $100 a year, which could purchase about $6,000 con-

---

[34] Legally, inducing a policyholder to drop an existing policy to take another *by misrepresentation*. However, whenever a policy is replaced an agent may be subject to accusations of twisting even if the technicality of misrepresentation was not present. The fear of having his motives misinterpreted, especially by his fellow agents, sometimes keeps an agent from recommending advantageous changes. In the A & S field, as in the fire-casualty field, it is more common to think of policies as being for a term of one year, and the suggestion that the policy be changed is considered "replacing," there being no cash values involved and, hence, no chance of loss of values to the policyholder. However, even in the A & S field, the agent who is concerned with his reputation "goes slow" before he suggests dropping a policy.

RECOMMENDED PROTECTION PICTURE

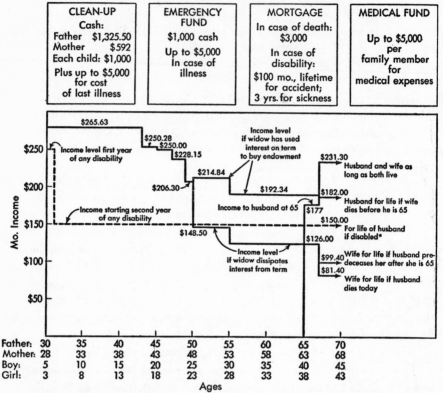

CLEAN-UP	EMERGENCY FUND	MORTGAGE	MEDICAL FUND
Cash: Father $1,325.50 Mother $592 Each child: $1,000 Plus up to $5,000 for cost of last illness	$1,000 cash Up to $5,000 In case of illness	In case of death: $3,000 In case of disability: $100 mo., lifetime for accident; 3 yrs. for sickness	Up to $5,000 per family member for medical expenses

(Chart: Mo. Income vs. Ages)

- $265.63
- $250.28
- $250.00 — Income level first year of any disability
- $228.15
- $214.84
- $206.30
- $192.34 — Income to husband at 65
- $182.00
- $231.30 — Husband and wife as long as both live
- $177 — Husband for life if wife dies before he is 65
- $150.00 — For life of husband if disabled*
- $148.50
- $126.00
- Income starting second year of any disability
- Income level if widow dissipates interest from term
- Income level if widow has used interest on term to buy endowment
- $99.40 — Wife for life if husband predeceases her after she is 65
- $81.40 — Wife for life if husband dies today

Ages:

Father:	30	35	40	45	50	55	60	65	70
Mother:	28	33	38	43	48	53	58	63	68
Boy:	5	10	15	20	25	30	35	40	45
Girl:	3	8	13	18	23	28	33	38	43

* To the disability income for the father would be added any benefit from Social Security, should the law be amended to provide these benefits (as appears possible).

tinuous-premium Whole Life insurance on the life of the father; this held at interest until the children were ready for college would pay each of them around $65 a month (depending on the interest guaranteed) over a four-year college period in contrast to the $21.85 they will get during those same years from their Endowments. Thus about $87 would be added to the family's income during college years when the money could be advantageously used. The $6,000 at interest until college years would add $12.50 a month to the family's income during the child-rearing period unless these funds could be left with the company to accumulate at interest until the children were ready for college. As stated, many companies will accumulate the proceeds of the policy at interest during the minority of the beneficiaries. Furthermore, the cash value of the two Endowments, assuming they were taken at ages 0 and 2, would now be better than $235. These funds could be used to pay part of the first premium on the new insurance. The first premium usually is a problem with any buyer since he has not been budgeting for it and, therefore, does not have it accumulated.

This recommendation is not shown on the chart of the new program because (a) the ethics of an agent suggesting it might be questioned, however wrongly; (b) it is not necessary to meet minimum requirements, although certainly it is advantageous planning; (c) having cash come in when the children are ready to start to college has a strong appeal to every father. The insured himself might react adversely to the suggestion and, hence, to all the recommendations. If, however, basic minimums could not be met with additional premium money available, adverse reaction should be risked in the interest of reaching those minimums.

Along the same lines, the 20-Pay Life policy is also open to criticism. The $68.50 premium could be better spent for continuous-premium Whole Life which, at age 30, would purchase over $3,600. The additional $1,100 of insurance could increase the family income or add to the emergency fund. It will be recalled that $1,000 of paid-up insurance was left in force at age 65 to pay Clean-up expenses at death following the retirement years. These plans will not have to be disturbed because the paid-up nonforfeiture option under the $3,600 continuous-premium Whole Life policy would give around $2,800 of paid-up insurance at 65. If only $1,000 were used, the rest would be available to supplement retirement income. The present $2,500 20-Pay Life policy could be surrendered for $400 in cash, exchanged for $1,000 of paid-up insurance, or kept in force at its full value for almost 30 years. The choice of nonforfeiture options would depend upon the attitude of the insured. If he did not need the cash to help pay the first-year premiums on his new insurance and his greatest interest was in building retirement protection and a cash value emergency fund, he could take the paid-up policy for $1,000. If he were interested in providing more income to his family in case of his premature death, he would take the extended term option.

This latter recommendation is not shown on the chart either—for practically the same reasons the Endowment recommendations were omitted.

The Options to Select. The program calls for the use of every commonly available option. The $5,000 Term and $2,500 20-Pay Life in the present program and the new $22,000 Term are held at *interest only*, switching to the *specified amount* (principal and interest to exhaustion) in later years. *Specified amount* is also used for the proceeds of the basic policy in the Family Income plan when it comes due. *Fixed period* is used for the college Endowments. *Life income* is used for retirement income. An important need for the accumulation of interest option was indicated and would

be used if any of the policies happened to be in one of the companies granting the option. Each option selected has been dictated more by the nature
of the income need than by nature of the option, which is usually the situation in programming.

Assuming the recommendations are followed and the new program is
set up, the question arises whether the insured himself should elect the
options in advance. Some authorities will recommend tying the program up
tight, especially when the incomes are marginal, as in this case. The withdrawal of a few thousand dollars could upset the whole plan. Then, also,
if options are elected now, the insured will be sure that there are no objections to the options on the part of any of the companies involved. For instance, some few companies might object to the interest only until a fixed
date and the subsequent switch to another option. The arrangement is rarely
covered by contractual provision. It depends, instead, on company practice.
Even if the company has no objections today, it might change its philosophy
years from now at a time before the beneficiary herself tries to make the
election.

Tying the program up now is safe, but it is inflexible. Conditions—living
costs, for example—might have changed drastically by the time the program
matures (since, despite admonition, insureds do not review their programs
frequently) making the incomes set by the pre-elected options wholly unrealistic, but leaving the widow powerless to change them.

The other plan is to draw up detailed recommendations for the widow
to follow and leave all proceeds at interest with the right to withdraw in
whole or in part, or to elect any other option. Some companies will require
that the widow make her election of another option within one or two years
after the policy matures as a death claim, although they will usually allow
her to elect a change from interest only to another option at some time in
the future if she will make the selection within the time limit. Other companies will allow the widow to elect any other option at any future time, a
much more flexible arrangement because she can then select other than the
suggested one if, at the time she is ready to change, the change is advantageous.

If the options are not selected by the insured but are left as recommendations to the widow, the instructions should be detailed, and each company
involved should be queried in advance to learn if it will allow the recommended selection—or at least whether it would under present practices, even
if it will not commit itself on what its practice might be in the future.

Whether to tie up the program in advance or leave it open for the widow
to elect the options depends on the philosophy of the agent and the in-

sured, the character of the beneficiary and, of course, the amount of insurance involved.

Checking for Policy Safeguards. A final step in programming is that of checking for policy safeguards. It is necessary to see that (1) primary and contingent beneficiaries are properly designated; (2) spendthrift trust clauses are used where desirable and permissible; (3) settlement options are properly selected; (4) wise use is made of any dividends; (5) common disaster clauses are used where necessary; (6) premiums are arranged so that they may be budgeted without paying interest; [35] (7) automatic premium loans are included where allowed by the company; (8) disability protection is provided if available; and (9) policy loans are repaid or hedged; (10) wise use is made of deductibles in major medical policies.

4. SUMMARY OF PROGRAMMING

Insurance needs are as individual as are people. It is no more possible to set up one formula by which everyone can determine how much insurance he should have than it is to concoct one prescription that will take care of the medicinal needs of everyone.

The only way to determine how much insurance is needed in any given case is to analyze the needs in that particular case. The process of analyzing needs and fitting policies to them is known as "programming."

Needs in Programming. The process of programming consists of several steps of which the first is the analysis of needs.

While needs vary with individuals, and the order of the importance of basic needs varies with the family situation and the philosophy of each individual, the following will be found to be basic in the program of almost every family man, and about in the order of importance in which they are listed here:

1. Cash needs for final expenses and outstanding debts, including any mortgage

2. Readjustment income to give the family a "breathing spell" before it has to cut its former standard of living to whatever standard will be provided by its income without the pay check of the head of the family

3. Family-period income; that is, income while the children are growing up

4. Life income for the widow after the children are grown so she can retain a measure of independence and not be a burden on the children

---

[35] If desirable, premiums may be paid annually but yet budgeted by arranging premium due dates on policies so that an annual premium is due each month. In this way, the policyholder can take advantage of monthly payments without the payment of carrying charges.

5. Educational fund

6. Wife insurance to offset the extra expense to which the family would be subject if someone had to be hired to run the home

7. Retirement income

In addition to these basic needs, a number of others might be listed. Most of them are, however, less than basic. In fact, they might be better described as "wants." These special needs, or "wants," are valid uses of life insurance *if* basic needs have been adequately covered. The trouble is that too often the appeal of one of the special uses leads to using premium money for it that should be used to cover basic needs.

The Tools of Programming. The tools of programming are the policy settlement options, most commonly these: *Interest only,* under which the company holds the policy proceeds and pays interest on them at a guaranteed rate, and, in some cases, at excess rates when earned. This option is the same in effect as a bank savings account, except that withdrawals cannot be made at will but only as specified when the option was selected. *Fixed period,* under which the proceeds are paid out in equal (usually monthly) amounts over a preselected period of time. *Specified amount,* under which the proceeds are paid out in preselected, equal installments until the principal, and the interest credited on it, are exhausted. This option is also called "principal and interest to exhaustion." *Life income,* under which the proceeds are paid out on annuity basis, the amount of each installment per $1,000 being determined by age at time the payments begin and lasting as long as the beneficiary lives. The option may usually be elected with a "period certain," which means that a fixed number of installments will be paid (usually 60, 120, 240) regardless of whether the beneficiary lives or dies. After that time, the income will be continued only if the beneficiary is living. *Joint and Survivor,* under which income is paid for the lifetime of either one of two or more beneficiaries, perhaps reducing the amount by one third or a similar fraction upon the death of the first or of each.

The Process of Programming. The process of programming consists, *first,* of determining the needs in a given case and the order of their importance. *Second,* it consists of determining how much income should be provided for each of these needs, tempered by what can be afforded. *Third,* it involves determining how far existing coverages and other assets go in covering the needs. *Fourth,* it consists of determining the extent of the gaps between estimated needs and the amounts now available to fill them. *Fifth,* it concerns making recommendations for filling the gaps as far as can be done with the money available for premiums. And, *finally,* it involves selecting and putting into effect all the settlement options and other policy safeguards necessary to the efficient functioning of the program.

Life and disability insurance policies may be looked upon as the materials with which a house of protection can be built. Programming is the process of building that house. The completed program is the shelter into which the family moves and under which it lives.

An income insurance program tells a family in advance not only how much insurance it has, but also what that insurance will do. It is the only real way of knowing whether or not one has enough income insurance, because face values mean little. It is much more important to think of insurance in terms of income than in terms of lump sums. Thinking in terms of face amounts is misleading; $10,000 is a lot of money. Few of us have ever held it in our hands. Yet $10,000 is pitifully small when it is the only source of income for a family whose earning power is gone.

Income insurance, properly programmed, provides something to take care of the family as long as the family takes care of it.

Questions for Class Discussion

1. Several formulas have been established to tell a man how much insurance he should own. How accurate do you think such formulas can be?
2. Which is more important, adequate disability income insurance or adequate life insurance?
3. In arranging an income insurance program, is it better to provide for *all* needs in part or *some* needs in full if the budget will not allow sufficient funds for a full program?
4. The Macmillan family, which is composed of the father age 35, mother 31, and two children, George age 5 and Caroline, age 3, budgets $500 a year for income insurance. Suggest a program for this family which will make the best use of this $500. Make whatever assumptions you wish about other property owned by this family.
5. Suppose the family could spend twice as much for insurance as indicated above ($1,000), what would you recommend as a program?
6. Suppose the family can spend only one half as much ($250), what kind of program would you recommend?
7. Develop the kind of income insurance program you feel you need for yourself. How much would this cost? If you cannot afford it (and you probably cannot) what economies will you make? Do you have this program? If not, why not?
8. Explain the importance of selecting the correct dividend options in programming life insurance.
9. Aside from selecting policies and assigning them to the various needs, what would you say is the job of the programmer?
10. In what ways would you handle the program developed in Chapter 16 differently from the way the authors handled it?

CHAPTER 17

INSURANCE IN ESTATE
AND TAX PLANNING

OFTEN THE MAN with a substantial estate is not afraid of what will happen to his family should he die prematurely. He is confident that his estate will take care of them. If approached on the subject of life insurance, he will say, "Why, do you know that if I were to die tonight there would be enough income from my estate to support my family for the rest of their lives?" He might be correct, but often he fails to realize that his death would reduce the amount of income available from that estate.

This man, therefore, does have a financial problem involving death but it is not one of estate creation. Instead it is one of estate conservation. He needs to plan his estate so as to protect it from the heavy losses that normally occur at death so that he can pass on to his heirs as much of his estate as possible.

Estates shrink upon the death of their owners; they do not pass intact from owners to heirs. Property must be insured against this type of loss just as it needs to be insured against loss resulting from fire or theft. It is a function of life insurance to provide this protection.

Estate planning involves two major objectives: (1) reduction to the minimum of the cost of estate transfer, and (2) arrangement for the most economical method of paying transfer costs which cannot be eliminated. Many plans and devices have been conceived and developed by attorneys, trust officers, accountants, and life insurance agents to help men achieve these objectives. Some of these devices include the use of life insurance.

380

It is the purpose of this chapter to describe briefly the job of the life underwriter as an estate planner and to show how life insurance may be used to protect estates. A discussion of the tax aspects of life insurance policies also is a subject of this chapter.

1. THE PLACE OF ESTATE PLANNING IN LIFE INSURANCE SELLING

Several types of selling techniques are noticeable in the life insurance business:

(1) Policy selling is the practice of offering a policy on the basis of its merits with little or no consideration of what need the policy is supposed to fill. For example, it is selling a 20-year Endowment policy because it pays face value "whether you live or die." This type of selling is undesirable, because it considers more what will induce a prospect to buy rather than any particular need he might have.

(2) Package selling is the practice of selling insurance by concentrating on one specific need. Each of the needs discussed in Chapter 15 can be a package. Thus an agent sells retirement income insurance, college education Endowments, or mortgage retirement. While this is a more desirable form of selling than policy selling, it is dangerous in that first needs are not always covered first. Agents often sell, and propects often insist on buying, the most attractive package first rather than the one which is most needed. An example would be selling Juvenile insurance before there is adequate coverage on the life of the father because it is easier to sell.

(3) Program selling is the type of selling discussed in Chapters 15 and 16. It involves the consideration of all needs along with the ability to pay. Programmers arrange to fill these needs in order of their importance. This is the professional way to sell life insurance to people seeking to create an estate.

(4) Estate planning is "upper-bracket" selling, involving the problems of estate protection rather than estate creation and liquidation. It is for the man whose problem is not so much that of acquiring a dollar, but rather of getting the most long-run value out of the dollar after he acquires it. It is with this type of client that estate planners work. This is the professional way to sell life insurance to people who seek to conserve an estate.

(5) Business insurance selling is also "high-bracket" selling. It is discussed in the following chapter. In so far as the business interest is a part of the estate of the deceased, it is also a part of estate planning. That aspect of business insurance is touched upon in this chapter.

2. THE LIFE INSURANCE AGENT
AS AN ESTATE PLANNER

Why has the life insurance agent entered a field so technical as estate planning? Why has he not left the field to the expert services of accountants, lawyers, tax consultants, and trust officers? A number of reasons justify the estate planning services of the life underwriter.

Life Underwriters as Advisers in Personal Finance. For years, life insurance men have undertaken the responsibility of motivating men to save. They have helped and encouraged men to create estates. It is only logical that they should help men conserve and protect their estates once they have been accumulated. Many people who are busy making money have no idea of the hazards to which their estates will be exposed or the methods of conserving them. They need the advice of those skilled in estate planning.

Life Underwriters Are Experts in Motivation. It is always the other person who is going to die. Just as a man must be motivated to protect his earned income against premature death, he must also be persuaded to protect his estate against postdeath shrinkage.

The code of ethics of the American Bar Association prevents an attorney from going to his clients. Instead, he must wait for the clients to approach him. Similarly, accountants abide by the code of ethics prescribed by the American Institute of Accountants. Both the legal and accounting professions feel, therefore, that it is not in good grace to communicate with clients and make suggestions regarding the clients' affairs, particularly with reference to their estate.

On the other hand, life underwriters can and are expected to be aggressive. It is perfectly proper for them to bring up the subject of estates and to urge that action be taken to put them in order. The life insurance agent fills a gap between counsel and client.

Estate Planning Means More Insurance Sales. Life insurance may be used in many ways in meeting the two major objectives of estate planning. It may be used to reduce the cost of estate transfer, and in most cases it may also be used to provide the most economical method of meeting estate settlement costs. How life insurance may be used in estate planning will be seen presently.

A working knowledge of estate planning can, and does, lead the underwriter to a different type of prospect. He calls on and talks with men of substantial means. He is able to help them distribute their assets in the most advisable way. He helps them arrange their estates to eliminate the probability that assets will have to be sacrificed at forced sale to raise the cash necessary to pay the costs of estate transfer.

Estate planning gives the life insurance agent an opportunity to conduct his business on a professional level. He creates prestige for himself and enlarges his sphere of influence. Even if a life insurance agent works hours on an estate planning case without obtaining any direct business, the chances are that he will not be the loser for he stands to gain new clients traceable to the reputation he has built as an estate planner.

All Life Insurance Men Are Not Estate Planners. Estate planning is a professional service requiring years of training and a vast store of knowledge. Not all underwriters are prepared to do a creditable job of estate planning. Many do not have the opportunity to develop contacts which call for estate planning jobs. Others do not have the ability to comprehend the specifics of the job. A competent estate planner must understand wills, laws of descent, trusts, investments, creditors' rights, estate and inheritance taxation, as well as income taxes, and gift taxation; in addition, he must have a full and complete knowledge of life insurance. He must also know how to use this knowledge to help his client preserve his estate.

3. THE COSTS OF ESTATE TRANSFER

Estates shrink as they pass from one individual to another. Several factors are responsible.

Administration Cost. Estates do not pass directly from a decedent to his heirs. They go first to the executor or administrator of the estate.[1] The services of executors and administrators of large estates cost money, for these men have time-consuming tasks to perform. Estimates have been made on the cost of estate administration. On the average they run from $2,500 on an estate of $25,000, to $250,000 on the estate of $5,000,000. For an estate of $50,000, the cost would be approximately $3,500, whereas the cost would be $7,500 for an estate of $150,000. On estates of over $500,000, the administration cost is about 5%.[2] Administration cost, then, is an important item of estate shrinkage.

Debts. Before estates may be passed to heirs, all debts must be paid. Since most people use credit facilities, there are usually debts to be paid out of the estate. The size of the debt will vary with the size of the estate,

---

[1] The executor is appointed to execute a will; the administrator is appointed by the court to administer an estate when there is no will.

[2] These are, at best, rough estimates. Obviously, they will vary widely from case to case and from time to time. They do show, however, that administration costs are no minor item.

the length of the last illness, and the habits of the deceased. On the average, debts run from 12% on estates of $25,000 to 5.4% on estates of $5,000,000.[3]

Taxes. One of the major causes of shrinkage in the transfer of estates is taxes, which cut deeper than most people realize. Commonly, the owner of a modest estate thinks of the Federal Estate Tax, at least, as being the problem of the millionaire. Yet a home, a car, a reasonable amount of life insurance, a few investments here and there, and estate taxes begin to be a problem. Anyone who will leave more than $60,000, including his life insurance, faces an estate tax problem, and while it may be possible to arrange his estate, so that the problem is eliminated,[4] even this modest estate owner needs to go into the matter thoroughly.

Federal estate taxes are not the only tax problem the estate owner faces. Only the state of Nevada imposes no death taxes whatsoever;[5] and while rates in most of the other states are low[6] in comparison to Federal Estate Tax rates, the exemptions even to Class A[7] beneficiaries are as low as $5,000 in some jurisdictions.[8]

Still other taxes can cause estate shrinkage: (1) accrued Federal income taxes in the case of a person whose income is not wholly subject to withholding and in the case of a person for whose salary the withholdings are insufficient;[9] (2) accrued state income taxes, these usually not being collected by payroll withholdings; (3) accrued personal and real property taxes.

Other Factors Causing Shrinkage. Two other factors cause shrinkage in an estate which contains general property holdings: (1) the loss of the

---

[3] The same comment may be made concerning debts as was make in Footnote 2 concerning administration costs.

[4] A Federal Estate tax "marital deduction" of up to 50% of the adjusted gross estate is available on transfers of estate property between husband and wife; however, not all such transfers will qualify, and care must be exercised by the estate owner to make sure that his transfers will qualify, provided, of course, he can (by having a wife living) and wants to take advantage of the marital deduction.

[5] States impose one or all of three of the following types of taxes: (1) an inheritance tax, (2) an estate tax, (3) an "80% tax." The first is imposed on the shares received by the individual beneficiaries. The second, like the Federal tax, is imposed on the estate before it is broken down into shares. The third is a device to make certain that the state retains an amount in taxes which is equivalent to the total amount of state taxes paid which may be deducted from the Federal tax payable.

[6] They range from 1% to 16% on Class A beneficiaries except that New York and North Dakota have top estate tax rates running up to 20% and 23% respectively.

[7] Usually the surviving spouse, children and grandchildren, parents, and grandparents. However, the definition varies from state to state, in some few instances including only the surviving spouse.

[8] District of Columbia, Hawaii, Louisiana, New Jersey, Ohio, and Virginia, for example.

[9] This is generally true in the case of annual incomes of about $10,000 and upward. However, much depends on the exemptions and, particularly, deductions in any given case, and also on the extent of prepayments made on the Declaration filing.

superior investment management ability of the estate owner and (2) the necessity of a changed philosophy of investment when the estate owner dies.

1. When an estate passes from the owner through the executor or administrator to heirs, it loses the benefit of the management of the original owner, whose knowledge of the peculiarities of the estate and whose management skill, particularly in the case of the estate containing business interests, may have been the major factor in making it profitable.

2. The beneficiary of an estate is interested primarily in income, not capital appreciation, as the estate owner may have been; consequently, estate property that is ideal for an active businessman may not be ideal for a widow. Few businessmen, if possessed of foresight enabling them to know they would die within a year, would leave the character of their estate unaltered. Such changes, made by the executor or the beneficiaries, often involve loss which must be offset with life insurance if the estate value is to be preserved.

In summary, a survey of shrinkage costs in estates of various sizes indicate the following: [10]

Estate Size	Percentage of Shrinkage
$25,000	19%
$100,000	23%
$250,000	31%
$500,000	37%
$750,000	40%
$1,000,000	42%

4. LIFE INSURANCE AND ESTATE PROTECTION

The major problem of estate protection is that of offsetting the shrinkage factors in estate transfer.

The Necessity of Planning for Shrinkage. The costs of estate transfer must be paid in cash in relatively short order, usually within a year, or they begin to incur interest costs. Estates, therefore, should remain liquid enough to meet these costs, or a forced sale of preferred estate assets might be necessary.

Forced liquidation often results in heavy losses to the estate. The amount of the losses, if any, depends upon two factors: (1) economic conditions at the time of the forced liquidation; and (2) the nature of the estate assets.

Economic Conditions. If death comes in a period of prosperity, the problem of forced liquidation of estate assets may not be difficult. At such times, market prices for most estate property are high, assuring adequate liquidation values for the major portion of estate property. Periods of prosperity, however, do not assure that *all* estate assets can be marketed without a sac-

---

[10] *The Insurance Salesman*, February, 1950.

rifice, for there may be some for which the market is down in spite of general prosperity.

If death comes in a period of depression, the forced liquidation problem becomes a major one. Estate transfer costs must be paid in cash, and to obtain the cash, estate assets may have to be sold at a sacrifice. Trust officers of banks can recall many estates with a high proportion of nonliquid holdings which were reduced to a fraction of their former worth because of the necessity of forced sale to raise money to pay estate settlement costs. No one knows what the economic conditions will be at his death; therefore, he must be prepared for the worst.

The Nature of the Estate. A liquid asset is one which can be converted into cash on a moment's notice and without any loss of value. Accordingly, cash is the most liquid of all assets. Government bonds and widely circulated stocks [11] are perhaps the most liquid of earning assets. If estates were made up in a large part of highly liquid assets, the problem of forced liquidation would not be so serious. Liquidity, however, costs money. As a general rule, liquid assets earn less than nonliquid assets. The majority of estate owners are reluctant to sacrifice yield for liquidity.

To avoid forced liquidation, estate planning in advance is necessary. It is strange how few people plan their estates to avoid forced liquidation; too few people really understand what forced liquidation means. Forced liquidation does not mean that the most undesirable assets of the estate will be liquidated, leaving the most desirable assets to the heirs. It means that the best part of the estate will be sold—the safest, the preferred investments are used to meet the costs of estate transfer. Cases are on record in which control of a business has been lost because of the necessity for the forced liquidation of a portion of its stock to pay estate transfer costs.

Liquidation losses may be avoided if a loan can be arranged to pay estate liabilities but an adequate loan may not be easy to obtain, and the interest costs may be as severe as the liquidation losses.

Handling Estate Transfer Costs.   If the owner of an estate does not want his estate assets sold to meet estate transfer costs, he must arrange in advance for their payment. One method would be to keep on hand a large cash reserve to meet estate liabilities. Obviously, this method is uneconomical. There is no reason to keep idle cash to pay expenses which have an uncertain due date if the uncertainty may be insured against. The most logical method of meeting estate obligations is through life insurance. Under a life

---

[11] Where one individual owns a large block of stock in any one company, the entire block may not be as liquid as a few shares since an effort to sell a large block of stock may depress the market for that stock.

insurance plan, the same contingency (death) which creates the estate liability will create an offsetting estate asset. The use of life insurance to pay estate settlement costs allows the insured to pay his death taxes as he goes, just as he pays his income taxes. With the use of life insurance to pay transfer costs, the current estate may be passed intact to the heirs.

Not only does the use of life insurance to pay estate obligations avoid liquidation losses in estate settlement, but it also reduces the cost of estate transfer. It makes it practical for the insured to maintain a less liquid but higher income-producing estate. It lessens the problems of estate settlement, thus reducing the cost of administration. The immediate cash provided by the insurance enables the executors to take advantage of all cash discounts for prompt payment. Finally, it is the least expensive way of providing estate liquidity, for it enables the insured to pay his estate liabilities with "fractional" dollars. For example:

With single-premium life insurance, a man, age 50, can pay a $10,000 estate clearance bill for just a little more than 60¢ on a dollar by purchasing a $10,000 single-premium Whole Life policy for $6,000 premium. If the insured is age 40, little more than 50¢ on a dollar will pay the bill. At age 60, it will take a little more than 70¢ on the dollar. If he uses a 20-pay Life policy, his premium will be about $472 a year for the $10,000 at age 50. The total cost of his tax bill will then depend on how long he lives. It cannot exceed $9,440 for the $10,000, which means he will never have to put up 100¢ on the dollar to pay the clearance bill.

Therefore, it would seem worth while for such a man to consider transferring part of his assets to single-premium life insurance or using income to buy annual premium. It is true that the above estimates of savings on the tax bill do not take into account the interest that assets were earning before being transferred to single-premium life insurance, or the interest the money put into annual-premium life insurance could earn if invested in other securities. However, an individual with such a clearance bill is undoubtedly in high income tax brackets. His interest earnings on investments will be subject to high rates; and the net amount of interest foregone by putting the money into life insurance will be small.

Furthermore, the value of the life insurance asset at the time cash is needed is greater than it has ever been throughout the life of the investment. For example, at age 45 a life insurance policy paid up at age 65 will cost about $43 a thousand annually on a nonparticipating basis. In ten years, this policy will be worth about $321 to the living policyholder and in 20 years it will be worth $754. The living values continue to increase every year but do not reach $1,000 until age 100. But immediately upon the death of the insured, the policy is worth $1,000. The maximum amount that can be paid for this contract is ($43 × 20) $860 since it is paid up in 20 years.

An earning asset which has a higher "death-liquidated" value than a living "going-concern" value is especially valuable in estate planning.

One problem, however, relating to the use of insurance to meet death costs merits careful consideration. If the insurance dollars are considered a part of the estate they will increase the estate tax bill. Therefore, if the insurance proceeds are taxed in his estate, a man age 50 who buys single-premium life insurance for 60¢ on the dollar will find that, at his death, the additional 40¢ will be taxed at the highest rate, perhaps 50% in a very large estate. The net result is a gain of only 20¢ per dollar. Only a very few estates, however, carry as much as a 50% estate tax liability. To do so, an estate must have a value well in excess of a million dollars.

In the small estate, the tax problem is not important, for the rate is relatively low. In the large estate, however, the tax problem is one which must be given serious attention. If at all possible, life insurance purchased to pay death taxes should be arranged in such a manner as to keep the insurance out of the estate of the deceased. Under present tax laws, in order to eliminate the possibility of the insurance becoming subject to estate tax liabilities, the insured must not own the policy nor have any rights in it. The insured must have no control over the policy whatsoever.[12] Incidents of ownership include the right to the cash values and proceeds, right to change beneficiary, right of assignment, and the like. If the insured has any such right either alone or acting with someone else the proceeds will be taxable in his estate.

Arranging Insurance for Estate Liabilities. The type of life insurance policy which should be used for estate protection purposes depends upon the nature of the estate. In large estates where the income is taxed in high brackets, there may be a tax advantage in buying single-premium life insurance to meet estate obligations. The annual interest increments to the cash value under the single-premium policy are tax free.

Where the estate is invested in the controlling shares of a business, it will not be desirable to liquidate them to buy single-premium life insurance. The best plan may be to use part of the income from these assets to pay premiums for annual-premium life insurance. The same may be true of other assets which the clients wish to hold.

The amount of life insurance needed would depend upon an estimate of

---

[12] Under the law as of this writing, who pays the premium on the policy does not matter. The insured may pay it himself, and proceeds will still not be in his estate if the beneficiary has ownership of the policy with no more than a 5% chance (actuarially calculated) of reversion to the insured.

(1) the costs of estate transfer and (2) the loss of income, if any, resulting from the change in estate management. These factors are not easily measured. They must be estimated. Trained life insurance agents are often able to estimate these costs on the basis of past experience within a reasonable margin of error.

Other things being equal, the executor of the estate should be the beneficiary of the policy, since he will have to pay all estate transfer costs. However, in many states, if the insurance is made payable to a named beneficiary, it will not be subject to state inheritance taxes. If this is the case, there is advantage in naming the widow as beneficiary.

5. LIFE INSURANCE AND TAX PLANNING

It is impossible in a text such as this to develop in detail all the problems of taxation as they relate to life insurance and estate planning. Only a few of the major problems can be demonstrated in order to show the importance of expert legal and tax counsel in planning estates.[13]

Income Taxation of Proceeds. Proceeds are payable in a lump sum, as fixed installments or a life income. They may also be held at interest. Proceeds paid as a lump sum by reason of death are exempt from *income tax* liability. The one exception to this rule involves policies transferred for value. If A purchases from B an existing policy for $10,000 on B's life, paying B $3,000 for it, and then pays another $1,000 in premiums before B's death, he is taxed on the $6,000 gain. The rule is that if a policy is transferred for value, income tax is payable on the difference between the proceeds and the purchase price plus premiums paid by the transferee. There are two exceptions to this rule: (1) If the transferee is the person whose life is insured, no tax is payable on the gain, and (2) there is no tax where the policy is transferred to a partner of the insured, to a partnership in which the insured is a partner, or to a corporation in which the insured is a shareholder or officer. Note, however, that a transfer between stockholders does not fall under the exception to the rule.

Proceeds payable under a fixed installment option involve some taxable income. Only that portion of the installment settlements that represents return of principal is exempt. The law seeks to tax only the interest and even here a surviving spouse is allowed an annual exemption of $1,000 in otherwise reportable income. For example, if the widow is to receive ten annual installments of $11,380 instead of a lump sum of $100,000 she will report only $380 annually as taxable income. Ten thousand dollars is excluded as

---

[13] For up-to-date information on Federal income, estate, and gift taxes as they relate to life insurance, see the *R & R Tax Handbook*, published by the Insurance Research and Review Service, 123 West North Street, Indianapolis, Indiana.

return of principal and $1,000 is exempted under the widow's exclusion, leaving only $380 as taxable income. If the beneficiary were someone other than a surviving spouse, taxable income would amount to $1,380 annually.

Proceeds payable as a life income also involve some reportable income. In this case the proceeds are divided by the life expectancy of the beneficiary [14] and the amount so obtained is the annual deduction. The excess is reportable as income subject to the $1,000 surviving spouse exclusion. If the life income option guarantees a minimum number of payments, as is customary, then before prorating the proceeds over the life expectancy, the actuarial value of the guaranteed payments is subtracted from the proceeds.[15]

If the proceeds are left at interest, the entire amount of the interest payable is subject to the income tax in the year paid. There is no $1,000 exclusion for the surviving spouse.

Any "excess interest" paid under any of the above options is treated as guaranteed interest, and will be taxable subject, of course, to the $1,000 surviving spouse exclusion where applicable.

In general, the $1,000 surviving spouse exemption applies only if the settlement option selected is a contractual right, either contained in the policy or made a part of it by endorsement prior to the insured's death. There is a possibility that if the beneficiary, subsequent to the death of the insured, negotiates a settlement not a part of the contract, the proceeds will be taxed as an annuity without regard to the $1,000 surviving spouse exemption.

Taxation of Endowment Policies. The difference between the amount paid by the insurance company when an Endowment policy matures and the total premiums paid for the policy represents taxable income to the insured when the policy matures.

For instance, assume a person buys a $10,000 20-year Endowment and his total premiums less dividends and charges for double indemnity, waiver of premium, and disability income over the 20 years amount to $9,000. The policy matures, and he receives a $10,000 check from the insurance company. The $1,000 gain is subject to the income tax as ordinary income, not as a capital gain. However, the tax cannot exceed the amount the tax would have been had the gain been taxed ratably over the taxable year in which received and the two preceding taxable years.

If the policyholder is in a high income tax bracket and a large amount of life insurance is involved, he may prefer to spread the gain over a period

---

[14] The life expectancy tables are furnished by the Treasury Department.
[15] The Treasury Department prescribes the tables for use in this computation.

longer than three years by taking the proceeds in installments. This is possible if the policy gives the policyholder the right to select an installment option and the policyholder exercises this option either before or within 60 days after maturity of the contract. Income tax will be payable on that part of each annual installment which represents interest. The amount subject to tax is computed in the same manner as the tax on annuity income is figured.[16] The basis for the cost of the contract is the sum of the net premiums paid.

If an option is exercised after the expiry of 60 days beyond the maturity date of the policy, the full gain will be taxed as ordinary income under the doctrine of constructive receipt. The basis for the cost of the contract for income tax then becomes the face of the contract rather than premiums paid.

Taxation of Cash Values. Two questions are important in discussing the taxation of cash values of life insurance policies: (1) The growing cash values of policies in force and (2) the cash values of policies upon surrender.

Annual increments in cash values are not subject to the income tax even though the entire increase in cash values is traceable to interest earnings. There can be no income tax on cash values until the policy is surrendered and then the excess of surrender value over net premiums paid is subject to the income tax as ordinary income. The tax on this gain, however, cannot exceed the aggregate of the taxes attributable to such gain had it been received pro rata over the past three years. Thus, if an insured surrenders a policy for $25,000 in which he has invested $16,000 net in premiums, he will be taxed on $9,000. The amount of the tax can not exceed the aggregate of the tax on $3,000 in the year received and that produced by a tax on $3,000 added to the income already reported in the two preceding years. It can, however, yield a lower tax. For example, if the year in which the policy is surrendered is one in which the tax bracket is much lower than that of the past two years, taxation of the full amount in that year might result in a lower tax liability than would be the case under the three-year distribution plan.

It is not necessary to subtract the cost of insurance from the premiums paid in computing the gain. Therefore, all the gain is not taxable, for that part which was used to pay premiums in effect is exempted. In the above illustration, if the actual cost of insurance protection received over the life of the policy was $8,000, then the insured actually gained $17,000 [17] rather than $9,000, although only $9,000 is taxable.

---

[16] Cf. Footnote 9, Chapter 5, and later discussion in this chapter.

[17] $25,000 − (16,000 − 8,000) = $17,000. The actual amount invested was only $8,000 since the other $8,000 was used to purchase the protection which the insured enjoyed over the life of the policy.

If the cash values are taken under an installment or annuity option, and a tax liability is involved, the rules governing the tax are the same as those applicable to Endowment proceeds settled under an income option.

Taxation of Dividends. Dividends on life insurance policies are not taxable as income, since they constitute a return of a portion of the premiums paid. If dividends are left with the company to accumulate at interest, the amount of interest credited is subject to the income tax in the year so credited. If, however, there are substantial restrictions as to the time and manner of payment or upon the payment of the interest, certain modifications have to be made in the application of this rule.

Dividends applied to buy paid-up additions create no tax liability. They are viewed as dividends received in cash and then used to buy single-premium insurance.

Taxation of Annuities. Receipts under an annuity policy are taxed each year according to the formula detailed in Chapter 5, Footnote 9. Briefly, the amount subject to the income tax is the annual annuity income less the amount which represents a proportionate return of principal or the expected return. The return of principal (called "annual exclusion") is found by dividing the purchase price by the number of fixed installments. The expected return in the case of a life annuity is found by dividing the purchase price by the life expectancy as determined by the commissioner. If payments are for a period certain and life, the cost is reduced by the value of the payments for the period certain. The values of payments certain and of refund features are calculated by use of tables provided by the commissioner. The annual exclusion continues throughout the life of the contract even though the annuitant has already received a full return of his investment tax free. The amount of the exclusions at that time actually represent insurance gains and as such are not taxable. They are gains from living too long.

Income Taxation of Accident and Sickness. Benefits payable under accident and sickness insurance contracts are not subject to the Federal income tax. Premiums paid on medical expense insurance (but not for insurance to provide income during disability) are includible as a medical expense and as such are deductible if medical expenses exceed 3% of adjusted gross income.

Premiums on Life Insurance. Premiums paid for personal life insurance are not a deductible expense. Interest paid on loans made to finance the purchase of life insurance is deductible except when single-premium policies or annuities are purchased. Interest on a loan to purchase single-premium policies is not deductible; and the law treats as single-premium any policy which is paid up in less than five years or on which a substantial number of premiums is either prepaid or deposited under a premium-deposit plan.[18] The question of the deductibility of premiums in connection with business insurance will be discussed later in this chapter.

Estate Taxation. The question of the taxability of life insurance in the estate of the insured has been discussed. Death benefits under A & S policies and refunds or period certain payments under annuities are taxed in the same manner as life insurance. An important consideration in estate taxation is the marital deduction.

The Marital Deduction. In the case of an estate passing between spouses by reason of the death of the one, a "marital deduction" is allowed. In life insurance planning, it is highly important that this deduction be clearly understood. The following illustration will help to clarify it.

Assume a married man worth $220,000 including securities, cash, business interests, real estate, life insurance and all other assets. When he dies and his estate tax is computed, the first step is to deduct all obligations he owes, the expenses of his last illness, such as doctors' and nurses' bills, and all other debts. Suppose these amount to $20,000, leaving a net estate of $200,000. The marital deduction is whatever the deceased leaves his wife *outright*,[19] up to *one half* of the *net* estate. If he leaves his wife $50,000, then that amount is the marital deduction, which may be deducted from the net estate. If he leaves his wife $75,000 outright, then $75,000 is the marital deduction. If he leaves her the entire $200,000 outright, then the marital deduction is only $100,000 because of the 50% ceiling on the amount of the marital deduction. Thus the marital deduction in this estate can be any amount up to $100,000.

In summary, the marital deduction is whatever amount a spouse leaves a surviving spouse *outright* but not more than 50% of the total net estate. It is most important that this be clear because usually the deduction is substantial and, consequently, should be conserved, if possible, by careful planning.

The marital deduction has an important application in life insurance and tax planning. If a married man worth $200,000 net leaves his wife half of his

[18] Restrictions on deductions with respect to annuities apply only to those purchased since March 1, 1954.

[19] In order for estate assets to qualify for the marital deduction, the surviving spouse must have the power to appoint the person to take the proceeds at his or her death or the power to dissipate the estate. Whether or not the surviving spouse ever exercises the right of appointment or dissipation is not the test. For instance, the insured may have named a contingent beneficiary which the surviving spouse never changes and who, then, receives the unpaid proceeds at the death of the survivor. However, if the survivor had the power during his or her lifetime to remove that contingent beneficiary and appoint any other of his or her choosing, the power to appoint existed for purposes of the marital deduction.

estate outright, the total estate tax under present rates after the marital deduction and the $60,000 estate tax exemption is $4,800. But what happens if the wife dies before the husband? What is the amount of the estate tax due when the husband subsequently dies? If the wife is not alive when the husband dies, there can be no marital deduction. In that case the tax is $31,500 instead of only $4,800.

Since there is no possibility of predicting who will die first, insurance on the wife might be purchased to offset the loss of the marital deduction.[20] The husband insures his wife for the amount of the excess tax liability payable upon his death ($26,700) or the children will buy that amount of life insurance on their mother's life. Then the children will have $26,700 of life insurance proceeds if the wife dies first. Subsequently, at the death of the father, the net estate received by the children will amount to $168,500 after taxes. Accordingly the children's inheritance will finally total $195,200, of which $26,700 came to them at their mother's death and $168,500 at their father's death.

The difference that planning can make in estate taxes is illustrated by the following examples.

Examples of Estate Tax Planning
Estate of $200,000, Married Man, Two Children

NOTE: The following plans assume that the husband dies first and that the wife's share received after the death of the husband is fully intact at her death. Also, in cases where the husband has not previously utilized his lifetime gift tax exemption, there would be no gift tax liability on the annuities purchased for the son and daughter.

Plan 1
  Leave $200,000 life estate [21] to wife by will

Tax when husband dies	$31,500 [22]	
Tax when wife dies	None	
Net retained by wife		$168,500
Net acquired by children		168,500

Plan 2
  Leave $200,000 outright by will to wife

Tax when husband dies	$ 4,800	
Tax when wife dies	30,136	
Net retained by wife		$195,200
Net acquired by children		165,064

[20] This is not to suggest that the marital deduction is the wife's only insurable value. Cf. Chapter 15.

[21] A life estate is an arrangement whereby the beneficiary has the right to enjoy the income as long as he or she lives. Upon death of the beneficiary, the property goes to a secondary beneficiary who has already been named by the husband.

[22] Tax rates used throughout this chapter are those in effect at the time of this writing.

Plan 3
    Leave $100,000 outright to wife by will
    Leave $100,000 life estate to wife by will

Tax when husband dies	$ 4,800	
Tax when wife dies	4,044	
Net retained by wife		$195,200
Net acquired by children		191,156

Plan 4
    Leave $100,000 life estate to wife by will
    Buy $150,000 single-premium life insurance on
        husband (Payable to wife)

Tax when husband dies	$10,700	
Tax when wife dies	14,508	
Net retained by wife		$239,300
Net acquired by children		225,808

Plan 5
    Leave $100,000 life estate to wife by will
    Leave $50,000 outright to wife by will
    Buy and give now $25,000 Annuity to son
    Buy and give now $25,000 Annuity to daughter

Tax when husband dies	$ 4,800	
Tax when wife dies	None	
Net retained by wife		$145,200
Net acquired by children		195,200

Plan 6
    Leave $75,000 life estate to wife by will
    Leave $75,000 outright to wife by will
    Give now $25,000 Annuity to son
    Give now $25,000 Annuity to daughter

Tax when husband dies	$ 1,050	
Tax when wife dies	1,050	
Net retained by wife		$148,950
Net acquired by children		197,900

Which Is Best?   Under Plan 1, the wife receives the income from the estate as long as she lives, and the children receive the remainder at her death. There is no second tax on a life estate where the wife has no powers of appointment of the remainder at her death.

In Plan 3, the husband leaves his wife half the estate *outright* and the other half in a life estate. When the husband dies, the half he leaves his wife outright qualifies for the marital deduction. From that figure is deducted the $60,000 estate tax exemption, with a final net taxable estate of $40,000 on which the estate tax is $4,800.

In a life estate where the children receive the corpus of the estate at the death of the wife, there is no second tax when the wife dies. She has a taxable estate of the amount her husband left her outright (assuming, for illustrative purposes, that she still has the entire $100,000 intact at her death), less, of course, the $4,800 estate tax she paid when the husband died. This leaves a taxable estate of $95,200, with a final taxable amount of $35,200 after the $60,000 estate tax exemption. The total of the $4,800 tax when the husband dies and the $4,044 when the wife dies is $8,844, leaving a net after taxes of $191,156 for the children.

Plans 1, 2, and 3 can be accomplished or arranged by the simple means of a will. Plans 4 through 6 involve the combination of a will and the purchase of life insurance on the life of the husband and the purchase of annuities for the children.

Which plan is best? The answer to this is a personal one. Decide first on objectives, and then develop the plan which best meets these objectives.

Danger in Tailor-Made Plans. These examples of estate tax planning are given as indications of the many combinations that can be made in estate planning with and without the utilization of life insurance to accomplish desired, specific objectives.

Life underwriters frequently hear: "I am much more interested in the welfare of my children than I am in the future of my wife. She may get married again; she is extravagant; and the plan I want is one where my wife will have enough income during her lifetime but in which she cannot touch the principal."

Such an arrangement can be made and in a way which will still save estate taxes. Two life estates or trusts may be arranged. In one of them the wife will get the income for her lifetime, and at her death the remainder will go to the children. In the second life estate or trust, the wife will get all the income during her lifetime and will have the power to leave the property to any one she chooses at her death.

These two different types of life estates contain different powers of appointment. In one, the wife is limited to leaving the corpus of the estate to persons designated by the husband. In the other, she may leave it to anyone.

When the wife has the power to leave the corpus to anyone she chooses, it will qualify for the marital deduction at her husband's death but will be fully taxable in her estate at her death. When she is restricted in appointing the persons to receive the corpus at her death (the children, in this case), the corpus will be taxed in her husband's estate, but it will not be subject to tax again in her estate when she dies.

By using the combination of the two types of power of appointment, the wife gets the income from both estates during her lifetime, but the entire principal is tied up beyond her reach.

Gift Taxes.   In Plan 6, if the husband has not previously used his lifetime gift tax exemption, there is no gift tax on the total of $50,000 he gives the two children in the form of annuities.

Every individual has a lifetime gift tax exemption of $30,000. In addition, he has an annual exclusion of $3,000 per donee. He can give away $3,000 a year to each of any number of people without incurring gift tax liability. However, if he gives away more than $3,000 in any one year to any *one* person, his annual exclusion will be exceeded and he must then turn to his $30,000 lifetime gift tax exemption. For example, if he gives away $5,000, the difference between that figure and his $3,000 annual exclusion per donee must be taken out of his $30,000 lifetime gift tax exemption, leaving an unused total of $28,000.

If he gives away, say, $33,000 to any one individual in a given year, he has entirely used up his $30,000 lifetime exemption, and from then on he will have only the $3,000 annual exclusion per person, per donee. Therefore, in subsequent years in which he makes a gift of more than $3,000 to any *one* person, the excess over $3,000 will be a taxable gift.

The foregoing rules apply to single men or women. In the case of married men and women, the rules are more favorable.

A married person may give away, with the consent of the spouse, a total per donee of $6,000 without gift tax liability and $60,000 over and above the annual exclusion of $6,000 per donee without gift tax liability. This can be done by taking advantage of the gift tax rule which considers a gift of property owned by either spouse as being made 50% by the wife as an individual and 50% by the husband.

Therefore, in *Plan 6*, where two children or two "donees" are involved, the husband can make a total of $72,000 gifts in one year without paying gift tax. From then on, of course, his lifetime exemption and his wife's lifetime exemption are entirely used, and he has only the annual exclusion of $6,000 per donee.

It is important to note, in connection with gifts made by a spouse, that the law requires the *consent* of the other spouse before the combined exemptions and exclusions will apply; that is, if the husband gives away, say, $6,000, he can claim only a $3,000 annual exclusion unless his wife consents to the gift. If she consents, the other $3,000 is considered as a gift from her. If the gift is one of $8,000, then $4,000 is considered as a gift from each spouse so that $1,000 is deducted from the $30,000 lifetime exemption available to each party.

Gifts in Estate Planning. It will be recalled that the function of estate planning is not only to provide liquid funds to pay the cost of estate transfer but also to arrange the estate in such a manner as to reduce these costs. One way to reduce the estate tax liability is to reduce the value of the estate. This can be done by making living transfers or simply gifts of assets to someone else. The motive for the transfer, however, must be strictly a living motive—that is, the transfer must not be made in contemplation of death.

The Revenue Act provides that transfers of property made more than three years prior to the death of a decedent shall not be taxed as a transfer in contemplation of death. If the death occurs during the three-year period from the date of the gift, the presumption is that it was made in contemplation of death. The burden of proof that it was otherwise is on the estate.

It is desirable, therefore, to establish clearly that a living motive exists when a transfer of property is consummated. Typical living motives include providing an independent income for dependents, the giver's withdrawal from business, lower income taxes for the donor, and the like.

Even when these gifts are subject to a gift tax liability, they are quite likely to be taxed at a rate far less than the same amount of property would have been taxed under the estate tax formula. For one thing, the gift tax rate is about 25% less than the estate tax rate. The actual differential, however, is much greater since both tax structures are progressive. For example, a taxable living gift of, say, $25,000 might be taxed in a 10.5% gift tax bracket instead of, say, a 32% estate tax bracket had the gift been postponed until after the death of the donor. By taking assets out of a high estate tax bracket and placing them in a tax free or low gift tax bracket via living transfers, more of the estate can be conserved for the beneficiaries.

Estate plans often include gifts of life insurance and annuities on the lives of the donee. It is especially popular to make these gifts to children and grandchildren. In the absence of conclusive evidence to the contrary, gifts of life insurance and annuities generally are considered as originating from a living motive. Insurance is a valuable and necessary asset for the donee. It is more likely to be held by the insured until needed for a given and necessary purpose rather than haphazardly dissipated in careless spending and investing. Also, a life insurance policy can be paid for on an annual basis so that the donor can take advantage of the annual $3,000 deduction available for each donee.

Short-Term Trusts. Short-term, reversionary trusts—that is, a trust under which the corpus (body) of the trust or the income therefrom reverts to the grantor after a specified period or event—were long the subject of litigation and confusing Revenue Bureau regulations until the Revenue Act of 1954, which clearly defined their taxable status. The 1954 law opened the way to effecting legal tax savings through such trusts, which savings can be combined advantageously with life insurance in a number of ways, some few of which will be mentioned by way of illustration.

Generally speaking, the 1954 Revenue Act provided that the grantor will not be subject to tax on the income of a non-charitable trust if the term of the trust is for at least ten years or until the death of the income beneficiary, whichever occurs first. (The term for a charitable trust is two years if the income is payable to a specified church, church organization, tax-exempt school, or tax-exempt hospital.)

The short-term trust, therefore, offers persons in higher income tax brackets a chance to transfer income from property or securities from their own, higher tax brackets to the lower tax brackets of the trust or trust beneficiary, or both, without the necessity of giving away the corpus of the trust permanently. Thus, for instance, a parent in a 50% tax bracket can save on his tax bill by placing some of his income producing property in a short-term, reversionary trust. Under this arrangement instead of half of the income from the property going for taxes as it would if received by him, the income is paid to the trust and is taxed at the lower rate applied to the lower income of the trust, say 20% instead of 50%.

Such a trust can be set up with the trustee directed to use the income to purchase various types of life insurance: educational insurance on a child; insurance on the wife of the grantor; insurance on a partner or co-stockholder; insurance on a son during the first few years of his marriage when his need for protection is high but his ability to pay low; etc.

It is even possible to set up such a trust to pay for life insurance on the life of the grantor if (a) the income is payable directly to a trust beneficiary who has (b) full authority to use the money in any way he or she sees fit. If there is no trust requirement or other binding agreement that the income is to be used to buy insurance on the grantor, but the trust beneficiary so uses it of his or her own free will, then the insurance so purchased will be considered to be owned by the beneficiary and not includible in the grantor's estate at the time of his death. Thus a temporary trust could be set up for 10 years and the income used by the trust beneficiary (voluntarily and entirely at the beneficiary's option) to purchase 10-pay Whole Life. At the end of the ten years, the insurance would be fully paid up and the property of the beneficiary, and the corpus of the trust, could revert to the grantor. The insurance would have been paid for out of favorably-taxed income (compared to the tax that would have been paid had it been income to the grantor) and yet the corpus of the trust not permanently lost to the grantor.

In essence, such a trust will be advantageous wherever the grantor has property, the income from which would be taxable to him at a higher rate than it would be taxable to a trust or trust beneficiary.

These trusts will constitute taxable gifts, the amount of which will vary with the exact provisions of the trust. However, inasmuch as any grantor has a $30,000 exemption a substantial trust can be set up without incurring any actual tax liability.

Business Interests. When the estate includes a business interest, life insurance can play a major role in estate plans. As will be discussed in Chapter 18, death of the owner can cause severe shrinkage in the value of the business interest. When the owner of a business dies, the business is either liquidated or reorganized. Estate planning considers these possibilities and in either situation, use is frequently made of life insurance.

If the decision is to liquidate the business, life insurance might be necessary to facilitate this liquidation and to protect the general estate from business debts. Estate planning for business liquidation is usually confined to sole proprietorships. In partnerships and close corporations, the plan is almost always one of reorganization. Life insurance is used in this case to finance a buy-and-sell agreement.[23] Each partner or stockholder (or the business itself) will insure the lives of the other so that upon a death, life insurance will be available to the survivors to purchase the interests of the deceased at the agreed-upon price. The plan assures that the business interest will be liquidated promptly and fairly.

The Importance of a Will. Typical of the genuine importance of the position of the life underwriter is the substantial service he can be to his policyholders by discussing wills.[24] Rarely will an attorney or accountant ask a client about his will. To do so is considered unethical. They must wait

---

[23] See Chapter 18.

[24] Bar associations are extremely jealous of any action on the part of laymen which they interpret as encroaching on the practice of law. For example, in a recent instance, a member of the Illegal Practices Committee of a bar association informed a leading life insurance agency specializing in the sale of insurance for estate-planning purposes that he considered it an illegal practice of law for a life underwriter to discuss with a client what provisions should be contained in his will even if the life insurance agent recommended that he consult his lawyer about the changes. The extent to which an agent can enter into a discussion of a will, according to the committee member, is to recommend that the client see his lawyer. Any recommendations as to provisions should be made only to the lawyer who, then, will pass them on to the client, if the client comes to see him. While this opinion is extreme, it does illustrate the care that agents must exercise in talking to prospects and policyholders about wills.

for the person to come to them—even if they wait so long the individual dies intestate with all the trouble and loss to dependents an intestacy can produce. But a life insurance agent, who understands what the absence of a will can mean in the case of the marital deduction, for instance, will invariably find out if there is a will.

Here is what it means. Under Illinois law, for example, in the case of a husband dying without a will and leaving children, the wife automatically is entitled to one third and the children to two thirds of the estate. It will be remembered that the marital deduction is whatever the wife receives outright from her husband's estate up to a maximum of half the total net estate.

Therefore, where a husband dies intestate (without a will) and the estate is, say, $200,000, the wife would get $66,666 outright from the husband and the children would receive the balance. This means that the marital deduction would be $66,666, with a resulting tax liability of about $13,000. By the simple expedient of a will leaving half the estate to the wife, the estate tax would be $4,800, a tax reduction of about $8,000.

6. TAXES AND BUSINESS LIFE INSURANCE PLANNING

Life insurance tax planning, while a major consideration in any type of life underwriting, is especially important in the field of business insurance. It is here that many pitfalls, unknown to the uninformed, can be avoided and that substantial reduction of income and estate tax liability can be accomplished.

Life insurance is usually purchased to back up agreements between partners or costockholders. Jones and Smith are partners. They come to an agreement between themselves and their wives that when one of the partners dies, the survivor will buy the partnership interest from the wife of the deceased. The deceased's wife agrees to sell at a price determined in advance.

To assure that the funds required are available and to obtain those funds at the lowest possible cost, life insurance is purchased. Jones buys a $10,000 policy on Smith's life, and Smith buys the same amount on Jones's life. When Jones dies, Smith has enough money from the proceeds of his insurance on Jones's life to provide him with the means of buying Jones's partnership interest from Jones's wife.

In absence of a trust agreement, most insurance authorities consider the best arrangement is for Jones to be the beneficiary on Smith's policy and for Smith to be the beneficiary on Jones's policy. Frequently, however, the men will make their own wives the beneficiaries on the policies on their lives. This can be expensive in taxes.

For example: Jones and Smith are partners, and each buys a $10,000 policy on the other's life. Jones's wife is beneficiary in the policy on his life, and Smith's wife is the beneficiary on the policy on his life. Jones dies, and his wife gets the $10,000 proceeds from the insurance company. She has signed an agreement to deliver Jones's interest in the partnership to Smith, and she delivers it.

Smith now owns a $20,000 business in which he originally invested $10,000. If he had been the beneficiary on Jones's policy, he would have received the proceeds from the insurance company and turned over the $10,000 to Jones's wife in exchange for the partnership interest.

However, since Jones's wife received the $10,000 direct from the insurance company, Smith still has only his original $10,000 invested in a business now worth $20,000 to him. If he later sells the business, he will have to pay income tax on the difference between his original $10,000 investment and whatever price he receives for the business. On the other hand, if he had been Jones's beneficiary, he would then have had a $20,000 investment in the business, and his cost basis for tax purposes would be $20,000, not $10,000.

The same principle would apply on an agreement to buy out costockholders in a corporation. Robinson owns 500 shares in a corporation and his associate, Hamilton, owns 500 shares in the same corporation. They sign an agreement to buy each other's stock in the event of the death of either. If Robinson is the beneficiary in the policy on Hamilton's life and Hamilton dies, the insurance company pays the life insurance proceeds to Robinson, who uses those proceeds to buy the stock from Hamilton's widow. Robinson has twice as much money invested in the business, and his cost basis of the stock for tax purposes is the total of his original investment in his 500 shares plus the cost of the 500 shares he acquired from Hamilton's widow.

On the other hand, if the corporation purchased insurance on the lives of the stockholders under a stock purchase plan and one died, the corporation would use the money to buy and cancel the stock of the deceased stockholder. The stock of the remaining shareholders would then increase in value. If a stockholder eventually sold this stock at its increased value, he would have an income tax (usually a capital gain) to pay on the profit with his original cost as the cost basis.

For example, the Consolidated Corporation receives $50,000 proceeds on the policy on the life of its president. The corporation then buys the president's stock from his widow at $50,000. There now being less stock outstanding, each share has a greater book value.

Circumstances alter cases, and in many instances it is advisable for the corporation to be the beneficiary; but it is important to consider whether the surviving stockholders would not fare much better if they themselves arranged a cross-insurance plan and paid the premiums on the lives of one another.

Brown, Jones, and Smith are the sole stockholders of a small corporation. Each owns 100 shares of stock. They enter into a cross-insurance arrangement under which each insures the other. Brown dies, and as beneficiaries on the life of Brown, Jones and Smith each receive $1,000 from the insurance company, which they use to buy Brown's stock from his widow.

Jones now owns 150 shares, and Smith, 150 shares. Their cost basis for those 150 shares owned by each is the original cost of their 100 shares plus the $1,000 they received from the life insurance company and which they used to buy Brown's stock. When, as, and if Jones or Smith sells his stock, his income tax liability will be on the difference between his original investment plus the $1,000 life insurance proceeds and the selling price of the stock.

On the other hand, if the corporation were the beneficiary and used the insurance proceeds to buy the stock from Brown's widow, subsequently retiring the stock from the corporate treasury, Jones and Smith would then own all the stock in a corporation whose book value had increased because of the retirement of Brown's stock, but both Jones and Smith would still have as their cost basis only their original investment in their respective stock interests.

Deductibility of Premiums. Life insurance premiums are not deductible when paid on the lives of partners or sole proprietors. Premiums are deductible as a business expense when paid by corporations only when the corporation is not the beneficiary and holds no incidents of ownership. If, for instance, the Consolidated Corporation pays the premiums on the life of an officer or other employee and that employee's wife is the beneficiary, the premiums are deductible by the corporation provided, of course, that the corporation has no incidents of ownership. The amount of the premiums, however, constitute additional taxable income to the employee whether he be an officer or a general employee. Group insurance, as it will be seen, is an exception to the rule.

It is important to bear in mind that the life insurance premiums, when added to other compensation, salaries and bonuses, for example, must be reasonable. The total must not be so out of line that the Bureau of Internal Revenue will consider it excessive compensation for the amount and type of services rendered by the stockholder or officer.

The premiums, moreover, must be clearly shown to constitute compensation to the employee. In one case, a stockholder-employee, a corporate officer, was paid a salary and, in addition, under an agreement among the stockholders, the corporation paid the premiums on his insurance. The court held that the premium payments were not additional compensation but were dividends, and therefore not deductible as business expense. In this case, the corporation might just as well have issued a check to the employee direct and let him pay the premiums out of his own bank account.

Section 303. While discussing this point, perhaps a word about Section 303 is in order. If a corporation buys back a part of the stock from a stockholder, the price paid to the stockholder usually will be treated as taxable distribution. This is the rule under Sections 301 and 302. But under Section 303, where stock is included in the gross estate of the decedent, a redemption of such stock by the corporation will not be considered a taxable distribution to the extent of the sum of the death taxes, funeral, and administrative expense. The value of the stock must be more than 35% of the value of the gross estate or 50% of the value of the taxable estate.[25] Life insurance on the principal stockholder purchased and owned by the corporation can provide the funds necessary to purchase the stock from his estate. The use of this plan enables the surviving stockholders to hold on to this business interest and thus help perpetuate the control of a family corporation.

Income Taxation of Group Insurance. Payments of premiums by an employer for Group life insurance are deductible business expenses and do not constitute taxable income to the employees. There are, however, certain restrictions and rules that must be applied. The employee must not name the employer as beneficiary, and there must be no blanket or individual assignment of the policies to the employer which will allow him to cancel the policies and receive the cash surrender value if any. Group insurance premiums on the lives of employees are deductible business expenses not only for corporations but also for partnership employers or employers who are sole proprietors.

Deferred Compensation Plans. One method of compensation to stockholder-employees, officer employees, and key employees has received con-

---

[25] If stock of two or more corporations is included in the gross estate, the combined stock may be treated as the stock of a single corporation for the purposes of applying the 35% or 50% tests provided that the gross estate includes more than 75% of the outstanding stock of each corporation.

siderable attention, favorable and unfavorable: Deferred Compensation plans.

Assume a key man with a salary of $25,000 a year. At that time, his tax bracket is high. After payment of taxes, his net, take-home pay is much less. So he might get together with his company (or like to) and say:

> How about paying me $20,000 a year instead of $25,000 a year for the next 20 years? At the end of that time, I'll retire, and you can pay me $10,000 a year for 10 years. Right now, I'm 45 years old. If you pay me $25,000 a year for 20 years, that will total $500,000. On the other hand, if you pay me $20,000 a year for 20 years, then that total will be $400,000, leaving a differential of $100,000. I'll draw that $100,000 by taking $10,000 a year for 10 years. In that way, I'll reduce my income tax liability for the next 20 years, and when I retire at age 65, I'll be in the lower $10,000 tax bracket and have more exemption. This will reduce the cost of financing my retirement to the extent of the tax savings effected.

The corporation could underwrite the future $10,000 a year liability by buying an Annuity or a 20-year Endowment policy for the employee. Either would provide the funds necessary to pay the key man his $10,000 a year.

However, such a plan will not save the employee any taxes at all, because if he was entitled to draw $25,000 instead of $20,000, and if he drew $20,000 instead of $25,000, he would nevertheless pay income tax on the entire $25,000 because of the "theory of constructive receipt." [26]

There is another angle to Deferred Compensation. An employer says to a key man or other employee:

> We should like to pay you a bonus, but we cannot afford to pay it now. We want you to be happy and satisfied with your earnings from this company, and we want you to stay with us. So here's what we'll do. We will continue to pay you your present salary which is all we can afford right now, and we will promise you that when you retire 20 years from now, we will give you $10,000 a year even though you are not actually working for us in an active capacity at that time.

In a case like this, since the employee was not entitled to receive the money in that year and could not draw it, the theory of constructive receipt apparently would not apply. This, then, would seem to be an opportunity for life insurance to underwrite the future bonus: to assure the employee he would get it, and to provide the funds for the employing company when the promise became due. However, the widespread interest in such plans came to the attention of the Treasury Department. It has indicated that if

---

[26] That is, any cash basis taxpayer who has money coming to him which he can get at his option must pay tax on that money whether he draws it or not.

an employee's right to future compensation is "vested," the commuted value of the employer's promise to pay will be construed as taxable income in the year the promise is made. By "vested," the Bureau appears to mean no *if's, and's,* or *but's* attached to the employee's right to get the money in the future.

If, on the other hand, the corporation said to the employee: "If you continue to work for us until you reach age 65, we will pay you $10,000 a year until your death *so long as you are not working for a competitor,*" then vesting is *conditional* and not *absolute* so that constructive receipt seems unlikely. Life insurance may be used to fund the obligation.

$5,000 Exemption. An employer may pay the family of a deceased employee up to $5,000 after his death and the family does not have to report the money as income for tax purposes. However, if the deceased employee had more than one employer, the exemption applies only to a total of $5,000. His beneficiary could not claim it for each $5,000 paid by each employer. The employer, of course, can deduct this $5,000 payment as a business expense.

Life insurance is used in this case to fund these payments. The employer insures the life of the employee and names himself as beneficiary. Premiums are not deductible nor are proceeds reportable for income tax purposes. The employer gains a tax advantage, however, when he collects the proceeds tax free and then deducts as an expense the amount paid over to the widow of the deceased employee.

7. REPLANNING A CONTINUING NECESSITY

Tax and estate planning for any given estate is not a one-time matter. Re-examination must be constant. In the first place, the situation and needs of the estate owner change constantly. Dependent children grow up. An heir dies. A new heir is born. The nature and character of estate assets change. In the second place, tax laws, regulations, and rulings constantly change. For instance, at one time life insurance up to $40,000 was exempt from Federal estate tax. That law was changed, requiring replanning of every estate which had taken it into account. At one time the test of whether a policy was to be included in the estate of the insured depended on who had the incidents of ownership; the law was changed to add to the test of ownership the question of who paid the premiums; now it has been changed back to the ownership test only; tomorrow it may be changed to some other basis. Before 1948 there was no such thing as a "marital deduction." [27] Once

---

[27] Except as such a deduction was obtained in effect in states operating under the Law of Community Property, which is of Spanish heritage, as contrasted to Common Law, which is of English heritage.

the interest element in limited installment payment of proceeds was non-taxable if the insured elected the option for the beneficiary prior to death; then for a few years it was nontaxable no matter who elected the option; currently it is taxable in any case except for the $1,000 exemption to a surviving spouse.

Unless frequent re-examinations of any estate plans are made, unnecessary taxes are almost inevitable, to say nothing of delays in estate settlement, losses on estate values, and increased administration costs.

8. SUMMARY

Life insurance and life insurance agents serve an important role in estate planning. As an estate asset, life insurance has many important attributes. Cash values increase free of income tax. Policies have the greatest liquid value at death when these values are needed to pay estate taxes and other transfer costs. Life insurance payable to a named beneficiary does not have to pass through probate court and it is free from the claims of creditors of the insured. Life insurance can be so arranged as to qualify for the marital deduction. The use of settlement options eliminates the need for costly trust arrangements. Life insurance is valuable for funding business interest buy-and-sell agreements. It is well qualified as a gift medium.

Perhaps one of the most important advantages of life insurance in the estate plans of anyone is that it makes it possible for a man to provide a comfortable living for his family in case of his death without accumulating a huge estate. With adequate life insurance, a man is free to concentrate more on enjoying what life has to offer rather than being so concerned with the acquisition of property that he loses sight of the importance of living itself.

Questions for Class Discussion

1. Why should a professional life insurance agent keep abreast of tax laws?
2. What does it cost to die? Where can accurate data be found on this subject?
3. Why might life insurance be a good investment for a man with a high income?
4. Can disability income insurance be used in estate planning?
5. Explain the Federal income and estate applications, if any, of the following life insurance transactions:
   a. "A" purchases a $300 monthly immediate life annuity for the single premium of $47,000. He dies after receiving an annuity income for ten years.
   b. "A" purchased a whole life policy of $20,000 for a single premium of $10,574. He surrendered the policy at the end of five years for $10,052.

  c. Assume that in the above case, "A" surrendered the policy at the end of ten years for $11,020.

  d. "A" dies, leaving the proceeds of a $25,000 policy payable to "B" under a life income option.

  e. Excess interest is paid on the guaranteed installments under the above policy.

  f. "A" dies and leaves the proceeds of his life insurance policy to his widow under the interest-only option subject to full withdrawal. Six years later, the widow asks the company to pay her the proceeds on a life income option. The company agrees.

  g. "A" gives his wife an allowance of $200 a month. She uses part of this money to purchase a $30,000 life insurance policy on A's life. After several years, "A" dies. She has full ownership of the policy.

  h. "A" left the dividends on his $20,000 life insurance policy to accumulate at interest. After four years, he drew out the entire dividend accumulation which amounted to $250.

  i. Veteran "A" died and left among other property $10,000 proceeds from National Service Life Insurance.

  j. "B" pays $400 a year on a life insurance policy to secure a debt to "A" who is the beneficiary of the policy. "B" dies with the debt unpaid.

6. Among the following statements, some are true; others are false. Ignore the true statements and explain briefly why you consider the others false.

  a. There can be no reportable loss for income tax purposes when a business surrenders a life insurance policy.

  b. If a limited payment policy is paid up, and year by year the dividends are taken in cash, no income tax is levied upon the dividends as they are withdrawn.

  c. Corporate dividends paid to stockholders out of insurance proceeds are not taxable as "dividends" for purposes of income taxation but are exempt as insurance proceeds.

  d. Premiums paid by a business concern for life insurance are not deductible as a business expense.

  e. Disability income benefits paid to the insured under a life insurance policy are not subject to income taxes.

  f. Disability income benefits paid to the insured under an accident and health policy are not subject to income taxes.

  g. Premiums on accident and health insurance are deductible as an expense for purposes of computing personal income taxes.

  h. Premiums paid by a creditor on policies held on the life of the debtor as collateral security for a loan or debt are usually deductible as an ordinary and necessary expense.

  i. If the surrender value of a life insurance or endowment policy is settled under a fixed amount or fixed period option pursuant to a right contained in the contract to do so, there will be no taxable income until the installments received exceed aggregate premiums paid, after which the full amount received is taxable.

j. The same rule as above would apply if the surrender value of a life insurance or endowment policy is settled under a life annuity option.

7. Aside from its principal function—that of providing for estate liquidity—life insurance can be used in a number of other ways as an instrument of estate planning. Describe briefly at least two ways in which life insurance can be used advantageously in estate planning other than that of providing for estate liquidity.

8. Under what types of settlement do life insurance proceeds qualify for the marital deduction for Federal estate tax purposes?

9. "A" dies and wills his property to his wife, one half outright and the other half in a life estate. How does this procedure save estate taxes upon the death of his wife? How might the same purpose be accomplished by means of life insurance instead of making a transfer of a life estate by means of a will?

10. Explain how the selection of dividend options, settlement options, and non-forfeiture options might be affected by the tax laws.

CHAPTER 18

BUSINESS USES OF LIFE
AND DISABILITY
INSURANCE

A SURPRISING number of businessmen are unaware of the uses of life and disability insurance in protecting their businesses.

The Bureau of Economic and Business Research of the University of Illinois interviewed 580 businessmen in seven Midwestern cities a few years ago. It found that 35% of them had never heard of the uses of life insurance to facilitate the transfer of business interests at death. More than 30% did not know about key man insurance. Less than 10% of the firms contacted had business interest liquidation life insurance; and less than 25% had any key man insurance in force in their organizations.

The businessmen interviewed were not selected at random. They were among the most successful and stable business units in the community, as recommended by the local Chamber of Commerce in each case. In other words, only businessmen who should have had a need for business life insurance were interviewed.

Based on the general business population, the percentage of businessmen unaware of the uses of business life insurance would probably be even more appalling.

While no similar survey has been made in the field of disability insurance, it is probable that the percentages there are much smaller, perhaps infinitesimal. Actually, at this stage of the development of disability insurance, few insurance men ever think to call to the attention of businessmen the need for business disability insurance.

410

The purpose of this chapter is to explain the principal ways in which insurance—life and disability—can be used to protect a business. The field of business insurance is a highly technical one. Legal complexities, such as the ramifications of the partnership buy-and-sell agreement, the stock repurchase agreement, and the details of tax questions involved, will be touched upon only to the extent necessary to explain basic principles. Students seeking an exhaustive treatment of these topics will find a number of specialized textbooks devoted exclusively to the subject.

The four basic uses of business insurance are:

1. To protect the business against financial loss in the event of the death or extended disability of a key man.

2. To salvage the value of a sole proprietorship upon the death or extended disability of the owner.

3. In a partnership, to prevent the liquidation of the business in the event of the death of a partner, and to preserve the value of his share. In the event of the disability of a partner, to prevent heavy financial drains on the partnership, and to preserve the value of his interest.

4. In a close corporation, to enable surviving shareholders to retain management control and to assure an equitable price for the shares in the estate of the deceased stockholder. In event of disability, to prevent the same type of losses mentioned in the case of partnership insurance.

In addition to these basic uses, business life and disability insurance offers collateral advantages in the form of business stability and improved credit. Business life insurance under certain circumstances also offers a source of capital, confidential borrowing, and tax free additions to surplus.

1. KEY MAN INSURANCE

Plants, equipment, and material do not make a business unless turned into a product merchandised by men of technical and executive ability. Wipe out the personnel and the business is destroyed. The purpose of key man insurance is to protect a business against financial loss resulting from the death or disability of a key employee. "What corporate purpose could be considered more essential than key-man insurance?" asked the Federal Court of Appeals for the Third Circuit in a case involving key man insurance.[1] "The business that insures its buildings and machinery and automobiles from every possible hazard can hardly be expected to exercise less care in protecting itself against the loss of two of its most vital assets—managerial skill and experience."

Who Are "Key Men"? The key men in any business are those em-

---

[1] Emeloid Co. v. Commissioner, *189F. (2nd) 230*, p. 233.

ployees whose loss by reason of disability or death would cause the business a serious financial loss. They are also those employees who are important enough to the business to merit a continuation of their salaries during periods of disability to an amount beyond that provided under the usual Group disability plan or sick leave arrangements established as the personnel policy of the company.

Examples of key men fall into many categories. Top executives are obvious examples. Less obvious but often equally important are research workers, sales managers and top salesmen, department heads, the company treasurer or accountant—any employee who will be costly to replace because (a) training a new man will take time and money, and/or (b) efficiency in his department will sag sharply while a replacement is being trained.

Determining Insurable Value. Determining the insurable value of a key man is rarely subject to precise formulae. Usually the value is arrived at in a largely arbitrary fashion—by guesswork. However, the value arrived at can be an "educated guess" if careful consideration is given to several factors:

(1) What would it cost to replace the key man if he were to die or become disabled? It is infrequent, except in small businesses such as the sole-proprietorship, that any employee, however valuable, cannot be replaced adequately, eventually; but such replacement will almost always cost money. If replacement comes from the "ranks" below him, it is rarely that the new man can step into the job with no loss of efficiency or production in the department. The probable cost of the reduced efficiency in terms of profit needs to be estimated. If the replacement must come from outside the company, a replacement of equal ability often will require a higher salary. In all probability the desired man is secure in his present position. A new job is a gamble. If nothing else, there may be conflicts of personality even though his work is eminently satisfactory. Therefore, to be attracted, he must be offered a large enough differential to compensate him for the risks of moving. A study of the personnel market might help in estimating the value of a key man in this connection.

(2) What portion of company profit is traceable to the key man? In most cases, this will probably be difficult to answer precisely; in others, such as that of a salesman, it may be relatively easy to estimate.

(3) How much investment would be lost if the key man died? Large sums might be invested in a research or developmental project which would be a total loss in event of the death of a key man. One man might be solely responsible for the development and operation of a specialized department, or he might be the guiding genius or even the sole worker on an expensive

advertising or merchandising campaign which would have to be scrapped entirely if he were lost.

(4) How much of the loss is the company willing to insure? Since the amount of probable loss in almost all cases is impossible to measure with any degree of accuracy, the amount of key man insurance will depend, not so much on a rough estimate of his value, as on the amount of money the company is willing to spend for indemnity in case of death or disability.[2]

In the case of disability there will be, in addition to the loss of the services of the key man, the cost of continuing the employee's salary for a period of time.

Taxation of Key Man Insurance. The customary arrangement in key man insurance is for the business to purchase the policy, retain all incidents of ownership, pay the premium, and name itself as beneficiary. The key man himself has only to give his permission for the insurance of his life by his employer for his employer's benefit. Aside from that, he is completely outside the transaction.[3]

Taxation of Premiums. Since the business is the beneficiary, it cannot deduct the premium.[4]

Taxation of Proceeds. The proceeds of a key man policy paid to the business are specifically exempt from income tax.[5]

Taxation of Surrender Values. The tax rules with respect to gains or losses on surrender of key man insurance are no different from the rules discussed in Chapter 17 in connection with personal insurance.

Taxation of Disability Income. Amounts received under an employer-financed accident and sickness plan are excludable from the taxable income of the recipient if they are reimbursement for medical care, payments for permanent injury or loss of bodily function, or wages or payments in lieu

---

[2] Actually, there are a number of cases in which key man insurance has more than offset a loss or where, actually, the expected loss did not materialize when the key employee died.

[3] The question of insurable interest and the requirements relating to consent of the person whose life is insured are discussed in Chapter 8.

[4] This, of course, seems inconsistent with the decision in the Emeloid case, quoted earlier, which upheld the purchase of business insurance as being for an essential business purpose, and likened its purchase to the purchase of property insurance. Yet premiums paid by a business on property insurance are deductible whereas those paid for life insurance are not.

[5] In Chapter 17, the $5,000 widow exemption was discussed. Key man life insurance on the employee is used in some cases to provide the funds for this payment. So that the premiums paid on the policy will not be reportable as income to the employee and the proceeds not includible in his estate, the employee must have no nonforfeitable right to receive the payment while living, and the proceeds of the policy must be payable to the employer. Under this arrangement, of course, the premiums are not deductible by the employer, nor are the proceeds taxable.

of wages during absence from work as the result of injury or sickness. This last exclusion has some qualifications:

(1) All payments made in lieu of wages during the first week of absence for sickness are includible for taxes unless the employee has been hospitalized for at least one day during the period of absence. All payments as a result of accident are excludable whether the employee is hospitalized or not.

(2) The maximum amount of the payments excludable is $100 per work week.[6] These exclusions apply whether the payments are funded by insurance or not.

Under the key man disability insurance arrangement, the proceeds could be paid to the employer who would, in turn, place them in his general funds. He does not have to report the insurance proceeds as income, and he may deduct as expenses, funds paid to the disabled employee. Whether or not the premiums paid by the employer are deductible is not clear as of this writing when regulations covering a recently-passed Revenue bill have not yet been announced.

Taxation of Premiums on Disability Insurance. Premiums paid by an employer on individual accident and sickness policies made payable to employees are deductible by the employer for income tax purposes if these payments are considered an ordinary and necessary business expense under Section 162(a) of the Internal Revenue Code.[7] The premiums paid by the employer do not constitute taxable income to the employee.

2. SOLE PROPRIETORSHIP INSURANCE

The predominant type of business structure in the United States and Canada is the sole proprietorship under which one man owns the business alone without partners or shareholders. From the standpoint of estate planning, it is one of the most dangerous of all types of business structure. Rarely, however, does the sole proprietor realize this fact.

Ask the corner grocer, druggist, garage-owner where the family support would come from if he were to die or become disabled. His answer almost always will be, "The business will provide an income." In many cases, the business not only would fail to provide an income, but it might also be an expense burden on the family and cut deeply into other available estate assets.

The Problem in Sole Proprietorships. The estate problem in sole pro-

---

[6] Thus, if the work week is five days, then the exclusion per day is $20; if it is 6 days, then the exclusion per day is $16.67, etc.
[7] They are usually so considered.

prietorship organization arises from the fact that *the law recognizes no difference between the business and the personal estate.*

The sole proprietor, however, usually thinks of his business as something apart from his personal estate. He thinks of the business as his "job," the source of income for his family needs and out of which he accumulates such property as a home, a car, a savings account, and, perhaps, securities or other investments of a "personal" nature not connected with the business.

Actually, his business and personal estate—the home, the car, the savings account—are one and the same thing. His business assets can be attached to pay his personal debts, and his personal assets can be attached to pay his business debts. They are interchangeable. Many are the cases in which errors in business judgment have caused losses of personal fortunes as well as instances in which extravagances in personal living have caused losses to business estates.

When a Sole Proprietor Is Disabled.   In most cases, the sole proprietor is not only the owner and manager of the business, he is also a full-time employee. Therefore, when he becomes disabled, the business is without the services of a key employee. If the disability is of lengthy duration, his services will need to be replaced.

One of two solutions is usual:

(1) Someone from the family steps in and does his work: his wife, perhaps. This, however, might not be satisfactory. If his disability is such that he cannot work, he might need full-time care at home. If his wife has to run the business, then she must hire someone to take care of the house. This will create an added drain on the family budget. It also is likely that the wife will not be capable of performing his job as efficiently as he did.[8] The probable result then is a squeeze: The amount of income will drop while, at the same time, the amount of expenditure will increase.

(2) A manager is hired. His salary will have to come directly out of profits, thus reducing the income to the family by a like amount. Further, unless the manager is as efficient as the proprietor, the income from the business will drop. If he is as efficient, he will be entitled to, and probably will demand, a high salary. In the case of most sole proprietorships, the business provides only one good income: that of the owner-manager. If a nonowner manager also must be paid a good income, what is left for the owner?

Disability income insurance on the sole proprietor can be used to help

---

[8] Not necessarily because of lack of intelligence but because of lack of experience and interest.

offset the financial problems involved in each of the above two courses of action.

If the proprietor's wife is capable of running the business, then there will be additional income to pay for the cost of her replacement in the home. If she is not capable of maintaining the level of business profits, the disability income insurance will help to offset the drop in family income.

If a manager must be hired (or an existing employee promoted to the position of manager), the disability income insurance will provide a fund which can be used to pay the additional costs of business management and to cushion a possible decline in profits resulting from the change in management. Inasmuch as disability insurance purchased on the proprietor is personal insurance,[9] proceeds from it will be income tax free. Therefore, the amount of insured income needed will be less than the amount of gross income to be offset.

Short-term disability [10] of the owner which produces inconvenience in the business but no serious financial loss to the business is not a subject for business insurance. The discussion above refers to disabilities of durations long enough to create a major financial problem.

If the disability is permanent, there should be sufficient coverage to enable the sole proprietor to dispose of the business. He might wish to sell the business to an outsider or, if he has a son, he might wish to continue the business until the son is ready to take over. Sole proprietorship disability insurance will enable him to (a) take his time in making a sale so that he can gain the most advantageous price, in contrast to a distress sale; (b) enable him to keep the business until a son is old enough and experienced enough to manage it.

When a Sole Proprietor Dies.   When a sole proprietor dies, the business does not pass immediately to his heirs. It becomes a part of his estate to be disposed of by the executor or administrator. Actually one of two things will

---

[9] Since the business and personal estate of a sole proprietor are one and the same, any sole proprietorship insurance is, in the final analysis, personal insurance. However, the existence of the business creates new insurance needs, a different viewpoint on the part of the insurance buyer, and a different basis for the evaluation of insurable needs. Hence it seems valid to classify sole proprietorship as "business insurance" even though there is no business ownership as encountered in some other forms of business insurance.

[10] What constitutes a "short-term" disability in such a case depends on how long the business could get along without the services of the proprietor without either (a) incurring additional expense for someone to perform his duties or (b) causing a serious drop in profits. In a one-man business, cost or loss might start almost immediately. When the total of that cost or loss mounts to a point which will be a financial hardship (as contrasted to inconvenience), then insurance should be available. In a larger proprietorship with a number of employees, it might be several months before the absence of the proprietor would have serious financial effects. The waiting period in the coverage is, then, a matter of the individual case involved.

happen: The executor [11] will sell or liquidate the business; or the executor will make an effort to operate the business.

(1) The executor will dispose of the business. Unless (a) the last will and testament of the sole proprietor contains express instructions "in direct, explicit, and unequivocable language" for continuing the business; [12] or (b) all the heirs are adults and agree to assume the responsibilities for the continuation of the business, the legal duty of the executor is to dispose of the business as rapidly as possible. He has no choice in the matter, for he has no right to leave the estate assets invested "in trade" [13] any longer than absolutely necessary. If he continues to operate the business beyond the time necessary for its sale or liquidation, he may be held personally responsible to the heirs for any loss.

Exactly how long an executor may leave estate assets in the business is a matter to be determined by the court in any given case. The executor, however, because of his exposure to liability, will tend to dispose of the business as quickly as possible. The sale, being a forced sale, will not be conducive to a favorable price. In any event, however, the amount realized from the disposal of the business asset is apt to be much less than the sole proprietor had expected. It is entirely possible that the liquidation losses will be so severe that the business estate will be inadequate to pay its own settlement costs. If this proves to be the case, then other estate assets will have to be used for this purpose: the bank account, the home, and, in some cases, family life insurance.[14]

The first need of the sole proprietor, then, is to protect his general estate against the debts of the business. He should provide enough cash through life insurance payable to his estate to meet all the business debts and estate administration costs without forcing liquidation of his so-called "personal assets."

(2) The executor will make an effort to operate the business. If there is an express provision [15] in the will permitting the executor to operate the

---

[11] Although there is a distinction between an *administrator* and an *executor* (cf. Chapter 17) the term *executor* will be used herein to mean either one.

[12] Thompson on "Wills," Sec. 142–43.

[13] Cf. 24 *Corpus Juris 55*, Sec. 474–5.

[14] If the family's personal life insurance is made payable to named beneficiaries, it will not be subject to the claims of the insured's creditors. If it is made payable to the insured's estate then it becomes a part of the estate and can be used to pay estate debts. Cf. Chapter 8.

[15] A typical provision might read: "I authorize my executors for the time being to carry on, during such period as they shall think fit, the trade or business of _____, now carried on by me, and for that purpose to retain and employ therein the capital which shall at my death be employed therein, and such additional capital as they shall think fit to advance from time to time out of my residuary estate, with power to employ

business, the executor may attempt to run it. Before he can do this, however, there must be enough cash available in the estate to pay estate debts, administration costs, and estate taxes, or the business might have to be liquidated for that purpose. It should be held in mind also that the existence of an authorization to continue the business is not a mandate to the executor. If he undertakes to operate the business, the courts will take the position that the decision was voluntary on his part and hold him personally liable for all debts incurred by him in the operation of the business.[16] If continuation of the business has been authorized, he is entitled to indemnification for any of these debts out of the general estate or out of any assets specifically earmarked in the will for the conduct of the business. However, should the business debts exceed available estate assets, the executor would have to pay the excess without indemnification. A cautious executor will be hesitant to operate the business, even when specifically authorized to do so.

How successful the executor's operation of the business will be also is problematical. The nature of the sole proprietorship is such that much of its value as a going business is traceable to the proprietor himself. The business is successful because the proprietor himself made it that way. If there were others in the business equally responsible for its success, the business undoubtedly would have been organized as a partnership or a corporation. The executor, however, rarely will be as effective in the management of the business as was the owner. Not only will he be less experienced in that particular business operation, but also he probably will have his own work to look after so that he would be able to devote only part time to his duties as executor. People who traded with the business because of the good will created by the proprietor are likely to drift away, and suppliers might be leery of extending additional credit. Creditors might demand immediate payment of all debts, a right which they have upon the death of the sole proprietor irrespective of the maturity date of the obligations.

Too often the continuation of the business by the executor results in a nightmare for the executor himself, accompanied by a steady reduction of business so that in the end he is forced to liquidate it anyway—and in view of the decline of the business, perhaps for even less than if the business had been liquidated immediately.

---

at such salary as they shall think fit, any manager of the said business, and generally to act in all matters relating to the said business as if they were beneficially entitled thereto; and my executors shall be free from all responsibility for losses arising in the prosecution of the said business." Quoted from *The R & R Advanced Underwriting & Estate Planning Service,* Vol. Two, p. 13–3. Copyright by The Insurance Research and Review Service, Indianapolis.

[16] Cf. *11 Ruling Case Law,* Sec. 147.

The need for sole proprietorship life insurance for business continuation (as distinguished from business liquidation) is to provide enough cash (*a*) to guarantee that the business will not have to be liquidated to raise cash for administration costs, debts, and taxes; (*b*) to provide the executor with working capital to carry on the business; [17] and (*c*) to guarantee sufficient assets to indemnify the executor for debts contracted in running the business. [18]

If the business passes to the heirs: If, as a result of successful planning and a fortunate selection of executors, the business does survive to pass to the heirs, sole proprietorship insurance can be of additional use:

(1) If the business passes to someone who will not be the active manager, such as the widow, an inexperienced or incompetent son or daughter, or heirs who already are engaged in activities which to them are more attractive than the business, there is the problem of hiring a manager. As already mentioned, the cost of hiring a manager can cut heavily into the profits of the business. If this is the case, it may be better to dispose of the business and invest the proceeds in assets yielding a better net return. If, however, for some reason there is a desire to continue the business (for example, to preserve it for a minor son or for a possible second husband for the widow), and the business income is insufficient to pay a manager's salary, life insurance can be used to provide the funds. Actually, however, no business unable to support an adequate managerial salary should be continued except under unusual circumstances. A sole proprietor engaged in such a business needs personal insurance to offset the loss of his own personal earning power, since a high proportion of his income actually results from his personal services rather than from the capital invested in the enterprise.

(2) If the heir does take over active management, he or she may not be able to earn as much from the business for the first few years, at least, as was earned by the deceased proprietor. Sole proporietorship life insurance can make up the loss. Also, the insurance proceeds will be useful in helping the heirs maintain the credit rating of the business and retain its employees.

Actually, there is serious question as to the advisability of turning over a sole proprietorship to the heirs to be held as income property. If the heirs are unsuccessful in operating the business, they might dissipate their inheritance from the general estate in an attempt to save the business. In this event, the business becomes a liability rather than an income producing asset. If they hire a manager competent enough to run the business as suc-

---

[17] To offset the possibility of more stringent credit conditions.
[18] So as to reduce or eliminate the possibility of personal loss to the executor.

cessfully as it operated under the proprietor, they may find that the manager requires a high salary which cuts heavily into what was formerly considered profits. In this event, the business will return a low yield on the investment, especially in view of the risk involved. Therefore, many sole proprietors recognize from the start that the most desirable plan of handling their business in event of death or permanent disability is to dispose of it.

Disposing of the Business. If the proprietor makes up his mind that disposal of the business is the best method of handling the estate problem relating to it, he may either (a) leave the disposal problem to the executor after his death or to the family in case of his disability, or (b) arrange for his own buyer in advance. In either case, sole proprietorship insurance is needed.

If the buyer is to be located after disability or death occurs, the proprietor should recognize two facts—

(a) It will take time to arrange a favorable sale. In the meantime, cash will be needed to keep the business going and retain customers and good will until a buyer is located. Customers and good will usually make up a good part of the value of a sole proprietorship. A going business is worth more than the liquidation value of its inventory and equipment. Life and disability income insurance can provide the needed cash to continue the business in operation and to preserve its values until it is sold.

(b) No matter how competent the effort to maintain the value of the business after the death of the owner, that value is almost certain to decline. As has been said, the sole proprietor himself is one of the most important sources of value in the business. When he is forced to disassociate himself from the business because of either disability or death, the value of the business is almost certain to decline. In estimating the value of his estate, the sole proprietor, therefore, must take this probable shrinkage into consideration and, if necessary, offset it with additional insurance protection so that his estate will continue to provide the income necessary for the maintenance of his family.

If the proprietor decides to arrange for a buyer in advance, all the problems incident to finding the buyer after disability or death will be eliminated, but two new ones will be introduced: *first,* assurance that the buyer will go through with the purchase, and *second,* guaranteeing that the buyer will have the money to pay the price agreed upon.

The first problem is a matter of contract. A contractual agreement can be drawn up under which the proprietor agrees to sell and the buyer agrees to purchase the business at a price to be determined by the agreement. Usually a trustee should be designated to handle the transfer.

When sole proprietorship life insurance involves post-mortem purchase of the business under a buy-and-sell agreement, a trust may prove advantageous. Proceeds of the policies are paid into trust, and the trustee handles all details of the transfer. The trust arrangement is more flexible and less complicated than paying the proceeds to the buyer who, in turn, must deal with the executor in effecting the transfer. For one thing, the executor will have a prejudicial interest in the transaction (the interest of the estate), whereas the trustee is impartial, interested in neither the buyer nor the seller, but only in carrying out the terms of the agreement.

The second problem is a matter of sole proprietorship insurance.

In its simplest form, the sole proprietorship buy and sell arrangement contemplates that insurance on the proprietor will be bought and paid for by the prospective purchaser of the business. If the buyer is not able to finance the premiums necessary to purchase all the insurance needed, provision may be made in the agreement for the insurance proceeds to be the down payment, the remainder of the purchase price, as fixed by the agreement, to be paid over a period of years out of the income from the business. If the proprietor wants his family to have a fixed sum in cash immediately on his death and that sum involves more insurance than the buyer can afford, the proprietor may arrange to advance part of the necessary premiums, to be paid back by the buyer in addition to the purchase price.[19]

Sole proprietorship insurance also can be used to fund a disability buy-and-sell agreement. The potential buyer purchases permanent and total disability income insurance on the owner. The insurance can be used to provide a tax free income [20] to the buyer which he can pay over to the seller if the seller becomes totally and permanently disabled. If the disability income payments are inadequate to pay the full purchase price over a reasonable length of time, as is likely to be the case, the payments can be supplemented out of business income. Since disability income insurance does not pay off in lump sums,[21] the terms of payment in the buy-and-sell agreement should

---

[19] It is sometimes contended that if the proprietor must advance part of the premiums to the prospective buyer, he might be better off to use the money to buy personal insurance and have, at his death, the insurance *and* the business. Actually each estate problem must be studied individually to determine the best solution for the objectives involved. Often the principal problem is to get the business out of the estate. Personal insurance does not assure that this will be done.

[20] The fact that the buyer gets the insurance proceeds tax free is a great help, especially since ownership of the business might put him in a relatively high tax bracket. The only part of the periodic payments made to the seller that is deductible is that allocated to interest.

[21] Except for disability from dismemberment or loss of sight, for which capital sum coverage is available.

not require a heavy down payment. The buyer might be able to raise a small down payment out of his own resources or through a loan.[22]

As for the type of policy to use in funding a buy-and-sell agreement involving death and disability, a Whole Life or long-term Endowment form with waiver-of-premium and monthly income disability is worth consideration. In case of death, the proceeds of the life insurance will provide the buyer with the cash to complete the purchase. In case of disability, the monthly income will provide the funds for the periodic payments, and the waiver of premium will continue the values of the policy which will be available at death to complete the payments, or at an earlier date if the cash values of the policy should equal the balance outstanding on the purchase price. The cash value could be borrowed at that time and turned over to the seller. Since the waiver of premium will keep the policy in force, the policy loan will never have to be repaid. Interest paid on the loan will be deductible as an expense for income tax purposes. The disability income will continue to be paid, and the owner of the policy will collect the death or endowment benefits, less the policy loan, when they mature.

Such buy-and-sell arrangements in the case of sole proprietorships most often are made between the proprietor and a key employee or employees. When so made, it ties the employees closer to the business and helps to eliminate turnover among key employees.

Occasionally the best solution to the problem of the disposition of the business is incorporation. Such a situation might arise where there is a minor child and the proprietor wishes to hold the business for him. If there is a key employee in the business capable of running it, a solution would be to incorporate the business upon the death of the proprietor, selling the key employee a portion of the stock and placing control of the business in a trust. The trust maintains control until the child reaches an age at which he is deemed capable of handling it himself.

This arrangement also might be worked out for disability. The agreement could provide for the key employee to carry a specified amount of Endowment life insurance on the proprietor (probably to endow at retirement age and thus cover the contingency of retirement as well) plus a specified amount of disability income insurance in the form of a separate A & S policy or rider on the life insurance. In event the owner becomes permanently disabled, the business would be incorporated and a portion of the stock sold to the employee. The disability income paid the proprietor could be handled as installment payments on the price of the stock with the proceeds of the

---

[22] The loan can be made against the business assets or against the cash values of the life insurance written to fund the agreement in case of death.

Endowment upon endowment date or prior death being considered the balance due. The stock retained by the proprietor might be held in trust until the child is ready to take it over; or, if the nature of the proprietor's disability were such that although it prevented him from active work in the business, he could comprehend what was going on, he might retain and vote the stock.

3. PARTNERSHIP INSURANCE

Corpus Juris defines a business partnership as *"a contract of two or more competent persons, to place their money, effects, labor and skill, or some or all of them, in lawful commerce or business, and to divide the profit and bear the loss, in certain proportions."* [23]

Two principles should be held in mind with respect to the partnership: (1) Each partner in a general partnership (the most common type) is fully liable for all debts and obligations of the firm to the extent of his personal estate, and (2) at the death of a partner, the firm is legally terminated as to future business irrespective of the desires of the surviving partners. Business problems can arise out of the disability or death of a partner, and life insurance can be of help in solving these problems.

When a Partner Is Disabled. Except in the case of a silent partner, disability of a partner deprives the firm of a key employee. If he is disabled for a long period of time, it will be necessary to hire someone to do his work. In the case of a personal-service partnership, the income of the firm may be reduced by the amount of business lost because of the inability of the disabled partner to handle it.[24] At the same time, the disabled man is entitled to his division of the partnership profits and, perhaps, a continuation of his so-called "salary" or drawing account. It is possible to draw the partnership agreement so that any partner's share of the firm income is in proportion to his active contribution to it. However, the partnership arrangement usually grows out of and cultivates a close personal relationship among the members of the firm. The chances are that even if partners are not contractually bound to continue income to a disabled partner, they will feel morally obligated to do so. As a result, the income of all partners will be reduced.

Such loss of income can be avoided by the use of partnership disability insurance under which each partner is insured for an amount necessary to reimburse the firm for increased expenses and/or decreased income.

---

[23] *47, 640*, Sec. 1.
[24] Some of the business attracted to the firm because of any given partner, of course, will continue and can be handled by one of the other partners.

When a Partner Dies. The partnership relation is a personal one. It subjects each partner to responsibility for the acts of the other or others. Because it is such a close relationship, the law protects the right of a person to select his partners. No one can choose a partner for another, nor can anyone elect to be the partner of another unless the other is willing. The entire act of effecting a partnership is *voluntary*. Therefore, unless there is an agreement or a statute to the contrary, the death of a partner dissolves [25] the partnership and leaves each surviving partner free to choose new associates.

The business must be either *liquidated* or *reorganized,* and the choice is not entirely up to the surviving partners. The law provides only for liquidation, except where the heirs of the deceased partner may agree to permit their inherited share of the business to remain in the partnership,[26] in which case they become partners. If the heirs are minors, if they are unwilling to join the firm, or if the surviving partners do not want them as new partners, liquidation usually is the only choice in absence of a partnership buy-and-sell agreement.

If liquidation is necessary the surviving partners become trustees in liquidation, saddled with the responsibility of trusteeship, bound to act promptly and honestly, and to render an accounting of their acts to the personal representatives (executors or administrators) of the deceased.[27]

Forced liquidation is an unfortunate solution, for rarely will the full value of the assets of the business be realized. The surviving partners may find themselves without a business or jobs. Business debts that cannot be paid from funds realized from the sale of the business assets can cut into the personal funds of the surviving partners and the estate of the deceased. The heirs of the deceased, therefore, may not only fail to realize anything from the business but also may find other estate assets depleted because of the business.

So, if for some reason it is decided that upon the death of a partner the business shall be liquidated instead of reorganized, sufficient life insurance on each partner will be needed to offset liquidation losses and to protect the other assets of the surviving partners and those of the deceased partner's estate against the debts of the business.

---

[25] It is sometimes stated that the death of a partner *terminates* the partnership. In the legal sense of the term, "terminate," it does not. After dissolution, a partnership remains as a firm as long as is necessary to wind up pre-existing obligations. However, dissolution —which is effected whenever a partner withdraws as well as when one dies—operates with respect to all future business transactions. A dissolved partnership may not take on new business commitments.

[26] 20 *Ruling Case Law 990,* Sec. 226.

[27] For a description of the role of the survivors as trustees, *cf. 40 American Jurisprudence,* Sec. 306.

If the firm is to be reorganized,[28] four courses are open:

1. The surviving partner or partners may be named heir of the deceased.

2. The survivors may take in the heirs of the deceased as partners.

3. The survivors may agree to take in as a partner purchasers of the heir's interest.

4. The survivors may purchase the interest of the heirs.[29]

(1) Inheriting the Share of the Deceased. Obviously, partners will name each other as heirs only where the survivor is a person to whom the deceased partner normally would make a bequest, such as in father-and-son partnerships. In these arrangements, unless the son also makes his father heir to his interest, a problem will result if the son predeceases his father. It is more customary for the father to leave his interest to the son, but for the son to pass his interest to his wife. Arrangements, therefore, should be made in the son's will to handle the son's interest in case he predeceases his father. In partnership estate planning, it is too often forgotten that fathers sometimes do bury sons.

(2) Taking in the Heirs of the Deceased as Partners. As mentioned, the nature of the partnership relationship is close and personal. The surviving partners wish to select their own partners. It would be unusual if the heirs had the same qualities that made the deceased partner attractive to the survivors. Further, the heirs rarely will want to go into the firm as active partners. Usually they have no experience in the business and no interest in working in it. They might be a little more willing to be "silent" partners (that is, nonworking partners), but the surviving partners may not be able or willing to support nonworking partners. Usually the survivors do not want new partners and the heirs do not want an interest in a partnership. They want money.

(3) Taking in the Purchaser of the Heirs' Interest as a Partner. The survivors are under no obligation to take in as a partner a prospective purchaser of the heirs' interest. Although occasionally the surviving partners and heirs might be able to agree on a purchaser, it is poor estate and business planning to leave the disposition of the interest of the deceased partner to a chance sale agreement.

(4) Purchasing the Interest of the Heirs. In most cases, the only satisfactory method of reorganization is for the surviving partner or partners to purchase the interests of the heirs. The problems involved here are

---

[28] Reorganization will almost always be the desire of survivors, whose jobs as well as money are tied up in the firm.

[29] Actually there is a fifth method of reorganization: The heirs may buy out the partners. Usually, however, the survivors will not be interested in this method of reorganization since it leaves them without a business; and rarely will the heirs want the business.

(a) reaching an agreement with the heirs as to the terms of the purchase; and (b) financing the purchase.

Reaching an agreement as to terms will prove no simple matter in the majority of cases. *In the first place,* the survivors will have to deal with an executor or administrator who is under obligation to obtain the best "deal" possible for the heirs. Usually, therefore, he will set a high price. If his asking price is refused, he has evidence that the interest of the heirs is not worth as much as they expected. If he compromises, the heirs may feel he made unnecessary concessions. *In the second place,* it is difficult for the heirs to realize that the business without the services of the deceased is worth less than it was while he was still alive. They tend to think of the value of the share in terms of what the deceased had earned from it. If he has been realizing $10,000 a year out of the business, they tend to think of the $10,000 as business profit, ignoring the value of the personal services he rendered to the firm. Since $10,000 a year is a return on $100,000 at 10%,[30] they think of the value of his share in terms of that figure; whereas the entire assets of the firm, and even its value as a going business, may be only a fraction of that amount.

Often the attempt to buy out the heirs *after* the death of a partner results in a stalemate over price that can be resolved only by liquidation; and liquidation is rarely to the gain of either the survivors or the heirs.

The solution is an advance agreement on the part of each of the partners that in the event of the death of one partner, the survivors shall have a right to acquire the deceased's interest and are obligated to purchase it at a price set in the agreement or determined by a formula established in the agreement. This is the partnership buy-and-sell agreement.

The buy-and-sell agreement also could be drawn to cover permanent disability. The agreement can specify that in the event disability continues beyond a certain period of time—two, three, five years, for instance—the disabled partner will be bound to sell and the others to buy his interest. Payments made to him under a disability income policy carried by the other partners or the firm will be considered installment payments on the value of his share. It may be that additional installments will be paid direct by the firm or by the individual purchasers, depending on whether the Cross-Purchase plan or Entity plan (to be discussed) is used. Any unpaid balance on the value of his share at the time of his death can be paid out of the partnership life insurance on his life.

---

[30] Assuming this is a type of business where 10% represents a reasonable capitalization figure.

Legally, two types of agreements are possible: the *survivorship* agreement and the *purchase* agreement.

The *survivorship* agreement provides that upon the death of a partner, his interest shall vest in and become the property of the surviving partners, either at his death or upon the payment of a stated amount. Since this type of agreement makes a direct transfer, it might be challenged as an attempt to make a testamentary distribution of property outside of a will.[31]

The *purchase* buy-and-sell agreement uses the language of purchase and sale. Each partner agrees that if he dies, his estate will sell his partnership interest at the price and terms set in the agreement. He also agrees that if he is predeceased by any other partner, he will purchase his pro rata share of the interest of the deceased. The agreement provides that the deceased's personal representative (executor or administrator) will make the necessary transfers. The legality of this type of agreement has seldom been successfully challenged.[32]

The buy-and-sell agreement offers a planned solution to the problem of disposal of a partnership interest. The price is established in advance by a formula which is likely to be equitable since it was determined by the partners under the most favorable conditions for achieving equity: The parties, in making the agreement, do not know on which side of the transaction they will find themselves when it is carried out. If they survive, they are the buyer. If they die, they are the sellers.

The agreement guarantees that the heirs will sell and that the surviving partners will buy the interest of the deceased partner. The only problem that remains is whether the buyers will have the money to carry out the agreement. The certainty of a buy-and-sell agreement losses its effectiveness if it is not funded.[33]

While there may be other methods of funding a buy-and-sell agreement, partnership insurance will almost always prove the best solution. The situation which creates the need for funds, death or disability, also creates the funds needed: the insurance proceeds. If insurance is used to fund the

---

[31] Most of the litigation concerning the legality of buy-and-sell agreements has been over the survivorship type. The preponderance of opinion has upheld its legality, starting with McKinnon v. McKinnon, 56 Fed. 409 (1893). There has been some contrary opinion; for example, cf. Ferrara v. Russo, 40 Rhode Island 533, 102 A. 86 (1917) or Gomez v. Higgins, 130 Alabama 493, 30 S. 417 (1900).

[32] An instrument that is testamentary in character operates only by reason of the death of the maker. The instrument of a purchase-type buy-and-sell agreement is operative the day it is signed. The element of present existing contractual rights distinguishes this type of agreement from the survivorship type. Cf. Ireland v. Lester, 298 Mich. 154, 298 N.W. 488 (1941).

[33] That is, if funds are not arranged to meet the obligations under the agreement.

agreement, the partners will not have to drain their personal resources, nor will they have to borrow to carry out the terms of the agreement. Partnership insurance provides the amount of money needed,[34] at exactly the time it is needed, and on the most efficient basis.

How the Insurance Is Arranged. The insurance to fund the buy-and-sell agreement can be arranged in several ways. The most popular plans are the *Cross-Purchase* or the *Partnership Entity*.

Under the Cross-Purchase plan, each partner individually buys and maintains enough insurance on the lives of the other partners to fund the purchase for which he is obligated.

The Cross-Purchase plan has a number of advantages; among them:

1. Since each partner owns and pays the premiums on the policies on the lives of the others, he pays exactly in proportion to his benefits.

2. The plan is free from estate tax complications, since the deceased held none of the incidents of ownership in the policy on his life.

3. The purchase price sets the cost basis for income tax of the share purchased in case of its later sale.

4. The plan is more flexible since, in the case of more than two partners, the survivor may purchase any amount of the deceased's share agreed upon rather than an amount which is in direct proportion to his share in the partnership. For instance, among three equal partners, one might wish to purchase only 25% of the interest of a deceased partner, leaving the other 75% to the other surviving partner. Under a Cross-Purchase plan in which each partner is acting as an individual buyer, this arrangement can be made.

The fact that one of the partners may be much older than another sometimes is considered a disadvantage of the Cross-Purchase plan, under which each pays the premiums on the life of the others.[35] The older man in such a case is paying a lower premium than the younger men. This arrangement,

---

[34] It is not necessary for the insurance to equal the full amount of the value of the deceased's share. In fact, where the price is to be set by a formula taking into account current financial factors, it is impossible to have the life insurance equal the exact amount, for that amount is unknown until after the death of a partner. If the full amount cannot be insured, the life insurance can be considered a down payment, with the balance to be paid under arrangements set forth in the agreement. This will give the heirs immediate cash, which is usually a consideration desirable to estate owners.

[35] Where there is a wide difference in age and proportionate ownership shares, it may sometimes prove impossible for younger members of the firm to pay the premiums on policies on older members directly as under the Cross-Purchase plan. In that case, premiums may be pooled: Either each partner contributes to the pool in proportion to his ownership interest or the total premiums are divided by the number of partners, each paying an equal amount. The buy-and-sell agreement should arrange, when necessary, for the reimbursement of the estate of the deceased for his premium contributions. Except under peculiar circumstances, the Entity plan, to be discussed later, usually will prove a better way of meeting the problem of premiums too high for some partners.

however, is not inequitable, since according to the laws of mortality the younger men are more likely to collect on the policies they have purchased.

The one serious disadvantage of the Cross-Purchase plan arises when there are a number of partners. Only two policies are necessary when there are only two partners. If there are three partners, six policies are necessary. A four-man partnership requires 12 policies. If there are ten partners, 90 individual policies will be necessary. For this reason and others,[36] where a partnership is composed of a large number of partners, the Entity-Purchase plan is most common.[37]

Under the Entity plan, the buy-and-sell agreement specifies that upon the death of a partner, the partnership itself will purchase the share of the deceased partner for the account of the surviving partners. The insurance on the life of each partner is owned by and made payable to the partnership. The partnership pays the premiums out of partnership income.[38] The cash values are carried as assets of the firm.

The following points regarding the Entity plan will be useful as a basis for comparing it with the Cross-Purchase plan:

(1) The indirect but real premium burden of the plan will rest more heavily on the older and on the larger-interest partners in contrast to younger partners and those with smaller interests. While this often makes the plan more acceptable to younger firm members, who usually are less able to pay the higher premiums required under the Cross-Purchase plan, it also results in an inequity, which has to be adjusted in setting the purchase price for the shares of the older firm members.

(2) The policies and proceeds are company assets and, as such, subject to the claims of creditors of the firm. Thus, payment of the funds intended for the purchase of the share of a deceased could be delayed or the amount depleted entirely.[39]

(3) The result of the payment of the premiums by the firm is exactly the same as though each partner had paid them in direct ratio to his interest in

---

[36] One of the "others" being that the sale of the Cross-Purchase plan calls for convincing each partner that he should spend money out of his pocket for premiums on insurance on the other partners. It is easier to sell a man on spending "company money," even when "company money" in the case of a partnership is actually the individual partners' money.

[37] A variation of the individual ownership Cross-Purchase plan is the joint ownership plan under which the policies on the lives of the individual partners are jointly owned by the other partners who pay the premiums jointly and are the joint beneficiaries.

[38] The premiums, of course, are *not* deductible as a necessary business expense for income tax purposes.

[39] If the financial situation of the firm is such that its assets are insufficient without the insurance, the insurance proceeds can be helpful in preventing the partners from being saddled with a personal liability for firm debts. (It must be remembered that a general partner has unlimited liability for the debts of the partnership.)

the partnership. Under the Cross-Purchase plan, each partner owns the cash values in the policies he has purchased on the lives of the other partners; but under the Entity plan, the cash values are owned by the partnership. Therefore, in setting the purchase price for a deceased partner's share, the formula must take into account both the cash values of the insurance owned on the lives of the surviving partners and the proceeds of the policy on the life of the deceased partner.

(4) The deceased's interest in the firm will be divided among survivors in exact proportion to their present interests, which may be an advantage or disadvantage.

Personal Service Partnerships.   The personal service partnership (such as a firm of lawyers, investment bankers, a medical partnership, and the like) often will use an income-continuation agreement instead of a lump sum payment. Under this plan, it is provided that for a specified number of years after the death of a partner, the firm will share a percentage of its profits with the heirs of the deceased. Sometimes there will be two agreements: one a regular buy-and-sell agreement covering tangible assets including receivables, and the other an income-continuation agreement covering the deceased's share in future earnings. Life insurance can be used to fund both agreements.

Who Shall Be the Beneficiary?   In the Cross-Purchase plan, the *surviving partners* usually are the beneficiaries, since they are the ones obligated by the agreement to buy the interest of the deceased. Under the Entity plan, *the partnership itself* usually is the beneficiary since it is the party obligated by the agreement to purchase the deceased's interest.

In either type of plan, *a trustee as beneficiary* will usually prove the most advantageous arrangement. The trustee receives the proceeds, turns the money over to the personal representative of the deceased, and secures the necessary transfers and releases. Not only does the trusteed plan provide for impartiality and relieve the survivors of the details of direct negotiations, but it also permits clear segregation of the partnership insurance proceeds from the proceeds of the personal life insurance carried by the deceased. As another function, the trustee can also serve during the life of the agreement for certain details such as collection and payment of premiums and as a depository for the policies.

It is possible for the *estate of the insured* to be the beneficiary; although such a plan has its dangers because the executor or administrator then has in his hands both the insurance proceeds and the partnership share. Unless the agreement is legally exact, he may seek to retain both.

It is possible to make the policy payable to the *widow or other named beneficiary* of the insured. The plan is often considered desirable by partners who wish to give their beneficiaries the advantage of the installment options in the policy or to avoid the expense and delays of having the proceeds go through their estate, as they will have to be if paid to other than the insured's beneficiary. This plan also is fraught with dangers. The beneficiary might claim both the proceeds and the partnership share. In fact, in one such case,[40] the agreement was held to be unclear, and the widow was allowed to keep both the proceeds of the policy and the partnership share. When the insured's beneficiary is named, the partnership interest is in the estate, but the purchase price for it goes directly to that beneficiary. Creditors with claims against the estate may object to the transfer of estate assets (the partnership interest) without any direct compensation to the estate. A number of companies make it possible for the heirs of the deceased to use the settlement options under the policy even though the policy is made payable to the surviving partner or the partnership. Various plans are available, for example, the "additional direct beneficiary" arrangement. Under this plan, after the terms of the buy-and-sell agreement have been executed, the direct beneficiary releases the policy proceeds for the "additional direct beneficiary" (the insured's beneficiary) who can take them under the settlement options.

4. CLOSE CORPORATION INSURANCE

In many corporations, the stock is owned by a limited number of people, most if not all of whom also are active in the business, usually as officers or executives. This type of organization is called, a "close corporation." [41]

The close corporation has an existence apart from the individual stockholders.[42] However, the relationship among the stockholders is almost exactly the same as that among partners. In fact, the relationship is so intimate and personal that the close corporation is often called an "incorporated partnership." Unlike the partnership, however, the withdrawal or death of a stockholder has no legal effect on the continuation of the business,

---

[40] Price *v.* McFee, *196 Maryland 443, 77 A (2nd) 11.*

[41] The use of the word "close" is a colloquialism and sometimes appears as "closed." The usage seems to come from definitions of the word as designating something either closely held or closed to the public: hence, a "close" corporation, whose stock is not available to outsiders, in contrast to a corporation whose stock can be purchased or is held by outsiders.

[42] Under the 1954 Revenue Act, for some purposes, at least, a partnership can be dealt with as an "entity" apart from individual owners; thus the "entity" plan referred to previously. The tax code says, "If a partner engages in a transaction with a partnership other than in his capacity as a member of such partnership, the transaction shall be considered as occurring between the partnership and one who is not a partner." *I.R.C.* Sec. 707 (A).

although it will necessitate a realignment of ownership which can create problems—unless proper plans are made to take care of the contingency.

The relationship among stockholders in the close corporation is so close that it breeds the same feeling of moral responsibility for one another as is often found in partnerships.[43] Further, the close corporation *is* closed because the existing stockholders do not want to admit new stockholders—at least not stockholders they cannot select for themselves.

Out of the close relationship of close corporation stockholders grows the need for close corporation insurance.

If a Stockholder Becomes Disabled. The effect of the disability of a close corporation stockholder who is also an employee of the firm is almost identical to that resulting from the disability of a partner. He will continue to share in the profits of the company although contributing nothing to them. A replacement for him will have to be hired, costing additional money. Very probably, the company will feel an obligation to continue his salary over a long period of time. If the stockholder is a key man, as is often the case, the firm may suffer a loss of income as well as incurring additional expenses. Partnership disability income insurance can be used in the close corporation to offset these extra expenses and the loss of profits in exactly the same way as it can be used in the key man situation or the partnership.

When a Stockholder Dies. When a close corporation stockholder dies, there is no legal effect on the company. His shares simply become a part of his estate, eventually passing on to the heirs. Here, however, is the situation in which trouble lies.

While a partner cannot be forced to take in a partner against his will, a close corporation can be forced to take in as a stockholder the heir of a deceased stockholder or the person to whom the heir has sold his inherited stock. Anyone who holds legal title to stock becomes a part of the company regardless of what may be the wishes of the surviving stockholders. The new "member" might even be a competitor. The surviving stockholders could do nothing to keep him out or to bar him from full information about the operations of the firm.

Such is the major problem created for the surviving stockholders at the death of a close corporation stockholder.

---

[43] This is not to say that all partners and close corporation stockholders feel a moral responsibility for the welfare of one another. Examples of partners and close corporation stockholders who live in absolute hatred of one another could be found. This is only to say that partners or close corporation stockholders usually become associated because they know and have an interest in one another. This close relationship usually is conducive to the development of a feeling of obligation for one another's welfare.

The heirs of the deceased minority stockholder are faced with problems, too. Stock in a close corporation in which one is not actively engaged usually is considered a speculative investment at best. Since close corporations are normally highly dependent on the skills and abilities of a limited number of stockholder-executives, the degree of safety of principal is usually low. Earnings on such stock are unpredictable for the same reason. Further, dividend earnings may be low because employee-stockholders are frequently more interested in ploughing profits back into the business rather than declaring dividends on the stock; and they may vote themselves salary increases and bonuses which take up a large part of the profits available for dividend distribution. The "old" stockholders with the controlling interests could freeze the "new," unwanted stockholder out of the business. It is true that minority stockholders have enforceable rights and can sue to force distribution of surplus or profits as dividends and to stop unreasonable salary and bonus payments; but any investment under which the owner must argue with others about return and resort to costly law suits is hardly the kind of investment to leave to an heir.

If the estate or heir wishes to sell stock in a close corporation, he has difficulty in finding a buyer, and, if lucky enough to find a buyer, has even more trouble establishing a price. The very factors that keep close corporation stock from being a good investment for heirs also prevent it from being a good investment for anyone who does not intend to work actively for the company or whom the firm would not accept as an employee even if he were willing. Since future earnings on the stock are unpredictable, and since there is no market price for the stock, its value is not clear. The seller is prone to value it high. The buyer is prone to value it low because of its inherent drawbacks. The gap between the two valuations is often too great for successful negotiation.

The heirs of a majority stockholder are also faced with problems. While it is true that by their control they can set what policies they wish and, in effect, say to the minority stockholders, "Do as we say or get out," the nature of the close corporation is such that often heirs of a majority interest cannot get along without the co-operation of the minority. As has been brought out, many if not all of the minority stockholders in the usual close corporation are also key employees in the firm. The heirs are often not acquainted with the business or not enough interested in it to risk losing the key men. Also, since the minority stockholders are active employees, they are in a position to sabotage the heirs, should they wish.

If the minority stockholders are left to run the business while the majority heirs act as "silent partners," the minority can conduct the business so dividends to the heirs become negligible. For instance, they can put profits back into the business, living on their salaries.

Further, as minority stockholders, the survivors have the same rights as heirs have when *they* are minority stockholders, and the law will guard the survivors' interest just as it would the heirs' in similar circumstances. Thus the minority survivors could cause the majority heirs embarrassment and trouble.

Finally, if heirs inheriting a majority interest wish to sell, the minority interests may not have the money to buy at a price that will give the heirs anything like what their proportionate share of the going business is; and the problems of finding an outside buyer have been discussed.

One more problem faces the heirs of a deceased stockholder: valuation of the stock for tax purposes. Since there is no yardstick in the form of established market price (and rarely a value established by a prior sale close enough in time to have any bearing), there can be a wide discrepancy between the value set on the stock for Federal estate tax purposes by the executor and the value set by the government. Trust officers report that the valuation problem of stock in close corporations for estate tax purposes represents one of the greatest difficulties in estate administration and often results in excessive administration costs. On the other hand, if the buy-and-sell agreement and the method of valuation used in it have been negotiated at arms' length and in good faith, the government will consider the valuation of the stock under the agreement as acceptable for tax purposes.[44]

Thus from the standpoint of both the surviving stockholders and the heirs, the best arrangement in the vast majority of cases will be for the survivors to buy, and the heirs to sell, the stock of a deceased stockholder. Again, in view of the problems encountered when an attempt is made to negotiate the sale after the death of the stockholder, which problems are the same as those in the case of the partnership, the best way to handle the sale is through a buy-and-sell agreement among the stockholders, put into effect while they are all alive. Such agreement is, of course, of little value unless there also is money to pay for the stock. The agreement can be funded in various ways but, as in the case of the partnership buy-and-sell agreement, life insurance offers the best method in the vast majority of cases.[45]

How the Insurance Is Arranged. The two most common types of purchase agreements are the *Individual* and the *Stock Retirement*.

Under the Individual plan, each stockholder agrees to buy a portion of

[44] May v. McGowan, 194 F. (2nd) 396. (Numerous other cases could be cited.)
[45] If one of the partners or stockholders is uninsurable, other funding methods will have to be used with him. Life insurance can continue to be used with the insurable partners or stockholders.

the stock of the deceased stockholder. Each purchases, owns, and maintains the insurance necessary to fund his purchase. The plan is exactly the same as the partnership Cross-Purchase arrangement and is, indeed, often known by that name. The advantages of the plan when used in connection with the close corporation are the same as those available when the plan is used with the partnership.

Under the Stock Retirement plan, the corporation agrees to purchase the stock of the deceased shareholder and purchases, maintains, and owns the insurance necessary to fund the agreement.[46] This plan is the counterpart of the partnership Entity plan. The advantages and disadvantages of the Stock Retirement plan are the same as those of the Entity purchase plan, except for the tax question. However, since corporations are not authorized in every state to buy their own stock, it will not always be usable.

In the partnership plans it makes no difference, taxwise, who pays the premium: the partners or the partnership. Since the partnership is not a separate tax entity, whatever the partnership earns is taxable as income to the partners. Premiums paid by the partnership are not deductible as an expense and, therefore, are considered as part of the partnership income taxable to the partners. In the corporation plans, who pays the premium can make a tax difference. Premiums paid by the corporation are not deductible by the corporation; but since a corporation is a separate tax entity, they are not reportable as income to the stockholder. Earnings of a corporation are taxable to the stockholder only when they are paid out as dividends. Therefore, the choice of plans can have a real effect on the tax burden. For example, the corporation can pay the premium directly or increase the salaries of the stockholders to allow them to pay the premiums.[47] The tax question can be important in the decision because the premiums on the insurance are a nondeductible expense for the corporation, whereas salaries are deductible for the corporation but reportable as income to the stockholder. Thus, which plan will cost less in income taxes depends on a comparison between the marginal tax rate being paid by the corporation and the marginal tax rates being paid by the individuals. If the corporation is

[46] Where the stockholder is also an employee, the agreement often calls for him to sell and the corporation or stockholders to buy his stock in the event he severs employment. The price for his stock is set in the agreement, either at an actual figure or through the establishment of a formula. Cash values in the insurance carried on his life can be used to fund the purchase. However, since cash values may be insufficient at the time he leaves employment, and since it might be financially impossible for the corporation or the individual stockholders to meet the agreed price, provision may be made to pay the balance in installments or to allow the stockholder to dispose of the stock himself if the buyers are unable to meet the established price or make a satisfactory settlement.
[47] Or reduce the salaries of the stockholders and pay the premiums themselves, as the case may be.

paying more than the individual shareholders, the individual stock repur-chase plan will cost less in taxes. If the stockholder is paying more than the corporation, then the Stock Retirement plan will cost less.

If the close corporation stockholder is also an employee, it may be desir-able to provide in the buy-and-sell agreement for the sale of his shares in the event of permanent disability, as in the case of the partnership agree-ment. If he is not an employee, there would be no reason for this provision.

The Trustee plan can be used in connection with the close corporation the same as with the partnership agreements and insurance.

Who Shall Be the Beneficiary? Problems of beneficiary designation under close corporation insurance are the same as those under partnership insurance. If the Cross-Purchase plan is used, the stockholders themselves can be made beneficiaries of the insurance they carry on each other. If the Stock Retirement plan is used, the corporation can be the beneficiary. The value of a trustee as beneficiary in the close corporation case is the same as in the partnership case. The problems and disadvantages of naming the heirs direct beneficiaries or naming the estate of the insured are the same as in the partnership case.

5. MISCELLANEOUS USES OF BUSINESS INSURANCE

In addition to the uses of life and disability insurance in business that have been discussed, several others might also be classified under the head-ing of "business insurance."

Collateral Uses. Many of these miscellaneous uses are actually col-lateral advantages of the uses of disability and especially, life insurance for key man protection, business interest liquidation, and business continuation. They serve as predeath or predisability advantages of the insurance which is purchased for postdeath and disability uses. These uses are:

(1) Key man insurance aids in establishing credit for a business. Cred-itors and lenders usually are more aware of the importance of key personnel to the financial standing of the business than is business management itself. Many a bank loan has been made or line of credit extended, not so much because of the physical characteristics of the business itself, but because John Doe is president, or general manager, or in some other key position. Creditors recognize the added strength key man life insurance gives to a firm.

The value of key man disability insurance is far less understood by cred-itors and lenders, largely because so little key man disability insurance is in force. Yet the effects are the same whether a man's services are lost to the business because of death or because of disability. Inevitably, as the use of business disability insurance spreads,[48] its value in strengthening credit will increase.

(2) Business life insurance makes cash and loan values available to the business. Life insurance policies other than Term are good collateral for loans. The life insurance company is contractually bound to make such loans up to the cash value of the policy at a contractually-set rate of interest regardless of the money market at any given time. Banks and other lending agencies always will accept life insurance policies as collateral for loans. If money is easy, they will usually lend at a lower rate of interest than that set in the policy.

Policy loans made by the insurance company have another value: They can be made confidentially. Occasions arise when a business firm may not want it known in banking or credit circles that a loan was needed. A policy loan can be effected without the knowledge of such circles.

(3) Business insurance can be used to fund retirement. If the key man lives to retirement, the cash or endowment values of a life insurance policy on his life may be used to help fund his retirement.

(4) Business insurance also can be used as an aid to corporate financing. Where the success of a business enterprise is recognized to be largely dependent on one man, or where a stock is being issued to finance a program of development the success of which will be largely in the hands of one man, it is possible to use key man insurance to back the issue and thus add a margin of safety that will make the issue more attractive to investors. In event of the key man's early death, proceeds from the policy can be used to retire the stock.[49] It might be possible also to take an Endowment policy on the life of a key man, designating the proceeds to be used for the retirement of a block of, say, preferred shares.

(5) Key man life insurance permits an accumulation of reserves that is less liable to criticism from stockholders. This is especially important where there are minority stockholders not actively engaged in the business. To them, the accumulation of reserves may seem a means of depriving them of dividends. Minority stockholders have distinct rights in law. They have

---

[48] Such spread is itself inevitable as sales activity in the A & S field grows. The uses of insurance expand·as competition becomes keener and agents reach out for new markets. The present state of development of business disability insurance is roughly comparable to the status of the use of business life insurance about 30 years ago.

[49] It appears from a study of court decisions in such cases (cf. Ellsworth v. Lyons, U.S. Circuit Court of Appeals. 6th dist., 181 Fed. 55 and Tweedie Footwear Corp. v. Fonville, Texas Court of Civil Appeals, 115 S.W. (2nd) 421), that the proceeds would have to be payable to a trustee for the specific benefit of the holders of the block of stock rather than to the corporation.

been known to cause a business embarrassment and expense by threatening or bringing suit against officers for alleged attempt to accumulate reserves to avoid payment of dividends. Such stockholders are less likely, however, to look upon the cash values in key man insurance as an unreasonable surplus accumulation. Life insurance as a means of accumulating liquid reserve funds has the same advantages for the business as it has for the individual, among them regularity of saving, automatic management of funds, safety of principal, high convertibility, automatic compounding of interest, tax-free interest increments during accumulation, and the like.

Other Primary Uses. A number of other uses of business insurance are available, which are primary rather than collateral uses. These are:

(1) *Credit Insurance.* Life insurance is widely used as security for credit or loans. The creditor or lender may require the borrower to assign existing life insurance as collateral; or the lender may himself purchase and maintain life and disability insurance on the borrower. Credit insurance is widely used to guarantee installment purchases, usually in the form of Group insurance, as discussed in Chapter 13.

(2) *Deferred Compensation.* The subject of deferred compensation and the uses of life insurance as a method of funding are discussed in Chapter 17.

(3) *Group Insurance.* Group life and disability insurance is an important use of life insurance in business. Group insurance is discussed in Chapter 13.

(4) *Insurance in Pension Plans.* The use of life insurance and annuities in pension and profit-sharing plans is discussed in Chapter 14. This is becoming a more and more important use of life insurance in business.

(5) The use of life insurance to fund the *$5,000 exemption* is discussed in Chapter 17.

6. SUMMARY

In addition to Group, Pension, and Profit-sharing uses of insurance in business, there are other situations in which life and disability insurance can be of value in guarding against business loss and disruption resulting from the disability or death of an employee or part-owner.

(1) Insurance can protect the business against the loss and extra cost that come when a key man is disabled or dies.

(2) It can protect the heirs of the sole proprietor against (a) the loss in value in his business resulting from his death or disability and (b) against the possibility that business obligations will siphon off other estate assets.

(3) It can protect the partnership against the drain that the disability of a partner will cause and assure continuation of the business in event of the death of one of the partners. It also protects the heirs of the deceased

from the loss that will come if the business cannot be continued and must be liquidated.

(4) It will protect the close corporation from the loss that disability of a stockholder-employee can occasion and against the entrance of unwanted interests into the business in event of the death of a stockholder. It also guarantees the heirs of the deceased a market for their shares at a fair price; and it sets the valuation of their shares for estate tax purposes.

In addition, life insurance has several miscellaneous uses in business: as credit, as backing for corporate financing, as a method of building reserves and for compensation plans designed to hold valued employees.

Questions for Class Discussion

1. Do you see any inconsistency in the taxation of key man insurance and the taxation of fire insurance purchased for a business? Discuss.
2. Alec Trician, the sole owner of a large electrical supply house, was shocked to hear of the untimely death of his best friend. When he learned of the shrinkage of his friend's estate, he immediately generated some interest in the problem of estate planning. Alec decided to conduct a study of his own problem and charged you with the responsibility of enlightening him on the avenues of approach to a solution. Since Alec's estate included little more than his business, the problem was simply one of preserving the value of this business interest. Alec, 39 years old, has a wife and two children, a son age 18 and a daughter age 16. Assume that Alec's son has his heart set on eventually taking over the business and is studying electrical engineering and business management at the university and that Alec's daughter is madly in love with a mediocre piano player and it looks like the real thing. His wife is a good mother without any business sense. With this set of facts, it becomes obvious that Alec would want his estate to hold on to the business interest in the event of his death. What plans, if any, should Alec make to protect his business after his death until his son is ready to take over? Would life insurance be helpful in these plans? Discuss.
3. What other problems should Alec consider in his estate plans if he should decide to will the business interest to his son? Would life insurance be helpful in handling any of these problems? Discuss.
4. A business might have uses for life insurance which are totally unrelated to the estate planning objectives of its owners. They are uses which are in no way connected with the life or death of the owners in their functions as owners. Discuss the ways in which life insurance can be used effectively by a business in improving employee relations.
5. Aside from the use of business life insurance in estate planning and employee relations, what other legitimate needs might a business have for life insurance?
6. Good business management principles dictate the use by most partnerships and close corporations of buy-and-sell agreements funded by life insurance. Any other arrangement except in unusual circumstances appears to be pure folly. It is important, therefore, that both the philosophical and the technical

aspects of buy-and-sell agreements financed by life insurance be understood by those who use them or advise their use. As to the philosophical aspects?

   a. Explain briefly why properly financed buy-and-sell agreements are so important to the surviving partners or stockholders, and

   b. Explain briefly why life insurance is the ideal financial instrument for use in funding these buy-and-sell agreements.

7. As to the technical aspects in arranging insurance to fund a partnership or close corporation buy-and-sell agreement, several decisions need to be made. For example, questions relating to policy *ownership*, policy *beneficiaries*, and *premium payments* have to be settled.

   a. Outline what you consider to be the best answer to each of the above questions for the rank-and-file business insurance case and give the reasons for your choice.

   b. Indicate what factors or characteristics of a given partnership or close corporation case would lead you to recommend some answer other than the ones indicated above and point out (with reasons) what your new answers would be.

8. A & B have entered into a partnership buy-and-sell agreement. The insurance was arranged so that A's wife would be the beneficiary on the policy on A's life and B's wife would be the beneficiary on the policy on B's life. Each has signed an agreement to deliver her husband's interest in the partnership to the surviving partner. Assume the partnership is worth $50,000—each partner owning a $25,000 interest and each partner being insured for that amount. A dies and his widow receives $25,000 from his policy and then turns over A's interest in the partnership to B as agreed. Can you see any *possible* income tax disadvantage in this arrangement to B if B subsequently sells the business? If so, what plan could have eliminated this disadvantage?

9. In the above case, would the $25,000 life insurance proceeds paid to A's widow upon A's death be subject to the Federal estate tax on A's estate?

10. A, B, and C are the stockholders of a close corporation, and own 100 shares of stock each. The corporation purchases $20,000 of life insurance on each stockholder (the value of each stockholder's share) and names itself as beneficiary. It enters into an agreement to purchase the shares of a deceased stockholder. A dies and the corporation purchases A's stock from his widow with the proceeds of the $20,000 life insurance policy. Can you see any income tax disadvantage of this arrangement to C if he should later sell his stock for $40,000? What plan could have eliminated this disadvantage? Can you see any income tax advantage in having the corporation purchase the life insurance? If so, what?

CHAPTER 19

UNDERWRITING
THE RISK

LIFE insurance rates are based on mortality tables. The tables used are a compilation of mortality experience among a group of people in average good health. Therefore, when new persons are added to the insured group, they must be in the same average good health if future experience is to approximate the past experience shown on the table.

The process used to determine average good health (and the other factors involved, such as habits and occupation) is known as "underwriting the risk" or "selecting the risk." The former is probably the better term. The latter implies that the process is one of choosing the best risks, which is not the case. Instead, the process is more that of making sure that no one is accepted who is an excessive risk. It therefore becomes necessary to reject some applications and to charge others an additional premium to make up for poorer health, occupational dangers, or the like.

Out of every 100 regular Ordinary life insurance policies applied for, three are rejected, eight are asked to pay an extra premium, and 89 are accepted at standard rates.[1]

Ideally, companies would like to be able to offer some type of coverage to everyone who applies, because rejections cause adverse public relations and often are both irritating and discouraging to agents.

Sometimes the applicant has just been examined by his own physician

---

[1] This is not a picture of the insurability of the American public at large, but only of people who apply for Ordinary life policies. Among those who don't apply, and, therefore, do not appear in this summary are (a) those who know they would not be accepted, and, hence, never apply in the first place; and (b) those agents know would not be accepted and whom, therefore, they never solicit.

and told he has "absolutely nothing to worry about." Too often the medical examiner, despite instructions, reminders, and cajolery from the company, pats the applicant on the back, and remarks, "You passed with flying colors."

In the case of the family physician, he is treating an individual patient. He may feel it is better not to frighten the patient about a condition, or he may consider whatever condition exists to be compensated. The home office medical director and underwriting department, however, are dealing with a mass of risks. They know that a given impairment about which the family physician is not concerned in the individual case will produce a greater mortality in the mass.

In the case of the physician making the examination, his function is not to "pass" any applicant. His function is only to report his findings to the company. Almost never is he even qualified to form a judgment. Insurance medicine is a technical branch of the profession in which few practicing physicians are qualified. Rarely, however, will an examiner making a remark about "passing" explain his limited role to the applicant. Perhaps it is the desire sometimes found in the various professions to be considered the fount of all wisdom that keeps him from admitting he has no authority to make any statement about "passing."

The whole situation can be aggravated by the fact that when a company rejects the three applicants out of 100, it is not always able to tell the applicant or agent the reason, since it may be confidential. The result can be a ex-applicant who publicly criticizes the company and an irritated agent, who spends time he should be using to solicit or service business, to engage in protracted correspondence with the company about the case.[2]

This chapter will describe the various classifications of acceptable applicants and the relationship of the information from various sources to the standards against which applicants are measured. It will also deal with the nature and expense of nonmedical life insurance and touch upon the importance of reinsurance.

1. THE NECESSITY FOR SELECTION

Adverse Selection. In any voluntary insurance program, there always will be selection. A life insurance company has the choice of selecting or being selected against.

If one knew he were going to die tomorrow, he would beg, borrow, or steal the largest sum of money he could get his hands on to buy life insurance tonight. But as long as death is not imminent, the average person thinks

---

[2] The author of the following poem (sung to the tune of "Oh My Darling Clementine") is unknown, but in a humorous and exaggerated manner it clearly depicts the gist of a

next week, next month, next year will be soon enough for him to insure his life. When the public is left to its own initiative to buy life insurance, among those who apply for it will be the poorer risks. As a result, mortality among a group that includes unsolicited and unselected applicants will be greater than the mortality anticipated among solicited and selected applicants. The company must, therefore, reject or rate up all applicants whom it can recognize as not measuring up to the standard assumed in the table of mortality. Were a company not to apply rigid selection standards, applicants who might be rejected by other companies would gravitate to that company. This would be an example of selection against the company and is known as "adverse selection." Adverse selection could well lead a company to eventual financial difficulties.

Inequity of Cost. It would be possible, of course, to compile a mortality table in which the death rate per thousand would be, within practical limits, the same as the rate among unselected and unsolicited applicants. However, since this group of unselected applicants would contain a number of poor risks, the mortality rate would be higher. If such a table were used in rate computation it would lead to a higher premium.

It is theoretically true that any rate is inequitable for every applicant except the average. Since the average is a statistic rather than a human being, it becomes technically correct to state that any rate is inequitable for

---

lot of correspondence in the files of the Medical Departments of many life insurance companies.

"My Dear Agent," wrote the Doctor,
"Application of Jim Brown
Is declined for valid reasons;
Sorry, but we've turned him down."
"My Dear Doctor," wrote the Agent,
"Your form letter just received,
And the information given
Makes me just a little peeved.
In the first place, my dear Doctor
I have known this man a year,
And I've never seen him drinking
Much of anything but beer.
He don't chew nor smoke tobacco;
He don't toddle to the Jazz;
I can't detail all the virtues
That this super-standard has."
"My Dear Agent," wrote the Doctor,
"You are certainly some kidder.
Case-of-Jim-Brown still is turned down;
Sorry; cannot reconsider."
"My Dear Doctor," wrote the Agent,
"Your decision makes me sigh—
Brown's entitled to a contract;
If he isn't—*tell me why.*"

"My Dear Agent," wrote the Doctor,
"Brown's case shows much albumin,
Mitral murmur, high blood pressure,
And the fat man's prize he'd win."
"My Dear Doctor," wrote the Agent,
"Brown has trivial ills, that's true,
But they're family characteristics;
So it's safe to pass him through.
Why, his father had a murmur
You could hear a block or more;
His old grand-dad had albumin,
And he lived to ninety-four.
Note the weight's good distribution;
Pressure shows the heart is strong.
He has never had a hemorrhage;
So please rush the contract on."
"My Dear Agent," wrote the Doctor,
"Application of Jim Brown
Is declined for valid reasons;
Sorry, but we've turned him down."
When the Agent got this letter
He just settled back and sighed,
For he couldn't argue further,
'Cause his "prospect" had just died.

all applicants. But the operation of the insurance principle depends upon large numbers. If there are too many classifications there will not be a large enough group of people in any one of them to assure the safe operation of the Law of Large Numbers. The companies must make their classifications sufficiently broad to produce stability of experience. Hence, while there are technical inequities in any practical rate, there is a limit to the extent to which they can be eliminated. The purpose of risk selection is to determine not only who is insurable but also what degree of insurability he possesses.[3]

2. BASES OF SELECTION

Several different selection factors are used by underwriting departments of life insurance companies. Among them are: (1) age, (2) sex, (3) plan of insurance, (4) occupation, (5) residence, (6) race and nationality, (7) family and personal history, (8) physical condition and physique, and (9) financial condition. Some discussion of the nature and importance of each of these bases will be helpful in understanding both the questions asked on a life insurance policy application and the reasons why some applications are rejected.

Age. Every company establishes maximum ages above which it will not issue policies. The maximum limit for new insurance usually is 65.[4] An increasing number of companies write new insurance up to age 70. An exception usually is made for term insurance where the maximum age commonly is set at 60.

Several explanations may be given for establishing maximum age limits. As a practical matter, the number of applications for life insurance which

---

[3] The degree of rate inequity for a given policyholder increases with the extent that he is above or below the *average* of the classification in which the underwriting standards place him. Very good risks, for example, pay proportionately more than is really necessary to uphold their share of the burden. In recognition of this fact, there has been a tendency among companies to segregate such risks by offering at lower rates a "special" or "select risk" policy, underwriting standards for which are higher than for other policies. This helps adjust the inequity for the "superstandard" risk but increases it for the average risk since, with the superstandard risks skimmed off the top of the group, mortality experience for the group now becomes poorer, and the mortality cost for the group now goes up. In effect, when the superstandard risk is taken off the top of the group, what was formerly the average risk in the group becomes a superstandard risk as far as that group is concerned, and the inequity which formerly fell on the new superstandard risks now falls on what had been the average risk. It becomes just as justifiable to remove him from the group into a class by himself, at once creating a new superstandard class in the old group, which becomes justifiably eligible for a group of its own . . . *ad infinitum.* The *reductio ad absurdum* of "select risk" underwriting is a violation of the Law of Large Numbers. Moreover, it can increase the cost of insurance for the average policyholder. As a practical matter, however, select risk underwriting offers a low-rate policy showing an extremely low net cost which makes competitive sales ammunition, especially when it is used as a "typical example" of the cost of the company's whole line of policies.
[4] Some companies set the maximum age for women at 60.

could be obtained above age 65 would be insufficient in the average company to constitute a group large enough for the safe operation of the Law of Large Numbers. At age 65, the need for new life insurance is almost nonexistent, the cost almost prohibitive, and the possibility of passing the physical examination negative. A danger in issuing policies to applicants over age 65 is the possibility that the purchaser may be buying the policy as a speculation. Companies find it good underwriting policy to decline insurance when no real need exists.

Some companies, however, recognize that there may be a need for new life insurance beyond the published maximum age limit. To meet this demand, they have a special set of rates for applicants up to, perhaps, ten years above the regular limit. These rates are confined to but one or two plans of insurance (usually continuous-premium Whole Life) and are loaded to take care of the problem of antiselection.

Age also is important in determining how much life insurance a company will accept on a given life. Usually companies will write their largest maximum amounts on applicants between ages 25 and 55 with the limits graded downward on each side of this age span. It is felt that the need for life insurance is greatest between the above ages and, too, that the ability to pay for large amounts of life insurance under age 25 is questionable. When policies are issued on infants under age one, companies often reduce the benefits for the first year.

Age may affect other factors used to determine insurability. For instance, a given degree of overweight after about age 25 (the actual age depending upon the opinion of the company's own medical and underwriting departments) is usually looked upon as less favorable to insurability than the same amount of overweight at younger ages. Underweight on the other hand is regarded more seriously at younger ages than at older ages.

Sex. In general, women are accepted for life insurance on the same basis and for the same rates as men, although this has not always been true. It was commonly considered, even well into the 1920's, that women were not as good risks as men and should either pay a higher rate or not be accepted at all. The childbirth hazard is now considered to be so minor as to have no practical effect upon mortality experience, being offset by the more sheltered lives of women.[5] Moreover, it is statistically observable that

---

[5] To avoid sarcastic annotation in the margin by the feminist contingent, we explain that by "more sheltered lives" we mean, for instance, that fewer women than men work outside the home; hence the statistically average woman is exposed to a smaller number of chances of traffic accident and contagion, to name just two hazards. Moreover, women show a smaller incidence of coronary breakdown, stomach ulcer, nervous breakdowns, and other disturbances generally considered to be aggravated if not created by the vicissitudes of business life.

women live more than five years longer than men. Today over one fifth of all insurance in force is on the lives of women.

In practical underwriting, sex affects the maximum amount of life insurance a company will allow on any one life. For a single woman, the judgment of what constitutes overinsurance becomes a matter of how much income she earns. Some companies may place a lower maximum limit on the amount of insurance on female lives than on the lives of males. There seems to be little justification for this discrimination, however, if all other factors are equal. Most companies have definite rules about the amount of insurance they will write on a married woman with no personal income. The limit generally is fixed in proportion to the amount of insurance owned by her husband. This rule is in keeping with the philosophy that the bulk of family premium dollars should be spent for coverage on the life of the breadwinner. If special reasons exist for a disproportionate amount of insurance, for instance, uninsurability of the husband, the rules usually will be waived, provided the husband has enough income to carry the insurance.

Some companies will not write disability insurance for women, and those that do restrict the coverage to single, self-supporting females. Some contracts provide further that the disability benefits are canceled upon marriage. In some companies, the dollar limit of monthly income disability benefits may be lower for women. Also, the maximum age to which the coverage is issued and the maximum age at which disability may occur (in some companies) are lower for women than for men. For example, a company may pay a maximum of $250 a month for a male and issue the policy up to age 50, requiring that disability occur before age 55. For a female, the maximum amount may be only $100 and the corresponding age limitations may be 45 and 50. For waiver of premium, typically the disability must occur before age 60 but some companies set the limit at age 55 for women.[6] The rate for waiver of premium for women in some companies runs 50% higher than the male rate. The reason for the stricter underwriting limitations on disability coverage for women is based simply on statistical evidence that women experience a higher rate of disability than do men. Also the moral hazards (i.e., malingering) is great when disability insurance is unrelated to earned income.

Plan of Insurance. Before the development of substandard underwriting, it was common practice for companies to be considerably more liberal in underwriting higher premium plans of insurance. Higher premium plans require higher reserves per $1,000 of insurance and, consequently, the com-

---

[6] The policy must be issued usually before age 55 for males and before age 50 or, in some companies, age 45 for women.

pany has progressivly less at risk under these plans. Hence, applicants who may have been considered uninsurable for a continuous-premium Whole Life plan may have been insured at standard rates under a fairly short term Endowment plan.

The practice of dealing with impairments by restricting the plan of insurance is in use today but on a more limited scale. For example, an applicant with a slight health or physical condition the effects of which are usually postponed until later years might be insurable at standard rates under an Endowment plan which expires prior to the years in which the impairment is likely to affect mortality. Thus, for illustration, an overweight person at age 25 under some conditions might be insurable at standard rates under a 20-year Endowment plan because the effects of overweight do not begin to be seriously felt until the middle years. However, this same applicant might be rated substandard for a continuous-premium Whole Life policy.

Finally, the plan of insurance is important in risk selection because the amount at risk is different under different policies; hence companies often have stricter underwriting rules for certain types of policies. Whereas a given applicant might be eligible for continuous-premium Whole Life insurance, he might not be eligible for a Family Income policy, Term policy, or a Preferred Risk contract.

Occupation. Certain occupations are considered extrahazardous and not to be written at standard rates. A list of occupations requiring extra rates covers 32 pages set in fine print in the rate book of a given company. Ap-

ROAD, HIGHWAY AND STREET CONSTRUCTION	LIFE INSURANCE	DIS- ABILITY	DOUBLE INDEMNITY
Superintendents, foremen, surveyors	Std.	W	Yes
Operators ditching, grader, steam roller, scraper and similar road building machinery, truck drivers	Std.°	W	2
Blasters and others handling explosives	$7.50	No	No
Paving brick, block and cement layers, stone setters	Std.°	1½	2
Asphalt layers, air hammer operators	A	No	2
Concrete mixer operators	Std.°	1½	2
Cement and concrete finishers	Std.°	1½	2
Power shovel operators and firemen	Std.°	1½	2
Stone crushermen	B	No	2
Traffic lane painters	Std.°	1½	2
Laborers	B	No	2

° Not eligible for 10-, 15-, and 20-Year Term, Term to 65, Family Income, Family Maintenance, Joint Life, Preferred Whole Life, and the Juvenile Payor Rider (Death or Disability).
1½ and 2. Eligible for Waiver of Premium or Double Indemnity at multiples of the Standard premium.
A & B refer to the substandard classification applicable. Class A is a better risk than Class B.
W means risk is eligible for waiver-of-premium but not eligible for disability income.

proximately 300 different employment classifications are listed, and under some of them, as many as 100 different jobs are designated and individually considered.[7] As an example, one small classification is reproduced here.

Note that, in this particular listing, some of the jobs may be standard for life insurance alone but substandard or uninsurable for Waiver of Premium or Double Indemnity riders.

What occupation and what duties are insurable or uninsurable and what ratings they will take if insurable vary from company to company; however, there is almost always agreement that certain obviously hazardous occupations—steeplejacks, to give an extreme example, or bartenders, race-car drivers, workers in plants manufacturing explosives, and sand blasters—are to be rated at least substandard. Even here there may be no general agreement among companies as to the extent of ratings, that is how much extra premium should be charged.

The hazardous nature of any particular occupation arises from either a greater incidence of accident in that occupation or from duties or working conditions of a nature which adversely affect health, or both.

For underwriting purposes, the company is interested in how long the applicant has been in his present job, and, if less than two years, the nature of his previous occupation. This information is necessary since a previous occupation might affect the present state of health of the applicant as well as having a bearing on the moral or morale hazard. A question of concern, too, is whether or not the applicant has an occupational history which suggests a return to a former hazardous occupation. Once a policy is issued it cannot be rated up should there be a subsequent change in occupation.

Residence. Although health and hence mortality may be adversely affected by various climates and sanitary conditions in different areas, these usually are not considered variations justifying extra rates, at least as among locations in North America. Among companies writing foreign business, however, permanent or long-term residence in unhealthful climates or in areas where sanitary conditions are bad may call for either higher premiums or complete rejection.

If the applicant has changed his residence within the past two years, the company wants to know the place of previous residences. This information is important since it can have a bearing on the present state of health of the insured and may indicate whether or not the applicant may be expected to settle permanently in a location which is undesirable from an underwriting

---

[7] Occupational mortality has been improving over the past years with the resulting tendency among life insurance companies to reduce or eliminate ratings on a number of occupations. Only about 20% of the extra-risk insurance written is rated up for occupation.

point of view. Also it has its value for purposes of identification and investigation.

Race and Nationality. Certain races can be shown statistically to have a mortality rate higher than that expected among "Caucasians." With an actuary's fine disregard for exactness in any science except his own, most rate books lump in with "race" certain nationalities whose environment and living standards are such that they may produce impairments that may continue through one or more generations even after these people migrate to a different country.

Commonly, a distinction is made between American-born and foreign-born in the case of any races and nationalities which any given company feels adversely affect standard mortality. For instance, in one rate book, American-born Japanese and Chinese who are professional men, chief officials of banking, mercantile, and manufacturing concerns, plantation owners, senior clerks employed by large concerns, or college graduates, teachers, "and others who are obviously of the same class and who are well established" are accepted as standard risks on any plan except Term insurance or insurance which has a large Term element. If they are foreign-born, but have no intention of returning to the Orient, they are accepted standard in this same rate book for Endowment at 65 or for a higher-rate plan; on less expensive plans, they are rated Table A, substandard. This table produces only a slight addition to the standard rate. Japanese and Chinese who are proprietors of small retail shops, manufacturing firms employing few people, owners of small plantations, clerical workers in offices, and those employed in similar occupations are accepted at standard rates for Endowment at 65 or higher-price plans, if American-born; Table A on Endowment at 65 or higher-price plan, and Table B on less expensive plans if foreign-born. Japanese or Chinese employees in stores, fish markets, restaurants and hotels, unskilled workers, *et al.* are insured under Table B on Whole Life or Endowment plans if American-born and Table B on 20-year Endowment and higher-price plans if foreign-born. Female Japaneses and Chinese, and children, are treated still differently in this particular rate book.

Since the mortality experience among the non-Caucasian races has been improving at such a rapid rate, race is becoming less important as an underwriting factor. In fact, there is a definite trend toward the elimination of special discriminatory treatment of certain races.[8] A reasonable period of

---

[8] Some states have laws forbidding any differences in rates based on race, thus confusing social discrimination with objective discrimination. There is no more social discrimination involved in setting a different rate for a race which shows a higher average mortality than there is in setting a different rate for any other statistical reason. It may be contended that setting different rates for a race as a whole discriminates against those

residence in this country, however, is usually required before life insurance may be written on new immigrants. This is to allow them time to adjust to a new diet and to establish a reliable medical and personal history.

Family and Personal History.   The health records of both the insured and his family are considered important in the selection of risks.

In general, family history is important only if it reveals something which might adversely affect the risk. Rarely will favorable family history offset the adverse effect of personal history. Age of parents is requested on an application blank since it is considered as having at least some bearing on longevity of the offspring. Death of the parents under age 60 usually is looked upon as an adverse factor; but it is never in itself justification for rejection, affecting underwriting only if early death resulted from something which could be transmitted to children by inheritance or childhood contact.

The personal history of the applicant himself is more directly important in appraising the risk: health record, habits, environment. All these are important in measuring not only the physical hazard involved, but also the moral hazard. In fact, the habits, environment, and reputation of the applicant are considered so important that there is an investigation of these history factors by professional and disinterested investigators, commonly employees of organizations conducting a credit investigation business. The nature and significance of the inspection report will be discussed later.

The application blank itself, by including a series of questions, also attempts to determine information relating to the personal history, habits, and environment of the applicant. Heavy drinking, excessive use of drugs, and dangerous living are grounds for rejection. Habits relating to air travel also are important. If there appears to be an *unusual* aviation hazard [9] the company will require more information. The final effect may be an extra premium added to cover the additional hazard. It should be noted here that as a general rule, life insurance policies do not exclude deaths resulting from aircraft accidents, although such a restriction occasionally might be found in policies issued in those states which permit the use of such a clause.[10]

---

members of it who could qualify as standard risks. However, if the number of "standards" in a classification is lower than average (as it is if the entire classification is lower than average), then the cost of selecting the few who qualify becomes higher than the average cost and can be met only by increasing the loading in the premium for expenses of operation. Antidiscrimination laws merely pass the cost of insuring substandard cases along to standard policyholders, which is in itself discrimination. This footnote is intended to discuss only the matter of rate discrimination without any comment or implication on the ethics of social discrimination—a subject not within the scope of a text on insurance.

[9] Travel on regularly scheduled air lines as a fare-paying passenger and even travel in a CAA-licensed plane is not considered to be an unusual aviation hazard. Usually the amount of such travel is ignored unless the policy involves large amounts of insurance.

[10] However, the disability and double indemnity provisions of these same policies commonly carry some aviation restrictions of their own.

Physique and Physical Condition. Physical condition, of course, has a direct effect upon longevity. Life insurance companies want to know about an applicant's sight, hearing, heart, arteries, nervous system, lungs, tonsils, teeth, kidneys, etc. They judge the applicant in the light of their knowledge of the effect of any discovered impairment or disorder on longevity in general, and not as it may affect any one individual's life span. Consequently, while a practicing physician might not consider a given impairment as serious in the light of an individual's health, habits, and environment, the life insurance medical department may consider it cause for rejection in view of statistics which show that out of a large group of persons with the impairment, more will die than standard mortality tables indicate.

For example, the practicing physician, with a chance to observe an individual over a period of time and with full knowledge of all his affairs, might consider an elevation of blood pressure a temporary functional disturbance brought about by a passing condition. On the other hand, the life insurance physician, having no chance to observe the individual over a continuing period of time or positive evidence as to his past history, but having before him only the report of an elevated blood pressure on one or a small series of examinations will give the matter serious consideration. He has statistical evidence that high blood pressure has an adverse effect on mortality in the mass. Even if he knows that the condition is functional rather than organic, he also has evidence that a certain percentage of functional cases will eventually become organic. He cannot judge by the individual case; he must judge by mass experience, for the whole principle of life insurance depends upon the operation of factors in the mass.

In general, impairments can be broken down into two classes: *static* and *progressive*.

A clear-cut example of a static impairment is an amputation (assuming that it was the result of a localized condition such as an injury and not of a general, progressive disease or disturbance which amputation cannot arrest). Amputation of one limb is usually not cause for rejection or for an extra premium, although it may have an effect upon waiver of premium or upon double indemnity.

A clear example of a progressive impairment is cancer. Progressive impairments, however, may eventually become static impairments. For instance, cancer, at least in the early stages, often can be completely arrested by X ray or operation. A history showing a successful cancer operation ten years ago with no evidence of recurrence can be considered in an entirely different light from existing cancer or cancer only recently operated upon. Diabetes is an impairment which some companies will consider as changing eventually from a progressive to a static stage. Within the past few years, a number of companies have begun to accept as substandard risks diabetic patients whose condition has proved to be completely controllable by the use of insulin.[11] At one time diabetics were universally rejected.

The general physique of the applicant is important. Marked variations from the average height and weight, for instance, are considered adverse factors, since such deviations affect mortality in the mass. The distribution of weight is a major factor for consideration. A rule of some companies is that if the waist measurement exceeds the expanded chest measurement, an overweight condition is present. Overweight is much more serious than underweight. The effect of underweight and overweight on mortality must be evaluated in the light of personal and family history. Generally speaking, underweight is not seriously regarded as a risk impairment; [12] however, particularly at younger ages and coupled with a family history of tuberculosis, it will cause more careful scrutiny.

Financial Status. Obviously, application for a policy calling for a total premium outlay (adding any existing insurance on the life) completely out of line with the size, source, and stability of the applicant's income is cause for underwriting suspicion. Either the policy is not going to be accepted by the applicant if issued, or there is a good chance that the policy will result in an early lapse. Also there might be speculation involved. Perhaps the applicant has knowledge of a serious impairment which he is trying to conceal. A life insurance company is not interested in speculative risks, and it is not eager to pay either for medical examinations or for the cost of issuing policies only to have them rejected when issued or lapsed before enough premiums are collected to permit the company to recover the acquisition costs in connection with them.[13]

What constitutes overinsurance in any income bracket is difficult to define. Much depends upon the psychology of the individual. Any two men in the same salary bracket and with the same responsibility are apt to have different ideas as to what constitutes a reasonable percentage of income to budget for life insurance premiums. Five per cent may be too much for one of them, if his sense of financial responsibility is not deep and his living standards are relatively high. Twenty per cent may seem to another man no

---

[11] The common practice is to assess a rather high mortality rating.

[12] Recent studies indicate that the group 10% to 30% underweight shows a better mortality experience past age 30 than do people of average weight. As for overweight, studies show a lesser improvement in mortality over the past years than has been experienced by those of average weight. Overweight, therefore, is becoming more seriously regarded by underwriters. On the other hand, underwriting philosophy is just the reverse in disability insurance.

[13] See Chapter 20 for discussion of acquisition costs.

burden at all if he feels strongly the responsibility of protecting his family and is willing to live conservatively. Here, again, the company must judge on the basis of averages.

Insurance equal to that amount which could be purchased under the continuous premium Whole Life plan with 20% of the applicant's income is considered acceptable. An application calling for an amount of insurance in excess of this figure may, in some cases, be considered overinsurance—or at least may be a cause for underwriting concern. At extremely low levels of income, even the 20% rule might produce overinsurance. For example, 20% of a $200-a-month income leaves only $160 for living expenses. At extremely high levels of income, the 20% rule might also produce overinsurance, since at that level of income 20% may buy an amount of insurance so large as to be undesirable from an underwriting standpoint. In such cases, however, the agent may supplement the application with unusual facts or the inspection may reveal an individual set of circumstances which will alter the underwriting attitude toward what constitutes overinsurance.

Even if the applicant's financial status clearly qualifies him for the amount for which he is applying, companies must place restrictions on the amount issued since concentration of large amounts of insurance in few policies is actuarially unsound. The maximum may be very high, several million, for instance, in the giant companies and correspondingly lower in the smaller companies.

Underwriting rules restricting the amount of insurance allowable on any one insured often are influenced by the ability of the company to get reinsurance, since most companies do not retain the entire face value of a large policy themselves, but reinsure part with other companies.

There has been a noticeable tendency among companies to increase the maximum limits of insurance allowable on a single life. Mortality experience among the so-called "jumbo" risks has improved so rapidly as to make possible this trend toward liberalization of underwriting rules.

Cases involving large amounts of insurance, either in the application or in the aggregate, are usually investigated more thoroughly. Commonly, if the application is for more than $25,000, two medical examiners must report on the applicant. If it is in excess of $100,000, the company may call for electrocardiogram tracings, heart X rays, and other supplemental data indicated by the case.

Aside from size, source, and stability of income, the underwriter wants information regarding the general business reputation of the applicant. His credit standing is important in the over-all picture in judging the fitness of the applicant for life insurance. This is especially true when life insurance is issued for credit purposes; i.e., to insure the creditor against the death of the debtor. Insurance on the life of a "dead beat" debtor may be classified as a speculative venture and, therefore, be grounds for rejection.

3. SOURCES OF UNDERWRITING INFORMATION

There are five principal sources of underwriting information: (1) the application, (2) the medical examination or statement of health,[14] (3) the agent's report, (4) the inspection report, and (5) the Medical Information Bureau.

The Application. A reproduction of the application is found in every Ordinary life insurance policy. A discussion of the more important questions included in the application will show how the information which forms the basis of selection is obtained and the purpose for which it is used.

Part I, Section A, of the application is filled out by the agent in the presence of the prospect.

One of the first questions asked is *date of birth.* The importance of this question is obvious, since the rate for insurance is based on age. In the case of Ordinary insurance, the age of the applicant for rate purposes is considered to be that of his nearer birthday.[15] Hence, for Ordinary insurance, age changes midway between calendar birthdays.[16] The applicant is considered age 25 from the time he is 24 years and 6 months until he is 25 years and 6 months. In the case of Industrial insurance, the age for the next birthday is used. The applicant is rated as age 25 as soon as he passes his 24th birthday. "Age change" is the term used to designate the date on which an individual becomes the next higher age for rate purposes.

Former as well as present address is asked in all applications in order to facilitate the inspection investigation if the applicant is too new in his present location for the inspector to find people who know much about him.

Occupation is asked in order to determine whether or not it is hazardous, and for the same reason, specific duties must be given in addition to "kind of business." If the applicant has been in his present occupation less than two years, he must give his former occupation. Applications also inquire regarding any aviation activities.

---

[14] In nonmedical life insurance, the statement of health is the substitute for the medical examination.

[15] A mortality table can be constructed on a basis of last birthday, next birthday, or nearest birthday. For the purposes of determining the applicable rate, the age-count rule must match that of the mortality table; that is, if the table is based on "nearest" birthday, then age must be counted, nearest birthday.

[16] The purchase price for a Single Premium Life annuity generally is based upon the number of full years plus full months of age which may be completed at the date of issue. The annual premium for a Retirement annuity is based upon the nearest age at issue, as in the case of regular life insurance. Cf. Chapter 5.

The application also asks whether or not there are *negotiations for other policies* now pending or contemplated. The overinsurance picture might change when all policies pending are added to those already in force. A question is included relating to whether or not the applicant has ever had an *application for life insurance declined or postponed,* or offered a policy with a rated-up premium, or on a plan other than applied for. If the answer is "Yes," space is provided for an explanation. Companies are especially careful of risks that have a history of rejection.

Applications often ask if the applicant is a *member of the reserve forces* of any branch of the United States Army, Navy, Marine Corps, or the National Guard. By itself, an answer in the affirmative is not considered cause for rejection, rating, or change of plan by most underwriting departments but may, together with other unfavorable factors, have bearing on acceptance, rejection, or rating.

Any contemplation of *change of occupation* or *change of residence* to a foreign or tropical country must be noted since such a change might materially affect the risk.

The final set of questions in Part I of the application concerns itself with the type of policy applied for, the amount, special benefits, methods of paying premiums, how dividends are to be applied (if a participating policy), and the beneficiary designation or designations.

Part I of the application closes (except for the agent's certification, to be discussed separately) with the details of total insurance already in force: year of issue, name of company, amount, and annual disability income, if any. The importance of this information has already been discussed.

Part II of the application is the medical report, to be completed by an authorized medical examiner for the company in the presence of the prospect. In the case of nonmedical policies, Part II consists of "statements in lieu of medical examination." Nonmedical policies are those underwritten without the benefit of a medical examination. Medical information as a basis for selection is obtained by means of a questionnaire. The advantage of nonmedical insurance to the agent is the elimination of one more obstacle to the sale of insurance. Some people object to the time and trouble involved in submitting to a physical examination. Some even are afraid of physical examinations.

We shall consider the questions in Part II, medical, first. Here the application goes into considerable detail regarding the prospect's past history and present health condition. There is a request for a statement of every illness, disease, injury, and operation since childhood and every physician or practitioner consulted in the last five years. A long series of questions to be answered "Yes" or "No" includes inquiries about such things as X rays, electrocardiograms, blood tests, other laboratory tests; whether or not the applicant has ever had albumin, sugar, etc.; whether he has ever been in a hospital, clinic, or the like for observation or treatment; whether he has ever changed occupations or residence because of health and whether he has been on a restricted diet within a year; whether he has made a claim for disability or compensation based on sickness or accident; whether his health is impaired, or whether he is in any way deformed or crippled; and whether he has ever had any one of a number of specific diseases or disturbances. Questions regarding his use of alcohol or narcotics are considered highly important in underwriting the risk, as are also the occurrence of tuberculosis or insanity in his household at any time.

The family record asks the age, health details, and cause of death (if death has occurred) regarding the applicant's spouse, father, mother, brothers, and sisters.

If the applicant is an adult female, there is a further series of questions regarding pregnancy, maternity, and disturbances indicative of trouble with the female generative organs.

The questions discussed above are those which are asked of the applicant by the medical examiner, and the signature of the insured certifies that the answers have been correctly recorded by the medical examiner. The signature also waives all provision of law forbidding a physician from disclosing any knowledge or information which he has acquired in examining or attending the applicant. This waiver permits the company to make inquiry of any physicians who have attended or treated the applicant in the past. As a practical matter, such inquiries are not made unless it appears that they would have a bearing on the risk.

Part II of an application for a policy issued nonmedically consists of "statements in lieu of medical examination" and covers many of the same questions as those asked by a medical examiner, except that they are asked by the soliciting agent: height, weight, all diseases, illnesses, etc.; physicians or practitioners consulted; X rays, electrocardiograms, blood tests, albumin, and various specific diseases and disturbances; the use of alcohol and drugs; family records; and the additional questions if the applicant is an adult female. Omitted, of course, are the questions to be answered as the result of a physical examination.

It will be seen from the list of questions that the impression occasionally found among insurance prospects that the physical condition of the applicant is disregarded in the case of a "nonmedical" policy is erroneous.

Both the number of companies issuing nonmedical policies and the limits in amount of insurance that will be taken on the plan from any one applicant have increased considerably in the past few years.[17] A principal reason for this trend is the accumulation of favorable experience with nonmedical insurance. Other factors are the lack of availability of medical examiners and the increasing cost of medical examinations. Nonmedical insurance was first tried in Canada, where the experiment was made because of the difficulty, in rural provinces, of getting the medical examiner and the applicant together. Its use in the United States was originally limited to rural districts for the same reasons. However, it has expanded steadily from the rural areas into the small towns and nonmedical is to be found, currently, being written by some companies even in large cities. There was a time when the average physician was eager to be appointed medical examiner for one or more companies, not only for the steady flow of fees but also to build his practice, for many applicants without a family physician when originally examined eventually become his patients. With the cursory examination that some physicians give a life insurance applicant today—and the proof of the cursory nature can be found in the taking of an examination—it seems unlikely that nonmedical applicants are any more poorly selected than a number of those who have submitted to medical examinations. This is especially true when the agent himself does a conscientious job of selection. Companies may limit the privilege of writing nonmedical to agents who, by past record, have proved their conscientiousness and their willingness to look at an applicant from a company rather than commission viewpoint. It would not be too surprising an evolution for the practice of medical examinations to be dropped entirely from the process of selecting risks, possibly making such an examination elective on the part of the company if the answers to Part II of the nonmedical application contain anything questionable, if the amount of insurance involved is large, or if the age of the applicant exceeds a given figure. Studies have indicated that at some ages and for reasonable amounts of insurance the cost of physical examinations exceeds their value in terms of mortality savings.

The Medical Examination. Part III of the application for a medical policy consists of the physician's answers to questions based on his examination of the applicant: marks of identification, general appearance, apparent age, race, height, weight, body measurements, the findings of a urinalysis, heart action, condition of nervous system, blood system, lungs, stomach, kidneys, muscles, joints, glands, eyes, ears, and all such matters. Finally, the examiner is asked if he knows anything in connection with the insured's

---

[17] The common practice is to write nonmedical insurance up to age 40 for a maximum limit of $10,000.

physical condition, family history, or past health not already recorded which would affect the insurability and if he does, whether he is sending confidential information on it to the home office. The physician also is asked about the applicant's habits with regard to the use of stimulants and narcotics. Finally he may be asked if he unreservedly recommends the applicant as a first class, average, or poor risk.

Agent's Certification. One of the sources of underwriting information is the agent's report or certification, which appears at the end of Part I of the typical application.

The certification asks how long and how well the agent has known the insured, if he has any unfavorable information regarding the insured's health, character, habits, and so on; the approximate amount of money the insured is now putting into life insurance; the agent's estimate of the applicant's net worth and annual income. An additional report is requested on women concerning source of income and who will be responsible for premium; whether the husband carries insurance on his own life and in what amount, and if he carries less than his wife, why; the maiden name of the married applicant and a question regarding the cause of her husband's death if she is a widow. This certification usually requires, also, that the general agent or manager name the soliciting agent in the case and give the names of several references who have known the insured for several years. The company wants to know, too, whether the applicant sought the insurance herself or whether the applicant was solicited by the agent. Companies are careful of adverse selection when the applicant is unsolicited.

The help of the agent in the selection of risks can be of great value to the underwriting department. If the agent is personally acquainted with the applicant, lives in the same area, and is acquainted with other people who know him, he may be able to provide useful information. In any event as one company states in its rate book, the following is true:

> The final responsibility of selecting risks necessarily rests upon the proper officials at the Home Office. The agent may, however, practice a preliminary selection which will be greatly to his advantage. One measure of an agent's worth to the company is the quality of gilt-edged business which is placed and paid for. In the long run, the agent will earn more money by spending his best efforts in finding prospects who are good risks than in spending this amount of effort in trying to argue the company into taking risks which should not be accepted or by trying to induce the company to reduce a rating.

Underwriters, however, find it unwise to place too much reliance on the agent's certification. The agent, in his zeal to increase his commission, might tend to color his judgment. Some agents have been known to conceal information (about an applicant) which they know would result in rejection or an extra rate. On the other hand, there are those agents who do co-operate with the underwriters and are helpful in risk selection.

Inspection Report. An important source of underwriting information on an applicant is the inspection report. The use of inspection reports for supplemental and confirming information on the applicant arises from an original practice of making inquiries among his friends regarding his reputation and habits in order to discover anything of a fraudulent or "off-color" nature about the application. However, both because the territorial activities of companies widened, and because friends often gave prejudiced information, companies began to check applicants through disinterested local correspondents who either knew the applicant or were able to collect information on him from his neighbors and business associates. Some companies eventually established their own inspection departments, and among the larger companies a few of these departments are still in existence.

Today the usual practice is to use a commercial credit investigation agency, or a bureau especially established for the purpose, to make inspection reports on applicants for life and disability insurance policies or applicants for agents' contracts. There are several of these commercial investigation agencies. They provide a means of gathering unbiased information, since inspection agencies have no interest, one way or the other, whether the information reported is favorable or unfavorable.

Inspection reports on smaller policies where there are no contradictions or complications in the application are simple and relatively brief. The making of credit investigations is so common a practice in everyday business transactions that an inspection agency usually will have data on the applicant even before the insurance company makes inquiry. It needs to do only a little checking to bring the data up to date or to find requested information that it does not already have. Among some of the life insurance companies there is a tendency to eliminate inspection reports on small policies as a move toward economy. Not only do inspection reports themselves cost money, but also there are costs involved in handling and using them.

In the case of larger policies or of questionable applications, a more detailed investigation may be requested. The ability of the large commercial credit investigation organization to find obscure facts is sometimes almost incredible. These organizations do not, of course, make criminal investigations, and the uses to which their services may be put and the purposes for which they may be called upon to make investigations are carefully specified in a contract with users.

Questions on the usual inspection report concern the identity of the applicant, his occupational duties, his participation in aviation, his finances,
health, habits, and reputation.

The inspection report is also considered the primary source of information relating to moral hazard. In a typical inspection form, this information
appears as follows under the classification, "reputation":

> Do any of the following apply to this applicant:
> Heavy debts?
> Domestic trouble?
> Drink habits?
> Connection with illegal liquor?
> Irregular beneficiary?
> Is his general reputation as to character and morals good?
> If not, give details.
> Do you recommend him for life insurance?

Specific comments are asked concerning the exact duties of the applicant's occupation and any part-time occupation; line of business in which he
is engaged and how long he has been so employed together with his previous
employment record and present financial standing; his marital status, number of children, home surroundings, and standing in the community.

The inspection report is considered an invaluable source of underwriting
data. It serves as a good check on information gained from other sources.
Sometimes the services of inspection companies also are used to clarify circumstances surrounding questionable death claims.

The Medical Information Bureau. A final source of underwriting data
is the Medical Information Bureau, known throughout the industry as the
"M.I.B." The Medical Information Bureau, an association of 327 life insurance companies,[18] is a clearinghouse for information relating to the physical
condition of prospects for life insurance. Its purpose is to enable life insurance companies to detect misrepresentations of fact and thus to guard the
interests of existing policyholders against imposition and fraud.

The Bureau obtains its information from member companies, who submit reports on all applicants showing any one of a given number of impairments. These impairments may be those affecting the health, any family
health history, or habits of the prospective insured. The information which a
company reports is limited to its finding of a medical impairment and does
not indicate the action taken. The Bureau is never told whether the insur-

---

[18] The M.I.B. was originally organized in 1902 by the Medical Directors Association. This
connection was terminated in 1946 when the M.I.B. was reorganized as an unincorporated
association of member life insurance companies. There is no longer any legal connection
between the M.I.B. and the Medical Directors Association.

ance was issued as applied for, declined, or rated. Moreover, it does not reveal the name of the reporting company.

The fact that a report has been made on the individual simply alerts another company to some impairment which might not otherwise be revealed to that company. Since the underwriting practices of life insurance companies are not the same, it is a common occurrence for one company to accept a risk that has actually been rated or declined by a previous company.

The information on individuals is reported in code by the M.I.B. and is available only to a restricted group of people in a subscribing company and chiefly for the purpose of processing an application for life insurance.

4. RISK CLASSIFICATION

Numerical Rating. The evaluation of the risk is the function of the underwriting department. For the most part, the process of evaluation is a matter of correlating information reported about the applicant with its statistically observable effect, if any, on longevity. Often, of course, the effect of any given factor will change over the years as pertinent statistics change. For instance, formerly most life insurance companies considered any participation in aviation as an unfavorable factor. With current improvements in air safety records, the effect of participation in aviation on mortality rates has decreased. Companies no longer consider the normal use of regularly scheduled passenger lines as affecting the risk. Again, as previously mentioned, diabetes was once considered cause for rejection. Statistical observation over a number of years now indicates that the malfunction under control does not produce as large a deviation from average mortality as was once thought to be the case.

Wherever human judgment enters in, there is always a residual margin of error despite the amount of training the human mind has been given. Consequently, there has been an effort in the science of underwriting to standardize its operations. Perhaps the most common method of standardization is the numerical rating system.[19]

Although there are many variations in use, the basis of the numerical system is the calculation and assignment of debits and credits for the various factors involved in the underwriting of a risk. A standard risk is assumed to have a rating of 100. A factor or condition which is known to cause a variation from average experience is debited if the deviation is adverse and credited if it is favorable. The extent of the debit or credit of specific items varies from company to company according to that company's own experi-

---

[19] Developed early this century by O. H. Rogers, M.D., and A. H. Hunter of the New York Life Insurance Company.

ence and according to its interpretation of published experience. An illustrative example which bears no particular relation to any one company's system follows.

Assume the application of a clergyman. The occupation of clergyman is considered a better than average risk. According to statistics available to the company (and remember that this is only an illustration), the mortality of clergymen is 25% better than average. Consequently, for occupation, the applicant is assigned a credit of 25. However, the application and inspection report reveal that the gentleman went into his profession as a result of a reformation from habits somewhat tipsy. All sources of underwriting information report that he has suffered no relapses in a considerable time. Although as a given individual he probably never will, the company has statistics which show that a certain percentage of chronic tipplers will go back and sign the pledge again, "for life, same as the last time." It has further determined statistically that in any large group of former alcoholics the mortality will be 25% above standard. Consequently it debits the application 25.

And so the process goes on down the list of underwriting factors, debiting some and crediting others. In the end, the total of the debits is added to 100, and from that total is subtracted the sum of the credits. The resulting figure, assuming that the schedule of value of debits and credits is accurate to begin with, will indicate the degree to which mortality can be expected to vary from standard. If the final figure is 95, for instance, then the mortality to be expected on this type of risk is 5% below standard mortality; that is, 5% better experience is expected than of standard risks; if the total is above 100, say 125, then 25% greater mortality is to be expected. Companies generally will accept, at standard rates, applications scoring not more than 125. Some companies are even more liberal.

The values and the inaccuracies in the numerical system have been a subject of discussion and treatise since 1906. There was extreme reluctance on the part of old-school medical directors and actuaries to agree that risks could be satisfactorily evaluated without individual scrutiny by those trained in medical and actuarial sciences. A particular criticism was that there is often an interrelationship among factors which will not be evaluated properly by use of the system, being in combination a greater risk than the sum of the two of them separately indicates, for example, underweight and tuberculosis.

Various modifications of the numerical system handle cases of interrelated factors more satisfactorily. In borderline cases, the application can be submitted to the medical director or the actuary, whereas the great mine run of applications can be processed smoothly by trained and experienced clerks with a minimum of expense and loss of time, and with a more uniform evaluation than even the most learned experts could give, considering the pressure of time and the element of human judgment.

Classes of Risks. Broadly, applicants may be classed either as insurable or uninsurable, although theoretically there is no such thing as an uninsurable risk.[20] A rate can be figured for any age and any physical condition. Every individual still alive has some life expectancy. Obviously, however, as this life expectancy decreases, the actuarially calculated rate for the risk will eventually become too high for the applicant and at this point insurance become economically impractical. Under these conditions, the applicant is, for all practical purposes, uninsurable.

As among companies, who is insurable and who is not depends also upon the extent to which the company issues extra-premium (substandard) policies. Some companies will write no substandard risks at all whereas others will issue substandard insurance up to rates as high as any prospects would ever want to pay in terms of extra premiums. Reinsurance facilities are available which will, as it is sometimes humorously put in the business, "figure a rate for a one-legged Spanish War veteran with TB." Among those companies that write substandard insurance, there are some that strictly limit the extent to which they will write this type of business. For reasons of management philosophy and administration, they may wish not to have too many rated-up cases on their books even though reinsurance facilities are available for them.

Insurable risks divide into three broad classes: standard, substandard, and preferred. Every company, however, does not use all three classifications. As stated, some companies do not insure substandard risks; probably less than the majority make any distinction between standard and preferred risks. When a distinction is made between standard and preferred risks, it usually is done for competitive reasons and is limited to the continuous-premium Whole Life policy. Many of the companies writing these so-called preferred risk contracts place a minimum on the size of the policy which they accept in this class. The resulting rate differential often is as much a product of expense savings on large policies as of mortality savings on better than average risks.

Extra premium charges as a result of specific diseases, or impairments are almost as old as *modern* life insurance, which may be said to have begun with the establishment of the Equitable Society of England. In 1762, Old Equitable was charging an additional premium to insure applicants who

---

[20] Except, perhaps, an individual on his deathbed.

had suffered from gout, for applicants with hernia, for applicants who had not had smallpox, for applicants with the "female hazard" (women under 50), and for beer retailers.

It was 134 years later, however, before the insurance of substandard lives made its appearance in the United States. In 1896, the New York Life Insurance Company entered the field on an extensive scale following a study of the mortality experience among applicants rejected over the previous 15 years. As a result of this investigation, a measure of the effect of certain impairments on the mortality of a representative group was devised. The company then issued policies written for an extra premium designed to cover the expense of the additional mortality.

New York Life was alone in the substandard field for a considerable period of time, and it was not until the publication of the "Medico-Actuarial" investigation in 1910, a joint project of the Actuarial Society of America and the Association of Life Insurance Medical Directors, that very many companies were willing to issue such policies. Subsequent studies have convinced an increasing number of companies that substandard insurance can be issued on a scientific basis.

There are several methods of rating substandard risks:

(1) *Lien Plan.* Under the Lien plan the standard premium is paid, but less than the full face amount of the policy is payable if death occurs within a certain number of years. This plan is rarely, if ever, used in the United States today; although it finds some employment in Canada and Great Britain.

(2) *Rated-up Age.* The rated-up age plan assumes that, for insurance purposes, the age of the applicant is a given number of years higher than his chronological age. For example, a man 35 years old may be charged the rate for a man 40 years old. The plan is suitable when the extra mortality increases in amount with age, that is, when the difference between the standard rate of mortality and the rate of mortality for the substandard group increases with increasing age. Reference to the death rate per 1,000 in the mortality table will illustrate that the differences in the mortality rates between any given age and the rated-up age increases as the ages involved increase. For example, consider the mortality rates per 1,000 at the following ages.

Age	Mortality Rate per 1,000
30	3.56
35	4.59
40	6.18
45	8.61
50	12.32

The difference in mortality rate at age 30 and at age 35 is 1.03 per 1,000. Betwen ages 35 and 40, it is 1.59; between 40 and 45, the difference is 2.43, and it jumps to 3.71 between ages 45 and 50. Thus although a Rated-up-Age policy carries a level premium, the insured would be in effect paying an increasingly higher extra mortality cost each year the policy is in force. Whereas the Lien plan of rating substandard risks is useful when the extra risk decreases with time, the Rated-up-Age plan is useful when the extra risk increases with time. Actually, however, few impairments increase in mortality rate to the extent of that assumed by the Rated-up-Age plan.

Simplicity is the principal advantage of the Rated-up-Age plan. It is easily understood and requires no special handling of reserves, cash values, and dividends. In spite of its simplicity, the Rated-up-Age plan is not widely used.

(3) *Flat Additional Premium.* Under the Flat Additional premium plan, a constant additional premium is added to the standard rate. For example, one company charges a flat additional premium of $5.00 for window cleaners. This means that although the standard rate for continuous-premium Whole Life insurance at age 30 is $23.80, a window cleaner at this age would be required to pay $28.80. On any policy with a terminal reserve (which includes everything except one-year renewable Term), the Flat Additional premium, like the Rated-up-Age method, provides for an increasing mortality hazard. The extra expense brought on by extra mortality applies only to the net amount at risk; the net amount at risk in any policy with a terminal reserve decreases with the age of the policy. The constant additional premium, therefore, results in a heavier mortality loading each year. Therefore when the extra risk is constant, it is necessary to calculate the average extra risk and load the premium accordingly.[21] Since the mortality exposure decreases faster under an Endowment policy, these policies generally carry a lower extra premium for the same impairment than would be carried by a Term or Whole Life policy.

For the policyholder, the Rated-up-Age plan is more favorable than the Flat Additional premium plan. Part of the extra premium collected under the Rated-up-Age plan is used to build up higher cash values.

(4) *Extra Percentage Tables.* A convenient device for substandard rating is the extra percentage table. This is perhaps the most common method of handling the majority of substandard risks. Applicants are classified on the basis of the extent to which the mortality of their group exceeds standard mortality. Tables of separate premium scales are then evolved which are

---

[21] It is felt that a decreasing extra premium charge would create too many problems of administration.

based on various brackets of percentages. The percentage tables are used to calculate the amount of additional premium which will be added to standard rates for various percentage classifications. The effect of this plan may be the same as that of the Flat Additional premium. In this case, standard values are used for reserves and the entire extra premium is used for additional mortality and other expenses. It is also possible for the percentage tables to be used as a basis for the Increase-in-Age plan. Here a proper new age is assigned the applicant that will correspond in mortality experience as nearly as possible to that indicated by the percentage table. Finally the extra percentage table may be used as the basis for rating without any particular reference to the other two plans. In this event, dividends and nonforfeiture values, as well as the rate, are based on the special mortality indicated by the percentage table.

Extra percentage tables are designated "Table A," "Table B," "Table C," and so on. One company may write only through Table C; another may write policies through Table F, etc. Each table represents a percentage of extra mortality: Table A, 25%; Table B, 50%, and so on.

The accompanying excerpts are illustrative of table ratings as published by one company for two different policy forms.[22]

Extra Premium Per $1,000 of Insurance at Illustrative Ages

Substandard Table A

Age	Continuous Premium Whole Life	10-Payment Life
20	1.63	2.82
25	1.71	3.02
30	1.98	3.25
35	2.42	3.51
45	3.83	4.22
55	6.55	5.63
65	12.01	9.17

Substandard Table P

Age	Continuous Premium Whole Life	10-Payment Life
20	15.67	25.61
25	18.64	27.45
30	22.68	29.71
35	28.25	32.62
45	47.01	42.58
55	85.86	67.77
65	169.26	140.79

Removal of Ratings.   It is common practice for a company to reconsider an extra premium rating for physical impairment at a designated future date in the light of a new medical examination, most frequently paid for by the

---

[22] Separate tables are constructed for different policy forms to reflect the decreasing amount at risk on higher premium forms.

insured. If the physical impairment is shown to have disappeared completely, the extra rating will be removed from the premium.

It could be contended that removal of a rating for an improvement in physical condition is not valid, for it constitutes selection against the company. In the operation of the insurance principle, the individual is a member of a group. The mortality for the group is based on the average of all entrants and assumes as many in the group who will prove to be better than the average as there are those who fall below it. If those whose condition improves are taken out of the group then the average mortality of the group will become higher.

As a practical matter, however, most companies will reconsider ratings and, if extra premiums are clearly no longer justified, will remove them. The technical error brought about is adjusted in advance by allowing a margin of safety in the calculation of the extra charge.

Removal of extra rates based on a hazardous occupation is theoretically sound if the insured has changed his occupation to one less hazardous. It is customary, however, to impose a waiting period before eliminating the extra charge in order to make sure that the change is not temporary. A medical examination may be required to determine whether or not the insured's health was affected by his former work.

Extra premiums are never refunded. The extra premium was charged to pay for the cost of the extra mortality in the group. It has been spent for that purpose and is not recoverable. Since extra premiums once removed cannot be reassessed, companies must give careful consideration before eliminating them.

Substandard insurance is socially desirable since it makes life insurance available to more people than could otherwise obtain it if only standard risks were assumed by the company. Properly rated substandard business does not jeopardize the financial strength of the company. Companies who refuse to write it do so principally to preserve simplicity of operations. It is often said that companies that write no substandard business sometimes are inclined to take at standard rates (rather than to reject it) business that should be rated up.

5. THE EFFECT OF SELECTION ON COST

The foregoing discussion of risk selection reveals clearly its direct effect upon cost. The cost of life insurance is determined by the mortality of the group, interest earnings, and cost of operation. The higher the mortality, the higher is the cost of insurance. Consistently poor risk selection will, in the case of participating insurance, cut dividends, which means that the existing policyholders will pay more for their insurance. In the case of nonpartici-pating policies, consistently poor risk selection cannot alter the contractually fixed premium charged any existing policyholder, but it will result in a dis-proportionate rate increase for new policyholders to make up the loss.

The purpose of selection is integral to rate-making, and upon good selec-tion depends not only adequacy of funds to meet contractual obligations, but also equity among policyholders, in so far as equity can be achieved without violation of the Law of Large Numbers. When selection is poor, the better risks pay part of the cost of the insurance of the poorer risks.

6. LIMITS OF RETENTION

All companies set maximum limits on the amount of life insurance they will retain on an individual life. This amount varies from company to com-pany and, in general, is in some proportion to the size of the company: usually the larger the company, the higher the limit of retention, since large claims affect small companies much more adversely than they affect large companies. The retention limit of small and new companies might be $5,000 or even less, whereas the large company might retain well in excess of a hundred thousand dollars.[23] Not only does the retention limit vary among companies, but also it may vary within a given company according to age of issue, type of policy, and class of risk. For example, for all types of policies issued at standard rates except Term and Modified life, a company might retain $200,000 for applicants between the ages of 21 and 55 but only $130,000 for those 56 to 60, and $100,000 for those between 10 and 20. These retention limits might be cut in half for Term and Modified life policies. For substandard risks, a lower schedule of retention limits might be in effect.

As a practical matter, however, a company does not like to reject an application from a desirable policyholder simply because the amount for which he may wish to insure legitimately is more than the company can handle. If the company refuses to accept the total application, it might end in losing the amount it is willing and eager to insure.

To solve the problem of low net retention limits on the one hand and large applications on the other, life insurance companies resort to a process known as reinsurance.[24]

Under the reinsurance system, a company accepts an application for whatever the amount may be, regardless of whether or not it exceeds the

---

[23] Three of the giant companies have net retention limits of $500,000 and two have limits of $400,000.

[24] Not all companies engage in reinsurance transactions. A few very large companies and some fraternals prefer to limit their writings to those amounts which they feel they can handle themselves.

company's retention limit, and issues the applicant a policy for that amount.[25] It then takes the amount of the policy in excess of its retention limit to a reinsurance company, which agrees to pay that amount when the policy becomes a claim.[26]

For a simple illustration of reinsurance, suppose the retention limit of a company receiving an application for $25,000, is $15,000. The company which has received the application (called the "direct-writing" company) issues a policy in its name for the full $25,000 and then reinsures $10,000, which is the amount in excess of its retention limit. If the policy becomes a claim during its first year, the direct-writing company will contribute $15,000 out of its own funds, while the reinsurer will make up the other $10,000.[27] The payment by the reinsurer, however, is to the company which issued the policy rather than to the policyholder's beneficiary. The full claim check is written by and signed by the company which actually issued the policy to the insured.

As far as the policyholder is concerned, there is no difference between a claim paid wholly by the company issuing the policy and a claim paid jointly by that company and its reinsurer. If the reinsurer fails to pay its share of the claim, the direct-writing company still is responsible to its policyholder. The policyholder himself is not a party to the reinsurance agreement, nor does he usually know anything about it.

An important reinsurance service to many companies is the underwriting advice and assistance given by the reinsurer. In other than highly specialized cases, the underwriting services of reinsurance are far more valuable to small companies than to the large companies which have their own expert underwriting departments.[28]

Types of Reinsurance. There are two types of reinsurance: (1) Yearly Renewable Term and (2) Coinsurance.

Under the Yearly Renewable Term plan the company reinsures only the net amount of risk in excess of its retention limit. The net amount at risk on any policy is the difference between its face value and the value of its terminal reserve. For example, if the terminal reserve on a $25,000 policy cur-

---

[25] There are limits on how much a company will write even with reinsurance. It would be more accurate to say, "A company accepts an application for any amount within reason in view of its underwriting philosophy and the reinsurance facilities it has.

[26] Many companies accept reinsurance, and a number actively solicit it. There are one or two companies which do not sell direct to the public at all but deal only in reinsurance.

[27] The distribution of the claim burden should the loss occur in a subsequent year will depend on how the reinsurance contract is written.

[28] For an excellent discussion of reinsurance practices, see W. M. Howard, *Reinsurance of Life Risks*, Philadelphia, *Journal of the Society of Chartered Life Underwriters*; Fall, 1954.

rently is $5,000, then only $20,000 is at risk. Thus a company with a net retention limit of $15,000 in this case would have to reinsure only $5,000 under the Yearly Renewable Term plan. The reinsurer simply multiplies the net amount at risk under the reinsurance agreement at the beginning of any year by the Yearly Renewable Term rate for the attained age in order to arrive at the reinsurance premium. In the case cited above, if the insured were now age 45, then the reinsurance company would charge the Yearly Renewable Term rate for age 45 and apply it to $5,000 of insurance. Under this plan the amount of the reinsurance decreases annually as the terminal reserve on the policy increases. The Yearly Renewable Term plan of reinsurance is preferred by the smaller companies since it enables them to keep a larger amount at risk on each reinsured contract.

Under the Coinsurance plan, the company reinsures the amount of the original contract that exceeds its retention limit and continues this amount of reinsurance in force throughout the life of the contract. For example, if a company with a net retention limit of $50,000 writes a policy for $75,000, it will reinsure $25,000 and continue this amount of reinsurance in force until the policy becomes a claim. The reinsurer will be entitled to one third of the premium less acquisition and certain other expense allowances and will be liable for a corresponding proportion of claims, non-forfeiture values, and dividends.[29] If a company wishes to reinsure on a coinsurance basis with a carrier not licensed in its state it may use a modified plan whereby the ceding company retains the entire reserve under the contract. Reserves held by nonlicensed reinsurance companies (unlike those of licensed companies) are not allowable as a deduction from the reserve liability of the direct writer.

Reinsurance Agreements. A company may handle each policy on which it needs reinsurance on an individual basis, that is, the company may wait until it has a need for reinsurance, then "shop" for a reinsurer. This method has the distinct disadvantage of delay in issuing the policy to the applicant. The company does not wish to accept the application until it determines whether or not reinsurance will be available. In the meanwhile, of course, the applicant may withdraw and purchase his insurance elsewhere. This method still finds some use in the life insurance business, particularly in

---

[29] Mortality experience under large policies generally is not as favorable as experience under smaller policies. Since dividends usually are based on average mortality experience, reinsurers often find themselves forced to pay dividends in excess of that which is earned by the larger risks which they were reinsuring on a coinsurance basis. Thus, there is a tendency for the reinsurers to prefer the decreasing term basis of reinsurance under which no dividends are guaranteed by the reinsurer.

locating reinsurance for that portion of the excess for which the direct writer does not have regular reinsurance contracts.

Because of the disadvantages of case-by-case "shopping," or "street reinsurance" as it is sometimes called, it is customary to provide for reinsurance facilities in advance of need with contracts or "treaties." There are two types of contracts: *Facultative* and *Automatic.*

The Facultative treaty is only a little more than a step away from individual shopping, for the reinsurer has the right to accept or reject any reinsurance submitted after a survey of each individual case. However, there is the advantage of agreement in advance regarding the form in which risks, premium terms, and other details are to be submitted, eliminating the expense of separate policies for each case since the memoranda data coupled with the terms of the contract serve the same purpose.

The disadvantage of the facultative treaty is that the direct writer does not know, in advance, whether or not it will be able to obtain the reinsurance sought, although by dealing with one reinsurer constantly it comes to know within reasonable limits what that reinsurer will and will not accept.

Treaties may also be Automatic; that is, the reinsurer agrees that it will assume liability automatically for the excess over the direct writer's retention limits (up to a certain maximum) on any application acceptable to the direct writer. Thus the policy may be written at once, and the direct writer knows in advance exactly how much reinsurance it will be possible to obtain. More than one reinsurer may be involved in a given reinsurance treaty in which case the basis for sharing the loss among them will be set forth in the treaty.[30]

The maximum reinsurance acceptable to the reinsurer usually bears a definite proportion to the retention limit of the direct writer.[31] The proportion decreases as the size of the net retention limit of the ceding company increases. To illustrate: With a $10,000 net retention maximum, the direct writer may be able to obtain automatic reinsurance for four times its own limit. It is then able to issue a $50,000 policy without any shopping for reinsurance. If, however, it were to raise its net retention limit to $25,000, the automatic treaty might not provide reinsurance for more than twice the

[30] Reinsurance arrangements involving reciprocal agreements among several companies to exchange reinsurance are known as reinsurance pools. Under such arrangements, each company is given an opportunity to take as much reinsurance as it cedes.

[31] In some situations involving special hazards, a reinsurance company might accept the entire risk if the ceding company does not want any of it. This procedure has made possible the development of adequate exposure units and underwriting experience to handle effectively business which otherwise might have gone uninsured. Cf. Chapter 2 for a review of the essentials of an insurable risk.

amount of the retention limit, making it possible to issue a policy for $75,000 without additional reinsurance facilities.

When an application is submitted for an amount which exceeds the maximum available through automatic treaties, the treaty may provide that the excess be submitted on a facultative basis, or it may be necessary for the direct writer to "shop" for it. Reinsurance treaties also are written in combination, being automatic for standard business and facultative for substandard business.

The use of reinsurance to write amounts in excess of the company's retention limit is not its only use; companies rather commonly reinsure a large part of their substandard business; Double Indemnity and Disability riders often are reinsured. Reinsurance itself may also be reinsured. The process of reinsuring reinsurance is called *Retrocession.*

7. SPECIAL ACCIDENT AND SICKNESS UNDERWRITING PROBLEM

Because intangibles such as habits, environment, financial responsibility, and character have much more bearing on the incidence, size, and duration of A & S claims than on life claims, a higher degree of underwriting is necessary, and some extra attention to the underwriting of A & S is called for here in addition to the general principles as developed earlier in the chapter.

This brief treatment of A & S underwriting will be broken down into four divisions: (1) The persons involved in A & S underwriting; (2) The tools of underwriting; (3) Factors of importance in A & S underwriting; (4) Handling the substandard risk.

Persons Involved. Three persons are involved in underwriting the A & S application: the agent, the lay underwriter, and the medical underwriter or department.

The *agent* is much more important in A & S underwriting than in life. In life insurance, the underwriting function of the agent is little more than being sure of the financial standing of the prospect and watching for obvious fraud. Even in the case of the nonmedical application, his job is hardly more than that of a reporter. Most of the underwriting of life insurance is done in the home office.

In A & S, because of the intangibles that are important to proper underwriting, the agent is actually the primary underwriter. As between him and the home office underwriting department, only he knows, sees, and talks with the applicant. He is in a better position to judge habits and attitudes than is the home office. In fact, A & S underwriting may be said to begin with the agent,[32] a fact it is often hard to get experienced life men who enter the A & S field to understand.

The *lay underwriter* in the home office handles most of the phases of the underwriting. He refers to the medical department only technical points regarding physical condition. The lay underwriter's job is not only to apply known experience and statistical data to the facts revealed by all sources of underwriting information on the application at hand, but also to attempt to evaluate the interrelationship of these facts and to go beyond the statistics into the human element involved.

The *medical department* establishes the underwriting rules, develops the statistics used in underwriting, and passes on technical questions of physical condition referred to it by the lay underwriter.

In general, the home office underwriting department is concerned not only with evaluation upon application but also with re-evaluation at time of renewal. In Commercial forms, such re-evaluation seeks to weed out bad risks, most commonly the moral risk as indicated by excessively frequent claims, unduly prolonged claims, and questionable claims. While the Noncan underwriter cannot cancel such risks, re-evaluation is a source of information for future selection.

Tools of Underwriting. The tools of underwriting, from which the underwriting information is obtained, are the application, information from the agent, the inspection report, physicians' reports, and the medical examination, if any.

The A & S *application* gives the picture of the applicant's occupation, age, sex, health history, etc. These are all prime questions in underwriting, which is the reason they are asked on the application.

Information *from the agent,* facts, impressions, etc., which he may have discovered aside from the questions on the application, are vitally important. As was stated, only the agent has seen and talked to the applicant.

The *inspection report* is disinterested, third-party reporting. The inspector talks to business and social acquaintances of the applicant to confirm details on the application. The inspection report is routine in Noncan and frequent in Commercial applications for the larger or broader coverages.

Physicians' reports are obtained where there is any recent history of medical treatment. The attending physician's report (and, sometimes, hos-

---

[32] A & S underwriting actually begins with the selection of agents. Since an agent solicits business among his natural contacts, the caliber of his applicants will rarely be higher than his own caliber. Underwriting continues through the training and supervision phases of handling agents, also.

pital records) are highly important because there is a vast difference between clinical medicine and insurance medicine, as discussed.

Medical examinations, as stated, are routine for Noncan but usually used only for higher limits of broader coverages in the case of Commercial.

Factors Affecting Underwriting. The chief factors considered in A & S underwriting (listed here in what is not necessarily their order of importance) are physical condition, including health history and the findings of the medical examination, if any; occupation; amount and plan of insurance applied for; other insurance owned; age; sex; financial standing; and character.

Physical condition is obviously important in writing insurance which covers sickness. It is sometimes not understood why it is also important in underwriting accident insurance. While health has little to do with the incidence of accident, it can prolong the disability resulting from accident, or intensify it.

Occupation has a direct bearing on the risk. While the introduction of plant safety devices has reduced the direct occupational hazard in many lines of work, there are still very definite differences in claim experience among occupations.

Each company uses a manual or system of occupational classifications. The A & S rate book carried by the agent lists occupations in alphabetical order and assigns a code to each. Here is an excerpt from a typical Commercial rate book—

AAA *Abstractor,* office duties only
AAA *Accountant*
B   *Acetlyene,* gas plant employee
B   *Acid* plant employee
B   *Actor,* actress, acrobatic, or gymnastic work
AAA *Advertising,* office or sales duties only

Some companies develop their own classification systems and manuals. Probably most companies use one of the systems developed by either the Bureau of Accident & Health Underwriters, New York, or the Health & Accident Underwriters Conference, Chicago, intercompany associations. The Bureau manual contains 14 classifications, coded A through M. The Conference has two manuals, one with 11 classifications and 6,200 listings, coded AA to J, and the other, a simplified classification with 1,380 listings, coded AAA, AA, A, and B.

Noncan occupational classification systems are usually simpler, partly because the higher rate of Noncan is in itself selective, limiting the great bulk of applications to the professional, executive, and white collar classes, and partly because there has never been any real statistical basis for such classifications. An illustrative Noncan classification system is as follows:

1. Office or clerical work in a stable business
2. White collar groups not meeting the requirements for Class 1
3. One-man occupations
4. Skilled manual workers
5. Insurable risks with some occupational hazard.

The agent fills out the application on the basis of the classification applying to the applicant at hand. The home office checks his classification.

Amount and Plan Applied For. The *amount* applied for is important in determining the possibility of moral hazard. Other insurance already owned is also important because the total amount of coverage an individual has can have a bearing on claim experience. Too much principal sum can be a source of future trouble. The line between natural and accidental death is often hard to draw. If the amount of death benefit is substantial, it becomes "profitable" for the question of the type of death to be taken to court. The amount of loss-of-time benefits owned is even more important. If it is sufficient to maintain a standard of living reasonably close to that being enjoyed on earned income, the incentive to get well may be lessened, increasing the duration of disabilities or the benefits may even come to be looked upon as a pension.

As a general rule, many underwriters hold that the maximum safe amount of monthly benefits where earned income exceeds $300 a month is one half of earned income plus $50. Example, if earned income is $500, the maximum benefit should be $300 (1/2 of $500 = $250 + 50). Also, there comes a point at which the disability income available is sufficient to live on comfortably regardless of its percentage in relation to earned income. This is particularly true because of high taxes. A $1,000-a-month disability income free from tax will maintain a very comfortable standard of living for a large family even though the head of the family may have been earning more than twice that amount.

The amount of loss-of-time coverage owned is also susceptible to some subjective evaluation. Assume two men, each earning $10,000 a year. One lives very frugally, far below a $10,000-a-year standard; his children are almost grown; and he has no outside responsibilities. All other things being equal, he would not be as good a risk as the other man who has a higher standard of living (but not in excess of his income), small children, and dependent parents. The first man might have to reduce his standard of living little at all if he had $500 a month, tax free disability income; the second couldn't possibly maintain his standard and keep up with his financial responsibilities on the same amount.[33]

The *plan* applied for is important since some types of plans can be issued to certain impaired risks, whereas others cannot. For instance, sometimes it is considered perfectly proper to issue an accident-only policy where coverage for both accident and sickness could not be issued.

Age affects underwriting because the incidence and duration of disability increase with age. Although for life insurance purposes, mortality rates increase each year beginning with about age eleven, increases in morbidity rates are more by age groupings. For instance, the rate is fairly constant up to age 50, at which time it jumps but remains relatively constant again for the next five or ten years.

Sex is important for two reasons: First, the rate of disability among women is 50% to 100% higher than that for men in the same age brackets. Second, loss-of-time coverages cannot be sold to unemployed women.

Financial standing is indicative of the character of the applicant. Is his credit standing good? Does he evidence integrity in his financial dealings? Is there indication that he "cuts corners" in financial matters—and thus might cut them on claims? Does his financial standing justify the amount of insurance applied for? What is the relation of his earned income to investment income—since loss-of-time insurance is meant to cover earned income?

Character of the applicant is one of the most important yet most intangible underwriting factors. What is his marital history? What are his business ethics? What is his general reputation? Does he show evidence of sufficient moral stamina to stand up in adversity? If not, physical adversity or economic adversity may make him an expensive policyholder.

Handling the substandard case. If the applicant does not fall in what are termed "standard" ranges, one of several things can be done:

(1) He can be declined. The company can refuse to issue him any insurance at all.

(2) He can be issued reduced limits. As a simple illustration, assume the applicant has applied for $400 a month disability benefits but already has $400, or a total of $800, whereas the company's limit of participation is $600. Instead of the $400 applied for, he could be offered $200.

(3) He can be issued a modified plan. As mentioned previously, the company might offer an accident-only policy where it could not offer accident and sickness.

---

[33] This is not meant to imply that the more extravagently a man lives, the better moral risk he is. Note that we said clearly that the second man does not live *beyond* his means. Extravagance is a moral hazard in itself.

(4) He can be offered a longer waiting period. An applicant with a history of severe hay fever who applied for first-day benefits might be acceptable only if the policy contained a waiting period of 30 days before benefits begin for any claim.

(5) He can be offered a waiver. The waiver is a provision attached to the policy excluding the company's liability for a stated condition or conditions. For instance, a prospect with a history of phlebitis might be acceptable standard with a waiver of liability for phlebitis and varicose veins.

(6) He can be offered coverage at an increased rate. This is the common type of substandard underwriting in life insurance but is not common in A & S. However, at least one attempt to work out tables of substandard ratings has been made, and limited experimentation with it is going on. It is complicated by the importance of the intangible factors in claims. While it is possible to compile statistics on the added hazard of certain conditions and, hence, possible to calculate the additional rate that should be charged, it is more difficult to determine what effect any given disability will have on the moral fiber of differing policyholders.

8. SUMMARY

Risk is the basis of insurance, and the reduction of the burden of risk for the individual is the function of the insurance company. All risks cannot be accepted, because not all risks are insurable. Moreover, even as among insurable risks, there may be wide variation in the chance of loss involved. In order to operate on any practical basis and with any practical degree of equity among policyholders, it is necessary for the company to choose from among the risks that may be submitted to it only those that fall within the limits of chance of loss which are assumed in the rate.

The selection of risk has a very direct relation to the cost of life insurance, since the cost of life insurance is made up of three factors: the mortality expense, interest earnings, and the cost of operation. Improperly selected risks will inevitably increase the mortality cost and, hence, the rate. Consistently bad risk selection could, theoretically at least, wreck a company, since it could lead to a greater mortality cost than is allowed for in the premium.

Certain intangibles are more important in underwriting the A & S case than they are in writing the life case; therefore, the process of underwriting will vary somewhat. It is one of getting a complete picture of the factors which affect the risk, analyzing those factors, equalizing the adverse ones by the various methods of handling substandard cases, and attempting to foresee the possibility of future unsatisfactory developments among factors satisfactory at the time of initial underwriting. For example, is there any foreseeable chance that economic conditions affecting the applicant's line of work may change to the extent that what is now a satisfactory relationship between income and coverage will in the future, be drastically altered?

A & S underwriting must also hold in mind that the agent is the primary underwriter, for only he knows and comes face to face with the applicant. It must also hold in mind that statistical evaluation can go only so far because, more than in almost any other form of insurance coverage, the underwriting is dealing with the human factor.

Questions for Class Discussions

1. Why is it necessary that an applicant for life insurance meet certain underwriting standards, whereas there are no selection standards applied by the government under the Social Security Act?
2. Why might an applicant be acceptable to one company yet unacceptable to another?
3. Why is the physical condition of an applicant important in the underwriting of accident insurance?
4. Is the amount of insurance applied for a more important factor in the underwriting of life insurance or disability insurance?
5. What information is needed for the underwriting of life insurance which is not needed for the underwriting of disability insurance? What information is needed for the underwriting of disability insurance that is not needed for the underwriting of life insurance?
6. Why do you suppose that substandard insurance has not developed in the disability insurance field as it has in life insurance? What can disability insurance underwriters do for applicants who are ineligible for standard contracts at standard rates?
7. Your friend Irma has a heart condition so she is not able to buy insurance at standard rates. One agent offers her a policy on a rated-up age plan whereas a second agent offers a policy on a flat additional premium basis. It so happens that the cost to friend Irma in either case would be $35 per $1,000 of insurance. Which plan would you advise her to take? Would any other method of substandard rating be more beneficial to her than either of these two plans?
8. What are the objections to an automatic reinsurance treaty on the part of the reinsurance company? What can a reinsurance company do to offset any disadvantages resulting from an automatic treaty?
9. For what purposes other than coverage for excess liability might reinsurance be used?
10. What are the economic and social benefits derived from reinsurance?

CHAPTER 20

THE TOOLS OF
RATE-MAKING

THROUGHOUT this book, constant reference has been made to rates and reserves. It is only logical to expect that curiosity might have been aroused as to how rates and reserves are computed. If so, this and the next three chapters should be of real interest. If not, perhaps these chapters can create that interest as well as explain the methods involved in computation of premium rates and reserves. These can be fascinating subjects.

As was stated in Chapter 2, the basis of insurance is found in that branch of higher mathematics known as the Theory of Probability. Fortunately for most of its readers, however, this is not a text in mathematics. It does not seek to instruct potential actuaries. Instead, it seeks only to explain basic rate-making principles so that the general student of life insurance will have at least a fundamental knowledge of the "whys" of rate calculation. Such knowledge is important to anyone seeking a broad background in life insurance principles and practices.

Three factors are involved in computing a rate: Mortality, Interest, and Operating Expenses. These three factors may be said to be the tools of rate-making and this chapter is about them.

1. MORTALITY TABLES

The mortality table is used in rate computation as a basis for predicting the probable amount of future claims. It enables the company to estimate within reasonable limits how much it will need to charge to be able to pay all claims as they mature.

479

The mortality table is not, as its form might suggest, the mortality history of a group recorded until there are no longer any survivors. It is, rather, the assembly of a series of relationships between the probable number dying and the number living at any given age. For example, the Commissioners' 1941 Standard Ordinary Mortality Table, commonly called the CSO mortality table, shows the relationships between the probable number dying and the number living at each age from 1 to 100. To illustrate: Of 939,197 people assumed to be living at age 25 the probability is that 2,705 will die before they become 26; of 906,554 living at age 35, probably 4,161 will die before 36; and of 125 living at age 99, probably all of them will die before 100.

In addition, since the mortality table is a series of relationships, the two components may be changed to meet the needs of the user of the table as long as these components are multiplied or divided by identical figures. To illustrate: If the calculation is being made on the basis of only 1/3 as many people living (313,066) at age 25 as shown in the table, probably 902 (1/3 of 2,705) of these individuals will die before they reach 26.

What's in a Mortality Table?   Table 1 is the Commissioner's 1941 Standard Ordinary Mortality Table. It is made up of five columns—"Age," "Number Living," "Deaths Each Year," "Deaths per 1,000," and "Expectation of Life." (Cf. pp. 482 f. for table.)

The "age" column runs from 1 through 99. Why does it stop at age 99? Why not include ages 100 and beyond? According to the table, out of 125 people alive on their 99th birthday, 125 will probably die before they reach 100 years of age. In other words the table states that probably all the people reaching age 99 will die before they reach 100. Since it is presumed that no one will live to be 100 there is no point in extending the table beyond age 99. There are some authenticated cases of people living past age 100, but statistically they are so few that they can be ignored for purposes of rate-making.[1]

The "number living" column starts with a group of one million individuals at age one. Any number, however, could have been used as a starting figure and any age as a starting age. In fact, the Commissioner's 1941 Standard Ordinary mortality table extends to age 0 by increasing the number alive at that age to 1,023,102. The American Experience mortality table (1843–1858) starts with 100,000 individuals at age ten. In 1900 it was extended to age 0.

The figures in the "deaths each year" column are the probable number of people out of the given group at that age who will die before reaching their next birthday. This figure is the other half of the relationship between

---

[1] Annuity tables, which are constructed with different mortality assumptions, extend to age 109.

the number living and the number dying. It is the difference between the figures for two successive ages in the "number living" column since the figures in the "number living" column are reduced each year by the probable number dying during the previous year.

By reducing the "number living" by the "deaths each year" the table makes it easy to determine the probable number of deaths over a period of years out of any starting group. For example, to determine the probable number dying over a five-year period out of 939,197 living at age 25, all that is necessary is to add the number dying at ages 25, 26, 27, 28, and 29—a total of 14,588.

In theory, the "deaths per 1,000" column is similar to the "deaths each year" column. The figures in both of these columns are the "death part" of the living-dying relationship. However, in the "deaths each year" column, the "living part" of the relationship is the *number assumed to be living* at the beginning of the year, whereas in the "deaths per 1,000" column, the living half of the living-dying relationship is always *1,000*.

The final column, "expectation of life" is the average number of additional years which those at any given age can be expected to live. For example, based on the CSO table of mortality, life expectancy at age 97 is 1.08 years. The table shows that there are 1,005 living at the beginning of age 97. Out of this group, 551 will probably die between ages 97 and 98; 329 between 98 and 99; and 125 between 99 and 100. The average age of death of the group is computed as follows:

Number Dying		Age of Death		Aggregate Age
551	×	97.5	=	53,723
329	×	98.5	=	32,406
125	×	99.5	=	12,437
1,005				98,566

The total aggregate age, 98,566 divided by 1,005, the number of individuals in the group, equals 98.08, which is the average age of death for the group. Life expectancy of the group, therefore, is 1.08 years. It should be noted that, contrary to the general impression of a large part of the public, life expectancy does not enter into life insurance premium calculations in any manner.

Constructing a Mortality Table. Possession of any one of the following sets of figures will make it possible to compute the first three columns in a mortality table: (1) The number of people surviving at each age from an original group of individuals. (2) The number of people dying during each age from an original group of individuals. (3) The number of people dying

Table 1. Table of Mortality (1930–1940)
(Ages 1–50)
COMMISSIONERS' 1941 STANDARD ORDINARY

Age	Number Living	Deaths Each Year	Deaths per 1,000	Expectation of Life	Age	Number Living	Deaths Each Year	Deaths per 1,000	Expectation of Life
1	1,000,000	5,770	5.77	62.76	26	936,492	2,800	2.99	41.24
2	994,230	4,116	4.14	62.12	27	933,692	2,904	3.11	40.36
3	990,114	3,347	3.38	61.37	28	930,788	3,025	3.25	39.49
4	986,767	2,950	2.99	60.58	29	927,763	3,154	3.40	38.61
5	983,817	2,715	2.75	59.76	30	924,609	3,292	3.56	37.74
6	981,102	2,561	2.61	58.92	31	921,317	3,437	3.73	36.88
7	978,541	2,417	2.47	58.08	32	917,880	3,598	3.92	36.01
8	976,124	2,255	2.31	57.22	33	914,282	3,767	4.12	35.15
9	973,869	2,065	2.12	56.35	34	910,515	3,961	4.35	34.29
10	971,804	1,914	1.97	55.47	35	906,554	4,161	4.59	33.44
11	969,890	1,852	1.91	54.58	36	902,293	4,386	4.86	32.59
12	968,038	1,859	1.92	53.68	37	898,007	4,625	5.15	31.75
13	966,179	1,913	1.98	52.78	38	893,382	4,878	5.46	30.91
14	964,266	1,996	2.07	51.89	39	888,504	5,162	5.81	30.08
15	962,270	2,069	2.15	50.99	40	883,342	5,459	6.18	29.25
16	960,201	2,103	2.19	50.10	41	877,883	5,785	6.59	28.43
17	958,098	2,156	2.25	49.21	42	872,098	6,131	7.03	27.62
18	955,942	2,199	2.30	48.32	43	865,967	6,503	7.51	26.81
19	953,743	2,260	2.37	47.43	44	859,464	6,910	8.04	26.01
20	951,483	2,312	2.43	46.54	45	852,554	7,340	8.61	25.21
21	949,171	2,382	2.51	45.66	46	845,214	7,801	9.23	24.43
22	946,789	2,452	2.59	44.77	47	837,413	8,299	9.91	23.65
23	944,337	2,531	2.68	43.88	48	829,114	8,822	10.64	22.88
24	941,806	2,609	2.77	43.00	49	820,292	9,392	11.45	22.12
25	939,197	2,705	2.88	42.12	50	810,900	9,990	12.32	21.37

at each age out of the number living at the beginning of the age. The following examples will illustrate how mortality tables are constructed.

Example 1: From an original group of individuals, the number living at the ages tabulated below is:

Age	Number Living	Age	Number Living	Age	Number Living
27	311,231	30	308,204	33	304,762
28	310,263	31	307,107	34	303,506
29	309,255	32	305,961	35	302,186

The first three columns of a mortality table (ages 27 through 34) may be constructed from these data as follows:

First, compute the "deaths each year" column: Since 311,231 individuals were living at the beginning of age 27 and only 310,263 were living at the

Table 1. Table of Mortality (1930–1940) *continued*
(Ages 51–99)

COMMISSIONERS' 1941 STANDARD ORDINARY

Age	Number Living	Deaths Each Year	Deaths per 1,000	Ex-pecta-tion of Life	Age	Number Living	Deaths Each Year	Deaths per 1,000	Ex-pecta-tion of Life
51	800,910	10,628	13.27	20.64	76	287,973	27,651	96.02	6.44
52	790,282	11,301	14.30	19.91	77	260,322	27,071	103.99	6.07
53	778,981	12,020	15.43	19.19	78	233,251	26,262	112.59	5.72
54	766,961	12,770	16.65	18.48	79	206,989	25,224	121.86	5.38
55	754,191	13,560	17.98	17.78	80	181,765	23,966	131.85	5.06
56	740,631	14,390	19.43	17.10	81	157,799	22,502	142.60	4.75
57	726,241	15,251	21.00	16.43	82	135,297	20,857	154.16	4.46
58	710,990	16,147	22.71	15.77	83	114,440	19,062	166.57	4.18
59	694,843	17,072	24.57	15.13	84	95,378	17,157	179.88	3.91
60	677,771	18,022	26.59	14.50	85	78,221	15,185	194.13	3.66
61	659,749	18,988	28.78	13.88	86	63,036	13,198	209.37	3.42
62	640,761	19,979	31.18	13.27	87	49,838	11,245	225.63	3.19
63	620,782	20,958	33.76	12.69	88	38,593	9,378	243.00	2.98
64	599,824	21,942	36.58	12.11	89	29,215	7,638	261.44	2.77
65	577,882	22,907	39.64	11.55	90	21,577	6,063	280.00	2.58
66	554,975	23,842	42.96	11.01	91	15,514	4,681	301.73	2.39
67	531,133	24,730	46.56	10.48	92	10,833	3,506	323.64	2.21
68	506,403	25,553	50.46	9.97	93	7,327	2,540	346.66	2.03
69	480,850	26,302	54.70	9.47	94	4,787	1,776	371.00	1.84
70	454,548	26,955	59.30	8.99	95	3,011	1,193	396.21	1.63
71	427,593	27,481	64.27	8.52	96	1,818	813	447.19	1.37
72	400,112	27,872	69.66	8.08	97	1,005	551	548.26	1.08
73	372,240	28,104	75.50	7.64	98	454	329	724,67	.78
74	344,136	28,154	81.81	7.23	99	125	125	1,000.00	.50
75	315,982	28,099	88.64	6.82					

beginning of age 28 (the end of age 27), then 968 must have died during the year. The process is repeated for each of the other years as indicated below:

Age	Living Beginning of Year		Living End of Year		Deaths During Year	Age	Living Beginning of Year		Living End of Year		Deaths During Year
27	311,231	−	310,263	=	968	31	307,107	−	305,961	=	1,146
28	310,263	−	309,255	=	1,008	32	305,961	−	304,762	=	1,199
29	309,255	−	308,204	=	1,051	33	304,762	−	303,506	=	1,256
30	308,204	−	307,107	=	1,097	34	303,506	−	302,186	=	1,320

Then compute the "deaths per 1,000" column by dividing the number dying during the year by the number living at the beginning of the year, and then multiplying the answer by 1,000. At age 27, 968, the number dying, is divided by 311,231, the number living. This gives .00311231, which represents the chance of death for any one member of the group. When this figure is multiplied by 1,000 it gives 3.11, which is the expected number of deaths from each 1,000 members of the group. This process is repeated for each age group as shown below:

Age	Deaths Each Year	Number Living				Deaths per 1,000	Age	Deaths Each Year	Number Living				Deaths per 1,000
27	968	÷ 311,231	×	1,000	=	3.11	31	1,146	÷ 307,107	×	1,000	=	3.74
28	1,008	÷ 310,263	×	1,000	=	3.25	32	1,199	÷ 305,961	×	1,000	=	3.92
29	1,051	÷ 309,255	×	1,000	=	3.40	33	1,256	÷ 304,762	×	1,000	=	4.12
30	1,097	÷ 308,204	×	1,000	=	3.56	34	1,320	÷ 303,506	×	1,000	=	4.35

The following are the completed first three columns of the table:

Age	Number Living	Deaths Each Year	Deaths per 1,000	Age	Number Living	Deaths Each Year	Deaths per 1,000
27	311,231	968	3.11	31	307,107	1,146	3.74
28	310,263	1,008	3.25	32	305,961	1,199	3.92
29	309,255	1,051	3.40	33	304,762	1,256	4.12
30	308,204	1,097	3.56	34	303,506	1,320	4.35

The "expectation of life" column is omitted since it cannot be computed unless the table is completed to the age at which all members of the group are dead. In the case of the CSO mortality table, this age would be 100.

Example 2: Raw data used in the construction of a mortality table usually are collected by age classes. From the following raw data, several steps are necessary to complete a section of a mortality table (from ages 35 through 40).

Age	Number Living	Number Dying	Age	Number Living	Number Dying
35	30,000	138	38	63,000	346
36	25,000	124	39	54,000	313
37	75,000	386	40	63,000	391

First, list the ages. Next, figure the "deaths per 1,000." The process would be identical to that used in the example above.

Age	Deaths Each Year	Number Living				Deaths per 1,000	Age	Deaths Each Year	Number Living				Deaths per 1,000
35	138	÷ 30,000	×	1,000	=	4.6	38	346	÷ 63,000	×	1,000	=	5.5
36	124	÷ 25,000	×	1,000	=	5.0	39	313	÷ 54,000	×	1,000	=	5.8
37	386	÷ 75,000	×	1,000	=	5.1	40	391	÷ 63,000	×	1,000	=	6.2

In constructing the table it is possible to assume any number as the number living at age 35; consequently 100,000 will be used. If 100,000 were living on their 35th birthday and 4.6 per 1,000 died before reaching 36, then 460 would be the probable number of deaths during the year out of 100,000, age 35. The probable number surviving to age 36 would be 99,540. The probable number dying during age 36 would be 498 (99,540 × 5.0). The process would be continued until the calculation of the number dying for age 40. The completed table is below.

Age	Number Living	Deaths Each Year	Deaths per 1,000	Age	Number Living	Deaths Each Year	Deaths per 1,000
35	100,000	460	4.6	38	98,537	542	5.5
36	99,540	498	5.0	39	97,995	568	5.8
37	99,042	505	5.1	40	97,427	604	6.2

Use of Mortality Tables. The following examples will illustrate how the mortality table is used as a tool for computing expected claims under life insurance contracts.

Example 1: How much should be charged (excluding interest and expenses)[2] for a one-year Term policy issued at age 35 assuming the CSO mortality table is used? This table shows that if 906,554 individuals were insured at age 35, 4,161 would probably die before they reached age 36. Furthermore, if each of these individuals was insured for $1,000 the expected claims would amount to $4,161,000. The proportionate share of these claims to be borne by each policyholder would be $4.59 ($4,161,000 ÷ 906,554), assuming, of course, that enough will be insured so the law of averages will operate to give an actual mortality approximately equal to the tabular.

Example 2: How much should be charged (excluding interest and expenses) for a $1,000 pure Endowment at 65 issued at age 30?[3] If 924,609 pure Endowments were sold, the probable number of claims would be 577,882. Since each claim would amount to $1,000, total claims would be $557,882,000. The cost per policyholder would then be $557,882,000 ÷ 924,609 = $603.37.

The first step in computing the premium for any type of insurance or annuity contract is to tabulate the amount of expected future claims. A mortality table is absolutely essential for this task.

Mortality tables also are important in the valuation of reserve liabilities and for the calculation of nonforfeiture values. Companies might, for ex-

---

[2] The role of interest and expenses in premium computations is deferred until later in the chapter.

[3] A pure Endowment at 65 is a policy which pays nothing if one dies before reaching age 65 and pays the face if one lives until age 65.

ample, use the CSO table for reserve valuation but a less conservative one for premium computation and nonforfeiture values. Especially is this true in figuring premiums for a nonparticipating policy where a dividend cannot be used to refund excess premiums resulting from ultraconservative safety cushions which have been built into the table or which have resulted from general improvement in mortality experience. Reserves are discussed in Chapter 23.

Safety Factor. Not only must a mortality table be based on adequate statistical data, but also it should provide a safety factor to allow for unpredicted increases in the death rate and for temporarily adverse mortality fluctuations.[4]

In some of the older mortality tables, a safety factor was assured by using data gathered from a period which had a higher mortality rate than the present or than was expected in the future.

The newer tables, however, are first computed on the actual expected mortality based, of course, on relatively recent data, to which is added a safety margin computed mathematically. For example, the following are the death rates per 1,000 from the CSO mortality table, first without the safety factor and then with that factor added.

Age	No Factor	With Factor	Age	No Factor	With Factor
20	1.40	2.43	50	10.05	12.32
25	1.74	2.88	55	15.24	17.98
30	2.28	3.56	60	23.21	26.59
35	3.15	4.59	65	35.37	39.64
40	4.53	6.18	75	81.23	88.64
45	6.69	8.61	85	179.54	194.13

Annuities. On first thought one might assume that a life insurance mortality table would work as well for annuities as it does for life insurance. Careful further analysis of the question, however, would reveal three reasons why this is not true.

First, the safety factors which are built into a life insurance mortality table, as mentioned previously, would have the opposite effect if the table were to be used for annuity rates, in that it would result in the establishment of an unsafe rate rather than produce a margin of safety.

Second, while a decreasing trend in mortality rates is a factor of safety for life insurance rate computation, it tends to make the table unsafe for annuities. If a life insurance policyholder lives longer than is expected, the

---

[4] Insurance companies, for example, witnessed a temporary mortality fluctuation during the influenza epidemic of 1918–1919.

company has a gain from mortality; [5] however, for every year annuitants live longer than the table predicts, the company has a loss from mortality.

For example, in 1940 the life expectancy at birth was 63.6 years. By 1950, it had risen to 68.4 years. Although some of this increase was brought about by an improvement in infant mortality, analysis shows that more than one half of it was a result of a decline in the death rate beyond age 25. Life expectancy at age 65 also has increased during this period from 12.1 to 13.0 for white males and from 13.6 to 15.3 for white females.

Third, in an annuity table, companies find it necessary to distinguish between the sexes. Mortality rates for females are much lower than for males. Since women are heavy buyers of annuities, companies want to take this mortality differential into consideration. This difference usually is handled by figuring male rates at an age four or five years younger than for females, avoiding the necessity of two tables.[6]

Until very recently, life insurance mortality tables have grouped the sexes together. As a result there has been no sex differential in life insurance [7] rates, except in some Retirement Income insurance policies.

Fourth, mortality among the people who purchase annuities is lower than that among those who purchase life insurance—for at least two reasons: (1) They are a select group as to environmental conditions. Single-premium annuities can be purchased only by people with capital, and the possession of capital often indicates that the owner has had the opportunity to enjoy superior environmental conditions and better medical care. The annuity income continues these environmental advantages to the group, thus creating a better mortality experience among them in general.[8] (2) People are not likely to buy annuities unless they are in good physical condition. This is not necessarily the case in life insurance, even though companies do make an effort to select carefully and charge extra for substandard applicants.

Annuity mortality tables will, therefore, show fewer deaths and a greater

---

[5] This gain is not a profit but is either (a) anticipated in advance in calculating a rate, (b) returned in the form of policy dividends, or (c) both.

[6] For example, a man age 30 would take the same death rate as a woman age 34 or 35.

[7] As women become more important holders of life insurance, the time will probably come when life insurance companies will recognize the inequity of charging women the same as men for life insurance while charging them more for annuities. In fact, just as this is being written, a major reinsurance company has reduced rates for women and an issuing company has followed suit, perhaps establishing a trend.

[8] It is often said that the way to live to a ripe old age is to purchase an annuity. While the longer life of annuitants is largely a result of the preselection described, there is an element of validity in the statement. The ownership of an annuity not only assures better environment and health care but also relieves the mind of one of the most ruinous of all worries of later years—whether money will last or whether the individual will have to become an object of charity, public or private.

expectation of life at any given age than will mortality tables used to compute rates and values for life insurance.

Types of Mortality Tables. Mortality tables are of four specific kinds: general, basic, select, and ultimate.

A general mortality table is one based on population statistics. The Census Bureau of the United States Government prepares, periodically, a group of mortality tables showing mortality rates of the country among males and females, among white and colored, among rural and city dwellers, and among native and foreign-born in various sections of the country. These tables are not used in rate-making since life insurance companies select risks rather than insure all applicants. Consequently, mortality experienced by the companies should be less than that stated in the general population tables. Table 2 shows the difference. If poor risks were not rejected, adverse selection would produce mortality experience higher than the general table.

General tables are aggregate tables as distinguished from select and ultimate tables.

Table 2. Deaths per 1,000

Age	CSO Basic * (Without Safety Factor)	1939–41 CENSUS	1949–51 CENSUS
20	1.40	2.17	1.35
30	2.28	3.07	1.79
40	4.53	5.24	3.68
50	10.05	10.76	8.76

* These mortality figures are based on mortality statistics for the period 1930–40. Were they based on the 1939–41 period used in the census figures quoted above for those years, there would be even greater disparity, since mortality experience is improving. Compare the 1939–41 census mortality figures with those of 1949–51. This comparison indicates clearly a large decrease in the death rate. A mortality table based on life insurance company experience in these years would show a lower death rate.

A basic table is one based on insurance company experience without the inclusion of a safety factor. Since 1934, a group of major companies has maintained a continuous mortality investigation on the basis of their combined experience. The statistics so obtained are used periodically by the mortality committee of the Society of Actuaries to construct basic tables. They are used also by company actuaries to construct tables to serve as standards with which they can compare their own company's experience. Both select and ultimate tables are prepared. Select mortality rates are provided each year for the preceding year. Ultimate mortality statistics are provided in five-year groups for policies in force for more than 15 years. In addition to select and ultimate mortality data for ordinary insurance, mortality investigations are made of the experience on juvenile ordinary policies,

policies of large face amounts, group life insurance, aviation, and when applicable, war. The main purpose of these investigations, and the resulting tables, is to study mortality trends and to serve as standards of comparison of mortality experience among companies. Since frequent changes in the mortality tables used for premium calculations, reserve computations, and nonforfeiture values are neither practical nor necessary,[9] such changes are made only at long intervals.

A select mortality table shows the rate of mortality among a group of recently selected lives, at age of entry and for each year thereafter. Two groups of insured individuals, both age 35, would not be expected to experience the same rate of mortality if one group was insured ten years ago and the other was insured last year. The second group will still show the effect of selection based on physical, occupational, and moral standards. However, when these same two groups reach age 40, five years hence, their mortality rates should be identical. It is estimated that the beneficial effects of selection wear off in five years.

Table 3 is an example of a select table. Notice that the table shows age (35), (35)1, (35)2, and so on, rather than age 35, 36, 37.[10] When the five-year select period has expired, the age will be age 40, not (35)5. At that age, the benefit of selection is assumed to have worn off, and select data are replaced with ultimate experience. Ages (36) through (36)4 are also shown for comparison.

An ultimate mortality table shows the rate of mortality at various ages for lives beyond the select period; that is, it shows the rate of mortality after the effect of selection has worn off. The mortality rate for a group age 35 on an ultimate table will show the expected mortality under policies which have been in force for more than five years. The CSO table, which has been

---

[9] Not necessary because, as mentioned, gains from mortality are (a) anticipated in calculating the rate; (b) returned as dividends; or (c) both. Not practical because the cost of computing new rates and issuing new policy forms and rate manuals based on them is high. Professional critics of life insurance—meaning people who make money out of yellow-journalism attacks on the business—often seek to make a point of the fact that the mortality table in use is "out of date." Although by definition these critics are correct in fact and always will be, they are not correct in their interpretation of these facts. Since a mortality table is a compilation of past experience, it is out of date from the date of the earliest statistic used in it. Practically speaking, life insurance rates are always based on current mortality since they are set with an allowance for anticipated gains from mortality. The Guertin Committee, which compiled the CSO table to replace the old American Experience Table, was appointed to study the need for a new table from a public relations standpoint as much as from an equity standpoint. Aside from public relations, the importance of a new table has far more significance in the regulation of reserves than in the computation of a premium rate.

[10] (35)1 is the symbol to show that the age of issue was 35 and that one year has elapsed.

Table 3. American Men Select Table

(Ages 35 & 36)

Age	Number Living	Number Dying	Deaths per 1,000
(35)	100,000	316	3.16
(35)1	99,684	428	4.29
(35)2	99,256	454	4.57
(35)3	98,802	474	4.80
(35)4	98,328	514	5.23
(36)	100,000	323	3.23
(36)1	99,677	441	4.42
(36)2	99,236	469	4.73
(36)3	98,767	495	5.01
(36)4	98,272	539	5.48

in general use since 1948, is an ultimate table, with a margin for contingencies.

Development of Mortality Tables. "Traditionally, the actuary has interested himself primarily in the measurement of the span of human life and the determination of the probabilities of death and survival over specific periods. From the first crude table of mortality constructed by Halley, of Comet fame, through the speculations on the possibilities of a mathematical law resulting in the empirical formulae of Gompertz and Makeham, to the modern actuarial techniques, we have seen a constant and continuing search for information which would reduce the risk of error in the making of estimates as to future mortality experience. Accuracy in these estimates is necessary in our business to reduce the risk of financial loss to the insurer and to increase the degree of fairness with which the losses insured against are apportioned among those insured." [11]

Four mortality tables have been used in the United States for Ordinary insurance. Until 1900, the actuaries' table, more precisely known as the English Seventeen Offices Table of 1843, was commonly used. This table was based on the experience of British companies.

After 1900 and until 1948, The American Experience Table was generally used. This table is chiefly the work of Sheppard Homans, who used as his basis the mortality statistics of a period from 1843 to 1858 taken from the experience of the Mutual Life Insurance Company of New York, of which he was at one time actuary. The table was first published in a schedule attached to an act passed by the legislature of the State of New

---

[11] Alfred N. Guertin, *Actuarial Trends in the Life Insurance Field*, University of Connecticut, *Insurance Lecture Series*; Spring, 1952.

York on May 6, 1868. It was the first table based upon American insured lives.[12]

Substandard or extra premium insurance for policyholders of impaired health has been made possible largely through a study of the experience on policies issued by some 39 companies between 1885 and 1927. This study was made by the Actuarial Society of America and the Association of Life Insurance Medical Directors through what is known as the "Medico-Actuarial Mortality Investigation."

The American Men's table, the American Women's table, the Canadian Men's table, and the Canadian Women's table were published in 1918 and were based on the work of the Actuarial Society of America with the co-operation of the American Institute of Actuaries and the National Convention of Insurance Commissioners. Experience in them covers the years 1900–1915 on policies issued from 1843 to 1914. These tables show more favorable mortality experience, especially at younger ages, than is reflected in the American Experience table. A comparison of the tables reveals the rapid strides made in mortality reduction over the period. While these latter tables were recognized and authorized by the Insurance Department of Canada and the provinces, they never came into general use in the United States. They were used by a few companies in the late 1930's and in the 1940's. The smaller companies in particular objected to the use of these newer tables for reserve valuation and successfully fought attempts to require their use. Companies did not want to use them because their use would have decreased the safety margin in rates and have led to increased reserves and surrender values.

Another modern mortality table is one prepared in 1939 by a committee of the National Association of Insurance Commissioners, known as the "Guertin Committee." [13] The table is known as "Table Z" and is an empirical table based upon the mortality experience of major companies, excluding a select period of five years, from 1924 to 1934. It was never intended for use by companies, but was constructed to provide a standard for comparative purposes.

The most modern mortality tables in use today are the Commissioners 1941 Standard Ordinary (CSO) and the 1941 Commissioners Standard In-

---

[12] For many years the use of this table was under attack. The principal charge was that it was not only old and out of date but was based upon the experience of only one company and the judgment of only one actuary. See Footnote 9, this chapter, for a discussion of these charges.

[13] Named after Alfred Guertin, chairman of the committee. See next paragraph.

dustrial tables, adopted by most states as the basis for reserves and non-forfeiture values in the mid-1940's.[14]

The CSO table was compiled by the Committee to Study the Need for a New Mortality Table of which Alfred Guertin, then Actuary for the New Jersey Insurance Department, was chairman. The committee was appointed in 1936 as a committee of the National Association of Insurance Commissioners. The table was based on mortality experience of a large group of companies between 1930 and 1940, and is weighted to give an adequate safety margin to companies which use it. Except at very low ages, it is similar to the American Men's table.

The 1941 Standard Industrial table is based on the mortality statistics of the Metropolitan Life Insurance Company from 1930 to 1940 and is also weighted to give an added margin of safety. It soon replaced the Standard Industrial table of 1907.

2. INTEREST

Two assumptions, which necessitate consideration of interest, are made in the computation of premium rates for life insurance: (1) Premiums will be paid at the beginning of the year. (2) Claims will be paid at the end of the year.

The first assumption is accurate because the first premium must be paid before the policy goes into force; and unless each of the following premiums is paid when due, the policy will not continue as originally written but, instead, will be placed on one of the nonforfeiture options.

The assumption that claims will be paid at the end of the year, however, is not true to fact. Actually, insurance companies pay their claims promptly upon completion of necessary forms. They realize that death creates costs that must be paid before the end of the policy year, and that widows and

---

[14] There were many efforts to encourage the development and adoption of a new mortality table long before the development of the CSO tables. The opponents, however, had always been successful in blocking the moves. The chief arguments for a new table were (1) the American Experience Table was out of date. (2) It did not represent the average of all companies. (3) A new table would show the fallacy of the contention that companies were overcharging by using the old tables. (4) The public demanded a new table. The principal objections as to a new table were (1) the present table was good enough so there was no need in going to the expense of developing a new one. (2) A newer table might create serious problems for new companies since it might result in higher reserves. (3) A new mortality table might give less margin for expenses under New York and Wisconsin laws since it will give lower net premiums. (4) A new table might cause stricter selection of risks which would not be in the public interest. (5) Lower net premiums resulting from new mortality tables might cause the public to demand lower gross premiums. For a good discussion of arguments over the desirability of a new mortality table and other matters relating to the history of mortality tables, see R. Carlyle Buley, *A Study in the History of Life Insurance*, New York, Appleton-Century-Crofts, Inc., 1953.

children do not wish to fast for the sake of simplifying actuarial computations. Despite this practice, the assumption is used to simplify calculations, and allowances may be made in the loading for gross premium to offset interest losses resulting from the assumption.

Since premiums are paid at the beginning of the year and claims are assumed to be paid at the end of the year, companies have the use of net premiums for at least one full year. These funds are invested and earn interest. Consequently, in rate computation, this interest must be taken into consideration.

Types of Interest. There are two types of interest: simple and compound.

Simple Interest. Under simple interest, the interest is paid to the investor each year as it is earned, and the investor has the problem of reinvesting it if he so desires.

For example, if $100 is invested at 2% simple interest, the earning is $2 a year and is actually paid to the investor. The amount of interest also is $2 in each of the following years. As a result the amount of interest earned in four years is four (number of years) times $2 (amount of interest per year) or $8.

Compound Interest. Under compound interest, the interest earned each year is added to the principal and reinvested for the next year. In this way, the principal constantly increases each year by the amount of the interest earned during the preceding year. Consequently, as the size of the principal increases each year so does the amount of interest earned each successive year increase.

For example, if $100 is invested at 2% *compound* interest, the return is $2 the first year. During the second year, interest is earned not just on the principal of $100, but also on the previous interest earning of $2 which has been reinvested. Thus, the second year the interest earned would be $2.04. During the third year, the interest would be $2.08 (2% of $104.04) and $2.12 in the fourth year. For the four years the total interest earned would be $8.24. This compares with $8 earned at *simple* interest.

Table 4 shows the value of $1 invested at 2% compound interest for the years indicated.

Present Value. Compound interest tables show how much one dollar at a given rate of interest will accumulate to at some specified future date. Present value tables show the reverse; that is, they show how much (assuming a given rate of compound interest) must be on hand now in order to accumulate to $1 at a specified date in the future.

For example, at 2% compound interest in order to have $100 at the end

Table 4. Amount of $1 at Compound Interest

Year	2%	Year	2%	Year	2%
1	1.0200	16	1.3728	31	1.8476
2	1.0404	17	1.4002	32	1.8845
3	1.0612	18	1.4282	33	1.9222
4	1.0824	19	1.4568	34	1.9607
5	1.1041	20	1.4859	35	1.9999
6	1.1262	21	1.5157	36	2.0399
7	1.1487	22	1.5460	37	2.0807
8	1.1717	23	1.5769	38	2.1223
9	1.1951	24	1.6084	39	2.1647
10	1.2190	25	1.6406	40	2.2080
11	1.2434	26	1.6734	41	2.2522
12	1.2682	27	1.7069	47	2.2972
13	1.2936	28	1.7410	43	2.3432
14	1.3195	29	1.7758	44	2.3901
15	1.3459	30	1.8114	45	2.4379

of one year, $98.04 must be invested. This figure cannot be found by simple subtraction. It might seem at first glance that since at 2%, $100 will earn $2 in a year's time, the present value of $100 due a year from now will be $100 − $2 or $98. The fallacy of this method of determining present values will be recognized at once if $98 is multiplied by 2%. This computation will yield only $1.96 interest. Consequently, the sum of the principal ($98) and the interest earned ($1.96) is only $99.96, not $100. The present value of a dollar due one or more years from now is found by the following formula: $P = \dfrac{S}{(1+i)^n}$. P is present value, S is the sum (in this case $1), i is the compound rate of interest, and n is the number of years. Thus the present value of $1 due five years from now at 2% is: $P = \dfrac{1}{(1+.02)^5}$ or .9057. Just as in the practical use of algebra no one ever stops to calculate a logarithm (or a square root), even though he might have been taught how to go about the calculation, so no one in the practical use of present values ever stops to calculate them as has been done here. Instead tables of present values are available. Table 5 shows the present values of $1 at 2% due in from one to 45 years.

Use of Interest in Rate Computation. The method of figuring the cost of two different types of insurance contracts, if interest and expenses are excluded, has already been explained. Interest can now be put into the picture. Under the assumption that claims are paid at the end of the year and premiums are paid at the beginning of the year, it becomes necessary to determine how much is needed at the beginning of the period, assuming a given rate of compound interest, in order to have enough to pay claims as they become due.

Table 5. Present Value of $1 at Compound Interest

Year	2%	Year	2%	Year	2%
1	.9804	16	.7284	31	.5412
2	.9612	17	.7142	32	.5306
3	.9423	18	.7002	33	.5202
4	.9238	19	.6864	34	.5100
5	.9057	20	.6730	35	.5000
6	.8880	21	.6598	36	.4902
7	.8706	22	.6468	37	.4806
8	.8535	23	.6342	38	.4712
9	.8368	24	.6217	39	.4619
10	.8203	25	.6095	40	.4529
11	.8043	26	.5976	41	.4440
12	.7885	27	.5859	42	.4353
13	.7730	28	.5744	43	.4268
14	.7579	29	.5631	44	.4184
15	.7430	30	.5521	45	.4102

Example A: How much (excluding expenses) should be charged assuming 2% interest for a one-year Term policy issued at age 35?

Reference to the CSO mortality table shows that if 906,554 individuals are insured, probably 4,161 will die before they reach age 36. In other words, if each of these individuals has a $1,000 policy, the probable amount of future claims for the group would be $4,161,000. The process thus far is identical with that used in the mortality examples; however, to take interest into consideration, it is necessary to find the present value of these future claims; that is, to find out how much money is needed now to have $4,161,000 at the end of the year. To find this figure, multiply the amount of future claims ($4,161,000) by the present value of $1 for one year at 2% compound interest (.9804). This computation gives $4,079,444.40 for the present value of future claims. To obtain the cost per policyholder, divide the present value of future claims by the number buying the policy (906,554). The answer is $4.50, which is the net premium for a one-year Term policy at age 35, CSO, 2%.

The above computation is shown below in tabular form.

Age	Number Claims	Amount of Insurance	Future Claims	Years of Interest	Present Value Factor	Present Value of Future Claims
35	4,161	1,000	$4,161,000	1	.9804	$4,079,444.40

Present Value of Future Claims		Number of Policies		Premium
$4,079,444.40	÷	906,544	=	$4.50

Example B: How much should be charged (excluding expenses) for a $1,000 *pure* Endowment at age 65 issued at age 30, assuming 2% compound interest? If 924,609 pure Endowments are sold, probable number of claims will be 577,882. Since each of these policies is for $1,000, the total amount of future claims would be $577,882,000. Next, find the present value of these future claims by multiplying this figure ($577,882,000) by the present value of $1 at 2% compound interest for 35 years (.5000). The reason for the 35-year discount period is that the premiums are to be collected at age 30 but benefits will not be paid out until age 65 (end of age 64). As a result, they will be earning interest for 35 years. This computation gives a present value of future claims of $288,941,000. Next, divide the present value of future claims by the number buying the policy (924,609) to get the single premium charged each policyholder. The result is $301.69.

The above computation is shown below in tabular form.

Age	Number Claims	Amount of Insurance	Future Claims	Years of Interest	Present Value Factor	Present Value of Future Claims
30	577,882	$1,000	$577,882,000	35	.5000	$288,941,000

Present Value of Future Claims		Number of Policies		Premium
$288,941,000	÷	924,609	=	$301.69

Importance of Interest in Premium Computations. The use of correct interest assumptions is of utmost significance in both the fixing of premiums and the valuation of reserves. Life insurance rates are established for the life of the contract and cannot be changed at any time. Participating companies can select a conservative rate and return as dividends to policyholders any excess interest earned. Nonparticipating companies must select an interest rate more nearly in line with expected earnings since no dividends are available to policyholders to offset excessive charges based on ultraconservative estimates. Competition forces Nonpar writers to keep their rates in line with the net rates (gross premium less dividends) of Par Companies.

It is no easy task to predict accurately the course of future interest rates. In the past 25 years, net interest earnings of life insurance companies have fluctuated from a high of 5.05% to a low of 2.88%. Currently, companies are earning about 3½% before income tax.[15]

It is common to try to discount the effect of declining interest rates on the cost of life insurance with the assumption that lower interest is offset by

---

[15] Companies have been able to adjust to the decline in the interest rate over this period by (1) reducing the assumed rate of interest on new policies; (2) decreasing the interest assumptions for purposes of reserve valuation on old policies; and (3) earnings on surplus and gains on mortality have been available to offset interest losses on contracts guaranteeing higher interest than is currently being earned.

improved mortality. For example, the net level premium figured on the old American Experience table at 3% for a continuous-premium Whole Life policy issued at age 30 is $18.28. A change to the new CSO table, with the same interest rate, would decrease the premium to $15.90, a drop of slightly over 13%. If the interest assumption on the CSO table were then reduced one third (from 3% to 2%) it would more than wipe out the savings produced by the change in mortality assumptions. When it is remembered that interest earnings of life insurance companies declined from 5.18% in 1923 to a low of 2.88% in 1947, it should be clear that it would take a drastic improvement in mortality to offset entirely the loss in interest. On the higher premium limited-payment and Endowment policies, the relative importance of interest as compared to mortality assumptions is even more pronounced.

3. EXPENSES

The premium computations illustrated in earlier paragraphs provided for enough money to pay expected claims. They allowed nothing for the cost of doing business. They were *net* premiums [16] and were computed taking only two factors into consideration: mortality and interest. The $4.50 computed in Example A is the *net* premium for a one-year Term policy issued at age 35. Likewise, the $301.69 computed in Example B is the *net* premium for a pure Endowment at 65 issued at age 30.

Only a subsidized insurance plan can operate on the basis of net premiums. Even a nonprofit carrier would have to allow for some expenses for handling the insurance. The expense addition is known as loading [17] and is spread among all policies. Also included in the loading is an allowance for taxes and for the creation of various contingency funds to meet adverse fluctuations in interest earnings and mortality experience. The loading when added to the net premium gives the *gross* premium, which is the premium quoted in the rate books of the companies.

The technique of loading involves three objectives: (1) to cover all expenses and contingencies, (2) to have the funds when needed, and (3) to spread the cost equitably among the policyholders. Loading is actually a problem in cost accounting rather than actuarial science.

Items of Loading. There are four main items of loading.

Immediate Payment of Death Claims. One of the items which might be

---

[16] The term "gross" and "net" as used here must be distinguished from the same terms as applied to (a) participating premiums before and after dividends or (b) premiums including and excluding commissions.

[17] This term is trade argot and disliked by some who consider that it connotes to the public an unnecessary addition to the premium. However, it is so widely used in all discussions of rates that there is no good way to avoid it.

added to the net premium in arriving at the gross premium is a charge to offset the loss resulting from the fact that death claims are paid throughout the year rather than at the end of the year as was assumed in the net premium computation.

Relying on large numbers, it is safe to assume that death payments will be reasonably uniform during the year, and, therefore, that on the average all death claims will be paid six months before the end of the year, or about six months earlier than is assumed in calculating net premiums. This means that in any year there will be a loss to the company of approximately one half of one year's interest on the funds used to pay mortality costs for that year. Allowance may be made for this loss by loading it into the gross premium, or it may be considered in the computation of the net premium by making assumptions which are truer to fact.

Acquisition Costs. By far the largest of all expenses to be considered are those in connection with putting new business on the books. For example, on a $1,000 policy issued at age 25, total costs of acquisition might be in the neighborhood of $30, while costs in connection with the administration of the policy after the first year may drop to $2.25 or $2.50. Acquisition costs could be loaded into the premium in the year incurred. However, this plan would involve a premium differential, making the first year's premium substantially higher than subsequent premiums. While such a plan is used occasionally, particularly in the case of mutual assessment and some A & S policies, it is usually not considered the best practice from the standpoint of life insurance selling. Companies do not like to emphasize the high acquisition cost nor does the public like to pay heavy first-year premiums. Hence costs of acquisition are amortized over the total premium-paying period, and a level amount is added to each year's premium.[18]

General Overhead Loading. All expenses designated as general overhead in any type of business—clerical salaries, furniture and fixtures, rent, management salaries, etc.—must be considered. The allocation of these costs is unaffected by the size of the premium, probably little affected by the face value of the the policy, but most likely is affected by the number of policies.

Loading for Contingency Funds. Once a level-premium legal reserve policy has been issued, the premium cannot be changed, even should unforeseen contingencies make the rate in the policy inadequate.[19] Assessment

---

[18] The difference between the amount charged against the first-year reserve and the amount of premium left after acquisition costs and death claims are paid is charged against surplus. The surplus account is built back out of subsequent premiums.

[19] A participating premium can be increased in effect, by paying a smaller policy dividend, but only up to the amount of the gross participating rate.

insurance plans can take care of such contingencies, theoretically, by levying an extra charge against the policyholders. Legal reserve companies, however, allow for the possibility of increased expense or decreased earnings by establishing various contingency funds.

The amount of loading for contingency funds will vary in relation to the type of policy and the amount at risk, that is, the difference between the cash value and face value of the policy. Contingency loading usually constitutes an amount per $1,000 of face value which, while varying among different types of policies, is constant within any one type.

Methods of Loading. In discussing acquisition costs, contingency funds, and general overhead loading, three classifications into which expenses of operation may fall have been considered. (1) Expenses which vary with the size of premium. (2) Expenses which vary with the face value of the policy. (3) Expenses which are constant regardless of size of premium or face value. The first problem in loading is to determine into which of the three categories each type of expense falls.[20]

Three methods of allowing for expenses are: (1) Add a constant amount to each policy for each $1,000 of face value. (2) Add to the net premium a certain percentage of that premium. (3) Add to the net premium a loading which is computed from a complicated combination of both of these.

Obviously it would be inequitable to lump all operating expenses and divide by the number of policies in force, since each policy does not contribute equally to company expenses. Just so it would be inequitable to assess all loading in proportion to the size of the premium or the face value of the policy. Hence, the system of loading used by any one company is a combination of a percentage of premium, percentage of face value, and a flat sum. In addition, there are necessary modifications to prevent inequalities between high age and low age policies.

As can be expected, the system of loading used by any one company will usually vary considerably from that of other companies,[21] and even the system of loading used by any given company for the calculation of present rates may not be the same as was used to calculate rates in the past, nor the same as may be used to calculate rates in the future.

Problems of Loading. There is a difference between the problems involved in determining the loading on participating policies and those involved in calculating the loading for nonparticipating policies. In the case of the latter, the company must attempt to figure more accurately the ex-

---

[20] A recent development is to separate policies of large amounts and to reduce the loading percentage on them. Reduced rates for large policies seem to be a coming change.
[21] Even though techniques among companies vary, results obtained are almost the same.

penses that will be involved, since once a policy has been issued at a given rate, that rate cannot be changed. However, in the case of participating policies, unless inequities and inadequacies in loading are far more serious than even mediocre actuarial ability might produce, these inequities and inadequaces can be adjusted by varying the dividend scale.

Term insurance also presents a special loading problem. An additional loading is usually charged against it under any system to take care of the initially adverse selection, to cover the cost of any renewal and conversion privileges, and to offset the fact that Term policies usually show the least gains from favorable mortality.[22]

There are special problems involved in calculating the loading for Industrial insurance since the premium is to be paid on a weekly rather than an annual basis and is to be collected at the door rather than mailed to the company. Additional loading must be included to cover these expenses.

Various technical formulas and loading systems attempt to solve these special problems. Any explanation of the processes involved in these solutions must go into theory of cost accounting and are outside the scope of this text.

Expense Ratios.   There is often an attempt, especially in competitive selling, to use a comparison between the expense ratios of different companies to indicate economy of operation. The expense ratio is essentially a relationship between operating expenses and premiums. Comparisons imply that if the ratio of actual expenses to total premiums is low, economy of operation is indicated.

Such comparisons are invalid because the statements of loading may contain figures arrived at on such differing bases as to render them useless for the purpose of comparing operating economy. Moreover, since acquisition costs are such a large part of loading, the company writing a large amount of new business—generally a desirable development, since the operation of the insurance principle depends upon the constant addition of new exposure units—will tend to show a higher percentage of incurred expenses to total premiums than will the company not writing a large volume of new business.

Expense ratios indicate the degree of accuracy with which the company has estimated its expenses, not the economy of operation. For example, if

[22] Among applicants for Term will be lumped all those who are suspicious of their health but can get by the medical examiner. Also, the man whose health fails after the policy is issued will be more likely to convert Term to a permanent policy plan than will be the man whose health remains sound. Hence, from these factors result adverse initial selection and slighter mortality gains in Term.

two companies had the same expenses and one used a higher estimate for loading, that company would have a lower expense ratio.

Actually, the cost of company operation and, hence, the size of the total loading factor in any gross premium, is held about as low as is humanly possible—and "humanly" is intended in the literal sense, for there are extravagances or waste somewhere in the operation of almost every company. They occur because human beings are not perfect, and they appear in varying degree in any large organization—insurance or otherwise—regardless of careful, capable, and sincere management.

4. SUMMARY

Three tools are needed to compute rates for life insurance—mortality, interest, and expense.

The purpose of mortality tables is to assist in predicting future claims. These tables can be computed from any one of three different sets of data: (1) the number living at each age from an original group; (2) the number dying at each age from an original group; and (3) the number dying each year out of the number living at the beginning of the year. After actual mortality rates are computed, a safety factor is added to allow for unpredicted changes in the future. There are four types of mortality tables—general, basic, select, and ultimate. The tables are used in estimating the present value of future claims and for reserve computations. The table commonly used today is the Commissioner's Standard Ordinary, which is an ultimate table.

In rate-making, three important assumptions are made: (1) premiums are paid at the beginning of the year; (2) claims are paid at the end of the year; and (3) that there will be a large enough number of exposure units so that actual mortality will approximate tabular.

Accurate compound interest assumptions are important in rate-making. Interest assumptions are used to find the present value of future claims. This figure when divided by the number insured is the net single premium for the policy.

There are two types of premiums: gross and net. The gross premium is the net premium plus loading. Loading covers four general items: (1) loss from immediate payment of death claims, (2) acquisition costs, (3) general overhead costs, and (4) contingency funds. Some of the expenses vary with the amount of the premium. Others vary with the amount of the insurance. Still others are constant, and depend only upon the number of policies issued.

There are three methods of loading: (1) a percentage of net premium,

(2) a constant amount per face value, and (3) a combination of the first two. The latter is the most equitable and is the one used by most companies.

The next chapter deals in the methods of determining the net level premium of life insurance and annuity contracts.

Questions for Class Discussion

Deferred until the end of Chapter 21.

CHAPTER 21

COMPUTATION OF
PREMIUMS

ALTHOUGH the vast majority of life insurance policies is purchased on a level premium basis, computation of a premium rate [1] begins with the computation of the net single premium. The net annual level premium is then figured from the net single premium. The two must be mathematically equivalent.

This chapter will first summarize the steps required in calculating the net single premium and the application of these steps to the computation of rates for the three basic forms of life insurance policies and for annuities. Then it will consider the problem of translating single premiums to level premiums. Finally, premiums for Accident and Sickness insurance are discussed.

1. NET SINGLE PREMIUMS

The net single premium of any life insurance policy is the equivalent of the present value of all expected future claims under the policy figured according to a mortality table and based on a given interest assumption, usually 2% or 2½%. For example, if 1,000 people of a given age are insured for $1,000 for a period of five years and ten are expected to die at the end of the first year; 11 at the end of the second; 12, the third; 13, the fourth, and 14, the fifth, a fund of $56,375 at the beginning of the period (assuming a 2% interest return) will be just enough to meet all claims expected during the term of the agreement. The cost for each of the 1,000 participants will be $56.38 per policy (56,375 ÷ 1000).

[1] Technically, a "rate" is the cost per $1,000; a "premium" is the total of the "rates" for the number of $1,000's insured by the policy.

Here is how this works out. The $56,375 collected in advance will earn $1,128 during the first year.[2] At the end of the year a total of $10,000 will be paid out in death claims, leaving $47,503 to be invested throughout the second year. This earns $950. After paying $11,000 in claims, $37,453 is available for investment the third year, and earns $749. Claims payments of $12,000 at the end of that year leave $26,202 to earn $524 interest during the fourth year. After subtracting $13,000 for claims, $13,726 is available to earn interest during the fifth year. This fund invested at 2% will amount to $14,000 at the end of the year, which is the exact amount needed to pay estimated claims at that time.

The question now is how was this figure of $56.38 computed? In Chapter 20, the use of mortality tables and interest assumptions in rate-making was described. The application of these tables and interest assumptions to specific problems can now be reviewed. The mortality assumptions to be used in the following pages are those contained in the 1941 CSO table. Remember that in actual practice, however, companies might not use the CSO table but instead they may use mortality assumptions that are more in line with their own needs. Nevertheless the use of the CSO 1941 assumption here does serve to illustrate the principle involved. The interest assumption used in this chapter is 2%. Here again, companies vary as to the interest assumptions employed. Some use 2¼%, others, 2½%, and still others might compute rates on the basis of a 3% assumption. But again the 2% assumption used here is sufficient to illustrate the principle involved.

Steps in Calculating Net Single Premium. Ten steps are involved in computing a net single premium:

1. Determine what constitutes a claim
   a. Living benefits
   b. Death benefits
   c. Combination of living or death benefits
2. Determine when claims are paid
   a. Beginning of year
   b. End of year
   c. During year
3. Determine the number of insureds
4. Determine the ages to be covered (that is, the duration of the policy)
5. Determine the probable number of claims per year
6. Determine the value of claims per year
7. Determine the number of years of interest involved and find the present value of a dollar for each of these periods
8. Determine the present value of the claims for each year

---

[2] Remember the assumption that premiums are paid in advance and claims are paid at the end of the year.

9. Determine the present value of all future claims
10. Determine the net single premium (present value of future claims divided by number assumed to be buying the policy)

Each of these steps requires additional explanation:

Step 1. Determining what constitutes a claim: Two types of contingencies are covered by life insurance: living and dying. The annuity is an example of coverage for the contingency of living for it pays only so long as the insured lives.[3] Term insurance is an example of coverage for the contingency of dying, for it pays only if the insured dies during the term of years insured.[4] In addition, certain types of life insurance policies pay if the insured lives to the expiry of a designated number of years *or* if he dies prior to that time. The Endowment policy is an example of the combination of living or death claim.

Step 2. Determine when claims are paid: Claims may be paid at the beginning of the year, at the end of the year, or any time during the year. For example, ordinary annuities pay claims at the end of the year; an annuity-due pays them at the beginning of the year. Life insurance policies pay claims as incurred. When claims are paid at the beginning or the end of the year, interest calculations can be exact. When they are paid at any time during the year, such accuracy is not possible. Therefore, the premium is calculated on the assumption that death claims will be paid at the end of the year.

Before the calculation of a rate for any policy form can begin, the amount of claims expected and the time of their payment must be known.

Step 3. Determine the number of insureds: As was discussed in Chapter 2, insurance operates by combining a large enough group of individual exposures to make the loss predictable under the Law of Large Numbers. The premium charged each individual in the group is his share of the group loss. Therefore, to calculate a premium, the group loss must be determined. In computing the premium it is assumed that the group insured is the number living as shown on the mortality table for the age at which the policy is issued. For example, in computing the rate for a Term policy to be issued at age 27, 933,692, the number living at that age (on CSO) is assumed to be the number in the group. Actually the group could contain any number of insureds sufficient to give effect to the Law of Large Numbers. CSO tabular assumptions are made for convenience since mortality experience can be ascertained without additional computations.

---

[3] The fact that some annuities have a cash or installment value after death does not alter this statement, as will become apparent in the calculation of an annuity rate.

[4] The Whole Life policy also is an example for it pays the face value only in the event of death. The cash values are not actually living "insurance" benefits as such but result from the level premium process. See Chapter 23.

Step 4. Determine the ages to be covered (that is, the duration of the policy): For example, a five-year Term policy issued at age 27 covers ages 27, 28, 29, 30, and 31.

Step 5. Determine the probable number of claims per year: If the number insured is assumed to be the number living at the age of entry, then the number of *death claims* each year must be taken from the deaths per year column for that year in the mortality table and for each succeeding year within the policy period. The number of *living claims* (if the policy covers that contingency) will be the figure in the number living column of the mortality table.[5]

Step 6. Determine the value of claims per year: Since life insurance rates are quoted in terms of $1,000 of coverage, the number of claims per year (Step 5) is multiplied by $1,000.

Step 7. Determine the years of interest involved and find the present value of a dollar for each of these periods: The calculation here depends on the time at which claims are to be paid. If they are to be paid at the end of the year, then the funds for first-year claims will earn one year's interest; those for the second year will earn two years' interest; etc. If claims are to be paid at the beginning of the year, funds for first-year claims will earn no interest; those for second-year claims will earn one year's interest; and so on. The present value of a dollar for each of these periods can be ascertained from a present value table.

Step 8. Determine present value of claims for each year: Multiply the amount of the claims for each year covered by the present value of $1 compounded annually for the number of years interest will be earned on the funds which have been earmarked to pay for the claims expected in each of those years. For instance, the funds earmarked to pay the claims at the end of the first year will be multiplied by the present value of $1 at the assumed rate of interest for one year; funds for the second-year claims will be multiplied by the present value of $1 compounded for two years; etc.

Step 9. Determine the present value of all future claims: The computation here is merely the sum of the present values of claims for each of the years insured.

---

[5] Whether the number of living claims will be the number living at the end of an age year or the beginning of the next age year depends on the time of claim payment. If claims are to be paid at the beginning of the year, the number living column for that age year is used; if they are to be paid at the end of the year, the number living column for the next year is used. For instance, at age 27, living claims paid at the *beginning* of the year will be taken from the number living column for age year 27. If they are to be paid at the *end* of the year, then living claims for age 27 will be the number living column as of age year 28.

Step 10. Determine the net single premium: The net single premium is the present value of all future claims divided by the number living at the age of entry.

How each of these ten steps is involved in calculating the net single premium for Term, Whole Life, Endowment, and Annuity policies can now be illustrated.

Net Single Premium for Term. The net single premium for a $1,000 five-year Term policy issued at age 25 is calculated as follows:

1. What constitutes a claim? Death.

2. When are claims to be paid? Although they are paid during the year, they are assumed to be paid at the end of the year.

3. How many are to be insured? 939,197 (number living at age 25).

4. What are the ages covered? Twenty-five through 29 (five years).

5. How many claims per year? Age 25: 2,705 claims; age 26: 2,800 claims; age 27: 2,904 claims; age 28: 3,025 claims; age 29: 3,154 claims.

6. What is the amount of claims per year?

Age (a)	Number Claims (b)	Amount of Insurance (c)	Amount of Claims (b × c)
25	2,705	$1,000	$2,705,000
26	2,800	1,000	2,800,000
27	2,904	1,000	2,904,000
28	3,025	1,000	3,025,000
29	3,154	1,000	3,154,000

7. How many years of interest? Since the assumption is that claims are paid at the *end* of the year, the following are the number of years of interest: age 25, one year; age 26, two years; age 27, three years; age 28, four years; age 29, five years.

The present value of $1 at 2% for each of the number of years involved is: one year, .9804; two years, .9612; three years, .9423; four years, .9238; five years, .9057.

8. What is the present value of the claims for each year?

Age (a)	Amount of Claims (b)	Years of Interest (c)	Present Value of $1 (d)	Present Value of Claims (b × d)
25	$2,705,000	1	.9804	$2,652,000
26	2,800,000	2	.9612	2,691,000
27	2,904,000	3	.9423	2,736,000
28	3,025,000	4	.9238	2,794,000
29	3,154,000	5	.9057	2,857,000

9. What is the present value of *all* future claims? $13,732,000

10. What is the net single premium of a five-year Term issued at age 25?

$$13,730,000 \div 939,197 = \$14.62$$

Whole Life Policies. A Whole Life policy is essentially a Term policy which covers for the life of the insured rather than for a limited period. To abbreviate the illustration, the net single premium for a $1,000 Whole Life policy issued at age 92 will be calculated.

1. What constitutes a claim? Death.

2. When are claims paid? Although they are paid during the year, they are assumed to be paid at the end of the year.

3. How many are to be insured? 10,833 (number living at age 92).

4. What are the ages covered? 92 until death (assumed to be age 99 under the CSO mortality table).

5. How many claims per year?

Age 92 — 3,506 claims	Age 96 — 813 claims
Age 93 — 2,540 claims	Age 97 — 551 claims
Age 94 — 1,776 claims	Age 98 — 329 claims
Age 95 — 1,193 claims	Age 99 — 125 claims
	Age 100 — 0 claims

6. What is the amount of claims per year?

Age (a)	Number Claims (b)	Amount of Insurance (c)	Amount of Claims (b × c)
92	3,506	$1,000	$3,506,000
93	2,540	1,000	2,540,000
94	1,776	1,000	1,776,000
95	1,193	1,000	1,193,000
96	813	1,000	813,000
97	551	1,000	551,000
98	329	1,000	329,000
99	125	1,000	125,000
100	none		none

7. How many years of interest? The years of interest are shown in step #8 for ages 92 through 99, the year when all members of the group are assumed to be dead.

8. What is the present value of claims per year?

Age (a)	Amount of Claims (b)	Years of Interest (c)	Present Value of $1 (d)	Present Value of Claims (b × d)
92	$3,506,000	1	.9804	$3,437,000
93	2,540,000	2	.9612	2,441,000
94	1,776,000	3	.9423	1,674,000
95	1,193,000	4	.9238	1,102,000
96	813,000	5	.9057	736,000
97	551,000	6	.8880	489,000
98	329,000	7	.8706	286,000
99	125,000	8	.8535	107,000
100	none			none

9. What is the present value of *all* future claims? $10,272,000

10. What is the net single premium for a Whole Life policy issued at age 92?

$$\$10,272,000 \div 10,833 = \$948.21$$

A more realistic Whole Life policy would be one issued at age 25 rather than at age 92. So that this figure will be available for use in computing a net level premium, the following is an abbreviated table showing the calculations of a net single premium for a Whole Life issued at age 25.

Age	Amount of Claims	Years of Interest	Present Value of $1	Present Value of Claims
25	$2,705,000	1	.9804	$2,652,000
26	2,800,000	2	.9612	2,691,000
27	2,904,000	3	.9423	2,737,000
28	3,025,000	4	.9238	2,795,000
29	3,154,000	5	.9057	2,857,000
95	1,193,000	71	.2451	292,000
96	813,000	72	.2403	195,000
97	551,000	73	.2356	130,000
98	329,000	74	.2310	76,000
99	125,000	75	.2265	28,000

Present value of future claims $422,276,000

$422,276,000 ÷ 939,197 = $449.61, the net single premium for a Whole Life issued at age 25.

Endowment Policies.   The net single premium for a $1,000 Endowment at 65 issued at age 55 is computed as follows:

1. What constitutes a claim? Combination: Claims are paid to those dying before age 65 and to those living at age 65.

2. When are claims paid? Although the death claims are paid during the year, they are assumed to be paid at the end of the year. The living claims are paid at the end of the endowment period.[6]

3. How many are to be insured? 754,191

4. What are the ages covered? Fifty-five through 64 for death claims, and to age 65 for the survival claims.

5. How many claims per year?

Age 55 – 13,560 claims	Age 60 – 18,022 claims
Age 56 – 14,390 claims	Age 61 – 18,988 claims
Age 57 – 15,251 claims	Age 62 – 19,979 claims
Age 58 – 16,147 claims	Age 63 – 20,958 claims
Age 59 – 17,072 claims	Age 64 – 21,942 claims

Age 65 – 577,882 claims (survival)

---

[6] If the policy reads Endowment at age 65, then the living claims are paid to those living at age 65. If the policy is a 20-year Endowment, for example, the living claims are paid to those living at the end of 20 years, or the *beginning* of the 21st year.

6. What is the amount of claims per year?

Age	Number Claims	Amount of Insurance	Amount of Claims
55	13,560	$1,000	$13,560,000
56	14,390	1,000	14,390,000
57	15,251	1,000	15,251,000
58	16,147	1,000	16,147,000
59	17,072	1,000	17,072,000
60	18,022	1,000	18,022,000
61	18,988	1,000	18,988,000
62	19,979	1,000	19,979,000
63	20,958	1,000	20,958,000
64	21,942	1,000	21,942,000
65	577,882	1,000	577,882,000

7. How many years of interest? Since the *death* claims are assumed to be paid at the *end* of the year, the years of interest are as shown in Step 8 for ages 55 through 64. However, since the *living* claims at age 65 are paid at the *beginning* of the year, there will be no interest earned during that year. As a result, only ten years of interest is earned the 11th year, as is shown in Step 8.

8. What is the present value of the claims for each year?

Age (a)	Amount of Claims (b)	Years of Interest (c)	Present Value of $1 (d)	Present Value of Claims (b × d)
55	$13,560,000	1	.9804	$13,294,000
56	14,390,000	2	.9612	13,832,000
57	15,251,000	3	.9432	14,371,000
58	16,147,000	4	.9238	14,917,000
59	17,072,000	5	.9057	15,462,000
60	18,022,000	6	.8880	16,004,000
61	18,988,000	7	.8706	16,531,000
62	19,979,000	8	.8535	17,052,000
63	20,958,000	9	.8368	17,538,000
64	21,942,000	10	.8203	17,999,000
65	577,882,000	10	.8203	474,037,000

9. What is the present value of all future claims? $631,037,000

10. What is the net single premium for an Endowment at age 65, issued at age 55? $631,037,000 ÷ 754,191 = $836.71.

Life Annuity Certain. The net single premium for a $1,000 Life Annuity, five years certain, issued at age 90,[7] is computed as follows: [8]

1. What constitutes a claim? Claims are paid annually for five years dead or alive and thereafter for each year so long as the annuitant is alive.

---

[7] This unrealistic age of issue is assumed for purposes of simplicity; i.e., to reduce the number of calculations involved.

[8] The CSO table will be used in this illustration, although more realistic results would be obtained by using an annuity mortality table. Nevertheless, the principle is the same regardless of the table used, and the principle is all that is of interest here.

2. When are claims paid? End of the year.

3. Number to be insured? 21,577.

4. Ages covered? Ninety until death.

5. Number of claims per year? The full number buying the policy (21,577) will be paid claims during the first five years, only those living thereafter will continue to be paid claims. Thus:

Age 90 – 21,577 claims	Age 94 – 21,577 claims
Age 91 – 21,577 claims	Age 95 – 1,818 claims
Age 92 – 21,577 claims	Age 96 – 1,005 claims
Age 93 – 21,577 claims	Age 97 – 454 claims
Age 98 – 125 claims	

6. Amount of the claims per year?

Age	Number Claims	Amount of Insurance	Amount of Claims
90	21,577	$1,000	$21,577,000
91	21,577	1,000	21,577,000
92	21,577	1,000	21,577,000
93	21,577	1,000	21,577,000
94	21,577	1,000	21,577,000
95	1,818	1,000	1,818,000
96	1,005	1,000	1,005,000
97	454	1,000	454,000
98	125	1,000	125,000

7. Number of years of interest? Since claims are paid at the *end* of the year, the following are the years of interest.

Age 90 1 year	Age 93 4 years	Age 96 7 years
Age 91 2 years	Age 94 5 years	Age 97 8 years
Age 92 3 years	Age 95 6 years	Age 98 9 years

8. Present value of claims per year?

Age	Amount of Claims	Years of Interest	Present Value of $1	Present Value of Claims
90	$21,577,000	1	.9804	$21,154,000
91	21,577,000	2	.9612	20,740,000
92	21,577,000	3	.9423	20,332,000
93	21,577,000	4	.9238	19,933,000
94	21,577,000	5	.9057	19,542,000
95	1,818,000	6	.8880	1,614,000
96	1,005,000	7	.8706	875,000
97	454,000	8	.8535	387,000
98	125,000	9	.8368	105,000

9. Present value of *all* future claims? $104,682,000.

10. What is the net single premium for a Life Annuity, five years certain, issued at age 90? $104,682,000 ÷ 21,577 = $4,851.55 (net single premium)

Temporary Life Annuity Due. The net single premium for a five-year Temporary Life Annuity Due of *one dollar* issued at age 25 is computed as follows:

1. What constitutes a claim? Claims are paid annually to those alive.
2. When are claims paid? Beginning of the year.
3. Number to be insured? 939,197.
4. Ages covered? Twenty-five through 29.
5. Number of claims per year? Age 25, 939,197; age 26, 936,492; age 27, 933,692; age 28, 930,788; age 29, 927,763.
6. Amount of the claims per year?

Age	Number of Claims	Amount of Insurance	Amount of Claims
25	939,197	$1	$939,197
26	936,492	1	936,492
27	933,692	1	933,692
28	930,788	1	930,788
29	927,763	1	927,763

7. Number of years of interest? Since claims are paid at the *beginning* of the year, the following are the years of interest: age 25, none; age 26, one year; age 27, two years; age 28, three years; age 29, four years.
8. Present value of claims per year?

Age	Amount of Claims	Years of Interest	Present Value of $1 at 2%	Present Value of Payments
25	$939,197	0	1.0000	$939,197
26	936,492	1	.9804	918,137
27	933,692	2	.9612	897,465
28	930,788	3	.9423	877,082
29	927,763	4	.9238	857,067

9. Present value of all future claims? $4,488,948.
10. What is the net single premium for a five-year Temporary Life Annuity Due issued at age 25? $4,488,948 ÷ 939,197 = $4.78.

As will become apparent in the next section, the present value of an Annuity Due of $1 is a useful device for converting single premiums into level premiums.

2. NET LEVEL PREMIUMS

Few people are able to purchase life insurance on a single premium basis, and even fewer are willing to do so. They want to budget their insurance into a series of annual payments, either for life or for a limited number of years. Broadly speaking, two budget plans are available for the purchase of life insurance: (1) the natural premium plan, and (2) the level premium plan.

Natural Premium Plan. The natural premium is one that increases each year with the increase in the rate of mortality. The net natural premium is the mortality cost per policy for each year, discounted for one year. Accordingly, the net natural premiums each year for a five-year Term policy of $1,000 issued at age 25 would be:

First year	$2.88 × .9804 =	$2.82
Second year	2.99 × .9804 =	2.93
Third year	3.11 × .9804 =	3.05
Fourth year	3.25 × .9804 =	3.19
Fifth year	3.40 × .9804 =	3.33

If this were a 30-year Term policy, the rate would rise to $17.98 × .9804, or $17.62 per $1,000, in the 30th year. The one-year discount factor is used in each of the above computations because, under the natural premium plan, the full natural rate is paid each year. Because premiums are paid at the beginning of the year and claims are assumed to be paid at the end of the year, more than one year's discount is never involved.

The vast majority of the insuring public not only does not like to pay for its insurance with a large single premium, but also it does not like a premium that increases each year. Thus, for five-year Term, the majority would prefer a net annual level premium rather than a net lump sum single premium of $14.62 or a net premium starting at $2.83 and progressing to $3.33. A net level premium becomes even more desirable in the case of long-term policies, for then single premiums are much higher and natural premiums advance to an almost prohibitive level. For example, the natural premium at age 70 is almost 17 times that at age 30.

Level Premium Plan. The level premium plan is a method by which the cost of insurance is paid for evenly over the period during which premiums are paid. Thus, instead of an increasing premium, the payment will be the same throughout the premium-paying period. This means that the insured must contribute more than the actual cost of the insurance in the earlier years of the policy and less than the actual cost of the insurance in the later years. The overpayments in the earlier years are held at interest to meet claims when they fall due and represent an obligation of the company to the policyholder. They are carried on their financial statements as legal reserves.[9] On a $1,000 continuous-premium Whole Life policy issued at age 20, the net level premium will be in excess of the natural premium until age 50, at which time the natural premium jumps ahead of the level premium.

Importance of Mortality and Interest in Net Level Premiums. Earlier in this chapter, a single premium of $56.38 was computed for a $1,000 five-

---

[9] See Chapter 23.

year Term policy based on given mortality assumptions. What would be the equivalent five-year level premium for this contract? What about a simple division of $56.38 by 5, or $11.28 a year? If the 1,000 living at the beginning of the period paid $11.28 each, the company would collect $11,280. Invested at 2%, it will amount to $11,505.60 at the end of the year. From this fund $10,000 will be paid out in claims. To the $1,505.60 left, a total of $11,167.20 will be contributed by the 990 alive at the beginning of the second year. This fund will accumulate to $12,926.26 at the end of the year from which $11,000 will be paid in death claims. The 979 people alive at the beginning of the third year will contribute $11,043.12 to bring the fund to $12,969.38, which at 2% will accumulate to $13,228.77 by the end of the year. Death claims amounting to $12,000 will reduce this fund to $1,228.77 but premiums paid by the 967 people alive at the beginning of the fourth year will bring the fund back to $12,136.53. Interest earned on the fund during the year will further increase it to $12,379.26 but this will be insufficient to meet the $13,000 in claims payable at the end of the year. Claims due the fifth year amount to $14,000; yet only $10,761.11 will be collected in premiums from the 954 still alive.

Why is there a shortage? Why will a level premium obtained by dividing a single premium by the number of premium-paying years yield an insufficient premium?

A simple division of this type ignores the two important factors in rate-making: interest and mortality.

In computing the net single premium, it was assumed that the company would collect the entire cost of the insurance in advance and thereby earn interest on it until paid out in claims, one, two, three, four, and five years hence. Under the level premium plan, only part of the cost of insurance is collected in advance so that there will be a substantial loss in interest on the unpaid portion. Allowance must be made in level premium computations to offset this loss.

The net single premium computation assumes also that the full premium is paid by everyone, whether he lives or dies. The level premium, however, is collected only from those who are alive on each succeeding premium due date. Therefore, there is a mortality loss with respect to premiums collected which also must be offset in level premium computations.

Neither the interest nor the mortality loss was taken into account in the above computation. How can allowance be made for these factors?

According to the mortality assumptions, 1,000 people will pay premiums the first year; 990, the second; 979, the third; 967, the fourth; and 954, the fifth. It is assumed that 2% interest will be earned. What will be the equivalent single premium if each annual premium is one dollar?

(1) Year	(2) Number Paying	(3) Amount Paid (Col. 2 × $1)	(4) Years of Interest	(5) Present Value of $1 at 2%	(6) Present Value of Payments (Col. 3 × 5)
1	1,000	$1,000	0[10]	$1.0000	$1,000.00
2	990	990	1	.9804	970.60
3	979	979	2	.9612	941.01
4	967	967	3	.9423	911.20
5	954	954	4	.9238	881.31
		Total Present Value			$4,704.12

The equivalent net single premium per person is $4,704.12 ÷ 1,000 or $4.70. Thus a lump sum of $4.70 paid in advance is equivalent to $1 paid at the beginning of the year for each of five years.

With this information it becomes simple to determine the level premium which is equivalent to a single premium of $56.38. The problem can be set up as one involving simple proportion: An annual level premium of one dollar bears the same ratio to the single premium just computed ($4.70) as the level premium to be determined (x) bears to the single premium for the policy in question ($56.38). In this problem, there are three knowns and one unknown. The equation appears as follows: $1 : \$4.70 = x : \$56.38$. Working out the equation, it is found that $\$4.70 \, x = \$56.38$. Dividing $56.38 by $4.70, x is found to equal $12. Therefore, a level annual premium of $12 rather than the $11.28 previously shown is the equivalent of a single premium of $56.38 for the policy involved. How this checks out is shown in Table 1.

The Annuity Due as a Concept of the Net Level Premium. Note the similarity between the computation of the net single premium equivalent of an annual premium of one dollar for five years and that computation on page 512 of the single premium of a five-year Temporary Annuity Due of $1. Actually, a level premium is an annuity payable to the company by the policyholder. The premium payments for a 20-year Term or for a 20-Pay Life represent a Temporary Life Annuity for 20 years, whereas the net level premium for a continuous-premium Whole Life policy is a life annuity payable by the policyholder to the company. Since it is the practice to calculate rates based on payment of the premium at the *beginning* of each premium period [11] the net level premium is an annuity-due. It will be remembered

---

[10] Since the first premium is due at the beginning of the year, no period of discount is involved.

[11] It was once almost universally the practice to compute premiums on an annual basis; that is, the premium was the amount due at the beginning of each policy year. Premiums payable at more frequent intervals were, under this method of calculation, merely installments on the total amount due. Calculation of the premium on an annual basis has one adverse public-relations effect: It means that premium installments not yet paid at the time of the death of an insured must be paid and therefore, are deducted from the

Table. 1. Validation of the Net Level Premium of $12

Number Paying Premium	Amount Paid per Person	= Total Amount Paid	+ Balance from Preceding Year	Amount Invested	+ Interest at 2%	= Total Amount Available for Claims	− Claims for Year	= Balance
1,000	$12	$12,000	0	$12,000	240	12,240	10,000	2,240.00
990	12	11,880	2,240	14,120	282.40	14,402.40	11,000	3,402.40
979	12	11,748	3,402.40	15,150.40	303.01	15,453.41	12,000	3,453.41
967	12	11,604	3,453.41	15,057.41	301.15	15,358.56	13,000	2,358.56
954	12	11,448	2,358.56	13,806.56	276.13	14,082.69	14,000	82.69*

* Results from rounding off figures.

that, by definition, an annuity-due is one on which "claims" are to be paid at the beginning of the period rather than at the end.

Previously, the net single premium for a Temporary Life Annuity Due of $1 for five years at age 25 was found to be $4.78. This means that, at age 25, payment of $4.78 is the mathematical equivalent of the survivors paying $1 at the beginning of each of the five years from age 25 to 29 inclusive. This is the value of $1 paid yearly after deducting mortality and interest losses. Consequently, if the net single premium for a five-year policy issued at age 25 (CSO 2%) is $4.78, it follows that the net level premium is $1. If the net single premium were $500, the level premium would be $500 \div 4.78$ or $104.60.[12]

To find the net level premium for any policy, the net single premium is divided by the present value of an annuity-due of one dollar for the premium-paying period. It should be stressed that the annuity-due is for the term of years *during which the premium is to be paid.* This may or may not be the same as the *period insured.* For instance, a Whole Life policy may call for continuous premiums or premiums may be limited to ten, 20, 30 (or any number) years; to age 65; to age 85; or the like. If it is a continuous-premium policy, then the present value of a whole life annuity-due is used. If it is a 20-pay policy, the present value of a temporary life annuity-due for 20 years is used.

Steps in Calculation of Net Level Premium. The following are the steps in calculating a net level premium:

1. Determine the net single premium for the policy.

2. Determine the present value of an annuity-due for the premium-paying period.

3. Determine the net level premium by diving Step 1 by Step 2.

To illustrate the steps, the net level premium for a limited payment and a continuous-payment policy are computed as follows:

Limited-Payment Life Policies. What would be the net level premium of a five-pay Whole Life policy issued at age 25?

---

claim. For instance, on an annual premium calculation, if an insured who is paying quarterly premiums dies in the first quarter, three premium installments are still due. However, few beneficiaries understand the mathematics involved and so often consider that the company has charged them for more protection than they received. As a result, more and more companies are computing semiannual, quarterly, and even monthly premiums. Under this method of computation, there is no unpaid installment due when the policy becomes a claim. The premium in such cases, however, still is an annuity-due, because it is due at the beginning of the premium period. For purposes of simplifying the illustration of the method of calculating a premium rate, the annual premium basis is assumed.

[12] The equation is $500 : x = 4.78 : 1.00. The formula for solving this equation is the means times the extremes. Thus, $4.78 x = 500 or $x = $500 \div 4.78$.

1. What is the net single premium for the policy? This has been calculated and found to be $449.61.

2. What is the present value of a five-year Temporary annuity-due? As previously calculated, $4.78.

3. Determine the net level premium, $449.61 ÷ 4.78 = $94.06 (net level premium).

Continuous-Premium Whole Life. What would be the net level premium of a continuous-payment Whole Life policy issued at age 92? [13]

1. What is the net single premium for the policy? This was computed previously and found to be $948.21.

2. What is the present value of a lifetime annuity-due?

   a. What is the starting age? 92.

   b. Determine the number of premium-paying years. Eight (age 92 through life—99).

   c. Determine the present value of the annuity-due. This is computed below and amounts to $2.64.

Age (a)	Number Payments (b)	Amount Per Payments (c)	Amount of Payments (b × c = d)	Years of Interest (e)	Present Value of $1 (f)	Present Value of Payments (d × f)
92	10,833	$1	$10,833	0	1.0000	$10,833
93	7,327	1	7,327	1	.9804	7,183
94	4,787	1	4,787	2	.9612	4,600
95	3,011	1	3,011	3	.9423	2,837
96	1,818	1	1,818	4	.9238	1,679
97	1,005	1	1,005	5	.9057	910
98	454	1	454	6	.8880	403
99	125	1	125	7	.8706	109
		Present value of future payments				$28,554

$28,554 ÷ 10,833 = $2.64, present value of life annuity due.

3. Determine the net level premium. $948.21 ÷ 2.64 = $359.17.

Endowment, Term, and Annuities. The procedure for calculating the net level premium for other than Whole Life policies presents no new problems. To find the net level premium, the net single premium for any policy is divided by the present value of an annuity-due for the number of premium-paying years. In the case of a ten-year Term policy, the annuity-due would be for ten years; in the case of a 20-year Endowment, the annuity-due would be for 20 years. In the case of a deferred annuity at 65 paid for on an annual premium basis from, say, age 35, the annuity-due would be for 30 years.

Special Policy Combinations. Rate calculation for the many special

---

[13] Again the late age is used to reduce the number of calculations and thus simplify the illustration.

policy combinations that will be found, such as Family Income, Family Maintenance, Double Protection, and Retirement Income, are based on the same principles as Term, Whole Life, and Endowment. To compute the net level premium for any of them, all that is necessary is to find the present value of all expected future claims per policy (net single premium) and divide this by the present value of an annuity-due of $1 per annum for the premium-paying period.

The future claims can be determined easily after studying (1) the promises of the company relating to death and any survival benefits; and (2) the number of insureds entitled to such benefits as shown by the mortality table in use. It then becomes a simple matter of finding the present value of these claims by applying the present value of $1 shown in the present value tables.

The net single premium on a Double Protection policy, for instance, is the present value of the Term and the present value of the Whole Life benefits that will have to be paid by the company. The net level premium can then be computed by using the appropriate annuity-due for the premium-paying period. In some cases, the premium-paying period for the entire policy will be for the whole of life, whereas in other cases the premium-paying period might be divided, part for the whole of life and part for period during which the Term protection is offered.

3. ACCIDENT AND SICKNESS PREMIUM RATES

Basically, the calculation of a premium rate for Accident and Sickness insurance coverage is the same as that for life insurance. A "pure" or net rate is determined, to which are added various loading factors.

Two things keep A & S rate-making from being as precise a calculation as life insurance rate-making: (1) lack of adequate morbidity statistics; (2) variables not found in any significant degree in life insurance, such as (a) the greater difficulty of defining disability as contrasted to defining death; (b) variations in average claim value; (c) cyclic variations in claim frequency following variations in the economic cycle.[14]

The gross rate paid by the policyholder is made up of the pure insurance premium (net rate) plus loading for expenses, taxes, a margin for contingencies, and a margin for profit or policy dividends. The first step in calculating the gross rate is, then, calculation of the pure insurance rate.

---

[14] A period of economic depression will greatly increase claim frequency and claim value. The man who is unemployed has less incentive to get well. As long as he remains disabled, his income from insurance will continue. When he gets well, he will have no income. Further, in periods of depression, salaries and wages drop so that income insurance purchased in better times may guarantee a net income close to or even larger than a man can earn on his job.

Pure or Net Rate. The number of claims occurring during a year among a given number of policyholders is the "claim rate." [15] The pure insurance premium is obtained by multiplying the claim rate by the average value of the claims. In the case of stated-value indemnities (death and dismemberment, for examples), the average value of the claims is the amount of the stated coverage. Where the benefit is an indemnity, claim values are variable depending on the length of the disability or the amount of expense incurred. In the case of a loss-of-time benefit for $100 per month, for example, the total claim amount will be the present value of $100 a month for the duration of the disability. Average claim values are determined by statistical analysis.

Most rate-making starts with the calculation of the pure insurance rate for a term of one year.[16] If the peril is accidental death, the pure insurance rate is the probability of accidental death at a given age, multiplied by the amount of insurance. For example, if the claim rate is one in 1,000 and the amount of insurance is $1,000, then the pure insurance rate for a term of one year is $1.

If the peril is loss of time from total disability, then the pure insurance premium is the claim rate multiplied by the present value of an annuity for the duration of the disability at the rate at which benefits are payable under the policy. For example, if the claim rate at a given age is 200 in 1,000, then the claim rate is .2. If the average claim is for one month at $200, the one-year, pure insurance rate is .2 × $200, or $40.[17]

Level Premium. If claim rates and average claim values do not vary greatly over the years covered by the benefit offered, then a level premium can be achieved simply by using the pure premium at all ages. If the claim rate and average claim value do vary significantly, benefits can be reduced at older ages, rates can be jumped at age groupings, or a level premium can be calculated in the same way as one is calculated for life insurance: Develop a single premium equal to the present value of the one-year premiums for all ages covered and then divide by an annuity-due payable to the maximum age.

This is the method usually used in figuring noncancellable, guaranteed renewable policy rates.

Loading. The pure insurance rate must be loaded for acquisition costs, expenses, regular and contingency reserves, and profit or policy dividends.

---

[15] Also called "claim frequency" and "probability of occurrence."

[16] If claim rate and average value of claims are the same at all ages, the pure insurance rate could be computed for the entire period of coverage.

[17] This ignores any discount for interest, which can be ignored safely in a one-year term calculation unless the maximum period for which the indemnity is payable is lengthy.

The largest item of acquisition cost is agents' commissions. Two types of commission plans are used in A & S: (1) *Level plan:* a relatively low (compared to life insurance) first-year commission of, say, 25%, followed by the same commission rate on each subsequent annual renewal. (2) *Unlevel:* a relatively high first-year commission as in the case of life insurance, followed by relatively low renewal commissions—say 50% plus 5% renewals. The level plan will produce a greater loading factor over a long term, whereas the unlevel plan will produce more of a loading factor if the average persistency of the business is low. For instance, the 25% level plan will cost 250% of one year's premium over ten years, whereas the 50%–5% unlevel plan over the same period will cost only 95% of one year's premium. On the other hand, if the policy persists only two years, the level plan will cost 50% of one year's premium; whereas the unlevel plan will cost 55%.

Making Up the Premium. Rates are usually calculated on a unit basis, say $1,000 units for accidental death and dismemberment and $5 a week units for loss-of-time benefits. A unit for hospital expense is usually $1 per day of benefit; whereas unit cost for surgical is based on the maximum benefit in the surgical schedule. The premium for any policy is made up by totaling the unit rates involved.

Rating Factors. The rate for an A & S policy is based on three factors: age, occupation, and sex. The occupational factor is important primarily for the rating of accident rather than sickness insurance. In fact, very few companies consider the occupational factor in determining rates for health insurance; however, they may limit their coverage only to those individuals in nonhazardous occupations.

The rate for accident insurance usually does not vary with age for men between the ages of 16 and 60 and for women between 16 and 55. In addition, men at ages 60–75 and women at ages 55–65 are considered for accident coverage at a higher rate. Health insurance rates are the same for men from 16 to 49, and for women from 16 to 45. For an additional premium, men can buy health insurance at ages 50–59. The increase of the morbidity rate at later ages is more significant in sickness than in accident insurance.

Studies have shown that women experience a lower incidence of accidental death, but a higher rate of accident and sickness disability than men. The cost of accident and sickness insurance for women has been about 50% more than for men, whereas the rate for accidental death is only about 2/3 the male rate.

Elimination Periods. It is common in A & S policies to provide for an "elimination" or "waiting" period for each disability—particularly for sickness coverage. Under such clauses, benefits do not begin until the end of the first few days or weeks (depending on the policy provision) of each period of disability. The elimination or waiting period essentially makes the insured a coinsurer since he bears all the cost of small losses and part of the cost of large ones. Thus the company pays and charges only for the larger, more uncertain part of losses, which actually should be the only losses insured. As a result (1) the pure premium can be greatly reduced because a smaller amount is paid out in claims, and (2) loading can be reduced because the expenses of handling numerous small losses is eliminated. This advantage is greater in health insurance than in accident insurance because small losses resulting from accidents are less frequent. Also, sickness insurance produces a greater moral hazard since illnesses are more easily faked than are accidents.

4. SUMMARY

The net single premium of a $1,000 life insurance policy is equal to the present value of all future claims expected under the policies issued to a given group divided by the number of participants in that group. Future claims are estimated from mortality tables and are discounted by use of compound interest tables. Both mortality and interest assumptions vary among companies.

As a rule, policyholders prefer to buy their insurance on the level premium plan. To compute the level premium, it is necessary to divide the single premium by the present value of an annuity-due of one dollar for the premium paying period, since actually a level premium is an annuity payable by the policyholder to the company.

Rate computation for accident and sickness insurance is much like that for life insurance. However, accident and sickness insurance faces the problems of inadequate data and the subjective nature of the terms accident and sickness. Both types of insurance use three criteria for risk selection: (1) age, (2) sex, and (3) occupation.

Questions for Class Discussion

1. Construct a mortality table from ages 35 to 39 from the following data.

Age	Number Living	Number Dying
35	40,000	143
36	35,000	129
37	. 85,000	390
38	73,000	350
39	64,000	395

2. A mortality table has been described as the picture of "a generation of individuals passing through time." Comment on the accuracy of this description.

3. Explain why life insurance rates are not computed upon the basis of life expectancy.
4. Explain why mortality tables used in annuity computations are different from those used in life insurance calculations.
5. Explain how interest rates enter into premium computations in life insurance.
6. "Loading is more a problem of cost accounting than of actuarial science." Explain this statement.
7. If rate-making is a science, how do you account for the fact that all companies do not charge the same rates?
8. Compute the net level premium, CSO, 2% for a 5-pay, 10-year Endowment issued at age 30. Explain each step in the computation.
9. Explain why the net level premium for a 5-year Term policy is *not* the net single premium divided by five.
10. Explain any significant differences between rate-making in A & S insurance and that in life insurance.

CHAPTER 22

FINANCIAL MANAGEMENT:
STATEMENTS AND
ASSETS

THE FINANCIAL management and condition of an insurance company are a concern of the law, which not only sets rigid standards for the company's investments and disbursements, but which also makes its transactions subject to constant review by state regulatory authorities.[1] In order for these insurance departments to obtain information which will enable them to judge whether a company is fulfilling the requirements of the law in its financial transactions and whether it is in sound condition as defined by the law, each company is required to submit a highly detailed annual statement. In the United States, these statements are filed with the insurance department in each state and territory in which the company is licensed to do business. In Canada, they are filed with the Dominion department, which assumes the primary responsibility for the solvency of companies licensed by it.

While the annual statements of companies licensed in a given state are on file with the department in that state and are public records, open to inspection by anyone on demand, the annual statement required by a state is designed primarily to provide information for the use of the department rather than to present the information in a form readily understandable by the layman. These statements are highly complex and do not always follow the form customary in ordinary corporate annual statements.

---

[1] Cf. Chapter 27.

The insurance company annual statement is further complicated by the fact that different state laws might require different information or different presentation of the same information. At one time in the history of regulation of the insurance business, every state had its own form, or "blank." Thus a company licensed in several states had to develop information for and fill out several different blanks. Since developing the information for and filling out an annual statement blank is a relatively expensive and complicated procedure, the use of different blanks, requiring different information, by different states was highly unsatisfactory. To remedy the problem, the National Association of Insurance Commissioners developed a uniform report known as the "convention blank," because the association was then called "The National Convention of Insurance Commissioners." This blank was developed in 1872, as one of the first projects of the newly-organized association. With the exception of the "Gain and Loss Exhibit," the 1872 convention blank was used without revision until 1951. The "Gain and Loss" blank was revised in 1939. In its present form, the convention blank is accepted by all states as providing the information needed or wanted.

While the convention blank is uniform for all states, the financial statement for any given company may vary from state to state. Certain assets may be admitted in one state but not admitted in another.[2] At times in the past,[3] different states have required different methods of valuing certain types of securities. Other differences could be cited; but the point here is that there can be a variation in the financial statement of a company from one state to another even though the annual statement *form* used is the same for all states.

Insurance companies have been criticized from time to time for the complicated nature of their annual statements. Critics charge that the statements cannot be understood by policyholders and the public. Two points need, therefore, to be stressed: (1) The form of the annual statement is prescribed by state insurance departments, not by insurance companies. (2) As stated, insurance departments are interested in developing information that will enable them to judge the condition and transactions of companies in relation to the law. The information desired by the departments and the form in which they wish it presented may or may not be of interest or significance to the general public.

---

[2] Admitted assets are those which the law of the state allows to be used to determine the excess of assets over liabilities. Nonadmitted assets are those which state law does not allow to be so used. Examples of the latter are cited later.

[3] As in the years 1917–1921 and 1931–1933 when, because market prices were abnormally low, many states permitted valuation of nonamortizable securities at higher than market value.

For policyholders and the public, all companies prepare and publish condensed annual statements in a form understandable to anyone who has a rudimentary acquaintanceship with corporate annual statements. Many companies develop attractive reports which have sound advertising and public relations values, while at the same time presenting general financial and operational information of interest to the policyholder. The information given in these reports includes the surplus position of the companies, mortality and expense rates, net interest earned, company's investment policy, and figures which show the extent of the company's growth. About all the typical policyholder gets from his perusal of the reports is some assurance that his company is well managed and financially sound. Actually he is not apt to give the report any more than a quick "thumb through."

In addition to the convention reports developed for the regulatory authorities and the annual reports developed for policyholders, the companies prepare interim financial reports for the use of management. This chapter is concerned only with the reports required by state officials.

1. THE CONVENTION BLANK

The convention blank as revised in 1951 calls for three different groups of statements: [4]

    I. Three financial statements
        1. Balance sheet
        2. Operations statement
        3. Surplus account
    II. Four miscellaneous statements
        1. Gain and loss exhibit
        2. Policy exhibit
        3. Interrogatories
        4. Deposit schedules
    III. Exhibits and schedules
        Detailed information with respect to the summary figures used in the three financial statements.

Each of these statements will be discussed briefly.[5]

---

[4] The principal difference in the old and the new blank is in the financial statements. The statements in the old form were more complicated and detailed. They included statements of income, disbursements, assets and liabilities, surplus, and other funds. The problem was one of reconciling the income and disbursement statements which were on a cash basis with the statements of assets and liabilities.

[5] A detailed discussion of each of the items of an annual statement requires a development of background of technical knowledge of both actuarial and accounting theory beyond the scope of this book, or the course for which it is intended as a text. The purpose of this discussion is to acquaint the student with the general nature of the blank in order to facilitate understanding of company assets, liabilities, and surplus, and the problems of financial management.

The Financial Statements.   As in any business, the three most important statements are the balance sheet, profit and loss statement, and allocation of surplus.[6]

The balance sheet for a life insurance company is given on pages two and three of the convention blank. In the form required, it is similar to the balance sheet of any type of business. Assets are given on the lefthand page and liabilities and net worth on the righthand page. Different sections of the balance sheet will be discussed later.[7]

The profit and loss statement is presented on page four of the blank in the form of a summary of operations.[8] Income applicable to the period is stated whether actually received or not and from it are deducted expenses applicable to the period whether actually paid out or not. Income items consist of premiums, investment income, and net capital gains. Disbursements consist of policy benefits paid or payable, interest credited on dividend accumulations or policy proceeds, increases in reserves, commissions, net capital losses, general operation expense, taxes, licenses and other fees, and dividends.

Allocation of surplus is shown on the bottom of page four of the blank as a double-column form. The lefthand column is a statement of the source of the surplus funds; for example, surplus carried over from the previous year, gains during the current year, capital gains not listed in the summary of operations. On the right is detailed the distribution of surplus funds; for example, dividends to stockholders (if any), increase in contingency reserves, unassigned surplus, capital losses not listed in the summary of operations.

The Miscellaneous Statements.   The four miscellaneous statements are:

The gain and loss exhibit, appearing on pages five and six of the convention blank, is divided into two sections: operations by classes of insurance issued, and increases in reserves.

Operations by classes or "lines" is a breakdown of the items in the summary of operations, the second of the two financial statements described above. The purpose of the exhibit is to show the contributions of each of the following classes of business to the surplus of the company for the year.[9]

---

[6] If a copy of the convention blank is available, it would help in the study of this section to refer to it so as to give some life to the following description.

[7] Assets are discussed later in this chapter. Liabilities and surplus are discussed in the following chapter.

[8] This "Summary of Operations" is handled on an accrual basis and replaces the old "Income and Disbursement" statements which were on a cash basis.

[9] Remember these figures are *after* the payment of policy dividends and therefore represent net gains or losses.

Industrial
Ordinary
   Life insurance
   Total and permanent disability insurance
   Accidental death insurance [10] ("Double Indemnity")
   Annuities
   Supplementary contracts
Group
   Life insurance
   Annuities
A & S
   Group
   Individual

The section on reserves begins with a statement of the previous year's reserves for each "line" or subdivision included above. To the previous year's reserves are added net premiums [11] collected, assumed interest, and other increases. From the total are deducted assumed mortality, other costs, and payments on terminations.[12] The remainder is the reserve as of the end of the year.[13]

The policy exhibit is divided into three parts:
Industrial
   Whole Life
   Endowment
   Term
   Dividend additions
Ordinary
   Whole Life
   Endowments
   Term
   Dividend additions
   Group
Annuities
   Individual annuities
   Group annuities
   Supplementary contracts involving life contingencies

The exhibit starts with a statement of the number of policies in force at the end of the previous year and the amounts involved. To this is added the

[10] Although the statement refers to "Double Indemnity" as accidental death it is technically death by accidental means.
[11] Net premiums refer to valuation premiums without the expense loading.
[12] Note the use of the terms *assumed* interest and *assumed* mortality. These mean that if the policy is written 2%, CSO then 2% and the CSO tabular mortality are used regardless of the actual interest earned or mortality experienced.
[13] This is known as the "retrospective method" of calculating a terminal reserve which will be explained in detail in Chapter 23. Except for the fact that it is a part of the "Gain and Loss" exhibit, it can be ignored here.

number and amount of policies issued, revived,[14] and increased [15] during the year covered by the statement.

From the total arrived at are deducted policies which have become claims, matured as endowments, expired, terminated, lapsed, decreased in amount,[16] withdrawals, and termination by disability.[17] The remainder is the number of policies and amounts of insurance in force as of the end of the year for which the statement is made.[18]

Under each of the divisions of the annuity section, the number of such annuities is listed, but, there being no "face amount" in the case of annuities, income payable, deferred payments fully paid, and deferred payments not fully paid are listed.

A note at the end of the exhibit gives the number of policies and the amount of insurance which has been reinsured.

The interrogatories section requests the answers to a series of 42 questions about the company and its operations. Often these questions are designed for the purpose of gathering statistics on trends in the business and have little or no actual bearing on the financial position of the company. They might even be asked in connection with a study by the NAIC Blanks Committee for use in deciding whether more schedules should be added or others dropped. Examples of questions in the interrogatory section are the number, kind, and amount of the company's stock outstanding; whether or not the company has a retirement plan for agents and employees; in what states, territories, and countries the company operates.

Deposit schedules are of two types: special and general. In the special schedule are included deposits not available for the protection of all policyholders, such as a deposit required of a United States company for the exclusive protection of Canadian policyholders. The general deposit schedule includes a schedule of all other deposits.

Exhibits and Schedules. The third and final group of statements required on the convention blank are exhibits and schedules showing in detail information supporting the figures used in the financial statements. Briefly, the *exhibits* called for are as follows:

---

[14] Lapsed policies reinstated.
[15] Increases may result from a change from a limited pay to a continuous premium for a larger amount of insurance carrying the same premium.
[16] Most of the decreases result from policies being put on the paid-up option.
[17] Such termination arises under a type of policy that provides for payment of the face amount in installments at the time of disablement or at age 65 in event the policyholder is continuously disabled prior to that age.
[18] The statement also will show transfers from one form to another, the most common of which are conversion of Term to Whole Life and the conversion of Whole Life to Extended Term.

1. Breakdown of premium receipts, dividends, reinsurance, and commissions into the following categories:

Industrial life
Ordinary
    Life insurance
    Total and permanent disability insurance
    Accidental death insurance ("Double Indemnity")
    Annuities
Group
    Life insurance
    Annuities
A & S
    Individual policies
    Group policies

Figures in each category are divided into first-year, renewal, and those based on single premiums.

2. An analysis of investment income, derived by subtracting taxes, licenses, fees (computed in Exhibit 6), and investment expenses (computed in Exhibit 5) from the total interest, dividends, and real estate income (computed in Exhibit 3).

3. A detailed report of total interest, dividends, and real estate income shown in Exhibit 2.

4. Breakdown of capital gain and loss on investments by showing the increase or decrease in book value and the profit and loss on the sale or maturity of all investments of the company.

5. Expenses and amounts paid during the year for life insurance and A & S investment operations, and the total. The total of investment expenses is one of the deductions used in Exhibit 2.

6. Taxes, licenses, and fees for life, A & S, and investment operations, and the total of the three. The total of the investment expense is the other deduction used in Exhibit 2.

7. Analysis of dividends to policyholders.

8. A detailed explanation of the reserves shown for the different types of life insurance policies outstanding.

9. A detailed explanation of A & S reserves.

10. Funds held by the company not involving life contingencies, such as limited installment option funds.

11. A report on all outstanding life insurance claims in process and as yet unpaid.

12. Determination of the amount of the company's ledger assets.

13. Breakdown of all assets into ledger, nonledger, nonadmitted, and admitted.[19]

14. An analysis of nonadmitted assets.

The 18 *schedules* are, briefly, as follows: [20]

A. A list of real estate owned and of real estate sold during the year. Real estate owned is divided into that owned at the beginning of the year and that acquired during the year. Information concerning description, cost, value, income produced, and expenses in connection with the property is required. Property is divided into farm and other and its value given by states in which it is located.

B. A report of mortgages owned and changes made during the year. These mortgages are classified according to the states and foreign countries in which they are held. Also farm and other mortgages are handled separately. A distinction is made too between purchase-money mortgages and all other mortgages. Loans more than three months overdue but not yet in process of foreclosure, mortgages over $250,000 or over one half of 1% of admitted assets, loans on which interest or taxes are delinquent for more than a year, and several similar items are listed separately. A detailed list of foreclosures during the year also is required.

C. A schedule of loans secured by collateral.[21]

D. A schedule describing the type, cost, book, market, par, and amortized values of stocks and bonds owned; purchased (or otherwise acquired); sold, redeemed, or otherwise disposed of during the year. Also included is the amount of income from stocks and bonds and the rate of earnings on stocks for the previous three years; a summary of bonds purchased during the year with their descriptions, name of seller, cost, and par value; a similar type of summary of securities sold during the year, including profit or loss.

E. Balance in each bank account as of the date of the statement plus the highest balance in each such account during each month of the year and interest received on such accounts. Amounts on deposit in any suspended banks or trust companies are listed separately.

F. A list of the amounts of all claims resisted or compromised during the year divided into (a) those disposed of and (b) those still in process at the end of the year. Claims are divided into death, disability, double indemnity, and other.

---

[19] These terms will be defined later in this chapter.

[20] For purposes of simplicity, these schedules are discussed in the order appearing on the blank. Notice, however, their illogical arrangement. For example, schedules H, N and O deal with Accident and Sickness insurance. Schedules A through E deal with assets and so does schedule X. The order of the arrangement of the schedules could be improved, at least from a logical point of view.

[21] Few companies have any such loans outstanding.

G. Payments over $500 made to trade associations, rating bureaus, service organizations; compensation paid to all officers and directors,[22] amounts in excess of $5,000 paid any individual, firm, or corporation except those included in Schedules I, J, and K. In the case of employees who are not directors or officers and who were paid under $10,000, it is necessary to show only the total number of such employees and the total amount paid them. In the case of any employee, whether an officer or director or not, who receives $10,000 or more, the individual and amount must be shown.

H. An analysis of A & S experience with respect to premiums, claims, and expenses. The analysis segregates group from individual policies and further divides these classes into types of coverage.

I. Commissions on loans and purchase or sale of property which exceed $5,000, including name and address of the person receiving the commission and amount involved in the transaction.

J. Names and addresses of persons paid legal fees of $100 or more and reason for which the fee was paid. Amounts under $100 are reported as a total.

K. Itemization of all expenditures made in connection with matters before legislatures, government departments, etc.

L. A report of the last annual meeting: names of candidates for director and votes cast for each, and a copy of the minutes of the meeting.

M. Examples of dividend rates paid during the year on the different classes of policies and a statement of the method by which the dividends were calculated.

N. Premium and loss experience on various types of A & S policies.

O. Analysis of A & S claims arranged by types of coverages and broken down into amounts paid, unpaid, and estimated.

S. A list of amounts recoverable from reinsurance companies.

T. Premium collections for life insurance and annuities classified by states.

X. Unlisted assets, consisting of assets of doubtful or no value, with particulars about any property acquired, sold, or transferred to or from this schedule during the year.

New York sets a limit on the amount which may be used for expenses.[23] In order to administer the law, the department in that state requires a "Schedule Q" showing details in connection with new business expense and, in the case of companies issuing participating forms, in connection with

---

[22] Except commissions paid to or retained by agents.
[23] Wisconsin also limits expenses. See Chapter 27 for a discussion of the New York and Wisconsin expense limitations.

expenses as a whole. "Schedule Q" is not a part of the convention blank but is a New York state requirement for all companies operating in that state.

As stated, many of the schedules are detailed breakdowns or listings of figures required in the statements. Others require the information called for as a part of the general policy of publicity for all insurance company transactions. In these cases, no restrictions are set by law. Instead publicity is relied upon as a deterrent to improper practices. Thus companies are allowed freedom of action in matters which might otherwise be subject to restrictions.

2. ASSETS

Although the policy reserve of a life insurance company often is referred to as a "fund," it is simply a bookkeeping figure, actuarially determined, to measure the liability of the company under policy contracts outstanding. Thus the reserve is a liability; and it is necessary for the company to hold assets to offset that liability if the company is to remain solvent. Assets represent the values owned by the company which are available to offset liabilities.[24]

The instructions for filling out the annual statement blank state that "Each class of assets should be entered . . . at its final value." To determine this final value, five terms relating to life insurance company assets must be defined: *ledger, nonledger, gross, nonadmitted,* and *admitted.*

Ledger assets result only from completed transactions. They arise from an excess of income over disbursements. They do not take into account values that may have been accrued as a result of the completed transaction. In addition, ledger assets reflect any write-up of the value of an asset (which shows as income) and the value of any write-down (which shows as a disbursement). Examples of items included in ledger assets are cash on hand, real estate, mortgage loans, stocks and bonds, policy loans, and furniture and fixtures.

Nonledger assets are those to which a value is attached but not yet reflected in completed transactions. Examples of nonledger assets are interest due and accrued but not yet collected, and uncollected premiums due.

Gross assets are merely the total of ledger and nonledger assets.

Nonadmitted assets are assets which cannot be included in determining the solvency of the company, that is, they cannot be counted in measuring the amount by which assets exceed liabilities.[25] Examples of typical non-

---

[24] And the ownership interest in the company.
[25] Admitted assets vary from state to state; i.e., an asset might be admitted in one state but not in another.

admitted assets are stock of the company which is owned by the company itself or loans secured by the company's own stock; supplies on hand; furniture; advances to agents; the amount by which the book value of any asset exceeds the valuation as determined by the state insurance department.

Admitted assets are the net after nonadmitted assets have been deducted from gross assets. Expressed as a formula, *ledger assets + nonledger assets − nonadmitted assets = admitted assets.*

Admitted assets are the final value of the assets asked for on the annual statement blank.

Valuation of Assets. The admitted assets of a life insurance company consist mainly of stocks, bonds, mortagages, other types of loans, real estate, and cash. For the purpose of the annual statement, each of these assets must be assigned a value. If they are overvalued the statement will not be a fair measure of the company's financial condition. Therefore care must be taken in ascertaining a fair value for admitted assets.[26] Since the surplus of life insurance companies rarely exceeds 10% of policyholders' reserves, it is also important that valuation standards for assets be flexible enough to prevent unnecessary insolvencies during adverse market reactions. In many cases, the state insurance department prescribes the method of valuation. Currently much attention is being given to valuation problems by both the industry and the regulatory authorities. The common methods of valuing assets today are:

Cash. Obviously, the value of cash, on hand or in banks, is the dollar amount itself.

Loans. Loans are valued at face value, i.e., the amount lent plus accrued interest. Policy loans are fully secured since any default cancels an equal liability on the part of the company. Collateral loans (which, as stated, are rare among life insurance companies) are secured by the assignment of collateral equal to or exceeding the amount advanced. Mortgage loans likewise are secured by a negotiable asset (the deed to the property), which is intended to be of value in excess of the amount of the loan. The amount advanced on the mortgage is always substantially less than the appraised value of the property to allow a margin for a possible decline in its value. FHA and "GI" mortgage loans, on which a higher percentage of the appraised value is advanced, not only are secured by the property itself but also are guaranteed against loss by agencies of the Federal government. If the value of the property at the time of a foreclosure is less than the unpaid balance on the mortgage, these agencies will, in effect, "make up the difference" to the lender.

---

[26] Liabilities must also be fairly valued. This is a subject for Chapter 23.

Real Estate. Real estate held by a life insurance company may be classified into three types: (1) Property necessary to the operation of the business. (2) Property acquired in satisfaction of a debt (such as property obtained through the foreclosure of a mortgage). (3) Property in the process of sale.

(1) Property necessary to the operation of the business—home office and branch office buildings, for example,—can be valued at cost, subject to write-ups and write-downs.[27] However, cost is not an altogether satisfactory method of valuation. In the case of a new building, the cost may have been excessive. In the case of an existing structure, the price paid might have been too high. As a matter of fact, property is often sold to the highest bidder and, therefore, technically at least, more was paid for it than the purchaser could realize from an early resale. The local demand for business property may have fallen or risen since the property was acquired. The building may not have wide use by other types of business without costly alterations.

A second method of valuation is by appraisal. However, an appraisal is only an "educated guess" of the value at the time the appraisal is made, and since so many factors affect value, it would be necessary to have frequent reappraisals.

A third method of valuation is the cost of replacement if the building or buildings were reproduced at the present time exactly as they stand. From reconstruction cost is deducted accrued depreciation.

Perhaps the most widely used method of valuation of home and branch office property is to take the lesser of the amounts arrived at by (*a*) capitalization of the earning power of the building and (*b*) original cost minus depreciation. It is in the valuation of their home and branch office buildings that insurance companies most often understate asset values.

(2) Real estate acquired to satisfy a debt is valued twice: at the time of entry, and at the time of the report.

For valuation at time of entry, several factors must be considered: (*a*) the amount of the unpaid principal on the foreclosure loan; (*b*) the cost of foreclosing; (*c*) the cost of clearing the title. Some authorities express the opinion that the amount of uncollected interest should also be included; but most hold that the interest, being a nonledger asset, should be included in a separate account so that the proper capital gain or loss can be determined.

For valuation at the time of the annual statement, reconstruction cost minus depreciation can be used, or the company may apply the same methods it uses in the valuation of its business property. If the property is resi-

---

[27] Rarely, if ever, does an insurance company write up the value of its home office.

dential and consists of less than four units, the reconstruction minus depreciation method is common; if it is a larger residential building or a commercial building or property, the method most common is that followed in valuing the company's own property (customarily book value less depreciation).

(3) Property in the process of sale; i.e., property being sold on installments with title remaining with the company until final payment, presents the problem of handling the difference between the value in the real estate account and the amount for which the property is sold. There are three possibilities:

1. Profit or loss can be withheld until the final payment is made.

2. Profit or loss can be claimed when the purchaser has paid enough so that the balance due can be classed as a loan on the security of the amount already paid by the purchaser.

3. The difference between the value in the real estate account and the amount for which the property is sold can be prorated over the life of the purchase, recording periodic changes in an account established for profit and loss on sales of real estate.

Nonamortizable Securities. Most states establish two classes of securities, nonamortizable and amortizable. A typical definition of nonamortizable securities includes all stocks,[28] bonds in default as to principal or interest, bonds not amply secured, bonds yielding in excess of a given percentage on the current market, and bonds without maturity date ("perpetual bonds"). Nonamortizable securities must be valued at their fair market price. The problem in this case is that of determining just what is the fair market price. Nothing reflects the market price of listed securities better than the stock exchange prices; so these are generally used as the valuation basis. Actually, valuation of listed securities is left to the Committee on Valuation of Securities of the National Association of Insurance Commissioners, which promulgates annual valuation rules based largely on ratings in security manuals and current market prices. In 1955, the Committee recommended the market quotations as of December 31. Directly placed preferred stocks usually are valued at cost or capitalized earnings, whichever is lower.[29] Unlisted stocks usually are valued at their last public sale price, or at the bid or asked price. If there have been no recent sales, common stock may be valued at book value.[30]

Amortizable Securities. In general, to be eligible for valuation on an

---

[28] Stocks are nonamortizable since they do not have a definite maturity date.

[29] Direct placements are discussed later in this chapter.

[30] Book value of common stock is found by dividing capital plus surplus minus preferred stock by the number of common shares outstanding.

amortized basis, a bond must not be in default as to principal or interest, must have a maturity date, must be amply secured,[31] and must fall into one of the following classes: (a) issued, assumed, or guaranteed by the United States or Canadian government; (b) special revenue bond of a political subdivision or corporation bonds in the four highest grades of a recognized rating agency; (c) corporate bonds on which the yields to maturities do not exceed a given figure; [32] (d) approved by the Committee on Valuation of Securities; and (e) foreign bonds approved by the Committee.

Amortizable securities [33] are valued according to a procedure under which their original cost is written up or down by gradual stages until the book value equals par at maturity date.

A bond is a document certifying a debt of a specific amount of money payable at the end of a designated period. For example, a $1,000 25-year bond shows that a debt of $1,000 is due 25 years from its date of issue. The debt carries an interest rate known as the bond or coupon rate. If the above illustrated bond has a 4% rate, it promises in addition to its maturity value to pay $40 a year during each of the 25 years of its life. The $40 is a fixed contractual obligation and will not vary during this 25-year period. Perhaps interest rates in the market might rise to 5% at one time and drop to 3% at another, depending upon conditions in the money market. If the market rate rises above the bond rate, the bond will sell at a discount; i.e., the bond-holder in a sale will have to accept less than $1,000 for his $1,000 bond. The reason is simple. If the purchaser paid $1,000 for the bond, he would get only a 4% return on money which has been assumed to be worth more than 4%. Therefore, he would be willing to pay for the bond no more than that amount which would make the entire transaction yield him the market rate of interest.

---

[31] The term amply secured does not necessarily mean secured by the pledge of specific assets but secured in the sense of being safe as indicated by a favorable working capital position and earnings record. The Commissioners set up certain tests for measuring the adequacy of the security.

[32] This is called the yield test. The test at this writing is that bonds based on association values in the current and preceding year should not yield more than 1.5 percentage points more than the yields on fully taxable U.S. Government bonds of comparable maturities. The theory behind this rule is that unusually high-yielding bonds often are not considered to be of good quality and for that reason their valuation on an amortized basis might be denied. The effect of this ruling is to require the use of market value. The yield on a bond is a function of the relationship between the interest payments and the market price. Since the interest payments are fixed, the yield increases as the price goes down. Therefore high-yielding bonds have low market values and these are the values which must be used for admitted assets.

[33] "Amortized value" actually refers only to bonds bought above par. The excess value is written down over the life of the bond so that the valuation at maturity date is par. However, the term is also used to cover the reverse process, i.e., writing up, the technical name for which is "accrual of discount."

For purposes of illustration, assume that the market rate of interest for this type of investment risk is 5%. What will be the price of the bond in question? The price is the function of three factors: (1) the bond rate (4%), (2) the market rate (5%), and (3) the length of time until the bond matures (assume this to be ten more years). Bond tables are published from which the price of the bond can be ascertained. A quick reference to one of these tables will give a price of approximately $922. If an investor purchases a $1,000 4% bond with ten years left to go and pays $922 for it, the investment will yield him 5%. The effective annual return will be $40 plus an annual write-up. On the straight line method which gives approximate yields only, the annual write-up would be $7.80. The $7.80 annual accumulation (or write-up) is computed by dividing the bond discount ($78)[34] by the number of years until the bond matures (ten). The $47.80 gives an effective yield of approximately 5% on a mean or average investment of $961.[35] For valuation purposes, the bond will be entered at cost ($922) when it is purchased but will be increased in value by the write-up each year so that by maturity it will have reached a value of $1,000.

If the market rate is 3% instead of 5%, the bond would sell at a premium. Assuming the other facts are the same as above, the bond would sell for about $1085.80. The annual amortization cost (write-down) would amount to $8.58 on the straight line method. This means that the effective earning each year is $40 minus $8.58 or $31.42, which on an investment of $1085.80 yields an effective return of approximately 3%. The bond will be valued at $1085.80 when purchased but will be written down each year so that on its maturity date its valuation will be equal to its maturity value.

Amortization and accrual are common terms in valuation of bonds for any purpose, but the simple procedure described above is not an exact method. In connection with the valuation of life insurance company assets, the more correct method is commonly used, i.e., one which does not involve the same write-up or write-down every year as in the straight-line method. The actuarial method calls for an exact determination of write-ups or write-downs. Under this method the actual amount of effective interest deemed earned on the book value is computed. If the bond is a discount bond, then the excess of the effective interest over the bond interest is the write-up for the period. If the bond is a premium bond, then the excess of

---

[34] The bond discount is the face of the bond ($1,000) minus the price of the bond ($922).

[35] The average investment ($961) is the average of the initial investment of $922 and the terminal investment of $1,000. The annual interest received plus the increase in the write-up of the investment value ($40 plus $7.80) makes the annual return $47.80.

the bond interest over the effective interest is the write-down for the period. The tables may help to clarify the point.

Table 1. Discount Bond Illustration

Bond $1,000—Bond Rate 4%
Purchase Price $922—Effective Rate 5%
(Ten years to maturity)

Years to Run	Initial Book Value	Bond Interest	Effective Interest	Write-up	Terminal Book Value
10	$922	$40	$46.10	$6.10	$928.10
9	928.10	40	46.41	6.41	934.51
8	934.51	40	46.72	6.72	941.23

Table 2. Premium Bond Illustration

Bond $1,000—Bond Rate 4%
Purchase Price $1085.80—Effective Rate 3%
(Ten years to maturity)

Years to Run	Initial Book Value	Bond Interest	Effective Interest	Write-up	Terminal Book Value
10	$1085.80	$40	$32.57	$7.43	$1078.37
9	1078.37	40	32.35	7.65	1070.72
8	1070.72	40	32.12	7.88	1062.84

In these tables, the value in the last column is the valuation used for the year in question. If the tables in these illustrations were to be carried to completion, the book value at the end of the tenth year would equal $1,000, the maturity value of the bond payable at that time.

Efforts currently are being made to devise new and more realistic methods of valuation. Much progress has been made with respect to bonds but a great deal of study needs to be given to stock valuation. More realistic valuation methods to many authorities mean methods that give less weight to liquidation values and more consideration to what might be considered long run stable values. After all, as will soon become apparent, life insurance company investment portfolios do not require the liquidity assumed in the valuation formulas.

3. INVESTMENTS

Life insurance companies are more than risk-bearing institutions. They are major financial institutions investing large sums of money every business day of the year. Their function as financial institutions is as important to the economy as their function as risk-bearing institutions.

The sources of funds available for investment by life insurance companies consist chiefly of:

1. Overpayments of premiums in early policy years required under the level-premium plan to offset deficits in premiums to be collected in late policy years.

2. The accumulation of funds under the pure endowment portion of Endowment and Retirement Income policies.

3. Funds left with the company under policy settlement options.

4. Various contingency funds accumulated out of expense loadings, excess interest earnings, investment profits, and mortality savings.

5. Capital stock [36] and paid-in surplus.

It is not absolutely necessary for companies to invest these funds in order for the life insurance principle to operate.[37] The funds could be held in cash to be paid out as required under policy contracts. However, because the interest that can be earned on these funds drastically reduces the cost of the insurance, the funds are invested to yield a return. In anticipation of this return, the company guarantees a minimum rate of interest on funds paid in advance and on funds left with the company.[38]

Investment vs. Speculation.   In order to understand the basic philosophy of life insurance company investment policy, a distinction must be made between *investment* and *speculation*.

The primary objective of speculation is a high rate of return, either in the form of large earnings or capital appreciation. Speculation has a definite place in the economy. It is a major source of developmental and entrepreneurial funds. For instance, it probably would be conceded that nothing is much more speculative than an investment in oil wildcatting. The over-all chance of a wildcat well coming in or of even hitting gas is one in nine; and the chance of hitting a large oil field, defined as one which will supply United States needs for one week, is one in 991.[39] Yet in view of the ever increasing needs of the country—and of the world—for oil and the limitations on known oil deposits, wildcatting is a necessity. Since the average cost of such wildcatting is $90,000 a drilling, speculative capital is important.

When money is placed primarily for possibility of large gain over a short period of time, the process is speculation. On the other hand, when the primary concern is for safety of principal with dividend or interest return

---

[36] Applies only to capital stock companies. See Chapter 24.

[37] The effects on the economy of a hoard of life insurance funds, however, would be drastic.

[38] Cf. Chapters 20 and 21 for an explanation of the importance of interest in rate computations.

[39] Chance ratios from *Bulletin of the American Association of Petroleum Geologists*, January, 1951.

a secondary consideration, then the process may be called *investment*. It is rare that a high degree of safety of principal and a high rate of return go hand in hand. They are usually at opposite poles.

The overwhelming majority of the assets of life insurance companies are funds held to meet contractual obligations under policies in force or under settlement options. In view of the guarantees made under these contracts, a life insurance company must be concerned first with safety of principal in dollars.

Legal Restrictions. The classes of investments permissible for life insurance assets are set by state law. In the main, they are confined to what may be called "first-lien" securities: bonds and mortgages. Limited investment in stocks and rental real estate have been authorized by many states in recent years.

The primary purpose of legal restrictions on life insurance company investments is to eliminate speculation and assure that the bulk of the funds, at least, will be placed in earning assets of a debt nature. This type of investment as a class is more likely to have a steady value. The law restricts investments in equities which as a class are subject to wide fluctuations in value. Such regulations also seek to prevent undesirable practices. For example, they prohibit officers or board members from making personal profits on any investment transaction they conduct for the company, and they prevent one individual from making secret investments by requiring that all investments be approved by the board or by a committee.[40]

Investment Qualities Required. Safety is not the only quality sought in life insurance company investment policy. In addition, companies want adequacy of yield, diversification, liquidity, and to some extent, a socio-economic purpose.

Safety. Inasmuch as the major portion of life insurance company assets is, as previously stated, held to meet reserve liabilities under contracts in force, the ability of the company to meet its policy obligations depends on the safety of its investments.

It is considered fundamental in life insurance company investment policy and the basic concern of laws relating to those investments, that investment should be proponderately "first-lien" securities. Any substantial investment in equity securities is opposed because the values which life insurance policies guarantee are in terms of fixed amounts of dollars, whereas the values

---

[40] Unfortunately state laws have, from time to time, sought to direct life insurance investments into channels of interest to state legislators without much regard for the welfare of policyholders. An example is the Robertson Law in Texas, requiring the investment of assets equaling 75% of the reserve liability on Texas policyholders in Texas securities.

of equity investments are not fixed.[41] Furthermore, as a rule principal is less safe in equity investments than in debt investments.[42]

Adequacy of Yield. Inasmuch as the guarantees in a life insurance policy contract and the premiums for it are based on the assumption of a given rate of interest, it follows that yield is an important investment consideration for life insurance companies. The company must seek the highest rate of interest compatible with the required degree of safety in order to hold down the cost of insurance to policyholders. Moreover, human judgment not being perfect, it is not unrealistic to expect occasional losses in an investment portfolio. Thus, to offset possible capital losses, it is necessary for the company to earn on the average a rate of return in excess of the amount guaranteed by the policy contract.

As indicated in Chapter 20, the problem of adequacy of interest earnings has been an acute one for many years. In 1922, the net rate of interest, earned on life insurance company investments was 5.18%. At that time, it was common to guarantee policy rates of 3½% and even 4%. Once such guarantees are made, they can of course never be reduced. From the high point in 1921, the net rate earned declined steadily to a low of 2.88% in 1947. This was below the average rate guaranteed on all policies outstanding in some companies. Some of the losses had to be made up by reducing policyholder dividends and increasing premium rates on new policies.[43] Policies being issued today contain guarantees ranging for the most part from 2% to 2½%. Although the interest rate has moved up somewhat since 1947 and is currently running between 3% and 3¼% net after income taxes, the margin between the interest guaranteed on all outstanding policies and the interest earned is small. The result is that adequacy of yield is a major concern in the management of life insurance company investments.

Diversification. Most states have recognized in their laws the fact that the safety of life insurance company investment portfolios is enhanced by diversification. Some states limit the proportion of assets which may be invested in any single type of investment. Companies have gone far beyond the requirements of law in securing diversification not only by classes of investments and within these classes, but also by geographical distribution

---

[41] The "variable annuity" of course is an exception; it does not need guaranteed value investments since it does not guarantee a return in terms of a fixed number of dollars. The basic theory of the "variable annuity" requires that funds be invested in equities.

[42] While the above is a general rule, the common stock of a corporation which has no other securities outstanding might well be safer than the junior bonds of another corporation with heavy senior commitments.

[43] Also used was the process of *reserve strengthening.* Under it, lower interest assumptions were used in computing the reserve liability. The result, of course, was an increase in reserves and a decrease in surplus. (This is nothing more than an accounting technique.)

and by maturity dates. In addition, investments of life insurance companies are diversified among industries, companies, types of security, and periods of the business cycle over which funds are committed.

Liquidity. Liquidity, the ability of an asset to be converted into cash immediately and without loss of value, is of relatively little importance as a standard for life insurance investments. In the first place, life insurance company commitments are long-term commitments, and therefore, the assets held to meet those commitments can be long-term investments. Life insurance company investments are not purchased to be cashed out but rather to be held to yield income. In the second place, since investments are made every day they mature at different times rather than all at once. In the case of any company in operation for any length of time, securities are maturing and are automatically converting into cash daily. In the third place, cash receipts arising from premium income and investment earnings continue to grow so that, except in an extreme economic emergency,[44] the company always has cash income sufficient to meet cash calls. Finally, almost every policy written today contains, as a result of state law, a "delay clause" permitting the company to postpone payment of any cash or loan value (except a loan to pay premiums) for a period of time, usually up to six months. The use of the delay could help to prevent a serious loss resulting from a forced liquidation of assets if cash calls suddenly exceeded the amount of cash readily available.

Socioeconomic Purposes. Life insurance assets today form the greatest and most rapidly growing pool of capital in the country. There has been and continues to be some public demand that at least a part of this pool be used to expand the facilities of production on a risk-sharing basis—that is, that it be put into equities. As previously mentioned, some states have authorized the investment of small amounts of assets in preferred and common stocks and in rental housing, but the percentage permitted is a minute portion of the total assets of any one company and, hence, of the combined assets of all companies.

Some companies are taking advantage of the opportunity to put money into venture investments although life insurance companies, on the average, are not investing as much in common stocks and real estate as the law permits. It is entirely possible, however, that the time will come when growth, competition, and market conditions will force life insurance companies to move away from traditional forms of investment into the more

---

[44] Such an emergency would have to be more extreme than the depression of the 1930's. During the depression years, total revenue of the business always exceeded total disbursements. In fact, premium income alone exceeded total disbursements in all but three years, 1932–33–34. Cf. Table 1, Chapter 1.

venturesome types. The trend already is discernible. The companies might find that the higher yields on successful ventures will more than offset the possible losses on those that prove to be unsuccessful. Since liquidity is not too important, companies can ride with temporary setbacks in investment values.

Types of Investments. Life insurance investments are distributed among government securities, corporate bonds, mortgages, real estate, stocks, policy loans, and a few miscellaneous investments. Although the law restricts investments to certain classes and in certain amounts, life insurance companies have wide discretion as to their choice of investments among these classes. Wide variation among company investment portfolios will be found. The suitability of each of these types of investment for life insurance funds deserves a brief discussion as a guide to an understanding of the composition of life insurance assets and the role played by life insurance companies in the capital market.

Government Securities. Traditionally, United States government bonds offer the highest degree of dollar safety of any investment; but they also offer the lowest investment yields. Prior to World War I, few United States government bonds were owned by life insurance companies. However, during both World War I and World War II, as part of supplying the tremendous wartime demands on the government for money, companies invested heavily in United States governments.[45] At one point during World War II, United States bonds represented about half of the total investments of the companies. Holdings of these bonds have decreased significantly since the war as safe and profitable private investments became available.

Canadian government bonds are eligible for life insurance investments. Some states, however, limit the amount of assets that can be placed in the obligations of foreign governments. For instance, New York restricts the amount to 10% of admitted assets unless the company has foreign policyholders, in which case, up to one and one-half times the assets necessary to offset the reserve liability on those policies may be invested in foreign bonds.

State, county, and municipal bonds vary in suitability. Many issues are acceptable, but they usually produce low yields. The income tax exemption of the interest earned on such bonds, which makes them a favorable investment for individuals, does not offer a similar tax advantage for life insurance

---

[45] Aside from patriotic motives, life insurance companies purchased large amounts of government bonds during the war because these bonds were available as an investment outlet for the huge amount of investment funds being built up in the companies. If more profitable, safe investments had been available, life insurance companies probably would have purchased fewer government bonds.

companies, whose Federal income tax liability is figured on a basis different from that applicable to individuals or other corporations.

Corporate Bonds. Corporate bonds have long been an important medium for the investment of life insurance company funds. There are few restrictions on bond investments.[46] The only questionable class of corporate bond is the collateral trust bond, which is secured by shares of stock. It is a suitable life insurance company investment, according to some experts, only if the corporate shares used as collateral would themselves be suitable for investment.

The only legal restrictions on bonds relate to those which are not fully secured or are in default as to the payment of interest.[47]

Mortgages. In general, the mortgage loan is well qualified as an investment for life insurance companies. If an adequate margin has been maintained between the amount lent and the appraisal value of the property, the loan is well secured. Mortgage lending offers an opportunity for both geographical diversification and diversification of credit risks. Furthermore, it offers a relatively high rate of return for the degree of security involved.[48] On the other hand, mortgaged loans are relatively expensive to initiate and to service, and foreclosure in case of default is costly and sometimes harmful to public relations. One other disadvantage is the relatively short term durations of many mortgages as compared with other investment media. Moreover, inasmuch as most mortgages can be paid off in advance, there is a tendency in times of falling interest rates for mortgage borrowers to "refinance" by paying off the old mortgage and making a new one at a lower rate of interest.

Prior to the depression of the 1930's, mortgages customarily were of the conventional type, that is, payable in a lump sum at maturity date. The depression popularized the monthly payment mortgage, which greatly increases the safety of the loan, since the margin between appraisal value and the debt constantly increases. Mortgage loan liquidity has also been enhanced since the depression by FHA insurance and the guaranteed "GI" mortgage of the Veterans Administration.

---

[46] In fact, the Armstrong Committee recommended no restrictions at all on the investments in bonds, which indicates the suitability of such investments inasmuch as the over-all recommendations of the Committee were for vast restrictions in every phase of life insurance company operations. See Chapter 26 for further reference to the Armstrong Committee.

[47] The New York law states that to be eligible, bonds must be adequately secured and not predominantly speculative. Bonds of corporations which have earned fixed charges 1¼ times over the three previous years are eligible per se.

[48] This is a comparative matter, of course. There have been times in the past when the spread of return between high-grade bonds and mortgages has not been as favorable as it has been in the last couple of decades.

In the eyes of most life insurance investors, the advantages of mortgage lending outweigh the disadvantages. The total of life insurance assets invested in both farm and nonfarm mortgages is second only to investment in the securities of business and industry.

Real Estate. At the present time, direct investment in real estate is the smallest of all classes of life insurance investments and few observers feel that it will ever become any more important.

Considered highly speculative, real estate was barred by law in almost every state as an investment for life insurance companies until the mid-1940's.[49] An insurance company was allowed to own only whatever real estate properties—such as home office and branch offices—it needed for the convenient transaction of its business plus any real estate it might have acquired by mortgage foreclosure. Foreclosed real estate had to be disposed of in a specified period of time—within five years, for example, according to New York law.[50]

Today, all but a few states have laws permitting investment in real estate. The percentage of assets which can be invested in real estate, however, is limited and many states prohibit investment in certain types of real estate, the exclusion list varying from state to state but including such prohibitions as hotels, agricultural property, mines, quarries, amusement enterprises, and clubs. The most liberal investment allowance made in any state is 20% of total assets, but this is the exception rather than the rule. Other states have much lower limits.

Types of real estate in which life insurance companies have invested include retail stores, industrial sites, suburban shopping centers, supermarkets, and the like. A popular type of investment transaction has been the purchase of industrial or business property from the industry or business, followed by a lease back to the former owner. The transaction releases working capital for the business [51] as well as offering it certain tax advantages.[52] Another type of investment, not widely used to date, is the purchase of the land upon which a building stands and then a lease back to the building

---

[49] Virginia was one of the first states to pass legislation permitting life insurance companies to hold investment real estate. The law became effective in 1943.

[50] An extension of time usually is allowed if market conditions are such that a sale within the five-year period would work a hardship on the company.

[51] The sale and lease back of property enables the corporation to realize in working capital the full value of the building whereas a mortgage loan would release only a given percentage of its value, usually not more than 50% to 60%.

[52] The tax advantage arises out of the right of the tenant to deduct rents paid as a regular business expense. The profit on the sale of the building, if any, is taxed as a capital gain. The insurance company can deduct depreciation anew on the building based on the cost of the building to the company regardless of how completely the building was depreciated by its former owner.

owner. For example, an insurance company purchased from the building owners the land on which the Empire State Building stands.

Some states now allow the acquisition and construction of apartment buildings up to a limited percentage of assets, 3% for example. Since housing developments create management problems, they are not considered desirable unless the size of the apartment or housing development is huge. Inasmuch as the limit on the amount of assets a company can invest in this type of project is small, only the largest companies have shown any particular interest in rental property investment.

A number of company investment men believe real estate in limited amounts has a proper place in a life insurance investment portfolio. It yields a higher return than almost any other investment the company can make and thus helps to offset the low return on fixed-yield investments. They feel that even though there is an element of speculation in real estate investments, large and diversified portfolios make it possible to assume the risk without serious loss—especially since the amounts that can be legally invested in real estate are small in comparison to total investments. Few, if any, however, contend that any substantial portion of assets should be invested in real estate.

Stocks. Stocks once formed a considerable part of life insurance company assets.[53] The Armstrong Investigation and the recommendations arising from it led to legislation that all but eliminated stock investment for many years. The investigating committee recommended that the state insurance law be amended virtually to prohibit investment of assets in any class of stock, common or preferred. That amendment was passed in 1906. Since most of the other states amended their insurance laws in light of the findings of the New York investigation, investment in stocks by life insurance companies was at a virtual standstill everywhere in the United States until 1928. In that year, New York amended its law to allow limited and restricted investment in preferred and guaranteed issues. During the 1940's, a number of states changed their laws to allow some investment in common stocks, and New York changed its law for that purpose in 1951. Today, only a few states prohibit investment in common stocks, although the percentage of assets that can be invested in common stock is restricted.

Stocks are generally considered to be speculative.[54] On the other hand, advocates of limited common stock investment point to the size and diversi-

[53] Fire insurance companies have long invested in common stock.
[54] However, the argument has been advanced that selected issues of common stock can be a more conservative investment than selected issues of medium and high-grade bonds. Cf. David McCahan, ed., *Investment of Life Insurance Funds*, Philadelphia, University of Pennsylvania Press, 1953, pp. 196 ff.

fication of life insurance company portfolios as a guarantee against any severe loss from common stock investing as well as from real estate investing.

One practical objection to investment in common stocks is the fact that they are not eligible for amortized valuation. They must be valued at the official market price as determined by the NAIC. Thus a severe drop in market prices could reduce the surplus margin to a point which would make the company technically insolvent.

Policy Loans. Policy loans are 100% secured. Default on the loan results in cancellation of a like amount of liability under the contract. However, policy loans are not encouraged by life insurance companies. In the first place, most of them are in the category of "small loans" which are expensive to handle. In the second place, a policy loan is likely to be a prelude to a lapse.[55] Moreover, banks will usually lend money on the security of assigned policies at lower rates than the loan rate set in the policy if the amount of the loan is reasonably large.[56] For all these reasons, policy loans are not considered as a primary investment medium.

Miscellaneous Investment. Various minor investments may be held by life insurance companies. One example is collateral loans, of which few are made. Another is investment in transportation equipment—for example railroad rolling stock leased back to the railroad. Life insurance funds have also been used in pipeline and toll-road financing and various other projects. Since the legislation of several states allows companies to invest a small percentage of assets without restriction, any type of investment or speculation might be found in the portfolios of companies controlled by these laws. For example, an Illinois company [57] once invested funds in a large quantity of cheese, hoping to make a profit from the increase in its value resulting from the aging process.

Problems and Trends. One of the primary problems facing life insurance companies is the need for ever increasing investment skill. Three factors are influential in creating the need.

First, low interest rates, which seem destined to continue into the foreseeable future, have the effect of decreasing the size of the return in relation to the investment risk.

Second, the funds available for investment by life insurance companies have grown to such proportions that today companies cannot pick and

---

[55] This is not to deny that some people borrow a number of times on their life insurance and pay it back.

[56] The life insurance company, setting a loan rate by contract, is bound to that rate no matter what the conditions of the loan market are at the time the loan is made. It is also bound to charge the same rate on small loans as on large ones. Therefore, the contractual rate must be large enough to handle the high cost of making small loans.

[57] Illinois companies may invest 5% of their assets in anything they wish.

choose among investments as they once could. In earlier days when there was not so much money to invest, the companies could find all the investment opportunities they needed among the fields in which the quality of investments was recognized and respected. There was no need to give minute and exhaustive study to the possibilities in fields where the qualities were not so clear. If the investment qualities in any field required intensive study and appraisal, it was easier simply to avoid that field. Today, the need for investment outlets and yield are such that every possibility must be scanned however exhaustive the study required.

Third, there is need for life insurance to invest with some eye toward the public interest, that is, toward promoting sound economic development. Wholly aside from considerations of the effect of life insurance investments on the economy, there is a public relations problem involved. As has been mentioned, there has been increasing public pressure over the years for life insurance to supply more of the economy's needs for venture capital. Unfortunately, there is often a conflict between socioeconomic needs and the sound investment of funds which, as in the case of life insurance, may be considered to have many of the characteristics of trust funds. A high degree of investment skill is needed to balance socioeconomic purpose with the type of investment required for life insurance funds.

The public demand for wider use of life insurance funds as venture capital also creates the problem of government interference. It creates a temptation for the politically minded to seek public attention by pressure or force on life insurance companies to comply with public demand. Life insurance already has felt such pressure. For example, it has been subject to government pressure to follow various courses in handling or acquiring government securities and has been subject to pressure to supply mortgage money at fixed interest rates.

Demands and pressures to employ investible funds in various ways seems to rise largely out of the public and political impression that life insurance funds dominate and can control the American investment market. The combined long-term savings of Americans in commercial banks, savings and loan associations, mutual savings banks, noninsured pension funds, United States savings bonds, and the like vastly exceed those in life insurance. Moreover, the Federal government itself is a bigger "insurance company" through Social Security, the Veterans Administration, Railroad and Civil Service retirement plans than all the private insurance companies combined. Finally, it is unrealistic to contend that life insurance through its investible funds can have anything like the effect on the economy that the Federal government with all its economic controls and powers can exert. Life insurance is only one of the forces influencing the economy. As powerful as it is, it is far from being all-powerful.

Valuation is another problem in the life insurance investment field, particularly if it is desirable to have more funds flow into venture capital. The effect of valuation of stocks has already been discussed.

Finally, life insurance investing always must hold in mind the fluctuation of economic cycles. As this is written, the cycle has been "up" for so long that there is a tendency to overlook the fact that downswings are possible. Furthermore, as the wealth of the country grows, the percentage of consumer spending going into nonnecessities and postponable items increases. Thus the business cycle becomes more subject to wider fluctuations and changes. A mere scanning of the curves for the past century will indicate that downswings have become increasingly more severe. Much reliance is placed today on government powers and controls over the economic system. It is often contended the system is now "depression-proof." It should not be forgotten that in the steady upswing of the 1920's there were also those who contended that the government's then existing economic controls meant there could never be a serious downturn.

Clear in hindsight, investment trends are difficult to see in foresight. The horizon is always too close. Certain opportunities that might create trends do seem to exist.

Despite the venerable age of the mortgage field, it may be an investment frontier. It has seen great innovations in the past two decades—the widespread use of the monthly payment mortgage, for an example. There is no reason to think that it may not see further developments. "Package" mortgages which include major household equipment along with the property itself already have made their appearance. There has been experimentation with mortgages containing a number of options, such as the option to make payments in excess of the regular schedule, to increase the loan without complete refinancing, to suspend payments under certain conditions. There seems also room for improvement in the mechanics of handling mortgages— in originating and servicing, and in the foreclosure process. Improvements here could make mortgage investing even more profitable and thus more attractive.

The importance of industrial bond investment seems to be growing, and there are possibilities for increased investing in real estate, transportation equipment, pipeline and tollroad financing, and other forms of investment which are now relatively so minor that they have been listed here under a "miscellaneous" classification.

Some expansion of investment in common stocks may be a trend, but it does not appear to be a major one. In the first place, the proportion of assets that can be invested in such issues is severely restricted by law. In the second place, stocks of all kinds entail artificial risks created by valuation methods that can expose surplus to wide fluctuations. In the third, and perhaps most important place, stocks call for management that requires a different type of investment skill from that traditionally developed by life insurance companies. It would seem, therefore, that as long as the interest available on fixed-return investments exceeds the contractual assumptions of the companies on their policies in force, there is but little incentive for them to take on the problems that stock investing entails.

There has been a tendency in the last decade or so for insurance companies to reduce the cost of acquiring securities. The common stock method of financing corporate issues for many years has been sale through an investment banker; that is, the issuing corporation sells bonds or stocks, en bloc, to an investment house at a price less than the investment house anticipates charging individual buyers. The procedure not only eliminates the expense of "peddling" an issue to the retail market, but also gives the issuer the cash at once. The investment house, in turn, advertises and sells to individual buyers. This is the old familiar processs of "manufacturer-to-wholesaler-to-retailer." The intermediary (investment house) justifies its existence and its profit by assuming the marketing functions of risk-bearing, financing, research, and selling. In general, the issuing corporation is not equipped to perform these marketing functions.

Recently insurance companies, especially the larger ones, have come to be such huge buyers of corporate issues that, alone or in combinations of two or three, they are often able to buy entire issues, en bloc, just as the investment house does. All the limited marketing functions required here can be performed by the issuing corporation and the life insurance companies without the aid of a middleman. Furthermore, the corporation does not have to go to the expense and inconvenience of filing with the United States Securities and Exchange Commission.

The procedure has met objections, of course. Investment houses, believing that they perform an economic function not only as middleman for the corporate security issuer but also in distributing corporate issues widely and thus diffusing ownership widely among the people rather than concentrating it in a few hands, regard the practice as undesirable and monopolistic. Both sides—that is, the insurance company, which sees itself forced in the interest of policyholders to obtain the most favorable investment return possible, and the investment broker, who sees the practice of direct buying of corporate issues as monopolistic and his existence threatened—have their arguments.

One important service investment bankers render to institutional investors that should not be overlooked in the appraisal of their importance is the role of a "finder." Many investment opportunities would never come to the attention of insurance companies were it not for the services of investment bankers in uncovering them.

There is room here, and perhaps place for, only a brief mention of the whole large and very controversial subject of direct placements. This discussion is not intended to be at all exhaustive.

4. SUMMARY

The summary of this chapter is deferred to the end of the next chapter, since that chapter continues and completes the discussion of financial management.

Questions for Class Discussion

Deferred until the end of Chapter 23.

CHAPTER 23

FINANCIAL MANAGEMENT: LIABILITIES AND NET WORTH

IN THE preceding chapter, the nature and problems of assets were discussed. The other side of the accounting equation, *assets = liabilities and net worth,* is the subject of this chapter.

The concept of a "liability" at first seems a bit tricky, for it is not something that can be touched or seen. It is simply a figure on paper which serves as a yardstick for measuring the adequacy of assets. If asset values are not equal to the valuation of liabilities, the company is technically insolvent.[1] A liability exists wherever a company is "liable" (bound or obligated) to pay out assets now or in the future. Thus the policy reserves of a company are not assets but liabilities. They measure the extent to which the company is obligated to policyholders for funds necessary to meet future death claims.

The concept of *net worth* is not at all difficult. It represents the ownership interest in the business. It follows that this figure is the difference between what the business owns (assets) and what it owes (liabilities). It is composed of two items: surplus and capital.

The nature of liabilities and net worth of a life insurance company will be clearer if the items which appear on the right hand (or liability and net worth) side of a condensed annual statement for a typical company are listed:

---

[1] It is true that a company could actually be solvent although its assets did not equal its liabilities, since asset valuation contains some element of uncertainty.

553

Policy Reserves (also called "policyholders'" or "technical" reserve). This is the amount required, together with interest to be earned and premiums to be collected, to pay all benefits under insurance and annuity contracts in force in the company.[2]

Policy Proceeds (and other amounts) left with the company. This measures the amount of proceeds payable but left with the company for future withdrawal under settlement options, dividends left to accumulate at interest, and deposits left with the company to pay future premiums. These are liabilities because they also measure the value of obligations of the company to its policyholders.

Policy Benefits in Process of Payment. This represents claims reported but not yet paid and estimated claims incurred but not yet reported. They are liabilities for they measure obligations of the company.

Dividends for Policyowners. Since policy dividends are declared at the beginning of the company's year but are not paid until the anniversary of each policy, and since policy anniversaries are distributed throughout the calendar year, the company is liable for dividends declared but not yet paid.

Taxes. Many taxes, particularly income taxes, are payable after the end of a year; thus the company will be liable in one year for taxes which have accrued in the preceding year.

Mortality Fluctuation Reserve. The policy reserve is calculated on the basis of a standard mortality table which does not necessarily represent actual mortality. Actual mortality might be higher or lower than tabular mortality. In other words, a company might be liable to pay out more for mortality claims than is allowed for in the policy reserve. As a conservative measure, it might set up an estimated liability to cover the possible discrepancy. Usually the mortality reserve is combined with a *policy revaluation reserve*. It might become necessary to set a new basis of valuation for older policies issued on bases no longer realistic, such as policies issued at relatively high interest assumption. Revaluation might call for increasing the policy reserve liability with an offsetting decrease in the revaluation reserve. This revaluation is simply a bookkeeping transaction, because once the policy has been issued, none of its provisions can be changed.

Investment Fluctuation Reserve. Estimated liability to offset adverse fluctuations in investment values. Actually, as will soon become apparent,

---

[2] Another way of explaining the concept of the reserve is to view it as the difference between the present value of future premiums receivable (an asset) and the present value of the future claims payable (a liability). Since the latter always exceeds the former on any anniversary date after the issuance of a policy, it is thus demonstrated that when the smaller asset is subtracted from the larger liability, the remaining liability is the reserve.

this reserve and the mortality fluctuation reserve are simply surplus reserves as distinguished from unassigned surplus.

Miscellaneous Liabilities. These include any liabilities not segregated under the above headings. The exact items any given company might include vary. For instance, expenses incurred in the past year but not yet paid is an example of the type of item that might be included. In a stock company, miscellaneous liabilities might include liability for dividends on stock declared but not yet paid.

Contingency Reserves. These are simply an estimated margin of safety over and beyond known liabilities. If at any time known liabilities should increase above estimates, the contingency reserve would be decreased correspondingly.

Capital Stock. The par value of the capital stock of a stock company represents the amount of funds or its equivalent paid in by the owners. It is not a liability but represents net worth.

Unassigned Surplus. Put in nontechnical terms, unassigned surplus is the margin by which the assets of the company exceed the liabilities, surplus reserves, and capital stock, if any.

1. THE POLICY RESERVE

Reserves make up the principal liabilities of life insurance companies, equalling roughly 85% of the liabilities of all United States companies.

Technically, there are two types of reserves: liability reserves and surplus reserves. *Liability reserves* are the obligation of a company to its policyholders and must be valued or set up according to the laws of each state. *Surplus reserves* are a restriction of surplus made for the purpose of conservative evaluation of unassigned surplus. They are not required by law but result from accounting practices designed (when used properly) to show the true financial position of the company. Companies that set surplus (or contingency) reserves too low tend to make their financial position appear better than it is, whereas those that are overconservative in the creation of these reserves by overestimating them tend to understate their financial position. Within certain ranges, the amount of surplus reserves is an individual company problem to be handled by management as it sees fit. In this section, liability reserves are discussed first, after which attention will be given to surplus reserves. Whenever the term "reserve" is used here, unless otherwise indicated, it shall mean liability reserve, or "legal reserve." [3]

---

[3] That is the reserve as valued under the rules or formulae prescribed by state law. It might be noted here that this formula can vary from state to state, since each state

Definition of Terms.   Several terms need defining: *terminal* reserve, *initial* reserve, and *mean* reserve.

The *terminal* reserve is the reserve at the end of any given policy year. It is sometimes called the "ending" reserve.

The *initial* reserve is the reserve at the beginning of a policy year. It is calculated by adding to the terminal reserve, as of the previous year, the net premium [4] collected. The initial reserve for the tenth year, for example, is the terminal reserve for the ninth year plus the net premium for the tenth year.

The *mean* reserve is the reserve at midyear. It is determined by averaging the initial and terminal reserves for a given policy year. Obviously, when a life insurance company prepares its annual statement, it has on its books policies issued every business day throughout the year. For the purpose of valuing reserves it is assumed that, on the average, all policies will have been in force during that year for six months. Therefore, the mean reserve is used in calculating the reserve liability entered in financial reports.

Definition of Reserve.   Because the reserve creates a need for assets, it is common to refer to the reserve as "a fund." For the purposes of a nontechnical discussion, the misnomer is of little consequence; in fact, it is often difficult and awkward to avoid such reference. However, the reserve is not a "fund" because it is a liability, and a liability is an accounting measure of obligations.

To amplify on the definition used at the beginning of this chapter:

> The Reserve measures that amount of assets which the company must have, and which, together with future premiums to be paid and future interest to be earned thereon will be required to meet all policy obligations as they fall due.[5]

Why a Reserve Liability Is Necessary.   If all life insurance policies were issued on a natural premium basis (one-year Term), there would be no need to calculate a reserve or to hold assets to offset the reserve liability.[6]

---

enacts its own laws; therefore, it is possible for a company to be on a "legal reserve" basis as far as its home state goes without necessarily being "legal reserve" by the standards of all other states. As a result of the activities of the National Association of Insurance Commissioners, wide variations among valuation laws and the number of discrepancies among them are held down.

[4] Gross premiums minus the expense addition or loading.

[5] If a company were to transfer assets to another company equal in value to the reserve together with the right to collect all future premiums on the policies outstanding, the new company could meet the obligations on these policies as they fell due, assuming that actual and tabular mortality coincided. For this reason, the reserve is sometimes called the "reinsurance reserve."

[6] Technically, there would be a need for a small *mean* reserve; although there would be no terminal reserves.

At the end of the year, there would be no further liability existing on the contract. However, the overwhelming majority of individual policies [7] in force are on the level-premium plan. The level-premium plan calls for premium payments in the earlier policy years which exceed the natural cost of the insurance. The overpayments are necessary so that the premium can remain level during the later policy years when the death rates become high and the natural cost of insurance rises sharply. The extra premiums collected in the early policy years are invested and are used in the future to help discharge policy obligations. In the collection of these excess premiums, the company incurs a liability—the obligation to use the money so collected plus interest earned on it to pay claims in the future when the premiums coming in are insufficient for that purpose. The liability so created is called the "policy," "policyholders'," or "technical" reserve.

One other source giving rise to the policyholders' reserve liability is the obligation under Endowment contracts to pay living benefits (the "pure Endowment" reserve).

The Pro Rata Concept of the Reserve. Because it is common to think of the reserve as a "fund," and to refer to it as a "reserve on a policy," laymen tend to think of the reserve as a fund divided pro rata into each individual policy. This misconception has plagued life insurance since the days of Elizur Wright.[8]

As insurance commissioner of Massachusetts, Wright kept an account book in which he computed the amount of reserve that should be set up for each policy written in the state. (Ohio still does this.) This book was open to the public, and since the amount of the reserve is stated in dollar terms, it led policyholders to assume that the reserve liability so calculated represented an amount of money in which each individual policy had a vested interest.

Actuarially there is no such thing as a reserve for an individual policy. Note again the definition of the reserve: "The Reserve is a liability representing THAT AMOUNT of assets [not "those amounts"] which . . . will be required to meet ALL policy obligations. . . ."

The assets held to meet the reserve liability are held *in the aggregate* and for the benefit of *all* policyholders. Wright's book of reserves led to tying surrender values of policies to the reserve. From then until the passage of the Standard Nonforfeiture Valuation laws [9] in the late 1940's, surrender values were calculated as a pro rata share of the funds offsetting the reserve.

---

[7] As distinguished from Group.
[8] Cf. Chapter 26.
[9] To be discussed later.

The concept of the reserve as a fund in which each policyholder has a vested, pro rata interest has led to another misconception which has plagued the business for years; that is, the misconception that the reserve is a fund *in addition* to the face value of the policy. Thus the argument often is heard that when a policy is paid as a death claim, the company "confiscates" the reserve. Actually there is no "confiscation of the reserve" when a claim is paid. The amount of excess premium payments in the early policy years is computed on an actuarial basis which assumes a normal distribution of deaths at various age levels. The premium payments above those required by the natural premium method made by those who die young are used to level the premiums and pay the death claims of those who live a long time. This is the principle of insurance, and is the theory upon which the level premium plan is based.

2. METHODS OF CALCULATING THE RESERVE

The reserve liability of a company on outstanding policies may be calculated in either one of two ways: *prospectively* or *retrospectively*. Either will give the same result.

Prospective Valuation. The prospective viewpoint considers the reserve from the standpoint of the deficiency in premiums to be collected at the later policy ages under a level-premium plan. So viewed, the reserve is the present value of all *assumed* (tabular) claims to be paid in the future minus the present value of all net premiums [10] to be collected in the future, both values computed on the basis of assumed rates of interest and mortality.[11] Obviously, the amount of the reserve liability will have to be the difference between the value of all claims that will be paid out and the value of future net premiums to be collected. The equation might be stated thus:

> *Present value of future claims minus present value of future premiums equals terminal reserve*

Steps in calculating the reserve by the prospective method on a group of identical policies issued at the same age are these:

Step 1. Determine the present value of future claims for the age at which the reserve is computed. (This is the same as the net single premium for a policy issued at this age.)

Step 2. Determine the present value of future premiums to be paid from

---

[10] "Net premiums" used here to mean gross premiums minus loading. (Net premiums on the valuation basis.)
[11] Assumed mortality and interest as distinguished from actual amount experienced.

the age at which the reserve is computed. (This is computed by multiplying the net level premium by an annuity due for $1 at this age for the remaining premium-paying period.)[12]

Step 3. Determine the reserve for one policy by subtracting the result of Step 2 from the result of Step 1.[13]

Step 4. Determine the reserve for all the policies of a given class by multiplying the result of Step 3 by the number of such policies outstanding.

The following are the steps involved in computing the reserve at the end of the second year on 5,000 Ordinary Life policies of $1,000 each issued at age 96. The net level premium on the policy using the CSO 2% mortality table is $521.87.

1. *Determine the present value of future claims for the age at which the reserve is computed.* At the end of the second year, the insured is age 98. So, it is necessary to find the net single premium for a continuous-premium Whole Life policy of $1,000 at age 98. This amounts to . . . . . . $976 [14]

2. *Determine the present value of future premiums for the age at which the reserve is computed.* To find this figure it is necessary to multiply the net level premium ($521.87) by the present value of a Whole Life annuity due of $1 a year issued at age 98.[15]

    Net level premiums $521.87
    Value of a Temporary annuity due of $1 per
    annum for remain period issued at age 98 . . 1.27
    Present value of future premiums ($521.87 × 1.27) . . 663

3. *Determine the reserve per policy.* This is found by subtracting the present value of future premiums ($663) from the present value of future claims ($976). It is equal to $313

4. *Determine the aggregate reserve.* This is determined by multiplying the reserve per policy by number of outstanding policies (5,000) giving an aggregate or terminal reserve of . $1,565,000

Retrospective Valuation. The retrospective viewpoint considers the reserve from the standpoint of excess premiums collected in the past rather than as a deficiency in premiums to be collected in the future. The equation might be stated this way:

---

[12] This computation is explained in Chapter 21.
[13] Remember that the reserve for one policy is a theoretical concept since, by definition, the insurance principle could not operate with only one exposure. It is shown here as an intermediate step in the calculation of total reserves on a group of policies of any given classification (type of policy by age of issue).
[14] Review Chapter 21 for method of computation.
[15] *Ibid.*

Initial Reserve [16] plus assumed interest earned minus assumed mortality costs equals the terminal reserve for the year

Steps in calculating the reserve by the retrospective method are these:

Step 1. *Assume (for simplicity of illustration) that the number of policies is the same as the number of people living as shown in the mortality table for the age of issue.*

Step 2. *Determine the reserve for the first year by:*

(a) Finding the initial reserve by determining the amount of premiums to be paid for the year. This is done by multiplying the net level premium by the number of policies involved. (The number of policies involved is assumed to be the number of people living at the beginning of the year as shown in the mortality table.)

(b) Compute the assumed interest earned on the initial reserve by multiplying the result of Step (a) by the *assumed* interest rate.

(c) Add Steps (a) and (b).

(d) Determine the amount of death claims by multiplying by $1,000 the number assumed to be dying during the year according to the mortality table.

(e) Determine the terminal reserve for the first year by deducting the figure obtained in Step (d) from that obtained in Step (c).

Step 3. *Determine the terminal reserve for the second year by the same method as that used in Step 2 to find the first year's reserve with but one exception.* In part (a) of Step 2, the terminal reserve for the previous year must be added to the premiums to be paid for the year in order to find the initial reserve.

Step 4. *Continue the process until the year desired is reached.*

Step 5. *When the desired year is reached, divide the reserve obtained by the number still living as shown in the mortality table to obtain the reserve per policy.*

Step 6. *Multiply the answer obtained in Step 5 by the actual number of such policies outstanding to obtain the aggregate reserve.*

The following is an example, using for illustration the 5,000, $1,000 policies issued at age 96 and again computing the reserve at the end of the second year. The net level premium based on the CSO table at 2% is

---

[16] Remember, "initial reserve" is the terminal reserve for the preceding year plus the net level premium for the current year.

$521.87. The reserve calculated by the retrospective method would be as follows:

1. Make the assumption that the company sold as many policies as there are people living in the mortality table for the age the policy is issued. At age 96 this would be   1,818
2. Determine the first year's reserve by the retrospecive method.
   a. Determine the amount of premiums to be paid during the year.
   Net level premium $521.87
   Number living   × 1,818 $949,000
   b. Determine the assumed interest earned—
   949,000 × .02 =   19,000
   c. Add Steps a and b $968,000
   d. Determine the amount of death claims.
   Deaths assumed during the year   813
   Amount per claim $1,000   813,000
   e. Determine first year's terminal reserve
   (968,000 − 813,000) $155,000
3. Determine the second year's terminal reserve.
   a. Find initial reserve by listing the amount of the previous year's reserve $155,000
   and adding to that the amount of premiums to be paid during the year.
   Net level premium $521.87
   Number living   × 1,005   524,000
                                                             679,000
   b. Determine the assumed interest earned—
   $679,000 × .02 =   14,000
   c. Add Steps a and b $693,000
   d. Determine the amount of death claims.
   Amount per claim $1,000
   Deaths during year   × 551   551,000
   e. Determine second year's terminal reserve
   (693,000 − 551,000) $142,000
4. Continue the process until the year desired is reached. In this case, the second year is the desired year; so the process can end here.
5. When the desired year is reached, compute the assumed share of each policy.
   Ending reserve of the desired year $142,000
   ─────────────────────────────────── = $313
   Number living at beginning of age 98   454
6. Determine the aggregate reserve.
   Assumed policy's share $313
   Number of outstanding policies   5,000
   Aggregate or terminal reserve $1,565,000

Note that the reserve is $1,565,000 whether computed prospectively or retrospectively. The excess premiums collected in the past will always be equal in value to the deficiency of premiums to be collected in the future because the premiums were set up originally to cover all assumed claims. Either procedure measures the reserve liability of the company.

Modified Reserve Systems. A problem in the practical operation of a life insurance company is the high first-year expense on a given policy as distinguished from expenses in subsequent years. These high first-year expenses exceed the loading on the first year's premium. Commissions to the agent, examination fee, inspection reports, policy issue—all these add up to an amount of money far in excess of the cost of maintaining the policy in any subsequent year. The valuation of the reserve, therefore, is tied up directly with the cost of acquisition for reasons that will appear in the following illustration.

Assume that the nonparticipating rate for an Ordinary life policy issued at age 25 is about $18. The total first-year commissions involved will be about $10.80; the medical examination, $6; the inspection report, $1; and the state premium tax, assuming a 3% rate, 54¢. These four items alone add up to $18.34, with no allowance for the expense incurred by the home office in writing the policy. On the CSO table, the net natural premium, that is, the mortality expense at age 25, is $1.74 without the safety factor added ($2.88 with the safety factor). Excluding home office costs connected with the policy but including the first year mortality cost of $1.74,[17] a total of $20.08 will be spent the first year. Since the premium collected is only $18.00, it is obvious that there will be nothing left to offset the required first-year terminal reserve for the policy. If a company values its reserves on the full net level premium system,[18] the sale of a new policy creates a reserve liability greater than the net addition to assets, thus reducing surplus. In subsequent years, the actual expense of operation is less than the loading, and the high first-year cost can be amortized over the premium-paying life of the policy.[19]

Thus, the more new business a company writes, the greater is the drain on its surplus. In an established company with a large surplus, the drain is of no consequence; but in a newer company with a small surplus and a high proportion of new business to business in force, the drain may be serious.

---

[17] The mortality cost on newly selected lives is likely to be less than this estimate.
[18] The full net level premium system of valuing reserves is the method used in the illustrations of either the prospective or the retrospective reserve computations made earlier in the chapter.
[19] Illustrating the fallacy of the criticism that companies make money from lapses.

Required use of the net level premium valuation system could force some companies to limit the amount of new business written.

The problem of disproportionate first-year expense could be solved by charging a higher premium the first year; but this solution is not practical since the sales forces and the buying public would object to it.

There appears to be no sound actuarial or accounting reason why a reserve valuation system that takes into account the unlevel incidence of expense cannot be used. The relationship of the reserve valuation to the expense incurred under any given policy is an arbitrary and artificial one anyway.[20] Actually, so long as the valuation system used produces a safe over-all reserve, it is sound.

In recognition of this fact and of the practical problems involved in the incidence of cost, various modifications of the net level premium reserve valuation system have been developed, authorized, and successfully used by companies throughout the years. The most important of these are the full *preliminary term, Illinois standard,* and the *Commissioners' Standard Valuation.* The full preliminary term standard has theoretical interest. The Illinois standard has historical interest, since it was the most popular plan until the mid-1940's and is still used extensively on old policies. The Commissioners' Standard Valuation system has current interest since it is the one most commonly used today by companies that do not use the full net level premium system. These three systems will be explained here, the first because an understanding of its principles will help in the explanation of the Illinois standard, and the Illinois standard because the Commissioners' Standard is but a slight modification of it.

Full Preliminary Term. Under the full preliminary term system of valuation, there is no terminal reserve at the end of the first year. Instead more will be charged to reserves in each of the future years than ordinarily would have been the case. For purposes of calculating reserves only, the policy is looked upon as a one-year Term policy for the first year. Thereafter it is regarded as the regular policy, issued one year later, for a period one year shorter. For example, a 20-payment Life policy issued at age 35 is looked upon as a one-year Term policy at age 35 plus a 19-pay Life policy issued at age 36. A continuous-premium Whole Life policy issued at age 35 would be looked upon as a one-year Term policy issued at age 35 plus a continuous-premium Whole Life policy issued at age 36.[21]

---

[20] In the sense that there is no such thing as an individual policy reserve.
[21] It should be stressed that it is erroneous to say that the policy itself is a one-year Term policy for the first year; it is only the reserve that is affected. The nature of the policy is that stated in the contract and is not determined by the method of valuing the reserve.

Since there is no terminal reserve as of the end of the first year, the entire amount of the first-year premium is released for expenses.

Many states did not permit the use of the full preliminary term reserve system under any condition, and very few states that did allow it permitted its unrestricted use. While the amount of premium released under this plan for first-year expenses under a continuous-premium Whole Life plan may be justifiable, the amount that will be released under a higher-premium policy may be excessive. The agent's commission is a large part of the first-year acquisition cost for any policy. Because the continuous-premium Whole Life policy and certain other Whole Life policies carry relatively low premiums, the standard practice is to pay the top commission scale on them and to pay smaller commissions on higher-premium policies. Thus the combination of a relatively high premium on, say, an Endowment form plus a relatively low commission will produce a large amount for expenses under the full preliminary term valuation—a larger amount than needed and might contribute to extravagance.

Illinois Standard. In view of the fact that the full preliminary term system of valuation is not satisfactory for all types of policies, modifications of it were developed. One of the most widely used in the days before the Standard Valuation laws was the Illinois standard. Under this system of valuation, policies were divided into two classes: (a) those for which the premium charged was equal to or less than that charged for a 20-pay Life policy issued at the same age for a like amount; and (b) those for which the premium charged was in excess of that for a 20-pay Life plan issued at the same age and for a like amount.

The reserves on all policies falling in class (a) could be valued on a full preliminary term basis if the company chose. Those falling into class (b) required a partial (as contrasted to net level) reserve at the end of the first year. This reserve was equal to that amount which, if credited annually to the preliminary term reserve on a 20-pay Life policy, would equal the full net level reserve on the policy at the end of the premium-paying period, or in 20 years, whichever was less. To put it another way, the first-year reserve would equal the net level premium of a pure endowment of an amount representing the difference between the full net level premium reserve on the policy in question at the end of 20 years or the premium-payment period, whichever was less, and the reserve on a full preliminary term basis of a 20-pay Life policy.

The Illinois standard valuation system can best be illustrated with a 20-year Endowment, the premium on which will exceed that of a 20-pay

Life and, therefore, must be valued in class (*b*). The method of arriving at the Illinois standard reserve on such a policy is as follows:

Step 1. Calculate the terminal reserve on the full net level premium basis for the 20th year for a 20-pay Life policy of like amount issued at the same age.

Step 2. Determine the terminal reserve on the 20-year Endowment for the 20th year. (This will be, of course, $1,000 for each $1,000 of face value because the policy endows at the end of the 20th year.)

Step 3. Subtract the reserve on the 20-pay Life policy from the reserve on the 20-year Endowment.

Step 4. View the difference between the two as the face value of a 20-year pure endowment, and then find its net level annual premium.

Step 5. The first-year reserve required for the Endowment policy will then be the equivalent of the net level premium for the pure endowment. Reserves for each succeeding year will be the reserve required for that year for a 20-pay Life policy valued on the full preliminary term basis, *plus* the accumulated net level premiums for the pure Endowment.

The explanation will be clearer if actual figures are used. Assume a 20-year Endowment for $1,000 issued at age 25, CSO 2%. Each step below is numbered to correspond with the same step in the explanation above.

(1) 20th-year terminal reserve for a 20-pay Life of same amount, issued at same age: $571.66.[22]

(2) 20th-year terminal reserve for a 20-year Endowment: $1,000.

(3) $1,000 − $571.66 = $428.34.

(4) To find the net level premium for a 20-year pure endowment of $428.34, first find the net single premium: Out of 939,197 living on the CSO table at age 25 (the age of entry), 852,554 will survive the 20 years to age 45. If each of the survivors receives $428.34, then the total to be paid in the endowment year will be $428.34 × 852,554 or $365,182,980.36. The net single premium for the pure Endowment will be $365,182,980.36 × .6730, the 2% discount rate for 20 years ÷ 939,197, the original number of premium payers or $261.68. To find the net level premium, the net single premium of $261.68 is then divided by the present value of an annuity-due of $1 per annum for 20 years issued at age 25 (which latter is found to be 16.1225). Thus $261.68 ÷ 16.1225 = $16.23.

(5) $16.23 is, then, the first-year reserve, Illinois standard, on a 20-year Endowment issued on CSO 2% at age 25 for $1,000. It is also the amount that must be accumulated and added annually to the full preliminary term valuation reserve on a 20-pay Life policy.[23]

---

[22] Calculated according to the methods explained earlier in this Chapter.

[23] For another example, the premium on a 15-pay Life policy is greater than the premium on a 20-pay Life. Therefore, under Illinois standard, there must be a first-year reserve

Commissioners' Standard Valuation. Under the Commissioners' Standard Valuation system in use on most policies issued since 1948, and many before that time, the *minimum* standard requires an interest assumption of not greater than 3½% (3% in New York) and the use of the Commissioners' mortality tables.[24]

The Commissioners' method is identical with Illinois standard except that in the case of Endowment policies running for more than 20 years, the full net level premium reserve does not have to be reached until the end of the premium-paying period instead of by the end of the 20th year as under the Illinois standard. This difference between the Illinois standard and the Commissioners' valuation system eliminates an inconsistency that arose under the Illinois standard method when premiums on some plans would be higher than 20-pay Life at young ages but lower at older ages (30-year Endowment, on CSO 2½%, for example).

It will be noticed that allowing the full reserve to be postponed to the end of the premium-paying period rather than requiring it to be equaled at the end of 20 years will result in a slightly lower valuation for such policies under the Commissioners' valuation system than under the Illinois standard. Thus the total company reserve under the Commissioners' valuation system will be slightly less (assuming a normal distribution of business and identical mortality and interest assumptions) than under the Illinois standard.

It should be stressed again that the Commissioners' valuation is the *minimum* reserve required. Any reserve valuation system which produces a larger reserve is acceptable.

One other point about modified reserve systems: Regardless of the system used, the reserve is always equal to the full net level reserve at the end of the premium-paying period.

Effect of Interest and Mortality on Reserves. The size of the reserve varies inversely with the interest assumed in its calculation. The reason, if not at once obvious, will become so after a glance at the accompanying table.

In other words, for each dollar of assets desired, say 50 years hence, it will be necessary to deposit today approximately 18¢, if the assumed rate of interest is 3½%; 23¢ if it is 3%; 29¢ if it is 2½%; and 37¢ if it is 2%. Thus, if interest rates move downward, reserves valued on the previously high rate

---

on the 15-pay Life policy. This reserve must be equal to the net level premium on a 15-year pure Endowment policy of an amount representing the difference between the full 15-year reserve on a 15-pay Life and the reserve required under the full preliminary term valuation method at the end of 15 years on a 20-pay Life.

[24] Note that this is a minimum valuation formula. A company may value its reserves more conservatively if it wishes, using any standard up to the full level premium system.

Present Value of $1 Due at End of
Designated Number of Years

End of year	If 2% is assumed	If 2½% is assumed	If 3% is assumed	If 3½% is assumed
5	$0.9057	$0.8839	$0.8626	$0.8420
10	.8203	.7812	.7441	.7089
20	.6730	.6103	.5537	.5026
30	.5521	.4767	.4120	.3563
40	.4529	.3724	.3066	.2526
50	.3715	.2909	.2281	.1791

will be inadequate. Conversely, an increase in interest rates will make reserves valued on the previously low rate redundant. Premiums also vary inversely with interest assumptions used in their calculation.

Reserve requirements (and premiums) *decrease* as mortality assumptions decrease. The reserve measures the amount of assets necessary to meet future claims. The fewer the claims, the less money needed to meet them. The use of the CSO tables for reserve valuation guarantees a conservative mortality assumption, because mortality has improved at some ages since these tables were constructed.

The reserve valuation as reported by any company is determined by both the interest and the mortality assumptions used. Unrealistically high interest assumptions or low mortality assumptions can reduce the effectiveness of reserve requirements by producing an unreasonable low reserve valuation. For this reason, the minimum valuation is specified by law. By specifying the method of valuation, the law controls the reserve and thus gives at least some assurance to policyholders that the company will be able to meet all contractual obligations as they fall due. Such is the etymology of the term, "legal reserve company"; i.e., a company which maintains assets equal to the reserves required by law.

Differing Bases of Calculation. For the sake of simplifying the foregoing explanation of the valuation of the reserve, it was assumed that the same interest rate and mortality table are used for both premiums and the reserve.

In actual practice, a company may assume a higher rate of interest in computing premiums than that used in computing the reserve. It might also use more conservative mortality assumptions in reserve computation than in premium computations.

Computation of Nonforfeiture Values. From the time of Elizur Wright until the passage of the "Guertin Laws," [25] completed in all states about 1948, it was common to tie the nonforfeiture values to the reserve. Roughly,

---

[25] Cf. Chapter 26.

the method of computing nonforfeiture values under the old plan was to return the terminal reserve minus, in the early years, a "surrender charge." The purpose of the surrender charge was to offset the higher first-year expenses which were to be recovered out of the premiums to be paid over a period of years.[26]

The Standard Nonforfeiture Valuation Laws ("Guertin Laws") take recognition of the fact that there is no pro rata relationship between the reserve and individual policies. The laws do recognize, however, the fact that a surrendering policyholder has made an "advance" premium contribution and should be entitled to a refund. This "refund," or nonforfeiture value, is determined according to a formula set forth in the law, which formula produces the *minimum* nonforfeiture value required by law. A company may grant a higher value if it wishes. Since the nonforfeiture values are now separate from reserves, the reserves can be changed without affecting nonforfeiture values—which are a matter of contract.

This minimum nonforfeiture value is based on an "adjusted premium" concept rather than on the net level premium used in reserve computations. The purpose of the adjusted premium is to amortize the high initial expense (acquisition cost) of a policy over the life of the policy and to add this amortization to the net premium in arriving at the adjusted premium. The adjusted premium is based on the three factors in rate-making: mortality, interest, and initial expense, in contrast to the net premium, which is based on only two: mortality and interest.

In order to determine the adjusted premium, the first year's expense must be figured. For the purpose of computing *minimum* nonforfeiture values the amount of these expenses is restricted by law. The maximum legal initial expense allowance is as follows:

(*a*) 2% of the face value of the policy, plus (*b*) 40% of the adjusted premium for the policy using the interest and mortality assumption employed in computing nonforfeiture values, plus (*c*) 25% of the adjusted premium for a continuous-premium Whole Life policy issued at the same age and under the same conditions, or 25% of the adjusted premium of the policy under consideration, whichever one is less.[27]

---

[26] Wholly aside from the actuarial weakness of tying nonforfeiture values to the reserve was the bad public relations of the term, "surrender charge." Uninformed critics constantly pointed to the "surrender charge" as evidence that the company "made money" when a policyholder dropped his policy.

[27] Since the expense allowance is needed to compute the adjusted premium and the maximum expense allowance depends upon the adjusted premium, an algebraic equation needs to be worked out to find the adjusted premium. These have been worked out for the usual line of policies, however, and tables of adjusted premiums have been published for them.

In no case can the adjusted premium used in the above formula exceed 40% or 4% of the face value of the insurance. In addition, the law requires that the CSO table with a 3½% [28] interest assumption be used in determining the legal minimum values.

The adjusted premium is determined first by adding the net single premium (computed under nonforfeiture interest and mortality assumptions)[29] and the amount of initial expenses. This total is then divided by the present value of an annuity-due of $1 for the premium paying period. The answer is the adjusted premium. It lies between the *net* premium and the *gross* premium. It is more than the *net* premium since it includes initial expenses. It is less than the *gross* premium since it includes only the initial expenses and not all expenses.

Minimum cash values are computed similarly to the prospective method of computing terminal reserves. Instead of subtracting the present value of future *net* premiums from the present value of future claims, the present value of the *adjusted* premium is subtracted. It gives a cash surrender value that makes allowances for high initial expenses, and returns to the policyholder what is considered to be his actuarial interest in the policy. If a surrender value is derived by the adjusted premium formula method before the end of the third year, companies are not required to pay it in cash under the 1948 law but, instead, may grant its equivalent in reduced paid-up insurance.

The other nonforfeiture options, extended term [30] and paid-up additions, are computed from the cash surrender values.[31]

The Standard Nonforfeiture Valuation law achieves several beneficial effects: (*a*) It eliminates the so-called surrender charge and substitutes for it nonamortized past expenses; i.e., the part of initial expenses which have not yet been amortized. (*b*) Under the previous practice of basing the surrender value on the terminal reserve, any company which, in the interests of safety, desired to carry a higher reserve than that required by law was forced to allow a higher surrender value. This at least partially defeated their effort to achieve greater safety. Under the new system, the two values are divorced completely. (*c*) Under the previous practice, the reserve valuation of a policy once issued could never be changed regardless of how

---

[28] 3% in New York.

[29] As distinguished from assumptions used in reserve computations.

[30] The Guertin laws allow the company to use mortality rates up to 130% of the rates for other nonforfeiture values in figuring extended term values. The allowance is made to enable a company to offset possible adverse selection under the extended term option. The additional mortality assumption, however, is seldom used by companies because of the complications created by the additional computations.

[31] Cf. Chapter 10.

unrealistic changes in mortality or interest earnings make it. Under the Standard Valuation system, the reserve basis can be changed any time without affecting the policyholder since the surrender values in the policy remain the same regardless of the reserve calculation. In fact, the reserve basis need not be mentioned in the policy.

Accident and Sickness Insurance Reserves. In addition to life insurance reserves, companies writing Accident and Sickness insurance (and Accident and Sickness companies) show several types of reserves for that class of business in their annual statements. The nature of these reserves depends on the nature of the coverages being offered. In general, the types of A & S reserves are (a) *policy reserve*, (b) *unearned premium reserve*, (c) *claim reserves*, (d) *uncompleted and unreported claim reserves*, (e) *disabled lives reserve*, and (f) *contingency reserves*.

Policy Reserve (sometimes referred to as "active life reserve"). If the claim rate or the average claim value increases with age but a level premium is charged, a policy reserve must be maintained. A policy reserve is required by law for Noncancellable Guaranteed Renewable policies and, although not always necessary, often is held for Commercial policies.[32]

Unearned Premium Reserve. Since premiums are paid in advance, companies are required to maintain a reserve equal to the premiums on the unexpired terms of all policies. On the assumption that policy anniversaries are distributed evenly throughout the year, half of all premiums are set up as the unearned premium reserve. This reserve is based on the business in force as a whole, not on the individual policy.

Claim Reserve. Since the policy reserve and unearned premium reserve provide only for losses occurring during the term of the policy, additional reserves must be maintained for claims on which, at annual statement date, full payment has not been made. If the loss is a known, stated-value benefit, such as accidental death, then the reserve is the stated value. If it is a period of terminated indemnity benefit, then the reserve is the amount of that benefit due. If it is an indemnity benefit still in progress (such as a current disability), then the reserve is the estimated benefit that will have to be paid for the disability in progress.

Unreported Claim Reserve. The claim reserve is for claims known to exist (but unpaid) at the time of the annual statement. However, there will be some disabilities incurred too close to statement date for the company

---

[32] Many of the costs for which premiums were loaded in the early years decrease as the policy remains in force, leaving the total available to meet pure insurance costs greater on older policies. It is for this reason that a policy reserve on Commercial policies is not strictly necessary.

yet to have received notice of them. The value of the claims resulting from these disabilities is estimated from past experience, and set up as a reserve.

Disabled Lives Reserves. Some states require that in addition to other claim reserves, a special "Disabled Lives" reserve be maintained for Non-cancellable, Guaranteed Renewable policies. For instance, according to the ruling of one such state, the company must set up a reserve equal to seven weeks of indemnity when a disability claim arises. This amount is corrected every 30 days thereafter so that during the first 27 months a reserve is created equal to three and a half times the amount already paid on the claim. At the end of 27 months, the reserve formula is set in accordance with a modification of a disability experience table.

Similar reserves are often set up on Commercial policies, especially where the duration of benefits is long-term.[33]

3. NET WORTH

The final section of a life insurance company balance sheet deals with net worth. This section also ties in with the other two financial statements: Summary of Operations and Surplus Account.

Net worth is made up of capital and surplus. The vast majority of life insurance is written by mutual companies in which there is no capital stock. Theoretically these companies are owned by their policyholders [34] and their net worth is represented solely by surplus. This section shall treat capital as a part of surplus since it is not an important item with most insurance companies.

While it is common to speak of Surplus as a "fund," and while it often requires circumlocution to refrain from doing so, it will be helpful in understanding the following discussion of Surplus to hold in mind that it, like the reserve, is not a fund. When combined with capital, surplus is an accounting figure showing the *net* ownership interest in the assets of the company.[35] In a financial statement, assets must equal liabilities and net worth. If after the liabilities and capital stock have been added together there are assets in

---

[33] Claim rates are not always even. They will vary seasonally, by business cycles, as a result of epidemics, and because of catastrophes. Companies, therefore, maintain contingency reserves to take care of these "peak loads" in loss experience. This type of reserve is a reserve of surplus and is not a liability in the sense of the other reserves mentioned. The question of surplus reserves is taken up in the next section.

[34] Cf. Chapter 24.

[35] In a mutual company the concept of surplus as an ownership interest seems cloudy since a policyholder, upon withdrawal, is not entitled to a pro rata interest in the surplus. The surplus represents the ownership interest only of those who remain. Actually it is difficult to say what it is in terms of ownership.

excess of them, then what might be called a "balancing factor" is set up to
"even accounts." That balancing factor is labeled "surplus."

Sources of Surplus. A company can experience gains or losses in surplus
from six sources: interest, loading, mortality, capital gains and losses, surrender of policies, and experience on disability contracts.

In the computation of its rates, a life insurance company tries to assume
lower interest, higher mortality, and higher expenses than it actually anticipates. As a result, the company is likely to earn excess interest and experience savings on mortality and expenses which all go to increase surplus.

The surrender of a policy may add to the surplus. As explained, when
a policyholder surrenders his policy, he does not receive the full terminal
reserve, but instead he receives an amount less than the reserve. The difference between the reserve and the cash surrender value is the addition to the
surplus. Naturally when a liability [36] is decreased more than an asset,[37] the
surplus (balancing factor) will increase.

As explained in the preceding chapter, certain assets periodically are re-
valued according to market prices. Thus from year to year the asset side of
the balance sheet may remain the same physically (that is, in actual items
in the asset section); yet its value may change yearly as the value of the
asset items rises and falls. When assets increase or decrease in value, so
must liabilities or net worth if the statement is to remain in balance. Since
surplus is the balancing item, any changes in asset valuation without a
corresponding change in liabilities will be reflected in surplus. When the
value of the assets goes up and there is a capital gain, the amount of this
capital gain increases unassigned surplus. When the value of assets falls,
the size of the surplus shrinks accordingly.

In addition to mortality coverage, many insurance companies also offer
certain types of disability coverages—waiver of premium and monthly income disability, for example. When a disability rider is attached to a life
policy, two additional assumptions are added: (a) A certain number of
policyholders will be disabled during the life of the policy. (b) After a given
period, a certain number of these disabled individuals will be fully recovered or dead. Thus, with companies doing a disability insurance business,
there can be gains and losses resulting from deviations between the actual
and expected frequency and severity experiences. These gains or losses will
increase or decrease surplus.

Surplus in the Balance Sheet. The surplus section of the balance sheet

---

[36] The reserve.
[37] The cash used to pay the surrender value.

is divided into three parts: special surplus funds, capital paid up, and unassigned surplus.

The *special surplus funds* are surplus reserves as differentiated from liability reserves. Such surplus reserves are set up to offset adverse mortality and investment experience. A liability reserve covers a future expenditure which the company knows it must pay. For example, the company might hold a reserve for taxes. This reserve would be a liability which has been incurred and which must be paid in the future, probably at the end of the year. A surplus reserve is one set up to cover a payment which *might* occur in the future. For example, a contingency reserve is a surplus reserve. It is held for safety purposes only, to meet any possible mortality fluctuations (which actually are not expected to occur). In other words a *liability reserve* is to cover a *known* future expenditure payment; whereas a *surplus reserve* is to cover a *possible* future cost.

The *unassigned surplus* is that part of the surplus section which is the most important to both the stockholder and the policyholder because it is from that item that dividends on policies and stock are declared. The unassigned surplus is the remainder of the surplus which has not been earmarked for any specific purpose.

The balance sheet indicates only how large the surplus is now. It does not show the nature and causes of any changes. The Summary of Operations and the Surplus Account section serve this purpose.

Gain and Loss in Insurance. In the computation of a gross level premium, the following items are taken into consideration: mortality, interest, and expenses. Thus, if a company experiences mortality and expenses as assumed, earns interest at the assumed rate, and increases or decreases its reserve according to the mortality and interest assumptions made, there would be no gain or loss from operations. This relationship can be shown as follows:

Gross Premiums + assumed interest − assumed expenses − increase in reserves [38] *− assumed mortality = no gain or loss*

Since life insurance contracts are long range and thus subject to unknown and unforeseeable future contingencies, conservative rate-making demands the assumption of higher mortality, lower interest earnings, and more expenses of operation than actually anticipated. As a result, there will be operational gains. For clarification, however, the term "gain" should be defined to eliminate misconceptions.

---

[38] Or plus decreases in reserves, as the case might be.

The immediate result of a gain is to increase surplus. In the case of nonparticipating policies, these gains actually represent earnings and correspond to profit of an industrial firm. Therefore, in rating nonparticipating policies, assumed and actual experience must be as closely identical as possible in order to develop gross rates which are competitive with net participating rates.[39] Whereas reserves on nonparticipating policies must be valued according to the highly conservative standards set by law, premiums are calculated on realistic assumptions.

However, in the case of participating policies, gains are not profits in the usual sense of the word because a certain portion is expected to be returned to the policyholder as an adjustment for an overcharge of gross premium. As a result, if a company assumes a high rate of mortality on participating plans and actually experiences a lower rate the gain is not necessarily a profit to the company at the expense of the policyholder, because the majority of the gain might be returned to him in the form of a higher dividend.[40]

A large gain from operations is no standard of operational efficiency, as untrained analysts will sometimes try to make it. Since gain comes largely from the difference between the conservative assumptions required for safety and actual experience, all that is necessary to show a large gain is to overstate assumptions. Since the gains of a life insurance company are the result of the difference between assumed income and disbursements and actual income and disbursements, the relationship can be rewritten as follows:

Gross premiums + *actual* interest [41] − *actual* mortality − *actual* expenses − increase in reserves [42] = gain or loss.

---

[39] Gross rates minus dividends.

[40] Thus it becomes obvious that the mortality table used for the valuation of reserve need only avoid *understatement* of actual mortality. Any overstatement is automatically adjusted as far as actual cost to the policyholder goes by (*a*) return of any overcharge through policy dividends in the case of participating plans; and (*b*) by the use of up-to-date tables in computing the premium for nonparticipating plans. It has never been possible to explain this point to the general public, which will listen avidly to charges from uninformed or deliberately sensational critics that life insurance companies are making "huge profits" by the use of a mortality table which overstates actual mortality. The bad public relations occasioned by the use of the old American Experience table was much of the motivation behind the appointment of the Guertin Committee by the National Association of Insurance Commissioners to study the need for, and eventually compile, the more recent CSO table. The adoption of the CSO table quieted criticism for a number of years. However, since it is now more than 15 years old, criticism is again heard and will probably increase until there undoubtedly comes a day when it forces the compilation of a new table with all the attendant expense.

[41] Including capital gains and losses.

[42] Or plus decreases in reserves, as the case might be.

The Summary of Operations. The above relationship is what is actually effected in the summary of operations.

First, the gross premiums accrued are determined by adding together the premiums on annuities, life, A & S, supplementary contracts with life contingencies, and supplementary contracts without life contingencies (period certain in settlement options, etc.).

Next, the interest actually earned is added to the gross premiums. This interest is determined by adding the net investment income (interest less taxes, investment management expenses, and other such expenses) and the net capital gains.

Then, mortality costs are deducted by subtracting payments made such as death benefits, matured endowments, annuity benefits, disability benefits, A & S benefits, and disbursements under supplementary contracts (with and without life contingencies).

Following this operation, general insurance expenses; taxes, licenses, and fees; commissions; and expenses of investigating claims are deducted.

Finally, allowance for increases and decreases in reserves is made by subtracting the decrease in reserve resulting from surrendered policies, and adding the increase in reserves for new insurance.

The result is the net gain from operations. The Summary of Operations section of the annual statement continues with a deduction for policy dividends.

Surplus Account. It is the job of the Surplus Account to tie the results of the Balance Sheet and the Summary of Operations together to show both the gain and loss and the size of surplus as of the time of the statement. The Surplus Account tells *first* the source of funds and, *second*, their application.

The account is a double-columned statement. The left-hand side shows the source of surplus. It starts with the surplus at the end of the previous year, listing the unassigned surplus and the special surplus funds for that year. To the sum of these two figures is added the gain determined in the *Summary of Operations* after the deduction of the policyholders' dividends. Next is added any capital gain not included in the *Summary of Operations*. Last is added the amount, if any, of surplus paid in [43] during the year. The total of these items tells the source of surplus during the year.

The right-hand half of the surplus account shows the application of surplus during the year; i.e., how the surplus was used. The first item is the

---

[43] Only in rare instances will there be any surplus paid in during the year. Surplus paid in is to be distinguished from earned surplus. It is much like capital in that it is paid in by its owners to strengthen the company.

amount of dividends to stockholders. Next is added any increase in reserves resulting from any change in the basis of valuation. After this, the amount of special surplus funds at the end of the year is added. The remainder necessary to balance the account is the amount of unassigned surplus at the end of the year.

Apportionment of Dividends. The apportionment of dividends to stockholders is merely a matter of dividing funds available for dividends by the number of shares outstanding. This is exactly the same process as in the case of any corporation, a stock insurance company being merely a corporation organized and chartered to do an insurance business in contrast to a manufacturing business, or any other type business for which a corporation is formed. Dividends on stock are equitably distributed when paid to stockholders in proportion to the money they have put up, as represented by their shareholdings.

Policy dividends are not, however, profits. They are returns of premiums overcharged.[44] To distribute them among policyholders as profits are distributed among stockholders would be inequitable since policyholders contribute in different proportions to the total of expense loadings, mortality costs, and the investment fund. The problem becomes one of constructing a formula for the apportionment of the savings among policyholders in a proportion equitable to the contribution of each to the source of unassigned surplus.

In apportioning the funds covering unassigned surplus, it would be unfair to distribute savings in expense loading on the basis of the face amount of the policy, for example. The amount any policy contributes toward savings in expenses of operation depends on the size of its premium.[45] Again, it would not be equitable to distribute excess interest earnings and investment gains among policies on a basis of either face value or size of premium. The contribution of each to the total of these gains is in proportion to its contribution to funds offsetting the reserve.[46] A policy with a high reserve and with correspondingly high offsetting cash values, for instance, certainly

---

[44] Thus, in the annual statement, the amount of policyholder dividends never actually enters surplus but is handled in the Summary of Operations.

[45] Policies of high face amounts usually contribute more than policies of low face amounts since quantity discounts have not been the rule. There is, however, a trend today, toward quantity discounts. Some industry leaders are predicting that before long companies will be required to develop special rates for policies of high face amounts. Cf. the discussion of special policies in Chapter 4.

[46] The usual way of putting this is "in proportion to its contribution to the reserve." While for all practical purposes such an expression is entirely adequate, the attempt here is to avoid implying the reserve is a "fund," as the expression "contributed to" does. Textbooks, like legal documents, must often resort to circumlocutions in order to preserve fine-line distinctions unnecessary in ordinary writing or conversation.

has contributed more to any excess interest earnings and investment gains than one requiring a low reserve or no reserve at all.

One more illustration:

It would be inequitable to distribute gains from mortality on a basis of total premiums, the face value, or the reserve. It might appear at first glance that distributions of mortality gains according to the face amount of the policy would be equitable. However, except in a one-year Term policy the face value will be paid partly from funds covering the reserve and partly from the mortality fund. In other words, the contribution of each policyholder to any mortality savings depends upon the amount at risk in his policy for that year; that is, the difference between the face of the policy and the amount of the reserve.

Inequities, then, will always exist if an attempt is made to divide funds available for dividends on the basis of any single factor, a fact that has not always been recognized. In the early days of life insurance in America, dividend funds were divided among policyholders either arbitrarily or on the basis of premium payments. One of the earliest methods of dividend apportionment was to credit each policy with an additional amount of insurance equal to a given percentage of gross premium paid.

The search for a more equitable method of distribution than a single-factor or arbitrary distribution method resulted, in 1863, in the introduction of the *pro rata* or *contribution* plan, worked out originally by David Parks Fackler, founder of the Actuarial Society of America, then assistant to Sheppard Homans, Mutual Life of New York and later actuary for the Equitable Life Assurance Society of New York. The plan was based on the theory that a policy's contribution to the earnings of a company can be found by the following process:

Credit the policy with

(1) The initial reserve.

(2) The excess of the loading for gross premiums over actual expense.

(3) Interest for the year on Items 1 and 2 at the *actual* rate earned by the company.

Debit the policy with

(1) The terminal reserve.

(2) The cost of insurance at the *actual* (experienced) rate of mortality.

Any credit balance resulting from this process is the basis upon which that particular policy is to share in the dividend.

The process involved in the Fackler plan (which originally provided directly for interest and mortality, being later modified to provide for loading as well) succeeded in giving the policyholder credit for excess interest earnings, excess loadings, and mortality savings in proportions equitable to to contributions made to those factors.

The *pro rata* or *contribution* plan continues to be the basis of almost every company's formula for the apportionment of policyholder dividends. In practice, a myriad of variations has arisen; but the basic Fackler principle carries through all of them. Most companies issuing participating plans make an attempt to distribute the dividends as equitably as possible so that dividends are apportioned according to the contribution of each policy to the funds available for dividends. Variations, company by company, among dividend formulas are mainly differences in actuarial philosophy rather than actuarial principle.

4. SUMMARY

Two types of reserves are found in the annual statement: liability reserves and surplus reserves. The liability reserves are to cover payments which *must* be made in the future; whereas surplus reserves cover payments which *might* have to be made.

There are two ways of computing policy reserves: *retrospectively* or *prospectively*. The *retrospective* method computes policy reserves by figuring the amount of net premiums collected, assumed interest earned, less tabular mortality claims. The *prospective* method looks at the future and considers as the policy reserve the difference between the present value of future premiums and the present value of future claims. These reserves are the *terminal* reserves, which are the reserves at the end of the year. The reserves at the beginning and middle of the year are the *initial* and *mean* reserves, respectively. However, these reserves, valued on a net level premium basis, are often modified to allow for the large amount of initial expenses in the first policy year.

Since passage of the Standard Valuation and Nonforfeiture laws, completed about 1948, nonforfeiture values are determined by the *adjusted premium* method. It uses premium adjusted for initial expenses instead of a net premium in figuring the nonforfeiture values. Cash values are the differences between the present value of the adjusted premiums and the present value of future benefits.

There are six sources of surplus: interest, mortality, expenses, capital gains and losses, surrendered policies, and disability insurance. The Balance Sheet shows the size of surplus as of the date of the annual statement; whereas the Summary of Operations shows the amount of change in surplus over the past year. The surplus account combines the results of these two statements and shows their interrelationship.

Dividends to policyholders in life insurance are not profits, as in industry, but merely an overcharge in premiums. The amount of dividends to policyholders is usually determined by the *pro rata* or *contribution* plan, which distributes dividends shared according to the amount that each policy has contributed the amount available for dividends.

Questions for Class Discussion

1. Select an annual report to policyholders of a life insurance company and explain the nature of each of the items contained in it, then take any two companies and compare them from the point of view of financial soundness.
2. Explain the following statement: "a life insurance company might be better off financially than its financial statements show."
3. Describe the nature and purpose of the *summary of operations* and *allocation of surplus* statements. Compare the reports of two life insurance companies.
4. Why is it important to have fair valuation standards for insurance company assets? Describe what you consider to be the major asset valuation problems of insurance companies today.
5. How do you account for the recent innovations of the insurance companies in the investment field?
6. Select an insurance company and appraise the general nature of its investment portfolio. Explain the standards which you have used in reaching your conclusions.
7. Compute the 5th year terminal reserve on 15,000 25-year Endowment policies of $10,000 written at age 25 using the CSO table at 2%. Use the full net level premium reserve and compute it first on the prospective method and then on the retrospective method. Explain why the answers are the same.
8. Compute the above reserve on the Commissioners' Standard Valuation method. Explain the theory behind this method of reserve computation, i.e., why is such a method allowed?
9. Explain why a company which pays the highest policy dividends is not necessarily the most economical company in which to buy insurance.
10. Explain the problems involved in achieving equity in dividend distribution.

CHAPTER 24

TYPES AND ANALYSIS OF
LIFE INSURANCE
CARRIERS

L I F E I N S U R A N C E is written by three types of carriers which may be broadly classified as *proprietary, mutual,* and *state.* The chief difference among them is in nature of ownership. Proprietary carriers are owned by investors, usually through the corporate structure of shareholding,[1] profits being distributed among the shareholders and losses being made up by them to the extent of the amount they have invested in shares. Mutual companies are in the nature of co-operatives, owned by the policyholders themselves, profits usually being distributed among them in the form of policy "dividends" and losses shared through reduction of "dividends." *State* carriers are owned by the government, Federal or state, as the case may be, which is, theoretically, ownership by all citizens of the state.

It is the purpose of this chapter to analyze each type of carrier for advantages and disadvantages to the insured and, further, to analyze the variations among carriers of the same organizational classes, not as they favor

---

[1] In other fields of insurance, notably Marine, proprietary carriers include unincorporated, individual underwriters, each taking a portion of the risk. The best-known group of such underwriters is that operating through the facilities of Lloyd's of London. The system of individual underwriters is not, however, adapted to life insurance (save to the hazard of accidental death) because of the long-term nature of life insurance and the necessity for funding all permanent forms of policies through constantly increasing reserves. Individual underwriting is adapted to "if" insurance; that is, insurance which pays *if* a contingency occurs. Life insurance is "when" insurance; that is, it agrees to pay *when* the contingency occurs, there being no question but that every life insurance policy (except Term) will someday be either a claim or a matured endowment.

any one company, but as they can be used to judge which is the "best" company for any given insuring situation.

1. PROPRIETARY CARRIERS

Proprietary insurance is issued by individuals operating through the structure of a corporation. Such corporations are usually called "stock companies." The individual shareholders of the stock company advance the money to organize an insurance carrier, and they share in the losses and profits as previously described. The stock life insurance company functions in exactly the same way as any incorporated business organization. Management control rests with the shareholders, who elect the Board of Directors which, in turn, elects the executive officers. The product of the company is the insurance it issues, just as the product of a corporation for the manufacture of automobiles is automobiles. The policyholders are the customers, just as the buyers of automobiles are customers of the corporation manufacturing them.

Advantages and Limitations. *Ease of Formation.* The majority of new life insurance companies organize as stock companies [2] because the statutory requirements for that type of carrier are more easily met than for a mutual carrier. For instance, under New York law a stock company must have a minimum of $300,000 capital and $150,000 surplus. Since the stock in well-conceived companies offers the possibility of both appreciation and investment income, it is not difficult to find the purchasers needed to set up the capital and surplus required. Once the stock has been subscribed and the various state requirements met, the company can begin to solicit business as a "going concern."

Management. Advocates of stock companies contend that their officers will tend to give more efficient management in response to pressures from stockholders for dividends, and that stockholders will be less likely to tolerate inefficient management than will policyholders who control mutual companies. This argument, however, is more theoretical than factual. The rank and file of stockholders, like the rank and file of mutual company policyholders, rarely exercises its voting privilege in person, leaving actual control in the hands of the few who are actively concerned in the management of the company.

Good or bad management depends upon executives and not upon the

---

[2] Often when a stock company is established and of fairly good size, it mutualizes. Some of the biggest of the mutual companies operating today organized as stock companies. At almost any given time, somewhere in the business a stock company is in the process of mutualization. On the other hand, there are extremely rare cases of companies which organized as mutuals changing to stock or mixed carriers.

type of company. A stock company may be and sometimes is run for the benefit of a few stockholders alone. On the other hand, stock company management which puts the interest of policyholders above the interest of the controlling bloc is not unique.

Financial Stability. In judging the financial stability of a life insurance company, four factors must be considered: (1) investments, (2) reserves, (3) surplus, and (4) underwriting.

(1) *Investments.* Since all legal reserve companies operate under the same investment laws, there seems to be no reason to assume that one type of legal reserve carrier makes safer investments than another. Any variations that exist among the investment portfolios of companies are based on differences in the investment philosophy and judgments of company management and not on type of organization.

(2) *Reserves.* Minimum reserve requirements for all legal reserve companies are the same in any given state. A company may qualify as "legal reserve" in some states but not in others. Therefore, there is no inherent advantage or disadvantage in the stock company as long as it is legal reserve.

(3) *Surplus.* Surplus to policyholders, to be compared among companies, must be reduced to a percentage of obligations. A company with reserve obligations of $20,000,000 and a surplus to policyholders (i.e., capital and surplus) of $1,000,000 would not appear in as favorable position as a company with reserve obligations of $10,000,000 and a surplus of $750,000. In the first case, surplus is 5% of obligations; in the second, it is 7½%. However, a small company to be equally safe would need a higher percentage of surplus than is needed by a large one because in a small company wide deviations of actual from expected mortality are more likely to occur. The greater the number of exposures, the less the uncertainty, and the less the need for relatively large surpluses.

There is nothing inherent in any type of organization that automatically assures a larger surplus to policyholders. This statement might be questioned by those who argue that the capital stock of a stock company offers an added margin of safety to policyholders. Except in the very small company, the capital stock is usually not a relatively large surplus factor.[3] The impor-

---

[3] On a recent annual statement, for example, a Texas company with $136,262,786 in force reported a total surplus of $900,000 with $250,000 capital stock. The ratio of capital to surplus was 27.8%. In a larger company reporting at the same time, insurance in force was $2,388,286,927 and total surplus to policyholders, $42,221,117. Capital stock amounted to $3,000,000. The ratio of capital to surplus here was only 7.1%. A smaller company reporting insurance in force as $217,994,380 and a total surplus of $2,968,630 had paid-up capital stock of $500,000. An Eastern company with $206,366,139 reported surplus as $2,900,123 and capital stock as $637,530. The ratios of capital to surplus in the latter two examples were 16.8% and 21.9% respectively. Only in small companies, then, is capital stock likely to offer any appreciable margin of safety.

ant factor in appraising the surplus position of a company is not the ratio of capital stock to surplus but the ratio of surplus and capital to policy reserves and other liabilities. For example, take two very large life insurance companies, one a stock company, the other a mutual. The mutual has a ratio of 8.36% of surplus to reserve liabilities whereas the stock company has a ratio of only 6.97%.[4] Another comparable mutual company has a ratio of only 4.67%. In the stock company, the capital stock represents only slightly more than 10% of the total surplus to policyholders. A quick glance at any compendium of life insurance reports will reveal both stock and mutual companies with high and low ratios of surplus to reserve obligations. There is no pattern indicating a stronger surplus position for either type of carrier.

While not always and invariably true, the general statement can be made that the capital stock available in stock companies is not an important advantage inherent in that type of carrier.

(4) As to *underwriting*, there is nothing in the structure of a stock company which adds any safety factor in underwriting. While underwriting practices and philosophies vary from company to company, these variations do not stem from the type of company.

Rates. Rate structures are a matter of plan of insurance rather than of type of company. There are two rating plans in life insurance: *participating* and *nonparticipating*. The participating rate is higher than the nonparticipating but is adjusted periodically by the payment of annual (and occasionally extra) policy "dividends." [5] Nonparticipating rates are not adjusted but remain flat throughout the premium-paying period. In quoting rates for participating policies, agents often speak of "net" premiums. "Net" premiums are the gross premiums as published in the rate book less the expected but not guaranteed dividend. For nonpar policies, gross rates and net rates are one and the same.

Stock companies can, and often do, issue participating policies. Mutual companies can, but rarely do, issue nonparticipating policies.[6] However, it is true that by and large nonparticipating policies are associated with stock companies; so for all practical purposes, it seems valid to discuss the advantages and disadvantages of the nonparticipating rate in connection with the discussion of stock companies.

Since in nonparticipating insurance the net and gross rates are the same, the policyholder knows when he purchases the policy exactly what his pre-

---

[4] This ratio includes capital stock and surplus to reserve liabilities.
[5] The policy "dividend" is not income in a mercantile sense, but a return of the unused portion of the premium; hence it does not have to be reported for income tax purposes.
[6] Usually the stock company issuing participating plans also issues a line of nonpar; and the mutual issuing nonpar also issues par.

miums will be each and every year. To measure future costs he does not have
to rely upon an assumption as to what future dividends may be.[7] Moreover
since the first-year rate in both par and nonpar insurance is the gross premium, the first-year premium for a given amount of insurance on a nonparticipating plan is lower than that on a participating plan. For instance
in the premium rate book of one stock company issuing both participating
and nonparticipating plans, the rates for continuous-premium Whole Life
issued at age 25 are $15.73 nonpar and $20.66 par. Thus a premium budget
of $250 a year will buy initially about $15,900 of nonpar insurance but only
about $12,000 of participating insurance.

The nonpar rate remains less than the net participating rate for a number
of years. For example, the difference between the gross par rate and the nonpar rate in the above company is $4.93. The present dividend schedule for
the participating contract is as follows:

Year	Dividend	Year	Dividend
1	$1.00	9	$5.23
2	3.04	10	5.59
3	3.32	12	6.19
4	3.62	15	7.11
5	3.92	17	7.44
6	4.23	18	7.99
7	4.55	19	8.23
8	4.89	20	8.48

Not until the ninth year will the dividend be large enough to bring the
net participating rate below the nonpar rate. By that time the total excess
paid on the participating contract will have accumulated to $10.87 so that
it will take eight more years until there is a net savings on this particular
participating contract.

The participating rate of a prominent low-cost mutual company for continuous-premium Whole Life at age 25 is $20.60. This is $4.87 more than the
nonparticipating rate of the above stock company. The present dividend
scale of this company is much more liberal so that the net premium on its
policy is less than that of the nonpar policy by the sixth year.[8] The total of
excess net premiums paid on the participating policy by that time equals
only $2.63, which will be more than recaptured by the tenth year. Another
prominent mutual charges $18.70 for its contract. Its dividends are lower
but exceed the $2.97 difference by the fifth year. By that time its contract

---

[7] Decreased interest earnings by the company or increased mortality will not increase
the premium rate of nonpar policies in force, as it will under the participating plan
where "dividends" can be reduced and, hence, net premiums increased.
[8] The stock company issuing both participating and nonparticipating plans does not
usually make its participating net premiums much different from its nonparticipating.

has cost a total of $1.96 more than the nonpar contract, but by the eighth year this excess will have been more than wiped out.

A final advantage claimed for nonparticipating insurance is the smaller amount of expense necessary to handle it when those expenses vary directly with the premium. Since agents' commissions are based on gross premiums and the participating plan usually has a higher gross premium than the nonparticipating, the same rate of commission on the participating plan will produce a higher commission than on nonparticipating. Another cost advantage of nonparticipating is the absence of dividend payments. It costs money to calculate dividends, notify policyholders of the amount of them, and make out checks for those policyholders taking their dividends in cash. Since premium taxes are based on net rates, nonparticipating policies have little advantage in that cost.

The nonparticipating rate has at least one potential disadvantage which may or may not be realized.

Life insurance rates are based on the best available estimates of mortality, interest, and expenses. If these estimates prove inadequate, present policyholders cannot be made to bear any part of the added burden. If the estimates prove too high, present policyholders do not get a return of the overcharge. Past dividend history on participating plans, as illustrated above, indicates that as a general rule in the past the total premium paid on the nonpar plan has been slightly higher.[9] This has been a disadvantage of nonparticipating, however, only to those who live long enough to realize it. Those who die early have provided for their beneficiaries a higher amount of insurance than would have been available under a par contract carrying the same gross premium.

2. MUTUAL CARRIERS

A mutual insurance company is distinguished from a stock company by the fact that voting control of a mutual organization is technically in the hands of the policyholders, who elect the board of directors, which, in turn, elects the officers of the company who supervise its operation. In case the premiums collected from policyholders prove to be more than needed to pay claims, establish legal reserves and needed surplus, and pay operating expenses, the excess is returned periodically as a policy "dividend" according to formulas devised to return to each policyholder his equitable share.

At this point, it becomes necessary to make a distinction between theoretical principle and practical effect.

---

[9] This is speaking in averages, not company by company. Whether or not it will be true in the future depends on economic conditions.

In a stock company, the individual stockholders technically control the company through their votes for the Board of Directors, which, in turn, elects or appoints the managing officers of the company. In practice, however, stockholdings are usually so widely scattered that the actual managers of the corporation are those who hold a "working majority," an amount of stock sufficient to provide the majority of votes ordinarily cast at any meeting of stockholders. Very often the "working control" is in the hands of the active management of the corporation. There are exceptions to this generalization, of course.

In a mutual company, control is technically in the hands of the policyholders through their vote for the Board of Directors. In practice, however, control is in the hands of a "working majority," just as in the case of a stock company. Few if any policyholders ever attend policyholders' meetings. Therefore, the control of the organization is usually in the hands of a relatively few policyholders—who are usually the active managers of the business. Translated into plain language, *stock companies* often are controlled by two or three officers (or relatives or friends thereof) who own a working majority of the stock. *Mutual companies* often are controlled by a few officers who have a working majority of votes by virtue of owning policies themselves and holding proxies from other policyholders. This is not to imply that the officers in either case cannot have a strong sense of trusteeship.

There appears, therefore, to be no practical difference between the methods of "control" in the usual stock insurance company and those in the usual mutual insurance company.

Few mutual companies have had at any time since the first few years of existence (when the number of policyholders was small) a sufficient number of individual policyholders at any annual meeting to outvote the existing management of the company. Policyholders do possess, however, what might be termed a "veto power." If management is bad enough to stir them up, they can step in and do something about it, a privilege they would not have in an annual meeting of a stock company unless also stockholders. Generally, however, from the standpoint of the policyholder, control creates no problem. Insurance is a regulated industry. A policyholder in either type of company can file a grievance with his state insurance department, which has the authority to correct any mal-practice. State departments have within very recent years forced the resignation of top company officers who, in the judgment of the department, were not conducting the business or their relationship to it in the full interest of the policyholders.

Advantages and Limitations. *Ease of Formation.* Mutual carriers are, by and large, a difficult type of carrier to form. In the first place, the laws of many states are very strict on their formation. In New York, for instance, the requirements for formation of a mutual life insurance company are so difficult as to make it almost impossible. The company cannot begin operation as a going concern unless it has bona fide applications for not less than $1,000 each from 1,000 people with the full amount of one annual premium for an aggregate amount of $25,000, plus an initial surplus of $150,000 in cash.[10] It takes an almost evangelical salesman to get people to buy and pay for life insurance in a company that does not even exist!

Management. Theoretically there is a great difference between the control of a mutual and the control of a stock company. These differences are, as discussed, almost purely theoretical. Actually both mutual companies and stock companies are subject to good or bad management. Which they have at any time bears little relation to the fundamental nature of their organization. It is sometimes said that in a mutual company the executives have less incentive to be economical or efficient in management since their only interest in the company is their salaries and they have no proprietary interest in the business; yet examples of carefully managed mutual companies are to be found in plentiful number. On the other hand, the mere ownership of stock by management is not, per se, a guarantee of efficiency.

Financial Stability. With respect to the four factors of financial stability, investments, reserves, surplus, and underwriting, the mutual like the stock company appears to show no advantages or disadvantages over the other types of private carriers. As for surplus, however, it is sometimes contended that the mutual company, not subject to pressure for stock dividends, tends to build up larger surpluses. However, the mutual life insurance company, most frequently issuing participating policy plans with their higher gross premiums, is under competitive pressure to pay large policy "dividends" and thus distributes surplus about as rapidly as does the stock company. Statistics are available to show that neither type of carrier predominantly has a larger surplus. Competition is a great equalizer.

Rates. Advocates of participating insurance insist that there is a margin of safety in their method of setting rates. Mutual carriers issuing participating policies charge a higher gross premium than they anticipate will be necessary, returning the overcharge at the end of the premium period as a "dividend." If mortality or investment experience is adverse, the premium overcharge is automatically available to offset it. Low interest yields and increased costs of administration in periods of inflation make it necessary for mutual companies to cut the dividend rate on existing policies. Thus increased costs of servicing business already on the books can be charged

---

[10] Requirements vary from state to state.

against that business instead of being charged only against new policy-holders, as is necessary with the nonpar policies usually issued by stock companies.[11] The participating feature has the double-barreled advantage of (1) giving an added safety cushion and (2) making equity among all policy-holders (new and old) possible.

A theoretical advantage of participating insurance is that it offers insurance at actual cost, that is, actual mortality cost plus actual cost of doing business. Competition within the industry is such, however, that the leading companies have to hold their rates in line whether they be participating or nonparticipating if they want to maintain their position in the industry.

Lower net cost is another advantage generally attributed to participating insurance. In the past it has been true that the *average* net cost [12] on participating insurance has been lower than the average on nonparticipating insurance. This is not true, however, company by company. Instances could be cited of nonparticipating policies showing a lower net cost in a given company than do participating policies in another company.

Another cost advantage of participating policies is the privilege of buying paid-up additions with the dividend. However, whether this is a cost advantage *of value* to policyholders depends upon how the policyholder wishes to use his dividends. The same is true of the privilege of allowing the dividends to be accumulated at a contractually guaranteed rate of interest, plus any additional interest above the guaranteed rate that the company may earn.

It is trite to say, but it is something of which insurance buyers, in particular, need to be continually reminded, that the least expensive issue is not always the best issue for that particular buyer. Whether the cost advantage of paid-up additions and a guaranteed interest rate on dividends left to accumulate is a real advantage for the policyholder depends on whether the policyholder lives or dies. If the policyholder lives, he is better off to have bought paid-up additions or to have left his dividends to accumulate at interest—for he then has higher values in cash to use for retirement purposes. On the other hand, if he dies while there are dependents who still need income, he would have been better off to have used the amount of the dividends each year as a premium on additional, installment-premium life insur-

---

[11] It will be recalled that one of the requisites of an insurable hazard is that it be possible to establish an equitable rate for it. Therefore, the claim that participating policies make for greater equity in rates is an important one. However, whether equity of rates is a cost advantage depends upon whether or not it favors the side you are on.

[12] Net cost is defined as total premiums paid, minus dividends if any, minus cash value at the end of the period over which the estimate is being made.

ince which is, in effect, what happens when a given premium budget is used :o purchase nonpar insurance.

One disadvantage inherent in participating insurance is that it too often leads to selling on a basis of projected net cost; that is, the agent leads the buyer to believe that the net cost of the proposed insurance over the policy period will be comparable to if not identical with the net cost computed either (1) over a period of past history (ten to 20 years usually) or (2) with the current dividend scale.

Few companies writing participating insurance can honestly deny that the majority of their agents sell on the basis of projected net premiums. Such carriers can and do defend themselves by pointing out that salesmen are warned to tell policyholders that projections of dividend scales are theoretical only and that nothing said should be implied as either guaranteeing or estimating that future net cost experience will compare with past net cost experience. They also will point carefully to statements accompanying all dividend illustrations that "dividend figures are illustrations only and neither imply nor guarantee future experience."

The use of dividend illustrations as a sales point may be bad public relations. No matter how carefully it has been explained to the policyholder that dividend projections do not imply future experience—and it is not too often carefully explained—the policyholder tends to be resentful when he finds his net premium greater in any one year or over a period of years than the rates suggested in the illustration he was shown as part of the inducement to buy.

3. MIXED COMPANIES

In addition to stock and mutual companies, there are in the business a few examples of what may be termed "mixed" companies. Such companies have aspects of both stocks and mutuals, but in combinations that vary so widely it is difficult to set up a general definition. For example, voting for directors may be shared between the stockholders and the policyholders. Sometimes voting by policyholders is restricted to those who own a certain minimum amount of insurance in the company; that is, each stockholder may have a vote per share or a fraction of a vote per share, whereas any policyholder with some such minimum as $5,000 of life insurance has one vote regardless of amount above the minimum. In other cases, the company may be technically stock but with a limit on profits to stockholders from participating issues; and the stock, or a large percentage of it, may be trusteed.[13]

---

[13] It is common to refer to companies which issue both par and nonpar as "mixed" companies. The authors do not feel issuance of both types of policies justifies the classifica-

4. OLD LINE COMPANIES

The term, "old line," has no real, technical significance. The designation was adopted by the regular companies during the latter half of the nineteenth century to distinguish themselves from the new and, at the time highly competitive fraternals.

The Old Line company on the one hand, and the fraternals on the other are organized under different sections of the insurance code. Since most of the fraternals were originally assessment insurance organizations, the term "Old Line" also is applied to indicate that the carrier is not an assessment company. "Old Line" is widely used to designate legal reserve companies writing business for the general public. An Old Line company may be either a mutual or a stock company.

5. FRATERNAL CARRIERS

A "fraternal" is an insurance carrier organized in most states under the section of the insurance code relating particularly to social organizations providing insurance for their members. State regulation and supervision of fraternal carriers generally are less strict than those applying to regular companies. Reserves may be computed on a less conservative basis than the Guertin legislation requires of regular carriers; that is, fraternals may use a combination of interest and mortality assumptions which yield lower reserve than the CSO table at $3\frac{1}{2}\%$.[14] Fraternals, however, are not allowed to issue "closed" contracts under which rates and policy provisions cannot be changed. Instead, they must issue an "open" policy (called "certificate") in which the bylaws and rules of the organization are a part of the contract and any amendment of them is automatically an amendment of the policy, as to rates and provisions. Also, fraternal sales representatives in many states need not be licensed and in others are subject to less stringent licensing requirements. Regulation pertaining to investment is the same for fraternals as for regular carriers.

To qualify as a fraternal, an insurance carrier must be nonprofit and must have a lodge system with a representative form of government. Fraternal insurance plans originally were organized on the full assessment principle.[15] As the average age of membership increased and assessments mounted, difficulties were encountered. Fraternals soon recognized the importance of

---

tion of "mixed." Instead, there must be some mingling of stock and mutual characteristics in the basic structure of the company to justify the classification. They admit their definition is an arbitrary one but feel it is less confusing than others which might be set up.

[14] 3% in New York.
[15] Cf. Chapter 26.

actuarially sound rate-making principles and began shifting to a legal reserve basis. When a fraternal has moved to a legal reserve basis, it may still continue to be a fraternal by virtue of holding on to its lodge system and its "social purpose." It is then known as a "Legal Reserve fraternal." When it has not only moved to a legal reserve basis but also has dropped its lodge system as a few have done, it becomes an Old Line company.

A "fraternal" always is a mutual. It may or may not be a pure assessment mutual. The usual metamorphosis of a successful fraternal is from an original assessment basis to a legal reserve basis (and some, eventually, to an Old Line basis). Often the lodge system of a fraternal is merely a token. This is particularly true of the fraternal which has reached a stage of development just short of "Old Line." At this stage, although only lodge "members" may be granted policies, anyone who wants to buy a policy automatically can become a member simply by purchasing the insurance.[16]

Advantages and Disadvantages. Although fraternals are not required to maintain legal reserves as rigid as those required of regular carriers, many of them value their reserves on a basis every bit as conservative as the leading Old Line companies. Therefore, if a given fraternal is a legal reserve carrier, whatever advantages are inherent in the mutual structure also are advantages inherent in the fraternal. Fraternals have an additional, theoretical safety advantage in the "open contracts" under which they reserve the right to increase the rates or modify the benefits of existing policies whenever such is essential to maintain solvency. The need for the safety clause, however, is questionable, especially when rates are computed and reserves are set up on an actuarially sound basis. Fraternals never make a point of emphasizing the open feature of their contracts because buyers, as a rule, do not favor such a contract. Were it not for the law, the open feature for all practical purposes could be eliminated from the contract since its value is largely theoretical. Rather than risk additional money in what would seem like a poorly managed operation, if the rate is increased, the insured is likely to discontinue his insurance in the fraternal if he is still insurable and buy a policy elsewhere. The number remaining with the company is likely to be too small to continue the operation, especially with the amount of adverse selection which would probably result.

Financial Stability. Obviously when fraternals are not on a legal reserve basis, they do not have the same margins of safety resulting from required reserves as do the legal reserve carriers.

---

[16] Restrictions on membership, however, still prevail among typical fraternals. Common restrictions are those limited to members of certain national, church, labor, and/or color groups. A few limit membership to men only and even fewer limit membership to women.

When fraternals are legal reserve companies, their surplus account may be similar to that of stocks and mutuals. However, many fraternals not on a legal reserve basis report "surpluses" which, in reality, are not "surpluses" at all in the true meaning of the word. Instead they represent future obligations to policyholders much as do the legal reserves in legal reserve companies, definitely a misleading use of the word "surplus."

Fraternals have varying underwriting standards. Some fraternals may be more lenient than some commercial companies, whereas other fraternals may be more strict. The term "fraternal" does not in itself imply any particular underwriting standard—lenient or severe.

Rates. Fraternal carriers are at neither an advantage nor disadvantage in the rates they charge for ordinary insurance. Just as among commercial carriers, there is a clear variation in rates charged by the different fraternals. It would be possible to find some commercial carriers which charge more and some which charge less than that charged by a fraternal selected at random. Fraternals, however, in general appear to offer insurance in low amounts (less than $500) at more attractive rates than those offered by the industrial departments of commercial carriers.

Taxation. Since fraternals are considered charitable institutions, they are exempt from taxation. They do not pay any Federal income tax nor do they pay the state premium taxes.[17] Those fraternals which actually do charitable and benevolent work are entitled to their tax-exempt status but it is feared that a number of fraternals are reaping the benefits of tax immunity without seriously performing any charitable or benevolent operations sufficient to justify their favored treatment.

6. ASSESSMENT COMPANIES

The assessment company may or may not be a fraternal; that is, it may write insurance only upon "members" of some type of lodge or social system, or it may write policies for virtually the general public. For instance, one small, Midwestern assessment company limits its policyholders to church members, interdenominationally, a definite "class" limitation but, at least in the United States, a broad class. The laws of many states now prohibit the incorporation of any new assessment associations.

The assessment life insurance company operates on the principle of practical as well as theoretical mutuality.

It will be recalled that, *theoretically,* mutual policyholders share not only in operational savings (as among Old Line mutuals) but also in losses. How-

---

[17] They do pay filing fees whenever they file required documents with the state.

ever, only in the assessment company do policyholders *actually* share directly in losses as well as in gains. In Old Line mutuals, the policyholder is paid or credited a return of the overcharge on his premium, which theoretically represents the operating savings of the company. However, the policyholder does not share directly in an operating loss of an Old Line mutual. Policy dividends may be zero, which means that the company has made no savings to share; but there can never be a request for more premium.

In the assessment company, the policyholder not only shares in the operating profit, through policy dividends, but also, in the event of loss, shares in that loss through an assessment—usually an additional premium.

The assessment mutual issues what is known as an "open-end contract." In effect, the carrier estimates the amount necessary for the operation of the business and the payment of claims during any premium-paying period and then establishes a premium rate in accordance with this estimate. It contracts with the policyholder to return any portion of that premium which is not required for operation. It also obligates the policyholder to pay additional premiums should they become necessary.

A "legal reserve assessment company," sometimes called stipulated premium company, is one which maintains the reserves required by law but which retains a "contingency clause" in policies in lieu of the required free surplus. Under the clause, it can then call for additional premiums through an assessment. Aside from the assessment feature, minimum rates and reserves are required by state law. These organizations, therefore, are hybrids since they have characteristics both of assessment associations and legal reserve companies. In some states, Illinois for example, the new company is required to have the assessment clause in all contracts until the surplus equals a certain minimum sum.

Perhaps in pure theory the assessment company is the safest of all, for the law permits them under their contracts to charge an additional premium whenever the original rate proves inadequate for a given operating period. Although a stock company cannot increase rates on existing nonparticipating policies and a mutual company has leeway only up to the extent of the dividends, an assessment organization can increase rates indefinitely or up to some maximum set in the contract. The advantage of the assessment feature is more theoretical than practical, however, for the task of collecting any sizable assessment is usually impossible.[18] While the assessment feature may

---

[18] A few instances can be cited of assessment carriers surviving an operating deficit or impairment of assets which would ruin a commercial company. The safety margin of the assessment feature proved to be the saving factor in those cases.

be a theoretical advantage of that type of carrier, it is generally considered to be a practical disadvantage from the standpoint of the insurance buyer who more than likely shudders at the mentioning of the word "assessment."

Assessment insurance cost advantages are mostly theoretical, whereas the disadvantages of assessment insurance are practical: (1) complete uncertainty as to the amount of premium that eventually will be required, and (2) less security as a result of inadequate surpluses and reserves.

Pass-the-Hat Assessment Companies. In addition to the assessment mutual there are still in operation today some examples of purely "pass-the-hat" insurance carriers. These are usually small racial, religious, or lodge organizations. Either they charge no premium in advance or charge only a small one designed to pay overhead costs. Each time a claim arises, members of the organization are requested to contribute an amount sufficient to indemnify the beneficiaries. These contributions generally are level among all members irrespective of age. It was this type of financing which caused much of the trouble fraternals experienced in the early days. Obviously, as members of the organization became older and the rate of mortality increased, the frequency of assessments had to be increased on the remaining members or the benefit had to be reduced. In the history of such insurance carriers, it has rarely been possible for a pass-the-hat organization to bring in the constant supply of new and younger members or contributors necessary to maintain financial health.

7. SAVINGS BANK LIFE INSURANCE

In recognition of the social and economic importance of insurance for the individual of modest income, it was suggested as early as 1874 that low-cost life insurance be written by savings banks. It was not, however, until after the Armstrong Investigation [19] that such a proposal was seriously considered.

Two of the findings of the Armstrong Committee disturbed Louis D. Brandeis, the father of Savings Bank life insurance: (1) that many companies at that time seemed to put the interests of the policyholders last on the list of considerations in the operation of the company, and (2) the comparatively high cost of weekly premium industrial insurance. So Brandeis, later Justice of the United States Supreme Court, worked out a plan for the issuance of life insurance by the nonprofit mutual savings banks of Massachu-

---

[19] An investigation by the State of New York, 1905, into many phases of life insurance company operations. Cf. Chapter 26.

setts. He convinced the legislature of the state that the banks would be a proper medium for the issuance of low-cost life insurance for the benefit of low-income groups. Originally, policies were to be limited to $500 in any one bank upon the life of an individual. This limit subsequently was raised to $5,000, although the insured could buy as many policies in different banks as he could get issued up to the statutory limitation of $36,000.[20] All the insurance, however, could be purchased through one bank. The originating bank serves as agents for the other banks. The $5,000 limitation does not apply to group insurance.[21]

In 1907 Massachusetts passed the laws necessary to permit the banks to establish insurance departments and required that the funds of the insurance department be kept separate from the banking funds. The insurance funds are not available to pay any obligations which might arise in the banking departments, nor are the banking funds liable for any obligations of the insurance departments.

Originally, in order to establish an insurance department, it was necessary for a Massachusetts savings bank to obtain, by subscription, a guaranty fund. A later provision in the law required each bank operating an insurance department to pay into a central fund 4% of the total premium it collected. The banks were required to continue to pay into this fund until it reached $100,000, which amount was reached in 1921. The purpose of the arrangement was to provide the guaranty funds for additional banks wishing to establish insurance departments. The effect was to eliminate the burden on each bank of raising its own guaranty funds.[22]

In order to hold down the cost of Savings Bank insurance, the use of agents is forbidden. Further, in the beginning, the expenses of the office of

---

[20] Although the statutory limitation is $36,000, underwriting rules of the banks restrict the maximum coverage to $25,000. Before July 24, 1951, the maximum limit available at any one bank was $1,000. There are 36 authorized banks in the system. When the maximum allowable in each bank was raised from $1,000 to $5,000 the total limit of $36,000 was left unaltered.

[21] The limitation on annual income from Deferred or Single Premium annuities is $200 per bank or $7,200 from all banks. Underwriting rules of the banks restrict the total to $1,800, which is far under the statutory limit. The banks are free to set whatever maximum they wish so long as it is under the statutory maximum.

[22] At the present time a Massachusetts bank voting to organize an insurance department must have as a cash advance to that department (1) a special expense guaranty fund of not less than $5,000 to be applied in payment of expenses, and (2) a special insurance guaranty fund of not less than $20,000 to assure the payment of claims. Under certain circumstances, in lieu of the special insurance guaranty fund, the General Insurance Guaranty Fund, with approval of the Commissioner of Insurance and the Commissioner of Banks, may contract to guarantee the risks of the insurance department of a savings bank until the bank's insurance department shall have accumulated a surplus of $20,000.

actuary and medical director were borne by the state.[23] The savings bank system in Massachusetts is supervised by the state insurance commissioner. A "Division of Savings Bank Life Insurance" employs "instructors" to present the insurance plan before employees and similar groups.

While the savings bank system does not use solicitors or agents, through the medium of a co-operatively supported Savings Bank Life Insurance Council it does carry on an extensive and continuous advertising and publicity program, employing all the usual advertising media: pamphlets, leaflets, radio, match folders, newspapers, etc. It cannot be said, therefore, that the system does not actively solicit business but only that it uses means other than agents.

Applications may be taken by nonissuing banks, employers, credit unions, and other types of authorized outlets which may retain a small collection fee. Employers authorized to receive applications are not entitled to the collection fee.

The Division of Savings Bank Life Insurance assumes such functions as calculations of rates, underwriting, and medical examinations. The individual banks have nothing to do with these operations. Through the medium of the General Insurance Guaranty Fund, mortality experience is pooled and distributed equally among the banks, thus creating a wider spread of risk than would be possible for an individual bank to achieve in view of the fact that it cannot use agents to gain an adequate distribution of risk.

All Savings Bank life insurance is issued on a participating basis. Types of policies and policy provisions are those customarily found in the commercial companies: Whole Life, limited-payment Life, Endowment, Term, and Annuities. Premiums are payable monthly, quarterly, semiannually, or annually. A popular plan of premium payment is for the policyholder to authorize his bank to pay his premiums regularly from his savings account.

The growth of business in force among the savings banks in Massachusetts was slow in the early years. Originally, banks were not enthusiastic about the plan. Up to 1922, only four banks had established insurance depart-

---

[23] Through the years 1907–1926, all expenses of the Massachusetts Savings Bank Division were borne by the state. During 1927–1933, an increasing portion was reimbursed to the state. For the period 1907–1933, the following figures relate to the expenses of the Division: Total actual expenditure, $670,248.43. Reimbursements to the state by banks from 1927 through 1933 were made in the amount of $119,102.21, leaving a net state expenditure of $551,146.22. Since 1934 there have been no out-of-pocket expense subsidies. From 1934 to 1938 the banks have reimbursed the state at the end of each year for the actual amount spent. From 1939 to the present banks have been paying into the State 1/12 of the annual appropriation each month in advance. The Massachusetts division is still housed, rent free, in the State House.

ments. Since that time, however, many new departments have been added and the volume of business in force has grown substantially.

Legislation to permit the establishment of Savings Bank life insurance in the State of New York was passed in 1938 and in the State of Connecticut in 1941.

The requirements for the establishment of a separate insurance department by New York mutual savings banks are much the same as those for Massachusetts banks with some technical exceptions.[24] In New York as in Massachusetts, savings banks have the same rights in general and are subject to the same limitations in their insurance operations as are other domestic legal reserve life insurance companies.[25]

Like the Massachusetts banks, New York savings banks write all the regular forms of life insurance. Individual annuities are not written. About 40 banks have insurance departments. About 26 more serve as agency banks for the receipt of applications and the payment of premiums.[26]

Similar regulations exist for the formation and operation of an insurance department in a Connecticut mutual savings bank.[27] Eight banks in Connecticut are qualified to issue insurance and about 23 serve as agency banks. The banks issue the usual line of policies. The maximum amount of insur-

---

[24] To establish an insurance department, a New York mutual savings bank must (1) establish a surplus fund of not less than $20,000 to meet operating expenses and losses occasioned by other causes and (2) invest $17,000 (formerly $20,000) in the Savings Bank Life Insurance Fund.

[25] The amount of insurance that may be written, however, is limited to $5,000 and insurance may be written only for residents or people regularly working in New York.

[26] The New York Savings Bank Life Insurance Fund, which is outside of the New York insurance department, administers the unification of mortality among the banks, determines premiums and policy forms, and prescribes underwriting rules and regulations. In general, the fund provides the services of the actuary and medical director. The fund is financed entirely by the issuing banks which, in addition to their original investments of $17,000, may be required to pay into the fund a given percentage of premiums received. The percentage has fluctuated between 1% and 4%. The approval of the Superintendent of Banks is required for any change.

[27] Here again are technical exceptions. The Connecticut statutes state that a mutual savings bank may establish a life insurance department by advancing a surplus fund of at least $5,000 to the insurance department of the bank and the investment in the Savings Bank Life Insurance Fund of not less than $1,000 for each $1,000,000 or fraction thereof of the book value of the bank's assets but not to exceed $50,000. No investment will be required in the Savings Bank Life Insurance Fund when the assets equal or exceed $100,000. Assets of the savings department of a bank and of the life insurance department shall be separate. At the end of each year the ratio of actual to expected mortality for all the savings and insurance banks combined and for each separately is determined and an adjustment is made accordingly by the Savings Bank Life Insurance Fund. Expenses of the Fund are apportioned among all the issuing banks. Banks are required to pay monthly an amount not to exceed 4% of all amounts paid to them as premiums or in the purchase of annuities during the preceding calendar month to the Savings Bank Life Insurance Fund.

ance that may be purchased on the life of one individual is $3,000—whether purchased all in one bank or divided among several banks.

The extension of the system of Savings Bank insurance into other states has been advocated from time to time, and bills authorizing Savings Bank insurance have been introduced in several state legislatures. To date, no additional Savings Bank insurance plans have been passed.

Commercial carriers and agents have charged Savings Bank life insurance with unfair competition, citing initial subsidies and favorable regulatory treatment, especially in Massachusetts. They charge particularly that Savings Bank insurance does not serve the function for which it was established: supplying the low-income worker with inexpensive insurance. They point out that the average size policy is indicative of the fact that purchasers are more often logical prospects for Ordinary policies rather than those for whom it was the original purpose to provide: the lower income, Weekly Premium policy buyer.

Agents' organizations profess that they would not oppose Savings Bank insurance if it were "fair competition" but feel that they must oppose it for what they see as *unfair* advantages. Savings Banks seek to dismiss these objections as attempts of agents to protect their market.

Advantages and Disadvantages. *Ease of Formation.* Savings Bank life insurance, in those states in which it is authorized is, perhaps, the easiest type carrier to organize. Applications to write Savings Bank life insurance will be entertained from any mutual savings bank willing to meet certain requirements.[28] These stipulations, inasmuch as the bank is already a going concern, are far less difficult to comply with than in the case of the organization of a company "from the ground up."

Financial Stability. Savings Banks operating insurance departments must invest insurance funds in the same way they invest banking funds, except they may make policy loans. Savings Bank investments are more restricted than the investments of commercial life insurance companies.[29]

---

[28] In Massachusetts, for example, a mutual savings bank may establish an insurance department by (1) securing the approval of (*a*) the Commissioner of Banks and Commissioner of Insurance and (*b*) a majority of two thirds of its trustees present and voting at a meeting specifically called for the purpose and the majority of its incorporators present and voting at a meeting duly called for the purpose, and (2) by providing the Special Expense Guaranty Fund and either the Special Insurance Guaranty Fund or the contract with the General Insurance Guaranty Fund referred to above. Formation is equally simple in New York and Massachusetts.

[29] In Massachusetts approximately 70% of assets are invested in bonds and 20% in mortgages. In New York about 65% is invested in mortgages and 25% in bonds. In Connecticut about 60% is in mortgages and 20% in bonds.

Legal Reserves required of Savings Bank insurance are the same as those required of private commercial insurers.

As for *surplus,* the laws of the various states differ for Savings Bank life insurance. In Massachusetts, for example, each bank must accumulate a minimum surplus of $20,000 out of its profits. After the minimum is obtained, the bank must pay out in dividends 85% of profits. Unless the state actuary approves a higher figure, the maximum surplus which a bank may hold is 10% of its reserve. Additional protection is provided in the bank's pro rata share of the assets held by the General Insurance Guaranty Fund. Without taking into consideration the General Insurance Guaranty Fund, the average surplus today for all banks is more than 9% of total liabilities. This is in excess of that of many mutual and stock companies.

As to *underwriting,* under the "unification of mortality" system, banks showing better than the average mortality experience for all banks pay into the General Insurance Guaranty Fund an amount determined by the actuary of the state. The banks experiencing higher-than-average mortality receive these contributions. However, since the underwriting is done centrally for all the individual banks, mortality experience is as uniform as the underwriting can make it. The pooling of mortality experience is not a matter of underwriting safety but is designed to iron out the expected fluctuations in mortality experience of the banks with a small volume of insurance. Although the mortality experience among savings banks is good, it can be matched by some of the well-managed stock and mutual companies.

Rates. Savings Bank life insurance offers policies at generally lower rates; [30] and the net cost of its policies has been generally lower than that of the typical commercial legal-reserve company. One factor contributing to lower rates is that some of the overhead charges common to all insurance carriers are lower because, as going concerns, banks provide the housing and the clerical staff at less cost to the insurance fund. For accounting purposes, a proportionate amount of the total overhead of the bank is chargeable to the life insurance department; nevertheless, the cost of two families living under one roof is not usually exactly double the cost of one family living under that roof. Also, actuarial and medical service is centralized in a cooperative bureau.

---

[30] The rates for Savings Bank life insurance are probably not as much lower than those for commercial carriers as Brandeis expected they would be. There are several commercial companies currently issuing policies at rates, dividends, and cash values that compare favorably with those of savings banks. For example, note the following table in which the average 20-year costs and the cash values of continuous-premium Whole Life and 20-Pay Life issued at age 25 are compared among Massachusetts savings banks insurance and several commercial life insurance companies.

Footnote 30 (*continued*)

Company	Continuous-Premium Whole Life Age 25				20-Payment Life Age 25			
	Total Premium	Total Dividend	Average 20-year Premium	Cash Value at End of 20 Years	Total Premium	Total Dividend	Average 20-year Premium	Cash Value at End of 20 Years
Massachusetts Savings Bank	$371.20	$90.84	$14.02	$288.48	$584.20	$108.76	$23.77	$558.24
Company A	331.40	68.46	13.15	268.00	600.80	122.99	23.89	535.00
Company B	412.00	116.47	14.78	303.19	675.80	140.16	26.78	616.45
Company C	349.20	69.75	13.97	261.11	574.80	88.61	24.31	551.37

Note that although Company B has a higher average net annual rate for the 20 years than shown by the Massachusetts savings banks, it also has a larger cash value. Note also that while Companies A and C have lower cash values they also have lower net rates than those reported for Massachusetts savings banks.

Savings Banks claim they can offer life insurance at generally lower rates also because they pay no salesmen's commissions.[31] Consequently loading for the servicing of Savings Bank life insurance policies is less than that for the servicing of commercial life insurance policies. Savings banks do not offer as much in the way of service to policyholders (advice, personal calls, etc.) as do regular companies. Finally, costs are lower because of a low lapse rate. Most of their policyholders are those with sufficient sense of responsibility to buy on their own initiative.[32]

Beyond these cost advantages, it need only be said that Savings Bank life insurance carriers issue participating insurance, and what has been said about the cost advantage and disadvantage of participating contracts applies to savings bank carriers as well as to commercial carriers.

Service. Since Savings Bank insurance operates without agents, it cannot offer as much service to policyholders as can the typical commercial company. True, Savings Bank outlets are well scattered throughout the three states, but the difference in service between Savings Bank insurance without agents and companies with agents is the same as the difference between the physician who won't make house calls and the one who will.

8. WISCONSIN STATE LIFE FUND

The Wisconsin State Life Fund is a life insurance carrier controlled and operated entirely by the State of Wisconsin.

The legislature of the State of Wisconsin, in 1911, authorized the Commissioner of Insurance to issue life insurance on residents of the State. The first policy was issued in October, 1913.

The maximum amount of insurance which may be issued by the Fund on one life is $5,000 and the minimum $500. The common types of insurance policies are offered. Only Wisconsin residents are eligible for insurance. Individual annuities are not issued.

The State assumes no liability other than through the fund itself. Administration of the fund is by the State Treasurer. The conduct of the business is left to the state insurance commissioner. The State Board of Health assists in medical selection, and the treasurer of the state is the treasurer of the fund. The secretary of state audits the accounts submitted to him by the

---

[31] There is, however, a sales cost factor in the loading for the rates for Savings Bank life insurance to pay the cost of advertising.

[32] If, however, these were the only people who ever bought life insurance, there would be far fewer American families with at least some insurance protection. The agent induces many who would never buy on their own initiative to provide needed protection. More of these "sold" policies lapse than among the self-selected, but many of those who do stick are people SBLI could never have covered.

audit board, members of which also are state officials.[33] The fund has no
agents and does not engage in the advertising which is undertaken by the
Savings Bank Council on behalf of Savings Bank life insurance. Applications
are taken by designated state, county, and city officials, and state banks, and
through them are forwarded to the commissioner.

Progress of the Fund has been minor, apparently from the lack of both
sales effort and advertising. The table shows the amounts of insurance in
force in the Fund:

Wisconsin State Life Fund

Life Insurance in Force by 5-Year Intervals Since 1913

End of Year	Amount in Force	End of Year	Amount in Force
1913	$ 146,400	1933	$1,426,550
1918	380,600	1938	2,122,090
1923	469,000	1943	3,071,270
1928	1,148,580	1948	3,643,385
		1953	5,152,385

9. UNITED STATES GOVERNMENT AND NATIONAL SERVICE LIFE INSURANCE

United States Government Life Insurance was established as a war measure in 1917. The Bureau of War Risk Insurance was organized within the
Treasury Department to handle insurance covering disability or loss of life
among members of the Armed Forces engaged in warfare, since the military
hazard is considered uninsurable by private companies during wartime.[34]
Policies originally issued by the Bureau of War Risk Insurance were on a
one-year Renewable Term basis, with the rate increasing each year on what
is known as the "step-rate" plan. Originally also, policies were renewable for
only five years. There were subsequent extensions of time, however.

The total War Risk Insurance in force was, at one time, in excess of
$40,000,000,000. By act of Congress in 1921 the Veterans Bureau was estab-
lished, and the functions of the Bureau of War Risk Insurance of the Treasury Department were taken over by it. At that time, only 651,054 policies
remained in force for a total face value of $3,849,375,735.

United States Government life insurance is the old War Risk Term converted to a permanent policy form. The Veterans Bureau also was authorized
to issue United States Government life insurance to veterans of World War I
and to members of the Armed Forces.

---

[33] The attorney general, state treasurer, and commissioner of insurance.
[34] The deviation of actual from tabular mortality could not be predicted within any
fair degree of accuracy and the hazard covered exposed the company to catastrophic
losses.

United States Government insurance is legal reserve life insurance issued on a participating basis and is backed by a trust fund set up from premiums collected and held in the Treasury Department, administered by the government as trustee. All costs of administration as well as claims resulting from the extra hazard of military or naval service are paid by the government.

Issuance of United States Government insurance was terminated [35] by passage of the National Service Life Insurance law.

National Service Life Insurance was created by act of Congress in 1940. The NSLI system provided policies for persons on active duty with the military and naval forces, including the Coast Guard. It was voluntary and available to those in active service. No evidence of insurability was required if application for the insurance was made within 120 days after entrance into the service. Policies were issued on a five-year level-premium Term plan on a participating basis and are convertible on any premium date into continuous-premium Whole-Life, 20-pay Life, 30-pay Life, 20-year Endowment, Endowment at age 60, and Endowment at 65.

The same freedom of beneficiary designation is allowed in National Service life insurance as in commercial insurance, and four settlement options are available under its contracts: The insured may elect a lump sum settlement, limited monthly installments, life income with 120 monthly installments guaranteed, or a refund life income (monthly installment for life—with total installments equal to face amount of the policy guaranteed). The insured may settle part of the proceeds under one option and the balance under another. If the insured has made no selection of any mode of settlement, the insurance is payable in 36 equal monthly installments under Option 2,[36] but the beneficiary has the right to elect to receive settlement under any installment option. Also, the beneficiary may change any mode of settlement designated by the insured as long as the change increases the period over which installments are to be paid.

Income options are not available to the insured himself as they are in most commercial policies, except Option 2 for matured Endowments.

In addition to the free waiver of premium disability provision included in National Service life insurance policies, the Veterans Administration offers a total disability income provision for the payment of an additional premium. On continuous-premium Whole Life at age 25, the additional premium per $1,000 is $2.49 a year. This disability provision grants, for each $1,000 of

---

[35] Except as to veterans of World War I in accordance with provisions of Sec. 310, World War Veterans' Act, as amended.

[36] Option 2, NSLI, pays the proceeds in equal monthly installments of from 36 to 240 in number.

insurance in force, monthly income payments of $5 as long as the insured is totally disabled after a six months' consecutive waiting period. On $10,000 insurance, a veteran may have up to $50 a month disability income protection.

While National Service insurance is available to disabled veterans, such policies are kept separate from the regular fund because of their high cost and are issued on a nonparticipating basis. This arrangement favorably affects the dividend potential of standard National Service insurance, which might otherwise have to share the losses of disabled veterans.

In National Service life insurance, all costs of administration, the cost of excess mortality as a result of the extra hazard of military service,[37] and the cost of waiver of premium on account of total disability traceable to extra hazards of military or naval service, are borne by the government. The maximum amount of NSLI any one individual may own (including any United States Government life insurance he may have) is $10,000. The insurance is backed by a trust fund held by the Treasury, similar to the fund back of United States Government life insurance.

Paralleling the history of World War I insurance, National Service life insurance has been dropped by policyholders at a startling rate.[38]

It should be mentioned that NSLI settlement options are particularly advantageous to the beneficiary in comparison to typical settlement options of commercial carriers. National Service life insurance pays the same benefits to women as to men and assumes a more favorable interest return and mortality experience than do most commercial companies; [39] so if National Service life insurance is used to provide installment payments rather than a lump sum, it has an additional cost advantage.

Issuance of new NSLI policies was terminated [40] by creation of the Servicemen's Gratuity system in 1951.

Gratuitous death benefits for members of the armed forces were estab-

---

[37] This includes death at any time after separation from service if evidence indicates the death was contributed to by service.

[38] The relatively slow progress of Savings Bank life insurance, the slow progress of the Wisconsin State Fund, and the tremendous decline of both War Risk insurance and National Service life insurance would seem sufficient evidence to justify the conclusion that in spite of low cost, life insurance either cannot be sold in volume or will not remain in force unless the sale of it is actively solicited and the business constantly resold. The expense of constant solicitation and continuous reselling would, of course, destroy the cost advantage which now exists for Savings Bank, Wisconsin State Fund, and National Service life insurance.

[39] American Experience, 3%.

[40] Except that upon separation from service, a serviceman may apply for a five-year Term policy, nonpar, renewable at attained age; or, if he has a service-connected disability rendering him substandard, he may apply for nonpar NSLI on a Whole Life or Endowment plan.

lished partly as a result of public pressure against what critics termed "the government in the life insurance business," and partly as a result of studies showing that it is actually cheaper for the government to provide a free indemnity than to finance the administrative machinery necessary to collect premiums, account for them, and then pay a good part of them back in dividends. The costs of administration of NSLI were greater than the net premiums retained.

Under the new system each serviceman is automatically covered for $10,000 without application from him and without any payment of premiums. The indemnity is paid in only one way: 120 monthly installments of $9.29 per $1,000. Eligible beneficiaries are a spouse, child, parents or persons *in loco parentis,* brother, or sister. If there is no designated beneficiary, or if the designated beneficiary predeceases the serviceman, payments are made to the next class of beneficiary in the order named. Unpaid installments at the death of any beneficiary also go to the next in line. If there are no eligible beneficiaries, the payments are waived since the money cannot be paid to the estate of the deceased.

From the $10,000 benefit must be subtracted any United States Government or NSLI insurance in force at the time of death. In order to get the full benefit of the free indemnity, any holder of United States Government or NSLI policies who is recalled to active duty may apply for a waiver of premium or may surrender his policy for cash. Within 120 days after separation from service, he may resume payment of premiums, may restore a surrendered policy, or may replace any five-year level premium Term policy which expired while he was in service.

The separated serviceman who did not have United States Government or NSLI policies before entering the armed forces may, if he has had at least 30 days of active service, apply for a five-year Term policy, provisions of which generally are the same as those of NSLI except that rates and values are based on the CSO table of mortality at 2¼% and annuity options on the 1949 Annuity Table at 2¾%. This insurance is nonparticipating nonconvertible Term but renewable for successive five-year intervals at the rate for the attained age.

If upon separation from service the serviceman has a service-connected disability rendering him unacceptable by the health standards of the NSLI act of 1940, as amended, he may apply for one of the permanent plans of nonparticipating NSLI, the only NSLI forms still issued.[41]

---

[41] Rates on "service-disabled veterans insurance" are based on the CSO 2¼% table. The policy is issued under conditions similar to but with settlement options lower than the former NSLI.

The Serviceman's Gratuitous Indemnity system is not based on the contributory principle but is included in the discussion because it includes insurance (although subsidized) in the form of five-year Term issued after separation from service and in the form of the nonpar, service-disabled veterans insurance.

10. SOCIAL SECURITY

The only compulsory insurance in the field of life insurance is Social Security. It might be contended that Social Security is not insurance. Rates and values are not a matter of contract between the insured and the carrier, but are set by legislation which may be changed at any time.[42] Social Security benefits are not mathematically based on premiums collected.[43] However, for all practical purposes, at least certain benefits under the Social Security Act bear a close resemblance to insurance, close enough to justify their classification as Social Insurance.

Three types of life insurance benefits are available under the Social Security Act: (1) retirement benefits, (2) lump sum death benefits, and (3) income for certain classes of survivors. These benefits are important enough in the financial plans of the typical policyholder to be given special consideration by the life underwriter in the programming of insurance. However, because they change so frequently, it is necessary to obtain details from sources other than a book.[44]

11. THE DOMINANT TYPES

Old Line mutual and stock companies dominate the business both in number of companies and volume of business. Of the total private life insurance in force in the United States, about one thirtieth is in fraternals, another one two-hundredth is in assessment associations, and about one four-hundredth is in Savings Bank Life Insurance. The amount of Servicemen's

---

[42] To this date, the Social Security Act has been amended five times: 1939, 1946, 1950, 1952, and 1954—each time liberalizing the coverage and benefits. Proposed changes for 1956 have already been announced, including addition of disability income benefits.

[43] Some economists feel that it would be sounder economically to pay all benefits from general taxation. They argue that nothing is to be gained by funding the benefits, either partially, as is now done, or fully, as is sometimes proposed. A funded Social Security system can hamstring the government in its efforts to promote economic stability through its fiscal policy. These economists, however, do recognize the psychological problems involved in eliminating the contributory feature from the Social Security Act. Eliminating it gives the impression that benefits are free.

[44] Current information on Social Security eligibility requirements, tax rates, and benefit formulas can be obtained from any local Social Security office. It also can be found in any of a number of standard reference works on life insurance, for example, the National Underwriter's *Diamond Life Bulletins, Unique Manual, Little Gem*; or Insurance Research and Review's *Advanced Underwriting Service*.

Life Insurance in force is equal to about one seventh of the total private insurance written. Of the insurance written by Old Line stock, mutual, and mixed companies about 65% is in mutual and 35% is in stock companies.[45]

12. DIFFERENCES AMONG CARRIERS OF THE SAME TYPE

From the buyer's standpoint, more important differences result from company philosophy and practice than as a result of type of organization. Significant variations exist among mutuals, stocks, and fraternals themselves.

Acceptability of Applicants. Not all companies accept the same classes of business. Some companies, regardless of whether stock or mutual, will accept juvenile applicants.[46] Others do not. Some companies, in order to restrict themselves to more favorable mortality groups and, hence, offer lower rates, will write only a certain type of applicant; for example, teachers, in the case of the Teachers Insurance and Annuities Association, or ministers, certain church officials, and their families only, as in the case of the Presbyterian Ministers' Fund.

There are, however, some variations in type of acceptable applicant that are the result of the nature of the carrier. These are, particularly variations among fraternal carriers. For instance, fraternals, because of their basic structure, write members only. They may further vary by imposing membership qualifications along religious, national, or occupational lines.[47]

Differences in Policies Issued. Companies also vary as to types of policies offered. In the main, every commercial company offers a continuous-premium Whole Life policy or a policy paid up at 85. They also offer at least one or two limited-payment policies, several Endowments, and one or two forms of Term.

Combinations and variations of the above more or less "standard" policy forms differ widely, as we have seen.[48] Some of this difference is a result of difference in underwriting philosophy. Policy forms one company considers sound another may not. Another part of the difference is a result of varying investment practices; one company may be more interested than another in

---

[45] Current information regarding the amount of insurance in force and the amount written by each type of carrier can be found in the *Life Insurance Fact Book*, an annual publication of the Institute of Life Insurance, 488 Madison Avenue, New York 22, N.Y.

[46] Ages 0 to approximately 10. The age at which applicants will be considered for adult policies varies from company to company.

[47] These racial and nationality qualifications, which to some fraternals, because of their basic organizational structure, make members of other racial or national groups unacceptable applicants, should be distinguished from underwriting practice which, in life insurance companies, sometimes makes certain racial or nationality groups unacceptable.

[48] Cf. Chapters 3 through 6.

bringing in investable funds; consequently, one company will feature policies with high reserve values, whereas another will feature those with lower reserve values.

Perhaps the greatest source of variation among types of policies offered is competition. Small and less widely known companies (and sometimes even the large and prominent companies) design special policy forms to offer in competition with the standard policies of their competitors. From the viewpoint of the issuing company, the special policy form also has the advantage of not being comparable to the policies of another company and so eliminating cost comparisons.[49]

Variations in Contract Provisions. In life insurance there are no "standard" policy forms. This statement is true despite the fact that the term "standard" is used to designate a certain group of policies which generally bear the same name among all companies and are alike in their major provisions. Rarely, however, are two life insurance policy contracts identical. A clause here or a clause there, even a phrase here or a phrase there, could make a difference in the value of the coverage at some future time. However, since no one knows at any given time what the future will bring, one's interpretation of what clause will prove of most value is in direct proportion to his ability to foresee the future.

In general, nevertheless, it is possible for the buyer to decide what clauses, phrases, and provisions of a policy are most needed in view of the major purpose for which he purchases the policy, that is, for instance, whether he purchases it for the retirement value, clean-up, or for income to his family in case of his death.

Perhaps the greatest variation among policies, even among those by the same name, is in optional modes of settlement. Options vary not only as to guaranteed amounts per installment, but also in nature.[50] For example, not all companies include the joint and survivor options. Some contracts contain life income options based on 5-, 10-, 20-, and 25-year-certain periods, whereas others limit the period certain to 10 and 20 years.

The options written in a life insurance contract at the time of its issuance

---

[49] Because of these variation in types of policies offered, it often becomes necessary for the buyer to look beyond one company to find a policy form best suited to his needs. The competitive special policies sometimes fit a particular life insurance need better than the "standard" form mentioned. *Who Writes What*, an annual publication of the National Underwriter Co., 420 E. 4th Street, Cincinnati 4, Ohio, is an excellent guide to companies by type of policy issued. It attempts no ratings or recommendations, confining itself to a listing of companies by policies. For an explanation of the provisions of these policies, it is necessary to seek the services of a qualified life insurance agent.

[50] Guaranteed amounts per installment vary among companies as a result of differing mortality and interest assumptions.

usually are not the only ones which the companies will write. Almost all companies will write special settlement options upon the request of the policyholder and attach the agreement to the policy as part of the contract. Many also will make special settlement agreements with the beneficiary. However, it should be remembered that the only options the company is obligated to grant are those which are either written in the policy or attached thereto as a part of the policy. Other options are issued according to "company practice," and company practice may vary from time to time. Moreover, there is a difference among companies in liberality in drawing up settlement agreements. Some companies will write virtually any type of legal settlement agreement requested. Others adhere to more or less standard forms.[51]

The differences mentioned in company practice in writing special settlement options carries over into variations in other matters as well. For instance, there is a variation among companies regarding the automatic premium loan. Some companies include it as a regular provision of the policy. Others include it only on request. Others will not write it at all. There is likewise a variation among the practices of companies in writing a "spendthrift" trust agreement.[52]

Special settlement agreements, spendthrift clauses, and the rest, represent trustee functions. The difference noted in company practices relating to them stem largely from differences in management philosophy among companies as to the extent the company feels it should engage in trust operations. Management thinking is not agreed on the line of demarcation between the life insurance and trust businesses.

Variations in Costs. Variations among companies as to cost of a policy always arouse the most interest among laymen, the greatest amount of discussion by "insurance advisors," and too much of many a sales presentation. Actually, in many cases it is almost impossible to determine what the differences in cost between policies and companies will be. The impossibility arises from the fact that no two policies ever are exactly alike. The policyholder, unable to predict the future, cannot determine which policy, in the final analysis, will offer him the most for his money.

Companies not using agents offer insurance at lower rates. The difference in rates is to a large extent the agent's commission. The agent's service to the policyholder, and especially to the beneficiary, has a definite value in money.

---

[51] For a good compendium of variations among settlement options and company practices relating to them, see the annual publication of the Flitcraft Company, *Settlement Options*.
[52] Under which the beneficiary is prohibited from invading the principal at all or for more than a set amount in addition to the installments elected.

Whether the service is worth the difference in premiums depends upon the kind and extent of service needed and rendered both to the insured and his beneficiary—something which, again, cannot be determined absolutely when the policy is purchased.[53]

The cost of a policy may depend also on its use. A company issuing a policy with a somewhat higher per-thousand premium rate may have in that policy more favorable settlement options than a company issuing an almost identical policy at a lower per-thousand premium rate. Which is the more expensive policy will depend upon whether the policyholder eventually uses it to provide a lump sum benefit (in which case the policy with the lower rate has cost him less) or for a periodic income (in which case the policy with the higher rate may actually cost less).

The cost of a policy may also depend on what is often referred to as the net cost, that is, total premiums paid, minus overcharges returned ("dividends") if any, minus the amount collected at either maturity or surrender of the contract. True net cost is something which can be determined only when the final payment has been made by the insurance company under the terms of the contract.

Unfortunately, there has developed the aforementioned practice of selling on an illustrative projected net cost basis. "Net cost" selling is not only misleading but also is invalid in determining the actual costs of a life insurance policy. In the case of most policy forms, it assumes that the policy is forfeited at some given point, the ultimate period of years used in the illustration.[54] Unless, therefore, the policy is forfeited at that time, the net cost will be other than what is shown in the illustration. If the policy is forfeited, then the protection against the peril, the major purpose involved in purchasing life insurance, is also forfeited.

It is meaningless to project the net cost of a life insurance policy on the basis of cash values while they remain in the policy. It is possible to determine ultimate cost only when the last penny of policy proceeds has been paid. Net cost selling also opens the business to adverse criticism, mis-

---

[53] It should be pointed out that cost is not always related to service. The fact that there is loading in the premium rate to take care of service to the policyholder does not always mean that the policyholder will receive that service. While this difference depends largely on the capability and sincerity of the agent with whom the policyholder deals, it also relates to some extent to the philosophy of the company. Once again, a good agent may render service of value over and beyond the loading factor in the premium—and so may his company. Another agent or company may not render service of value equivalent to the loading factor.

[54] Net cost illustrations published in life insurance compendiums usually are based on 10- and 20-year periods.

understandings, and misinterpretations which persist long after being disproved.[55]

Net cost illustrations are falacious. For instance, if carried for enough years, they often show that life insurance can be purchased free. These net cost illustrations eliminate the whole question of interest. If interest on premium deposits were considered in net cost illustrations, the picture would be entirely different. In the way net cost figures currently are presented, it would not be impossible to find a high net cost for a company charging a low rate or a low net cost for a company charging a high rate. In fact, it would be possible for an insurance company to charge a high enough premium so that interest earnings themselves could pay the cost of insurance right from the start.

Finally, net cost selling often induces policyholders to purchase insurance on a "cost" basis alone, which may ultimately prove to be the poorest possible basis for buying; and it paves the way for borderline companies to write a startlingly low-rate policy by restricting benefits. To say that one policy is "overpriced" whereas another is "correctly priced" on the basis of the premium rate alone is equivalent to stating that one make of car is overpriced simply because it costs more than another make. It may be that the more expensive car is overpriced; again, it may be that for value received, its price is less than that of the cheaper car.

Variations in Underwriting Practices. So many variations exist among companies in underwriting practices that it is difficult to cite representative examples. One company may accept a health condition that another would not accept. Again, some companies write insurance only at standard rates, whereas others accept substandard risks. Even among those who write substandard business, there is a variation as to how many degrees of substandard risks will be written. Some companies will write disability income protection in connection with life insurance; some will attach riders agreeing to waive future premiums in case of permanent or total disability; some will attach double indemnity riders under which the face value of the policy will be doubled in case of death by accidental means; some will write one

---

[55] One of the best examples of persistent criticism appeared during the depression of the 1930's in the form of Mort and E. Albert Gilbert's *Life Insurance, a Legalized Racket,* Philadelphia, Marlowe Publishing Co., 1936. While most of the criticisms contained in the book were met and some of the logic at least challenged by Paul Speicher in *The Truth About Life Insurance,* Indianapolis, Insurance Research and Review Service, 1936, and M. Albert Linton in *Life Insurance Speaks for Itself,* New York, Harper & Brothers, 1937, there are still probably many among the public who have studied and accept as indisputable the Gilberts' very catchily entitled book without ever having heard of the answering publications.

or another of these riders; and some will write none at all. Some companies will write Pension Trust and Group insurance, and some will not. There is also a difference among companies as to what are considered hazardous occupations and subject to an extra rate or not acceptable at all. The well informed life insurance agent knows which company is most apt to accept any given type of case.

Variation in Investment Practice. Variations in underwriting practice are equalled by variations in investment practice. The insurance code of each state limits the types of securities in which a life insurance company may invest funds; but within the limit of the law it is possible for practice to vary widely. For instance, some companies will invest more heavily in real estate mortgages than will others. Even among those who invest heavily in mortgages, there may be variation as to type of mortgage, some leaning more to the monthly repayment residential mortgage, while others prefer lump sum repayment building property mortgages. Others like farm mortgage investments. Some companies invest more in United States Government securities; others buy more heavily the securities of business and industry.

Variations in investment philosophy and practices rise out of differences of opinion among competent investment men as to future earnings and investment trends of the whole investment field. Investments are a specialized study, requiring a high degree of knowledge and skill. Investment practice, unlike mortality, is not subject to mathematical formulas. It is impossible to say today which investment will turn out to be best in the future. Investment men can only apply their knowledge and understanding to deciding individually which security has the best outlook at the moment.

Certain types of investment are universally recognized as "risk" investments—important in the creation and expansion of business and industry, but unsuitable for the "trust" investment purposes of life insurance companies. The cardinal principle of life insurance investing is security. Earning is second. Variations in investment practices affect interest earnings and consequently influence the cost of insurance in any given company. However, it is impossible to select with accuracy the "lower cost" companies of the future on the basis of an analysis of today's investment portfolios. Differences of opinion will be found among the most astute investment men.

Variations in Size, Surplus, and Reserves. Perhaps the most noticeable variation among life insurance companies is that of size. They run the gamut from companies with a few *millions* in force to companies with many *billions* in force. Not only do companies vary in size according to the amount of insurance in force but also according to assets.

Contingency reserves and surpluses also vary among companies, for the most part as a result of different actuarial philosophies. The actuaries of one company may be able to marshal irrefutable arguments and mathematical formulas to prove the adequacy of the size of their contingency reserves and surpluses, whereas those of another company of almost exactly the same size will be able to marshal equally irrefutable arguments and formulas to prove that a contingency reserve of a different size is correct. Mathematics go so far; human judgment must then enter in.

Differences in reserves depend upon the system adopted for their calculation. State laws set up minimum reserve standards. Companies may use higher standards than the minimum, and many do. The old and established companies usually use formulas yielding higher reserves than those used by the new companies which may lack the necessary surplus to establish higher reserves.

13. FACTORS TO CONSIDER IN THE SELECTION OF A COMPANY

Most of the factors which should be considered in selecting a company from which to purchase insurance have been implied in the discussion of variations among companies that arise out of both the type of organization and the type of management. This concluding section of the chapter, therefore, is actually little more than a summation.

Factor of Service. In selection of both company and agent, the buyer should consider the matter of service. In the case of companies, variations are a matter of management philosophy rather than type of carrier. Some companies are more bound by red tape, which can slow down service. Others so restrict the authority of agencies that matters that might be handled locally must make the long trip to the home office. There is a wide variation in company flexibility in the handling of special settlement agreements essential to programming and estate planning. There is an even greater variation in service rendered by agents. The amount and adequacy of service from any agent depends largely on his ability and desire to serve.

The Type of Policy. It is necessary for a buyer to limit the selection of a company to that company offering the type of policies which fit his particular insurable needs. Too often the need is fitted to the policy rather than the policy to the need. For instance, the need calling for a Family Income policy may be improperly fitted with a Family Maintenance policy; or the need for yearly renewable Term may be improperly met by the use of a ten-year renewable Term policy. These are but two obvious examples. Usually there is no reason to compromise a need simply because a given company does not write the policy that exactly fits that need. Chances are that another equally good company does write it.

The Factor of Cost. Price buying is not only dangerous but also can often be disastrous. While differences in cost do exist, they are difficult to ascertain and determine. Emphasis on cost or price buying inevitably results in judging cost by the only apparently variable factor: the premium rate. The fact that one premium rate is lower than another does not mean necessarily that in the end, the low-rate policy costs less than any other.

There are some instances in which the determination of variations in cost among carriers is clearer. National Service Life Insurance, Savings Bank life insurance, and the Wisconsin Life Fund have certain cost advantages which may or may not be offset by their inability to render the same service as life insurance companies. Some buyers of insurance do not feel the need for the services of agents. It should be pointed out, however, that even in these cases a policy purchased on a basis of price alone can prove, in the end, to be far more expensive than a policy of higher rate. The primary consideration is whether or not the buyer understands his need, and whether or not the carrier has available the type of policy needed. The policy that best fits the need will prove to be the cheapest policy in the end, even if the rate is somewhat higher than that for another policy not exactly suited to the need.

The Factor of Safety. In the matter of safety, it is again hard to lay down general rules as to what makes a safe company, and this despite the fact that company safety is an important factor to consider in buying.

The amount of insurance a company has in force has little to do with safety. Insurance in force is a liability; it represents the amount of money the company has contracted to pay at the maturity of all existing policies. At first glance, it might seem that the amount of insurance in force in a given company could be so small as to render the Law of Large Numbers inoperative. However, the smaller the company, the lower its retention limit. Thus, through reinsurance, it gains the spread of risk unavailable on its own policy account.

The size of admitted assets has little to do with safety in legal reserve companies. Assets are offset largely by policy reserves, and the amount of those reserves is established by law. It can be assumed that the assets of any legal reserve company are adequate to make up that portion of future claims and maturities which it is their purpose to pay.

The real factors in safety are underwriting standards and the degree to which they are achieved in selection; quality of investments; and the relative amount of surplus to policyholders.[56] The law sets the minimum safety standard for investments. It can be assumed, therefore, that any company's investments are as safe as the objective factors which can be used to judge them are able to make them. The extra margin of safety is in the skill of the investment men employed by the company.

Any legal reserve life insurance company may be said to be as safe as mathematical formulas can make it, since governmental regulation sees to that degree of safety. When there is actually doubt about the margins of safety of a given company, the insurance department of the state will provide the most accurate factual information available. It, however, is unable to pass objective judgment on the subjective element of safety, that is, the human factor, which takes up where mathematical formulas leave off. The impossibility of judging this factor of safety is illustrated by two things:

(1) Were objective measurement of safety possible, failure of a life insurance company would never occur, for the state department would know when to step in and order a change in practice.

(2) Orgainizations which rate life insurance companies as to their soundness would not make the mistake they have made in the past, of giving a company one of the highest possible ratings at the beginning of the very year in which the company failed.

A bad rating either by an insurance department or a rating institution is to be given serious consideration by the buyer. A good rating means nothing except that as far as objective measurements of safety go, the company is operating soundly, but objective measurements are not conclusive when it comes to judging safety.

Company Prominence. The prominence of a company is often given consideration by the public when choosing a company from which to buy. Prominence indicates that the company is well advertised and well represented. It indicates little more. It is well for the prospective buyer to remember that there are approximately 1100 legal reserve life insurance companies in the United States alone, and that the average layman does well to name more than half a dozen. It certainly would be fallacious to say that all those he cannot name are not sound. It would be much the same as saying that anyone a man can't call by name is not worth his knowing.

---

[56] The exact nomenclature for items making up "surplus to policyholders" varies from company to company. The most common names are "surplus funds," "general contingency reserve," "mortality fluctuation reserve," "unassigned surplus," "capital stock" (if any), "special surpluses." The ratio of policyholders' surplus to total assets is one measure of safety.

14. CONCLUSION

As was said in the beginning, there are many variations among companies. These variations usually arise because the business is competitive, and each company, therefore, differs in some measure from any other company.

It is possible to take the many variations among companies and with them prove that any one company is better than any other company and that all companies are better than each company. The task of choosing a "best company" is so shot full of "if's," "and's," "but's," and other qualifications that even for the expert the task is impossible. Much more impossible, then, is the task for the layman. No man will get lost quicker than the man who sets out to find the "best" company.

Finding the "best" life insurance company is like trying to solve a puzzle. It looks easy in the beginning. But an hour later you throw the puzzle out the window and in exasperation declare, *"I give up!"*

You start on the theory that if you find a company paying high dividends, your search will be ended. Then someone suggests that you had better find out if the dividends are being paid out of actual savings. Next you start to find the lowest net cost company, and someone suggests that you find out if the low net cost is offered at the expense of a constant decrease in the safety margin. Then you start out to find the company with the lowest mortality, and someone suggests that perhaps low mortality is offset by high expense ratios. Finally you find a company with a rate five cents lower than the company of your second choice and are about to buy, when suddenly you discover a clause in the second-choice company's policy which is *worth* five cents more. So you start all over again to find the "best" company, and you end at the same baffling conclusion.

The answer is that unless you find a good life insurance agent and believe him, you'll pursue your phantom search for the "best" company until it is too late for protection to do your family any good. The strength of the strongest company, the lowest net cost of the lowest net-cost company, mean nothing to the widow and family of the man who was so intent on buying insurance in the *best* company that he failed to buy it in *any* company at all.

Questions for Class Discussion

1. A friend of yours asks you whether he should buy his life insurance in a mutual company or a stock company. What advice can you give him?
2. Your brother-in-law wants to know whether he should buy participating or nonparticipating life insurance. Could you help him make a decision?

3. How does a fraternal life insurance company differ from an assessment carrier? Are they in any way alike? Discuss.

4. Which of the following types of carriers are legal reserve carriers: stock companies, mutual companies, fraternals, assessment companies, National Service Life Insurance, Wisconsin Life Fund, Savings Bank Life Insurance, Social Security? Which of the above are so-called Old Line companies? What is the significance of the two terms?

5. From which of the above types of carriers would you expect (a) better service, (b) lower cost, and (c) greater security?

6. The following is a quotation from a speech before a group of life insurance men: "People think most of the time that life insurance costs money, and you want to dissuade them of that erroneous impression. Life insurance is absolutely free." Why did the speaker make such a statement? Do you agree with the statement? Why or why not?

7. Is it better to assume that good companies are represented only by good agents or that good agents represent only good companies?

8. Under what circumstances is $10,000 NSLI insurance worth more than $10,000 benefit under the Serviceman's Insurance and Indemnity Act?

9. A friend of yours tells you that he has been approached by a salesman from the Blank Life. Since he knows you are studying life insurance, he asks you what he should know about that company. What would you tell him?

10. Some people criticize Social Security because it is too much like insurance; others criticize it because it is not enough like insurance. If you had to take sides, which side would you take?

CHAPTER 25

COMPANY ORGANIZATION
AND AGENCY MANAGEMENT

T H E O R G A N I Z A T I O N of a life insurance company breaks into two distinct divisions: Home Office and Field. The purpose of this chapter is to discuss the basic patterns of organization in each division, together with variations in their use among companies.

1. HOME OFFICE ORGANIZATION

Fundamentally, the organization of a life insurance company home office follows the basic principles of any business organization. It may be *line* organization with all authority tracing back to one individual, usually the president; it may be *line and staff*, with executive officers assisted by advisory staff officers or departments; it may be *functionalized*, with staff officers empowered not only to advise but also to act; or it may be *committee*, with major decisions being made by the heads of interested or concerned departments, each contributing his specialized knowledge to any given problem.

As do all businesses, life insurance home offices vary as to which of the types or combination of types of organizational structures they adopt. Commonly, the organization in any given company is a combination of several if not all four of the basic types. This is a result of the fact that a company rarely selects any one type of organizational structure consciously. Patterns grow as a matter of evolution.

Source of Authority. Stockholders in a stock company, or policyholders in a mutual company, are the primary source of authority. They bear responsibility for the formulation and administration of company policy. The stockholders (or policyholders) delegate their authority to the Board of Directors.

618

The Board of Directors, in turn, will usually retain some of the authority and delegate the rest to the executive officers of the company. It is these officers who exercise the direct, working control of the business.

Where authority goes after leaving the executive officers depends upon the individual company, and usually upon the size of that company. The larger the company, the more numerous are the levels of authority.

The *Board of Directors*, sometimes called "trustees" in mutual companies, is elected by stockholders in a stock company or by the policyholders in a mutual company. The Board of Directors, in turn, appoints the executive officers of the company, who perform the functions indicated in the company charter and bylaws.

Members of the Board also may serve on committees which pass on certain phases of company administration or action. This is particularly true in the larger companies where the Board of Directors has, otherwise, little or no direct contact with the business. The committees of the Board of Directors, not to be confused with administrative committees at the executive officer level, are delegated special authority by the Board of Directors.

The most common Board committees are the *Executive Committee*, which considers questions of general business methods, rates, types of policies, territories; the *Finance Committee*, which concerns itself with questions of investment policy and practices; and the *Auditing Committee*, which audits the accounts of the company periodically, usually by the employment of a professional auditing firm. Additional Board of Directors' committees may be found in various companies, their nature depending upon the special needs of the company or, often, upon the special interests of certain members of the Board.

The *company president* generally is the operating head of the business since usually not all members of the Board of Directors are full-time employees.[1] The president has general administrative supervision over all departments. Sometimes, especially in smaller companies, he may retain the actual control of the department through which he has risen to the presidency, and sometimes he may perform active duties in several or even all departments. Practically speaking, the president exercises most of the authority delegated by the stockholders to the Board of Directors between meetings of the Board. In truth, as in other kinds of companies, it is not uncommon for the Board of Directors to be, actually, under the control of the president. It will be seen in the chapter on the history of life insurance that one of the criticisms by the Armstrong investigating committee in New

---

[1] Occasionally the chairman of the Board of Directors (who may be the immediate past president of the company) exercises the operating control of the business.

York in 1905 was that directors and trustees did not check effectively on management and that Board committees "rubber stamped" approval of management requests or actions. The Armstrong committee recommended steps aimed at the elimination of this situation. Practically speaking, however, it is only natural that in some instances the president is in actual control of the company, since life insurance companies, like other businesses, may be organized and built mainly through the impetus of some one individual who naturally gravitates to the position of control. He commonly exercises that control from the position of the presidency regardless of the fact that technically he is subordinate to the Board of Directors.

Often, in cases of domination of the company by one man, the primary qualification of a candidate for the Board of Directors is amenability to the wishes of the president or controlling management bloc. Secondarily, the consideration will usually be the prominence of the candidate and, hence, his publicity or public relations value. Actual control of a company by the president is neither the general rule nor the exception; moreover, such control is not necessarily an unhealthy condition. While it can lead to ill effects, it can also, if the president is a man of outstanding ability, be even more efficient control than that of a less efficient Board of Directors. Whether such control exists and whether it is good or bad is an individual matter in every case.

The *vice-presidents* in most life insurance companies exercise active supervision over one or more departments, according to the size of the company. In a small company, a vice-president may have to "double in brass," and serve as the head of more than one department. In line of authority, a vice-president acts in the absence of the president. In larger companies vice-presidents are usually co-ordinated by an executive vice-president, the "vice-president in charge of vice-presidents." Now and again, a company will be found in which the executive vice-president actually performs the functions of the president, the position of presidency in that particular company at that particular time being more honorary than active. There have been instances in the past of the appointment of a well-known public figure as president of a company [2] even though he knew little about life insurance operations and did not necessarily exercise active control. In such cases control is in the hands of an executive vice-president or, perhaps, is split among several vice-presidents.

Especially in the larger company having a number of vice-presidencies,

---

[2] Former president Calvin Coolidge, for an example. However, sometimes such an appointment is made to capitalize on the person's organizational ability, which can be utilized effectively even if he is not trained in life insurance technicalities.

the title of vice-president is sometimes conferred as an honor upon a department head of long and faithful service who is never expected to function in the capacity indicated by the etymology of the title "vice-president."

The *company secretary* usually has responsibility for correspondence (in the sense of directing authority for official correspondence), the issuance of policies, which are usually signed by the secretary, and the records of the Board of Directors and committee meetings. In a company of any size, these duties may be wholly supervisory. Policies are actually issued by a Policy Issue or similar department with the secretary's signature printed on the form; and the transcript of the business of the meeting of the Board of Directors or of a committee is usually made by a professional stenographer.

As a result, functioning duties of a company secretary vary widely among companies, ranging anywhere from active charge of a department in no way concerned with his bylaw duties to the function of general manager or even executive vice-president. Actual duties of a secretary may go as far afield as serving as personnel manager. Moreover, as an outgrowth of this wide variation in the active duties of a company secretary, "assistant secretaries" will be found to be numerous, especially among larger companies, with duties varying as widely as can be imagined within one company.

The charter or bylaws of any given company may add other executive officers. For instance, the treasurer or controller, medical director, and general counsel (attorney) may be executive officers.

Other officers, unlike the officers so far named (who are executive officers) are common among most companies. They are what might be termed "functional officers." While the duties of functional officers may be necessary in the operation of the company, they are not officers of the corporation or organization. They do not have power directly delegated by the charter or bylaws to bind the company, as do executive officers.

Usually functional officers head various departments. For instance, the company treasurer or controller may be a functional officer rather than an executive officer. The same may be true of the medical director or the legal counsel. Often functional officers eventually are elevated to positions as executive officers by promotion to a vice-presidency. Thus, while the office of medical director may not be recognized by the charter of the company as an executive office, the medical director may be made an executive officer by promotion to the position of "vice-president *and* medical director." The assistant secretaryships previously mentioned are, in most companies, an example of functional officers who are not executive officers.

Functions of Standard Departments. The bases of departmentalization vary from company to company, and they may vary within any one company. Most of the departments of a company are organized along functional lines, although there may be one or two departments organized along product or territorial lines, or lines of executive interest.[3]

The Agency Department. In every life insurance company having a field agency organization, there is an agency department. It is usually headed by an executive officer, often the "vice-president in charge of agencies." He may, however, leave the actual working operation of the department to a "director of agencies," "superintendent of agencies," or functional officer of similar title. Sometimes there is no executive officer directly in charge of the agency department, the operation of it being in the hands of a functional officer who is responsible to some general executive officer, usually the president.

The primary function of the agency department in most companies is to recruit, train, supervise, and handle most of the affairs in connection with general agents, branch managers, and agents. The agency department usually is supreme in all matters concerning the field organization. The legal department, however, operates as staff adviser to the agency department in such things as the drawing up of contracts for use with general agents and subagents and in similar matters involving purely legal technicalities. The actuarial department advises concerning the scale of commissions.

The agency department may be supplemented by an educational department, a sales promotion department, an advertising department—one or all.

Certain staff departments sometimes take over active direction of specific phases of agency operation. This is particularly true in the case of educational departments. As the training of field men is increasingly stressed by companies today, more and more educational or training departments are assuming charge of the training of agents. Their authority then becomes direct instead of simply advisory.

More often than in the case of any other department in the home office

---

[3] Functional departments based upon functions performed, for example, are a medical department, a legal department, an investment department, an agency department, an advertising department, a purchasing department, an accounting department, etc. Product departments are based on type of product with which they deal, for example: an accident and health department, an ordinary department, an industrial department. Territorial departments, determined by the territory over which they exercise jurisdiction, for example, may be an East Coast department, West Coast department, a Southern Atlantic department, a Latin American department, or European department. Customer departments, established by the nature of the class of customers with which they deal, for example, are reinsurance (which deals with sales to other insurance companies) and group, often including salary savings and pension trusts (which sells only to employers and in the mass rather than to individual policy buyers). Finally, departments may be organized along the lines of the interest of any given executive or executives in the business, even though those interests may be somewhat diverse.

organization, the agency department operates virtually autonomously. This usually is a result of the departmental evolution of the company. Although it is by no means a common practice, it is not an unknown practice for a small or new company, formed by interests who are primarily acquainted with investment matters, to make a contract with another organization, usually formed for the purpose, to be the agency organization of the company. This corresponds to a recognized practice in general business. A manufacturer or processor may contract with a sales organization to be its exclusive selling agent. The sales agent then becomes the field organization of the manufacturer or processor, just as one may become the agency department and field organization of a life insurance company. While such an agency may long ago have become an integral part of the home office organization, much of its original autonomous nature may be preserved in the functioning of the agency department.

Another line of evolution produces a virtually autonomous agency department, the process of the absorption by one company of another mainly because the company absorbed or purchased has a more extensive and better functioning field organization than does the purchaser. In such a case the president of the absorbed company may become vice-president in charge of agencies of the dominating company; but because the field organization was originally his, he may operate virtually autonomously.

Finally, an agency department may derive a degree of autonomy from the disinterest of the top level of company management in field operation.[4] Life insurance companies are frequently headed by men who are, by training and experience, actuaries, investment men, or lawyers. They may know nothing about the operation of a field organization or about field problems, both of which involve understanding and skill in human relationships rather than in technical knowledge. Agency departments are sometimes left to run themselves more by default than by design.[5]

Underwriting Department. The function of the underwriting department is to set the standards of selection and to pass judgment upon applicants for

---

[4] Important exceptions weighted heavily in favor of agency operations are found in some companies where former field men have risen to the presidency.

[5] There is an attitude in many home offices that runs up the scale of seriousness to the point at which the field organization is considered merely a necessary nuisance—and sometimes not even a "necessary" one. Some degree of this attitude is most noticeable among rank-and-file employees, who will often actually make the illogical statement that their jobs would be much more pleasant if the field organization were not constantly demanding this or that information. To some extent, this is merely failure to see the relationship between the details of a clerical job and the over-all operation of the company, a failure not necessarily peculiar to life insurance home offices. One of the authors has actually overheard the remark in an organization with which he was associated, "If those orders just didn't keep coming in, we could all get our work out better."

insurance. In some companies, the underwriting and the medical departments are one and the same; in other companies, the medical department is a subdivision of the underwriting department, or vice versa. They are usually headed by a functional officer known by a title similar to "chief underwriter" or "medical director." In some instances he may be an executive officer by virtue of holding the title and position of vice-president. Again, the functional office of chief underwriter may be under the co-ordinating supervision of a vice-president in charge of underwriting, a general vice-president, or the company president. The department is staffed not only with physicians but also with specialists known as "lay underwriters," to distinguish them from physicians. Most underwriting decisions do not depend upon a physician's opinion.

Actuarial Department. While by derivation the term, "actuary," can designate a registrar or a clerk, it is now almost exclusively applied to a specialized mathematician in an insurance company who calculates insurance rates, dividends, reserves, and commission scales. He also works in the development of new policy forms and settlement options. The term is little known outside the insurance business and means nothing to the average layman. The functions and duties of an actuary are perhaps more clear if he is called, as in some Canadian and English companies, "Chief Mathematician."

The functions of the actuarial department in any company are merely those of the aforementioned calculation of degree of risk and their interpretation in terms of rates through the application of level premium formulas. The actuarial department determines the reserve necessary, advises as to what it considers sound contingency reserves and surpluses, sets the basis for installment settlements of proceeds, determines proper expense loadings, works out dividend formulas and, in short, performs all those functions in the business which are fundamentally matters of mathematics. Since life insurance is founded on mathematical principle, the basic importance of an actuarial department can be easily understood. Because of the specialized and technical skills required for the job, actuaries command one of the best salary scales in a home office. Often only the salaries of one or two higher executives and the earnings of a few of the top general agents and agents of a company will exceed those of the actuary who, if not an executive officer by virtue of his function, is usually one through a vice-presidency.

To the purely mathematical duties of actuarial departments of a small company are often added duties which in larger companies devolve upon a "policyholders' service" department. It is the duty of this latter department to handle matters relating to special optional settlement or trust agreements requested by policyholders. Since the nature of such agreements is fundamentally mathematical, the performance of these duties often lodges in the actuarial department.

Legal Department. The title of a legal department virtually explains its duties. While the basis of life insurance is mathematical, its operation is primarily legalistic. Since a life insurance policy is a contract and, as such, is subject to all the law pertaining to contracts in general as well as to those phases of the law and judicial opinion which apply particularly to life insurance, a legal department is of prime importance to a life insurance company.

Not only does the department concern itself with the legal problems involved in the development of policy forms; it often is assigned the duty of drawing up contracts with general agents and subagents (if terms of a subagent's contract are within the scope of the company's authority rather than the general agent's [6]), assuring conformance of the company's operations to the domestic insurance code, to the foreign insurance codes of those states in which the company operates, and to any alien insurance codes involved. It is the further duty of the legal department to defend the company in the case of any informal complaints brought against it through various insurance commissioners and in actual litigation, and to prosecute the company's case wherever it may be the plaintiff. The legal department also renders a service to the investment department of the company. It checks on real estate titles, bond indentures, and corporate charters, and it aids in any foreclosure proceedings.

Investment Department. As in the case of the legal department, the functions of the investment department are almost fully explained by its name. It concerns itself with the creation, maintenance, and liquidation of the investment portfolio of the company.

Other Departments. The above are the major departments common to most life insurance companies. In some companies one or more of these departments may be amalgamated, or one may be a division within another; moreover, in many companies, there are additional, well-defined and well-organized departments—the policyholders' service department mentioned previously, the policy issue department, the controller's department, the secretary's department, *et alia.* Larger companies may departmentalize such functions as advertising and sales promotion (usually subdivisions of the agency department); public relations; publications (company magazines, bulletins, sales literature), purchasing; personnel; and many others.

---

[6] This point will be clarified in the discussion of field organization.

2. FIELD ORGANIZATION

The field organization of a life insurance company is primarily a sales organization. Its purpose is to sell new business, to maintain old business in force, and to service policyholders. Of these three purposes, the first is by far the most emphasized.

The life insurance agent is integral to the sound operation of the business and to the functioning of the principle of insurance. It is through him that policies in sufficient number to yield average experience are written; it is through him that the exposure units are spread over a wide enough area to prevent local conditions from creating disproportionate deviations from average mortality and lapsation; and above all, it is through him that the flow of premiums is kept constant, making it unnecessary for the company to liquidate securities in bad times when cash calls are heavy and liquidation would mean a loss. Life insurance could not have attained its present dominant position in the American economy without the life insurance agent and without the type of field organization which, while not altogether peculiar to this continent, is, nevertheless, more emphasized here than elsewhere in the world. The life insurance business in America today is truly a monument to the genius and the perseverance of thousands upon thousands of often-derided life insurance salesmen.

The field organization of a life insurance company is under the direction of the home office agency department. For the organization of the field forces, one of two systems may be used: the general agency system or the branch office system. While rarely does a company organize its field forces any more under a *pure* general agency or branch office system, before adaptations of the two systems can be understood, it is necessary to know the nature of each.

General Agency System.   Under the pure general agency system, which is only theoretical in most cases, a contract is signed with an individual giving him exclusive rights to represent the company and solicit new business in a specific territory. The contract calls for a fixed scale of commission payments and, sometimes, a collection fee to be paid to the general agent. The general agent is empowered to appoint subagents, or what are known as "special agents" or simply "agents," within that territory and to make contracts with them under which he agrees to pay them a certain portion of the commission he receives from the company. The difference between what the general agent receives from his company and the amount he pays his agents is known as his "override" or "overriding commission."

It should be noted that agents' contracts are made with the general agent and not with the company. In the pure general agency contract, the company, theoretically, has no control over the contracts made by the general agent with his agents, although in actual practice the company usually specifies the form of contract to be used and reserves the right to reject agency appointments.

In the pure general agency contract, the company does not obligate itself to pay any part of the cost of establishing the agency, of operating it, or of developing the territory. On the other hand, it assumes no authority over the methods of operation except within the broad limits of company policy, and no authority or part in the selection, training, supervision, or disciplining of the agency force appointed by the general agent or over the personnel of his agency office. The general agent is responsible for collecting premiums, being obligated under his contract to submit only the "net"[7] to the company. He is responsible also for the collection of interest on loans as well as the servicing of policyholders and, in fact, of every and all company operations within the territory granted in his contract.[8]

It will be seen, then, that the general agent is an independent operator and that a general agency is an independent business owned and operated by the general agent under his contractual arrangement with the home office. He pays all his own expenses; he finances agents when financing is required; he pays all clerical salaries for the agency and all furniture, fixture, and rental expenses involved. The only actual control the company has over him is its right to void his contract. Usually such cancellation can be for violation of contract terms or without cause upon due notice from either party.

Branch Office System. The branch office system is the direct counter-type of the general agency system. The branch manager, corresponding in function to the general agent, is not an independent operator and his office is not an independent business. He is a salaried employee of the home office, hired to manage a particular territory. He may receive commissions in addition to his salary as an incentive wage; but this does not alter his status as an employee. He appoints and supervises the agency force on behalf of the company. Sometimes he supervises the clerical personnel of the agency; although in larger branch offices it is the practice for the company to employ

---

[7] The difference between the premium collected from the policyholder and the commission owed the general agent. This is not the "net premium" described in the chapter on premium computation.

[8] Earlier general agency contracts went even further in their grant of authority. One between the Northwestern Mutual Life Insurance Company and Dr. Henry Martin, dated August 22, 1861, not only authorized the doctor to solicit business, appoint agents, receive premiums, and service policyholders but also to make mortgage loans and *examine his own applicants!*

a cashier as the manager of routine business and collections. The cashier may or may not be subject to the authority of the branch manager.

In the branch office system, the company pays all expenses of operation, trains the agents or supplies the branch manager with the facilities for training them, issues contracts for subagents, and passes upon the qualifications of new agents whom the branch manager may propose. Branch offices are sometimes called "managerial agencies," and the branch office system is sometimes called the "managerial" or "manager system."

Home Office Contracts. Occasional examples of soliciting agents who have contracts direct with the home office rather than with a branch office or general agent may be found. The arrangement might be said to constitute another type of field organization, although rarely used. Actually this type of organization simply is but one step removed from the branch office.

Selling Without Agents. There is a third method of organization which is, actually, no field organization at all: mail-order or "over the counter" selling. Several carriers write insurance without the use of agents. Included in the groups are legal reserve carriers such as the Teachers Insurance and Annuity Association, the Presbyterian Ministers' Fund, Savings Bank life insurance, and the Wisconsin Life Fund. A number of assessment insurance societies also write life insurance by mail. Many of these latter have been the subject of severe criticism by various state departments of insurance. The use of the mails, however, cannot be restricted by state law, and a mail-order company may solicit business in a state in which it is not licensed as long as it does not appoint agents in that state or send agents into it.[9]

Comparison of Field Systems. In actual practice, pure general agency systems and pure branch office systems are difficult to find. There is a growing tendency for the company to assume more and more responsibility for the financing and operation of the general agency, thus bringing the general agency system closer to the branch office system for practical purposes, even though the basic relationship between the general agent and his company is unchanged. Several advantages and disadvantages of the two types of field organization in their pure forms are apparent.

Advantages of the Pure General Agency System. The primary advantage of the pure general agency system from the standpoint of the company is its lower initial cost. Since the company assumes no part of the financial burden of operation, theoretically it can open new general agencies without limit as

---

[9] A degree of Federal control over mail-order insurance has been established by the FTC, and there has been some pressure in Congress for legislation effecting even greater Federal control.

to number. If the agency established does not prove successful, the company has lost no money.

A second advantage of the pure general agency is that business often comes in more quickly after the establishment of the agency. In the first place, the general agent, paying expenses out of his own pocket, may be more aggressive in soliciting business. In the second place, the general agency system, offering a man a chance to have his own business, attracts an enterprising type of person. In the third place, the general agent, being in full authority, can cut through the red tape that sometimes delays the production of business in the new branch office. The branch manager often must refer many matters to the home office for decision before he can go ahead.

A third advantage of the pure general agency system is the flexibility with which it can adapt to local conditions. Usually the general agent is himself from the territory and knows what is required for successful operation in that territory. Being in a position to make his own decisions without consultation with the home office, he can make them on a basis of what he knows local conditions to be. The branch manager can simply report local conditions to the home office, which may or may not give them consideration. Finally, among advantages of the general agency system, and, it must be said, not the least of the attractions of the system, is that it is far less trouble and work for the home office. The entire job of training, supervision, and motivation can be lifted completely out of the home office and put into the hands of the general agent.

From the standpoint of the individual general agent, the big attraction is the independent nature of his operation. Not only is he the supreme authority in the operation of the agency and within the territory, but also he builds a financial equity in the agency as a business enterprise. He can take his entire field organization to another company should his own sever its contract with him or should he become dissatisfied with his present relationship. He can use his own ideas for selling, promotion, training, supervision, and every and all operations of the agency. He risks his own money, it is true, but he builds equities in his renewals; and America from the beginning attracted the type of individual who was willing to risk what he had in the hope of large gains and, especially, for the independence of operating as he saw fit.

Disadvantages of the Pure General Agency System. There are several disadvantages. The first lies in the fact that the company, under a pure general agency system, has virtually no control over its field forces. It cannot select its own agents, and it cannot train them. Those men to whom the general agent has delegated certain powers of agency on behalf of the company are employees of the general agent and not of the company. Yet the company is legally bound by their acts.

A further disadvantage of the general agency system is that it can lead to conflicts in sales policy. Whereas the company may recommend conservative sales practices, the general agent may use his own judgment; instances could be cited from the past in which highly promotional (or "high-pressure")[10] types of selling, not judged to be of the best professional standards, have been practiced by a general agency without the sanction of the company. Without very close control over its general agents, the company is unable to "police" the sales policy of its field organization.

The general agency system may, also, limit the financing of new agents. Since the financing under this system in its pure form must be out of the pocket of the general agent, it will often have to be more limited than the company could undertake. Often the general agent will neither be willing nor able to give new agents the kind of financial backing that is required to attract the calibre of men which the company might like to have.

Advantages of the Branch Office System. Since the pure branch office system is the counterpart of the pure general agency system, its advantages and disadvantages may be discussed in terms of the disadvantages and advantages of that system. Whatever appears as an advantage in one system shows up as a disadvantage in the other.

Under the branch office system, the company has direct control over the agents because those agents are hired, trained, and supervised by a salaried employee of the company, the branch manager. Since the company usually has greater facilities and resources than are available to any of its agencies, it is able to formulate and administer, or at least assist in the administration of, more carefully worked out systems of selection and training. Since the company works directly with the agents, it has closer contact with its policyholders. Sales policy can be more uniform because the company not only can establish a sales policy but also see that it is carried out. There is more uniformity of operations among all branches because the company can formulate the operational policy of the branch and, having direct salary control over the manager, make sure that the policies laid down are fol-

---

[10] The term, "high-pressure selling," as used here, means the inducement of the prospect to buy without either giving adequate consideration to his needs for the product purchased or bringing him to see his need clearly even though completing the sale. By "high-pressure selling" we do not mean the use of persistence, persuasion, and emotion to prod into action the individual who has a clear need, who sees that need, but who delays buying simply because he does not want to sacrifice the small luxuries the premium money will buy today.

lowed. Thus the same set of rules and regulations will be found in every branch of the company rather than widely differing sets of rules and regulations, as may be the case under the general agency system.

Disadvantages of the Branch Office System. Since under the branch manager system the company underwrites not only the income of the manager but also all expenses of operation, rent, furniture and fixtures, clerical salaries, and operating costs, the branch manager system is much more expensive, at least at the outset. Moreover, the operation of a branch office field organization demands a stronger home office agency department than would be necessary if all matters relating to the operation of the field offices were left to the judgment of a general agent.

Finally, the branch office system is less responsive to local conditions. By nature of organization, a greater proportion of the decisions are made by the agency department in the home office, where the knowledge of local conditions cannot be as complete as that of those who are "on the ground." There is always a chance that what may seem a perfectly logical decision to the home office will not take into account important local conditions. Theoretically this danger is offset by the fact that the branch manager is on the ground and should be able to advise the home office regarding peculiar local matters. Practically, however, many a branch office manager could tell at least one or two stories of decisions made without or against his advice which had not taken local conditions into full consideration.

Conclusions on Field Organization. Just as every football play is designed to carry the ball for a touchdown, if properly executed,[11] so either the general agency system or the branch office system is designed to yield perfect results in field organization. The fact that relatively few plays in any football game do go for a touchdown is not the fault of the play as planned but of its execution. Similarly, the degree by which either the general agency system or the branch office system fails to achieve perfection is a result of execution rather than inherent nature. Therefore, which may be the better system for any given company and in any given territory depends upon the company and upon the available personnel to man the offices. In recognition of this fact, some companies use general agencies in certain localities and branch offices in others; and further recognition of it lies in the current tendency to combine some of the advantages of both while retaining the outward form of one, usually the general agency system where this combination is attempted.

---

[11] The athletic member of the class will undoubtedly point out that there are certain football plays the purpose of which is to put the ball into a desired position and which cannot be diagrammed as touchdowns. However, we prefer that he keep that little matter to himself since revelation of it will spoil an otherwise perfectly good analogy.

As has been stated previously, this discussion of the two systems has been of their pure form. Actually, the distinctions between them, once clear, are now blurred. There could undoubtedly be found examples of general agencies which are more closely controlled by the home office than are some branch offices. In general, at the present time, there is a trend toward more and more staff services from the home office for both general agencies and branch offices—and often, even in the case of general agencies, of functional assistance out of the home office—home office trainers being a widespread example.

Appraisal of the Nonagency System. In the main, selling without agents has not proved effective in producing business in volume.[12] The Wisconsin Life Fund is an example.

The total of Savings Bank life insurance in force is usually quoted on a state-wide basis. Taking Savings Bank life insurance in any one state, the volume of business produced will be reasonably good. If each bank is considered individually, the volume will prove to be very small. Even then, it must be remembered, Savings Bank life insurance puts substantial effort behind the sale, through advertising and various forms of sales promotion, even though it has no soliciting agents.

The original in-force totals of National Service (and United States Government life insurance) [13] are not true examples of what may be done by direct writing. In the first place, National Service life insurance used a field organization which consisted of "insurance officers"; often these men were professional life insurance men in private life. Moreover, groups of professional men were often used as "flying squadrons" who put all the sales motivation they could behind talks to mass groups of servicemen to get them to apply for the maximum allowable. Finally, not only was the sale of National Service life insurance helped by the pressure of the imminent hazard of

---

[12] Some years back, Sears, Roebuck, and Company, usually considered to be one of the most experienced merchandisers by mail, established a life insurance company and attempted for several years to sell insurance, as well as its merchandise, by mail. Its success as far as life insurance was concerned was not outstanding enough for the company to feel it could continue the plan. Sears is, however, one of the country's largest direct writers of automobile insurance.

[13] At the peak over $140,000,000,000 of NSLI was in force. Right after World War II the amount of NSLI was less than $35,000,000,000. Factors other than the lack of agents have played their part in the disheartening lapsation record of service insurances, particularly NSLI. Perhaps principal among them was the way the coverage was often sold: "Some of you guys in this unit haven't yet applied for the full $10,000. We're going to be a 100% unit or else!" Perhaps better than saying NSLI is an example of what happens to insurance in force when there are no agents is to say that NSLI is an example of what happens when life insurance is forced on people by high pressure and subsequently not serviced.

actual combat but also by the pressure often put on servicemen by superior officers.

Another disadvantage of writing without agents is that service is more difficult to render. An advantage of the agentless system is lower cost, but this lower cost is often false economy. The wide and almost universal use of the agency system in American marketing indicates its strong hold on the insurance business. It is a hold that companies without agents have to date found impossible to break.

Internal Organization of a Field Office. The over-all objectives of a field office are to service old policyholders and to secure new policyholders.[14] These functions may be classified under two headings, the office functions and the sales management functions.

Office Functions. The internal organization of any field office will depend upon what is best suited to its size and available personnel. In general, however, the office functions in any agency, whether a general agency or a branch office, are the collection of premiums, the maintenance of policyholder records, and policyholder service in such matters as the negotiation of loans, the extension of premium payment date, execution of change of beneficiary request papers, answering inquiries, and communicating with the home office. In most cases such services are not sought by the policyholder direct, but through an agent. The details of handling them are most often left within the scope of the cashier's department.

The administration of the purely clerical affairs is a function of the cashier's department. In most branch offices and in many large general agencies, the management of all clerical personnel will be within the scope of the duties of the cashier. Often in the branch office system these functions are exclusively the province of the cashier, who may be on virtually the same level of authority as is the branch manager himself. In the general agency, of course, all employees are employees of the general agent.

Sales Management Functions. In addition to the clerical functions performed by a field office, there are the sales management functions, which include hiring, training, and supervising field personnel, and all phases dealing with the promotion of new business.

"Recruiting" is the term used commonly not only in the life insurance business but also in all types of selling to denote the process of finding and

---

[14] There are in the business some few examples of field offices, usually called "collection offices," whose duties are primarily and even exclusively the maintenance of policyholder records, collection of premiums, and any in-office service requested by policyholders calling at the office.

hiring new men.[15] Practically every life insurance company field office is always on the alert for new sales personnel and is considered by many agency men as not functioning properly unless it is actively searching for such men.

To some extent, this continual search is a result of the turnover in agents, that is, of agents leaving the business. Much criticism has been made of this turnover, which is sometimes quoted as 50% of first-year men. In the past, the lack of valid criteria by which to judge the potentialities of a prospective agent, poor training, poor supervision, and the fact that, under some types of agency contracts, the general agent stood to make an immediate gain if a man left the business before his renewals were vested [16]—these factors have undoubtedly contributed heavily to the turnover. They are becoming less a factor as companies take a firmer stand on the qualifications of men hired by their field offices, as agency heads realize the cost of turnover, and as aptitude and vocational interest tests become more widely used, and especially as life insurance education and training become constantly stronger.

It might be pointed out that turnover in personnel is not peculiar to life insurance field offices or to sales work in general. Large industrial concerns often have unbelievably high rates of turnover, especially among hourly workers. The fact that high rates of turnover are to be found in other businesses also, is, of course, no justification for such turnover among life insurance agents. However, there has been a tendency, perhaps, to emphasize turnover among agents in such a way as to make it appear to be a problem peculiar to the insurance business.

Selection is, of course, a part of the recruiting function. While rule-of-thumb judgment of the fitness of men for the job of life insurance selling is still too often practiced (as it is still often practiced in general business), valid and reliable aptitude and interest tests have been worked out and are widely used for preliminary screening of applicants for jobs as life insurance

---

[15] The term is held by some as not properly descriptive of the function and actually objectionable. However, it is nearly universally used.

[16] Under the terms of many contracts between general agents and subagents, the subagents' renewal commissions were not vested until the agent had filled certain conditions of (1) length of service and, especially, (2) amount of production during a given period. (Renewal commissions are said to be "vested" when the agent is guaranteed payment of them regardless of whether he leaves the general agent.) Under what was once the common type of general agent's contract, nonvested renewals reverted to the general agent when a man left the business. (That is, the general agent, having a contract with the company calling for the payment to him of 7½% renewals, say, and having himself granted an agent 5% of the 7½%, would, when an agent quit the business, again receive the entire 7½% on all nonvested renewals which the agent left behind.) Consequently, it was to the general agent's profit to recruit agents who would write their friends and relatives and then, unable to write others, would leave the business.

salesmen. The tests have been more useful in predicting failure than in predicting success; that is, one can be more sure of the failure of a man scoring low than he can be of the success of a man scoring high. These tests, therefore, do not guarantee success but do eliminate from further consideration men who are not likely to succeed.[17] Tests will not measure a man's willingness to apply himself, or his ability to build a market.

Training is an important sales management function. To be successful, an agent must have not only a reasonably good understanding of a fairly technical subject—insurance—but also intensive training in how to present the subject so that the prospect will buy. The values purchased in life insurance are future values, but they take money away from present uses. Moreover, the values are intangible. When the prospect has paid the first premium due, he has nothing but a piece of paper in his hand to show for his money. It is not easy to induce even intelligent people to give up present luxuries in return for life insurance, which promises tangible benefits only at some time far in the future when they are dead or have retired.[18]

Training in the life insurance business consists of (1) acquiring technical knowledge and (2) developing skill in selling. Knowledge alone will not make a life insurance salesman. The home office actuary, for an example, has more pure knowledge about life insurance than the most successful agent; but few are the home office actuaries who could keep up the sales pace of even a mediocre agent. On the other hand, sales skill without knowledge rarely leads to permanent success in life insurance selling.

Ideally, the acquisition of knowledge should come from formal education, and the application of that knowledge (which is "skill") should be taught in the business. Unfortunately, despite the vast increase in academic courses in life insurance since World War II, there are still too few people with formal education in life insurance to satisfy the need for agents. Therefore, training plans and courses offered by agencies, companies, and at the institutional level have to start off with imparting knowledge.[19]

---

[17] Sometimes there may be extenuating circumstances which will encourage an agency manager to contract an agent even though he scores low on a test.

[18] The difficulties involved in selling life insurance are much the same as those involved in "selling" religion. Both call for giving up present pleasures for future rewards. The job of the life insurance agent, like the job of the minister, priest, or rabbi, is to convince men that the satisfaction that comes from having done what they know is right will be greater than the satisfaction from the present pleasures that must be foregone. In truth, selling life insurance calls for a touch of evangelism on the part of the agent. The authors have never known a career life insurance agent who wasn't evangelistic about his work, determined to convince people for their own salvation. No sacrilege is intended by this comparison. It was first brought to the attention of the authors by a minister of the gospel.

[19] Unfortunately, since it is easier to impart knowledge than to teach skill, too many training courses concentrate on the former to the neglect of the latter. Whereas part of

In contrast to an earlier day in the business when training consisted of giving the new man a rate book and a pat on the back, there is today a plethora of training "plans" and "programs." These programs are of several kinds: agency or company, commercial, campus, and institutional.[20]

Supervising and motivating agents also are functions of a field office. Supervisory efforts are aimed at directing and controlling the business activities of the agent. They include working with the men in the field, perhaps actually accompanying them on their calls to observe their methods and technique and to offer suggestions for improving them; requiring reports from the agents regarding their work; analysis of reports with suggestions and criticisms; and the handling of special problems which arise and which may be brought to the attention of the agent's supervisor or unit manager, or directly to his general agent or manager.

The function of motivating the agent consists of building and maintaining his morale, creating job satisfaction, and developing in him a feeling of importance by constantly reminding him of the prestige that goes with the job of high-level professional life insurance selling. The general agent often must stimulate interest through agency meetings, study groups, sales contests, production clubs (in which membership is based on a number of qualifications, chief among which is usually a stated level of new business) and sales quotas.

Certain *sales promotion* functions also are a part of the duties of a field office. The extent and intensiveness of operation in this area depend much upon the type of agency system. In the pure general agency system, virtually all the sales promotion functions connected with life insurance devolve

---

the turnover among agents can be attributed to inadequate training, some turnover can be attributed to too much concentration of "education" to the neglect of "training." Life insurance training could take a lesson from medical training. While imparting a high degree of knowledge, medical training also concentrates on the development of skill, usually starting with practical work in obstetrics in the junior year. Even after medicine has imparted knowledge up to the highest academic degree, the doctorate, it does not allow the possessor of that knowledge to practice medicine until he has had at least a year or two of internship—which is training in skill as contrasted to knowledge. Unfortunately, there is in life insurance too great a body of thinking which considers knowledge alone enough for agent training.

[20] Agency or company training plans run up the scale from nothing more than a booklet of questions and answers designed to help the new man qualify for a state license, to a well-conceived series of training courses extending over a period of several years. The principal institutional programs are those of the Life Underwriters Training Council (L.U.T.C.), the Disability Insurance Training Council (D.I.T.C.), and the American College of Life Underwriters. The American College of Life Underwriters, the oldest of this group, offers a study course and a series of examinations leading to the award of the professional designation "Chartered Life Underwriter," usually abbreviated as "C.L.U."

upon the agency. On the other hand, sales promotion services or functions performed within the field office will be limited in the pure branch office organization to those functions which can be performed only locally. For example, in the pure general agency not only the decision regarding how much local advertising is to be done but also the creation and placement of that advertising will be the responsibility of the field office. In the pure branch office organization, however, perhaps the only function the field office will perform in connection with local advertising is the actual placement of advertisements—the number, nature, and media will have been prescribed by the home office. In truth, the only purpose in leaving the placement of the advertising to the branch office is to enable the branch manager to make a personal contact which will be of value in the public relations of the office in the local territory.

The sales promotion services in a field office may consist of the preparation of sales literature and visual aids, the drawing up of personal or business life insurance proposals for the agents or assistance in drawing them up, the building of prospecting lists, the aforementioned creation or placement of advertising, and the operation of a direct mail system of advertising. Which of these will be performed in any given field office depends, as stated, on the nature of the organization of the field forces and the policy of the company.

Compensating agents is another major sales management function. As with salesmen in general, the basic method of compensating life insurance salesmen is the commission contract. Compensation plans designed for Ordinary agents differ from those designed for Industrial [21] agents. The distinction is sufficient to justify discussing the two separately.

Ordinary Agent Compensation. Compensation contracts of Ordinary agents usually call for high commissions on the first year's premium with a much smaller commission on future premiums. For instance, what is commonly called the "New York scale" provides first-year commissions of as high as 55% on policies such as continuous-premium Whole Life and 20-Pay Life (the "top-commission" contracts varying with companies) down to as low as 15% on short Term and 3% on single-premium forms. Renewal commissions are 5% but are not graded—that is, they are the same for all policy forms and are payable for nine years.[22] Thus under the "New York contract" the

---

[21] Today the Industrial agent is more commonly called a "Combination" agent in view of the fact that he almost always sells Ordinary as well as Weekly Premium insurance.

[22] There are of course variations in these plans with some few companies paying slightly lower first-year commissions and slightly higher second- (and sometimes third-) year renewals.

total commission payable during the life of top-commission policies is 100% of one year's premium (55% first year, plus 9 × 5%, or 45%).[23]

Renewal commissions usually become "vested" (that is, his renewals will continue to be paid to him even if he leaves the company) if the agent achieves certain levels of production within time periods stated in the compensation contract or completes a requisite period of service such as five, ten, 15, or perhaps 20 years.

In recent years, in recognition of the fact that agents are often called upon to give service to policyholders long after the renewal commissions have expired, many companies have augmented the system of first-year and renewal commissions with "service fees" to be paid as continuing compensation after renewals stop. These fees are paid on the basis of the life insurance the agent has in force and are paid as long as the agent is with the company. They usually represent a lesser percentage of the policy premium than do renewal commissions and are level in amount.

Many companies also pay additional commissions or bonuses per $1,000 of new business paid for,[24] basing the bonus on a satisfactory average-size policy or rate of persistency, or a combination of both. There may also be additional compensation, usually in the form of a bonus, for cash with the application or for policies written on an annual rather than a quarterly premium plan. Some companies pay a bonus for larger policies, say $2,500 and over, as an example, by the reverse process of reducing the commission on smaller policies.

The presence of and nature of additional compensation in the form of various bonuses differ widely among compensation contracts and depend on the operating philosophy of the company involved; however, it is usual for

---

[23] First-year and renewal commissions totaling 100% of an annual premium are the maximum that can be paid under New York law. Any company licensed to do business in New York must comply "substantially" with this maximum in every state in which it operates. A company not licensed in New York might pay more, especially if it is a small company which feels that its competitive situation is such that it must pay more to attract agents. Contracts of these smaller companies often range as high as 90% of first-year commission with some such renewal arrangement as nine at 7½% and five at 5%.

[24] New business may be referred to by the status of the application at any given time. *Written business* consists of applications which have been signed by the applicant but on which no premium has yet been paid. *Examined business* has not only been "written" but also had the medical examination. *Paid business* has settlement for the first premium. *Issued business* consists of policies actually made out by the company but not yet delivered to the applicant. *Delivered business* consists of issued policies delivered to the policyholder but not yet paid for. *Placed business* has not only been delivered to the policyholder but also paid for by him. Business is "paid for" if there is settlement for the first premium at any of the above stages. It is not "placed," however, until both paid for and delivered, or delivered and paid for, whichever is the sequence in the particular case. The only business on which the agent actually collects the commission is "placed" business.

one or more of these extra compensation features to be found in any given agency contract.

In addition to straight compensation are various fringe benefits in the form of retirement pensions and Group life and disability insurance. In so far as these benefits are available, they represent, in effect, additional compensation.

Only a few United States and Canadian companies of any size use other than the commission plan of compensation. These contracts provide salary in lieu of or in addition to commission. The salary is weighted by and must be validated by production. It is, therefore, tantamount to commuting the commissions of a basic commission contract.

Under the commission contract the Ordinary agent earns nothing until he starts making sales. As a result, building up a satisfactory volume of production, and, hence, income, comes slowly for the average new agent; therefore, it has become common for companies or general agents to finance a new agent's first months or years in the business until his sales rise and especially until he begins to get the benefit of renewals.

Financing plans are of infinite variations. Several examples are as follows:

(1) *Drawing Account*. The agent is advanced money either on a stipulated weekly or monthly basis or as he needs it. The money is to be paid back—usually whether the agent terminates his contract or not.

(2) *Stipulated Weekly or Monthly Payments in Lieu of Commissions.* Under this plan, the agent's earned commissions are credited to his account to offset the stipulated payments. Usually the arrangement is to continue for a period of months or even several years, with the agent having the right to stop the payments and take his commissions whenever the latter exceed the former. In case of termination of employment, he may or may not be liable for any deficit of payments over commissions actually earned. The trend is toward the "forgiveness" plan (where the agent's debit balance is forgiven).

(3) *Stipulated Payments Plus Partial Commissions.* The agent is guaranteed a weekly or monthly income. In addition, he is guaranteed part of his commissions. In some plans he has this guarantee regardless of amount of the commissions and in others only if the commissions exceed a certain amount. These plans provide level income during the starting period plus incentive for increased production. Again, in case of termination of employment, the agent may be liable for any deficit or the deficit may be canceled. As stated, the trend is toward "forgiving" the deficit.

It should be emphasized that whatever the compensation arrangement established for the new agent, he must show signs of impending success or he will not last. In other words, one has to sell life insurance in order to make his living selling life insurance.

In addition to company financing plans, it is possible for agents to help finance themselves. One method is to borrow against renewals; that is, as soon as an agent has placed a case, he can borrow some of the money which he expects to be paid in the future from that sale. The actual value of the renewals, of course, will not be 100% of their maximum value possible since a certain percentage of policies will not continue in force until all renewals have been paid. However, banks, loan companies, general agents, and sometimes insurance companies will lend or advance money on the estimated present value of expected future renewals.

Whatever glowing pictures may be painted (and recognizing that exceptions are found), getting established in life insurance selling calls for expenditure of capital by the agent.[25] Either he uses up some of his savings or he has to borrow the necessary capital. The job of life insurance selling is equivalent to going into business for oneself. The established agent is a self-employed businessman.[26] While he may, in a sense, "work for" a given company, he is much freer to change companies than is the typical salaried man. If employment conditions with his company do not satisfy him, he can form a new connection almost overnight, and as far as new business goes, retain virtually all his clients. Moreover, if he has been with his company long enough for renewals to be vested, he also retains income from past business produced for that company.

Combination Agent Compensation. The theory of compensation for the agent who collects and services a debit is different from that for the Ordinary agent. The debit agent performs a salaried-type function in his collection activities; hence, he is paid a basic salary expressed as a percentage of collections on his assigned debit. One large industrial writer pays 12% of weekly premiums and 6% of monthly debit premiums. This basic salary compensates for the time the agent spends in making collections and the necessary bookkeeping. The fundamental difference between his compensation and that of the Ordinary agent is that the man who collects a debit starts out with a "salary" emanating from business previously sold, whereas the new Ordinary agent receives compensation only if and when he produces new business.[27]

In addition to his basic salary, the debit agent receives a commission on

---

[25] The young college man often is an exception. If he has no fixed obligations and can live on a close budget for a year or two, he may be able to earn his way while getting established.

[26] Except for Social Security purposes.

[27] Except those, of course, who are on one of the financing plans already discussed.

all new Industrial business sold. On new debit business, the agent's compensation consists of a graded commission scale with allowances for persistency. In one large industrial writer, the first-year commission rate is 37%, except that for Endowments of 30 years or fewer the rate is 28%. Also, when he writes Ordinary insurance, he receives the customary Ordinary commission payable for this business.

A third source of income to the Combination agent is a conservation commission. For example, in one large Industrial writer, this ranges from $3 to $7 a week, the exact amount depending upon the agent's lapse ratio in comparison with that of the company as a whole.

Some companies pay in addition an annual service bonus, the amount of which varies with the years of service. For example, one company pays $50 for service of from ten to 14 years on up to $200 for service of 25 or more years.[28]

Accident and Sickness Compensation. The basic method of compensating agents for the sale of Accident and Sickness insurance is also the commission contract; however, two different types of commission arrangements are in use.

Whereas the predominant practice in the life insurance is to "bunch" the bulk of the total commission payable into the first year, in the casualty insurance field the predominant arrangement is equal first-year and renewal commissions, with renewal commissions being payable as long as the policy is on a premium-paying basis. Inheriting, as it does, from both the casualty and the life fields, the A & S business uses both types of commission plans, varying from company to company.

The trend among life insurance companies is toward the "unlevel" commission plan to which their men are accustomed, although a different distribution of the renewal commissions is made. For instance, one of the largest life companies uses a 40% first-year commission, 15% second, 10% third, and 5% for the life of the contract. Another life company pays 40% the first year, 10% the second through the tenth years, and 5% thereafter for the life of the contract. On hospitalization contracts, both pay a 25% first-year commission, 8% the second through the tenth year, and 3% thereafter.

In contrast is the level commission plan of another large life insurer. It offers 25% flat for the first year and on all subsequent renewals. Usually neither this plan nor the graded plans cited above vary the commission scales

---

[28] While the top 10% or so of Ordinary agents will earn more than the average of the top 10% of Combination agents, it is not unlikely that the earnings of the average Combination agent would exceed those of the average Ordinary agent.

for different policies, as is done in the life field, except for the lowered commission on hospitalization noted in the one example.

The graded commission plan tends to emphasize new business, whereas the level plan emphasizes business that remains in force. Under the level plan, the agent who writes a policy which lapses the first year loses more than does the agent under the graded plan. However, as between the scales illustrated above, if the policy remains in force for as few as three years he is better off. Although the level commission plan seems to emphasize persistent business,[29] it does postpone compensation and this might make it harder for the new man in his first year or two. On the other hand, the level plan permits the building of a larger renewal income, thus giving him more vested interests in his business.

Which is the better plan of compensation—level or graded—is a subject much discussed in the business.

3. INTERCOMPANY AND FIELD ASSOCIATIONS

In the life and Accident and Sickness insurance business there are a number of intercompany co-operative organizations and agents' associations, some of which have been mentioned briefly elsewhere in the book but which might be summarized here.

The Life Insurance Association of America, usually abbreviated "L.I.A.A.," is an intercompany association devoted to an exchange of information of aid and value at company level, especially in the areas of investments, company management, and company taxation. With headquarters in New York and an office in Washington, it is highly active in watching legislative trends, suggesting legislation in the field of income taxation affecting life insurance, and offering expert testimony before congressional committees when called upon to do so. Originally considered the "big company" association, it now contains members representative of companies of all sizes.

The American Life Convention, usually abbreviated "A.L.C.," with headquarters in Chicago, covers the same fields of activity as L.I.A.A. Originally considered the "small companies'" association, like L.I.A.A., it has broadened its membership until it is representative of all classes.

Institute of Life Insurance, usually called "The Institute," has to date escaped the alphabetical designation that is the lot of most other associations. The Institute, with headquarters in New York, is primarily a public relations organization supported co-operatively by member companies. It prepares news releases on life insurance information of public interest, conducts a constant institutional advertising program in newspapers and farm journals

---

[29] That is, business which persists—stays—on the books.

throughout the country, prepares articles and booklets for distribution to the public and women's groups and through schools, and seeks to answer adverse criticism of life insurance in the medium in which the criticism was published. It also serves as a central source of information and statistics. The Institute, by sponsoring summer workshops for teachers, contributes toward proficiency in family finance and consumer education. The workshops are conducted by universities.

Bureau of Accident & Health Underwriters, usually called "The Bureau," is an intercompany association of carriers—life, casualty, or monoline—writing A & S. In addition to performing much the same functions for the A & S writers as the L.I.A.A. and A.L.C. do for life companies, it carries on research in occupational ratings and has developed a classification system. Once considered primarily the "Eastern company" association, it is now more representative of all geographical areas. Headquarters are in New York.

Health & Accident Underwriters Conference,[30] usually called "The Conference," functions much the same as the Bureau, including the development of a classification system of its own. Headquarters are in Chicago. Once considered the "smaller company" or "Western company" association, it is now representative of all geographical areas and size classifications of A & S writers.

Life Insurers Conference, often thought of as the "small companies'" association, includes a preponderance of Combination (Industrial and Ordinary) companies, particularly from the Midwest, South, and Southwest. Its purposes are exchange of information and experience in all areas of company operations and management. Headquarters are in Richmond, Virginia.

National Fraternal Congress of America, an intercompany association of fraternal companies for exchange of information and experience and study of investment and actuarial problems peculiar to fraternal operation. Headquarters are in Chicago.

National Insurance Association, an intercompany association of companies specializing in Negro risks, with Chicago headquarters.

The Life Office Management Association, abbreviated to "L.O.M.A.," has executive offices in New York City. Its primary objective is to assist in improving life office management through an exchange of experience and

---

[30] As this is written, a new intercompany association has been formed under the name of "Health Insurance Association of America." This organization has the approval of the boards of directors of both the Bureau and the Conference to solicit memberships from companies which are members of those two organizations, which will then cease to exist, leaving their present functions to the new organization. Memberships will also be solicited from several other intercompany associations which now perform some functions in the A & S field but are not devoted exclusively to A & S. The intention is to combine all intercompany A & S functions in the one, new association.

research among member companies and the development and administration of an educational program for office employees. Organized in 1924 by a group of officers of 83 life insurance companies, its membership now stands at approximately 100. L.O.M.A. organized the Life Office Management Association Institute in 1932 to administer an educational program and series of examinations. Close to 30,000 home office employees have pursued the courses offered.

Life Insurance Agency Management Association, usually abbreviated "L.I.A.M.A.," is devoted to research in and preparation of aids for life insurance sales management. It is supported co-operatively by companies and has headquarters in Hartford.

National Association of Life Underwriters, usually abbreviated "N.A. L.U.," is an agents' association, active (voting) membership being confined to agents, general agents, and managers. N.A.L.U. is active in all areas affecting the interest and welfare of agents, including state and Federal law and legislation. Headquarters has been in New York City for many years, but the association is now building a new office in Washington, D.C. N.A. L.U. operates through state associations which, in turn, are made up of local associations in cities and towns having enough life insurance agents to support a local organization.

General Agents & Managers Conference, usually abbreviated to "G.A. M.C.," is an organization within N.A.L.U. It grew out of the criticism of agents that general agents and managers tended to "dominate" N.A.L.U. and the criticism of general agents and managers that while N.A.L.U. derived much of its financial support from them, it devoted little of its attention to them. At the time of the formation of G.A.M.C. in 1952 there were throughout the country many local general agents and managers' associations unaffiliated with any national organization. G.A.M.C. has sought to bring members of these organizations into G.A.M.C. membership, and the local associations are beginning to adopt the requirement that all local members be members of G.A.M.C. Headquarters of G.A.M.C., which has its own executive director, are with N.A.L.U.

International Association of Accident & Health Underwriters, sometimes abbreviated "I.A.A.H.U.," is the agents' association for men who sell A & S. Membership among life insurance men whose companies sell A & S is overlapping with N.A.L.U. However, I.A.A.H.U. includes casualty and monoline A & S men who do not normally belong to N.A.L.U.

In addition to these broad company and agents' associations are a number of special-purpose associations with members from all companies—or at least with membership open to representatives from all companies. The following is a list of the better known of them. The name of each is reasonably descriptive of its nature:

Association of Life Insurance Counsel
Association of Life Insurance Medical Directors
Home Office Life Underwriters Association
Institute of Home Office Underwriters
Insurance Accounting & Statistical Society
International Claim Association
Life Insurance Advertisers Association (made up of home office advertising
    men)
Society of Actuaries

Membership in intercompany associations is not mutually exclusive. Thus a company might belong to L.I.A.A., A.L.C., Conference, Bureau, Institute, and L.I.A.M.A. There is, however, no such thing as company "membership" in N.A.L.U. or in I.A.A.H.U., although home office personnel may belong as associate members.

4. SUMMARY

The organizational problems of a life insurance company are not peculiar to that particular type of business but in the main duplicate those of all business. In other words, sound general principles of business organization apply to the organization of a life insurance company home office as well as to any other type of business operation. Departments may vary, but the bases of organization and the bases of departmentalization are the same in principle.

Since each business is a personality in itself—the reflection of the personalities which make it up or dominate it—no general rules can be laid down regarding the best type of organization for any given home office. Any two home offices, virtually identical to the casual observer, will prove upon examination and analysis to contain differences which make one or another type of organization more suitable. Moreover, no rules can be laid down as to the type of organization which may be most efficient throughout the history of the company. Companies change in size, and as they change, their organizational needs alter. Available personnel and executive interests always must be taken into consideration. The major consideration is flexibility.

In any home office, whatever its organization, authority will always move downward. It begins with the stockholders or policyholders, depending upon the type of company. These are the last court of appeal and the beginning of all authority. By their votes, they can exercise all control over the entire organization. From these stockholders or policyholders, authority moves downward to the Board of Directors, which may retain part of it in committees of its own and delegate the residual authority to executive officers who have the power to bind the company.

Authority leaving executive officers diffuses through the various departments in a pattern which varies from company to company. Perhaps it goes to appointed executives—who are called "functional" executives to distinguish them from those who exercise authority over operations rather than practical direction of them. From appointed officers it may go to divisional heads or unit supervisors and eventually finds its way down to the lowest level of authority: the individual worker who has responsibility only for his job and not for the work of any others. In a smaller company, lines of authority may flow directly from the executive officers to the individual workers; and in larger companies, they may go through even more steps than those detailed above.

The principal function of departments in a home office are agency, underwriting, actuarial, legal, contract, and investment. Insurance companies also may be departmentalized on the bases of products, territory, or class of customers.

Most businesses have production departments and sales departments. The function of the sales department is to sell the product produced by the plant. In life insurance, the sales department is also the production department, for the act of selling life insurance is the act of producing life insurance. The sale of a $10,000 life insurance policy automatically produces an additional $10,000 of insurance in force. The agent who sells $1,000,000 worth of life insurance is called a million-dollar "producer." It is the primary function of the field organization of a life insurance company to "produce" business.

In general, there are two basic systems of field organization: (1) the general agency system, and (2) the branch office or managerial system. Under the former, field offices are under the control of men to whom has been granted the power of agency not only for the conduct of business between the company and the policyholder, but also between the company and those who represent it in direct contact with the public, the subagents. The general agent is an independent operator who has a contractual agreement with the company under which he operates as a fully independent contractor, subject to the control of the company only within terms of the contract. Under the branch office system, each field office is under the direction of a salaried employee of the home office, resident in the territory over which his field office has authority. The company has direct control over him as over all employees and, hence, more direct control over the agents under him than it does over the agents under the general agent.

Neither the general agency system nor the branch office system can be called the "better" system for every given company in every given territory. Each has its merits, and each has its drawbacks. For one company in one territory, one may be the better, while in another territory or for another company the other may be the better. In actual practice, the distinction between the two is often hard to perceive except for the nomenclature. There is a tendency among all companies, at the present time, to reserve for themselves more and more control over their field offices, even though they may technically retain the general agency system of field organization. On the other hand, companies which use the branch manager system must frequently add to the manager's contract phrases or clauses which more accurately belong in a general agent's contract, particularly incentive arrangements in the way of bonuses and commissions above salary.

The main functions of a field office are the selection, training, supervision, and motivation of agents, and sales promotion. Although life insurance might function and survive without an extensive field organization, it could not have become the factor in the American economy and American business that it is today. This seems thoroughly proved by the experience of those American carriers which do not have extensive field organizations, as well as by the experience in Great Britain, for instance, where well-developed field organizations are not as common as in America.

Questions for Class Discussion

1. How does the job of the president of a life insurance company differ from the job of the president of the local bank?
2. Why do large insurance companies often have so many vice-presidents?
3. What is the most important department in an insurance company?
4. In which department of a life insurance company would you most like to work? Why?
5. If you were going into life insurance sales management, which would you prefer to have, a general agency or a branch office? Why? Suppose you were president of the company. Which would you prefer for your company? Why?
6. If you were going to sell life insurance, would you prefer to work for a general agent or for a manager? Why? If you were buying life insurance, would you prefer to buy from a general agency or a branch office? Why?
7. Is it the job of the colleges and universities to teach men how to sell life insurance? Discuss.
8. Do you think life insurance agents are overpaid? Discuss.
9. Why are there so many different kinds of organized associations in the life insurance business?
10. An important attribute of a job with a life insurance company home office is stability. Why? Is this true in the field (selling)? Why?

CHAPTER 26

DEVELOPMENT OF THE BUSINESS

THE ORIGINS of life insurance are obscured in the mists of antiquity. Nevertheless, since the principle of insurance is an evolution rather than an invention, life, accident, and sickness insurance can be traced back to any number of forebearers. The Chinese had forms of sickness, life, fire, crop, and war insurance from time immemorial. Sections 23 and 28 of the Code of Hammurabi show that ancient Babylon had various forms of government theft and crop insurance as well as an adoption-annuity plan. A Babylonian could adopt a son, rear him, and, for old age security, depend upon his adopted son's legal obligation to provide the necessary funds.

First Contribution Principle. The first evidences of personal insurance on the contribution principle are found in the *Eianoi* or *Thiasoi* of ancient Greece. These benevolent societies, supported by contributions from members, developed into common devices for paying burial expenses of members and the immediate cash needs of their survivors.

Rome early evolved the *Collegia* of the soldiery and the *Collegia Tenuiorum* of the civilians. The funds of the *Collegia* of the soldiery were used to meet unexpected expenses for the soldier such as those of a costly transfer to a distant post, new equipment necessitated by a promotion, disability and old age pensions, burial, and living expenses of his widow and children. The funds of the *Collegia Tenuiorum* were used to pay for the burial of the nonmilitary citizen and to provide for the most pressing post-burial necessities of his family.

The Guilds of medieval England were in a direct line of descent from the *Eianoi, Thiasoi,* and *Collegia.* In their beginnings, the Guilds seem to have had as their main purpose, the relief of brethren and their families in time of distress. When the Guilds collapsed under the rising tide of nationalism, their places were taken by the Friendly Societies. Without these societies the artisan class of Great Britain, in the first quarter of the nineteenth century, would have found it difficult to provide for even the simple necessity of burial. When the scientific laws of mortality were introduced into the life insurance business, the Friendly Societies became the framework on which the new life insurance companies were developed.

1. FIRST RECORDS IN ENGLAND

While continental theorists and mathematicians [1] contributed much to the development of the science of life insurance, the practical application of these principles to insurance developed there so slowly that it is better to look to England for background on the development of the life insurance business in America.

Marine insurance had long been established in England when, on June 18, 1536, Richard Martin turned to companions in the Old Drury Ale House, a gathering place for marine underwriters, and suggested that the practice of marine underwriting be extended to the underwriting of the risk of a human life, in this case a fellow drinking companion named William Gybbons (described as a "hale-fellow-well-met sort of individual, rubicund of jowl, healthy of person, and apparently destined to live to the full biblical 'three score and ten'"). Martin, with confidence in his judgment elevated by either a series of lucky underwritings or the ale, proposed to insure the life of William Gybbons for twelve months in an amount of $2,000 for a premium of about $80. Fifteen underwriters joined in the proposal. Mr. Gybbons accepted and, as fate would have it, died on May 29, 1537.

Now Richard Martin and his cohorts, and William Gybbons, for that matter, might forever have escaped the notice of history had not the underwriters been so upset by their bad selection that they decided to contest the claim on the grounds that the policy had been written in terms a year of twelve lunar months of 28 days each. Therefore, they contended, the policy had expired on May 20. The defense fell when the court laid down the principle of holding against the insurer who draws up an ambiguous contract and ordered the claim paid.

After the litigation over the Gybbons claim, the idea of underwriting lives

---

[1] To name a few: *John DeWitt* (1625–1672), Dutch pioneer in the mathematics of annuities; *Jean Bernoulli* (1667–1784), Swiss publisher of the first comprehensive book on probabilities; *Leonard Euler* (1707–1783), Swiss annuity mathematician.

seemed to have become more popular, for there followed 160 years of ever increasing activity in this field. Gradually life underwriting became a specialty rather than just a side line of the marine underwriters. Eventually life underwriters moved from coffee and pot houses to Exchange Alley where, despite Puritan antagonism and rumors of the sudden, sad, and suspicious demise of many an insured, life underwriting throve and prospered.

First Life Offices. The first registered life office in England was the Hand-in-Hand Society, established in 1696 by 100 incorporators.

In 1698, the Mercers' Company inaugurated a scheme for granting life annuities to the nominees of member-insurers. The venture, undertaken at the instigation of a Lancashire divine, Dr. William Assheton, author of such delightful Calvinism as *The Certainty and Eternity of Hell Torments,* finally had to be bailed out by the government. The mortality table on which the Mercers' Company proceeded seems to have had little of the certainty the worthy doctor saw in hell's torments.

The Society of Assurance for Widows & Orphans, founded in 1699, was the earliest life insurance association projected in England. It proposed to have members contribute $1.20 a week for life insurance of $2400. The Society, the first of the mutual life offices, introduced selection of risks with regard to health and age; contract exclusion of such hazards as military, naval, and sea service; a grace period (seven days) for payment of premiums; and waiver of liability in case of legal execution. The ultimate fate of the Society is unknown, although there is evidence that it had obtained only 600 of its proposed 2,000 membership by 1704, and only 1,104 by 1707. Thereafter it dropped from the horizon of recorded life insurance history.

Several other "companies" were projected in the early 1700's but faded quickly from the record. However, in 1706 the Amicable Society for a Perpetual Assurance Office received a charter from Queen Anne and set about with the purpose of correcting an abuse of private underwriting. Notably, as its name implies, it offered insurance for the whole of life instead of for a specific term as was common up to that time. However, it was not until 100 years later that the Society attempted to write whole life policies with a fixed face value. During the first century, the death benefit payable was the amount in the fund at the end of a year divided among the beneficiaries of members deceased during the year. The amount payable therefore fluctuated with variations in mortality experience and interest earnings.

Amicable was the beginning of the end of the dominance of the individual underwriter or underwriting syndicate in the life field.[2] Amicable was merged with the Norwich Union Life Office in 1866.[3]

"Old Equitable." The Society for the Equitable Assurance of Lives and Survivorships, familiarly known as "Old Equitable," was established in 1756 to offer whole life, level-premium insurance for a fixed face amount, the mathematical formula for which had eluded actuaries up to that time. When Old Equitable issued its first policies in 1762, life insurance as we know it today was born. The company offered a grace period of 30 days, a 90-day reinstatement provision, premiums graded according to age, and a refund of any overcharge on premiums—which set the pattern for the "dividend" system used today under what are called "participating" policies. The "Old Equitable" continues to flourish to this day.

Coming Of Surrender Values. The Scottish Widows' Fund and Equitable Assurance of Edinburgh added surrender values in 1851, and paid dividends in the form of additional, paid-up insurance, one of the dividend options in modern, participating policies. By the latter half of the century, the Fund had established branch offices throughout the British Isles and is, today, a representative British company.

In 1801 there were eight going companies in England, and policy transactions amounted to some £17,500,000 with premium income of £650,000.[4] By 1850, the amount in force had jumped to £130,000,000 with annual premiums amounting to £5,000,000. Although it has never attained the proportions it has in the United States, British life insurance has continued a steady growth.[5]

---

[2] Early insurance was written almost entirely by individuals, alone or in syndicates, who placed their personal resources behind the policy. For years they fought all efforts made by groups to obtain charters to operate as corporate insurers. The stories of these battles make interesting reading. A good brief account of them will be found in William D. Winter's *Marine Insurance*, New York, McGraw-Hill Book Co., 1952, pp. 14–19.

[3] Two other of the early life offices call for mention: London Assurance and Royal Exchange, chartered as stock companies to write marine risks in 1720 and to write fire and life in 1721. They did little in the last-named field.

[4] Names and dates of establishment of companies as of 1801: Amicable, 1706; Union, 1714; London Assurance, 1720; Royal Exchange, 1722; Equitable, 1762; Westminster, 1792; Pelican, 1797; Palladium, 1797.

[5] Concentration on the historical beginnings of life insurance in England does not imply no activity on the European continent. There, development was slower, despite the fact that among the names of contributors to the mathematical development of the life insurance principle are many of Swiss, Dutch, and Italian derivation. As early as 1630, the idea of developing joint stock companies to write insurance was presented in Holland. The Dutch, because of the prevailing high taxes and low investment yields, investigated life insurance and annuities. The idea soon died. A true life insurance company was founded in France in 1787 (*Compagnie Royale d'Assurances*). The trail-blazing company in Italy was founded in 1826 and was, coincidentally, the first successful operator in

2. EARLY LIFE INSURANCE IN AMERICA

Colonial America seems to have given little thought to life insurance, even though Benjamin Franklin is quoted as considering it more important than fire and marine insurance.[6] Only a few scattered life insurance policies were written on colonists and those were by individual underwriters.

A record of the opening of a public insurance office in Philadelphia in 1721 is available. This office served as headquarters for marine underwriters who occasionally also wrote life insurance policies. Offices such as that in Philadelphia became rather common in Providence, New York, and all the principal cities of the Atlantic seaboard. The usual life insurance policy was written for a six- or twelve-month term, or for the duration of a sea voyage. Premiums were 5% of the amount of insurance. No medical selection was utilized. Life insurance was purchased only for short-term, extrahazardous adventures. The average colonist had no way of protecting his family against the less dramatic everyday risks of death. In fact, to do so through insurance was looked upon with disfavor. As late as 1809, a Massachusetts court argued the legality and morality of life insurance.

First Companies. The first corporation in North America to insure lives was the Presbyterian Ministers' Fund, Philadelphia, founded in 1759, using a charter granted by William Penn. It continues to operate today. The Episcopal Corporation was founded ten years later.

Between 1790 and the 1800's, five insurance companies were chartered to write life as well as fire and marine risks. As far as can be determined, only one of these, The Insurance Company of North America, 1794, wrote any life insurance policies at all—six in five years, all of them short-term life and pirate ransom contracts written at very high premiums and containing severe conditions and restrictions. Although the Insurance Company of North America dropped its life department in 1804 the company holds the distinc-

---

Austria, since no domestic commercial company was formed there until 1830 (*General Assurance Company of Trieste*), and that, a company writing life insurance as a side line. The first German life company came in 1829 (*Die Lebensversicherungsbank für Deutschland in Gotha*), while in 1835, Pope Gregory XVI founded the *Societa Pontisicia d'Assicurazoni Nello Stato Tontisicio*, a short-lived venture, significant as the first corporate attempt in Eastern Europe to set up a general insurance company to write both life and property insurance.

[6] Benjamin Franklin is reputed to have said, "*It is a strange anomaly that men should be careful to insure their houses, their ships, their merchandise, and yet neglect to insure their lives, surely the most important of all to their families, and more subject to loss.*" Frankly, the authors have never found a source citation for the quotation, but they don't see why a little thing like that should keep them from using it. No one has ever found a source citation for the quotation usually attributed to Voltaire, "I do not agree with a word that you say, but I shall defend to the death your right to say it"; but that doesn't keep proponents of free speech from using it.

tion of being the first American commercial corporation to write life insurance.[7]

At the close of the eighteenth century, there were only 160 policies in force in the United States.

The first commercial corporation to write life insurance exclusively was the Pennsylvania Company for Insurance on Lives and Granting Annuities, organized in 1812. It wrote only a handful of policies but is credited with being the first American company to employ scientific principles in underwriting and rating risks. Today, with a simplified name, it confines its activities to trust operations.

The first life insurance selling agency in the United States seems to have been that of Israel Whelen, agent of the Pelican of London, who announced in newspaper advertising in 1807 that he was prepared to issue insurance on lives.

Another interesting side light is that the Girard Life Insurance and Trust Company, a stock company organized in 1836 in Philadelphia, was the first American company to allow policyholders to share in profits. Its first dividend was distributed in 1844 in the form of paid-up additions to the face value of the policy.

The New England Mutual, chartered in 1835, was the *first of the commercial companies still writing life insurance to be chartered*. However, New England Mutual did not issue its first policy until February, 1844. In the meantime, the Mutual Life of New York had been incorporated in March, 1842, and issued its first policy in February of the next year. It is *the first of the mutuals still in existence to write a policy*.

The first health insurer in the United States was the Massachusetts Health Insurance Company, Boston, established in 1847. The first accident company was the Franklin Health Insurance Company of Massachusetts, founded in 1850. It offered 24-hour coverage for railway and steamboat injury. Injury carried compensation up to $200; total disability was covered for two months for up to $400; and the premium was 15¢ a day.

3. ELIZUR WRIGHT

One of the outstanding personalities in the history of life insurance in America was Elizur Wright, an abolitionist who turned his crusading drive toward life insurance after a visit to England where he attended an auction of existing life insurance policies.[8]

---

[7] The North America Insurance Companies are today one of the nation's largest fire, marine, and casualty groups.

[8] Wright was graduated from Yale University in 1826 and soon thereafter became a teacher of mathematics at Western Reserve College. His interest in the antislavery move-

Since surrender values in a life insurance policy were rare, it was a common practice in England for old people who could no longer pay their premiums to offer their policies for sale.[9] The buyer made himself the beneficiary of the policy and took over the premium obligations in the hope of eventually collecting more from the policy than he had put into it. At auctions where old policies were sold, the insured would "mount the block" to be inspected by prospective buyers who were interested in speculating on how much longer the policyholder would live and, hence, how much they should pay for the policy. Usually the price paid for the policy was only a fraction of its actuarial value.

This practice smacked so much of American slave auctions that it aroused the evangelical wrath of Wright. He returned from England later to become a lobbyist in the Massachusetts legislature for laws requiring nonforfeiture values in life insurance policies. Furthermore, Wright was convinced that reserves on whole life policies often were so inadequate that the solvency of the companies was endangered. He wanted a law establishing a state insurance commission which would calculate not only proper policy reserves but also would have the power to enforce these reserve liabilities upon the companies. In other words, he wanted what is called today a "legal reserve."

Wright calculated a monumental set of net reserve valuation tables which were adopted by Massachusetts in 1850 as a basis for judging the solvency of companies. In 1858, Wright was appointed as one of a two-man board of insurance commissioners.[10] By 1861 he witnessed the passage of his nonforfeiture law by the Massachusetts legislature. While in office as insurance commissioner, Wright started and maintained a registry book in which he listed every single policy issued in the state together with yearly calculations showing what the reserve should be at that point. He kept this registry open to any policyholder who wanted to see what the reserve on his policy should be. He published financial statements of companies and kept the public informed generally on the state of the insurance business. In his eight years in office, Wright forced 14 companies out of the state on the grounds of dishonest practices. Wright's capacity for irritating legislators, his candor, his constant barrage of questions about profits, expenditures, dividends, salaries, and his life insurance registry—all these and more kept the companies

---

ment led him to abandon teaching in 1833 to go to New York to write for and edit abolitionist journals.
[9] The Institute of Actuaries of Great Britain and Ireland later fostered a law on the assignment of policies which brought about the end of this practice.
[10] The other member was G. W. Sargent, who was greatly overshadowed by Wright.

frantic, and irritated all who did not want sound practice and many who did. As a result, he was finally forced from office in 1867; but his labors had for all time made their impression on the course of life insurance in America. His annual reports as commissioner had been carefully studied by insurance men in England as well as in America; and those reports, together with his mathematical computations, laid the foundation for the sound development of life insurance.

4. ERA OF ESTABLISHMENT

The decade of the 1850's was notable not only for Elizur Wright and for the rise in life insurance sales but also for the establishment of modern marketing practices. In 1843, Morris Robertson, founder-president of Mutual of New York,[11] broke with previous American life insurance marketing traditions and became one of the first important users of the agency system. His demonstration of the value of aggressive selling through personal solicitation was instrumental in making the agency system, in time, almost universal practice in American life insurance marketing.

As the value of the agent became apparent, companies began to treat agents more liberally by increasing commissions above the original 5% and removing restrictions on their earnings, such as that placed by one company which required that an agent's earnings in excess of $1,500 a year be reverted to the company. By the time of the War Between the States,[12] the most common commission schedule called for 50% of the first year's premium on a Whole Life policy and a renewal commission of 5% for each of the subsequent nine years the policy remained in force.

The Decade of the Sixties. As might be expected, the Civil War brought the development of life insurance to a standstill. Northern companies had difficulties servicing southern policyholders. Many claims were disputed. But contrary to predictions at the beginning of the conflict, the war did not bring disaster to the business.

In 1863, J. G. Batterson, Hartford architect, intrigued by the widespread practice in England of issuing a travel accident policy as an extra stub on a

---

[11] This company (Mutual Life of New York) likes this shortening of its name. In the 1950's, an advertising man discovered that the initials of the shortened form spell "MONY," which, for any advertising man, is near enough to "money" to make an advertising slogan for a company which deals in money.

[12] The Southern background of one of the authors prevents his agreeing to the exclusive use of the term, Civil War. Therefore, there has been a compromise. In some paragraphs, the Civil War will be referred to as the "War Between the States." In others, the War Between the States will be referred to as the "Civil War."

railroad ticket, established the Travelers Insurance Company. A year later, the company decided to extend its coverage to more than travel accidents. So it had its charter amended to include all types of accident coverage. The establishment of the Travelers marked the beginning of modern accident insurance.

By 1866, there were 60 companies and associations in the Accident insurance field, and competition was so intense that it was endangering the rate structure. In 1865, Travelers chartered the Railway Passengers Associations of Hartford and consolidated the ticket business of 10 companies. Of the 70 companies organized between 1865 and 1869, only the Travelers was left by 1871. In 1878, it dissolved the Railway Passengers Associations and transferred the business to its own ticket department.

Accident insurance particularly received great impetus from the disasters of the decade following 1864. In 1864 alone, 140 railroad accidents took 404 lives and injured 1,846 persons. In the four years, 1867–71, there were 526 steamship disasters in American waters that took 1,437 lives.

Claims arising from these disasters almost ruined the companies, but they were able to pull through with a certain amount of borrowing. The companies, however, capitalized on the publicity that made the public more accident-conscious.

Post Civil War. As soon as peace was declared ending the War Between the States, a period of general economic prosperity set in, and life insurance gained materially from it. From 1864 to 1869, for instance, premium income increased from $16,163,138 to $98,507,319 and assets rose from $49,027,297 to $229,097,425. One of the factors accounting for this increase was the abnormally high interest rate of about 30% which effected a reduction in the cost of insurance, and made it possible to pay high commission rates.

Although the British Friendly Societies had found their way into America much earlier, it was not until 1868 that the first fraternal society was established in the United States. In October of that year John Jordan Upchurch, a railroad master mechanic, organized the "Ancient Order of United Workmen." His motivating idea seems to have been to offer working men greater privileges than they found in the usual trade unions of that time. Included in the Upchurch program was a plan to provide members with protection for dependents cheaper than commercial companies were offering it. Unfortunately Upchurch did not profit by the experience of the British Friendly Societies but, instead, fell victim to the lures of the assessment principle, which had appeared earlier in the development of the life insurance business. Miles M. Dawson, referring to the experience with assessment plans, wrote some 37 years later, "The subject . . . represents the pathological side, if I may express it, of life insurance." [13]

Upchurch's method of accumulating benefit funds was unsound, for there was no attempt at scientific rate-making. The plan called for the payment of $1 by each member into the insurance fund. When a member died, his dependents were paid up to a limit of $2,000 in death benefit out of this fund, and another dollar was collected from each member to prepare for the next death. This was a simple, pass-the-hat assessment plan. No reserves were accumulated. However, the idea of fraternalism appealed to the notoriously gregarious nature of Americans, especially since it seemed like cheap insurance.[14] The A.O.U.W. became not only popular but also the inspiration for a multitude of other societies. Some of these societies, to make the plan more practical, changed the method of levying an assessment at each death to a plan of "flat assessments" at regular intervals, but invalidly uniform for all ages. After that followed the "graded assessment" plan, which varied the assessments according to age of entry. Nevertheless, all these assessment plans resulted in rates which were inadequate to provide funds sufficient to meet all obligations as the society membership grew older. The inevitable result was a high failure rate among such societies which eventually led to the formation of the National Fraternal Congress in 1886. One of the first actions of the congress was to seek remedial legislation in the states relating to fraternal insurance. It actively sponsored a movement for a bill regulating the business and defining the status of fraternal societies. Known as the NFC uniform bill, it was submitted to the various state legislatures and passed by several of them. An amendment adopted in 1897 called for the creation of a reserve; and in 1899, the National Fraternal Congress Table of Mortality was adopted. In 1912 the New York Conference Bill was formulated, which is now generally the basis of fraternal regulation throughout the country.

Under the various insurance codes modeled after the New York Conference Bill, a considerable range is permitted in establishing solvency. Legal solvency and actuarial solvency, however, are not necessarily one and the same thing. Since theoretically all death benefits could be covered by assessments, a fraternal organization may be insolvent as measured by

---

[13] *Annals of the American Academy of Political and Social Science*, XXVI, 1905, p. 120.
[14] Competition between commercial companies and fraternals was bitter. The assessment fraternal, not using the reserve system, could offer much lower premiums than the commercial companies. The term "old line," still widely used, came into being at this time. It was probably coined by the older commercial companies to emphasize the "old" and thus "tested." Some historians claim, however, that the fraternals coined it and that it was originally "old lyin'" companies—lying about the need for higher premiums. Professional critics of life insurance say the term refers to companies which persist in giving the public the "same old line."

the standard for a legal-reserve company and yet solvent as measured by statutory requirements.[15] It should be noted, however, that in the past decade particularly there has been a trend among fraternals to establish themselves upon a basis which is actuarially as well as legally solvent. They handle their insurance transactions on the same basis as an "old line" company, differing from a mutual only in the fact that they have a lodge system.[16]

Since mortality cannot be less among the policyholders of a fraternal than among those of a regular company, it follows that if the test of actuarial solvency is to be met, rates cannot be markedly lower than those of the commercial companies. The narrowing of the margin of difference between commercial rates and fraternal rates, brought about by the trend of fraternals toward actuarial solvency and legal reserves, has lessened their special appeal as insurance carriers—apart from their appeal as social organizations. The proportion of life insurance in United States written by fraternals has dropped markedly from its peak in the earlier days when "rates" among the societies were set without relation to the scientific principles of rate-making.

The pressure after the Civil War among the old line companies and their agents for new business brought on new problems. The drive by the agents for commissions brought about less interest in renewals and more interest in new business. This encouraged high-pressure selling, misrepresentation, and "twisting." [17]

To take advantage of the expanding and prosperous market for life insurance, many new companies were formed, too often on unsound bases so that with the coming of the panic of 1873 and the ensuing hard times, there was a high incidence of company failure.

The accident insurance business also ran into trouble in the 70's. The original simple policies had now, because of adverse court decisions, become highly complicated and hedged with all sorts of restrictions. Unscrupulous promoters, interested only in long profits, were sharp in their claim practices. Discriminatory legislation had reached harmful proportions. Heavy license

---

[15] In order to be actuarially solvent, there must be a scientifically calculated reserve equal to the difference between the discounted value of future premiums and the discounted value of future claims figured on an adequate mortality table with conservative interest assumptions. If adequate reserves are not required, a company remains solvent so long as it can meet current claims; and in order to do this it must continue to grow with young policyholders.

[16] There are still, of course, many small fraternals operating on a pure assessment basis and many larger ones operating under the special laws applying to fraternals.

[17] Twisting is the giving of untrue information about existing policies in order to encourage clients to drop these policies and take new ones. Commissions on new policies were well in excess of renewal commissions. Many "trades" were in evidence where agents exchanged clients and practiced the "twist."

fees were often imposed on out-of-state carriers; and state laws forced too much investment in weak state bonds.

Yet in the period from 1870 to 1890, the business was beginning to find itself. A number of strong companies were formed, and right at the end of the period, in 1891, Aetna Life opened an accident department.[18]

While, as noted, there was activity in the sickness insurance field as early as 1847, all the early insurers failed or expired, leaving nothing on which to build. For all practical purposes, the development of sickness insurance began in the 80's. The mutual associations led the experimentation in sickness coverage, beginning about 1885. In 1890, the St. Lawrence Life Association issued a combination accident and sickness policy, and in 1891, the Federal Life & Casualty, Chicago, introduced the same form.

5. ERA OF FRENZIED FINANCE

From about 1870 on, the line of cleavage that had always been apparent between companies operated exclusively for the benefit of the operators and those operated with a sense of trusteeship became increasingly wide. Elizur Wright, now 64, began a 15-year battle to get legislation to drive the "brigands" out of the business.

A variety of strange, new practices came into the life insurance business. Tontine, which had swept France, Holland, England, and certain German states a century before, was revived in a modified but, as Wright saw it, equally vicious form.[19] Among other objections, he foresaw that Tontine "kitties" would build up huge sums of loose money which might tempt companies with a weak sense of ethics to investment speculation.

Tontine was but one of the evils of the business in this period. There was trickery in company management. Other transactions among those companies on the misty side of the cleavage line related to questionable high finance. Loans were made to banks in which insurance company trustees were interested; concealed loans were made to state commissioners; a state commissioner was paid $3,000 to foster a bill to crush the smaller rivals of one

---

[18] The accident and sickness business was pioneered principally by casualty insurance companies. For example, one of the earlier accident and sickness insurance carriers was the Knickerbocker Casualty Company, 1876, renamed Fidelity and Casualty Company of New York in 1883 and a leading company to this day.

[19] The Tontine system used in the United States put a fixed amount of gross premiums into a "kitty" each year. Those maintaining their policies in force and living to the end of the Tontine period shared the "kitty." Those who dropped out or died did not. Hence, the fewer remaining to the end of the Tontine period, the bigger the share of each survivor. Sheppard Homans, compiler of the American Experience Table of Mortality and one of the great actuarial names in life insurance history, is credited with developing the American Tontine plan; and D. Parks Fackler, still another actuarial great, described it in glowing terms as "the staff of life," providing increasing security as age advances.

large company; lobbying reached such proportions that in one instance, $60,000 was paid to a lawyer for "work" in the state capitol of New York—and there being few regulations regarding the accounting practices of companies, the expenditure was carried on the books as "taxes." Newspapers were offered (and many accepted) a dollar a line to publish attacks on Elizur Wright, who was constantly goading the companies with prophecies of disaster. Nepotism of the worst order was rampant, and in the 1870's and early 1880's, financial buccaneers repeated in America all the most unsavory details of the English bonanza days. Among agents there was widespread rebating, misrepresentation, and twisting. Those companies that stuck to conservative ways and ideals of trusteeship were sneered at, abused, and assailed when they dared speak out, and were forced into setbacks from which they did not recover for years.

Beginning of Trouble. In 1880, the trouble that was to result in the Armstrong investigation 25 years later began. The Tontine bubble broke. Over 100,000 policyholders had dropped their policies, and thousands bombarded the companies in person and by mail. Treated to the high-handed dismissal of their complaints, many instituted suits against the companies. They found no redress in law, for in the absence of insurance regulations to the contrary, the courts were forced to hold to the terms of the Tontine contracts. Public ill will, a feeling that "something ought to be done," faced the companies.

Overextension abroad, questionable financial transactions, heavy lapsation [20] weakened the position of the companies to the place where what had been easy morality in the annual statements of many companies became serious prestidigitation. Perjury in reports became a "smart trick," a sign of dexterity. A variety of subsidiary financing brought companies into the field of investment banking. In the end, the whole sorry mess in the life insurance business was forced on the reluctant New York legislature by a terrific internal battle for the control of one of the major New York companies.

Although the accident and sickness insurers were not caught up in the New York investigation, conditions in that field were not good, either. Policies were restricted and filled with complicated clauses. There was little or no co-operation among companies to improve the condition—or conditions in the business in general.

Legal requirements were lax, and so was supervision. Competition, as in the field of life insurance, was cutthroat. There was little constructive thought or vision for the future. Policies of up to $150,000 on one life were

---

[20] In 1895, the net gain in insurance in force for the year was one eighth of the new business written.

issued without adequate underwriting, and monthly indemnities totaling well beyond the bounds of good underwriting practice were assumed.

In disability insurance, the period was not wholly one of trouble. It saw the spread of insurance against sickness. In 1897, the stock companies began to write sickness coverage, Fidelity & Casualty leading by introducing a conservative combination accident and sickness policy restricted to about 15 specified diseases and containing a seven-day waiting period and 26-week benefit provision.

By 1900, the accident and sickness form had broadened. In 1903, all excluded diseases were eliminated and surgical benefits added. Step-rate premiums were abandoned for a flat rate with an increase between 51 and 60. By 1908, the seven-day waiting period had been generally dropped by most companies, questionable progress to say the least.[21]

6. THE ARMSTRONG INVESTIGATION

On July 20, 1905, the New York legislature in accord with a resolution adopted by the respective bodies established a joint Senate and Assembly committee to investigate the life insurance companies in the state.[22] According to the resolution, the appointment of the committee stemmed from the conclusions in the preliminary reports on a major New York company. These reports indicated that policyholders and their beneficiaries were not being properly safeguarded by existing laws and that a review of the insurance laws of the state was necessary because of the limited power of the Superintendent of Insurance. The Superintendent's powers were limited to examination with the chief view toward assuring solvency, whereas the reports indicated the necessity of investigating the companies more fully. The committee was organized on August 1, 1905, and began public hearings the following September 6. It continued in session consecutively for 57 meetings, closing on December 30, 1905. The committee became known as the "Armstrong Committee," and hearings were conducted by a brilliant counsel, Charles Evans Hughes, later to be justice of the Supreme Court.

---

[21] Waiting periods exclude the small losses, and therefore are desirable from the viewpoint of good insurance theory. Cf. Chapter 2.

[22] "The committee shall . . . proceed to investigate and examine into the business and affairs of the Life Insurance companies doing business in the State of New York, with reference to the investments of said companies, the relations of the officers thereof to such investments, the relation of such companies to subsidiary corporations, the government and control of such companies, and any other phases of the Life Insurance business deemed by the committee to be proper, for the purpose of drafting and reporting to the next session of the legislature such a revision of the laws relating to Life Insurance in this state as said committee may deem proper." *Concurrent resolution adopted by the Senate and the Assembly of the State of New York, July 20, 1905.*

The committee found even more than it had expected. Chicanery, manipulation, unholy alliance, squandering of funds stalk like nightmares through the seven aging volumes of testimony and exhibits known as *The Armstrong Report*.

Committee Findings. The Armstrong investigation centered around four phases of the business: regulation, investments, expenses, and dividends, and its findings can be summarized as follows:

1. *Regulation.* Directors and trustees were failing to serve as a check on management, their committees acting as mere "yes men" to officers. Policyholders, who are the theoretical control of mutual companies, actually had no voice in management.

2. *Investments.* Some companies were doing a banking business through ownership of bank stocks and were generally guilty of carrying uneconomically large balances with such banks. Still other companies were selling securities as investment bankers for industrial corporations. Many life insurance companies were holding real estate illegally and constructing extravagant home office buildings. The committee recommended that investment in stock be prohibited and investment banking operations by life insurance companies be discontinued.[23]

3. *Expenses.* The committee found widespread extravagances. They felt that commissions to agents and salaries to officers were too high and that too much money was being spent on lobbying. They recommended a limit on acquisition expenses (the amount spent to put new business on the books) and on total expenses, and that lobby expenditures be reported in detail.

4. *Dividends.* The committee opposed deferred dividends (an adaptation of Tontine), holding that the system built up huge surpluses which contributed to waste and extravagance. It recommended that annual dividends be required.

Result of the Report. A committee on Uniform Legislation (the Committee of Fifteen) was appointed by a conference of governors and insurance commissioners in Chicago in 1906 to study methods of strengthening insurance regulations. The New York Insurance Code of 1906, a result of the work of this committee, included just about all the recommendations of the Armstrong Committee and set the pattern for all state regulation throughout the country.[24]

---

[23] New York now permits some limited investments in stock. Cf. Chapter 22.

[24] Not only does the New York Code set a regulatory pattern for the country, but also it has an extraterritorial effect for it requires that any company licensed to do business in the state, whether New York domiciled or not, "substantially comply" with the New York code, especially in matters of acquisition costs and agents' commissions, in its operations in all other states in which it does business. Admission of a company to do busi-

The final result of the investigation was not only strengthened legislation but it also brought about a general housecleaning in the life insurance business. In the end, the most staunch advocates of the reforms that came from the Armstrong Investigation were the life insurance companies themselves. In 1906, the institution of life insurance reached maturity. It soon found itself in a position of public confidence and stability from which it could advance, unhindered by irresponsible, self-seeking management. Those companies which had held to the line of the trusteeship concept throughout the era of Frenzied Finance were vindicated.

Never before nor since has the business been subjected to as searching an inquiry and examination as the Armstrong investigation—nor one as beneficial to its future welfare and development.

7. FROM THE ARMSTRONG INVESTIGATION TO WORLD WAR I

The first effect of the Armstrong Investigation was to decrease business in force, but this result was only short-lived. From 1900 to 1925, the number of companies in the country increased 364% and the amount of insurance in force, 737%. In 1900, only 24 states had life insurance companies domiciled within their borders. By 1925, there were domestic companies in all except two states.

The years from the Armstrong Investigation to the first World War also were a period of growth in the Accident and Sickness business. Disability provisions were extended from 26 to 52 to 104 weeks. Then, in 1913, Fidelity & Casualty introduced lifetime disability.

Noncancellable, guaranteed renewable policies were introduced in January, 1907, by the National Masonic Provident Association. The Pacific Mutual Life followed suit in 1915—which was the beginning of a period in which life insurance companies were highly active in the accident and sickness field and, as it turned out, were storing up serious trouble that broke out a little more than a decade later.

Many new accident and sickness carriers were formed in this period. In addition to the entrance of many life companies in the field there came the rise of companion casualty companies for existing fire insurance carriers. Perhaps the most progressive step of the period was the introduction of the Standard Provisions laws in 1911.[25]

---

ness in the state of New York is still considered to be almost conclusive proof of stability and sound operation. Not one dollar of investment in life insurance was lost in the great depression of the 30's by policyholders of companies licensed in New York.
[25] Cf. Chapter 11.

8. WORLD WAR I

The first interruption in the life insurance business following the Armstrong Investigation was World War I, 1914–18. The interruption is now generally considered to have been a stimulus to life insurance both because of the creation of War Risk insurance,[26] which introduced millions of soldiers to life insurance for the first time and raised their sights from $1,000 policies to $10,000, and also because of the period of prosperity that lasted virtually uninterrupted through the 1920's.

The war did not reflect unfavorably on the mortality experience of life insurance. Military death rates were not too high; companies had proportionately little in force on the young men who made up the armed forces; and war exclusion clauses were included in new policies issued during the period of hostilities.

However, in the accident and sickness field, lack of foresight during the early years of the century when large single policies were written, unsoundly high monthly indemnities insured, and war exclusion clauses overlooked, caused World War I to throw the business into doldrums which lasted throughout the prosperous 1920's. This period of doldrums was made even worse by the fact that the business had not foreseen the growth of the automobile hazard in the earlier years of the 1900's.

About the most than can be said for the period from the entrance of the United States into the war in 1917 to the coming of the great depression of the 1930's is that there was a trend toward adaptability and some attempt to meet the needs of the public. Casualty and monoline A & S companies were also affected competitively by the heavy activity of the life companies in the disability field through the writing of disability income riders on life insurance policies, usually providing $10 per month per thousand of face value in event of total and permanent disability.

Immediately following World War I, the United States was struck with the world-wide influenza epidemic, which was of plague proportions. There were over 450,000 deaths in the United States alone, and mortality increased 50% to 100%. Moreover, the greatest increase in mortality was among young policyholders whose policies had not yet built up substantial reserves, and many companies had to draw heavily on contingency reserves, thus demon-

---

[26] War risk insurance is discussed in more detail in connection with National Service Life Insurance. During World War I servicemen were eligible to buy from $1,000 to $10,000 life insurance on a yearly renewable term basis from the Bureau of War Risk Insurance. The policies were convertible into permanent policies within 5 years after the end of the war. Some of these policies, known as United States Government Life Insurance, are still in existence.

strating the value of such reserves, which had often been criticized as unnecessarily large.

9. THE GREAT DEPRESSION

In October, 1929, the New York stock market crashed. The effect on new life insurance sales was not felt immediately, but loan and surrender calls on existing policies started an upward movement. As the general economic depression lengthened and deepened, loss of old business through policy termination and surrender accelerated, and by 1933, new business had been materially reduced.[27] When the attitude of the public toward all financial institutions indicated the possibility of a "run" on cash values similar to the "runs" then harassing banks, the various insurance commissioners instituted temporary restrictions on the companies in the payment of cash and loan values. Such payments, however, were never completely stopped, and maturity benefits, disability incomes, and supplementary contract incomes were paid as usual except, of course, during the bank holiday when all normal facilities for money transactions were shut down.

Depression factors which hurt the life insurance business most were decreased interest earnings and increased mortgage defaults. The amount of property held on foreclosed mortgages continued to be a problem to the life insurance companies until World War II, when a vastly increased demand for real property enabled companies to reduce their holdings markedly. Declines in the value of corporate stocks and failure of corporations had little investment effect on life insurance companies because stock investments had, since the Armstrong Investigation, been greatly limited by law.

Suicides went up—an increase of 30%; but even more costly was the increase in claims under the disability income provisions so widely written into life insurance policies during the 1920's and under A & S policies providing loss-of-time benefits. There was widespread exaggeration of the extent of disability, and court tests resulted in judicial interpretation of policy provisions that underwriting had never contemplated. The back of the noncancellable A & S business was broken and life insurance companies experienced serious problems with total and permanent disability income riders. All but a handful of companies ceased writing these forms.

The life insurance business was able to come through the depression with an enviable record of investment safety. This record was partly the result of the traditionally conservative investing of life companies, partly the result

---

[27] In 1929 the total insurance in force in the country had topped $100,000,000,000. In 1933, it receded below that mark and continued to decline until 1935.

of a widespread investment risk, and largely the result of the fact that company cash income kept coming faster than cash calls.[28]

There were life insurance company failures during the depression,[29] but most of them were reinsured by other companies so that the total loss to policyowners, percentagewise and in comparison with the field of general investments, was negligible.[30] The depression gave the institution of life insurance an opportunity to meet a difficult test with spectacular success and to prove the soundness of its structure.

Social Security.   One of the important developments of the depression years was the Social Security Act of August 14, 1935. It contained a system of retirement benefits for workers in certain designated classifications, to be financed by a special payroll tax levied on both employees and employers.

In 1939, the original act was amended to add a system of benefits for widows and dependent children. The act labels these benefits, "Old Age and Survivors' Insurance." They are not insurance benefits in either an actuarial or a practical sense.[31] Actuarially, the accrued liability at the present time is approximately $200,000,000,000 [32] whereas the offsetting "reserve" fund is approximately $18,000,000,000. In a practical sense, OASI is not insurance because the covered worker has no vested or contractual rights. What he will get from the system and under what circumstances depends on legislation and not contract. The OASI portion of the Social Security Act has been changed a number of times since 1939. The formula for calculation of benefits has been changed; benefit rates have been increased; new classes of employment have been added. Such changes can be expected throughout

---

[28] Cf. Chapters 1 and 22.

[29] In the light of hindsight, it is possible to argue that some of the failures were unnecessary. In several instances, regulatory authorities seem to have stepped in too quickly to close up a company on a rigid test of liquidity on the basis of actual market values of its investments when, because no company is ever called upon to turn all asests into cash at once, it might have ridden out the situation.

[30] Company failures involved less than 3% of the total life insurance in force. In a number of instances, death claims were paid in full in even these cases, confining any loss to impairment in cash values. M. A. Linton, *Life Insurance Speaks for Itself*, New York, Harper & Brothers, 1937.

[31] That is, they do not meet the requirements for insurance as set up in Chapter 2 of this text. If it can be argued that social insurance does not have to meet the tests set up, then it might be possible to contend the benefits are "insurance."

[32] "Accrued liability is the dollar amount necessary as of a given date to pay in the future all accrued benefits if the system should then terminate. . . . If the intent were not only to pay all beneficiaries in current payments status but also to make proportional payments to all others who have contributed, then the accrued liability at the present time is about $200,000,000,000 of which $18,000,000,000 is funded." U.S. Department of Health, Education, and Welfare, *Actuarial Study 36, Long Range Cost Estimates for Old Age & Survivors' Insurance*, p. 19.

the future inasmuch as Social Security and politics seem now to have become Siamese twins.[33]

Hospital Insurance. Perhaps the most important development in the disability insurance field during the depression years was Hospitalization insurance. To the public, the depression dramatized the cost of hospital and medical care. This fostered the development of Hospitalization insurance springing from prepayment plans fostered by hospitals in an attempt to fill empty beds.[34]

TNEC Investigation. Beginning in 1938, a Congressional committee, *The Temporary National Economic Committee,* commonly called "TNEC," undertook a study of the life insurance business with particular reference to monopoly power.[35] While the final report of TNEC called its investigation of life insurance the "most extensive study since the well-known Armstrong investigation," [36] the investigation was not undertaken because of trouble within the business, as in the case of the Armstrong investigation, but as part of the TNEC's over-all study of concentration of economic power.

While starting out merely to study the relationship of the funds of life insurance companies to their use as an instrument of economic power, the investigation eventually went far afield, covering such unrelated ground as agents' training and compensation; comparative rates and costs of Industrial, Ordinary, and Savings Bank Life Insurance; annuity reserves; and technical operations.

Final recommendations of the TNEC committee regarding life insurance dealt largely with the need for strengthening of state supervision; for better

---

[33] This comment is not to be taken as an indication of the attitude of either author on Social Security. It is simply a recognition of the fact that increasing Social Security benefits has come to be looked upon as "smart politics."

[34] There is at present severe conflict between regular insurance carriers and the Blue Cross and Blue Shield hospital-sponsored "insurance" plans, both of which provide prepayment of hospital and medical care. Nevertheless the hospital plans led the way in the field of Hospitalization coverage. The conflict today arises, among other things, from the successful effort of Blue Cross and Blue Shield to have themselves thought of as a "community service" instead of insurance carriers. The ability to "sell" themselves as a "community service" often results in the various Blue Cross plans obtaining the use of prominent names in a community, and, in some instances, getting community leaders and organizations to go out and sell Blue Cross policies as a public service. You can say either that the ability of Blue Cross to get such free services is good salesmanship on its part or that it is unfair competition, depending on which side of the fence you stand.

[35] The study was conducted by the TNEC for the Securities and Exchange Commission which was, at the same time, studying other allegedly monopolistic institutions, such as public utilities.

[36] While it is generally conceded that Hughes conducted the Armstrong investigation on a basis of strict impartiality, seeking to find facts whether unfavorable or favorable, some observers charge the TNEC investigation was conducted "in an atmosphere of antagonism to the companies." Cf. J. B. Maclean, *Life Insurance,* New York, McGraw-Hill Book Co., 7th ed., 1951, pp. 559–561.

qualification, training, and methods of compensating agents; for prohibiting a company from soliciting business by mail in a state in which it is not licensed; and for prohibiting intercompany agreements that reduce competition.

10. WORLD WAR II TO PRESENT

World War II brought no setback to life insurance. New business exceeded prewar figures in every year except 1942, the first full year the United States was in the war. Between 1942 and 1945, inclusive, the total life insurance in force rose from $130,332,848,315 to $155,722,777,547.[37]

Unlike World War I, when war mortality showed little or no increase, World War II had a serious mortality effect. War-caused deaths between 1940 and 1945, not excluded by military-service riders or covered by extra rating, amounted to over seven per cent of all death claims.[38] However, because of extremely favorable civilian mortality experience during the same period, few companies showed an increase in total mortality rates.

The war did, however, have a direct effect upon the cost of life insurance. The greater part of all investments during the war period was in government bonds, which bore a lower rate of interest than available on other investments. The result was an acceleration of the already downward trend in interest earnings of life insurance companies which of course meant an increase in cost to policyholders.

National Service Life Insurance. Starting in 1939, companies again began issuing policies with riders waiving the hazard of war-incurred deaths. To cover the hazard of war death, the Federal government again made insurance available to servicemen. Written originally as 5-year Term (with the term period subsequently extended), this insurance (commonly known as "NSLI") was available to all servicemen up to a maximum of $10,000, convertible any time after one year to one of several forms of permanent insurance.[39]

---

[37] The job of the life underwriter was facilitated by (1) increased national income, (2) decreased goods and services upon which to spend this income, and (3) rationing and price control of vital necessities, all of which meant more money available to buy life insurance.

[38] Causes: Greater number of military deaths than in World War II, far greater number of men and women in service, much greater ownership of life insurance among service personnel—partly because of greater use of life insurance and partly because of older draft ages.

[39] The fact that people will not purchase adequate life insurance without the urging of an agent is illustrated by a reputed episode in the history of NSLI: In the final hours before the fall of Bataan, radio facilities were cleared to send to Washington the names of those wanting NSLI coverage. Despite the fact that no immediate outlay of money was demanded (the premium being a deduction from service pay), and despite the fact

At the end of 1944, the total servicemen's life insurance in force was $123,754,000,000, rivaling the total commercial insurance in force in United States companies at the beginning of the war (1941: $124,673,237,570). However, at the end of the first full year after the war, despite strenuous efforts of the government to keep NSLI in force, the amount of servicemen's life insurance outstanding declined to under $37,000,000,000.

Upon the outbreak of the Korean War, the government substituted for its insurance system a gratuitous indemnity program for members of the armed forces. It was the thought that a gratuitous system would be less expensive to administer and would certainly meet with less objection from life insurance companies. The new plan, known as the Servicemen's Indemnity and Insurance Acts of 1951, did not replace the government insurance then in force but provided free indemnity of $10,000 for the death of any person on active duty with the armed forces.[40] Protection was extended for 120 days following separation from service. The veteran within these 120 days may apply for a five-year nonconvertible but renewable term policy which will be issued nonmedical on a nonparticipating basis. Disabled veterans may obtain on a nonparticipating basis any policy form, permanent insurance included, offered under the amended NSLI act of 1940.

The Guertin Legislation. Throughout the 1930's, the depressed economic condition made the public receptive to any type of criticism of business. One of the points that made best-selling articles, and even books, was the use by insurance companies of the American Experience Table of Mortality. This table had been compiled in 1863, reputedly on the experience of one company. Medical advancement throughout the twentieth century has greatly reduced infant mortality and mortality at younger ages, and this has resulted in an increase in life expectancy. Thus life insurance company reports were constantly showing mortality far under estimations in the table, as much as 50% under in the case of relatively young companies and 25% or even more in the case of older companies with older policyholders. The implication—and often the statement—of criticism was that the gain in mortality was an illegitimate profit to the companies and that the rates were excessive.

As a result of this criticism, the president of the National Association of Insurance Commissioners appointed a committee to study the need for a new mortality table and related matters in 1937. Chairman of the committee

---

that the defenders of Bataan knew they faced a most uncertain future, many did not request coverage and some that did requested less than the $10,000 maximum available.
[40] From this $10,000 was subtracted any NSLI or USGLI benefits payable.

was Alfred Guertin, then actuary of the New Jersey insurance department, and his committee subsequently became known as "The Guertin Committee" —and legislation based on the committee recommendations as "The Guertin Legislation."

The committee constructed two new mortality tables [41] and made recommendations for standard valuations which, in effect, broke the illusion that Elizur Wright had started that cash values are a mathematical equivalent of the individual policy proportion of the reserve.[42]

The Guertin Committee recommendations were embodied in model legislation, which by 1950 was passed in all states. The changes required by the Guertin legislation, as adopted in the several states, were extensive as far as the actuarial departments of home offices were concerned. Their over-all effect upon the life insurance product itself, the policies each company issues, was negligible from the buyer's point of view. The use of the CSO basis of mortality brought about some adjustment in rates, particularly at earlier ages where mortality gains had been heaviest, and nonforfeiture values at several ages.

Insurance and Interstate Commerce. Another development of the World War II years (1944) was the Supreme Court's reversal in the SEUA case of its 75-year-old holding that insurance was not commerce. Therefore, it could not be interstate commerce. This Supreme Court decision had little effect on life or Accident and Sickness insurance, except that it exposed it to possible future federal regulation.[43] The question of State vs. Federal control of insurance is deferred to the next chapter.

Mass Selling Developments. The war years also fostered the rise of mass selling techniques in life and disability insurance as contrasted to the sale of individual policies by agents. Tax laws, giving favorable treatment to Group insurance premiums paid by employers,[44] cost-plus government con-

---

[41] "Commissioners' Standard Ordinary," popularly known as "CSO," and "Commissioners' Standard Industrial."

[42] To recapitulate, the standard valuation laws dissociate the nonforfeiture values (which become merely contractual provisions) from the reserve, to which they had always been tied. Current actuarial thought holds that a withdrawing policyholder should be entitled to such share of the funds of the company as he has built up. The artificiality of expressing this amount as a reserve less a "surrender charge" has been eliminated by authorization of a direct calculation of that amount in the Guertin Legislation.

[43] In the Fire insurance business, however, rates had been set for all companies by a rating bureau. In many states, the law recognized only the rates set by such bureaus; yet under the Anti-Trust laws, such action constitutes restraint of trade. The conflict between the requirement of state laws and the Federal Anti-Trust law created a condition so chaotic that it was necessary for Congress to pass emergency legislation declaring a moratorium until January, 1948, later extended to June, on the application of the Sherman and Clayton Acts to the insurance business.

[44] In general, Group premiums paid by an employer were tax-deductible.

tracts, greater consciousness on the part of business management for good industrial relations, and union demands caused Group insurance to sky-rocket. Where this particular trend leads is still undetermined as this is written.

A & S Developments. In addition to developments already mentioned, several others in disability insurance deserve special attention.

The early 1940's saw the cautious re-entry of life insurance companies into the field of Accident and Sickness coverages from which they had almost all withdrawn after the debacle of the 1930's.

While the reentry was timid in underwriting practices, rating, and variety of coverages, it was somewhat of a rush in number of companies. Over a period of approximately 18 months at the start of the new decade, some 50 life insurance companies came out with a line of policies. Also, there was an increase in the number of companies writing disability income riders on life insurance policies.

One major development of the early 1950's, pioneered by a casualty insurer but quickly taken up by increasing numbers of life insurers, was the "Catastrophe" hospital and medical expense policy (also called "Major Medical"). Some "Catastrophe" policies cover only medical expenses if hospitalization is required. Others cover expenses in or out of the hospital. At the present time, coverages offered and premiums charged vary in extremes unusual in insurance policies. Such variation is understandable in a period of experimentation, such as the "Catastrophe" policy is undergoing.

During the first half of the 1950's, the A & S business was subjected to an intensity of public criticism, the effect of which it is not yet possible to appraise objectively.[45]

Throughout the latter part of 1953 and the early part of 1954, the business was subjected to a bombardment of criticism in periodicals, by syndicated newspaper columnists, by news service writers in the daily press, and by congressional and other governmental inquiry. For the most part, the charge of all of these sources, actual or implied, was trickery and deceit in advertising and sales practices. In quick succession, the business faced an investigation by the House Committee on Interstate and Foreign Commerce, hearings inquiring into mail order operations by the chairman of the Senate Committee on the Judiciary, and an investigation by the Federal Trade

---

[45] "The health of the nation has become a political issue of major significance. To some it is the early sign in this country of a trend toward some form of Government participation in meeting the problem. This may come as a surprise to those who interpreted the last Presidential election 1952 as a rejection of any form of Federal health program." Eugene Thoré, general counsel, Life Insurance Association of America, before the Health & Accident Underwriters Conference, May 5, 1954.

Commission into the advertising and sales literature of all companies, not just mail order.

11. SUMMARY

No summary has been prepared for this chapter. The chapter itself, covering over four centuries of life insurance history in about a quarter of a century of pages, is itself only a summary.

Questions for Class Discussion

1. Compare present-day policy restrictions with those found in the policies issued by the Society of Assurance for Widows and Orphans.
2. Why was the introduction of corporate underwriting in England so vigorously opposed by those in the insurance business?
3. What contributions to life insurance theory or practice were made by (1) The Amicable Society for a Perpetual Assurance Office, (2) The Society for the Equitable Assurance of Lives and Survivorships and (3) The Scottish Widows' Fund?
4. What United States insurance companies still in existence today can lay claim to the title of "first"?
5. In what ways has Elizur Wright influenced the life insurance business in America? Can you see any connection between the work of Elizur Wright and the work of the Guertin Committee?
6. From 1915 until 1953, the amount of Fraternal insurance in force increased from $9,444,000,000 to only $9,913,000,000, whereas life insurance in force of all kinds increased from $16,650,000,000 to $186,710,000,000. How do you account for the fact that Fraternal insurance did not maintain a dominant position on the American life insurance scene?
7. What was the status of the Accident and Sickness insurance business in America at the time of (a) the Armstrong investigation, (b) TNEC investigation?
8. Compare the nature, purpose, and results of the Armstrong investigation with the TNEC investigation.
9. Compare the effects of World War I, World War II, and the great depression on (1) the life insurance business and (2) the disability insurance business.
10. Compare United States Government Life Insurance of World War I, National Service Life Insurance of World War II, and Servicemen's Indemnity and Insurance of the Korean War. How do you account for the differences?

CHAPTER 27

THE REGULATION
OF COMPANIES

LIFE INSURANCE is one of the few American institutions engaged every day in operations that extend over three centuries. At any given time, life insurance companies are paying off contracts made in the last century while making contracts that will not be paid off until the next century.

Such long-range operations invite and require public regulation. Even if the majority of policyholders had confidence in their ability to keep constant watch on developments that affect the business, they would not have that same confidence in the ability of their beneficiaries to do so. It is natural, therefore, for them to seek what they consider the diligent and searching observance of public or governmental regulation.

Furthermore, insurance is a technical business, based on higher mathematics. Because of legal requirements, it is necessary to express the terms of insurance in complicated, legal phraseology which is incomprehensible to most laymen, and even to lawyers who are not specialists in the field. Since the buyer of insurance cannot hope to understand the technicalities involved, the judgment of technicians is necessary to keep constant watch on the business to prevent the companies from ill-advised attempts to take advantage of technical language to limit severely the coverage offered in a policy. Technicians also are needed to see that the companies maintain standards conducive to long-range solvency so that they will be in a position to deliver on their contracts when they mature.

For the individual policyholder to hire experts to provide these necessary technical services for him individually would be financially impossible even if insurance companies were willing to give the same co-operation to private

673

examiners as they are required to give to state authorities. The natural solution was public supervision in interest of the individual policyholder. As a result, the institution of insurance in both the United States and Canada is today under the surveillance of a complicated network of governmental— and, occasionally, political—supervision and control. In the United States especially, this regulation is complicated by the dual system of state and Federal government authority and the inevitable clash between the two.

1. HISTORY OF REGULATION

While the history of modern insurance begins in England, the history of insurance regulation begins in the United States. Modern supervision of life insurance had its beginnings in the establishment of the insurance department of Massachusetts in 1858, prior to which regulation consisted largely of restrictions and requirements in the charters issued by the states to the companies. The Massachusetts department was an outgrowth of the lobbying activities of Elizur Wright,[1] who became a member of its original two-man commission. For Wright, the establishment of a state insurance department was but the first step in his dream of a "National Insurance Bureau" or "Inter-State Valuation Commission."[2]

Subsequent to the establishment of the Massachusetts department and the adoption of an insurance code in that state, the question of legislative regulation of life insurance came before the British Parliament.[3] Investigation revealed to the satisfaction of Parliament that while there were evils in the business,[4] the degree of self-regulation being practiced by the companies was already more strict than anything the Parliament of the time would consider imposing by law. It pronounced as demogogic and dangerous any legislative interference with the business. However, in acquiescence to criticism, it did pass a law making it mandatory for companies to engage the services of an actuary to investigate their financial condition not less than once every ten years. The results of such "investigations" were to be set forth in a report published by the Board of Trade for the information of the public.

---

[1] Cf. Chapter 26.

[2] So convinced was Wright of the superiority of Federal as contrasted to state supervision that he characterized the court decision in Paul *v*. Virginia, holding that insurance was not commerce and, hence, not subject to interstate regulation, as "a blow to the sound regulation of the business."

[3] As late as 1851, Old Equitable, with 89 years of sound operation behind it, approached Parliament for a long-denied charter. It was informed that as an organization it was too ephemeral in nature to be granted the dignity of a charter.

[4] Evils bitingly satirized by Dickens in the "Anglo-Bengalee Disinterested Loan & Life Insurance Co." of *Martin Chuzzlewit*.

Currently, life insurance in the United States is regulated by the individual states and territories. Each state or territory has a department of insurance presided over by either an elected or appointed official, depending on the state. The department of any given state has jurisdiction over and regulates not only domestic companies, but also all foreign and alien companies licensed to do business in that state.[5]

In Canada, the business is subject to a dual system of federal and provincial control, both of which began at about the same time in the late 1860's. Conflicts and most of the duplication between the two systems have been adjusted in the past. The federal Insurance Department takes the primary responsibility for safeguarding the solvency of companies; whereas the provincial governments concern themselves primarily with the provisions of contracts, licensing of agents, and the regulation of general operations.

State Regulation. The pattern of state regulation of the business in the United States had its origin in the evolution of the political structure of the country. Originally, the regulatory activities of states in all areas exceeded those of the federal government. As early as 1866, however, a bill was introduced into the United States House of Representatives to create a national Bureau of Insurance in the Treasury Department. The Senate had a similar bill before it in 1868. One year later, the United States Supreme Court temporarily put an end to moves designed to bring about Federal regulation of insurance. In Paul v. Virginia it held that "issuing a policy of insurance is not a transaction of commerce" and, hence, not subject to the interstate commerce clause of the Federal constitution even when it extends across state lines.

The case of Paul v. Virginia [6] was, interestingly enough, not an attempt of the Federal government to regulate insurance but of a Fire insurance agent to escape state regulation. The Virginia law required out-of-state companies to be licensed by the state and as a condition precedent to receiving a license to deposit a given amount of securities with the state treasurer. Samuel Paul, a native Virginian, was appointed an agent in Virginia for a group of New York companies. He refused to comply with the deposit requirements and was therefore refused a license. Upon his continuing to

---

[5] A "domestic" company is one organized under the laws of state in which it is being classified. A "foreign" company is one organized under the laws of a state other than the one in which it is being classified. An "alien" company is one organized in a country other than the country of reference. Thus to a citizen of Illinois, an Indiana company is a "foreign" company and a Canadian company, an "alien" company. On the other hand, to a Canadian, a U.S. company is an "alien" company.

[6] 8 *Wall, 183* (1869).

transact business without a license, he was arrested, brought to court, convicted, and fined $50. After the highest court of Virginia upheld the decision the case was taken to the United States Supreme Court on the grounds that the Virginia law violated the constitutional requirement imposed on states to grant all the privileges and immunities of state law to citizens of all states, and that insurance was commerce and, hence, state regulation of a foreign insurer was interference with interstate commerce.

On the question of granting citizens of each state all the privileges and immunities of citizens in the several states, the court said that this constitutional provision was for the protection of human citizens and not corporate citizens which are creatures of state law only. On the question of the commerce clause, the court decided that issuing a policy of insurance is not a transaction of commerce within the meaning of the Interstate Commerce clause. The court had these interesting things to say on this point:

> Issuing a policy of insurance is not a transaction of commerce. The policies are simple contracts of indemnity against loss by fire, entered into between the corporations and the insured, for a consideration paid by the latter. These contracts are not articles of commerce in any proper meaning of the word. They are not subjects of trade or barter offered in the market as something having an existence and value independent of the parties to them. They are not commodities to be shipped or forwarded from one State to another and then put up for sale. They are like other personal contracts between parties which are completed by their signature and the transfer of consideration. Such contracts are not interstate transactions, though the parties may be domiciled in different States. The policies do not take effect—are not executed contracts—until delivered by the agent in Virginia. They are, then, local transactions, and are governed by the local law. They do not constitute a part of the commerce between the States any more than a contract for the purchase and sale of goods in Virginia by a citizen of New York whilst in Virginia would constitute a portion of such commerce.

Hence, the Paul *v.* Virginia decision upheld the right of the states to regulate insurance and virtually closed the door on Federal regulation for the next 75 years.[7]

Regulation Prior to 1906. As previously stated, regulation of the business prior to the establishment of the Massachusetts insurance department in 1858 and before the establishment of an insurance department in any given state was through corporate charters containing regulatory provisions. Usually these provisions related to capital required, investments, and finan-

---

[7] There were, however, some feeble attempts to introduce Federal regulation. For example, in 1892 HR 9629, 52nd Congress, First Session, a bill for the creation of a Federal office of Commissioner of Insurance was prepared, but failed to reach the floor of the House.

cial reports. Insurance companies were subject to the same type of regulation imposed on all monied corporations.

The incorporation of insurance companies by special act of the legislature was discontinued by a number of states by the middle of the nineteenth century in view of the formulation of incorporation statutes covering the various classes of carriers. Such legislation usually provided for reports of various kinds, but no special state official was designated to inspect such reports exclusively.

The step of selecting a special person or commission to examine insurance company reports, the next development in the history of insurance regulation, was taken by New Hampshire when it established in 1851, an ex officio commission for that purpose. Massachusetts in 1852 became the first state to provide specifically for the supervision of insurance and to appoint officials charged with that supervision. One of the earliest acts of the commissioners of Massachusetts was to establish standards of solvency for life insurance companies.

Many of the failures of life insurance companies in the decade from 1865 to 1875 may be attributed to extravagant, inefficient methods and, in some instances, dishonesty. However, many others may be attributed to strict enforcement by the new state insurance departments of requirements regarding valuation of reserves and valuation of assets. Thus state regulation, while filled with inadequacies, had been actively and widely operating for 36 years prior to the Armstrong Investigation in New York.

Results of the Armstrong Investigation. The Armstrong Investigation in New York turned attention in almost all states and in Canada to the inadequacies of insurance regulation as practiced up to that time. As a result of that investigation, the State of New York passed a new insurance code early in 1906. This code, and subsequent amendments—still considered the most exacting among state insurance codes—furnished the pattern for all state codes since established or amended. It ran the whole gamut of management, officers, directorate, publicity and kindred activities, administration, and investments. For instance, it required an annual statement from each company on elaborate forms; the following of specific regulations concerning policy forms, valuations, etc.; the adherance to expense limitations; the observance of limits on the amount of new business; [8] the strict construc-

---

[8] As explained in Chapter 23, acquisition costs usually exceed first-year premium plus the establishment of the required first-year reserve. The extra money required is charged against surplus. The more new business written, the greater the drain on surplus. However, on those occasions in the past when any New York company has reached its "quota" of new business prior to the end of the year, its surplus usually has been sufficient for the Department to waive the limitation.

tion of contingency reserves; the regulation of dividends; the prohibition of stock holdings; [9] limitations on the powers of officers; the insertion of nonforfeiture values and incontestable clauses; avoidance of practices resulting in nepotism; limitations on agents' commissions. Every phase of the business, those mentioned and others, was covered by the code resulting from the Armstrong investigation.[10]

Other states amended and strengthened their own codes to take advantage of the lessons taught by the New York investigation, resulting in a strong body of state insurance law throughout the country.

The first broad-scale investigation of the Accident and Sickness business was conducted in 1911 by the National Association of Insurance Commissioners. It resulted in the 1912 Standard Provisions Law,[11] concerned primarily with contract changes, policy reinstatements, notice of claim requirements, proof of loss requirements, time within which claim payments must be made, requirements as to whom benefits should be paid, and other administrative provisions.

Significantly, the Standard Provisions law, subsequently enacted in almost all states, did not restrict the companies from experimenting with new policy forms and coverages. They simply set up the "ground rules" under which the business should be conducted.

In addition to the Standard Provisions, state departments have general regulatory powers which, typically, prohibit unjust, unfair, inequitable, misleading, or deceptive policy provisions.

The SEUA Case. Paul v. Virginia stood for 75 years. It was tested time and time again, most often by insurance companies seeking to escape state regulation.[12] The power of the Federal government specifically to regulate insurance was not tested in any of these cases. Then, on November 20, 1942, the South-Eastern Underwriters Association, an organization controlling the rates for Fire and allied lines in its territory, was indicted for violation of the Sherman Anti-Trust Act.

The charge against SEUA [13] was that it restrained interstate commerce

---

[9] Amended in 1928 to allow investment in certain preferred and guaranteed stocks, and in 1951 to allow investment in common stocks to a restricted degree.

[10] Cf. Chapter 26.

[11] Cf. Chapter 11.

[12] See, for example, Hooper v. California, *155 U.S. 658* (1895); Noble v. Mitchell, *164 U.S. 367* (1896); Hopkins v. United States, *171 U.S. 578* (1898); New York Life v. Cravens, *178 U.S. 389* (1900); New York Life v. Deer Lodge County, *231 U.S. 495* (1913); Northwestern Mutual Life Insurance Co. v. Wisconsin, *247 U.S. 132* (1918); Bothwell v. Buckbee Mears Co., *275 U.S. 274, 276–77* (1927); Colgate v. Harvey, *296 U.S. 404, 432* (1935).

[13] Made against about 200 of its member companies and 27 individuals.

by fixing and enforcing arbitrary and noncompetitive premium rates, controlling agents' commissions, and using coercion, boycott, and intimidation to force nonmember companies into the conspiracy by preventing them from obtaining reinsurance facilities.

Agents who represented nonmember companies were denied the right to represent member companies, and buyers of insurance from nonmember carriers were threatened with boycotts and withdrawal of patronage. The Association maintained a staff to police the agencies and companies.

SEUA relied on the defense that since the Supreme Court had held that insurance was not commerce, the Sherman Act did not apply. The district court of Georgia upheld this view, pointing out that if the finding that insurance was not commerce were to be reversed, then the reversal would have to be by the Supreme Court which itself had established the ruling in 1869. The Federal government then appealed the case to the United States Supreme Court.[14]

In a four to three decision, two justices excusing themselves from the case, the court held on June 5, 1944, that when the transaction of insurance business crosses state lines, it is interstate commerce.[15] It explained that the business of insurance included many more operations than the issuing of policies for it included "transmission of great quantities of money, documents, and communications across dozens of state lines," and these activities had been held in other decisions by the court to be a part of interstate commerce. Even the three dissenting justices agreed that Congress has the power to regulate insurance. Their dissent was based on the contention that Congress did not intend the Sherman Act to apply to insurance companies.

On the same day it handed down the South-Eastern Underwriters decision, the Court held unanimously that a fraternal benefit society is subject to the National Labor Relations Act because it is an insurance company and its operations affect commerce.[16] Had the United States Supreme Court in 1869 upheld the right of the State of Virginia to regulate the insurance business on the grounds "that states may regulate interstate affairs so long as they do not improperly burden interstate commerce, and so long as Congress has been silent," [17] it would have been spared the embarrassment of a reversal after having held steadfastly to an awkward decision for three quarters of a century.

---

[14] Fearing the impact of a reversal on state regulation, 36 states joined in opposing the appeal.
[15] 322 U.S. 533 (1944).
[16] 32 U.S. 643 (1944).
[17] Cf. annotations to U.S.C.A. Constitution, Article 1, number 8, clause 3, note 1157.

Thus in two cases decided about the same time the court changed the ground rules established in Paul *v.* Virginia and opened the door to federal regulation. It should be pointed out, however, that these decisions did not affect the power of the states to regulate the insurance business but simply nullified those state laws which were contrary to Federal regulation.

Inasmuch as the laws of many states required the use of co-operative rate-making organizations in the Fire and allied lines, the immediate situation was confusing since the SEUA decision made co-operative fixing of rates a combination in restraint of trade. In order for a company to comply with the state law, it had to violate the federal law, and vice versa. The resulting confusion as well as the sweeping implications of the SEUA decision made it obvious that many readjustments would be required. As a result, the McCarran Act [18] was passed by Congress and approved on March 9, 1945.[19] The McCarran Act did three things:

1. In order to give the states time to enact the legislation necessary to bring state law into conformity with Federal law, a moratorium period was established (originally until January 1, 1948, later extended to June 30, 1948) during which the Federal antitrust laws would not apply to the business of insurance except as to boycott, coercion, and intimidation.

2. It established that even after the expiration of the moratorium period, the Federal antitrust acts should apply to the insurance business only "to the extent that the business is not regulated by state law."

3. It contained a declaration that the continued regulation and taxation of insurance by the states is in the public interest and that silence on the part of Congress should not be construed as a barrier to state regulation or taxation.

The National Association of Insurance Commissioners and the All-Industry Committee, made up of 19 national insurance organizations representing all branches of the business, initiated activity to bring state laws in line with Federal requirements, and many states passed rate-regulatory laws and "fair-trade" laws prohibiting unfair competition and practices in the business and giving their insurance commissioners power to issue "cease-and-desist" orders.

To date, the Federal government has enacted no special laws to supersede state regulation, although it has not completely ignored the insurance business since the passage of the McCarran Act. There have been several cases involving suits under the boycott, coercion, and intimidation clause of

---

[18] Public Law 15, 79th Congress.

[19] The insurance industry had previously sought to have Congress pass a law specifically exempting insurance companies from the Federal Antitrust Acts.

this Act.[20] Also the Federal Trade Commission has conducted several investigations into the insurance business.[21] Whether any special Federal laws relating to insurance will be passed in the future remains to be seen. A strong warning that "attempts" at regulation by the state are not enough, however, was contained in a report of the Subcommittee on Antitrust and Monopoly Legislation of the Committee on the Judiciary, United States Senate, 83rd Congress, Second Session, 1955.

Under the heading, "A Final Admonition," [22] the report warned "To those individuals who abhor the thought of Federal interference with the business of insurance, who desire the continued regulation of the industry by the several states, the subcommittee has this final admonition: . . . this subcommittee will not forever accept 'attempts' at regulation as a substitute for regulation of the business of insurance by the States. The patience of the Federal Government with those who would abuse the good name of insurance may someday come to an end."

Federal v. State Regulation. It is not the function of this discussion to argue the question of Federal versus state regulation, especially since the argument becomes involved in the traditional schism in political thinking in this country: states' rights versus Federal union.

That there is much to be criticized in the system of individual state regulation is not to be denied. Chief complaints against it have been:

1. Lack of uniformity among insurance codes, creating innumerable complications for companies operating in more than one state. For instance, the biggest "headache" of every company is obtaining the approval of new policy forms in all the states in which it operates. Legal departments, actuaries, and underwriters often are completely frustrated by having one state absolutely forbid a certain clause which another state requires.

2. The additional expense involved in filing financial reports in different states and the cost of maintaining more than 48 separate insurance departments.

3. Ill-advised legislation proposed and even passed in various states

---

[20] U.S. *v.* Investors Diversified Service, *102 F. Supp. 645* (1951) and U.S. *v.* Insurance Board of Cleveland, *Civil Action 28042, U.S.P.C.* for the Northern District of Ohio, for example.

[21] One investigation was of the practices of certain mail-order insurance companies. Another was one to determine whether or not marine insurance companies should continue to receive the protection afforded under the Webb-Pomerene Act which allowed combinations for foreign trade. Another was an investigation for the Federal Trade Commission by the Celler subcommittee to determine the effectiveness of state regulation in eliminating monopoly in the life insurance business.

[22] *The Tie-in Sale of Credit Insurance in Connection with Small Loans and Other Transactions,* Washington, U.S. Government Printing Office, 1955, p. 14.

where legislators are not "professionals" as are the members of the United States Congress, but part-timers often so underpaid for their work that in some cases the only reason they seek a seat is to be in a position to introduce special-privilege or retaliatory legislation.

4. The political nature of the appointment or election of insurance commissioners, which has too often produced commissioners who have few qualifications for the job.

5. Conflict with Federal regulations and rulings which, while not aimed exclusively at the insurance business, do affect its operations and transactions.

6. The business is national in scope. The fact that the vast majority of companies operate in more than one state would seem, logically, to call for national regulation.

On the other hand, strong arguments have been advanced for the system of state control:

1. State regulation is better able to give special consideration to local conditions where such consideration is needed.

2. Federal regulation, which would involve a much larger department than required by any single state, would tend to become cumbersome and involved in red tape.

3. State regulation is closer to the individual citizen and hence more subject to his observation and control.

4. Conflicts in state law and practices are steadily being reduced by the activities of the National Association of Insurance Commissioners. This organization, formed in 1870, has as a primary function the elimination of conflicts and the promotion of uniformity in state regulation. The association has, over the years, demonstrated its ability to accomplish its objectives so that today the complications resulting from company operations in several states have been minimized and are less annoying to the companies.

The thinking of the industry itself has not always been on either side of the question of state versus Federal control. As previously pointed out, Elizur Wright was a staunch advocate of Federal regulation, and most of the cases testing Paul v. Virginia were attempts by members of the industry to have insurance declared commerce and, hence, not subject to state regulation. Many writers in the field, even well into the 1930's, indicated belief in Federal as opposed to state control.[23] Some have since changed their stand.

---

[23] Cf., for examples, S. S. Huebner, *Life Insurance*, New York: D. Appleton & Co. (now Appleton-Century-Crofts, Inc.), 1915; J. B. Maclean, *Life Insurance*, New York, McGraw-Hill Book Co., 1932, p. 393; C. K. Knight, *Advanced Life Insurance*, New York, John Wiley & Sons, Inc., 1926, p. 26; J. H. Magee, *Life Insurance*, Chicago: Business Publications, Inc. (now Richard D. Irwin, Inc.), 1929, p. 604.

Moreover, as among company executives throughout history, there has been a difference of opinion as to the desirability of Federal regulation of insurance. As state legislation became bothersome, Federal regulation gained more and more support. The greatest drives for Federal regulation were made during the years immediately preceding the Paul v. Virginia case. The most opposition to these drives seemed to have stemmed from the insurance commissioners of the states. The large companies in the East seemed to have favored Federal control, whereas the small companies in the South and West seemed to have favored state control. Throughout the history of insurance in America the question of Federal supervision of insurance came up time and time again in the form of proposed congressional measures, suggested constitutional amendments, institutional resolutions, and public statements by company executives. Those who opposed the move always won out. At the present time the insurance industry seems to be more closely united in opposition to Federal control, especially after studying the New Deal and Fair Deal regulatory practices of two recent administrations.[24]

Exactly where the future of the regulation of the business lies is not clear at this point. Many believe that the business will see an "inching forward" of Federal power in the area rather than any superimposition of a system of Federal control on top of the present state system. In other words, they believe that if Federal regulation comes, it will be by slow evolution rather than the abrupt passage of a Federal insurance "code." Many see signs that the "inching forward" process is already well under way.[25]

Recent Developments. A development which has greatly strengthened the system of state supervision was the Supreme Court's decision in 1950 [26] upholding the validity of what is known as the "service of process" laws. Prior to the enactment of these laws, now in effect in the majority of states and anticipated for all of them, it was impossible for claimants to obtain service of a process on unlicensed companies in the claimant's own state.

---

[24] For an interesting discussion of the history of attitudes towards Federal regulation of insurance see A Study in the History of Life Insurance by R. Carlyle Buley, New York: Appleton-Century-Crofts, Inc., 1953, selections (see Index). President Theodore Roosevelt exerted strong pressure for federal regulation. History shows companies were lined up on "both sides of the fence." Two U.S. senators who were also presidents of life insurance companies were on opposing sides of the issue. Senator Dryden, who was president of Prudential, favored Federal control whereas Senator Bulkeley, president of Aetna, opposed it.

[25] For a discussion of developments that suggest the way Federal power might be exercised in certain areas of the insurance business, cf. E. M. Thoré, "The Government and Life Insurance," Insurance Lecture Series, Spring, 1953, Storrs, Conn., University of Connecticut, School of Business Administration, p. 69.

[26] Travelers Health v. Virginia, 339 U.S. 643 (1950).

To sue, he had to go to the state of domicile of the company. This was a grave handicap to the state regulatory system. Under the service of process law ("Unauthorized Insurers Process Act"), any insurance company mailing policies into a state or collecting premiums therein automatically appoints the insurance commissioner (or other appropriate state official) as its agent for the service of process in any legal action by domiciled insureds. Thus an insurer operating by mail in a state in which it is not licensed can be sued in that state.

In 1950, the National Association of Insurance Commissioners introduced the Uniform Individual Accident & Sickness Provisions to replace the old Standard Provisions. The Uniform Provisions are discussed in detail in Chapter 11.

What was viewed by many observers as one of the first definite moves of the Federal government into the regulation of the insurance business came when the Federal Trade Commission assumed jurisdiction over mail-order insurance and, in 1950, adopted a Fair Practices Code for that business. Then, in 1954, the FTC announced an investigation of Accident and Sickness insurance company advertising. It called for submission of all advertising material and the policies to which it related to the commission for review. Late in 1954 and during 1955, the FTC issued complaints against a number of companies, based on advertising practices during the calendar year of 1953.

As of this writing, these charges are still being heard. Companies involved have adopted two types of defense: (1) denial of the charges of misleading advertising; (2) rejection of the charges on the ground that the FTC has no jurisdiction. What the outcome of these cases will be remains to be seen. It would appear, for two reasons, that denial of the charges is the stronger of the two defenses: (1) If some companies are engaging in sharp practices or are misleading the public, the fair-minded companies should encourage attempts to restrain them. It seems probable that if the contention that the FTC has no jurisdiction is sustained (and there is serious doubt as to that), Congress will immediately pass legislation giving the FTC the desired jurisdiction. (2) If these charges are really untrue, then in the interest of public relations, they should be strongly denied and proved false.

2. CHANNELS OF REGULATION

There are four channels of regulation of the insurance business: legislative, administrative, judicial, and self-regulation.

Judicial Regulation. Much insurance regulation is established by the

THE REGULATION OF COMPANIES 685

judicial branch of the government through court decisions. In the American form of government, it is the function of the legislative branch to pass laws, the administrative branch to carry out their provisions, and the judicial branch to interpret legislation when its application to any particular situation is not clear. Consequently, the law of the land originally stemmed from two sources: the legislative bodies and the courts—legislative law and judicial or "case" law.

The insurance industry is subject to both types of "law." For instance, should the court be called upon to rule regarding the powers or the limitations of the power of the insurance commissioner, that decision, at least until reversed, becomes a part of the body of insurance regulation. The same is true when the court decides on the interpretation of a policy contract, the constitutionality or unconstitutionality of insurance legislation, the liability of a company in borderline cases, and in all the host of decisions which may be handed down in the cases of litigation directly or indirectly affecting the insurance business.

Legislative Regulation. The second branch of the various state governments to have a hand in insurance regulation is the legislative, the legislatures and assemblies of the 48 states, Alaska, Hawaii, and the Congress of the United States when serving as the legislative body for the District of Columbia. As has been seen in the discussion of the history of insurance regulation, each of the states and territories has a large body of law—usually referred to as the "insurance code"—directly pertaining to the operation, administration, and investment of the various companies domiciled or licensed within the state.

Drafting of legislation in the various states has not been left solely in the hands of the legislators. As in the case of most legislation, interested individuals and groups offer "proposed" bills which they seek to have sponsored by some legislator who will introduce them for possible passage in the legislature. In general practice today, new legislation or amendments to the insurance code are usually sponsored by the insurance companies themselves, either directly or through associations, and by the various insurance departments and commissioners. It is a widespread practice, when the state insurance commissioner is considering the sponsorship of insurance regulation in the legislature or assembly, for him to hold hearings at which interested parties such as the companies, company associations, and agents, as well as the general public, may express their views or make recommendations.

Legislation is also introduced at times by labor unions or other organized lay groups. One of the most bothersome sources of new legislative proposals is "spite bills" introduced by legislators who have a grudge against insurance resulting from a personal experience or that of a constituent.

As a general rule, state legislative bodies lean heavily on the insurance department both for the sponsorship of any needed regulation and for approval or disapproval of proposed regulation. The Attorney General of the state also frequently if not commonly assists in the drawing up of proposed laws affecting insurance in the same manner that he does with many other types of law. The National Association of Insurance Commissioners is another source of proposed "model" legislation as, for instance, the aforementioned Guertin standard valuation and nonforfeiture laws, the Uniform Provisions laws, and many others.

Administrative Regulation. Administrative regulation of the insurance industry is accomplished in the various states and territories by an official or department specifically appointed to see that the provisions of the law are carried out. The official is known as the commissioner or superintendent of insurance and his department the department of insurance.

The operations of insurance commissioners are an early American example of what is now known as administrative law. Today this type of law has become identified with a multiplicity of agencies concerned with regulation of economic activity. Prominent examples include the activities of the Interstate Commerce Commission, National Labor Relations Board, state utilities commissions, the Securities and Exchange Commission, and many others. Administrative law evolved out of the necessity for both flexibility and technical understanding inherently impossible in either the normal legislative or judicial processes.

The essence of administrative law has been the granting by the legislative branch of a field or scope of authority to an administrative agency which both makes and enforces rules within the limits of the initial grant and subject to judicial review. For example, as noted below, insurance commissioners are given powers to regulate the valuation of insurance companies' assets. These powers are effected by the establishment of particular rules of valuation which he can change from time to time as economic conditions and knowledge of investment principles change.

Discretion in enforcement is also available when power to revoke a company's license is given in such language as "whenever in the judgment of the Superintendent of Insurance it will best promote the interests of the people of this state. . . ." The insurance commissioners in some states have the power to levy fines after a formal hearing of the charges. Obviously, in making decisions, the commissioner is setting up rules of conduct; that is, creating administrative law. Of course, such rules must always lie within the general scope of powers granted by the legislature to the administrator, and the courts stand guard to see that these are not exceeded and that neither wilfulness nor arbitrariness appears in their application.[27]

An insurance commissioner combines the functions of an official clerk, of a judge, of a legislator and, often, of judge and jury. Partly judicial, partly legislative, and partly administrative, he is not confined within any of these areas.

The powers of a commissioner are broad and discretionary and are intended to be. By direct or indirect means he can bring about compliance with almost any rule he promulgates.[28] In fact, the powers of a state commissioner may even be extraterritorial. For instance, no company has successfully challenged the right of the New York department to require "substantial compliance" with New York law in all other states in which a company operates as a condition of licensing in New York. Thus, for one example, a company licensed in New York must observe the maximum commission allowances set by New York in every state in which it operates no matter in which state the company is domiciled.

Self-Regulation. The final channel of regulation of the insurance business is self-regulation; that is, those restraints imposed on the business from within the industry both through individual company conscience and through group pressure and associations. Self-regulation was the first type of insurance regulation in America and is the predominant type in Great Britain.

There is a sense of trusteeship in the insurance business that acts as what might be called the "individual company conscience." The cynic will say that good behavior is a result of necessity, that the business is under such intense public scrutiny in all phases of its operation that it is "the better part of valor" to act in the public interest. However, the source of such operating philosophy matters little to the fact that it does exist.

Through trade associations, business conscience becomes even more

---

[27] Some judicial authorities are seriously concerned by the great advances in administrative law. Judge Brennan in a court opinion had this to say, "concern with the problem of merger of the powers of prosecutor and judge in the same agency springs from the fear that the agency official adjudicating upon private rights cannot wholly free himself from the influences toward partiality inherent in his identification with the prosecuting aspects of the case . . . in a sense the combination of functions violate the ancient tenet of Anglo-American justice that 'No man shall be a judge in his own cause.'" (In re Larsen, 86A2D 430, 436.)

[28] It would seem that Federal regulation of even mail-order business is unnecessary if state regulatory powers were effectively applied. Every mail-order company is licensed in at least the state in which it is domiciled. By direct or indirect means, the commissioner in that state could regulate its practices in other states. The difficulty arises from the fact that domestic companies, being "home business," are usually able to get the ear of state legislators and other officials, who often can tie the hands of a commissioner.

important as a foundation for self-regulation. All the associations discussed in Chapter 25 serve to regulate the business, both by their very existence and through "codes of ethics" and similar statements and agreements adopted by them. For instance, in 1950, the National Association of Insurance Commissioners took action to approve and adopt a "Statement of Principles for Personal Accident & Health Insurance" drawn up by an industry committee. It includes principles for the construction of policy forms; principles applying to policy provisions and their uses, particularly exclusions, qualifying and waiting periods, and disability definitions; and principles applying to advertising and soliciting materials. As another example, in 1954, prior to the release of the FTC complaints, members of both the Health and Accident Conference and the Bureau of Accident and Health adopted voluntary codes of advertising standards for individual A & S policies and required members to agree to the codes as a condition of membership.

As further self-regulation, the agents' associations such as the National Association of Life Underwriters, the General Agents & Managers Conference, the American Society of Chartered Life Underwriters, and the International Association of Accident & Health Underwriters all have codes of ethics for their members.[29] Unfortunately, however, as in other business and professional groups some members of these associations fail to take the codes seriously enough.

3. WHAT IS REGULATED?

A list of duties or powers of an insurance commissioner actually constitutes a list of those aspects of the business which are subject to government regulation. At least four of these regulatory areas deserve specific treatment. They are the formation of new companies, financial solvency, product regulation, and field practices of agents and brokers.[30]

Organization of New Companies. It is the function of the insurance department or commissioner to supervise and act upon the formation of new companies, making certain that they conform to the requirements established by the insurance code and interpreting that code whenever such interpretation is needed.

---

[29] Not all agents belong to these professional societies, however. Whereas there are upwards of 225,000 full-time agents and managers in the life insurance business, fewer than 60,000 belong to the National Association of Life Underwriters, the largest of four organizations listed. The combined membership of all four would not greatly exceed that figure since there is much overlapping of membership among them.

[30] It should be borne in mind that all branches of insurance are regulated by the various commissioners and departments. The discussion here concentrates mainly on the details of regulation pertaining mainly to life and accident and sickness insurance companies.

Since the New York Code has been widely copied and used as the model in many other states, it will serve to illustrate the details of regulation dealing with the formation of new companies.

The New York law requires those contemplating the formation of a new life insurance company to draw up a charter giving among other data the name of the company, the location, the kinds of business it plans to write (life, life and annuities, annuities, life and accident and health, or the like); the power of the company officers and how these powers are to be exercised; methods of internal government, and if a stock company, details of stock arrangement. Next, the founders must advertise their intention to incorporate as an insurance company and file a certificate of intention and a copy of the charter.

After the charter is approved, and the certificate recorded, a stock company may sell stock or a mutual company may solicit applications for insurance, but neither can yet issue policies. Organization under the New York law is complete in the case of mutuals, when the premiums on a necessary minimum of insurance have been paid, when the necessary statutory surplus has been cleared with the superintendent of insurance, and when the directors who are elected have authorized the issue of the policies. A stock company organization is complete and policies can be issued when the total amount of capital and surplus has been paid in, when the statutory deposits have been placed with the superintendent of insurance, and when the directors have been elected and have authorized the issuance of the stock.[31]

Under New York law, since it is easier to organize a stock company than a mutual, companies sometimes are formed as stock corporations and then later mutualized. When Hyde formed the Equitable Assurance Society of New York, he referred to it as a mutual; but he had to organize it as a stock company.[32]

In both types of companies, internal management is regulated by the bylaws.

There is a difference between the *organization* of a company and the *licensing* of a company. Consequently, regulation covers not only organization but also licensing. The control of the insurance business by the state is exercised chiefly through its licensing power. The primary purposes of the requirements of licensing today is not revenue-raising, as was probably the original intention, but regulation. A license is a document stating that the company involved has complied with the laws of the state and is authorized

---

[31] Cf. Chapter 24 for minimum financial requirements for the organization of stock and mutual companies under New York law.

[32] The company has long since been mutualized.

to engage in the kind of business or businesses specified. A license might well be called a certificate of authority. Although life insurance underwriting by an individual rather than a corporation is not everywhere prohibited, little if any such business is written in the United States today.[33]

A license to write life or A & S insurance may be issued to a domestic company, an alien company, or a foreign company. The state has the right to make requirements for the issuance of a license to foreign or alien companies which are more stringent than those required of a domestic company. For instance, in New York and Massachusetts domestic companies are required to obtain licenses only once, and they need not renew them. Moreover, the grounds for the revocation of a domestic company's license are usually more limited in comparison with the grounds for the revocation of the license of a foreign or alien company.

While such discrimination might appear to be local favoritism, it must be remembered that the assets of a domestic company are domiciled within the borders of the state and subject to the control of the commissioner of insurance of that state through court procedure. However, the insurance commissioner in any given state has no power to seize assets domiciled in another state, and often he cannot even sue in the other state for that purpose except when acting as a liquidator or receiver.[34]

Financial Solvency. A second important area of insurance regulation is that pertaining to the financial condition of the company. Regulation for that purpose breaks down into four categories: (1) the power to compute reserve liabilities, (2) the power to value securities, (3) the power to approve investments, dividends, and expenses, and (4) the power to require a deposit of security.

Computation of Reserve Liability. The Guertin Standard Valuation Nonforfeiture legislation, which has become virtually standard in all states, requires that the life insurance company reserves must be those calculated from the Commissioners' Standard Ordinary mortality table at 3½% or a mortality table and interest rate giving, *in the aggregate,* higher reserves. Accident and Sickness insurance carriers must set up unearned premium reserves, loss reserves, and in the case of noncancellable contracts, an active life disability reserve.[35]

---

[33] Frankly, no statistical compilations show any, and the authors never heard of any; however, the authors have also found that it is unwise to make categorical statements to college students. Someone always comes up with an exception.

[34] Since the SEUA decision declaring insurance interstate commerce the courts have consistently held that a differential imposed on a foreign carrier as contrasted to a domestic carrier is not in restraint of trade, as might appear.

[35] Cf. Chapter 23.

The Evaluation of Assets. Any company may be made to appear solvent if its securities are evaluated high enough. Consequently, state commissioners are empowered to determine the method of evaluating securities of an insurance company for the purposes of determining whether or not that company is in a sound condition. Formulas for the evaluation of securities are both complicated and lengthy. They are designed to make certain that life insurance companies do not overvalue assets in reporting them. As a result, a more than ordinary amount of reliance may be placed in the financial statements of insurance companies in determining their financial strength.[36] Without formulas for the evaluation of assets, requirements for reserves would be meaningless.

Investment Regulation. Regulation restricts the types of investments in which an insurance company may place its money. For example, companies doing business in New York are restricted to the following types of investments: (1) obligations of the Federal, state, or municipal government; (2) obligations of solvent American corporations with a long earnings record or secured by specific property; (3) mortgage loans secured by unencumbered real property; (4) stock and debts of housing companies; (5) Federal home loan bank stocks; (6) obligations issued or guaranteed by the International Bank; (7) savings and loan association shares; (8) investment in housing projects; (9) limited investments in income-producing real estate; and (10) limited investments in preferred and common stocks.[37]

Interesting variations are found in laws of other states. For example, the Illinois law allows companies to invest 5% of admitted assets without restriction.[38] Texas requires that life insurance companies licensed there must invest in Texas real estate and securities at least 75% of their assets which offset the legal reserve required on policies written on the lives of Texans.

In general, laws regulating life insurance company investments are designed to restrict the investments, not only into certain given classes of securities, but also to the proportion of funds that may be invested in any given type of asset in order to assure diversification. Even with the numerous restrictions of the investments of life insurance company funds, carriers have

---

[36] An insurance company has more freedom in understating its strength if it wants to, say, depress the value of its stock or conceal the size of its surplus.

[37] Investments in preferred stocks were first permitted in New York in 1928, and investment in common stock was first authorized in 1951. The amount which a company operating in New York may invest in common stocks is limited to 3% of admitted assets or 1/3 of its surplus to policyholders, whichever is less. There are other restrictions on the investment in particular issues. Preferred stocks constitute about 2¼% of all assets of life insurance companies, and common stocks constitute about another 1%. Investments in real estate, almost nothing prior to about 1945 when most states passed laws permitting such investment, now amount to about 2½% of total assets.

[38] Connecticut allows 8%.

wide latitude for use of discretion in how these funds will be invested among the permissible classes. For example, a study of the issues of *The Life Insurance Fact Book* will reveal major changes in the distribution of investments with a wide shift from Governments to Industrial being the most in evidence during the last decade.

Regulation of Expenses. Only two states have laws limiting the amount that life insurance companies may spend on expenses. However, inasmuch as one of the states is New York,[39] whose regulation as previously mentioned has an extraterritorial effect, the limitations imposed have widespread application.[40]

The New York expense limitation requirements grew out of the findings of the Armstrong investigation which revealed extravagance in amounts spent, especially for the acquisition of new business. The limitation is placed on a specific list of items involving first-year expenses incurred in issuing a policy, the total of which must not exceed the first-year expense allowance. These items include first-year commissions; additional compensation paid in obtaining new business but not included in commissions nor forming a part of supervision costs; advances to agents; compensation and expenses of home office personnel who spend more than one third of their time in the field; a percentage of advertising cost; and the amount by which (1) renewal commissions, (2) service or collection fees, (3) special compensation, (4) cost of agency supervision, (5) agents' pension plans, and (6) certain branch office and agency expenses exceed the sum of a given amount (based on specified percentages) of the renewal premiums on life insurance and annuities plus flat amounts for each $1,000 of all insurance in force and each $1,000 of insurance in force not paid up.[41]

Rate Regulation. Life and Accident and Sickness insurance rates are not regulated in the same sense that rates are controlled in certain fire and casualty lines. Reserve requirements in life insurance assures the adequacy of rates whereas competition assures that the rates will be reasonable. Unfair

---

[39] The other state is Wisconsin, where the total expense of commissions, agents' advances, medical examinations and inspection, and the proportion of other expenses chargeable to new business must not exceed the loading added to net premiums and the excess of the net premium for a 20-pay Life policy over the net premium for a one-year Term. The Wisconsin law also includes a limitation which usually will be inoperative since life insurance is generally written on a level-premium basis. This limitation, to be added to those listed above, is the excess of the first year's premium over the largest renewal premium.

[40] Although companies licensed in New York are, by number, only about 10% of all companies in the United States, they represent about 85% of all assets held by U.S. life insurance companies.

[41] Smaller companies (less than $500,000,000 in force) are allowed to increase their expense limits over those for the larger company.

rate discrimination among buyers of the same policy is prohibited. In the A & S field, rates and loss ratios sometimes are checked indirectly before the department approves policy forms. The majority of states require that A & S rates and occupational classifications shall be filed with the commissioner. Some few states require that rates as well as policies be approved by the commissioner. A number of states provide that the commissioner's approval shall be withdrawn if the benefits payable are unreasonable in relation to the premium charged, but no exact standards of "reasonableness" are set. In another small group of states, the filing of a policy form for approval must be accompanied by an estimate of loss ratios expected under the coverage. Since about 1945 a majority of states have been requiring the filing of an annual statement of loss ratios by policy forms at the suggestion of the National Association of Insurance Commissioners, which in that year expressed the desirability of A & S loss ratio information. No action, however, has ever been taken on the statistics so gathered.

Product Regulation. In almost all states, policy forms in both life and A & S must be filed with the insurance commissioner. In some states, approval is required before the policy can be issued. In others, if not disapproved within a certain period of time, the policy may be issued. Generally speaking, the commissioner may disapprove if a life or A & S form contains provisions that are unjust, unfair, inequitable, misleading, deceptive, or encourage misrepresentation. His authority is highly discretionary.

In addition, policy forms in both the life and A & S field must contain a number of "standard" provisions.[42] Standard provisions have advantages to both company and policyholder by making for some degree of uniformity among insurance policies. They eliminate the necessity of bargaining for each individual policy and make mass production possible. They facilitate the gathering of statistics to measure costs accurately. They assure fair and equal treatment to policyholders, and lead to a better understanding of policies and their meaning.[43] The advantages of standard forms have been so accepted in the insurance industry that standard forms have been adopted in some lines of insurance without any requirement to do so by the state.[44]

---

[42] These standard provisions are discussed in Chapters 8 (for life insurance policies) and 11 (for Accident and Sickness policies).

[43] Dr. J. E. Hedges, of Indiana University, writing in *Law and Contemporary Problems* XV p. 358, says of the advantages of eliminating the doubt in the minds of buyers of the meaning of interest contracts: " . . . much of the mystery with which insurance seems to be shrouded in the public mind tends to disappear. With the disappearance of mystery, there tends to come the confidence so necessary if insurance is to provide the peace of mind which is one of its greatest services."

[44] In some cases the adoption of a standard form under self-regulation was done to discourage the state from developing a standard form of its own to spring on the companies.

As a result of a great body of law, judicial, legislative, and administrative, relating to insurance policy contracts, they have become so complicated in wording that it is virtually impossible for the layman to understand all their provisions; therefore, analysis and approval of them by technicians such as are available in state insurance departments is essential in safeguarding the public interest.[45]

Group Regulation. In general, much that has been detailed above in regard to rate regulation and policy forms relates to individual and family policies. Policy provisions required in individual policies generally do not apply to Group policies. In most states, Group insurance is regulated by a special set of laws. Laws relating to group insurance usually include: the definition of a group, the minimum size of a group, the percentage of participation required in contributory plans. Approximately 25 states have established special Group policy form requirements. They cover such things as the definition of a contract, representations, issuance of certificates to individuals covered, new admissions, remittance of premiums, time limit on notice of claim, proof of loss, time limit on filing proof of loss, payment of claims, physical examination and autopsy, time limit on legal actions. Provisions relating to all these issues, however, are not found in every state Group insurance law.

In Group life insurance, some states set the minimum first-year premium. After the first year, premiums may be adjusted to the loss experience of the particular group. Minimum first-year premiums are not required in A & S, although in practice filed rate schedules are usually followed the first year, the rate being adjusted thereafter by experience of the group.

In the field of A & S, special legislative and regulatory consideration is also given to Blanket and Franchise forms.

Regulation of Field Practices. As previously mentioned, agents and brokers must be licensed by the state.[46] Qualifications for obtaining a license as an agent or broker vary widely from state to state. Applicants may or may not be subject to any particular qualifications or examination. The agent must, of course, be authorized by the company. The very term, "agent," indicates that he has been designated by his principal (the company) to act as its representative in the transactions specified in his contract. In a growing number of states, written examinations are required. In other states, the law

---

[45] How effective this analysis is in practice as contrasted to theory is questionable. Most insurance departments operate on such limited budgets that they are without funds to hire sufficient trained personnel to give the multitude of policy forms submitted to them more than a "quick once-over."

[46] Some states make a distinction between brokers and agents for purposes of licensing. In other states, the same license is issued to brokers as to agents.

assumes naïvely, or more probably with a wink, that in view of the fact that the agent has extremely broad power to commit his principal, the company can be depended upon to use care in selection of agents.[47]

Agents' licenses may be refused or revoked by the insurance commissioner, but not without "cause," such as dishonesty, twisting, rebating, fraud, etc.[48] Dishonesty or fraud in the past is usually grounds for rejection of an application for a license. Some few states appear to regard incompetence or ignorance as grounds for rejection of a license. If serious qualification laws ever are adopted or if licenses ever are to mean more to the public than a source of state revenue these two elements (incompetence and ignorance) will have to be given more recognition and weight than it seems are being given to them today.

Penalties are usually provided in state insurance codes for doing business as an agent in the state without a license. In general, these penalties are similar to those applied to a company that operates in a state without a license. They usually are of two types: criminal and civil. Criminal penalties may run as high as $2,000 fines and jail sentences up to one year. Assessment of these penalties can be made only after due trial as provided for all criminal offenses. Such trials are infrequent. More deterring than criminal penalties are the civil penalties, which may include the refusal of the court to allow the agent to recover against the policyholder for nonpayment of premiums or to recover against his company for nonpayment of commissions.

In most states, licenses must be renewed annually, such renewal usually being made on application and payment of the proper fee. Some states issue perpetual licenses, but an annual fee is still required. Also, some few states license insurance counselors, auditors, or analysts. In most states, however, such "counselors" are usually self-appointed.

High among causes considered sufficient for license revocation are *rebating, misrepresentation,* and *twisting.*

Rebating is the practice of returning part of the premium or giving a valuable consideration in return for the application for the policy. Rebating generally takes the form of a refund of part of the commissions on the business. Regulation of rebating is aimed at maintaining a fair plane of competition among agents, the philosophy being not *free* competition, but *fair* competition. The prohibition against rebating also is designed to protect the

---

[47] The law may simply require certification from the company or field office head that the agent has completed one of several training courses previously approved by the insurance department. These types of requirements offer scarcely any protection to the public against poorly trained agents, although perhaps they are no worse than many of the state examinations which, according to any academic standards, are farcical.

[48] There is always appeal from the rulings of a commissioner to the courts.

career agent from the avocational agent. The career agent, that is, the agent who earns his entire livelihood from the life insurance business and who contemplates remaining in that business throughout his career, is to be encouraged in favor of the man who "picks up a little money on the side," the avocational agent. The latter, of course, not depending for his living on his life insurance sales, may be more prone to return part of the premium to the applicant as consideration for buying insurance.

Rebating is not clearly defined by law. State laws usually provide that a rebate may consist not only of part of a premium, but also any inducement, favor, or advantage not specified in the policy. In some jurisdictions, it is illegal for an employer to accept a commission for a policy issued to an employee, or for an employee to accept one for insurance on an employer. Sometimes, attorneys are prohibited from accepting fees for inducing a client to take insurance. Rebating may even extend to an agreement to render certain tangible services, say, for example, to do a specified amount of work for the applicant in return for his application. The acceptance of interest-bearing notes instead of cash, however, has been held not to constitute a rebate.[49] The acceptance of noninterest-bearing notes would be open to question as well as would the waiving of interest charges on interest-bearing notes, a practice sometimes used especially in connection with student business. As a further precaution, agents are expected to write a fair amount of business for people other than themselves and their immediate family so that commission payments do not indirectly become a rebate.

In many states, rebating is a legal offense (usually a misdemeanor) for the agent, and in others, it is an offense for both the agent and the person receiving the rebate. Few rebating cases actually appear in court. A rebating case is difficult to prove, especially since under the law of some states both parties, the buyer and the seller, are guilty. Neither is desirous of testifying against the other and hence incriminating himself.

Misrepresentation involves the making of any unfair, misleading, or incomplete comparison of two policies, or any misleading statement about the financial condition or reputation of another company or of any of the relationships between the insured and the company.

Twisting refers in general to misrepresentation in order to induce a policyholder to drop a contract he already has and to replace it with a new one. The practice generally relates to dropping a policy in one company in favor of taking a policy in a different one, although twisting might also consist of inducing a policyholder to drop a policy in the agent's own com-

---

[49] Diehl v. American Life Insurance Company, *204 Iowa 706, 213 N.W. 753* (1927).

pany in order to take another one in that same company.[50] Twisting is difficult to define; and inasmuch as there are on rare occasions valid reasons for having a policyholder drop one policy and replace it with another, the definition of twisting must include failure to disclose all the facts. Regulations against twisting are fostered and encouraged by the companies inasmuch as twisting increases the incidence of lapsation and the ratio of acquisition costs to total expenses.

Unfair discrimination is another prohibition in most states, although it is not an act usually committed by an agent. The word "unfair" must be stressed, for in a sense the very practice of the insurance business is discrimination. Good underwriting practices require that a difference be recognized among risks and that unlike risks be treated differently. "Unfair" discrimination usually is interpreted as treating like risks differently.

A large number of states have made twisting, misrepresentation, unfair discrimination, and the like a part of their unfair insurance practices act in an attempt to render the Federal Trade practices act inapplicable to insurance.[51]

4. TAXATION OF LIFE INSURANCE[52] COMPANIES

The life insurance business is subject to both Federal and state taxation. In fact, taxes, licenses, and fees take about 2¢ out of each dollar received by life insurance companies either as investment or premium income. The total paid in taxes runs over $400,000,000 a year.

Federal Income Tax. Because of the special nature of the life insurance business, the Federal income tax imposed on that branch of the business has been under constant revision ever since the passage of the sixteenth amendment. For purposes of discussion, the history of the income tax problem needs to be broken down into several broad periods.

Prior to 1921, the life insurance companies were taxed in the same way as commercial corporations. All earnings from whatever source were considered gross income. All expenditures, including charges for reserves, were deductible from gross income. The corporate rate was applied to the net, taxable income so determined.

---

[50] The fact that first-year commissions on new policies exceed the renewal commissions on an old one might tempt an unscrupulous agent to twist his own policies to the disadvantage of his client.

[51] "Whether this attempt will be successful remains to be seen." *Government Regulation of Insurance Marketing Practices* by Robert B. Ely III, Conference on Insurance, University of Chicago Law School, Conference Series 14, p. 129.

[52] Reference is made here to taxes imposed at company level, not to the even broader field of taxes imposed on life insurance proceeds.

The 1921 law set up special tax provisions for life insurance, recognizing that in effect a life insurance company is a depository of funds which are received in the form of premiums and invested for the benefit of policy-holders. The investment earnings of the company are credited to the accounts of the policyholders and these funds are paid back to the policyholders under the terms of the contract. The assets which the company holds are largely offset by policy reserves, on which the company is contractually obligated to pay a given rate of interest whether its investments earn that rate or not.[53]

Under the 1921 law, net taxable income was considered to consist of gross investment income minus investment expense, minus interest necessary to maintain legal reserves. Gains from sales or redemptions of securities, interest from tax-exempt securities, and dividends received on stocks of corporations subject to Federal income taxes were not taxed.

From 1921 to 1942, the interest required for maintaining reserves was set at 3¾% to be applied to the *mean reserve* for the year. During the latter part of this period, companies, because of declining interest earnings, began reducing interest assumptions on new policies with the result that the exemption produced by this formula proved to be too high. The government failed to get what it considered to be a reasonable tax income, so the formula was changed in 1942.

From 1942 to 1948, the interest required for maintaining reserves was computed on an industry-wide basis giving a weight of 35% to the actual rate assumed by each company on its reserves and 65% to an assumed rate of 3¼%. A ratio was then worked out each year by the Secretary of the Treasury between this figure and the total investment earnings of the companies. This ratio was known as the Secretary's Ratio and when subtracted from 100% measured the investment income subject to taxes. For example, the ratio in 1942 was 93%; so 7% of investment income was subject to taxes at regular corporation rates. The application of this formula provided additional tax income to the government, and at the time, seemed satisfactory. But a continued decline in interest earnings and an increase in deductions resulting from reserve revaluations produced a situation in 1947 in which the secretary's ratio exceeded 100% so the formula produced virtually no taxable income, and ever since, companies and the government have been occupied with attempts to find a new formula.

In 1950, a new averaging formula was established, using the 1942 system, except it discarded the 35%–65% weighting system in favor of the *average*

---

[53] This description is not actuarially correct but represents the concept of life insurance for income tax purposes.

valuation rate of interest for all companies, treating individual company ratios of valuation rates to investment earnings over 100% as 110% to eliminate negatives.[54]

In 1951, the companies developed a new formula. The investment income of companies without deducting the interest necessary to maintain the reserve was to be taxed at a flat rate. The rate imposed was 6½%.

As of the time of this writing, new income tax legislation was pending before Congress, the exact nature of which had not yet been determined. The 1951 legislation, which was regarded as "stop-gap," had expired, resulting in automatic reinstatement of the 1942 statute. This statute would have entailed higher taxes and was considered as outmoded. It seemed unlikely, at the time this was written, that Congress would allow the 1942 tax formula to be applied but would pass a new law based on what would be considered a more equitable formula. Most likely seemed to be a tax levied on a percentage of the net investment income at the going corporate rate. The tax rate probably will be applied to 12.5% of the first $1,000,000 of the net investment earnings of the companies; and to 15% of the remainder. This formula would give an effective maximum tax of about 8% of investment income.

The variety of tax formulas developed and the frequent changes in them indicate the difficulty of devising an equitable basis for taxing life insurance companies. A fair tax formula should consider (1) the fundamental differences and marked similarities between stock and mutual companies (2) individual company experience independent of national averages (3) avoiding discrimination against companies using conservative bases for valuation of reserves (4) the inadvisability of using purely arbitrary tax rates which cannot be related to general corporate tax rates (5) eliminating the discrimination against insured in favor of uninsured retirement plans. Experts are continuing to look for the ideal plan.

In addition to Federal income taxes, life insurance companies are subject to all other Federal taxes imposed on business generally, such as Social Security taxes, transfer taxes on securities, and the like.

State Taxes. The major tax imposed on life insurance companies by state governments is a tax on premiums, usually about 2%. Originally the tax was a tariff on out-of-state companies designed to protect home companies. Later it became a retalitory measure against taxes imposed by other states on out-of-state companies. Still today, some states make a differential between the rate charged home companies and that charged foreign and alien companies. In fact, some states do not impose a premium tax at all on domestic companies. In addition to imposing the tax on life insurance pre-

---

[54] The 1950 formula was to apply to 1949 and 1950 taxes, only.

miums, an increasing number of states is also imposing a tax on annuity premiums, although often at lower rates.[55]

The premium tax has developed into a revenue measure and is an important source of state funds in many states. It has been estimated that no more than 5% of the total premium tax collected by states is used for the regulation and supervision of the business.

The premium tax levied against life insurance companies is subject to question on the basis of tax theory. The question is controversial, however, because there are many different theories regarding taxation and also taxation itself is potentially not only a revenue-raising medium but also a tool for social adjustment. Some economists hold to the theory that taxes should be levied on the ability to pay and that they be levied directly; that is, recognizable as a tax. If these are the tests of a "good" tax, then premium taxes applied against life insurance are not theoretically acceptable.

If, on the other hand, this theory is cast aside and the question is looked at historically, it becomes clear that throughout history some taxes, at least, have been levied with two thoughts in mind: the amount of revenue they will raise and the ease with which they may be collected without objection by voters.[56] If these tests are used to determine what is a fair tax, then the life insurance business is properly taxed.

In addition to the premium tax, insurance companies are subject to various miscellaneous state taxes and fees such as license fees, filing fees for annual statements and other required documents, fee for certification of valuation, cost of triennial insurance department examinations, general property taxes, and the cost of required public advertising of annual statements.

At the present time taxes take more than $3.50 out of every $100 collected in premiums. More than half of this amount is paid to states. This tax burden has been termed as "a capital levy on the process of saving one's own money for one's own family" and is reported to have "no counterpart . . . in any other field of taxation."[57]

5. SUMMARY

Because of its effect on the public, the large scale of its operations and the technical nature of the business, life and Accident and Sickness insur-

---

[55] In addition to the states, some cities levy a premium tax.

[56] In recent years, especially, an additional test has been added, that of whether or not the tax helps redistribute wealth or serves as a desirable instrument of social control.

[57] Testimony of R. L. Hogg and Claris Adams representing company interests before the House Ways and Means Committee in Dec., 1954. They also declared, "Life insurance savings are taxed much more heavily here than they are either in Canada or Great Britain."

ance are subject to a high degree of governmental regulation. Such regulation, aside from the regulation involved in restrictions in corporate charters, begins with the establishment of an insurance department in Massachusetts in 1858. An assumption of the authority for regulation by the states as opposed to the Federal government was implicit from the beginnings of the business until 1869 when the Supreme Court of the United States rendered a definite decision that insurance was not commerce and, hence, not subject to Federal regulation.

State regulation was greatly tightened after the Armstrong investigation in New York and the passage in that state in 1906 of a "tight" insurance code. Other states following the lead of New York subsequently strengthened their codes. Then, in mid-1944, the Supreme Court reversed its decision of 75 years' standing and, in two cases decided the same day, declared insurance interstate commerce and hence subject to Federal regulation.

The decision immediately threw state and Federal law into conflict. These conflicts were resolved when Congress passed the McCarran Act, Public Law 15, declaring a moratorium on the application of the Federal antitrust laws to permit states to bring their laws into line with the Federal requirements and declaring (a) that no practice required by a state should be held in violation of Federal laws and (b) that it was the intent of Congress to leave the regulation of the insurance business to the states, with the Federal government entering the regulatory picture only where state regulation might be inadequate. To date, the Federal government has passed no specific laws superseding state regulatory law; but many observers feel that Federal regulation is coming by an evolutionary rather than a revolutionary process. They point to moves to regulate insurance practices by such federal agencies as the Federal Trade Commission. The question of Federal versus state regulation of the business can be argued endlessly and eventually becomes mixed up in the traditional political schism in the United States: states' rights versus Federal union.

Four channels of regulation are in evidence in the insurance business: judicial, administrative, legislative, and self-regulation. In the field of administrative regulation, power is chiefly in the hands of state insurance commissioners. These powers are broad and discretionary and cover almost every phase of operation, with possible exception in the life and A & S fields of rate regulation. There is neither rate regulation nor standard policies in either the life or A & S field; they are found in the Fire-Casualty fields.

The life and A & S business are subject to Federal and state taxation. The Federal income taxation of life insurance is difficult because of the nature of the special policy reserves peculiar to the business. In effect, the company acts as a depository of funds, which it invests in the interests of policyholders, and which it returns to them as required under the terms of the policy. Therefore, it becomes difficult to determine what actually is taxable income. The result is that ever since the passage of the income tax amendment to the constitution, the formula for imposing Federal income tax liability on the life insurance companies has been subject to constant revision. At the present time it consists of imposing a flat rate on investment income without allowing any credit for interest the companies are required to earn on assets to maintain policy reserves. Companies do not seriously object to the formula for arriving at taxable income, but they do insist that the rate charged is too high and has no counterpart in any other field of taxation.

The major tax imposed by states is a tax on premiums, usually around 2%. Such a tax is held by many to be unfair because it is a tax on savings, but the ease with which it can be collected is in its favor as a revenue producer. Few policyholders understand that such a tax merely increases the premium they must pay and, therefore, few of them object as voters.

Government regulation of the business, while at times onerous, irritating, and obviously containing inequities, has resulted in a high degree of public confidence in the insurance business. Furthermore, it has protected the ethical company against ruinous competition from the promotional company. Weighed in an over-all balance, regulation seems to have been of more benefit to the business than it has been a detriment, and there is little question but that it has had much to do with the stability and security for which the business is noted in this country.

Questions for Class Discussion

1. The life insurance business is one of the most closely regulated of all businesses. Is this unfair discrimination against the life insurance business?
2. Do you agree with Elizur Wright that the decision in the Paul v. Virginia case was "a blow to the sound regulation of the business?"
3. If you were a member of the Supreme Court would you have voted to reverse the Paul v. Virginia decision in the SEUA case?
4. How effective are state antitrust laws?
5. Are life insurance rates regulated? Are A & S rates regulated? Do you think these rates should be regulated?
6. Do you agree or disagree with the following statement? "I submit that it is the function of the Judge only to interpret the law as it is, uninfluenced by his own idea of what it should be, or by his desires to render his own ideas of alleged justice. It is not for the courts to rewrite the law or subvert its meaning. The Legislative branch enacts law. The Judicial branch should only

interpret it." From *Trends in Life Insurance Law*, Daniel J. Reidy, Insurance Lecture Series, University of Connecticut, Spring, 1953.

7. If the above quotation read: "I submit that it is the function of the insurance Commissioner to execute the law as it is, uninfluenced by his own idea of what it should be, or by his desires to render his own ideas of alleged justice. It is not for the Commissioner to rewrite the law or subvert its meaning. The Legislative branch enacts law. The Executive branch should only administer it," would you agree or disagree with the statement?

8. Why do you suppose that state qualifying examinations for prospective life insurance agents are not made more difficult?

9. Are life insurance companies fairly taxed by the Federal and state governments?

10. If you were elected to the State legislature would you recommend any changes in the regulation of insurance companies?

APPENDIX

A SPECIMEN AGENT'S
CONTRACT

The Stock Mutual Life Insurance Company

THIS AGREEMENT, made the ———— day of ————————, 19——, to take effect the ———— day of ————————, 19——, between the Stock Mutual Life Insurance Company, hereinafter called the "Company", and ———————— of ————————, State of ————————, hereinafter called the "Agent," WITNESSETH: That the Company, in consideration of the agreements of the Agent hereinafter contained, hereby agrees that the Agent may solicit and procure applications for life insurance and annuities in said Company within the territory of the ———————— Agency (No. ————) of said Company; and that the Company will allow the Agent, in accordance with the following schedule and subject to the provisions of this Agreement, first year's commissions, renewal commissions and fees upon payment of premiums on policies issued upon applications procured under this Agreement.

Form of Policy and Premium Period	Commissions on			Fees on 1st and Subsequent Renewal Premiums
	1st Year Premiums	1st and 2nd Renewal Premiums	3rd, 4th and 5th Renewal Premiums	
	Vested in any event	Vested in any event	Vested as provided later	Non-vested
Ordinary Life Age at Issue:				
Under 56	50%			
56	49%			
60	45%	10%	5%	2%
65	40%			
70	35%			

For ages at issue between 56 and 70 the first year commission rate is decreased by one percentage point for each increase of one year in the age at issue.

*No commission allowed on amount paid at terminal date to cover cost of conversion.

Form of Policy and Premium Period	Commissions on			Fees on 1st and Subsequent Renewal Premiums
	1st Year Premiums	1st and 2nd Renewal Premiums	3rd, 4th and 5th Renewal Premiums	
	Vested in any event	Vested in any event	Vested as provided later	Non-vested
Limited Premium Life and Life Paid-up at 85				
30 Payments or over	50%			
29 Payments	49%	10%	5%	2%
15 "	35%			
14 Payments	33%			
13 "	31%			
12 "	29%	10%	5%	2%
11 "	27%			
10 "	25%			

For durations of premium payments between 29 and 15 the first year commission rate is decreased by one percentage point for each decrease of one year in the duration.

nating at Age 70 *
(Ages 15–65)

Modified Whole Life with Reduced Paid-Up at 70
(Ages 15–55)

		10%	5%	2%
Age at Issue:				
Under 51	50%			
51	49%			
55	45%			
60	40%			

For ages at issue between 51 and 60 the first year commission rate is decreased by one percentage point for each increase of one year in the age at issue.

	10%	5%	2%
61	38%		
62	36%		
63	34%		
64	32%		
65	30%		

Modified Life Terminating at Age 65 *
(Ages 15–60)

Graded Death Benefit Modified Life Terminating at Age 65 *
(Ages 15–60)

		10%	5%	2%
Age at Issue:				
Under 51	50%			
51	49%			
52	48%			
53	47%			
54	46%			
55	45%			
56	43%			
57	41%			
58	39%			
59	37%			
60	35%			

nating at Age 60 *
(Ages 15–55)

		10%	5%	2%
Age at Issue:				
Under 51	50%			
51	48%			
52	46%			
53	44%			
54	42%			
55	40%			

Modified Whole Life with Reduced Paid-Up at End of 15 Years (Ages 56–70)

Modified Life Terminating in 10 Years *
(Ages 51–70)

Graded Death Benefit Modified Life Terminating in 10 Years *
(Ages 56–65)

		10%	5%	2%
Age at Issue:				
51	49%			
55	45%			
56	44%			
60	40%			
65	35%			
70	30%			

For ages at issue between 51 and 70 the first year commission rate is decreased by one percentage point for each increase of one year in the age at issue.

* No commission allowed on amount paid at terminal date to cover cost of conversion.

Commissions on

Form of Policy and Premium Period	1st Year Premiums — Vested in any event	1st and 2nd Renewal Premiums — Vested in any event	3rd, 4th and 5th Renewal Premiums — Vested as provided later	Fees on 1st and Subsequent Renewal Premiums — Non-vested
Graded Premium				
Ordinary Life				
With Family Income, Defered Survivorship Annuity, or Decreasing Term Insurance Agreement	35% ⎫			
Without above Agreements	40% ⎭	15%	15%	2%
Annual Premium Endowment				
For the term of:				
45 yrs. or over	50% ⎫			
37–44 yrs., incl.	47%			
36 years	46%	10%	5%	2%
30 "	40%			
25 "	35%			
20 "	30% ⎭			

For durations between 36 and 20 the first year commission rate is decreased by one percentage point for each decrease of one year in the duration.

19 years	28½% ⎫			
15 "	22½%	4%	2%	2%
10 "	15 % ⎭			

For durations between 19 and 10 the first year commission rate is decreased by one and one-half percentage points for each decrease of one year in the duration.

9 years	13% ⎫			
8 "	11%			
7 "	9%	2%	1%	2%
6 "	7%			
5 "	6% ⎭			

Commissions on

Form of Policy and Premium Period	1st Year Premiums — Vested in any event	1st and 2nd Renewal Premiums — Vested in any event	3rd, 4th and 5th Renewal Premiums — Vested as provided later	Fees on 1st and Subsequent Renewal Premiums — Non-vested
20 Premium Endowment				
Maturing in:				
40 yrs. or over	37% ⎫			
35–39 yrs., incl.	35%	10%	5%	2%
30–34 " "	33%			
25–29 " "	31% ⎭			
15 Premium Endowment				
Maturing in:				
40 yrs. or over	32% ⎫			
35–39 yrs., incl.	30%			
30–34 " "	28%	4%	2%	2%
25–29 " "	26%			
20–24 " "	25% ⎭			
10 Premium Endowment				
Maturing in:				
40 yrs. or over	25% ⎫			
35–39 yrs., incl.	23%			
30–34 " "	21%	4%	2%	2%
25–29 " "	19%			
20–24 " "	18%			
15–19 " "	17% ⎭			

Retirement Income Endowment
Maturity Age 70

Age at Issue:				
5–25, incl.	46%			
26–33 "	43%			
34	42%			
40	36%	10%		
41	36%		5%	
50	27%			2%

For ages at issue between 34–40 and 41–50 the first year commission rate is decreased by one percentage point for each increase of one year in the age at issue.

51	26%			
52	25%			
53	24%			
54	23%			
55	21½%	4%	2%	2%
56	20%			
57	18%			
58	15½%			
59	13%			
60	10%			
61	9%			
62	8%			
63	7%	2%	1%	2%
64	6%			
65	5%			

Retirement Income Endowment
Maturity Age 65
  (Ages 5–60)
Graded Death Benefit
Retirement Income Endowment
Maturity Age 65
  (Ages 15–60)
Annuity Income Endowment
Maturity Age 65
  (Ages 15–60)

Age at Issue:				
5–20, incl.	43%			
21–28 "	40%			
29	39%			
35	33%	10%	5%	2%
36	33%			
37	32%			
45	24%			

For ages at issue between 29–35 and 37–45 the first year commission rate is decreased by one percentage point for each increase of one year in the age at issue.

46	23½%			
47	23%			
48	22½%			
49	22%			
50	21%			
51	19%	4%	2%	2%
52	17%			
53	15%			
54	12½%			
55	10%			
56	9%			
57	8%			
58	7%	2%	1%	2%
59	6%			
60	5%			

Retirement Income Endowment — Maturity Age 60

Form of Policy and Premium Period	Commissions on 1st Year Premiums — Vested in any event	Commissions on 1st and 2nd Renewal Premiums — Vested in any event	Commissions on 3rd, 4th and 5th Renewal Premiums — Vested as provided later	Fees on 1st and Subsequent Renewal Premiums — Non-vested
Age at Issue:				
5–15, incl.	40%			
16–23 "	37%			
24	36%			
30	30%			
31	30%	10%	5%	2%
32	29%			
40	21%			

For ages at issue between 24–30 and 32–40 the first year commission rate is decreased by one percentage point for each increase of one year in the age at issue.

Form of Policy and Premium Period	1st Year Premiums — Vested in any event	1st and 2nd Renewal Premiums — Vested in any event	3rd, 4th and 5th Renewal Premiums — Vested as provided later	Fees — Non-vested
41	20%			
42	20%			
43	19½%			
44	19%			
45	18%			
46	17%	4%	2%	2%
47	16%			
48	14%			
49	12%			
50	10%			
51	9%			
52	8%			
53	7%	2%	1%	2%
54	6%			
55	5%			

Retirement Income Endowment — Maturity Age 55

Form of Policy and Premium Period	Commissions on 1st Year Premiums — Vested in any event	Commissions on 1st and 2nd Renewal Premiums — Vested in any event	Commissions on 3rd, 4th and 5th Renewal Premiums — Vested as provided later	Fees on 1st and Subsequent Renewal Premiums — Non-vested
Age at Issue:				
5–10, incl.	37%			
11–18 "	34%			
19	33%			
24	28%			
25	27%	10%	5%	2%
26	27%			
27	26%			
35	18%			

For ages at issue between 19–24 and 27–35 the first year commission rate is decreased by one percentage point for each increase of one year in the age at issue.

Form of Policy and Premium Period	1st Year Premiums — Vested in any event	1st and 2nd Renewal Premiums — Vested in any event	3rd, 4th and 5th Renewal Premiums — Vested as provided later	Fees — Non-vested
36	17½%			
37	17%			
38	16½%			
39	16%			
40	15%			
41	14%	4%	2%	2%
42	13%			
43	12%			
44	11%			
45	10%			
46	9%			
47	8%			
48	7%	2%	1%	2%
49	6%			
50	5%			

Retirement Income Endowment
Maturing in 10 Years
(Ages 46–70)

Graded Death Benefit Retirement Income Endowment
Maturing in 10 Years
(Ages 56–65)

Age at Issue:

46–70, incl.	10%	4%	2%	2%

Annual Premium Retirement Annuity
For the term of:

20 yrs. or over	20%			
19 "	19%	} 4%	2%	2%
15 "	15%			
10 "	10%			

For durations between 19 and 10 the first year commission rate is decreased by one percentage point for each decrease of one year in the duration.

9 years	9%			
8 "	8%			
7 "	7%			
6 "	6%	} 1%	1%	2%
5 "	5%			
4 "	4%			
3 "	3%			
2 "	2%			

Term

2 Yr. Initial Term	20%	8%	—	—	2%
3 " " "	25%	8%	—	—	2%
4 " " "	30%	8%	4%	4%	2%
5 " " "	30%	8%	4%	4%	2%

If the Agent is entitled to commissions upon automatic conversion of an Initial Term policy, the commission rates after conversion shall be those shown herein for the plan to which the conversion is made.

5 Yr. Term	30%	8%	4%	2%
10 " "	30%	10%	5%	2%
15 " "	30%	10%	5%	2%

5 Year Renewable Term

Original Term Period	30%	8%	4%	2%

Term to Age 65	30%	10%	5%	2%

Decreasing Term Insurance Agreement — 10, 15 and 20 Year Plans
Commissions and Fees will be payable at the rates currently payable to the Agent on the policy in connection with which such agreement is issued, except that where the 10 Year Plan is issued the first year commission rate on both the policy and the agreement shall be decreased by 2* percentage points.

*This adjustment does not apply when the 10 Year Plan is attached to a G.P.O.L. policy. See G.P.O.L. rates for proper adjustment.

Single Payment Contracts

Life	2½%			
End. (10 or more yrs. duration)	2½%			
Annuity*	2%			

*Other than Annuity Contracts issued in pursuance of options applicable to the proceeds of life insurance policies or annuity contracts.

Deferred Survivorship Annuity Agreement — Family Income Agreement — Supplementary Protective Contract
Commissions and Fees will be payable at the rates concurrently payable to the Agent on the policy in connection with which such agreement or contract is issued.

Commissions on any form of policy or contract not specified above will be allowed under this Agreement at the rates announced by the Company for such form of policy or contract.

The Agent agrees to deliver policies and other vouchers, and make collections on such receipts as shall be furnished by the Company, and to account, according to the instructions of the Company, or the General Agent or other representative of the Company in charge of said agency, for all policies, premium and other receipts, vouchers, drafts, moneys and valuable papers received by the Agent from the Company or from any person for the Company's account; and further agrees that all collections made by him for the Company shall be considered as trust funds. The Agent has no authority to make, alter, vary or discharge any contract, or extend the time for payment of premiums; or to waive or extend any obligation or condition; or to take payment of premiums other than in current funds; or to incur any liability in behalf of the Company; or to deliver any policy unless the applicant therefor is at the time in good health and insurable condition; or to receive any money due or to become due the Company except on receipts sent him for collection. The Agent shall be free to exercise his own judgment as to the time, place and means of soliciting and procuring applications for insurance and annuities under the authorization contained in this Agreement.

Termination of Former Agreements

The execution of this Agreement shall terminate as of the date of the taking effect hereof any outstanding agency agreements between the parties hereto, the same as if either party had given the other notice thereof in writing, without prejudice (a) to the Agent's rights, if any, to commissions accruing under any previous agreement, or (b) to any lien or right to a lien against such commissions.

Production Standards

This Agreement will be terminated by the Company upon the failure of the Agent to meet the standards set forth below.
Definition:
"Paid-for insurance" referred to in the following standards shall be credited according to the rules governing the Company's "Paid-for Bulletin" — excluding annuities.
I. The amount of paid-for insurance credited by the Company to the Agent from the effective date of this Agreement to the expiration of the first twelve full calendar months must be at least $50,000.
II. The amount of paid-for insurance credited by the Company to the Agent in any full calendar year must be at least $50,000; or must be at least $25,000, if such amount when added to the amount of paid-for insurance credited in the two preceding calendar years during the continuance of this Agreement totals at least $150,000.
III. The Agent shall conduct his business in such a manner as continuously to meet the Company's standards for classification as Full-time.

Exceptions:
The above production standards shall be waived for any year during which the Agent has been granted a leave of absence by the Company for at least six months, or during which the Agent shall have been temporarily disabled in the opinion of the Company for at least six months; and in either of such cases, the production standards set forth in II above shall be computed as though the calendar years preceding and succeeding the year in which the standards were waived were consecutive. Production standards set forth in II above shall be waived absolutely after the completion of fifteen consecutive full calendar years by the Agent under a full-time agency agreement or agreements with the Company, if the Agent has attained the age of 60 years; or in any event when the Agent shall commence to receive a pension under the Agent's Retirement Plan; or in the event that the Agent has, in the opinion of the Company, become totally and permanently disabled.
The foregoing provisions shall not prejudice the right of the

Company or the Agent to terminate this Agreement in accordance with the following paragraph.

Termination

It is hereby mutually agreed that the death of the Agent shall terminate this Agreement, and that this Agreement may be terminated at any time by either party by giving the other party notice thereof in writing.

Commissions After Termination

The Company agrees to pay to the Agent, his executor or administrator, after the termination of this Agreement, on policies issued upon applications procured under this Agreement by the Agent—

(a) First year's commissions at the rates stated above, on such of the first year's premiums as shall be paid after such termination;

(b) If this Agreement is terminated by reason of the Agent's death, renewal commissions at the rates stated above, on such of the 1st to the 5th renewal premiums, inclusive, as shall be paid after such termination;

(c) If this Agreement is terminated under any other conditions, renewal commissions at the rates stated above, as follows:

(1) If such termination takes place before the completion of 5 consecutive years by the Agent under a full-time agency agreement with the Company, on such of the 1st and 2nd renewal premiums as shall be paid after such termination;

(2) If such termination takes place after the completion of 5 consecutive years by the Agent under a full-time agency agreement with the Company, on such of the 1st to the 5th renewal premiums, inclusive, as shall be paid after such termination.

(d) If upon termination of this Agreement, the Agent shall thereafter continue immediately as a full-time salaried employee of the Company, or any of its General Agents, or under an agency agreement as a full-time field representative of the Company, then the Company will pay to him as long as he continues without interruption in any such capacity renewal commissions at the rates stated above on such of the 3rd to the 5th renewal premiums, inclusive, as shall be paid after such termination, whether or not he has qualified for such renewal commissions under the terms of sub-paragraph (c) of this provision, and in the event of his death while he is qualified for renewal commissions under this sub-paragraph, the Company will pay such renewal commissions to his executor or administrator. If he shall cease to act in any such capacity for any other reason than his death, he shall be entitled only to such further renewal commissions, if any, as he was qualified for under sub-paragraph (c) of this provision at the time of termination of this Agreement.

The Agent shall have no right to fees upon the termination of this Agreement.

It is mutually agreed that all of the provisions stated on the following page are and shall be considered as part of this Agreement the same as though fully set forth over the signatures of the parties hereto.

This Agreement shall impose no obligation upon the Company until it is executed on its behalf by a General Agent and countersigned by an Authorized Officer of the Company. No modification or any change in the terms hereof shall be made on behalf of the Company except in writing and signed by an Authorized Officer; but this Agreement may be terminated by any Authorized Representative of the Company.

IN WITNESS WHEREOF the said parties have executed this Agreement in triplicate on the day and year first above written.

THE STOCK MUTUAL LIFE INSURANCE COMPANY

By _____

General Agent

_____

Agent

Countersigned at Urbana, Indiana, on behalf of The Stock Mutual Life Insurance Company this _____ day of

of _____, 19____.

_____

Supervisor of Agents' Contracts

Entire Compensation

The Agent agrees that the commissions and fees herein provided shall constitute his entire compensation for his services hereunder; and that should the Company for any reason refund any premium on any policy covered hereunder, any commission and fee paid on such premium shall be refunded upon demand.

Advertising

The Agent agrees that he will comply with the rules and instructions of the Company now in force or issued during the continuance of this Agreement in regard to the use of all advertising matter, and any printed material which the Company may furnish.

Applications, When Procured

Any application shall be considered procured on the date of Part "2," thereof, or on the date of Part "1," when Part "2" is not required, or on the date of the written request for additional insurance where such insurance is issued on the basis of a former application.

Conversions and Other Matters Governed by Rules and Practice

The allowance of commissions and fees to the Agent in connection with the following matters shall be governed, irrespective of any other provisions of this Agreement, by such rules and practice as shall be set forth from time to time in the Company's Rules and Practice Letter and amendments thereto:

(a) conversion into Life or Endowment policies of Convertible Term policies, Annual Premium Retirement Annuities, and other changes in plan;

(b) premium payments on any insurance issued in exchange for or which, in the judgment of the Company, takes, or is to take, the place of insurance previously issued by the Company on the same life;

(c) premium payments made to establish any premium due date on a date other than the Policy Date and premiums paid within one year from such new premium due date, or premiums to effect a change of any premium due date;

(d) all other extra payments;

(e) premiums paid by automatic premium loans;

(f) upon each renewal of a 5 Year Renewable Term policy.

Fees and Records

The Company agrees to assume the cost of fees for licenses obtained, and medical examinations made, in accordance with the instructions and rules of the Company; to furnish such books and card systems of record or account to the Agent as the Company shall deem proper, which shall be the property of the Company; and to furnish such necessary blanks and canvassing documents as are issued by the Company.

Changes in Commission Rates

The Company reserves the right to change the rates of commissions set forth in this Agreement by giving notice in writing of such change; but such change shall not affect any business issued upon applications procured prior to the date when such change becomes effective.

Indebtedness

Any indebtedness or liability of the Agent to the Company, whenever and however incurred, shall constitute a first lien upon and may be charged against commissions and fees due at any time under this Agreement.

Any indebtedness or liability, whenever and however incurred, of the Agent to any General Agent in charge of said Agency during the continuance of this Agreement, shall constitute a lien upon and may be charged against commissions and fees due at any time under this Agreement on policies issued upon applications procured hereunder while such General Agent shall have been in charge of said Agency.

INDEX

This index consists of four parts—

INDEX OF SUBJECTS

INDEX OF AUTHORS CITED

INDEX OF BOOKS & ARTICLES CITED

INDEX OF COURT CASES CITED